The Money Behind the Screen

For my Llewella . . . forever

The Money Behind the Screen
A History of British Film Finance, 1945–1985

James Chapman

EDINBURGH
University Press

Edinburgh University Press is one of the leading university presses in the UK. We publish academic books and journals in our selected subject areas across the humanities and social sciences, combining cutting-edge scholarship with high editorial and production values to produce academic works of lasting importance. For more information visit our website: edinburghuniversitypress.com

© James Chapman, 2022, 2019

Edinburgh University Press Ltd
The Tun – Holyrood Road
12(2f) Jackson's Entry
Edinburgh EH8 8PJ

First published in hardback by Edinburgh University Press 2022

Typeset in Garamond MT Pro by
Manila Typesetting Company,
and printed and bound by CPI Group (UK) Ltd,
Croydon, CR0 4YY

A CIP record for this book is available from the British Library

ISBN 978 1 3995 0076 0 (hardback)
ISBN 978 1 3995 0077 7 (paperback)
ISBN 978 1 3995 0078 4 (webready PDF)
ISBN 978 1 3995 0079 1 (epub)

The right of James Chapman to be identified as the author of this work has been asserted in accordance with the Copyright, Designs and Patents Act 1988, and the Copyright and Related Rights Regulations 2003 (SI No. 2498).

Contents

List of Abbreviations	vii
Acknowledgements	ix
Introduction	1

Part I: An Industry in Crisis: 1945–1950
1 A Short History of the British Film Industry	11
2 Bogart or Bacon	31
3 Capital and Commerce	46
4 Producers and Profits	62
5 The National Film Finance Corporation	77
6 The Eady Levy	95

Part II: A Fragile Stability: 1951–1969
7 The Road to Recovery	109
8 The British Lion Film Corporation	128
9 Film Finances and the British Film Industry	143
10 Rise of the Runaways	161
11 New Waves, New Crises	179
12 Hollywood, UK	196
13 Backing British	214
14 Decline and Fall	228

Part III: Crises and Contraction: 1970–1985
15 Restructuring the Film Industry	243
16 The Changing Landscape of Film Finance	260
17 The National Film Finance Consortium	274
18 The Prime Minister's Working Party and its Aftermath	287
19 Revising Eady	300
20 The British Are Coming!	312
21 The Retreat of the State	330
Conclusion	347

Appendix I: Production Costs and Revenues of Selected Feature Films in the Late 1940s — 353

Appendix II: National Film Trustee Company: Production Costs and Receipts — 357

Appendix III: Budgets and Costs of Selected British First Features Guaranteed by Film Finances — 358

Appendix IV: National Film Finance Corporation: Accounts, 1950–1985 — 363

Appendix V: Feature Films supported by the National Film Finance Corporation, 1949–1985 — 365

Bibliography — 372

Index — 381

Abbreviations

ABFD	Associated British Film Distributors
ABPC	Associated British Picture Corporation
ACC	Associated Communications Corporation
ACT	Association of Cine Technicians
ASFM	Association of Short Film Makers
ATP	Associated Talking Pictures
BBFC	British Board of Film Censors
BEA	Bank of England Archive
BFA	British Film Authority
BFI	British Film Institute
BFM	British Film Makers
BIP	British International Pictures
BLPA	British Lion Production Associates
CEA	Cinematograph Exhibitors' Association
CFC	Cinematograph Films Council
DTI	Department of Trade and Industry
EMI	Electric and Musical Industries
FCI	Finance Corporation for Industry
FFA	Film Finances Archive
FFI	Finance for Industry
FIDO	Film Industry Defence Organisation
GBPC	Gaumont-British Picture Corporation
GCFC	General Cinema Finance Corporation
GFD	General Film Distributors
GFI	Goldcrest Films International
ICFC	Industrial and Commercial Finance Corporation
IFD	Independent Film Distributors
JARO	J. Arthur Rank Organisation
KRS	Kinematograph Renters' Society
LFP	London Film Productions
MGM	Metro-Goldwyn-Mayer
MPEA	Motion Picture Export Association (US)
MPPDA	Motion Picture Producers and Distributors Association (US)
NATKE	National Association of Theatre and Kinematograph Employees

NFFC	National Film Finance Corporation
NFFCo.	National Film Finance Company
PEP	Political and Economic Planning
TNA	The National Archives
UA	United Artists

Acknowledgements

This book – like some of the British films it includes – has been a long time in the making. The seeds of the project were sown during the summer of 2013 when I first undertook research at the Film Finances Archive in London: the initial outcome of this research was a special issue of the *Historical Journal of Film, Radio and Television* in 2014. The bulk of the archival research for the book was undertaken during a year's sabbatical leave in 2016–17: I should like to record my thanks to the Study Leave Committee of the College of Social Sciences, Arts and Humanities at the University of Leicester for approving that sabbatical. I had completed all but two chapters when the Great Coronavirus Lockdown of 2020 brought about the temporary closure of archives – the sort of contingency that even Film Finances' production consultant John Croydon could not have foreseen among the likely causes of delay to a project as it neared completion.

The research for this book has been entirely self-funded: it would seem that the subject of British film finance is not worth financing as far as the UK research councils are concerned! Nevertheless I treasure the comment of one reviewer for the Arts and Humanities Research Council (who described themselves as 'highly qualified' to assess the proposal) that an application to research the history of the National Film Finance Corporation (1948–85) would have more impact if it included 'new digital platforms' that did not exist until several decades after the corporation's demise. Perhaps the 'highly qualified' reviewer thought that the failure of the NFFC-funded Group Three in the 1950s was due to its films not being distributed by Netflix or Amazon Prime? Still, it is reassuring to know that applications for publicly funded research are subject to a level of 'expert' scrutiny that has not always been applied to the provision of film finance. If nothing else, *The Money Behind the Screen* demonstrates that external funding is not the be-all and end-all: the research just takes a little longer to complete without it. In this regard I am mindful of the comment attributed to Hannibal: *Aut viam inveniam aut faciam*.

As the late Professor Arthur Marwick once remarked: 'Without the sources contained in archives and libraries, the historian is nothing. Without archivists and librarians to guide him/her, the historian is a blunderer, high on purpose, low on achievement.' If I am the producer/director of *The Money Behind the Screen*, then the equivalent of the production managers, unit secretaries and accountants are the many librarians and archivists who have helped me in putting together the budget and managing the costs. The two main archive sources for this book have been The National Archives and the Film Finances Archive. I would like to thank

The National Archives' grants manager Jack Caswell and Contemporary Records specialist Mark Dunton for their enthusiastic support for our (ultimately unsuccessful) AHRC application. And the book would simply not have been possible without the co-operation of the London office of Film Finances, especially James Shirras (joint managing director), David Korda (chairman) and Thoko Mavolwane (PA to the managing directors), who have not only facilitated my research but have tolerated with unfailing good humour researchers occupying their boardroom and consuming their biscuits! Others who have provided invaluable assistance are Jonny Davis, Victoria Bennett, Storm Patterson and the Special Collections Unit of the British Film Institute; Hannah Cleal and the Bank of England Archive; James Darby and the Barclays Group Archive; Natasha Swainston and the Lloyds Banking Group Archive; John Porter and the Prudential Group Archive; and Georgina Orgill and the Stanley Kubrick Archive at the University of the Arts.

Many academic colleagues in the British cinema history community have contributed (some without knowing it) to the gestation and writing of this book: they include Professor Tony Aldgate, Dr Guy Barefoot, Dr Anne Bolton, Dr Llewella Chapman, Professor Sue Harper, Dr Lawrence Napper, Professor Julian Petley, Professor Duncan Petrie, Professor Vincent Porter, Dr Melanie Selfe, Professor Justin Smith, Professor Andrew Spicer, Dr Jenny Stewart, Professor Sarah Street and Professor Melanie Williams. Several 'work in progress' papers deriving from the research were presented at the conferences of the British Association of Film, Television and Screen Studies (BAFTSS) and the International Association of Media and History (IAMHIST) and at research seminars and symposiums at the Institute of Historical Research, University of Exeter, University of Leicester, University of St Andrews and University of Warwick.

I am grateful to Gillian Leslie and her colleagues at Edinburgh University Press for their highly positive response to a manuscript that did not conform to a standard monograph length and to EUP's readers for their generous and supportive comments on the proposal.

This book is dedicated to my wife Llewella: my soulmate, my best friend, my technical guru, my social secretary, and occasionally pressed into service as my research assistant. At times the writing of this book may have seemed more like grinding out the runs on a low seaming track at Headingley than crashing it to the boundary on a flyer at The Oval. The fact that I ever got off the mark is due entirely to her love and support. *Te amo sempre.*

Introduction

> Some people are fond of saying that you cannot measure artistic achievement in terms of the investment of money. That is true. But no film can be made without finance, and in my view the acid test of whether a film production company believes in its industry lies in its readiness to put its hand in its pocket. (John Davis)[1]

It would be fair to say that most general histories of British cinema – from pioneering works such as Raymond Durgnat's *A Mirror for England* and Charles Barr's *Ealing Studios* to more recent studies such as Brian McFarlane's *The Cinema of Britain and Ireland* – have focused primarily on films rather than on the film industry. This is no criticism of those works nor of the many excellent studies of British directors, studios, genres and stars that have enriched British cinema scholarship over recent decades; but it does point to a significant lacuna in the critical historiography of British cinema that this monograph seeks to address. As John Davis – who as managing director of the Rank Organisation for over a quarter of a century knew a thing or two about the film industry – put it: no film can be made without finance. *The Money Behind the Screen* therefore is a history of the financing of British films – and of the wider fiscal politics of the British film industry – from the end of the Second World War to the 1980s. It explores the contexts for the provision of film finance, the relations between producers and financiers, and the role of the different agencies involved in funding films.

One does not have to be a Marxist to recognise that the film industry exemplifies the capitalist model *par excellence*: the economic base and structure of the industry not only determine the organisation of film-making but also influence the nature and content of the films produced. There is now a very comprehensive historical map of what (in Marxist terms) might be termed the cultural superstructure of films and film-makers in British cinema: genres and production cycles including the Ealing comedies, the Hammer horror films, the 'Carry On' series and the James Bond movies have all been accorded their place in the sun, while directors as thematically and stylistically diverse as Anthony Asquith, Michael Powell, Carol Reed, David Lean, Tony Richardson, Joseph Losey, Lindsay Anderson, Ken Russell, Richard Attenborough and Ken Loach (and many others besides) have been acknowledged for their contribution to British film culture. But there has been significantly less attention given to the economic base of financing and production: and, in particular, the fiscal contexts of film-making remain largely hidden from view in a critical and scholarly literature that has focused more on genres and *auteurs* than the actual business of making movies. For example, there is no real British equivalent of Janet Wasco's *Movies and Money: Financing the American Film Industry* or Gorham Kinden's anthology *The American Movie Industry: The Business of Motion Pictures*. Nor is there yet a comprehensive history of the National Film Finance Corporation, the government 'film bank' set up in 1948 which played an important role in supporting the British film production industry for nearly four decades.

The history of film finance in Britain therefore remains largely unmapped. Rachael Low's *History of the British Film* – published in seven volumes between 1948 and 1985 – is the foundational work of British cinema history: Low provides the bedrock of an industrial history upon which others have built. Low is concerned to trace the key trends in the film industry and to document the structure and organisation of the production sector in particular. Her narrative extends from the origin of the cinematograph film industry in the mid-1890s to the end of the 1930s: in the event only one of the several commissioned continuation volumes – Robert Murphy's *Sixties British Cinema* – was ever published and that particular book is more concerned with films and film-makers than with the economic and fiscal structures of the industry. Alexander Walker's triptych – *Hollywood England*, *National Heroes* and *Icons in the Fire* – provides an overview of what in the author's view amounted to the long, slow decline of the British film industry between the 1960s and the end of the twentieth century: Walker was a journalist rather than a historian, but the books are informed by interviews with key industry figures and demonstrate an insider's knowledge of the film business and its personalities. And Margaret Dickinson and Sarah Street's *Cinema and State* remains the only full-length history of British government policy towards the industry from the Cinematograph Films Act of 1927 to the dismantling of state support in the mid-1980s: the availability of official records at the time of the book's publication (1985) means that its detailed coverage extends to the late 1940s. These books nevertheless remain rare examples in a historiography that has usually preferred to focus on the films themselves rather than on the institutions and structure of the film industry.[2]

How might the absence of film finance from much of the existing historiography of British cinema be explained? On the most basic level it is probably the case that the nitty-gritty nuts-and-bolts of film finance – budgets, distribution guarantees, front and end money, completion guarantees, gross receipts and producers' shares – seem rather dull in contrast to intellectually more exciting critical-interpretative approaches, such as analysing the form and aesthetics of *The Red Shoes*, the gender and sexual politics of *Dracula* or the construction of national identity in *Skyfall*. Who is really interested in the budgets and cost reports of, say, *Tom Jones* when we can revel in the narrative and visual pleasures of the film itself? This might also reflect something about the nature of film studies as an academic discipline. A consequence of the cultural and aesthetic emphasis of much film history has been the relative marginalisation of the economic and industrial contexts of film-making. The prevalence of the *auteur* theory has privileged individual agency and artistic creativity at the expense of economic considerations: we are interested in Joseph Losey or Ken Loach for the politics of their films rather than for the fact that they were economical directors who usually made their films on budget and schedule. The ascendancy of high theory during the 1970s and 1980s also had the effect of shifting attention away from questions of finance: semiotics and structuralism make uneasy bedfellows with budgets and box-office returns.

Another reason for the neglect of film finance in British cinema history has been the dearth of primary sources. There are no real equivalents of the Hollywood studio archives for British cinema. The Special Collections Unit of the British Film Institute tends to hold personal collections rather than corporate archives: some collections – such as the papers of Gerald Thomas, Karel Reisz, Sandy Lieberson and David Puttnam – include more details of budgets and finance than others, but these are far from being a full or representative record. The British trade press did not regularly publish details of production costs or box-office returns until the 1980s. Otherwise the archival record is patchy. The National Archives includes the records of the Board of Trade and its successor bodies: this material highlights the political and economic contexts that have shaped government policy towards the film industry and documents how this policy has changed over time. There is some material in the Bank of England Archive relating to the initiative to establish a films bank in the late 1930s and early 1940s. And the Prudential Assurance Company's archive holds corporate records relating to Alexander Korda's London Film Productions in the 1930s.[3] However, it was not until the Film Finances Archive was opened to researchers in 2013 that a fuller picture of the fiscal landscape of the post-war British film industry has begun to emerge. Film Finances provides guarantees of completion: its extensive archive – including distribution and financing agreements, budgets, cost reports and production correspondence for over 800 British feature films produced since 1950 – is the most comprehensive archival source for the post-war film production industry.[4]

But why should we be interested in the fiscal politics of the British film industry – or any film industry for that matter? I would contend that there are two main reasons. The first is that no film has ever been made outside of an economic context: this is as true for a low-budget independent film as it is for a major studio blockbuster. Film critics and historians may value films for their artistic, cultural or social significance, but all films have to raise the production finance. Therefore a history of film finance is one that includes all films rather than privileging only those that have been deemed culturally significant (what might be termed the *Brief Encounter* or *Kind Hearts and Coronets* version of British cinema history). And the financing arrangements for every film are unique: the budgets, contributions of the equity investors and share of the profits (if any) often vary significantly even for otherwise similar films. The study of film finance therefore identifies different patterns and connections from other histories. For example, accounts of British cinema of the early 1970s often link films such as *Straw Dogs* and *A Clockwork Orange*, which challenged the norms of representing screen violence and highlighted the changing culture of censorship.[5] From a finance perspective, however, *Straw Dogs* has a much more direct link to *Cabaret* than to *A Clockwork Orange*: the two films had the same executive producer (David Melnick) and were cross-collateralised against each other for their finance and completion guarantees.

The second reason why finance matters is that there often is a relationship between money and quality. John Davis was correct to say that artistic achievement cannot be measured by investment alone: the history of British cinema is littered with the corpses of expensive white elephants – *London Town*, *Bonnie Prince Charlie*, *Raise the Titanic!* and *Revolution* are among the most notorious – that did little to enhance the reputation of British films but nearly sank the production companies responsible. And of course there have been lower-budget films that turned out (often against expectations) to be box-office hits: *Genevieve*, *Saturday Night and Sunday Morning*, *Monty Python and the Holy Grail*, *My Beautiful Laundrette*, *Four Weddings and a Funeral*. However, such films are exceptional rather than usual: by and large there has usually been a correlation between the costs and production values of films and their performance at the box office. This is borne out by both statistical and anecdotal evidence. In 1939 the Cinematograph Films Council – an advisory body set up to monitor the film industry on behalf of the Board of Trade – undertook an investigation into film finance which analysed the costs and returns of 61 British feature films of the late 1930s and concluded that it was the more expensive films that were likely to make the larger profits. In particular, the higher-cost films tended to earn a higher percentage of their revenues from overseas markets.[6] And in 1963 the trade journal *Kinematograph Weekly* suggested that much the same situation persisted: 'The really big pictures – big at the box-office that is – are attracting larger audiences and more money in cinemas than ever before, but the run-of-the-mill films, the type that only a year ago were the bread and butter of the business, are barely yielding a crust.'[7]

The relationship between cost and quality is best demonstrated by a specific example. *Tom Jones* (1963) was one of the most successful British films ever made: it won critical plaudits – including the Academy Award for Best Picture – and was a major hit that took over £7 million at the box office worldwide and made large profits for its distributor (United Artists) and producer (Woodfall Films). For director Tony Richardson and screenwriter John Osborne, *Tom Jones* marked their move away from the social realist films they had made hitherto to a more flamboyant and expressive style of film-making. *Tom Jones* was originally to have been made for Bryanston, the independent British distributor which had backed *Saturday Night and Sunday Morning*, *A Taste of Honey* and *The Loneliness of the Long Distance Runner*. However, the maximum budget that Bryanston was willing to accept was £300,000 and even then its distribution guarantee would cover no more than 70 per cent of the cost of the film, leaving Woodfall to find the remainder from its own resources. In the event *Tom Jones* was financed by United Artists, which accepted the budget of £412,000 and was able to offer a distribution guarantee for 100 per cent of the budget. The switch from a small British distributor to a major Hollywood corporation raises important questions around economic and cultural capital in the film industry: it was the higher budget – and also the greater autonomy extended to him by United Artists, which adopted a very *laissez-faire* approach to costs – that allowed Richardson to make the film as he wanted.[8]

The Money Behind the Screen (the title is a conscious reference to the pioneering study of film finance published by F. D. Klingender and Stuart Legg in 1937) is based on extensive archival research: the sources include The National Archives, the Bank of England Archive, the Film Finances Archive and the Special Collections of the British Film Institute. In privileging the importance of archive materials I should make it clear that I do not regard these as neutral or unmediated: all sources need to be approached in a spirit of sceptical inquiry with due regard to their provenance and an awareness of both what they do tell us and what they do not. Archival sources do not necessarily reveal the 'truth': but what they do illuminate are the contexts in which policy takes shape and the various determinants upon the provision of film finance. On a more basic level they also provide a bedrock of factual detail. For example, while the press speculated that Alexander Korda's *Bonnie Prince Charlie* (1948) might have cost anywhere between £500,000 and £1 million, the Board of Trade records reveal that the actual recorded cost was £760,000.[9] I have endeavoured to consult a wide range of archival sources and to consider how different collections can complement and speak to each other. For example, while the records of the Board of Trade Manufactures Department and the Treasury held by The National Archives document the macro level of official policy-making, such as in the formation of the National Film Finance Corporation in the late 1940s, it is the boxes on individual films guaranteed by Film Finances that reveal the micro-level stories of how producers put together the finance packages for their films.

I have supplemented unpublished archival materials with published primary sources, including official reports on the finances of the film industry and trade year books which provide statistical data relating to investment in the film industry, the volume of domestic production and cinema attendances. The annual reports of the National Film Finance Corporation are revealing not only about the number of films it supported but also about how its economic and cultural priorities changed over time. I have also drawn extensively upon both the business press (*The Economist*, *The Financial Times*) and the film industry trade press.[10] This is a source that needs to be treated with caution. Some commentators are dismissive of the trade papers. A civil servant at the Board of Trade once remarked: 'No one, of course, treats these trade papers at all seriously; it is well recognised that they only exist for the sake of their advertising, and that their news columns have no value at all and are not to be relied upon.'[11] Nevertheless the trade papers can be valuable sources for the historian. In particular, their editorial matter reveals how the different sections of the trade responded to the major issues affecting the industry: there were often differences of opinion between producers, distributors and exhibitors over the extent to which the domestic production sector should be supported and what form that support should take.

A word of explanation is needed for the period covered by this book. It begins at the end of the Second World War: this was a paradoxical time when British cinema was at the height of its popular appeal – cinema attendances reached their all-time high in 1946 – but when most British films were losing money and producers were finding it increasingly difficult to raise their finance. There was a widespread sense of crisis in the film industry: the government responded by setting up the National Film Finance Corporation (1949) in order to provide loans to producers, and by establishing the British Film Production Fund (1950) which supplemented the income of producers through a levy on ticket sales. These measures – along with the quota established by the Cinematograph Films Act of 1927 – were the cornerstones of official film policy until they were abolished in the mid-1980s. The book is arranged chronologically. Part I covers the crisis of the late 1940s, exploring the sources of film finance, showing how the structure of the industry contributed to the unprofitability of films, and documenting the measures taken to support the British production sector. Part II covers the period between the early 1950s and the late 1960s when the British film industry enjoyed periods of relative prosperity punctuated by moments of crisis. The main narrative across this period in relation to film finance was the gradual decline of wholly British-financed production and the rise of American investment in the British production sector, to the extent that by the end of the 1960s American finance accounted for around 85 per cent of British films. Part III covers the period between 1970 and 1985: this began with one crisis (the sudden and large-scale withdrawal of American capital from the British production industry) and ended with another (the nadir of cinema admissions in Britain and the lowest level of indigenous production for sixty years). It was a period during which the structure of the industry and the landscape of film finance underwent far-reaching changes. The book ends with the dismantling of the support apparatus put in place in the late 1940s: the NFFC and the Eady levy – along with the quota – were abolished in 1985.

The Money Behind the Screen therefore seeks to fill an important gap in the history of British cinema. It considers three interrelated themes: 1. The institutional and economic structure of the British film industry, focusing especially on the production sector and highlighting how producers including both the major groups and independents raised their capital. This also mandates consideration of the costs of film production and the financial returns to producers. A recurring feature of the history of the British film industry is that more films have lost money for their producers than have made a profit; but to what extent has this been due to poor decisions by producers or to the nature of an industry in which the structure of distribution and exhibition is weighted against them? 2. The sources of film finance, including both private and public capital and domestic and foreign investment. The period covered by this book is not only one which saw the entry (and later the retreat) of the state into the provision of film finance, but also one in which the sources of private equity capital for film production changed gradually from mostly British to largely foreign (predominantly American) sources. In short this was a period during which the political economy of the British film production industry was entirely transformed. 3. The role of government in supporting the domestic production sector. The period covered by the book encompasses the history of both the National Film Finance Corporation and the British Film Production Fund: an important aspect of the history of film finance involves the decision of the government to become involved in assisting the industry and how that policy adapted over time in relation to changing economic and political circumstances.

British cinema has long ceased to be (in Alan Lovell's oft-quoted phrase) 'the unknown cinema': but it is still a cinema with hidden facets and unknown narratives.[12] The history of film finance is one of those. My aim in this book, therefore, is to shed light on an aspect of British cinema history that until now existed mostly in the shadows.

Notes

1. 'Co-production – key to future success?', *Kinematograph Weekly*, 9 September 1965, p. 7.
2. Much of the historiography of British cinema has been chronological by decade. Among the histories that include some account of the fiscal politics of film-making for their specific periods are: Sue Harper and Vincent Porter, *British Cinema of the 1950s: The Decline of Deference* (Oxford: Oxford University Press, 2003); Richard Farmer, Laura Mayne, Duncan Petrie and Melanie Williams, *Transformation and Tradition in 1960s British Cinema* (Edinburgh: Edinburgh University Press, 2019); Sue Harper and Justin Smith, *British Film Culture in the 1970s: The Boundaries of Pleasure* (Edinburgh: Edinburgh University Press, 2011); and John Hill, *British Cinema in the 1980s: Issues and Themes* (Oxford: Clarendon Press, 1999).
3. Sarah Street, 'Alexander Korda, Prudential Assurance and British film finance in the 1930s', *Historical Journal of Film, Radio and Television*, 6: 2 (1986), pp. 161–79.
4. One example must suffice to illustrate the riches of the Film Finances Archive. *Dr No* (1962) – the first of the James Bond films that would become the most successful series in the history of British cinema – is probably the most famous of the films guaranteed by Film Finances. The archive reveals that the film was financed 100 per cent by United Artists, with the production loan provided by the Bank of America and the profits shared fifty-fifty between United Artists and the producers after deducting distribution fees and expenses and repayment of the loan. The film was originally budgeted at £317,359, which was raised to £321,227 following an evaluation by Film Finances' production consultant John Croydon. *Dr No* went over budget due to overrunning its location schedule and overspending on sets. The final audited cost of the film was £392,022: United Artists provided an additional £10,122 on top of the budget and Film Finances advanced a total of £59,890 towards its completion, with the producers finding the balance from their own resources.
5. See, for example, Charles Barr, '*Straw Dogs*, *A Clockwork Orange* and the Critics', *Screen*, 13: 2 (1972), pp. 17–32.
6. Bank of England Archive (BEA) SMT 2/40: Cinematograph Films Council: 'Costs and receipts in respect of 61 British feature films produced in the period 1 January 1937 to 30 June 1938.' The data reveals that the most expensive films (there were thirteen costing over £75,000) earned total distributors' net receipts home and overseas of £1,190,803, representing an average of £91,600 per picture. In contrast, twenty middle-budget films (costing between £36,000 and £75,000) earned net receipts of

£1,094,840 (£54,742 per picture average) and twenty-eight lower-cost films (under £36,000) earned net receipts of £376,643 (£13,452 per picture average). The more expensive films tended to earn a greater percentage of their revenues from overseas markets: 41 per cent for films over £75,000 compared to 19 per cent for the middle-budget range and only 4 per cent for the lower-cost pictures.

7. 'British Films Again Ahead on General Release', *Kinematograph Weekly*, 19 December 1963, p. 5.
8. Sue Harper, 'The Price of Oysters: *Tom Jones* (1963) and Film Finances', *Historical Journal of Film, Radio and Television*, 34: 1 (2014), pp. 72–84.
9. The National Archives (TNA) BT 64/4493: 'British First Features released through British Lion Film Corporation Ltd during 30 months to 30 June 1949.'
10. In 1945 there were four British trade papers representing different sections of the industry: *The Cinema News and Property Gazette*, *Daily Film Renter*, *Kinematograph Weekly* and *Today's Cinema*. *The Cinema News and Property Gazette* ceased publication in 1957, the same year that the *Daily Film Renter* and *Today's Cinema* merged to become the *Daily Cinema*, with *Today's Cinema* re-emerging in 1969 when *Daily Cinema* ceased. In 1971 *Kinematograph Weekly* and *Today's Cinema* merged to become *CinemaTV Today*, which in turn became *Screen International* in 1975.
11. TNA BT 64/4521: Sidney Golt to George Calder, 7 December 1950.
12. Alan Lovell, 'The British Cinema: The Unknown Cinema', typescript of seminar paper held by the British Film Institute Reuben Library, 13 March 1969. A slightly revised version was published as 'The Unknown Cinema of Britain', *Cinema Journal*, 11: 2 (1972), pp. 1–8.

Part I

An Industry in Crisis: 1945–1950

CHAPTER 1

A Short History of the British Film Industry

> From time to time during the past few years the public has been made aware of recurring crises in the British film industry . . . Those of the public with long memories may have remembered that this state of affairs has been almost perennial. The crisis in British film-making – where lies the main problem of the industry – started long ago, and only at rare intervals during the past forty years have there been short periods of prosperity to lighten an otherwise depressing canvas. Of a stable production industry there has been no sign. (Political and Economic Planning)[1]

In the late 1940s there was much talk of a 'crisis' in the British film industry: film production was in a perilous state, costs were increasing, revenues were falling, studios were closing and the sources of capital investment had all but dried up. Although British films enjoyed much cultural prestige – this was the era of such classics as *Great Expectations*, *The Red Shoes*, *Hamlet*, *Oliver Twist*, *The Fallen Idol* and *The Third Man* – relatively few of them made a profit and film production overall was losing money. In 1948 the government was obliged to bail out the ailing British Lion Film Corporation to the tune of £3 million in order to prevent it from going out of business.[2] And in 1949 the Rank Organisation – the largest producer-distributor-exhibitor in Britain and the only British corporation operating on the same scale as the major Hollywood studios – announced that it would be cutting back its production programme after recording a loss of £3.3 million on film production and distribution over the previous financial year.[3] Rank was widely seen as a barometer of the state of the industry and the extent of its losses sent shockwaves through the trade. An editorial in the trade paper *Kinematograph Weekly* described it as 'a major tragedy for the British film industry'.[4]

However, as the report into the film industry published by the independent think tank Political and Economic Planning in 1952 correctly pointed out, there was a sense that the British film industry was almost perpetually in a state of crisis. The crisis of the late 1940s followed others in the mid-1920s when the domestic production industry nearly collapsed and in 1937 when a period of over-production on the wave of an investment boom was followed by the near-inevitable bust as producers were unable to pay back their loans and investors sought to cut their losses. And there would be other crises after the 1940s as cinema audiences declined and the production sector contracted. As one trade commentator observed in 1958:

> Crisis is a word that has become almost endemic in the film industry. In my experience I can hardly remember a time when we were not either in the middle of a crisis, recovering shakily from a crisis, or riding high upon a boom with one eye swivelled nervously in the direction of the next potential crisis.[5]

Much the same point was made by Eirene White MP in the course of a parliamentary debate on the film industry in 1963: 'The industry is suffering from a very severe crisis of confidence. We have had crises in the film industry before . . . But in some way the present crisis is deeper and more worrying.'[6] And in the late 1970s the Interim Action Committee on the Film Industry – chaired by former Prime Minister Sir Harold Wilson to consider proposals for government assistance for production – observed: 'The British film industry has been having crises for over 50 years, for most of its long life. So often, indeed, that the description of its current problems as constituting a "crisis" is perhaps misleading.'[7]

The narrative of crisis has also informed both journalistic and scholarly histories of British cinema. Charles Oakley's *Where We Came In: Seventy Years of the British Film Industry*, for example, compared it to a terminally ill patient who stubbornly refuses to die: 'It has been virtually written off several times. But the industry's recuperative powers asserted themselves. Something stirred, somewhere, somehow, and there it was once more.'[8] Ernest Betts echoed the PEP report in his book *The Film Business: A History of British Cinema 1896–1972*: 'The film industry is well known as "the crisis industry", for it has, for most of its history, failed to solve its problems and put its affairs in order.'[9] George Perry's *The Great British Picture Show* concurs that the history of British cinema has been one of 'consistently recurring crises throughout its long history'.[10] Julian Petley's account of state intervention in the British film industry understands the problems of the late 1940s as 'an intensification of the industry's long-term state of crisis'.[11] And Sarah Street's *British National Cinema* – one of the few general histories to devote a full chapter to the fiscal politics of the film industry – describes how the industry 'lurched from boom to crisis without a stable infrastructure'.[12]

To understand the nature and causes of the crisis in British film production in the late 1940s therefore requires us to take a long-term view: it necessitates a wide-angle establishing shot before moving in to a series of close-ups. While there were historically specific factors in the late 1940s, the underlying reasons for the crisis were rooted in long-term structural and economic weaknesses that may be traced back to the early history of the industry. One of these was the institutional structure of the industry itself. In their book *Film History: Theory and Practice*, Robert C. Allen and Douglas Gomery point out that every film industry needs to devise its own way of organising the 'three fundamental tasks' of production, distribution and exhibition.[13] In the US film industry between the early 1920s and the 'divorcement' ruling of 1948 this took the form of a process of vertical integration whereby the major Hollywood studios – MGM, Paramount, Twentieth Century–Fox, Warner

Bros. and RKO – combined interests across all three sectors of the industry. There were clear advantages to this model of industrial organisation: producers were guaranteed distribution for their films and exhibitors could depend upon a regular supply of product. In practice the Hollywood majors could not produce enough films to fill their own cinemas, so they showed each other's films on favourable terms: hence the US film industry developed into a mature oligopoly in which power resided with a cartel of vertically integrated corporations. In Britain, however, the film industry was more fragmented and took longer to embrace vertical integration – and even then it did so on a lesser scale. Until the late 1920s there was 'no British producing company with a sufficiently large and stable output to constitute the production end of an integrated group'.[14] Only two British combines – the Rank Organisation and the Associated British Picture Corporation – ever achieved full vertical integration: for much of its history the landscape of the British film industry was dominated by this unequal duopoly.

A specific problem for British cinema, furthermore, is the nature of the home market. Even at the height of cinema-going in the 1940s, the British market was only around a quarter of the size of the North American market. The US film industry always had the advantage that it would usually recover the costs of all but its most expensive films in the home market: any overseas earnings therefore generally represented a profit. The British market, however, was not large enough to guarantee a profitable return for anything but the most modestly budgeted films. Rachael Low concludes her history of the British film industry in the 1930s:

> It has been argued in this study that although it is sometimes possible, with a lot of talent, to make good films on modest budgets, in general a constant level of high quality is expensive and needs to be sure of a big market not just for isolated films but as a matter of course. The Americans had one and the British did not, and underlying the history of the British film industry is its struggle to come to terms with that fact.[15]

British producers have historically followed one of two strategies: either concentrating on the production of low- or medium-budget films that would recover their costs in the home market or producing more expensive 'international' films that would depend on overseas revenues in order to return a profit. The former strategy was relatively safe during the 1930s and 1940s, but it became more precarious as the home market contracted from the late 1950s. And any profit from the home market was usually quite modest. The latter strategy was potentially more lucrative, but it also represented a bigger risk. A recurring feature of the history of British cinema is that the ambitious producers who set their sights on the international market – Alexander Korda in the 1930s, the Rank Organisation in the 1940s, Lew Grade in the 1970s and Goldcrest in the 1980s – have invariably ended in failure.

Another reason for its underlying weakness is that historically the production sector of the British film industry has been under-capitalised. In 1925 the film industry statistician Simon Rowson calculated that total capital investment in the

British film industry was around £35 million but that only £500,000 was invested in production.[16] In contrast, total investment in the American production sector in the same year amounted to US $62 million (equivalent to £12.9 million at the time).[17] One of the reasons that American films were generally more popular with audiences was their superior production values: Hollywood was able to make more lavish and expensive films because its large home market could support the expenditure. British producers have been unable to match the production values of American films: this puts them at a competitive disadvantage in an industry that equates cost with quality. This point was made by the screenwriter Angus MacPhail in 1930 in relation to what he called 'spectacular dramas': 'Generally speaking, we cannot compete with America in this class on the score of expense ... Apart from the fact that America can (and does) almost always outbid us in this class, drama requires more than any other type extreme technical polish, and to assemble a unit of really first class technicians is beyond our means.'[18]

The structural and economic weaknesses of the British film industry can be traced back to its formative period. The standard accounts of the early years of cinema in Britain present it as a narrative of unfulfilled talents and lost opportunities.[19] Britain was one of the leading producers of cinematograph films before the First World War, and early British film-makers such as R. W. Paul, Birt Acres, William Haggar and Cecil Hepworth made important contributions to the development of film form and technique. Films were initially shown in music halls and travelling fairgrounds, but as it became apparent that moving pictures were more than just a short-lived novelty the first purpose-built cinema sites began to appear by around 1907–8. The exhibition sector of the industry expanded rapidly: a total of 1,998 cinema exhibition companies were registered in Britain between 1906 and 1914.[20] The best estimates for the total number of permanent cinema sites are between 3,000 and 3,500 by 1915.[21] However, the rapid growth of cinema exhibition was not matched by innovation in film-making technique as British producers failed to keep pace with their competitors. British cinema's struggle to adapt was exemplified by the career of Cecil Hepworth. In 1905 Hepworth had made *Rescued by Rover* – now regarded as a landmark in the development of film narrative as important as the films of Edwin S. Porter and D. W. Griffith in the United States. But a decade later he was making a series of static, stagey theatrical and literary adaptations – beginning with *Hamlet* (1913) – which 'had some warm patriotic reviews but limited box-office appeal'.[22] Even before the First World War there were signs that British films were being squeezed out of their home market by imports. Low calculates that in 1910 British films accounted for only 15 per cent of all those released in Britain compared to 17 per cent from Italy, 28 per cent from the United States and 36 per cent from France.[23]

It has often been maintained that it was the First World War that dealt a fatal blow to the British film industry in so far as it brought about the conditions in which American films came to dominate the British market. This, certainly, was the official view. According to Sir Philip Cunliffe-Lister, the President of the Board of Trade, in moving the Cinematograph Films Bill of 1927: 'It was during the four long years of War when the whole effort of this country was concentrated on winning the War, that our competitors in the film industry in America forged ahead, very often by using British talent in production in their acting, writing and technical skill.'[24] With the supply of films from continental Europe disrupted by the war, and with British domestic production affected by material shortages and by the recruitment of industry personnel into the army, American renters were able to secure a strong foothold in Britain. American film exports doubled between 1914 and 1916, and Britain accounted for over half of those exports.[25] Furthermore, American films were generally adjudged to be of superior quality to the indigenous product. British cinema audiences seem to have preferred American films: the films of Charlie Chaplin were the most popular attractions in Britain.[26] However, Low contests the narrative of wartime disruption, arguing that the impact of the war merely exposed the existing structural weaknesses within the industry that had already become apparent before 1914: she argues that 'the shortage of capital for British film production, its fundamental weakness, dated from before the war. There is no reason whatever to suppose that, had there been no war, British production would have been able to withstand the irresistible growth of the American output.'[27]

Regardless of the impact of the war, it is incontestable that by the 1910s the British production industry was falling behind its chief rival in terms of filmmaking technique. At a time when an embryonic studio system was emerging in the United States – exemplified by companies such as Universal Pictures (formed in 1912) and the Fox Film Corporation (1916) – British producers were slow to adopt the new streamlined production methods and were reluctant to embrace the trend for longer 'feature' films. British films seemed parochial and technically impoverished in comparison to extravagant American super-productions such as D. W. Griffith's *The Birth of a Nation* (1915) and *Intolerance* (1916). This situation persisted into the 1920s. The US film industry was now represented by a powerful trade organisation – the Motion Picture Producers and Distributors of America (MPPDA) – which embarked upon an aggressive overseas sales drive to ensure that it maintained its hegemony of world film markets.[28] All that Britain could offer in return was a series of lacklustre 'British Film Weeks'.[29] British producers tried various ways of differentiating their films from the American product. The Stoll Film Company was probably the most dynamic force in British production in the early 1920s: it produced a series of adaptations of contemporary novels under the label of 'Eminent British Authors' but its adherence to the short form – exemplified by the series *The Adventures of Sherlock Holmes* (1921) – was regressive as this was a mode of film practice that was already losing ground to the feature film.[30]

A combination of its own underlying structural weaknesses and the ineffective strategies of British producers meant that by the mid-1920s the British production industry was on the verge of collapse. British studio output had been declining for some years: while in 1920 there had been a total of 145 British feature films, and 136 in 1921, the numbers then fell sharply – 95 in 1922, 75 in 1923, 56 in 1924, 45 in 1925 – before hitting a low of 37 in 1926.[31] In the 'Black November' of 1924 the industry 'reached such a state of affairs that not a single foot of film was being exposed on any British floor'.[32] This was the context for the Cinematograph Films Act of 1927: the first – it would not be the last – intervention by the British government to assist the native production industry.[33] It was a protectionist measure that instituted a minimum quota of British films for both exhibitors and distributors (renters): the exhibitors' quota was set initially at 5 per cent, the renters' quota at 7.5 per cent, with phased increases over the ten-year term of the legislation until they reached 20 per cent by the mid-1930s. A British film was defined as one produced by a British-registered company where the studio scenes were shot in Britain or the British Empire and where 75 per cent of labour costs (excluding the salary of one foreign artiste or technician) were paid to British subjects. The reasons behind the Quota Act (as it became known) were both economic and cultural. Economically it was intended to provide a stimulus for domestic production by ensuring screen time for British films. From a cultural perspective it was seen as a means of ensuring that the representation of Britain in what was widely recognised as a powerful medium of public entertainment should not be left entirely in the hands of foreign (i.e. American) interests. This point was forcefully made by Sir Philip Cunliffe-Lister:

> I think the importance of securing greater production and wider distribution of British films is generally recognised throughout the country . . . The cinema is today the most universal means through which national ideas and national atmosphere can be spread, and even if these be intangible things, surely they are among the most important influences in civilisation . . . Should we be content for a moment if we depended upon foreign literature and upon a foreign Press in this country? At any rate the greatest proportion of the Press is British, and we should be very anxious if the proportion was in the opposite sense as it is with British films.[34]

To this extent the Quota Act may be seen within the context of a narrative of resistance to 'Americanisation' that informed political and cultural discourses around film and popular culture in Britain for much of the twentieth century.

The effects of the Cinematograph Films Act were mixed. It succeeded in its primary aim of boosting British production: the number of British feature films increased from 37 in 1926 and 45 in 1927, before the quota came into force, to 72 in 1928, 92 in 1930, 143 in 1932 and 182 in 1934.[35] And British films' share of their home market also increased from a mere 4 per cent in 1926 and 1927 to 12 per cent in 1928, 19 per cent by 1930 and 24 per cent by 1932. Simon Rowson concluded that '[the] quantity of British films registered has been largely in excess of the minimum quantity required to meet quota liabilities'.[36] However, the quota also had an unforeseen consequence in so far as the increase in the quantity of British production was not necessarily matched in terms of quality. The creation of what amounted in effect to a guaranteed market for British films was the context for the emergence of what came to be dubbed 'quota quickies': low-budget films churned out by smaller producers at minimum cost in order that distributors (particularly the American distributors operating in Britain) could meet their quota obligations. As trade journalist P. L. Mannock observed in 1930: 'A deplorable and rather sinister consequence of the shortage of quota films available . . . has been the demand for British films of any grade. Shoddy, contemptible and cheap pictures have been hurriedly made, and old films formerly too bad to show have been raked out of the vaults simply to enable American firms to comply with the law.'[37] The critical reputation of the much-derided 'quota quickies' has since come in for long-overdue critical rehabilitation – they provided a training ground for future film-makers including Carol Reed and Michael Powell as well as representing a distinct mode of low-budget film-making in their own right – though the volume in which they were produced did little to dispel the notion that most British films were cheap and shoddy affairs.[38]

By the 1930s cinema-going had become (in the oft-quoted words of historian A. J. P. Taylor) 'the essential social habit of the age'.[39] In 1934 (the first year for which reliable statistics are available) there were 4,448 cinemas in Britain and 963 million admissions, while the total paid at the box office was £41,125,000.[40] While cinema was an enormously popular entertainment, however, there is contradictory evidence regarding the popularity of British films. On the one hand contemporary sources seemed to suggest that American films were the most popular: with a few exceptions – notably the extravagant costume pictures of Alexander Korda and the polished contemporary thrillers of Alfred Hitchcock – British films were regarded as lacking the technical qualities and entertainment value of their American competitors.[41] On the other hand revisionist scholarship on British cinema of the 1930s has suggested that British films were more popular with audiences than their critical reputation would suggest. John Sedgwick, for example, has calculated the market share of British films employing a statistical method based on the length of their run in selected cinemas and the optimum seating capacity of those cinemas: he concludes that 'by 1934 significant numbers of British films were being made which were genuinely attractive to domestic audiences'.[42]

The standard narrative of the British film industry during the 1930s presents it as a period of boom and bust: the first half of the decade saw the expansion of the production sector, the building of new studios (including Sound City, Denham and Pinewood) and a dramatic increase in the volume of production which reached a high of 221 feature films in 1937, only to be followed by an equally dramatic slump precipitated by a financial crisis and the withdrawal of investment from the City of London. The high point of British production during the decade was Alexander Korda's *The Private Life of Henry VIII* (1933): this was an ambitious film costing £93,710 – five times the average cost of a British feature in the early 1930s – which is estimated to have grossed over £500,000 at the box office worldwide.[43] It had been a calculated gamble by Korda as such a high-cost film would never be able to recover its costs from the home market: its receipts in Britain (£81,825) were less than its production cost. Nevertheless the gamble paid off: *The Private Life of Henry VIII* did exceptionally good business for a British film in the United States.[44] George Perry contends that it was the 'extravagant success' of *The Private Life of Henry VIII* that 'set in train a period of excessive speculation with City firms almost falling over themselves in the rush to get a stake in the new booming business'.[45] Korda – bankrolled by the Prudential Assurance Company – embarked upon an ambitious programme of expensive films including *Catherine the Great*, *The Private Life of Don Juan*, *The Scarlet Pimpernel*, *Sanders of the River*, *The Ghost Goes West*, *Things to Come*, *The Man Who Could Work Miracles*, *Rembrandt*, *Knight Without Armour*, *The Drum* and *The Four Feathers*, as well as building a state-of-the-art studio complex at Denham.[46] Korda was not the only producer to set his sights on the world market. The Gaumont-British Picture Corporation – the largest of the two British combines of the 1930s – produced a series of lavish musicals starring the 'dancing divinity' Jessie Matthews, while Herbert Wilcox sought to match Korda with a cycle of historical pictures starring his wife Anna Neagle, including *Nell Gwynn*, *Victoria the Great* and *Sixty Glorious Years*. And other independent producers – including Ludovico Toeplitz, Paul Czinner, Max Schach and Erich Pommer – also sought to cash in on the boom at a time when it was easier than at any time in the history of the industry to raise finance for film production.

The production boom of the mid-1930s had been sustained by a system of speculative financing whereby producers were able to borrow money from banks and investment groups without adequate security or safeguards. The loans were guaranteed by insurance companies with no knowledge or experience of the film industry. This precarious system of finance fell apart following the scandal of Max Schach and the Capitol group.[47] Schach was an Austrian émigré who came to Britain in 1934 at a time when investment was pouring into the film industry following Korda's success with *The Private Life of Henry VIII*. He founded Capitol Film Productions and obtained a loan of £15,000 from the Westminster Bank to produce *Abdul the Damned* (1935). Over the next two years Schach borrowed heavily, most of the loans being arranged through a firm of insurance brokers known as Aldgate Trustees. By 1937 Schach was in serious trouble: the Capitol group had debts of over £1.3 million. An investigation into film finance by sociologist F. D. Klingender and documentary film-maker Stuart Legg published the same year identified 'a financial situation which bears all the characteristics of a highly speculative trade boom'.[48] It was largely as a consequence of the Schach case that the City became wary of further investment in film production. As the Bank of England observed in 1939: 'The British banks and insurance companies, having burnt their fingers over film finance, are now extremely shy of it, and producers here have considerable difficulty in getting finance. Film finance requires experience of trade practice and special knowledge of the actual people in the trade. It was lack of these qualities (in the opinion of the trade) that got British film financing into trouble.'[49]

The outbreak of the Second World War marked yet another moment of crisis for the British film industry.[50] An immediate consequence of the war was that all cinemas – along with other places of public entertainment including theatres and sports venues – were closed in anticipation of air raids. This was a precautionary measure that was not intended to be permanent – cinemas were allowed to reopen over the following two months and would remain open throughout the war even at the height of the Blitz – but it naturally caused much disquiet within the trade. The production sector was also disrupted. Alexander Korda had embarked upon a lavish Technicolor film of *The Thief of Bagdad* at Denham when the war started: he closed it down and – pausing only to produce a quickly made propaganda film called *The Lion Has Wings* that was released within two months of the outbreak of war – relocated his production activities to Hollywood.[51] However, perhaps against expectations, the film industry prospered during the war. In one important respect this would turn out to be a boom period for the industry as attendances increased by around 50 per cent: cinema admissions increased from 1,027 million in 1940 to 1,585 million by 1945.[52] And this was despite increasing ticket prices due to several increases in Entertainment Tax. To some extent the wartime increase in cinema-going was down to the fact that consumer goods were scarce due to wartime austerity. It also reflected the fact that cinema-going was particularly suited to the leisure needs of a transient population including servicemen and mobile workers.

The British production sector contracted significantly during the war: there were 51 British features in 1940, 47 in 1941, 45 in 1942, 50 in 1943, 36 in 1944 and 42 in 1945.[53] Several studios, including Pinewood, Elstree and Amalgamated, were requisitioned as storage facilities or temporary factory accommodation, while Teddington was put out of action when it was hit by a 'doodlebug' in 1944.[54] While the quantity of British films declined, however, the consensus was that the quality had improved: critics detected a renaissance in British film-making that was directly attributed to wartime conditions. In 1943, for example, the *Kine Year Book* noted 'how the war has provided a stimulus for the achievement of a higher average level of quality than ever existed in the days of peace'.[55] The canon of British wartime films – including such titles as *49th Parallel, In Which We Serve, One of Our Aircraft is Missing, Went the Day Well?, Fires Were Started, Millions Like Us, The Gentle Sex, San Demetrio, London, This Happy Breed, The Way Ahead, Waterloo Road* and *The Way to the Stars* – are notable for their realism: they eschew the melodrama of Hollywood in favour of emotional restraint and a sober visual style. It was as if the conditions of war, with its material shortages and economic retrenchment, created the conditions for the emergence of a national cinema that was similarly pared-down and lacking in extravagance and excess. The post-war Arts Enquiry survey *The Factual Film* (written by members of the documentary movement which represented the progressive wing of British film culture and had a particular commitment to social realism) contended that 'the success of films such as *Millions Like Us, The Way Ahead, Waterloo Road* and [*The*] *Way to the Stars* during the war, has shown that there is another way of overcoming Hollywood domination by producing films which reflect the British scene realistically in a way that would be impossible for Hollywood'.[56]

From 1942 the Rank Organisation was the dominant force in the British film industry. The Methodist flour magnate J. Arthur Rank had first become involved in the industry through his sponsorship of the Religious Film Society. In the mid-1930s he joined the consortium that built Pinewood Studios and was the biggest investor in the General Cinema Finance Corporation. At the end of 1941 Rank acquired a controlling interest in the Gaumont-British Picture Corporation and in early 1942 he became the majority shareholder in Odeon Theatres following the death of its founder Oscar Deutsch.[57] Rank now controlled half of the total studio capacity in Britain, the largest British distributor (General Film Distributors) and over 500 cinemas. Growing concerns over the extent of Rank's interests were sufficient for Hugh Dalton, the President of the Board of Trade, to appoint a committee (chaired by banker Albert Palache) to investigate 'Tendencies to Monopoly in the Cinematograph Film Industry'. The Palache Report was published in July 1944: it was a compromise in so far as it expressed concern that two combines (Rank and the Associated British Picture Corporation) controlled a quarter of all cinemas in Britain but drew short of advocating the dismantling of the duopoly.[58] Rank – partly in order to counter the critics of monopoly and partly to enhance his own production programme – bankrolled a group called Independent Producers, which brought together leading independents including The Archers (Michael Powell and Emeric Pressburger), Individual Pictures (Frank Launder and Sidney Gilliat) and Cineguild (David Lean, Anthony Havelock-Allan, Ronald Neame). According to David Lean: 'J. Arthur Rank is often spoken of as an all-embracing monopolist who must be watched lest he crush the creative talents of the British film industry. Let the facts speak for themselves, and I doubt if any group of film-makers in the world can claim as much freedom.'[59]

At the end of the Second World War, the British cinema industry seemed to be in a state of rude economic health. Cinema attendances reached their peak in the first full year of peace: in 1946 there were 1,635 million admissions and total box-office receipts reached £121 million.[60] The trade accepted that the wartime increase in cinema-going had arisen from a combination of unique and specific circumstances and there was an expectation that 'business as normal' would resume after the war; but even so, cinema admissions remained above their pre-war levels for a full decade after 1945. *Kine*'s first post-war British studio supplement saw 'signs of a virile Industry, eager to break loose from the tangle of restrictions and embargoes, and get on with the job for which all its members believe it to be fitted – the job of producing a spate of finely made films expressing all that is best in British life'.[61] Other economic indicators were also positive. Cinema industry equity prices were on the rise: the *Kine* reported that the total share value of the film industry had appreciated by £20 million in 1945 and attributed this to the ambitious international strategy of the Rank Organisation: 'J. Arthur Rank's attempts to put British films on the international map have caught the public fancy, both here and in the U.S.'[62] Alexander Korda also announced his return to Britain when he acquired controlling interests in Sound City Studios and the British Lion Film Corporation.[63] For the first time in a decade British film companies were finding it easier to raise capital through new share issues. The *Kine Year Book* reported that 1946 was 'the most active financial year in the entire history of British films and kinemas'.[64]

There were also encouraging signs that British films – for so long regarded as inferior to their American competitors – were now more than holding their own at the box office. Gainsborough's *The Seventh Veil* was the 'biggest winner' at the British box office in 1945: this was the first time that a British film had taken the number one spot since *49th Parallel* in 1941.[65] Gainsborough took the top spot again in 1946 with *The Wicked Lady*, while Herbert Wilcox's *Piccadilly Incident* was one of two 'runners-up' (the other was *The Bells of St Mary's*).[66] And in 1947 it was three in a row for British films as Wilcox's *The Courtneys of Curzon Street* took the top honour, with four other British pictures – *Great Expectations*, *Odd Man Out*, *Frieda* and *Holiday Camp* – among the six runners-up.[67] (The strong showing of British films in 1947 was due in some measure to a temporary boycott of the British market by Hollywood in retaliation for the imposition of an *ad valorem* duty on imported films meaning that no new American films arrived in Britain for nine months: nevertheless it was also part of a trend rather than an isolated year.) It is notable that the most successful British films of the immediate post-war years marked a return to the escapist melodramatic fare that had not been so prevalent during the war. The sequence of British successes was broken in 1948 by *The Best Years of Our Lives* (a film arriving late in Britain following the embargo), though Wilcox's *Spring in Park Lane* took second place.[68] *The Third Man* – a co-production between Alexander Korda and David O. Selznick – was the top film of 1949.[69]

Another encouraging development in the mid-1940s was that there also seemed to be evidence that British films were gaining a foothold in the lucrative American market. Rank spearheaded what came to be known as the 'prestige film experiment': the production of culturally ambitious films with budgets equivalent to the best that Hollywood had to offer.[70] This trend emerged towards the end of the war with *Henry V* (1944) – produced and directed by Laurence Olivier for Two Cities Films and supported by Rank to the extent of £475,000 – which earned over US $1.2 million when it was released in America in 1946 and won Olivier a special Academy Award for his 'outstanding production achievement ... in bringing *Henry V* to the screen'.[71] Over the following few years, Rank backed a number of expensive super-productions: these included Gabriel Pascal's historical drama *Caesar and Cleopatra* (1945), Wesley Ruggles' revue musical *London Town* (1946), Powell and Pressburger's artistic extravaganza *The Red Shoes* (1948) and Olivier's *Hamlet* (1948).[72] *The Red Shoes* and *Hamlet* returned large profits from the American market, and *Hamlet* also became the first British film to win the Academy Award for Best Picture.[73] However, it was acknowledged that this was a high-risk strategy. The writer and producer R. J. Minney, for example, citing *Men of Two Worlds* (reportedly costing £600,000), *A Matter of Life and Death* (£600,000) and *London Town* – all released in 1946 – argued that Rank 'has been recklessly lavishing large sums on production, spending far above the possibility of a return from the market within his own domination'.[74] And in hindsight Michael Powell – responsible with his writing partner Emeric Pressburger for some of the most artistically ambitious of Rank's prestige pictures, including *A Matter of Life and Death*, *Black Narcissus* and *The Red Shoes* – recognised that it was a risky strategy: 'Emeric and I had made twelve films together, nearly all from original stories, and each one a little more ambitious than the last. Costs had mounted proportionately . . . Obviously, if we couldn't get the world market, then we were heading for disaster.'[75]

The production of more high-budget films raised once again the spectre of production extravagance that had bedevilled the industry in the 1930s but had lain dormant during the war. One film in particular became a byword for the excesses of the film industry: Gabriel Pascal's costly production of *Caesar and Cleopatra* (1945). This film – Pascal's third adaptation of George Bernard Shaw, following *Pygmalion* and *Major Barbara* – ended up costing a massive £1.3 million. It was shot in Technicolor and involved overseas locations in Egypt as well as over a year on the floor at Denham Studios. Pascal's extravagance apparently knew no bounds: he sent a large-scale papier-mâché model of the Sphinx to Egypt and reportedly shipped sand to the Sahara Desert as the Saharan sand was deemed to be the wrong colour.[76] It was not just the film's excessive cost that outraged critics but the time it had taken to complete. For P. L. Mannock, '*Caesar and Cleopatra*'s 80 shooting weeks, attended by farcical extravagance, is something that should never have been allowed to go on so long, and an example never, I hope, to be repeated.'[77] Documentarist and union activist Ralph Bond described *Caesar and Cleopatra* as 'a positive scandal . . . It prevented at least 10 other British films being made.'[78] The Association of Cine Technicians even proposed a motion that 'Gabriel Pascal should not be permitted to make any further films in this country'.[79] In the event *Caesar and Cleopatra* did good business in the United States, where its receipts amounted to over US $2 million.[80] Even so, it recorded an overall deficit of £981,678 and Pascal never did make another film in Britain.[81]

The main problem facing the British film industry at the end of the war was that the production sector remained depressed. It had been expected that the contraction of production during the war would be reversed once the industry returned to normal conditions. However, this was dependent upon the requisitioned studios returning to commercial use. Early in 1945 the Associated British Picture Corporation had warned that it 'is very considerably handicapped in making plans for post-war film production in this country by reason of absence of studio space'.[82] The Bank of England – which was keen to see the quantity of British films increase in order to reduce the volume of American imports – reported that 'the great bottleneck is lack of studio space and has now become so serious that the two larger groups in this country are seriously considering restricting production absolutely in order to reduce overheads'.[83] However, the process of returning studios to civilian use was hampered by shortages of material and labour: the film industry naturally ranked some way behind housing and reconstruction projects in the allocation of scarce resources. A full year after VE day the active production capacity of the British film industry was thirteen studios totalling 46 sound stages, of which nine studios (39 stages) were equipped for major feature production: another eleven studios (26 stages) remained closed.[84] Amalgamated Studios (four stages) and Elstree (seven) had officially been 'demobbed' during the summer of 1945 but remained out of action over a year later. Pinewood (five stages) reopened in April 1946 but was not yet operating at full capacity.[85] In July 1946 the *Kine* predicted that only 40 features would be made during the year and concluded that 'it is now inescapably obvious that we are running into a period of temporary but acute famine of British films'.[86]

The diminished capacity of the production sector was compounded by the lengthening studio schedules of British films. *Caesar and Cleopatra* had been an extreme case, but it exemplified a wider trend across the industry. *London Town* was on the floor at Sound City for 'nearly ten months'.[87] Among the other films of the late 1940s that clogged up space on the studio floor were *Cardboard Cavalier* (18 weeks), *Scott of the Antarctic* (19 weeks), *The Fallen Idol* (19 weeks), *The Passionate Friends* (19 weeks), *The History of Mr Polly* (20 weeks), *Queen of Spades* (22 weeks) and *Bonnie Prince Charlie* (30 weeks).[88] To be fair to producers, the long schedules were not necessarily due entirely to their own extravagance. Ronald Neame, pointing out that the average shooting schedule of an American feature was between 8 and 10 weeks compared to the 12- to 16-week average for a British feature, blamed longer schedules on inadequate studio space and inferior equipment: 'Years ago Hollywood realised that money spent on stages and equipment was an excellent long-term investment which would pay handsome dividends in shorter schedules, and for the sake of the future of the British film Industry we, too, must learn that lesson.'[89] This was confirmed by Ealing Studios' head of production Michael Balcon, who told star John Mills during the production of *Scott of the Antarctic* in 1947: 'It is true that we are really a single-picture outfit here and there is always a little difficulty in raising two absolutely first-class units at the same time, but we thought we had done everything possible in the case of "Scott".'[90]

It took some time for the production sector to revive after the war and even then the volume was still well below pre-war levels: British studios produced 39 features in 1946, 48 in 1947, 68 in 1948 and 77 in 1949.[91] The Cinematograph Exhibitors' Association felt that 'the output of British films needs to be doubled, if not trebled, before the sufficiency can be regarded as satisfactory'.[92] Richard Eadle, chairman of the CEA's Northern branch, felt that high-end prestige films were the wrong type of product ('Does the industry really need these elephantine epics so expensive to everyone concerned? . . . I say that we can well do without these lyrically-belauded leviathans, so frequently box-office "lemons"') and that what exhibitors needed 'are more medium-cost quota films and featurettes from which all superfluous padding has been removed'.[93] The Cinematograph Films Act of 1948 caused an outcry from exhibitors when it raised their quota from its current level of 30 per cent to 45 per cent for first features (a lower level of 25 per cent was set for supporting features and shorts) while removing renters' quota entirely. Sir Alexander King, a leading independent exhibitor in Scotland, described the 45 per cent quota as 'the most ridiculous thing I've ever heard'.[94] An increase in the number of quota defaults by exhibitors was an almost inevitable consequence: the Board of Trade responded to exhibitors' concerns by reducing the quota to 40 per cent in 1949 and back to 30 per cent in 1950. *Kine* welcomed the reduction: 'After three years of trying to solve the film crisis, he [Harold Wilson, President of the Board of Trade] is forced to the conclusion that the industry is right and that legislation alone cannot make pictures nor compel the patron to pay good money to see indifferent pictures.'[95]

By early 1948 the sense of crisis was becoming acute. At the beginning of the year the *Kine* noted 'the appearance of seasonal chilblains in the City of London, where an outbreak of cold feet has occurred on the subject of film finance'.[96] A combination of factors – including the mounting evidence of a decline in cinema admissions, the abolition of renters' quota and the effects of the *ad valorem* duty – made investors wary. Industry share prices fell heavily: the market value of the 'big five' – Gaumont-British Picture Corporation, Associated British Picture Corporation, British and Dominions Film Corporation, Odeon Theatres and Provincial Cinematograph Theatres – had lost £10 million in February 1948 compared to the same time the previous year and 'the paper loss to investors in the same companies has been something like £20,000,000'.[97] *Kine* identified the causes of the 'monetary crisis in British production' as being costs ('Production costs are fantastic, and are geared in expectation of a boom in box-office receipts at a time when the boom is past'), the misguided international strategies of British producers ('Fortunes have been spent chasing the shadow of the American market and the money returned does not justify the increase in production budgets') and a general culture of mismanagement ('The industry still employs many of the wrong people in the wrong jobs').[98] Another warning was sounded later in the year when the British Lion Film Corporation delayed the publication of its accounts: although it reported a profit before tax of £344,784, the fact that its board called an extraordinary general meeting to secure shareholders' consent to borrow £2 million from the newly instituted National Film Finance Company cannot have done anything to reassure investors.[99] Associated Talking Pictures, the parent company of Ealing Studios, reported a 'very heavy adverse balance in the profit and loss account'. The chairman's report blamed the increasing cost of film-making: 'Production costs at present are far too high to enable an economic balance to be maintained in the production side of the industry by itself . . . As yet, however, we have not succeeded in making any appreciable impression on the American market.'[100] At the end of 1948, ABPC ordinary shares were a third down on 1946 prices, GBPC ordinary shares were 50 per cent down, while British Lion and Associated Talking Pictures were listed as having only 'nominal' value.[101] One trade commentator suggested that 'shareholders are beginning to ask whether it is not possible to do less talking and produce more pictures – decent pictures'.[102]

The industry's response to the crisis was to look to cut costs: this meant reducing overheads and laying off staff. Several smaller studios closed – some temporarily – in 1948 and 1949. British National ceased production activities in April 1948 and closed its studios at Elstree (Powell and Pressburger's *The Elusive Pimpernel* was the last film on the floor). It was followed by Highbury Studios in June 1948, Nettlefold Studios in January 1949, Islington and Shepherd's Bush in March 1949 and the Riverside Studios at Hammersmith in July 1949.[103] Ernest G. Roy, the managing director of Nettlefold Studios, blamed the lack of production finance: 'It is finance which prevents our company from going on the floor. We have subjects ready, but we are held up owing to lack of backing.'[104] In November 1948 the *Kine* reported that 'more studio space is dark than at any time since the end of the war': thirteen studios and 26 sound stages were empty and only fifteen films were in production compared to twenty at the same time the previous year.[105] The closure of studios also impacted on employment: the Cinematograph Films Council reported that the number of permanent studio employees fell from 7,253 in March 1948 to 4,104 by March 1950.[106]

By the end of the decade it was apparent that even the largest production groups were experiencing severe difficulties. In April 1949 the British Lion Film Corporation announced that it expected to lose £700,000 on film production for the financial year.[107] In August 1949 the Associated British Picture Corporation reported a 'satisfactory' profit of £2 million, but acknowledged that it had increased its provision for loss on production and felt that 'net receipts cannot be expected to increase'.[108] The nadir of the crisis came in November 1949 when the Rank Organisation revealed that it had lost £3,350,000 on film production and distribution over the previous financial year and that the group overall was running an overdraft of over £16 million. J. Arthur Rank announced a significant retrenchment in his production activities and even hinted that he might have to withdraw from film-making entirely if there was not some reduction in Entertainment Tax:

> We have decided to plan for the shooting of between six to ten films during the six months ending June 1950, which will keep our studios turning over and in first-class condition, and enable us to maintain the nucleus of our production organisation ... I hope that before a decision has to be made on the period following June, the Government will have considered the problems of the industry and will have announced an alleviation of the burden of entertainment tax.[109]

Rank was the flagship of the British cinema industry as a whole and its woes were a matter of grave concern: 'The organisation launched so courageously and with such high hopes to be the spear-point of the British assault on world markets is now floundering in a financial morass from which apparently only the Government can extricate it.'[110]

The narrative of crisis has pervaded the critical historiography of British cinema to the extent that it has become something of a *praesumpseram*. Nevertheless there was a sense that the problems of the production sector in the late 1940s were as serious as at any time in the history of the industry. Harold Wilson remarked in a speech to the British Film Producers' Association in March 1949: 'While the industry is generally prone to exaggeration and the word "crisis" is often used in it to denote any event that may attract the attention of the Press, it must be admitted that there exists today serious under-employment of the resources of film production.'[111] On the one hand some of the industry's problems arose from the specific conditions prevailing at the time: the drought of British films, the rising costs of production and the consequences of the failure to secure a foothold in the American market. But on the other hand the crisis was also rooted in the long-term structural weaknesses of the industry: the instability of a production sector that depended on short-term finance and the fact that the home market was too small to guarantee a profitable return for British producers. As the Cinematograph Films Council observed in its report for 1950: 'During the year the difficulties of the British film industry have continued and its fundamental economic problems seem unfortunately to be no nearer to a solution'.[112]

Notes

1. Political and Economic Planning, *The British Film Industry: A report on its history and present organisation, with special reference to the economic problems of British feature film production* (London: Political and Economic Planning, 1952), p. 11.
2. 'Loan from Film "Bank"', *The Financial Times*, 23 September 1948, p. 1.
3. 'Films and the Future', *The Economist*, 12 November 1949, p. 1076.
4. 'A Victim of Circumstance', *Kinematograph Weekly*, 10 November 1949, p. 4.
5. 'Production Will Live If Tradition Dies – says J. K. Morris', *Kinematograph Weekly: Studio Review*, 27 March 1958, p. iii.
6. *Parliamentary Debates: House of Commons*, 5th Series, vol. 686, 20 December 1963, col. 1665.
7. *The Financing of the British Film Industry: Second Report of the Interim Action Committee on the Film Industry*, Cmnd. 7597 (June 1979), p. 1 (1).
8. C. A. Oakley, *Where We Came In: Seventy Years of the British Film Industry* (London: George Allen & Unwin, 1964), p. 7.
9. Ernest Betts, *The Film Business: A History of British Cinema 1896–1972* (London: George Allen & Unwin, 1973), p. 12.
10. George Perry, *The Great British Picture Show* (London: Pavilion, rev. edn 1985), p. 9.
11. Julian Petley, 'Cinema and State', in Charles Barr (ed.), *All Our Yesterdays: 90 Years of British Cinema* (London: British Film Institute, 1986), p. 35.
12. Sarah Street, *British National Cinema* (London: Routledge, 1997), p. 197.
13. Robert C. Allen and Douglas Gomery, *Film History: Theory and Practice* (New York: McGraw-Hill, 1985), p. 132.
14. Political and Economic Planning, *The British Film Industry*, p. 49.
15. Rachael Low, *The History of the British Film 1929–1939: Film Making in 1930s Britain* (London: George Allen & Unwin, 1985), p. 270.
16. Margaret Dickinson and Sarah Street, *Cinema and State: The Film Industry and the British Government 1927–84* (London: British Film Institute, 1985), p. 10.
17. Gerben Bakker, 'The Decline and Fall of the European Film Industry: Sunk Costs, Market Size and Market Structure, 1890–1927', *Economic History Review*, 58: 2 (2005), p. 327.
18. BFI Balcon A/59: Angus MacPhail, 'Memorandum on types of production', 7 May 1930.
19. The historical and critical literature includes Rachael Low and Roger Manvell, *The History of the British Film 1896–1906* (London: George Allen & Unwin, 1948); Michael Chanan, *The Dream That Kicks: The Prehistory and Early Years of Cinema in Britain* (London: Routledge & Kegan Paul, 1980); and Andrew Higson (ed.), *Young and Innocent? The Cinema in Britain 1896–1930* (Exeter: University of Exeter Press, 2002). A summary of the current state of research can be found in Bryony Dixon, 'The Origins of

British Cinema 1895–1918', in I. Q. Hunter, Laraine Porter and Justin Smith (eds), *The Routledge Companion to British Cinema History* (London: Routledge, 2017), pp. 23–33.
20. Jon Burrows, *The British Cinema Boom, 1909–1914: A Commercial History* (London: Palgrave Macmillan, 2017), p. 20.
21. Ibid. p. 2.
22. Charles Barr, 'Before *Blackmail*: British Silent Cinema', in Robert Murphy (ed.), *The British Cinema Book* (London: British Film Institute, 1997), p. 15.
23. Rachael Low, *The History of the British Film 1906–1914* (London: George Allen & Unwin, 1949), p. 54.
24. *Parliamentary Debates: House of Commons*, 5th Series, vol. 203, 16 March 1927, col. 2044.
25. Kristin Thompson, *Exporting Entertainment: America in the World Film Market, 1907–1934* (London: British Film Institute, 1985), p. 216.
26. Michael Hammond, *The Big Show: British Cinema Culture in the Great War 1914–1918* (Exeter: University of Exeter Press, 2006), pp. 174–215.
27. Rachael Low, *The History of the British Film 1914–1918* (London: George Allen & Unwin, 1950), p. 49.
28. Thompson, *Exporting Entertainment*, pp. 100–47.
29. However, for a more sympathetic assessment, see Olly Gruner, '"Good Business, Good Policy, Good Patriotism": The British Film Weeks of 1924', *Historical Journal of Film, Radio and Television*, 32: 1 (2013), pp. 41–56.
30. Nathalie Morris, 'An Eminent Series: *The Adventures of Sherlock Holmes* and the Stoll Film Company', *Journal of British Cinema and Television*, 4: 1 (2007), pp. 18–36.
31. Dickinson and Street, *Cinema and State*, p. 13.
32. S. G. Rayment, 'The Story of 1924', *Kinematograph Year Book 1925* (London: Kinematograph Publications, 1925), p. 12.
33. The contexts of the Quota Act are discussed in Dickinson and Street, *Cinema and State*, pp. 5–33; Simon Hartog, 'State Protection of a Beleaguered Industry', in James Curran and Vincent Porter (eds), *British Cinema History* (London: Weidenfeld & Nicolson, 1983), pp. 59–73; and Low, *The History of the British Film 1929–1939*, pp. 33–53.
34. *Parliamentary Debates: House of Commons*, 5th Series, vol. 203, 16 March 1927, col. 2039.
35. Linda Wood (ed.), *British Films 1927–1939: BFI Reference Guide* (London: British Film Institute, 1986), p. 117.
36. Simon Rowson, 'A Statistical Survey of the Cinema Industry in Great Britain in 1934', *Journal of the Royal Statistical Society*, 99: 1 (1934), p. 117.
37. 'Will British Films Improve?', *Kinematograph Weekly*, 2 January 1930, p. 67.
38. Lawrence Napper, 'A Despicable Tradition? Quota Quickies in the 1930s', in Robert Murphy (ed.), *The British Cinema Book* (London: British Film Institute, 1997), pp. 37–47; Linda Wood, 'Julius Hagen and Twickenham Film Studios', in Jeffrey Richards (ed.), *The Unknown 1930s: An Alternative History of British Cinema, 1929–1939* (London: I. B. Tauris, 1998), pp. 37–55; and Steve Chibnall, *Quota Quickies: The Birth of the British 'B' Film* (London: Palgrave/British Film Institute, 2007).
39. A. J. P. Taylor, *English History 1914–1945* (Oxford: Oxford University Press, 1965), p. 313.
40. Rowson, 'A Statistical Survey of the Cinema Industry in Great Britain in 1934', p. 115.
41. Jeffrey Richards, *The Age of the Dream Palace: Cinema and Society in Britain 1930–39* (London: Routledge & Kegan Paul, 1984), pp. 24–33.

42. John Sedgwick, *Popular Filmgoing in 1930s Britain: A Choice of Pleasures* (Exeter: University of Exeter Press, 2000), p. 101.
43. BFI London Films Collection Box 5: Memorandum listing production costs and revenues of London Films productions by Sir David Cunynghame, 7 January 1946.
44. Sarah Street, 'Stepping Westward: The distribution of British feature films in America, and the case of *The Private Life of Henry VIII*', in Justine Ashby and Andrew Higson (eds), *British Cinema, Past and Present* (London: Routledge, 2000), pp. 51–62.
45. Perry, *The Great British Picture Show*, p. 76.
46. Sarah Street, 'Alexander Korda, Prudential Assurance and British film finance in the 1930s', *Historical Journal of Film, Radio and Television*, 6: 2 (1986), pp. 161–79.
47. Low, *The History of the British Film 1929–1939*, pp. 199–208. See also Naomi Collinson, 'The Legacy of Max Schach', *Film History*, 15: 3 (2003), pp. 376–89.
48. F. D. Klingender and Stuart Legg, *Money Behind the Screen: A Report prepared on behalf of the Film Council* (London: Lawrence & Wishart, 1937), p. 48.
49. BEA EC 4/248: 'Films: Note on Suggested Policy', 25 October 1939.
50. See Anthony Aldgate and Jeffrey Richards, *Britain Can Take It: The British Cinema in the Second World War* (Oxford: Basil Blackwell, 1986); Philip M. Taylor (ed.), *Britain and the Cinema in the Second World War* (London: Macmillan, 1988); Robert Murphy, *Realism and Tinsel: Cinema and Society in Britain, 1939–48* (London: Routledge, 1989); and James Chapman, *The British at War: Cinema, State and Propaganda, 1939–1945* (London: I. B. Tauris, 1998).
51. Karol Kulik, *Alexander Korda: The Man Who Could Work Miracles* (London: W. H. Allen, 1975), pp. 232, 240–5.
52. *Kinematograph Year Book 1953* (London: Odhams Press, 1953), p. 519.
53. Linda Wood (ed.), *British Film Industry: Reference Guide No. 1* (London: British Film Institute Information and Education Department, 1980), Appendix A, unpaginated.
54. 'Warner Bros. Closing Film Studios', *The Financial Times*, 27 October 1944, p. 3.
55. *Kinematograph Year Book 1943* (London: Kinematograph Publications, 1943), p. 263.
56. The Arts Enquiry, *The Factual Film: A Survey Sponsored by the Dartington Hall Trustees* (London: Geoffrey Cumberlege/Oxford University Press, 1947), p. 201.
57. The best summary of the growth of the Rank empire is Geoffrey Macnab, *J. Arthur Rank and the British Film Industry* (London: Routledge, 1993), pp. 17–34.
58. The Palache Report is discussed in Dickinson and Street, *Cinema and State*, pp. 139–49.
59. David Lean, 'Brief Encounter', *The Penguin Film Review*, 4 (October 1947), p. 34.
60. Political and Economic Planning, *The British Film Industry*, p. 93.
61. 'Trade is Poised for its Biggest Production Drive in History', *Kinematograph Weekly: British Studio Supplement*, 6 June 1946, p. iii.
62. 'Kinema Equities Rise by £20,000,000 During 1945', *Kinematograph Weekly*, 3 January 1946, p. 5.
63. 'Korda Completes Deal for Control of Sound City', *Kinematograph Weekly*, 4 April 1946, p. 29.
64. V. J. Burtt, 'Financial Review of 1946', *Kinematograph Year Book 1947* (London: Kinematograph Publications Ltd, 1947), p. 438.
65. '1945 Box-Office Stakes: A Very Exciting Race Ends With a Photo-Finish', *Kinematograph Weekly*, 17 January 1946, p. 50.
66. 'The Most Momentous Year in the History of the Industry', *Kinematograph Weekly*, 19 December 1946, p. 27.

67. 'What the Box Office Returns Show for 1947', *Kinematograph* Weekly, 18 December 1947, p. 13.
68. 'Box-Office Return for 1948', *Kinematograph Weekly*, 16 December 1948, p. 15.
69. 'Tops at Home', *The Courier-Mail* (Brisbane), 31 December 1949, p. 4.
70. Political and Economic Planning, *The British Film Industry*, pp. 96–8.
71. Sarah Street, *Transatlantic Crossings: British Feature Films in the United States* (London: Continuum, 2002), p. 99.
72. Robert Murphy, 'Rank's Attempt on the American Market, 1944–9', in James Curran and Vincent Porter (eds), *British Cinema History* (London: Weidenfeld & Nicolson, 1983), pp. 164–78.
73. According to information provided by the Rank Organisation for the Board of Trade, *The Red Shoes* earned £1,291,300 for the producer against a production cost of £505,600 and *Hamlet* returned £1,352,200 against a production cost of £572,500. TNA BT 64/4490: J. Arthur Rank Organisation Ltd: Memorandum regarding Film Production and Distribution, Schedule IV, 26 January 1950.
74. 'Minney and costs', *Kinematograph Weekly*, 6 February 1947, p. 20.
75. Michael Powell, *A Life in Movies: An Autobiography* (London: Heinemann, 1986), p. 664.
76. Valerie Pascal, *The Disciple and His Devil* (London: Michael Joseph, 1971), p. 105.
77. 'Kinematograph Studios', *Kinematograph Weekly*, 24 January 1946, p. 37.
78. '"Caesar" – A Scandal', *Kinematograph Weekly*, 7 March 1946, p. 26A.
79. 'ACT Will Criticise High Film Production Costs at AGM', *Kinematograph Weekly*, 25 April 1946, p. 13. In the event the motion was watered down to declare that Pascal 'be severely censured and only allowed to make pictures in this country subject to special control'.
80. Street, *Transatlantic Crossings*, p. 106.
81. Anne Bolton, 'Independent Producers Ltd: A Case Study of an Independent British Production Group of the 1940s' (PhD thesis, University of Leicester, 2020), p. 152.
82. TNA BT 64/95: E. Lightfoot to Board of Trade, 18 January 1945.
83. Ibid.: G. L. F. Bolton to E. Rowe-Dutton, 26 March 1945.
84. 'British Studios', *Kinematograph Weekly: British Studio Supplement*, 6 June 1946, p. iv.
85. 'Pinewood Studios are Reopened: £2,000,000 Budget This Year', *Kinematograph Weekly*, 11 April 1946, p. 6.
86. 'British Film Famine', *Kinematograph Weekly*, 11 July 1946, p. 4.
87. 'Ruggles' problems', *Kinematograph Weekly*, 11 July 1946, p. 18.
88. 'British Production Survey', *Kinematograph Year Book 1949* (London: Odhams Press, 1949), pp. 152–4.
89. 'Shorter Schedules Are Essential If We Are To Reduce Film Production Costs', *Kinematograph Weekly: British Studio Supplement*, 6 June 1946, p. xv.
90. BFI Balcon G/79: Michael Balcon to John Mills, 22 October 1947.
91. Wood (ed.), *British Film Industry: Reference Guide No. 1*, Appendix A, unpaginated.
92. 'CEA Says: We Want Three Times As Many British Films', *Kinematograph Weekly*, 7 March 1946, p. 3.
93. 'Ten Films Could Have Been Made for the Price of One: Medium-Cost Quota Subjects Needed', *Kinematograph Weekly*, 3 January 1946, p. 17.
94. 'Film Booking Crisis Intensifies', *Kinematograph Weekly*, 10 June 1948, p. 3.
95. 'The First Hurdle', *Kinematograph Weekly*, 16 March 1950, p. 4.
96. 'The Dangers of Abolition', *Kinematograph Weekly*, 8 January 1948, p. 4.

97. '£2,500,000 Drop in Film Shares', *Kinematograph Weekly*, 26 February 1948, p. 3.
98. 'Long Shots', *Kinematograph Weekly*, 26 February 1948, p. 4.
99. 'British Lion Film', *The Financial Times*, 13 October 1948, p. 2.
100. 'Associated Talking Pictures', *The Financial Times*, 28 December 1948, p. 7.
101. *Kinematograph Year Book 1949* (London: Odhams Press, 1949), p. 531.
102. 'Shares Fall Heavier – Holders Growing Restless', *Kinematograph Weekly*, 24 February 1949, p. 18.
103. 'London Films Pulls Out of British National', *Kinematograph Weekly*, 17 February 1949, p. 22; '"Highbury Studios Closing Down" – Elvin', *Kinematograph Weekly*, 10 June 1948, p. 3; 'Riverside Studios Shut Down', *Kinematograph Weekly*, 28 July 1949, p. 3; 'Two Rank Studios for Sale', *Kinematograph Weekly*, 15 September 1949, p. 3.
104. 'Nettlefold Studios to Close Unless –', *Kinematograph Weekly*, 6 January 1949, p. 3.
105. 'Production Crisis in Figures', *Kinematograph Weekly*, 18 November 1948, p. 3.
106. *Twelfth Report of the Cinematograph Films Council relating to the Year Ended 31 March 1950*, Paper No. 62 (May 1950), p. 1 (4).
107. 'All British Lion Films Except Two Showing a Loss', *Kinematograph Weekly*, 28 April 1949, p. 3.
108. 'Associated British Picture Corporation', *The Economist*, 13 August 1949, p. 381.
109. 'Rank Tells the Story of His Losses', *Kinematograph Weekly*, 10 November 1949, p. 6.
110. 'A Victim of Circumstance', p. 4.
111. TNA BT 64/4515: 'Present State of the Film Industry', speech prepared for the President of the Board of Trade, March 1949.
112. *Twelfth Report of the Cinematograph Films Council*, p. 1 (4).

CHAPTER 2

Bogart or Bacon

> In any conceivable circumstances the available supply of dollars for this country will be extremely limited; and the continuing expenditure of over $80,000,000 a year cannot be justified, in my submission, on any ground. I would like to confess to the House that I have great admiration for the acting of Mr Humphrey Bogart; and for the same reason as applied to every film fan, that I can see in him on the screen the presentation of the man I would like to be. Nevertheless, if I am compelled to choose between Bogart or bacon, I am bound to choose bacon at the present time. (Robert Boothby)[1]

The Labour government elected in 1945 faced a possibly unprecedented degree of economic problems. While the end of the war came quicker than expected – Japan surrendered in August 1945 following the destruction of the cities of Hiroshima and Nagasaki by US atomic bombs – many difficulties lay ahead as Britain adjusted from war to peace. The country was to all intents and purposes bankrupt after six years of total war: the National Debt had quadrupled and capital assets worth around £1,300 million had been liquidated.[2] The lifeline offered by Lend-Lease – through which the United States had provided Britain with war materials and other goods – was cut off by President Truman immediately at the war's end. The Treasury's influential economic adviser John Maynard Keynes warned that a perfect storm of adverse economic conditions – a weakened manufacturing base, dependence upon imports and a massive trade deficit – had left Britain facing 'an economic Dunkirk'.[3] Keynes was a member of a Treasury team that negotiated a loan of £938 million from the US government in November 1945 (US $3,750,000 million) but it was exacted at a high price: as well as annual interest of 2 per cent it came with the condition that sterling would become freely convertible against the dollar from July 1947.

At the same time as facing its economic Dunkirk, however, the Labour government had committed itself to an ambitious (and expensive) programme of social and economic reform. This included the introduction of a comprehensive welfare state 'from the cradle to the grave', a National Health Service free at the point of use and the nationalisation of key industries and public utilities. It also maintained wartime levels of spending on defence: the Labour government still regarded Britain as a global power – despite the early incidences of decolonisation signalled by independence for India, Pakistan and Burma – and in 1946 it decided to embark (secretly) upon the development of a British atomic bomb at an estimated cost of

£1,000 million. Historian Paul Kennedy summarises the underlying problem facing the post-war government in his book *The Realities Behind Diplomacy*: 'Given the pressing need to restore a balanced economy and the perceived threats to British interests during the Cold War, this inevitably meant that the political nation was again faced with a choice between guns or butter. By and large, as we shall see, the nation chose butter.'[4]

Or – as Robert Boothby, the Labour MP for Aberdeenshire and Kincardineshire, put it during a parliamentary debate on the film industry in November 1945 – between 'Bogart or bacon'. This was the first major debate on the British film industry since the end of the war and it came to focus on the question of the amount spent on film imports. The timing of the debate was significant as it coincided with the negotiation of the American loan. A consequence of the condition of the loan that currency controls should be liberalised was the need for Britain to reduce its balance of payments deficit in order to protect sterling when it became convertible: to do this it needed to curtail dollar expenditure. The trade in films reflected in microcosm the wider balance of payments deficit: not only did Britain spend more on importing films than it earned from exporting them, but the deficit had increased significantly during the war. In the late 1930s Britain had spent around £9 million a year on American films: this was the amount remitted back to the United States by American distributors from the receipts of their films in the United Kingdom.[5] Between 1940 and 1942 the US film industry had agreed a voluntary freeze on a proportion of its British revenues in return for a reduced renters' quota: the American companies were able to use their blocked sterling to invest in producing films in Britain. However, the Bank of England was never happy about this arrangement. According to its Governor, Montagu Norman: 'We have always disliked blocked sterling in principle and only accepted the procedure because of our difficult exchange position at the time. In particular we have disliked blocking current earnings which only means deferring a liability.'[6]

This was the context for the 'Bogart or bacon' debate. While films accounted for only around 4 per cent of Britain's total dollar expenditure – this was much less than the sums spent on foodstuffs and tobacco – it was inevitable that non-essential items should come under scrutiny. The debate in the House of Commons touched upon a wide range of issues relating to the film industry, including the lack of studio space in Britain and the value of film as a medium of national projection, but it was Boothby's emotive linking of film imports to food shortages that really caught the mood of politicians and set the terms of the debate. Boothby saw the problem in the context of the pursuit of economic aid from the United States: 'If the Government have decided to borrow a very large sum at a considerable rate of interest from the United States, and to go back to the gold standard and multilateral free trade without discrimination at the price, then I suppose the film industry will have to be included in the general "sell-out" of Great Britain.'[7] The debate suggested that both sides of the House understood the problem, though suggestions for constructive solutions were notably lacking. Conservative MP Derek Walker-Smith summed up the issue as being 'the relationship between two very important matters, dollars and films – dollars which this country badly needs, and of which it has all too few, and films which this country greatly likes, and of which it has a tolerably sufficient supply of extraneous origin'.[8]

The Treasury had in fact drawn up plans for a total freeze on film imports as early as August 1945: it was not introduced for fear that it would upset the Americans at a time when Britain was negotiating its loan from the US government.[9] It was also recognised that the British production sector was depressed at the end of the war and would be unable on its own to meet the public demand for films. In February 1947 Hugh Dalton, the Chancellor of the Exchequer, stated that 'for the moment the production of British films is not sufficient to fill the screens and the filmgoing public must, I think, count on seeing films from the U.S., and other places as things stand at present'.[10] Other members of the government were also keen to reassure the cinema trade. Sir Stafford Cripps, the President of the Board of Trade, told the Cinematograph Exhibitors' Association that he did not want to see restrictions on film imports: 'It is not that we want to close our markets to films from other countries – far from it. Let our people see the best of the films from any country and every country, but we must not, because of our weakness and inability, hand over a monopoly of our own market to foreign producers.'[11] Cripps's rhetoric of protecting the British film industry from control by foreign interests was consistent with the political discourses around British cinema since the Cinematograph Films Act of 1927: it was coupled with the usual bland statements about ensuring the production of high-quality British films. Hugh Gaitskell, Parliamentary Under-Secretary at the Ministry of Fuel and Power, demonstrated a more nuanced understanding of the problem. He pointed out that 'it's the important films that really take the money. Probably 90 per cent of what we pay goes in respect of about 20 per cent of the films imported.' Simply reducing imports would make little difference 'because the real moneymakers would still come in'.[12]

The alternative strategy for redressing the balance of payments was to increase the export of British films to the United States. The American market was four times the size of Britain's: in 1946 there were an estimated 18,000 cinemas in the United States and around 90 million admissions per week compared to 4,800 cinemas and 30 million admissions a week in Britain.[13] At this point J. Arthur Rank was of the view that producing British films for American screens was the best way of addressing the dollar shortage:

> Now that the screens of the American kinemas are open, it is up to us of British films to put into our motion pictures every possible element that will attract greater numbers of American picture goers to the box-office. This will increase our dollar intake and thus give us the means of buying more foodstuffs, machinery and other items for our own people at home.[14]

However, the extent to which American screens really were open to British films needs to be qualified. Some British films did well but they tended to be exceptional; and for much of the time their exhibition was limited to cinephile audiences in large metropolitan centres rather than the so-called 'mom and pop' theatres of the

Midwest.[15] In truth there never was a realistic prospect that British film exports would make any significant reduction in the dollar balance. In 1946 the value of American films exhibited in Britain amounted to US $60 million, whereas British films drew only $600,000 from the American market.[16]

With the prospect of reducing the film payments deficit through increased exports an unrealistic proposition, Whitehall considered different ways of controlling imports. One was to establish a state company for film imports: however, this was politically problematic as it would effectively give the state a monopoly over distribution and would undoubtedly create problems with the Americans. A second option – supported by the Inland Revenue – was to tax the profits of American companies at a higher rate. A third option – and the one eventually adopted – was the introduction of an *ad valorem* duty on imported films. There were two drawbacks to this scheme. One was that an import duty was paid up front rather than as a tax on receipts: as it was impossible to estimate the value of individual films whose worth would be revealed only by their box-office receipts this would necessitate setting the duty at a fixed amount. American trade interests estimated this would probably be around 30 per cent. The other potential problem with the import duty was that it might provoke the US film industry into taking retaliatory action against British films in America or even, in a worst-case scenario, boycotting the British market.

The Board of Trade believed – mistakenly as it turned out – that the Americans would not resort to a full boycott: 'The Americans will not like it; but the Board of Trade do not fear that they will refuse to supply films. It will not help our films in the U.S. but, on a long-term view, the American interests have more to lose from open hostilities.'[17] This view was not necessarily as hubristic as it seems in hindsight. The US film industry no longer held the same hegemony over world markets that it had enjoyed before the war: it had lost most of its continental European markets during the war and, while there was a concerted effort by the Motion Picture Export Association to open these up again after 1945, Hollywood had to contend with protectionist measures introduced in European countries that sought to revitalise domestic industries by imposing quotas or tariffs. In April 1947 the US trade paper *Variety* reported that the film industry was 'engaged in a desperate struggle to maintain its position in the international market against the triple threat abroad of a hard money famine, social chaos and a violent nationalism'.[18] Britain remained by some distance Hollywood's most lucrative overseas market: some estimates were that during the war it had accounted for 90 per cent of Hollywood's foreign revenues and even following the opening up of other European markets after the war Britain was still worth over 50 per cent of the total. And the US film industry was also facing difficulties at home: cinema attendances were declining and a sword of Damocles was hanging over the industry in the form of an anti-trust case lodged by the Department of Justice in 1938 that had been suspended during the war but was about to be reopened. The consequent Supreme Court decision in 1948 ruled that the vertically integrated studios should separate their exhibition interests from their production and distribution arms.

Hence the US film industry was facing up to the prospect of fundamental structural changes: this did not seem the moment for a boycott of its biggest overseas market.

It was over the summer of 1947 that the possibility of a duty on imported films gained momentum. The immediate context was that 15 July 1947 was the date at which sterling became convertible against the dollar: the government feared a run on its gold and dollar reserves if the trade deficit was not reduced. At the end of June Dalton tabled a motion that would allow the government to tax foreign films. Initially the film trade was not unduly concerned: 'It is improbable that anything drastic is contemplated immediately in the tabling of the motion. The realistic view is to assume that it is merely an enabling measure so that any time the Government could impose a tax if they decided on one.'[19] There were assurances that any tax would not be passed on to renters and exhibitors. *Kine* editor Connery Chappell predicted that if an import duty were imposed, it would almost certainly prompt a tit-for-tat response from the United States but that such an action might benefit the British film production industry by forcing it away from uneconomic superproductions: '[It] is a fact that more and more companies are realising that they cannot continue spending, say, £250,000 on pictures which are guaranteed nothing but their home market . . . This duty, if applied, would most probably close the American door, and this might result in a compulsory economy in picture costs over here.'[20] By the middle of July – when Dalton and Sir Stafford Cripps met MPEA president Eric Johnston on a trip to Europe – continuing speculation over the duty had caused cinema share prices to fall.[21] By early August the trade seemed to accept that a film duty was more likely than not: while it disliked the idea, it accepted that the nation faced 'an economic crisis as serious in its way as was Dunkirk. The whole standing of Britain as a first-class power is in danger; so is the whole standard of living of its citizens.'[22]

The industry therefore braced itself for the imposition of a duty; but what it did not expect was the level at which the duty would be set. On 6 August Dalton announced that an *ad valorem* duty of 75 per cent would be introduced with immediate effect on all imported films.[23] For once it was not hyperbole when the *Kine* remarked that the news hit the industry 'with all the impact of an atom bomb' and 'brought about the greatest crisis which the British film industry has had to face'.[24] It soon became apparent that the government had seriously miscalculated the American response. The MPEA retaliated by announcing that it would send no new films to Britain until the duty was lifted: the embargo came into effect on 29 August.[25] At the time of the embargo American distributors in Britain were holding 125 films as yet unreleased: this was estimated to be enough to last for six months.[26] Exhibitors were concerned that they would be stuck with an insufficient diet – in both quality and quantity – of British films and reissues. W. R. Fuller, the general secretary of the CEA, put it starkly: 'If the American withdrawal continues, it is only a matter of time before all the British kinemas close.'[27] The immediate economic impact of the duty and the boycott was that the market value of the three main British cinema chains lost £5 million.[28]

It has sometimes been suggested that the 'Dalton duty' (as it soon became known) was an attempt to provide additional protection for the British production sector. British producers seemed on the face of it to have been presented with an opportunity to claim back their home market as their main competitor had been removed. However, it soon became apparent that British producers would be unable to step up production to fill the void left by American films. In January 1948 the *Kine* reported that British studios had produced only 56 feature films during the previous year and that 'all the British subjects are not first features, many being in the "featurette" class'.[29] This was wholly insufficient to supply exhibitors with a steady stream of new product. In fact, the US boycott had an adverse affect on British production as the consequent contraction of the exhibition sector meant that box-office revenues were expected to fall. This in turn made investors wary of loaning money to the film industry. *Kine* reported that 'there has been something of a full stop in the financing of independent British films and the British studio picture generally is not an expanding one at that very moment when it is most important that the utmost possible stimulus should be given to British production'. It suggested 'that it is very desirable – to British producers as well as to Americans – that free traffic in films be resumed as early as possible'.[30]

The fallout from the Dalton duty had implications far beyond the film industry. The Board of Trade's miscalculation over the likelihood of a retaliatory boycott had embarrassed the British government at a time when its loan from the United States was nearly exhausted and when Britain was trying to negotiate further aid. The *Kine* was on the button when it pointed out that 'the British film tax was a political shock to the American nation. They gave us a loan and they did not expect to be taxed out of their trading in a key industry.'[31] It has been suggested – for example, by Margaret Dickinson and Sarah Street in their account of the film duty crisis in their book *Cinema and State* – that the real motive behind the duty was to impress upon the US government the extent of Britain's economic problems in order to procure more aid: 'The overriding consideration behind both the imposition of the duty and the management of the boycott seems to have been not the hope of obtaining some trivial dollar savings on film imports, but the need to bring home to the Americans the serious nature of Britain's economic predicament and to put pressure on them to provide more assistance.'[32] This is supported by contemporary accounts which suggest the duty was so punitive that it must have been imposed with a view to securing some other concession. *Kine* speculated: 'The new tax is so impracticable that it has resulted in the immediate withdrawal of all American films from the market . . . So far-fetched and grotesque is the situation that has arisen that there is even a school of thought that this industry is in fact something of a chip in an elaborate political poker game.'[33] It may be that there is some credence to this argument. Within only a few weeks of the boycott, the trade was able to report 'a qualified and guarded optimism . . . that the present 75 per cent import duty on foreign films reaching Britain will be modified as a result of the economic talks now proceeding between British spokesmen and the United States Department of

State in Washington'.[34] Sir Wilfrid Eady, the Second Secretary to the Treasury, was a member of the British negotiating team in Washington in August 1947. Eady met Eric Johnston and Allen Dulles (at the time a partner in the law firm Sullivan Cromwell who was engaged in lobbying the State Department on behalf of the MPEA) and sent a positive report of the meeting back to London: 'There were a number of points on which there need be no dispute, but they all came down to one point – that they needed earnings from our market and it was quite likely that our people needed their films.'[35]

Several rounds of negotiations followed between the autumn of 1947 and the spring of 1948. Dalton was no longer involved: the worsening economic situation had compelled his resignation in November 1947. He was replaced as Chancellor of the Exchequer – via a short tenure as Minister for Economic Affairs – by Sir Stafford Cripps. Cripps's replacement at the Board of Trade was Harold Wilson. Connery Chappel was initially sceptical about Wilson: he felt that 'the present Government brings to the film trade the approach of the school teacher and the *New Statesman* reader. I don't suppose Harold Wilson has ever queued up for Betty Grable in his life.'[36] In fact, Wilson would prove not only to have a good understanding of the problems of the film industry but would also be instrumental in the introduction of two key measures to support it: the National Film Finance Corporation and the British Film Production Fund. For the time being, however, his foremost concern was finding a resolution to the film duty crisis. Wilson bore no responsibility for the duty and was keen to distance himself from it. He felt the consequences had been 'most unfortunate for our producers. The American industry chose to regard the duty as an act of war against themselves.'[37]

The negotiations were nevertheless fraught with difficulties. Eady outlined the main issues in a memorandum in late August 1947:

> In relation to the present situation we have to remember three things about this industry:
> 1. It is an extremely powerful lobby in the State Department and capable of very considerable malice.
> 2. Our primary tactical objective with the United States Administration is to regain early access to the frozen United States credit. It is scarcely conceivable that the United States will release the credit without making some conditions to meet American interests: e.g. either reduction or repeal of the film tax.
> 3. Behind all this lies the Marshall Plan and what we may hope to get out of it. Here again one must expect this powerful lobby to be exercised against us in the discussions that will take place on the Marshall Plan.[38]

Eady's coupling of the repeal of the film import duty to the British government's application for credit again lends substance to the view that the duty had been a negotiating tool, albeit a drastic one, rather than being seen as a solution in itself. The Marshall Plan (or European Recovery Programme) was an initiative for the economic reconstruction of post-war Europe that would provide cash loans which European nations could use to buy goods from the United States: it was devised by

US Secretary of State George C. Marshall. Britain would benefit from Marshall Aid to the tune of £1,775 million between 1948 and 1952.[39]

The main stumbling block in the Anglo-American negotiations was that the British needed to bring home a very substantial dollar saving: the balance of payments had already worsened to the extent that the convertibility of sterling was temporarily suspended only a few months after coming into effect. The first initiative came from the American side. Fay Allport, the London representative of the MPEA, suggested that in return for removing the duty the US interests would agree to a blocked sterling arrangement similar to that which had been instituted during the war. Eady was opposed on the grounds that blocked sterling might be to the detriment of the British production industry: 'We were not anxious to have very large sums of American money invested in film production in this country. The pressure of large amounts might inflate costs in the industry and press out British producers while destroying the national character of British films.'[40] Eady suggested reducing the duty to 50 per cent and allowing 25 per cent of Hollywood's British earnings to be remitted. Wilson insisted that any agreement on film remittances should be linked to an undertaking from US distributors to make better efforts at promoting British films in America.

The British were still holding out for maintaining the duty at some level when Eric Johnston, evidently tiring of the stalling tactics of the British negotiators, took the drastic step of approaching Lord Inverchaple, the British ambassador in Washington, to enlist his 'help in seeking ways whereby negotiations could be resumed and a settlement reached before further harm was done to both United Kingdom interests and to those of the motion picture producers of America'. Inverchaple duly informed Foreign Secretary Ernest Bevin of Johnston's approach and summarised the arguments the Americans made against the duty:

1. It hurts the British producers. Banks, as you know, are loath to lend money on new British productions at a time when British theatres may have to close and when the world market is shrinking through threat of retaliatory taxes in other countries.
2. It will hurt the British Government, which stands to lose more than 36 million pounds annually in box office taxes on the American products.
3. It has hurt the British cinema owner, who will probably have to close through lack of pictures.
4. It has hurt the American film producer, whose product has been geared to a world market. Great Britain has been the American industry's most important foreign market.
5. It will hurt all the world, because if this new form of tariff in the guise of a tax on anticipated earnings is allowed to stand, it becomes a pattern for the taxation of numerous other products in many countries. The far-reaching work done at Geneva and Havana will thereby be vitiated.
6. Last, but most important, the British Government has allowed other countries to send in single prints of films not subject to the tax without extending this same privilege to the United States. In my book, this is rank discrimination.[41]

Johnston added 'that he had recently been to the White House and had told the whole story to President Truman. The President had commented that if this film tax procedure persisted and spread to other things and other countries, the USA and the United Kingdom might as well throw their Havana Charter into the waste paper basket.' The Havana Charter (formally the Final Act of the United Nations Charter on Trade and Employment) was an agreement setting out the basic rules for international trade due to be signed in March 1948.

Johnston's intervention had the desired effect. The Treasury backed down on the question of a blocked sterling arrangement. Early in March 1948 a basis of agreement was reached whereby the import duty would be removed and instead a proportion of American film revenues earned in the United Kingdom would be frozen, with a schedule of permitted uses to be agreed. There were still some eleventh-hour manoeuvres. The Treasury tried (unsuccessfully) to insert a clause whereby an unremitted balance remaining unspent at the end of the financial year would be ceded 'voluntarily' to the Exchequer.[42] Rupert Somervell, Permanent Under-Secretary at the Board of Trade, was still concerned about the blocked sterling arrangement: 'The inevitable result will be that, after the maximum of friction, the Americans will get the spending of all their sterling – in meal or malt – and we shall have accepted a grave burden on our balance of payments.'[43] At the same time, however, the Foreign Office had reason to believe that there was pressure on the Americans to conclude an agreement: 'We gather from Drew Middleton of the *New York Times* that the future of the American film industry depends absolutely on reaching an agreement with us. His opinion is that if we stand firm we should be able to secure an agreement on our own terms.'[44]

The Anglo-American Film Agreement was announced on 11 March 1948. Its main provisions were that the *ad valorem* duty would be removed (it was repealed on 3 May); that for two years from 14 June the American companies could remit jointly up to US $17 million of their earnings from the United Kingdom (a sum that represented 25 per cent of their total UK earnings based on the revenue figures for 1946–7); that this could be increased by a sum equivalent to the revenues of British films in the United States for the same period (this was referred to as the 'B Pool'); that the American companies' blocked sterling could be invested in film-making activities in Britain, or for a range of other permitted uses; and that half of any unspent revenue could be carried forward to the next two-year period. The inclusion of the 'B Pool' revenues above the basic $17 million was an attempt to persuade US distributors to make greater efforts to secure screen time for British films in the United States. The Agreement was to run for four years and would be subject to review after two. The permitted uses for blocked sterling were quite broad: they included investment in film production, purchase of studios and equipment, purchases of literary, dramatic and musical properties and rights, costs of prints and advertising in the United Kingdom, pensions and insurances, loans and credits to companies, and payments 'in respect of personal services rendered'.[45]

The response to the Anglo-American Film Agreement on both sides of the Atlantic was mixed. In Britain the trade associations were broadly positive. Wilson told Eady: 'I always felt that it was extremely important that we should reach an agreement with Hollywood at this stage and I am convinced, particularly in light of the comments of my colleagues and the messages of congratulations I have had from all sections of the industry, that we really have secured a good agreement.'[46] Cinema exhibitors were naturally relieved that they would once again have a supply of new American films: indeed, the lifting of the boycott would create a backlog of American product. W. R. Fuller averred that Wilson 'has negotiated an outstanding successful deal for this country for which he deserves the greatest credit'.[47] And Sir Alexander King felt that 'it is the most sensible arrangement that could have been achieved'.[48] However, there were voices in the national press who maintained that Wilson had 'sold out' the British film industry to the Americans. Randolph Churchill, a somewhat improbable film correspondent for the *Daily Mail* in the late 1940s, deplored 'Mr Wilson's surrender of British interests' and suggested that 'the whole episode would seem to be only another example of the bad judgement for which Mr Attlee's Government has become notorious'.[49] And an editorial in the *Financial Times* suggested that Wilson had been out-negotiated by the Americans: 'Had the Marx Brothers represented Britain in the negotiations with Mr Eric Johnston they could hardly have produced a more absurd agreement . . . Surely our innocent economist-socialist President of the Board of Trade should not have been allowed to play poker with the hard-shelled negotiators from Hollywood.'[50] Interestingly, however, the view among some of the Hollywood trade interests was that the MPEA had been 'out-traded and out-maneuvred by the British' because it had accepted limitations on remittances rather than maintaining the embargo and holding out until British exhibitors were so short of films that Hollywood could have negotiated better terms.[51] In particular there was a view that the blocked sterling arrangement meant that the British had successfully engineered conditions in which American investment would bolster their own industry. The *Motion Picture Herald* pointed to 'the unencouraging prospect of a flow of films bearing American trademarks which, made in England with English players, settings, etc., will actually be British pictures in all visible respects'.[52]

On balance it would probably be fair to say that the Anglo-American Film Agreement was a compromise that gave something to both sides. For the British it achieved the object of saving some dollars while restoring the supply of American films needed to satisfy the public's demand for entertainment: to this extent the main beneficiaries were the exhibitors. For the production sector the outcome was more equivocal: the blocked sterling arrangement clearly facilitated more American investment in film-making which kept studios occupied and workers employed but it also meant more competition for British producers. It was for this reason that producers felt the Agreement necessitated an increase in the level of the quota: the British Film Producers' Association was 'alarmed at the amount of money which US companies will in future have to invest in British production' and urged that 'the best safeguard for the British industry is now an assurance from the Board that the highest possible quota is put on exhibitors as soon as the Films Act becomes operative'.[53] A month after the signing of the Agreement, the new Cinematograph Films Act did indeed raise exhibitors' quota to 45 per cent. In the short term the Americans might seem to have lost more: they had ensured they kept their most important overseas market but had to accept withdrawing only a quarter of their revenues from that market for the foreseeable future. What could not have been foreseen at the time of the Agreement, however, was that the value of Hollywood's blocked sterling would be reduced from July 1949 when the continuing economic crisis forced the British government into currency devaluation: sterling was devalued by approximately one-third from a rate of $4.05 to $2.80. The Bank of England explained that 'the amount of dollars they are entitled to remit is not affected by devaluation but the dollars will cost them more in unremittable sterling'.[54] What it meant in practice was that Hollywood's US $17 million of remittable revenues now cost £6,070,000 rather than £4,250,000 before devaluation.[55]

There were some 'matters of interpretation' to be cleared up after the Agreement was signed. One important question was whether the American companies would be able to trade their blocked sterling between themselves. The Bank of England opposed transfers between companies because it feared US interests might deal among themselves at less than the official exchange rate: 'I feel I should confirm our strong view that, quite apart from the damage done to sterling transactions in "film sterling" at a depreciated rate, HMG could not avoid the charge that they had, in effect, blessed such rate or rates of exchange.'[56] However, the Board of Trade was not averse to the suggestion on the grounds that 'we are committed by the Agreement to make it easy for them to spend their unremittable sterling, provided that we are not injured by the way in which they do it'.[57] In the event it was agreed that the US companies could transfer up to £10,000 between themselves subject to approval by the Bank of England's Exchange Control Committee. Walt Disney Productions – one of the smaller American interests which held less blocked currency than the majors – was the first to take advantage of this arrangement when it bought additional sterling from RKO Radio Pictures to finance the production of *Treasure Island* (1950) in Britain.[58]

In the wake of the Agreement it was clear that the American interests in Britain had no intention of leaving any of their blocked sterling unspent. Among the more imaginative applications were the purchase of a motor car in Britain to be shipped to New York for the use of a Hollywood producer (rejected as outside the terms of the schedule of permitted uses) and the bulk purchase of chocolate bars to ship to New York for sale in cinemas (approved). More typical applications were United Artists' purchase of the distribution rights in a Finnish film for £7,500 and the purchase of French currency to finance a production in France (agreed subject to approval by the Exchange Control Committee).[59] Columbia Pictures in particular tested the limits of the Agreement. On one occasion they applied to repay a loan made to an Indian subsidiary from blocked sterling.[60] Another time they wanted to borrow £70,000 from the Chase Bank of New York to finance the production of a film in Britain with the intention of repaying the loan from blocked sterling:

this was declined as Columbia was deemed to have sufficient blocked currency to finance the film locally. These applications highlighted the fact that the Anglo-American Film Agreement 'is not a legal document, but a basis of understanding which must be interpreted by both parties with a good deal of give and take. Looked at from this point of view, the Columbia application might be regarded as a borderline case.'[61]

Another problem arose specifically in relation to the production of *Under Capricorn* (1949), produced and directed in Britain by Alfred Hitchcock. This was the second of two pictures that Hitchcock and Sidney Bernstein made for their company Transatlantic Pictures: the first – shot in Hollywood – had been *Rope* (1948). There was some question regarding the 'British' status of *Under Capricorn*, which was produced by the British-owned subsidiary of the Capricorn Corporation, an American company jointly owned by Hitchcock and Bernstein. Harold Wilson was obliged to explain the situation to Eric Johnston:

> The film is being financed almost entirely from America, dollars being remitted here to cover the production expenses in England. This money is to be recouped from a first charge on the receipts (less distribution fees, print costs, advertising, etc) arising from world distribution of the film by Warners, and the dollars brought into this country to cover the production costs will be returned to the United States to the extent of the film's net earnings in the normal UK territory of Warners Ltd. As it is anticipated that the net UK earnings will be considerably less than the cost of the picture, it follows that there should be no net dollar liability on the foreign exchange resources of the UK; on the contrary, there should be a net dollar gain.[62]

Wilson argued that the film fell outside the terms of the Anglo-American Film Agreement as the financing arrangements were 'virtually complete' when the Agreement was signed: Johnston seems to have accepted this.

After eighteen months – and with the two-year review of the Agreement looming – it had become apparent that there were some difficulties in the working of the Agreement. There was a view in Britain that the Americans had not done anything to support British films in the United States. Cripps – who had been sidelined by illness during the summer of 1949 – believed 'that the Film Agreement has not worked very satisfactorily. Apart from considerable friction on points of detail, the British film companies have not had any real co-operation from the Americans in showing British films in the United States, and the prospects of establishing a market for our films which would persist after the expiry of the Film Agreement seem as remote as ever.'[63] This verdict was borne out by data suggesting that in the first six months of the Agreement the total net billings of British films in the United States were US $1,793,257, of which only $609,307 was payable to British producers after deduction of distribution fees and expenses.[64] Wilson concurred that 'the chief American film companies have done nothing to promote the exhibition of British films in the USA ... The idea that the Americans would make a real effort to increase the earnings of our films in their market was one of the cardinal points in the Agreement and the fact that it has been a dead letter must influence our attitude in considering the terms of any renewed agreement.'65

However, the fact was that by the time the Agreement came up for renewal the domestic context had changed. One of the consequences of the devaluation of sterling was that exports had increased and the trade deficit had narrowed. The British could afford to make some concession to the Americans by increasing the allowance of remittable revenues. At the same time they were able to hold out the carrot of a reduction in the quota. The MPEA had objected to the 45 per cent exhibitors' quota as they felt it disadvantaged their films. The Board of Trade had already reduced the quota to 40 per cent in April 1949 and there would be a further reduction to 30 per cent in March 1950. A Treasury memorandum summarised the situation prior to Wilson's visit to Washington in late 1949:

> There are many internal considerations within the President's province, which are going to affect Anglo-American relations on films. It is clear that the volume of British production will fall off even though the quality of the best films may be maintained. This will surely lead to American demands for a decrease in the quota of British films which must be shown in our cinemas. This may be a valuable bargaining point when we come to negotiate on the dollars they may take out; but even on this we cannot yet be dogmatic since the Film Agreement when made was independent of the quota figure.66

In the event the renewal of the Anglo-American Film Agreement in 1950 proved to be much less contentious than the original negotiations: the main sticking point was the level at which remittable revenues should be set. The British wanted to maintain the level at US $17 million per year while the Americans wanted to increase it to $25 million: a compromise amount of $21 million was agreed with effect from October 1950. In addition, the American companies would also be allowed to remit additional revenue in proportion to the amount they had invested in British production: this was clearly a further incentive to encourage investment at a time when the US interests collectively had already used up most of their blocked sterling. The British also agreed, albeit reluctantly, to removing the 'B Pool' revenues from the Agreement: this amounted to an acceptance that the attempt to encourage better distribution of British films in America by relating it to American earnings in Britain had failed.67 There would be further minor revisions to the Agreement in 1952 and 1956 until it expired in 1960.

Notes

1. *Parliamentary Debates: House of Commons*, 5th Series, vol. 415, 16 November 1945, cols 2540–1.
2. Paul Kennedy, *The Realities Behind Diplomacy: Background Influences on British External Policy, 1865–1980* (London: Fontana, 1981), pp. 315–21.
3. Kenneth O. Morgan, *The People's Peace: British History 1945–1990* (Oxford: Oxford University Press, 1990), p. 65.

4. Kennedy, *The Realities Behind Diplomacy*, pp. 323–4.
5. BEA EC 4/248: 'Films' (undated but late 1939).
6. BEA EC 4/251: Montagu Norman to Armitage (Commonwealth Bank of Australia), 12 November 1942.
7. *Parliamentary Debates: House of Commons*, 5th Series, vol. 415, 16 November 1945, col. 2539.
8. Ibid. col. 2557.
9. Margaret Dickinson and Sarah Street, *Cinema and State: The Film Industry and the British Government 1927–84* (London: British Film Institute, 1985), p. 185.
10. 'Chancellor: "We must have US films"', *Kinematograph Weekly*, 6 February 1947, p. 3.
11. 'Cripps Favours Open Market', *Kinematograph Weekly*, 14 March 1946, p. 3.
12. 'The Truth About Those Film Imports', *Kinematograph Weekly*, 14 February 1946, p. 10.
13. Thomas Schatz, *Boom and Bust: American Cinema in the 1940s* (Berkeley: University of California Press, 1999), p. 29.
14. 'The Rank Dollar Earning Policy: "Films Will Buy More Food"', *Kinematograph Weekly*, 10 July 1947, p. 3.
15. Sarah Street, *Transatlantic Crossings: British Films in the United States* (London: Continuum, 2002), pp. 91–118.
16. TNA BT 64/4509: 'Film rentals from British films billed before 14 June 1948'.
17. TNA BT 64/2283: Hugh Dalton to Sir Stafford Cripps, 15 May 1947.
18. 'US Films in Global Crisis', *Variety*, 30 April 1947, p.1.
19. 'New Tax on Film Imports?', *Kinematograph Weekly*, 26 June 1947, p. 3.
20. 'An Import Duty on Films – What It Would Mean to our Industry', *Kinematograph Weekly*, 3 July 1947, p. 6.
21. 'Dalton proposal continues to have adverse effect in market', *Kinematograph Weekly*, 17 July 1947, p. 18.
22. 'The Industry's Attitude', *Kinematograph Weekly*, 7 August 1947, p. 4.
23. Statutory Rules and Orders 1947, No. 1680: Customs Additional Import Duties (No. 2). The amount of the duty was actually 300 per cent levied on 25 per cent of the distributor's gross receipts: this meant it would take 75 per cent of all US film revenue in Britain.
24. 'How the import duty will operate', *Kinematograph Weekly*, 14 August 1947, p. 12.
25. 'The Film Tax and After', *The Economist*, 16 August 1947, p. 289.
26. 'In Six Months the Cupboard May Be Bare', *Kinematograph Weekly*, 14 August 1947, p. 8.
27. '"A Collapse of All Film Trading in This Country" Foreseen by CEA', *Kinematograph Weekly*, 14 August 1947, p. 3.
28. 'Share Slump: "Big Three" drop £5,000,000', *Kinematograph Weekly*, 14 August 1947, p. 3.
29. '628 Features Offered in 12 Months: 155 Reissues', *Kinematograph Weekly*, 1 January 1948, p. 3.
30. 'In Being Pound Wise We Must Not Be Dollar Foolish', *Kinematograph Weekly*, 1 January 1948, p. 6.
31. 'The Washington Meeting', *Kinematograph Weekly*, 21 August 1947, p. 4.
32. Dickinson and Street, *Cinema and State*, p. 187.
33. 'A Tax That Cannot Work', *Kinematograph Weekly*, 14 August 1947, p. 4.
34. 'Film Crisis May Be Eased in Washington This Week', *Kinematograph Weekly*, 21 August 1947, p. 3.

35. TNA T231/509: Memorandum by Sir Wilfrid Eady, 23 August 1947.
36. 'Long Shots', *Kinematograph Weekly*, 4 March 1948, p. 4.
37. TNA BT 64/4515: 'Present State of the Film Industry', speech prepared for the President of the Board of Trade, March 1949.
38. TNA BT 64/2283: Sir Wilfrid Eady to R. G. Somervell, 29 August 1947.
39. Morgan, *The People's Peace*, p. 58.
40. TNA T231/509: Note of meeting with Fay Allport at the Treasury, 4 November 1947.
41. Ibid.: Lord Inverchaple to Ernest Bevin, 24 February 1948.
42. Ibid.: 'Anglo-American Film Remittances: Outline of Possible Settlement', n.d.
43. Ibid.: R. G. Somervell to Eady, 6 March 1948.
44. Ibid.: John Henry Patch to Eady, 6 March 1948.
45. Ibid.: F. W. Allport to Somervell, 4 March 1948.
46. Ibid.: Harold Wilson to Eady, 17 March 1948.
47. 'Harold Wilson Has Scored an Outstanding Success for His Country in the Negotiations', *Kinematograph Weekly*, 18 March 1948, p. 6.
48. TNA T231/509: Sir Alexander King to W. Glenvill Hall, 13 March 1948.
49. 'The triumph of Mr Johnston', *Daily Mail*, 12 April 1948, p. 2.
50. 'Men and Matters', *The Financial Times*, 15 March 1948, p. 4.
51. 'Did London "Out-Trade" H'Wood?', *Variety*, 17 March 1948, p. 36.
52. 'Impact of British-US Deal on Production is Worrying Hollywood', *Motion Picture Herald*, 15 May 1948, p. 27.
53. 'Producers: Pact Makes High Quota Essential', *Kinematograph Weekly*, 25 March 1948, p. 3.
54. TNA T 231/512: G. R. Hamilton to P. S. Milner-Barry, 1 February 1950.
55. 'Mr Wilson versus Hollywood', *The Financial Times*, 19 July 1950, p. 4.
56. TNA T231/510: G. L. F. Bolton to Eady, 8 June 1948.
57. Ibid.: Somervell to E. C. R. Kahn, 29 June 1948.
58. 'US Find Way of Using Frozen Dollars, Says Johnston', *Kinematograph Weekly*, 19 January 1950, p. 10.
59. TNA BT 64/2396: Digest of applications to the Anglo-American Film Agreement Control Committee, 1 March 1951.
60. Ibid.
61. T231/511: P. S. Milner-Barry to C. R. P. Hamilton, 4 November 1948.
62. TNA T231/512: Harold Wilson to Eric Johnston, 24 May 1948.
63. Ibid.: Sir Stafford Cripps to Harold Wilson, 11 November 1949.
64. TNA T231/511: 'British Film Revenues – Paragraph 2(c) of Anglo-American Film Agreement. Period: 13 June–13 December 1948.'
65. TNA T231/512: Wilson to Cripps, 17 November 1949.
66. Ibid.: G. R. [?] to Sir Henry Wilson Smith, 10 November 1949.
67. 'Britain, U.S. Set Up Film "Bonus" Plan', *New York Times*, 3 August 1950, p. 35.

CHAPTER 3

Capital and Commerce

> The perennial crisis in British film finance has shifted its ground since 1940 when Oliver Lyttelton was President of the Board of Trade and I was asked to write a memorandum for him on a Films Bank. In those days the Board of Trade was fearful lest the precious few capitalists financing British films – Lady Yule, Arthur Rank, Stephen Courtauld – should suddenly die. To-day their deaths would be regretted but not feared. Indeed, the different nature of the present crisis in British film finance was revealed a year ago in the death of Mr J. W. New, the forceful manager of the Piccadilly Branch of the National Provincial Bank who was the real financier of British films. (Nicholas Davenport) [1]

In 1939 it was estimated that the total capital invested in the British film industry amounted to some £97 million: the largest proportion of this investment (£77,750,000) was in cinema properties.[2] The exhibition sector, while subject to seasonal fluctuation, was the most stable part of the industry. It was also the most profitable: in 1934 – the first year for which reliable statistics are available – the British public spent an estimated £41.1 million at the box office.[3] The production sector was the most unstable part of the industry and tended to be subject to cycles of boom and bust. However, following the financing and production crisis of 1937, the revised Cinematograph Films Act of 1938 – which introduced a minimum cost threshold for British quota pictures and allowed renters to claim double or treble quota for higher-cost pictures – brought a degree of relative stability to the production sector until the outbreak of war in September 1939 once again plunged the industry into uncertainty. The Cinematograph Films Council reported that a total of £5.7 million had been invested in film production in the first year following the Act.[4] And the Bank of England estimated a total cost of £8,186,500 for all the British films released in the eighteen months following the Act. Around half of that total (£4,214,333) was from American companies producing films in Britain.[5]

It is evident that significant capital sums were invested in the film industry, but where did the money come from? Most major film corporations raised their working capital through a combination of public share and debenture issues and long-term loans from banks and commercial investment trusts. The two vertically integrated combines that emerged in the late 1920s – the Gaumont-British Picture Corporation (GBPC) and Associated British Picture Corporation (ABPC) – were the best capitalised outfits in the British film industry. In the mid-1930s GBPC had an authorised share capital of £6,250,000 and held another £5,160,000 in debentures with an additional credit of £1,149,785 from the National Provincial Bank. However, GBPC had incurred losses on film production and was in a weakened position. In 1936 the Bank of England reported: 'The Gaumont Company is at present seriously pressed for finance but unless plans which are now being considered for the internal reconstruction of their capital set-up can be brought to a satisfactory result it will be quite impossible for them to raise further finance.'[6] ABPC held authorised capital of £4 million with a further £3.5 million in loans and debentures: its major backers included the Clydesdale Bank and the Commercial Bank of Scotland. For the smaller production units there was often an imbalance between capital and loans. Alexander Korda's London Film Productions (LFP) is a case in point. LFP was registered in 1932 with a nominal capital of £100. Following the success of *The Private Life of Henry VIII* (1933) – which he financed through a loan from the Italian bankers Ludovico and Giuseppe Toeplitz secured against a distribution guarantee from United Artists – Korda embarked upon an ambitious programme of international films. For this he needed capital: even the profits of *The Private Life of Henry VIII* were insufficient to sustain his production plans. He therefore turned to the City to increase LFP's share capital, which by 1936 amounted to £428,799 with another £1,502,853 in loans and debentures. The largest shareholders were the Prudential Assurance Company, Lloyds Bank Nominees, the Midland Bank and the insurance firm C. T. Bowring & Co.[7] Finally, some production units were heavily dependent upon wealthy individual patrons. The jute heiress Lady Yule held a majority shareholding in British National Films as well as loaning it £30,000 of working capital.[8] And the philanthropist Stephen Courtauld, chairman of Associated Talking Pictures, was 'responsible for the equity of the Company and helped to procure an overdraft from the N. P. Bank amounting to £600,000 at one time'.[9]

The major new entrant into the field of film finance in the 1930s was the General Cinema Finance Corporation (GCFC). This was incorporated in March 1936 with a share capital of £1,225,000 for the specific purpose of acquiring 90 per cent of the share capital of General Film Distributors, the largest independent British distributor, set up in 1935.[10] GCFC brought a wealth of financial and business expertise to the film industry: its original directors were the flour-milling millionaire Joseph Arthur Rank, the paper magnate Lord Portal of Laverstoke, banker Paul Lindenberg and chartered accountant Leslie Farrow. In their contemporary study of film finance, F. D. Klingender and Stuart Legg doubted 'whether any other English film group could present a similar array of finance-capital magnates'.[11] GCFC was a well-capitalised operation whose backing came from a group of investment trusts (major corporate investors included the Heathfield Investment Society, Laverstoke Investment Trust, the Industrial Finance and Investment Corporation and Midland Bank Nominees, which each held over 200,000 shares) and individuals (including publisher Harold Macmillan and several men listed as 'company directors' by profession such as Lord Luke of Favenham, Lord Dulverton of Batsford, Aubrey Hyman and Major John Leslie).

The financing crisis of 1937 impacted most severely on those independent producers who lacked significant capital resources and were dependent upon loans for their production finance. Such producers tended to operate on a single-picture basis, unlike the larger units which could spread their risks across a portfolio of films. The Bank of England reported that '[the] financing of film production had until now been carried out by the Clearing Banks, the underlying security for their advances being insurance policies'.[12] The producer would raise their budget through loans from one or more sources: the loans (including interest) would be repaid from the producer's share of box-office receipts. The bank therefore held a mortgage or first charge on the film's receipts until the loan was repaid. The loans would be guaranteed by insurance companies or (occasionally) by 'persons of substance'. In the mid-1930s a private company called Aldgate Trustees acted as a specialist insurance broker for the film industry: it was responsible for arranging insurance for loans to producers totalling £2.8 million.[13] The major lender for independent producers was the Westminster Bank, which loaned nearly £1.5 million for the production of 22 films between 1935 and 1937. In March 1939 the Westminster Bank brought a group action against 15 insurance companies which had guaranteed loans for producers who had been unable to repay the bank's advances and most of whom had subsequently gone into liquidation.[14]

The outbreak of the Second World War brought the problems of film finance into sharp focus. The immediate catalyst was the near-collapse of financing for Gabriel Pascal's production of *Major Barbara*, a major film based on the play by George Bernard Shaw. General Film Distributors had agreed to finance the film at a budget of £125,000, but shortly after the declaration of war it got cold feet and cancelled a contract 'verbally agreed but not actually signed'. The American distributor United Artists then came forward with an offer to distribute the film 'on exceptionally favourable terms', offering to pay 70 per cent of the distributor's gross receipts. Pascal therefore needed to find a lender who would advance the budget against the distributor's guarantee. Nicholas Davenport, one of the directors of Pascal Film Productions, explained the problem to the Treasury:

> [It] is necessary to discount immediately the United Artists guarantee to pay $200,000 or the sterling equivalent on delivery of the negative in New York. There is unfortunately no financial organisation in existence to meet such discounting. At one time Lloyds Underwriters used to guarantee the performance of the film contract, which enabled the Joint Stock Banks to advance money against an approved distributor's contract, but on account of losses incurred through guaranteed performance of film contracts by unproved producers, Lloyds Underwriters no longer undertake this risk . . . With the protection of the Lloyds Producer's Indemnity Policy, distribution contracts have been discounted in private finance houses or financiers, but this channel has no doubt been closed by the outbreak of war.[15]

The Bank of England intervened to enable the National Provincial Bank to discount United Artists' distribution guarantee (its approval was necessary due to wartime currency controls) and to prevent *Major Barbara* from being lost to Hollywood.[16]

At the same time as its intervention over *Major Barbara*, the Bank of England was asked to consider the establishment of a film bank to support British production.[17] There were a number of factors at play. The Treasury supported the idea as a means of reducing the balance of payments deficit: more quality British films would displace American films at the box office and therefore reduce remittances of film distribution revenues to the United States. To this extent the Treasury reasoned that 'it would pay the Treasury better to lose money on financing British Films than to continue to spend dollars on renting American ones'.[18] The Board of Trade had a different concern: that without adequate finance, the British film industry would not be able to sustain production at a sufficient level to meet the quota. Rupert Somervell, the Permanent Under-Secretary of State at the Board of Trade with specific responsibility for film policy, told the Bank of England that 'recollections of the debacle of three or four years ago, coupled with political uncertainty culminating in the outbreak of war, have prevented and still prevent the natural development of new financial facilities'. A further issue was 'that a considerable proportion of the finance for existing film production is being provided by private individuals and may at any moment cease to be available through the death of the patron concerned or his unwillingness to continue his support'.[19] However, Montagu Norman, the Governor of the Bank of England, was implacably opposed to the idea: he responded 'that he does not see any present prospect of being able to raise finance in the City for a film bank, nor would he wish for his part to sponsor such an undertaking'.[20]

Nevertheless the proposal for a government-backed film bank or finance corporation remained under consideration throughout 1940. In January 1940 the Cinematograph Films Council – the statutory body set up under the Cinematograph Films Act of 1938 to advise the Board of Trade on film-related matters – recommended the establishment of a Film Finance Corporation with an initial capital of £2.7 million, of which two-thirds would be provided by the Treasury and one-third from commercial loans. The role of the corporation would be 'to provide finance on reasonable terms for the *British* Film Industry in so far as it cannot procure this itself on more favourable terms': it was suggested that the corporation would lend up to 70 per cent of the total production cost, with loans from the joint stock banks to make up the remainder.[21] The Council reckoned that the British production industry needed to supply around 150 feature films a year to meet the needs of the quota: with American distributors financing around 15 pictures a year this left British producers needing to provide 135 films. The Bank of England was asked again '[to] examine the present state of the British Film Industry and to ascertain what steps and finance are required to put it onto a satisfactory basis and what support from HMG would be necessary to that end'.[22] The Bank could no longer evade the issue. In May 1940 Montagu Norman personally signed off on a plan to establish a Film Finance Corporation on a 'temporary and experimental' basis for five years. It was an ambitious plan which proposed a working capital of

£2,750,000, of which £1 million would be raised from the City by offering five-year debenture stock at 4 per cent interest, the industry would provide £500,000 through a combination of share issues and ordinary capital, and the Treasury would provide a fund of £1 million as a guarantee against losses and a further reserve fund of £250,000. Any profits made by the corporation would be divided between shareholders (25 per cent) and the reserve fund (75 per cent).[23]

The change of government following the fall of Neville Chamberlain and the German invasion of France and the Low Countries pushed the film bank down the legislative agenda. The initiative was in abeyance for several months. Ironically it was *Major Barbara* that again brought it back into play. Pascal's film had run over budget: in August 1940 he approached the Board of Trade to seek its assistance in finding another £25,000 to complete it, otherwise it would be necessary to 'ask United Artists . . . to take over the film and complete it in America'. The Treasury felt there was 'a prima facie case for thinking that the possibility of finding further money from non-Government sources to complete the film ought to be considered . . . Presumably the idea of starting a Film Finance Corporation has not advanced far enough to make it possible to arrange temporary financing on the basis that the liability will be taken over by the Film Finance Corporation when it is constituted.'[24] However, Sir Andrew Duncan, the new President of the Board of Trade, had cooled on the idea: 'If this film is taken to America for completion, the consequences might be to bring about the formation of a Film Bank under political pressure. And that is not the way Sir Andrew wishes to work . . .' There was also a concern that 'public assistance' to bail out one film would 'open a door which would be difficult to close'.[25] In the event, the National Provincial Bank came forward again to furnish the completion money.[26]

However, the film bank initiative was overtaken by events. Two factors contributed to its demise. One was the insistence of Sir Andrew Duncan that any financial support for film production should also involve statutory regulation. Duncan was concerned that the film industry 'has a bad history, it lacks co-ordination, and there is little or no recognition by any of those engaged in it of the common interests either of the individual sections of the industry or of the industry as a whole'. He therefore felt that 'it is vital to set up an independent Films Commission, somewhat on the lines recommended by the Moyne Committee'.[27] However, this proposal was not welcomed by trade interests, who feared that a statutory body would be too interventionist. Arthur Jarratt, the senior film booker for the Gaumont circuit, 'felt it was quite possible that if this Commission was the only means by which the industry could get money they might prefer to do without the money'.[28]

The other factor that helped to kill the film bank was that by the winter of 1940–1 it had become apparent that the basis on which the bank had been proposed – that the British production industry needed to provide around 150 features a year – was no longer a realistic ambition. The Cinematograph Films Council advised: 'The limited studio space and film production man-power which now remain for producing British feature films are unlikely to suffice for an output of more than 75 feature films a year . . . Indeed it is by no means certain that even this output can be obtained under existing conditions.'[29] The requisitioning of film studios and the recruitment of technicians into other industries meant that the production sector was working at a significantly reduced capacity. Duncan's successor Oliver Lyttelton told Norman that 'present circumstances make it difficult to expand film production and it might be thought that it was out of place to revive the idea at the present time'.[30]

The contraction of the domestic production sector during the war had the effect of concentrating film-making in the hands of fewer production groups. The four leading British producers during the war were the J. Arthur Rank Organisation, the Associated British Picture Corporation, Ealing Studios and British National Films. Two American studios maintained production facilities in Britain: Warner Bros. at Teddington and Twentieth Century–Fox at Wembley. MGM closed its British studio operation in 1940 but continued to sponsor occasional high-end quota films from British producers such as *The Adventures of Tartu* (1943). While the costs of film-making increased during the war, especially in relation to studios, material and labour, these were offset by more economical production methods and the elimination of extravagance. The Board of Trade records include estimated production costs for 64 British first features made between 1941 and 1943: the average cost was £56,000.[31] Hence in an odd sort of way the war eased some of the financial pressures for British producers. According to the *Kine Year Book* for 1942: '[No] longer does the production chief concern himself on the subject of finance ... When it comes to studio space the supply is so much less than the demand that rents have soared beyond all reason; man-power is a painful problem; good stories want finding; but the lack of money, which has in the past ruined many promising ventures, is no longer a worry.'[32]

The major structural development during the war was the consolidation of the power of the Rank Organisation. At the outbreak of war Rank was already the dominant force in the industry. He was the major shareholder and chairman of the General Cinema Finance Corporation, which owned the major British distributor (General Film Distributors) and three of the biggest studios (Pinewood, Denham and Amalgamated: the latter had never been used for film production and had been leased to the Ministry of Supply before the outbreak of war). In October 1941 GCFC acquired control of the Gaumont-British Picture Corporation, and in January 1942 Rank became chairman of Odeon Theatres following the death of its founder Oscar Deutsch. From 1942 the Rank Organisation was responsible for around half of all British feature film production: this included films from its own subsidiary Gainsborough Pictures as well as from leading independents attached to Rank such as Filippo Del Giudice's Two Cities Films, which made a number of important British wartime films including *In Which We Serve* (1942), *This Happy Breed* (1944), *The Way Ahead* (1944), *Henry V* (1944) and *The Way to the Stars* (1945). (*In Which We Serve* – the second film at the British box office in 1943 – was actually distributed by the British Lion Film Corporation when GFD's chairman C. M. Woolf inexplicably passed it up.) Rank's generous provision of production finance allowed him to play the patriotic card whenever criticism of monopoly emerged. His biographer Alan Wood averred that Rank 'was resolved to keeping British production going during the war, however much he had to pay for it'.[33] The Bank of England similarly felt that 'Arthur Rank really does seem to have the interests of the industry at heart, otherwise he would not have risked so much money in it'.[34] In 1941 GCFC sought to increase its capital by selling part of its shareholding in Universal Pictures: the Bank of England averred that GCFC 'is a good company and a good influence in the industry and merits support'.[35]

The internal structure of the Rank Organisation was unwieldy in the extreme: this reflected the *ad hoc* process by which it had been built. Altogether the Rank group comprised around 100 companies and held fixed assets of around £60 million. At the top of the superstructure was Odeon Theatres: John Davis – formerly the chief accountant of the Odeon circuit whose expertise was in the administrative rather than the creative side of the film business – became managing director of Odeon Theatres in 1946.[36] Odeon Theatres had an authorised capital of £6 million: its major shareholders were four holding companies – Manorfield Investments, Foy Investments, Group Holdings and Odeon Cinema Holdings – which each had the same chairman (Rank himself) and several of the same directors (John Davis was common to all four). Odeon Theatres had several subsidiaries including Odeon Associated Theatres (which owned the group's cinemas in the United Kingdom), Odeon Properties (which controlled its cinemas overseas including in South Africa, Canada and New Zealand) and the General Cinema Finance Corporation. GCFC itself had three subsidiaries – General Film Distributors, J. Arthur Rank Overseas Distributors and the Metropolis and Bradford Trust – the last of which held a controlling interest in the Gaumont-British Picture Corporation. GBPC had authorised capital of £7,125,000 – major shareholders included the Eagle Star Insurance Company, Prudential Assurance Company and Bankers Investment Trust – and multiple subsidiaries including Gainsborough Pictures, the General Theatre Corporation, Provincial Cinematograph Theatres and British Optical and Precision Engineers (which manufactured cinema equipment such as projectors and lenses).[37] In 1944 Rank proposed a new holding company to finance its production activities: this did not progress, as the Bank of England's Company Law Committee was 'not much attracted to the idea'.[38]

The internal structure of the Rank Organisation may have been unwieldy, but this was one of the factors that explained its resilience during the economic crisis of the late 1940s. On the one hand losses sustained in certain areas could be offset by profits in others; on the other hand the structure of separate companies meant that profits could be accounted separately to minimise tax liabilities. In Rank's *annus horribilis* of 1949, for example, the headline figure was that the group had sustained a loss of £3,350,000 on film production and had total overdrafts amounting to £16,286,581. Within the group, however, GBPC made a net profit of £1,020,423 and Odeon Theatres a net profit of £546,142. In fact the group as a whole made a trading profit of £1,587,356: the problem was that this was around £4 million less than the previous year.[39] Rank's recovery over the next two years was based on reducing its losses on production and increasing profits from exhibition and from its manufacturing companies. In 1951 Rank lost £1,314,829 on production but was still able to report increased trading profits of £5,125,230 overall and was able to pay off £7 million of its overdrafts.[40] Rank's principal creditor was the National Provincial Bank, which held most of its loans and overdrafts. In 1952 a Board of Trade official noted: 'Mr Williams (Piccadilly Manager of the N. P. Bank) and Mr John Davis were both vulnerable when the Rank Organisation came so near to collapse in 1948. In these circumstances they apparently decided that their only hope was to back one another up and this they have, I think, done consistently ever since.'[41]

The Associated British Picture Corporation was the smaller of the two vertically integrated combines. It had a much less complicated internal structure than the Rank group. It consisted of one parent company and less than a dozen subsidiaries, including Associated British Cinemas, Union Cinemas, Associated British-Pathé (its distribution arm) and British Instructional Films. In 1945 ABPC had fixed assets of £24 million (less than half the fixed assets of the Rank Organisation) and authorised capital of £9 million. In the same year ABPC recorded a trading profit of £2,135,890, which was reduced to £494,463 following tax.[42] ABPC owned slightly over 400 cinemas in the United Kingdom and studio facilities at Elstree and Welwyn: the latter was deemed 'rather too small for economical production of feature films' and would be sold in 1950.[43] ABPC's founder and chairman John Maxwell had held 51 per cent of the ordinary shares: following his death in 1940 his shareholding passed to his widow Catherine. In 1941 the American company Warner Bros. bought 49 per cent of Mrs Maxwell's shares for a reported sum of £903,150.[44] Other major shareholders were Branch Nominees, chairman Sir Philip Warter and fellow directors Colin Saunders and Hugh McCreath, and the Commercial Bank of Scotland. There were evidently some tensions within the board. A. G. Allen, a director of the company between 1941 and 1943, told the Board of Trade that Mrs Maxwell 'was attempting to interfere in "certain essential matters of control". She and her family still tended to think of the concern as "Daddy's Company". The late John Maxwell had been a most dominating personality. All his assets were in ABPC and he had left considerable debts as well as having to meet heavy death duties.'[45]

Unlike the Rank Organisation, ABPC sometimes tended to slip under the radar of the critics of monopoly. As the *Kine* observed in 1946: 'Associated British is a quiet company that seldom makes the big headlines . . . [It] would be an excellent thing if Associated British adopted a forward looking, forthright policy in its public relations and assumed a position as a mouthpiece of the industry proportionate to its size.'[46] For its part, ABPC maintained:

> As the owners of the largest circuit of cinemas in this country, we desire to make a substantial contribution to building up British film production on a scale and by a series of pictures that will both commend themselves to the British film-going public and will compete with other films in the American and the world market.[47]

The Board of Trade's main concern in respect of ABPC was that Mrs Maxwell might sell her remaining shares either to Rank or to Warner Bros.: the former was the lesser of two evils but neither outcome was desirable.[48] In October 1943 it secured a voluntary undertaking from Mrs Maxwell not to sell her interest without prior approval of the Board of Trade: 'My husband took great pride in building up the Associated British Picture Corporation and I am very sensible of the opinion expressed in your letter as to the part which the Corporation can continue to play in the film industry in this country.'[49] This compromise did not prevent Warner Bros. from buying out other shareholders: in 1946 it paid £1,125,000 for a further million shares that increased its stake in ABPC from 25 per cent to 37.5 per cent.[50]

The end of the war saw the emergence of another major production group in the form of the British Lion Film Corporation. British Lion had originally been set up by the novelist and playwright Edgar Wallace in the late 1920s to produce films of his works: following his death in 1933 it focused mostly on distributing American second features though it also produced some British quota pictures. It emerged as a more significant presence during the war as the British distributor of *In Which We Serve*. Early in 1946 Alexander Korda acquired a controlling interest in British Lion, and a few months later acquired a 75 per cent interest in Sound City Studios at Shepperton. *Kine* put the combined purchase price of British Lion and Sound City at 'not less than £500,000' and there was some speculation in the trade where Korda had got the funds: 'All this adds up to very big money, and it has not all come from the profits of *Lady Hamilton*. Although Sir Alex is a rich man, I do not see him using his own coin to this extent.'[51] Korda's biographer Karol Kulik suggests that he raised the cash from selling his shares in United Artists and from the sale of Denham Laboratories to Rank.[52] The British Lion Film Corporation had three subsidiaries – British Lion Production Associates, the British Lion Studio Company and Shepperton Productions – and was itself owned by Korda's London Film Productions. Korda raised further capital by a share issue in the British Lion Film Corporation in 1947, which increased its authorised capital to £1.1 million.[53] Korda explained the funding of British Lion's film production programme in a letter to Sir Wilfrid Eady at the Treasury: 'These films were financed partly by the Bank loans, the Bank putting up about 75 per cent of the cost of the pictures, and partly by British Lion which put up the remaining 25 per cent. The only exceptions to this are *Anna Karenina* and *Ideal Husband* to which I, myself, put up a substantial sum of money.'[54]

British Lion was more severely affected by the crisis of the late 1940s because unlike Rank and ABPC it could not offset its losses on production against exhibition as it owned no cinemas. The problem was exacerbated by the fact that British Lion's production programme included a higher percentage of loss-making films. It was not only Korda's expensive vanity projects *An Ideal Husband* (1947), *Anna Karenina* (1948) and *Bonnie Prince Charlie* (1948) that lost money but also critically acclaimed films such as Carol Reed's *The Fallen Idol* (1948) and Anthony Asquith's *The Winslow Boy* (1948).[55] In April 1949 British Lion reported that it had spent

£4.5 million on film production over the last year and had lost £700,000.[56] It subsequently turned out that its losses had been underestimated: the total was revised upwards to £1,388,797.[57] The Board of Trade was particularly concerned about the fate of British Lion because it was the main supporter of independent producers who did not wish to be tied to either Rank or ABPC. James Lawrie, the managing director of the National Film Finance Corporation which would loan British Lion nearly £3 million in 1948–9, explained its importance: 'There is little doubt that the Korda producers represent a very important element in the British film industry, and a minimum programme of four films a year from them is probably desirable, both to keep Shepperton studios working at capacity . . . and to provide a reasonable number of high-class films for the international market.'[58]

The losses sustained by the main production groups in the late 1940s, especially Rank and British Lion, would have a significant impact on the provision of film finance. One of the consequences of the economic crisis in the production industry was that the major combines shifted from producing their own programmes of films to providing distribution guarantees for producers who would then be required to raise the finance themselves against the security of the guarantee. In 1949, for example, the Rank Organisation had backed a total of 20 films: ten were wholly financed by the group itself, five were partially financed by the group and five were through distribution guarantees. In 1950, however, Rank backed 18 films: only one was wholly financed, seven were partially financed and ten were distribution guarantees. Similarly, in 1950 ABPC produced nine films, of which six were financed by the corporation itself and three were distribution guarantees: an additional two films (*Stage Fright* and *Captain Horatio Hornblower, RN*) were produced at ABPC's Elstree Studios by Warner Bros., though these were 'Hollywood British' productions funded by the American studio's frozen capital rather than by ABPC itself. By the early 1950s ABPC was wholly financing a handful of films per year and was otherwise operating as a studio facility for independent producers for whom it provided distribution guarantees or cash advances.[59]

A Board of Trade-commissioned report published in November 1949 under the title *Distribution and Exhibition of Cinematograph Films* (informally known as the Plant Report after chairman Sir Arnold Plant) explained how the system of raising the production finance by discounting against a distribution guarantee worked in practice:

> It is the usual practice for the production of British films also to be largely financed by the renter. The extent of this finance has varied from about 50 to 100 per cent of the cost, a percentage of about 75 per cent now probably being the most common. As an alternative to actually putting up the money, distributors of standing have given guarantees to pay a stated sum within a given time after delivery or general release of the film, e.g. 75 per cent of the budgeted cost of production within one year of its general release date. The production company can take this guarantee to a bank and discount it, thus raising a large proportion of the money required for the production of the film. These advances and guarantees are recoverable by the renter from the receipts of the hire of the film to exhibitors, and the renter is

liable for any shortfall. This is important when considering the charge made by the distributors for their services, for the financial arrangement is usually covered by the overall contract which they enter into with the producer.[60]

The bank loan was known as the 'front money' as it was the first to be repaid from the producer's share of the receipts. For producers attached to one of the major combines, the provision of the distribution guarantee was usually a relatively straightforward matter. Rank was also prepared to loan the 'end money' – the amount of the budget not covered by the distribution guarantee – albeit 'on stiffish terms'.[61] For independent producers not aligned with one of the major groups and lacking working capital, however, the 'end money' would have to be found from their own resources: this would often involve the producer deferring part or all of their fee to be recouped from the box office after the other investors had been repaid. The producer Anthony Havelock-Allan advocated using deferments to make up the difference between the distribution guarantee and the total cost on the grounds 'that the participation of the very highly paid members of an independent production company in this manner is highly desirable, and that the earning of the large fees that are customary in this industry should be conditional upon the financial success or otherwise of the picture'.[62]

The retreat of the major combines from direct production at the end of the 1940s created the context for the re-emergence of more independent producers: examples included – but were not limited to – Pilgrim Pictures (Filippo Del Giudice), Constellation Films (Anthony Havelock-Allan and Robert Garrett), Pinnacle Productions (Edward Dryhurst), Javelin Films (Edward Baird and Anthony Asquith) and the Mayflower Pictures Corporation (Aubrey Baring and Maxwell Setton). The usual practice was to register a company with nominal capital to undertake the production of a single film: the enterprise would be self-liquidating and would be wound up after a few years. In 1951 the Treasury's Capital Loans Committee 'expressed some surprise at one or two proposals in which substantial expenditure was contemplated for the purpose of making a film where the ordinary capital of the Company formed for the purpose was disproportionate: e.g. £100 where the total expenditure contemplated was over £100,000.' Nevertheless it concluded that the system was appropriate because it shared the risks among different parties: 'There is no "capital" in the ordinary sense in this venture, which is self-liquidating... This elaborate form of financing is not unreasonable when it is analysed, since the risk is fairly distributed. It will be noted that the banks are in a guaranteed position and are properly putting up self-liquidating funds.'[63]

The withdrawal of many banks and insurance companies from the field of film finance in the late 1930s meant that the provision of production loans was left in the hands of a few financial institutions. In 1948 Anthony Havelock-Allan intimated that 'the discounting of these guarantees is performed almost exclusively by one bank – an American bank – though in special circumstances one of the big five English banks has been known to undertake this form of discount'.[64] Early in 1949 the newly established National Film Finance Corporation reported that 90 per cent of the front money loans for British films came from just two lenders: the National Provincial Bank and the Bank of America.[65] The National Provincial Bank was the main creditor for the Rank Organisation and the British Lion Film Corporation. Nicholas Davenport, who sat on the board of British Lion and acted as a financial adviser to Alexander Korda, explained the bank's role thus:

> The practice of the N. P. Bank is to advance an approved producer 75% of the estimated production cost against an approved distributor's guarantee to repay that advance within twelve months of delivery of the negative. A first mortgage on the film revenues is, of course, held by the bank until the advance is repaid. 4½% interest is charged (2% above Bank rate). The N. P. Bank insists that producers put up in cash and credits – it prefers, of course, cash to credits – the balance of 25% of the production cost. It even tries – as it did once with me – to get the directors of the producing company to give individual and personal guarantees of the bank overdraft. Finally, it puts a ceiling to its total advances. It limits its advances to the Rank group to about £12 millions and to the Korda group to about £1½ millions.[66]

There was some suggestion that the National Provincial was looking to reduce its lending to other producers in the early 1950s. According to Robert Garrett, the managing director of Film Finances, a company established in London in 1950 for the purpose of providing guarantees of completion, 'the National Provincial . . . these days does little or no business with independent producers'.[67] Of the first dozen films guaranteed by Film Finances, all the production loans were from either Lloyds Bank or the Bank of America.[68] In February 1950 Lloyds Bank had decided that it 'should undertake the financing of film production within certain limits': it agreed to make front money loans of 70 per cent to three producers – Romulus Films, Concanen Films and Pinnacle Productions – subject to the end money being put up by the National Film Finance Corporation and an overall loan ceiling of £2 million.[69] However, other sources suggest that the National Provincial was fully committed to supporting the Rank Organisation. 'Incidentally,' reported Sir Frank Lee, Permanent Under-Secretary at the Board of Trade, 'it is interesting that Mr Davis went out of his way to praise the helpful attitude of the National Provincial Bank, whereas as I recall Messrs [Richard] Stopford and [James] Lawrie told us that only Lloyds Bank was really a fully and effective part in the financing of film production.'[70]

The provision of loans secured against distribution guarantees was a system that in the long term worked to the advantage of the 'big three' distributors: Rank, British Lion and ABPC. It was the independent producer who was most disadvantaged by the system: there was no continuity in finance from one picture to the next, and they were dependent upon the patronage of the major distributors who were able more or less to set their own terms. The experience of independent producers in the late 1940s is exemplified by the case of John and Roy Boulting. The Boultings were twin brothers who had joined the Army Film Unit (Roy) and RAF Film Unit (John) during the war before resuming their career in the commercial film industry: they were among the most successful independent producers of the post-war period. They had made films in association with all three of the major British distributors – General Film Distributors (*Fame is the Spur*, 1947), Associated British-Pathé (*Brighton Rock*, 1947; *The Guinea Pig*, 1948) and British Lion (*Seven Days to Noon*, 1950) – and in the process became experienced in negotiating financing, distribution and studio contracts. It was an experience that left the Boultings with a highly jaundiced view of the industry:

> At no time has the independent producer been more dependent or less free . . . In the event of the film proving profitable, by the time the producer has distributed shares of profits due to the different parties helping to finance the film, the distributor, the [National] Film Finance Corporation, the completion guarantors, and many other interested bodies, what remains is all too frequently a meager return for his investment of money and effort, of blood, toil, sweat and tears. And as things are, the emphasis is very much on tears.
>
> In the event of loss every financial interest has priority protection before the producer himself. Guarantees exist for the strong, and not for the weak. The armour of 'orthodox' finance envelops the mighty. The humble stand naked and are expected to feel ashamed.[71]

A particular bone of contention was that the price of a distribution guarantee from one of the major corporations was that the producer was obliged to use (and pay for) studio space and contract artistes owned by the group:

> It will thus be seen that for this guarantee of 70 per cent of the cost, the 'independent' producer will be occupying studios which might otherwise be dark, employing artists who might otherwise be a burden on the group's finances, supplying the distributor with a film to sell to his own and other theatres at a fee of 20 per cent of the gross revenue (after the deduction of entertainment tax) and the theatre circuit with a film with which to meet its quota obligations and, let it be hoped, improve its balance sheet.[72]

The final insult for the Boultings was that, if the film was successful, 'the poor little producer will only be expected to PAY, say, 20 per cent of the profit to the distributor, who will already have received the fee referred to above, the share of the profits being in respect of the guarantee of 70 per cent'.

In short the whole structure of film finance was weighted against the producer, who bore most of the risk but was the last to share in the box-office receipts of their films. The distributor's risk was significantly less than the producer's in so far as the distributor offered no cash up front and reclaimed the amount of their guarantee (70–75 per cent of the budget) and their distribution fee before the producer received their share (from which they still had to repay the bank loan including interest). Any money that the producer had invested from their own pocket stood to be recouped last: hence most producers preferred to take deferments rather than put up the 'end part of the end money' in cash. In view of this it is hardly surprising that independent producers not attached to one of the main production groups often struggled to raise their finance. Furthermore, the producer's access to finance was only one part of the problem affecting the production sector: the other was that even when finance was forthcoming, film production was often still a loss-making activity.

NOTES

1. TNA BT 64/2366: 'Film Credits Corporation: A Memorandum by Nicholas Davenport', 20 February 1948.
2. Linda Wood, *British Films 1927–1939: BFI Research Guide* (London: BFI Library Services, 1986), pp. 138–43.
3. Simon Rowson, 'A Statistical Survey of the Cinema Industry in Great Britain', *Journal of the Royal Statistical Society*, 99: 1 (1936), p. 71.
4. *Cinematograph Films Council: First Report for the Year Ending 31 March 1939*, Paper No. 160 (July 1939), p. 16 (38).
5. BEA SMT 2/42: 'British Features: 1.4.39 to 30.11.39'. The ledger lists the statutory costs of 180 British quota films.
6. Ibid.: Unsigned memorandum dated 30 January 1936, though from its relation to other documents probably 30 January 1937.
7. BEA SMT 2/39: Document listing capital and major shareholders of London Film Productions, 27 May 1937.
8. TNA BT 31/39574/290703: British National Films: Particulars of a mortgage or charge created by a company registered in England, 12 January 1937.
9. TNA BT 64/4529: Simon Rowson to Hugh Gaitskell, 10 May 1943.
10. TNA BT 31/434851: Agreement between General Cinema Finance Corporation Ltd and General Film Distributors Ltd, 8 April 1936.
11. F. D. Klingender and Stuart Legg, *Money Behind the Screen: A Report prepared on behalf of the Film Council* (London: Lawrence & Wishart, 1937), p. 39.
12. BEA G14/80: Minutes of the Committee of Treasury, 3 June 1936.
13. Klingender and Legg, *Money Behind the Screen*, p. 59.
14. '£1,000,000 Claim Over Film Finance', *The Financial Times*, 2 March 1939, p. 7.
15. BEA EC 4/248: Nicholas Davenport to Secretary to the Treasury, 23 October 1939.
16. Ibid.: 'W. L.' to Deputy Governor, 1 November 1939.
17. BEA G14/233: T. K. Bewley to C. F. Cobbold, 24 October 1939.
18. TNA BT 64/58: Sir William Brown to R. G. Somervell, 9 February 1940.
19. Ibid.: R. G. Somervell to E. H. D. Skinner, 1 March 1940.
20. BEA G14/233: C. F. Cobbold to Bewley, 5 December 1939.
21. TNA BT 64/58: Cinematograph Films Council: Report of the sub-committee appointed to consider the financing of British film production, 27 January 1940.
22. Ibid.: 'British Films', 5 February 1940.
23. BEA G14/233: 'Film Finance Corporation', 7 May 1940, initialled 'M. N.'.
24. BEA SMT 2/31: Woods to Cobbold, 13 August 1940.
25. Ibid.: E. D. H. Skinner to C. F. Cobbold, 21 August 1940.
26. Ibid.: Handwritten note by 'M St P', 26 August 1940.
27. TNA BT 64/58: 'Proposals for legislation on films', n.d.
28. Ibid.: Report of a meeting of the Finance Committee of the Cinematograph Films Council, 13 August 1940.

29. TNA BT 64/117: Cinematograph Films Council: 'Resources now available to United Kingdom producers for the production of long and short films', n.d.
30. TNA BT 64/61: Oliver Lyttelton to Montagu Norman, 11 December 1940.
31. TNA BT 64/130: Estimated costs of British feature films, n.d. (mid-1943). As ever the average disguises a wide variation between the top and lower ends. Five films on the list cost over £100,000: *The Demi-Paradise* (£185,176), *The Life and Death of Colonel Blimp* (£163,502), *The First of the Few* (£141,626), *The Flemish Farm* (£115,971) and *Flying Fortress* (£102,848).
32. 'A Year of Struggle', *Kinematograph Year Book 1942* (London: Kinematograph Publications, 1942), p. 9.
33. Alan Wood, *Mr Rank: A Study of J. Arthur Rank and British Films* (London: Hodder & Stoughton, 1952), p. 153.
34. BEA SMT 2/31: E. Skinner to Cobbold, 30 April 1941.
35. Ibid.: Skinner to Cobbold, 23 January 1941.
36. 'Davis has key Rank position', *Kinematograph Weekly*, 11 April 1946, p. 3.
37. Political and Economic Planning, *The British Film Industry: A report on its history and present organisation, with special reference to the economic problems of British feature film production* (London: Political and Economic Planning, 1952), p. 135.
38. BEA SMT 2/31: 'Films', 14 July 1944.
39. 'Rank Tells the Story of His Losses', *Kinematograph Weekly*, 10 November 1949, p. 6.
40. 'Rank Pays Back £7 Million', *Kinematograph Weekly*, 6 September 1951, p. 3.
41. TNA BT 258/1945: Additional minute by S. Golt, 21 May 1952.
42. 'Associated British Picture Corporation, Ltd', *The Economist*, 29 September 1945, p. 466.
43. TNA BT 64/4531: Philip Warter to R. G. Somervell, 17 April 1947.
44. Political and Economic Planning, *The British Film Industry*, p. 86.
45. TNA BT 64/452: 'Mr Allen' – note by Hugh Dalton, 19 May 1943.
46. 'Long Shots', *Kinematograph Weekly*, 28 February 1946, p. 8.
47. TNA BT 64/95: E. Lightfoot to Board of Trade, 18 January 1945.
48. TNA BT 64/4529: Hugh Gaitskell to Liesching, 20 May 1943.
49. TNA BT 64/4531: Catherine Maxwell to Hugh Dalton, 25 October 1943.
50. TNA BT 64/94: File note – 'Undertaking by Messrs Warner Brothers to the President of the Board of Trade', n.d.
51. 'Long Shots', *Kinematograph Weekly*, 4 April 1946, p. 4.
52. Karol Kulik, *Alexander Korda: The Man Who Could Work Miracles* (London: W. H. Allen, 1975), pp. 286–7.
53. 'British Lion Film Expansion', *The Financial Times*, 12 March 1947, p. 1.
54. TNA BT 64/2366: Alexander Korda to Sir Wilfrid Eady, 7 July 1948.
55. TNA BT 64/4493: British First Feature Films Released Through British Lion Film Corporation during 30 months to 30 June 1949. This ledger reveals that *An Ideal Husband* cost £506,000 and returned distributors' receipts of £149,559; *Anna Karenina* cost £553,000 and returned £135,241; *Bonnie Prince Charlie* cost £760,000 and returned £155,570; *The Fallen Idol* cost £397,568 and returned £203,000; and *The Winslow Boy* cost £425,915 and returned £216,000.
56. 'All British Lion Films Except Two Showing a Loss', *Kinematograph Weekly*, 28 April 1949, p. 3.

57. 'State Money Saves British Lion from Receivership', *Kinematograph Weekly*, 5 January 1950, p. 30.
58. TNA BT 64/5156: Draft of letter from James Lawrie to Harold Wilson, n.d. It is not clear whether the letter was sent.
59. Vincent Porter, 'All Change at Elstree: Warner Bros., ABPC and British Film Policy, 1945–61', *Historical Journal of Film, Radio and Television*, 21: 1 (2001), pp. 5–35.
60. *Distribution and Exhibition of Films: Report of the Committee of Enquiry appointed by the President of the Board of Trade*, Cmd. 7837 (November 1949), p. 8 (15).
61. TNA BT 64/2366: 'Film Finance', n.d.
62. Ibid.: 'Memorandum on Independent Production'. The memo is undated but was included with a letter from Robert Garrett to Harold Wilson, 1 March 1948.
63. TNA T266/77: 'Film Finance', 1 December 1951.
64. TNA BT 64/2366: 'Memorandum on Independent Production'.
65. 'Back to the Banks Move for Film Finance', *Kinematograph Weekly*, 20 January 1949, p. 3.
66. TNA BT 64/2366: 'Film Finance', n.d.
67. Film Finances Archive (FFA) General Correspondence (Financial) Box 100: Robert Garrett to W. B. Cullen, 7 July 1952.
68. FFA Minute Book M.104: Minutes of the seventh meeting of Film Finances Ltd, 19 July 1950.
69. Lloyds Banking Group Archives: Advances and General Purposes Minute Book, 23 February 1950.
70. TNA BT 258/1945: Sir Frank Lee to Rupert Somervell, 19 May 1952.
71. 'Bewitched, Bothered and Bewildered', *Kinematograph Weekly: Studio Review Supplement*, 9 November 1950, p. 3.
72. Ibid.

CHAPTER 4

Producers and Profits

> The making of a film is the world's greatest gamble – and the most expensive. The stakes are too high, the odds far too long. And the hardest part of all is to find out whether you have won or lost – and exactly how much. (Sydney Box)[1]

In 1948 the British public paid a total of £109 million at the box offices of the approximately 4,800 cinemas in the United Kingdom.[2] For those unfamiliar with the peculiar structure and economics of the film business this did not obviously suggest an industry in crisis. And yet it was also estimated that in the same year the British film industry had lost £5 million on film production.[3] The combined producers' shares for all British films – the amount returned to producers following deduction of Entertainment Tax and after exhibitors and distributors had claimed their share of box-office receipts, and from which producers still had to cover their costs and overheads – amounted to £7.5 million in total. However, this was rather less than the £12.5 million estimated to have been invested in domestic production.[4] Even some very popular films did not make a profit. An example widely cited at the time was *The Courtneys of Curzon Street* – reported by the trade press as the top box-office attraction of 1947 – which 'collected for the Exchequer £406,250 in Entertainment Tax. Yet the Producer did not recover his production costs, which were on a very reasonable level.'[5]

There is much anecdotal evidence from producers' memoirs and the trade press that film production was an unprofitable business. On one level the film industry was like any other commercial enterprise: put simply, the return from sales must be greater than the cost of manufacturing and distributing the product in order to make a profit. But on every other level the film industry was unlike other businesses. For one thing the cost of production was much greater than the individual unit of revenue (the price of a single cinema ticket): therefore it depended on a very high number of individual sales which in turn required a large market. Britain had the largest domestic market for films outside the United States: in 1947 there were an estimated 1,514 million cinema admissions per year in Britain compared to 525 million in Italy and 419 million in France.[6] However, the domestic market was still not large enough to guarantee a profitable return for anything more than a modestly budgeted film. J. Arthur Rank had identified this problem in a memorandum for the Board of Trade in 1944:

> The disadvantage of an inadequate financial margin arising from the smallness of the Home market, however, remains. The cost of making films in this country has

risen greatly during the war. It is true that in spite of this, owing to the vast demand for entertainment, it is possible at present for a British picture costing in the region of £100,000 to £150,000 to make a profit. This state of affairs, however, is unlikely to continue and when peace comes most films costing up to these figures will be a risky speculation if they have to rely on the Home market alone.[7]

Other sources confirm this assessment. Maurice Ostrer, head of production at Gainsborough Pictures during the Second World War, averred that 'any subject made at a cost of more than £100,000 is liable to be an economic failure'.[8] Arthur Jarratt, the senior film booker for the Gaumont circuit, felt 'that the most a feature film could expect to gross in this country was £300,000'.[9] A maximum distributor's gross of around £300,000 seems to have been accepted as the trade's benchmark for a successful film. In 1946 the *Kine* reported that *The Wicked Lady* was expected to top £300,000, but that was regarded as exceptional.[10] As the cost of production and the distributor's fees and expenses had to be deducted from this amount before any profits could be calculated, it will be clear that the financial margins for British producers were very tight.

However, the film industry was also something of a paradox. On the one hand there was a maximum economic cost at which a film could be expected to return a profit; on the other hand the industry believed that it was the more expensive films that tended to have the higher market value. It is a truism that not every film is of equal quality: the industry has always maintained that there is a correlation between production values and popular appeal – hence the popularity of American films which generally had higher budgets than British films. A survey of the estimated costs and box-office appeal of 70 recent British films undertaken by the Cinematograph Exhibitors' Association in March 1949 suggested that this correlation was broadly correct, though there were some exceptions. The CEA's assessment of popular appeal was not based on statistical evidence but on which films its members reported were popular with their patrons. The CEA estimated that there were thirteen 'good' first features which 'could be offered as first features in the USA': *Hamlet* (Rank), *The Red Shoes* (Rank), *The Fallen Idol* (British Lion), *Oliver Twist* (Rank), *Scott of the Antarctic* (Ealing), *The Winslow Boy* (British Lion), *Spring in Park Lane* (British Lion), *The Guinea Pig* (ABPC), *Miranda* (Gainsborough), *Portrait from Life* (Gainsborough), *No Orchids for Miss Blandish* (Tudor), *Here Come the Huggets* (Gainsborough) and *No Room at the Inn* (British National).[11] Most of these films were from one of the major production groups, and most were estimated to have cost over the £150,000 regarded as the maximum for a film to return a profit from the home market (the last three on the list were the exceptions, each costing under £125,000). A further 31 films were identified as being first features of 'middling quality to poor, some of which would be acceptable as second features in [the] USA': around half of these were from the major production groups – most costing between £150,000 and £230,000, though there was one expensive Korda epic (*Bonnie Prince Charlie*) that cost substantially more – but there were also more independent producers towards the lower end of the budget range. The average cost of films in this category (excepting the Korda film) was £163,900.[12] Finally there were 26 second features, 'most of which are unacceptable to the US market' though some might be shown in Britain as first features: most of the films in this category cost under £50,000 and all of them were from smaller independent producers. The most prolific of the low-budget specialists was Rank's second feature unit Production Facilities which turned out seven films in 1948–9 – *A Song for Tomorrow*, *Colonel Bogey*, *Penny and the Parnell Case*, *Trouble in the Air*, *Fly Away, Peter*, *Love in Waiting* and *A Piece of Cake* – all costing between £20,000 and £25,000.[13]

Most sources suggest that the average cost for a British first feature in the late 1940s was between £125,000 and £150,000. The average cost disguised a wide variation between expensive 'super productions' and the routine programmers that remained the bread-and-butter of the industry. A Board of Trade Working Party on Film Production Costs in 1948 investigated the costs of 43 British first features by sixteen different producers made between 1946 and 1948. It grouped them into five categories: class 'A' (costing under £100,000), class 'B' (£100,000–£150,000), class 'C' (£150,000–£250,000), class 'D' (£250,000–£350,000) and class 'E' (over £350,000). It found that the largest number of films in the sample (14) were in the middle-cost range (£150,000–£250,000), with four in the lowest cost bracket and nine costing over £350,000.[14] The report does not mention specific titles, but other sources indicate that five films from the Rank Organisation (*Great Expectations*, *The Red Shoes*, *Hamlet*, *Blanche Fury*, *Oliver Twist*) and three from the British Lion Film Corporation (*Anna Karenina*, *The Fallen Idol*, *The Winslow Boy*) released between 1946 and 1948 cost over £350,000.

The industry acknowledged that production costs had escalated to the point where they were no longer economic. Even J. Arthur Rank acknowledged this in a speech to the Oxford University Film Society in 1946: 'Most films cost far too much. I am not only referring to *Caesar and Cleopatra*. Pictures are far too costly to-day, and that is keeping people back from going into production.'[15] British producers accepted that reducing costs was essential to return the industry to profitability. There was also a growing awareness that budgeting in the expectation of significant overseas revenues was a mistaken strategy. Herbert Wilcox – commercially one of the most successful British producers of the late 1940s – told the *Kine* in 1949: 'I am trying to trim production costs which are far too high. Export markets have almost gone and no British feature should cost more than £150,000 and mine have cost more than this. We have been trying to make not just box-office successes but "smash hits" and that is a bad policy.'[16] Frank Launder concurred: 'There have been cases of producers over-spending on a vast scale, perhaps in the mistaken belief that the American market was open to them, or perhaps just because they were the type of people who would over-spend anyway. At the same time the bulk of experienced British producers have tried very hard to keep rising costs down and to combine quality with economy.'[17]

There were different assessments of the reasons for the increasing costs of film production. One – favoured by politicians and journalists – was the charge of 'extravagance'. Harold Wilson raised this point in his speech to the British Film

Producers' Association in March 1949, though he accepted that producers also needed to take economic risks:

> The extravagance of the film industry is proverbial and much of the criticism is justified. Not only will the City hold completely aloof from the industry unless it can be shown to be taking radical steps to eliminate waste, but even such limited assistance as the Government is giving will be liable to criticism so long as it can be said that we are merely underwriting the continued supply of fur coats and other luxuries to the film moguls. At the same time it must be realised that a certain degree of extravagance is probably inseparable from this industry. Every film is an adventure and any attempt to tie down too tightly the somewhat flamboyant personalities concerned is more likely to end in the production of bad films and the loss of what has been spent on them.[18]

Wilson's characterisation of the extravagance of the 'film moguls' was probably somewhat unfair: for every spendthrift such as an Alexander Korda or a Gabriel Pascal there was an economically minded producer such as Michael Balcon of Ealing Studios or Sydney Box of Gainsborough Pictures. Nevertheless he was putting down a marker that assistance from the government would be dependent upon the industry putting its own house in order.

And in fairness, much of the escalating cost of production was not down to the excess of producers. The war had seen significant increases in wages, studio rents and the cost of raw materials. The Working Party on Film Production Costs found that average wages for film industry workers (excluding actors) had risen by 124 per cent between 1938 and 1949, and that the cost of some raw materials (such as timber for set construction) had increased by 300 per cent.[19] The introduction of a five-day 44-hour maximum working week by agreement with the film trades unions also meant that shooting schedules had become longer. Another factor was identified by producer R. J. Minney: that production costs were inflated by studio overheads. Following his resignation from Gainsborough Pictures in 1947, Minney complained that the Rank Organisation 'is too top heavy, and being over-centralised all the films cost more money to make because they have to carry the very large overheads. For example, a film which I could produce for £100,000 costs £40,000 to £50,000 more when made under the Rank Organisation – but you don't see this extra money on the screen.'[20] This was tacitly acknowledged by Rank's managing director John Davis, who confirmed that between July 1947 and December 1949 the combined studio overheads (£1,887,327) and production overheads (£1,644,510) amounted to 39 per cent of the total spent on production (£7,828,532) within the group. Davis was keen to point out, however, that 'the weekly cost of overhead expenditure has decreased very substantially over the period of 2½ years'.[21]

From information on film costs provided for the Board of Trade, it is possible to see where the budget was spent on a typical first feature in the post-war period. *Queen of Spades* (1948) – a costume drama directed by Thorold Dickinson for the Associated British Picture Corporation starring Anton Walbrook and Edith

Evans – cost £232,500: the major budget items (those costing over £5,000) were 'story and script' (£5,720), 'production and casting' (£7,126), 'artistes and extras' (£54,479), 'direction' (£13,025), 'camera' (£13,025), 'art direction' (£10,098), 'sets' (£37,195), 'set dressing and props' (£8,545), 'wardrobe' (£11,977), 'film stock and laboratory charges' (£8,150) and 'studio rent' (£32,000).[22] No single film can ever be entirely representative, of course: *Queen of Spades* was a studio picture so the cost breakdown featured minimal location costs but as a costume picture more was spent on wardrobe. The cost allocated for the camera operator (Otto Heller) is higher than usual for this period, while much of the cost of artistes was probably accounted for by the presence of Anton Walbrook. In contrast, *The Guinea Pig* (1948) – produced and directed by John and Roy Boulting for Pilgrim Pictures at a total cost of £252,418 – had significantly lower costs for camera operator Gilbert Taylor (£3,146) and for a cast headed by Richard Attenborough and Sheila Sim (£33,410) but higher costs for story and script (£16,961) and production and casting (£23,251) as well as £10,000 allocated for producer overheads.[23]

There were a number of industry initiatives to reduce costs in the late 1940s. In 1948, for example, the Rank Organisation introduced a process known as Independent Frame, which was intended 'to streamline production and reduce costs': the first picture completed using the process was *Warning to Wantons* (1949).[24] Independent Frame had been developed by a team led by art director David Rawnsley and arose from his experience of working on David Lean's *In Which We Serve* in 1942, for which he had created illusions of seascapes behind the partial set of a Royal Navy destroyer at Denham Studios.[25] The process was based around more detailed planning during pre-production in order to make more effective use of back-projection in preference to building large sets. Rawnsley explained the philosophy thus: 'Economy must begin in the fundamental design of a film . . . The colossal set helps to inflate the ego of the art director, just as a producer imagines his prestige is increased if he is allowed to spend a fortune on production.'[26] The fact that Independent Frame never really took off was due to a number of factors. Michael Powell was the only major director to embrace it in principle: most others remained sceptical. Nor did it help that the first group of films produced using the process in 1949, including *Stop Press* and *The Astonished Heart*, were hardly among Rank's finest. The process was overtaken by events: Gainsborough Pictures – responsible for around half of Rank's output and the Rank subsidiary that would have benefited most from the streamlining of production – was closed down as part of Rank's retrenchment in response to the economic crisis of 1948–9.[27]

The Board of Trade's intervention was no more successful. The Working Party on Film Production Costs had no fixed terms of reference: it interpreted its remit as being 'to examine ways and means of reducing production costs'. The Working Party was chaired by Sir George Gater, a former civil servant who had been Permanent Under-Secretary of State at the Colonial Office during the war and a senior officer at the Ministry of Supply. Its membership included representatives of production interests – John Davis of the Rank Organisation, Robert Clark of ABPC, Harold Boxall of London Film Productions and Sir Henry French of the British Film Producers' Association – and of the unions: George Elvin of the Association of Cine Technicians, Tom O'Brien of the National Association of Theatrical and Kinema Employees, Fred Haxell of the Electrical Trades Union, and actress Rosamund John representing the British Actors' Equity Association. The Working Party concluded that the overall increase in production costs was due in part to a 'substantial increase in costs of labour and raw materials since 1939' – something that was common to most industries – but that it also reflected the improving quality of British films, which was 'recognisably higher [and] has necessarily played its part in increasing production costs'.[28] It accepted that there was evidence of 'extravagance', which around 1945–6 had been 'allowed to go beyond all reasonable bounds'.[29] However, the Working Party was so concerned to balance the various factors at play that its conclusion was blandly equivocal:

> In reviewing the evidence submitted to us we find that producers tend to attribute present high costs to the increase in the cost of materials; to higher wage rates combined with a shorter working week; to the high level of studio rents; to 'restrictive practices' and to a decline in the team spirit. Studio workers, on the other hand, tend to stress high administrative expenses, top-heavy production executive staff (sometimes swelled by the introduction of 'passengers'), high salaries of 'stars', faulty planning, extravagance in sets and properties, and exaggerated standards of perfection.[30]

There were some specific recommendations – these included setting up joint production committees of management and unions to resolve industrial disputes (a strategy that was being adopted with some success in other industries) and the introduction of wage caps for artistes and 'higher technicians' in return for a share of the profits – though there was little enthusiasm for any of these measures in the industry itself. *Kine* felt that the Gater Report 'amounts to little more than a row of beans, except for the rather illuminating figures of labour costs it represents ... Apart from the emphasis given to the need for better industrial relations, they present no practical solution to the present situation.'[31]

The underlying reason for the unprofitability of British films, however, was not costs or quality but the economic structure of the film industry. The structure of distribution and exhibition was such that other parties all claimed their share of box-office receipts before the producer, who saw only a small proportion (usually less than 20 per cent) of the total taken by a film at the box office in the home market. From the total paid by cinema-goers at the box office, there were various deductions before the producer received their share. First there was Entertainment Tax (35 per cent of box-office receipts), which was sliced off the top. Then cinema exhibitors took their share of the net box-office receipts: this amount was variable (except for films hired for a flat rate – usually second features or reissues) but would not usually start at less than 60 per cent. In practice, several 'break points' were agreed between exhibitors and distributors at which different percentages were applied on a sliding scale, with the amount returned to the distributor increasing the more the film took at the box office: for example, exhibitors might pay 37.5 per cent of net box-office receipts to the distributor at the first break point up to £250; when the net receipts exceeded £250 the exhibitor would then pay 40 per cent until the next break point was reached, and so on. The maximum break point of 50 per cent was agreed between the Cinematograph Exhibitors' Association and Kinematograph Renters' Society in 1940 when American distributors were asking for 70 per cent for *Gone With the Wind*. In 1949 it was reported that the distributor (British Lion) had asked for 70 per cent for a booking of the popular *Spring in Park Lane* from an exhibitor who wanted to show it in preference to other films he regarded as 'unsuitable for his area'.[32] The amount returned to the distributor – already significantly less than half the total paid at the box office – was the distributor's gross: from this the distributor claimed their fee (usually around 20 per cent) and their expenses including the costs of prints and advertising. Whatever was left over was the producer's share, from which the producer had to repay the production loan (plus interest at 4.5 per cent) and cover their own overheads before any profit could be calculated. And the profit was not all the producer's: usually this would be shared with other financially interested parties (such as private investors) and with the distributor if the film had been financed through a distribution guarantee.

A single example will serve to demonstrate the division of box-office receipts. The case of *Spring in Park Lane* (1948) reveals how the producer's profits might be quite modest even for a very successful picture. *Spring in Park Lane* was one of Herbert Wilcox's cycle of romantic dramas starring Anna Neagle and Michael Wilding. It was the 'runner-up' at the British box office in 1948 (behind the American film *The Best Years of Our Lives*) and is held to have been one of the most popular British films of all time: its estimated domestic box-office gross of £1.4 million was 'a record for a British picture' at the time. Yet following the deduction of Entertainment Tax (£560,000), exhibitors' share (£462,000), distributor's fee (£75,000) and the costs of prints and advertising (£15,000), the producer's share of £280,000 was only around one-fifth of the total taken at the box office. From this Wilcox still had to repay the cost of production including interest (£238,000), which left him with a profit of £42,000.[33] Wilcox's share therefore amounted to 17 per cent of the total taken by the film at the box office: his profit in return to the cost of production was 17.6 per cent.

In short, the whole structure of distribution and exhibition was weighted against producers, who were the last to share in the box-office receipts of their films. This was highlighted by an inquiry commissioned by the Board of Trade in 1949 'to consider, against the background of the general economic situation of the film industry, the arrangements at present in operation for the distribution of films to exhibitors and the exhibition to the public in the commercial cinemas'. The committee was chaired initially by Lord Portal – who had been one of the original investors in the General Cinema Finance Corporation – and included two independent experts on the film industry in the form of Sir Arnold Plant (chairman of the Cinematograph Films Council) and James Lawrie (managing director of the National Film Finance Corporation): Plant became chairman of the committee following Portal's death during the course of the inquiry. The committee took evidence from the trade associations: the British Film Producers' Association (which highlighted Entertainment Tax as the main reason for declining profits), the Kinematograph Renters' Society (which declined the invitation to submit evidence and referred the committee to its previous comments on the Palache Report of 1944) and the Cinematograph Exhibitors' Association (which echoed the BFPA in blaming Entertainment Tax, though it argued simply for a remission of the tax rather than diverting it to supplement film production as the producers wanted). Alternative views were heard from the Association of British Independent Film Producers and from Jill Craigie of Outlook Films, who argued that the major circuits discriminated against independent producers by offering them less remunerative dates and locations.[34]

The Plant Report was particularly illuminating on the relationship between exhibition and film revenues. It presented evidence that an 'average' film might be expected to receive around 1,500 cinema bookings – which 'would normally mean a certain loss for a feature film made for the general market' – and that 2,000 bookings would be considered 'above average' and 2,500 as 'exceptional'.[35] The most profitable cinemas were controlled by the two combines: Rank and ABPC owned 974 cinemas in total and these included over two-thirds of the largest cinemas (those with a capacity over 1,000 seats). Therefore a release on one of the three main circuits – Rank's Odeon or Gaumont circuits or the ABC circuit – was highly desirable if not essential for a film to be able to make a profit. However, there was much anecdotal evidence that the circuits privileged films by producers within their own groups at the expense of independent producers, who 'were not satisfied that the circuit bookers would be allowed by the two groups to exercise complete impartiality even when deciding whether to offer a booking at all, to say nothing of the allocation of the most remunerative dates in the most important circuit cities'. 'In such circumstance,' the report suggested, 'independent British production was an exceedingly risky business.'[36]

The Board of Trade had the authority – under the Cinematograph Films Act of 1948 – to require the circuits to show up to six films a year 'by reason of their entertainment value'. It exercised this authority only once, in respect of *Chance of a Lifetime* (1949), produced and directed by Bernard Miles for Pilgrim Pictures. Pilgrim was an independent producer set up by Filippo Del Giudice following his break with Rank: its two previous films – *The Guinea Pig* and *Private Angelo* – had both been loss-makers for ABPC. In January 1950 Miles wrote to Harold Wilson to protest at the decision by ABC and the Circuit Management Association (parent organisation of the Odeon and Gaumont circuits) not to book *Chance of a Lifetime*: 'As it cost nearly £150,000 of independent money and represents the best part of a year's work by some of the finest film-makers in England, I would naturally welcome any assistance you could give me in smoothing its path towards general distribution.'[37] It was suspected that the circuits objected to the film not on grounds of quality but because of its political content: *Chance of a Lifetime* was a socialist-themed drama about a factory owner who lets the trades unions take over the running of his business.[38] Wilson referred *Chance of a Lifetime* to the Film Selection Committee under Section 5 of the Cinematograph Films Act.[39] The trade representatives all voted against a mandatory release (Sir Philip Warter averred that it 'had no entertainment value') but they were outnumbered by the independent members who felt that 'it was surely this kind of film that the Committee should try to protect'.[40] The committee resolved that *Chance of a Lifetime* should be accorded a circuit release and lots were drawn as to which circuit should take the film: it was allocated to the Odeon circuit. It did only moderate business at the box office: it is a moot point whether this was because it was poorly promoted (possibly deliberately) or because it was just a poor film.[41]

The most complete evidence regarding film costs and revenues for this period is to be found in the information provided by the four main production groups – Rank, British Lion, ABPC and Ealing Studios – at the request of the Board of Trade early in 1950. The context for this was that the Board of Trade was considering some form of 'special assistance' for the production sector: it was particularly interested in the share of box-office receipts returned to producers in relation to the amount invested in production. The Rank Organisation provided the most comprehensive data: John Davis compiled a memorandum summarising Rank's expenditure on production for the period between June 1947 and December 1949. He also included a schedule of 30 films with their production costs, the producer's share (including domestic and overseas receipts) and the margin of profit or loss. Rank had the most diverse portfolio of the major production groups: the schedule of films includes prestige pictures from its Independent Producers group – *Great Expectations, Oliver Twist, London Belongs To Me, The Passionate Friends* and *The Blue Lagoon* – and regular first features produced by its Gainsborough Pictures subsidiary. It also included two 'specials' costing over £500,000 – *The Red Shoes* and *Hamlet* – which were listed separately 'on the grounds that they are exceptional. The profits estimated on these two films are by reason of the fact that they both succeeded in the United States market. Otherwise, significant losses would have been made.'[42] The average cost of Rank's films (excluding *The Red Shoes* and *Hamlet*) was £233,176 (significantly more than the £150,000 which Rank deemed the upper limit for a film to return a profit from the home market), the average combined producer's share (including both home and overseas) was £150,386 and the average producer's share from the home market was £102,990. The average return from the home market was therefore only 44 per cent of the average production cost. The average costs of course covered a wide budget range: the lowest-cost film was *My Brother's Keeper* (£113,600) and the highest-cost film in the regular schedule was *Great Expectations* (£391,600).

The Rank data is revealing in several important respects. Only eight of the 30 films in the regular schedule returned a profit – *Great Expectations* (+£21,200), *The Upturned Glass* (+£45,000), *Holiday Camp* (+£16,000), *Easy Money* (+£2,200), *Miranda* (+£5,600), *Oliver Twist* (+£8,900), *Portrait from Life* (+£4,100) and *The Blue Lagoon* (+£40,000) – and the average profit was a little over £18,000 per film. In contrast, the average loss on the 22 unsuccessful films was £119,000. The losses were particularly severe on high-budget films costing over £250,000: these included *The Hungry Hill* (-£201,200), *Mr Perrin & Mr Traill* (-£194,600), *Blanche Fury* (-£135,000), *London Belongs To Me* (-£168,200), *The Passionate Friends* (-£127,400) and *Esther Waters* (-£305,706). And middle-range films costing between £125,000 and £250,000 were also often unprofitable: *Green for Danger* (-£26,200), *Take My Life* (-£84,900), *The Brothers* (-£55,200), *The End of the River* (-£78,000), *The Mark of Cain* (-£77,800), *Broken Journey* (-£63,900), *One Night With You* (-£173,000), *The Bad Lord Byron* (-£179,200), *The Weaker Sex* (-£69,400) and *The History of Mr Polly* (-£172,100). The figures suggest – contrary to the received wisdom in the industry – that there was no direct correlation between the cost of films and their box-office returns. Of the films costing over £300,000, three made a profit – *Great Expectations*, *Oliver Twist* and *The Blue Lagoon* – but the others in the same budget range all incurred heavy losses. At the same time, much cheaper films such as *My Brother's Keeper* and *Marry Me* also lost money: *Easy Money* was the only film costing under £150,000 to make a profit. The overall loss on the films on Rank's regular schedule amounted to £2,484,000: this was reduced to £918,00 when the two 'exceptional' films – *The Red Shoes* (+£785,700) and *Hamlet* (+£773,700) – are included.

However, none of the Rank films would have made a profit in the home market alone. The biggest producers' shares from the domestic market were for *Oliver Twist* (£277,300), *Great Expectations* (£222,600), *The Blue Lagoon* (£186,500), *Hamlet* (£187,800), *The Red Shoes* (£179,900), *The Upturned Glass* (£156,000), *Blanche Fury* (£145,300), *Miranda* (£143,400), *Holiday Camp* (£141,900), *The Hungry Hill* (£133,200) and *Green for Danger* (£114,700): in each case this was less than the cost of production of those films. The largest producers' shares from overseas distribution by some distance were for *Hamlet* (£1,164,400) and *The Red Shoes* (£1,111,400): the next biggest were for *Great Expectations* (£190,200), *The Blue Lagoon* (£164,900), *The Passionate Friends* (£135,900), *Oliver Twist* (£103,100) and *Blanche Fury* (£101,500). *The Passionate Friends* was the one film in the regular schedule where the overseas producer's share was significantly more (£52,400) than the domestic share: the only other regular film to make more overseas was *The End of the River* but this was by a negligible amount (£200). Otherwise the two 'exceptional' films each returned over five times more from overseas markets than from the home market. All the profitable films were therefore dependent upon overseas revenues for their profits, though the fact of significant overseas revenues (as for *The Passionate Friends* and *Blanche Fury*) did not necessarily translate into a profit overall. However, there was no correlation between overall profit and the differential between domestic and overseas revenues. For example, *Holiday Camp* earned 85.2 per cent of its revenues in the home market and *Miranda* earned 81.5 per cent: both were modest successes. In contrast, *The History of Mr Polly* earned 87.1 per cent in the home market and *The Mark of Cain* earned 92.3 per cent at home: both were significant loss-makers. David Lean's two Dickensian adaptations were both profitable, but while 46 per cent of the total producer's share for *Great Expectations* came from overseas, the equivalent figure for *Oliver Twist* was only 27 per cent.

It was a similar picture for the British Lion Film Corporation. British Lion submitted costs and revenues from the home market for seventeen films released between January 1947 and June 1949: *The Shop at Sly Corner*, *White Cradle Inn*, *The Courtneys of Curzon Street*, *Man About the House*, *An Ideal Husband*, *Mine Own Executioner*, *Nightbeat*, *Call of the Blood*, *Anna Karenina*, *Spring in Park Lane*, *The Winslow Boy*, *The Fallen Idol*, *The Small Voice*, *Bonnie Prince Charlie*, *Elizabeth of Ladymead*, *The Small Back Room* and *Forbidden*. The average cost of these films was £294,209, with a lowest cost for *The Shop at Sly Corner* (£76,715) and a highest cost for the historical epic *Bonnie Prince Charlie* (£760,000). British Lion had three films costing over £500,000 (*An Ideal Husband*, *Anna Karenina* and *Bonnie Prince Charlie*) and another four between £300,000 and £500,000 (*The Courtneys of Curzon Street*, *Man About the House*, *The Winslow Boy* and *The Fallen Idol*). It is no coincidence that the three most expensive films were all personal projects of Alexander Korda and were all big loss-makers: *An Ideal Husband* (-£356,441), *Anna Karenina* (-£457,313) and *Bonnie Prince Charlie* (-£665,673). However, British Lion also lost money on critically acclaimed films such as Carol Reed's *The Fallen Idol* (-£247,035) and Anthony Asquith's *The Winslow Boy* (-£266,382). Its only profitable films of those for which it provided data were *The Shop at Sly Corner* – a low-cost feature by quota producer George King which returned a modest profit of £16,162 – and Herbert Wilcox's *Spring in Park Lane*.[43]

Ealing Studios provided data on the costs of sixteen films released between 1947 and 1950 – *Nicholas Nickleby*, *Hue and Cry*, *The Loves of Joanna Godden*, *Frieda*, *Against the Wind*, *It Always Rains on Sunday*, *Saraband for Dead Lovers*, *Scott of the Antarctic*, *Another Shore*, *Passport to Pimlico*, *Whisky Galore!*, *Kind Hearts and Coronets*, *Train of Events*, *A Run for Your Money*, *The Blue Lamp* and *Dance Hall* – with the producers' shares for those released in 1948 and 1949: another film (*Eureka Stockade*) was listed in the revenues but not in the costs.[44] In 1944 Ealing had switched from its own distributor (Associated British Film Distributors) to General Film Distributors, which provided 50 per cent of the finance in return for worldwide distribution rights.[45] Although there were some differences in the calculation of costs (the Ealing data includes both 'direct costs' and 'negative costs'), a familiar picture emerges. The average negative cost of the Ealing films was £197,180: this was inflated by two high-cost pictures in *Scott of the Antarctic* (£371,588) and *Saraband for Dead Lovers* (£371,205), without which the average was £172,924. Ealing's head of production Michael Balcon advocated a policy of economic production for the home market:

> Much of the present crisis in British film production may be laid at the feet of the policy of costing films on an expectancy of proper American returns, thus making films with star and production values to compete with the best American product in our own domestic market. It is easy enough to advocate that we should make films costed on an expectancy of domestic returns only, but inevitably this diminished the appeal of such films in our own British kinemas.[46]

However, Ealing's policy of costing films for the home market was no more successful than the international strategies of Rank or British Lion. Only two films returned a profit – *Frieda* (+£15,620) and *It Always Rains on Sunday* (+£7,311) – whereas there were heavy losses on *Saraband for Dead Lovers* (-£312,171), *Passport to Pimlico* (-£251,938), *Scott of the Antarctic* (-£205,261) and *Another Shore* (-£155,990). In 1949 Ealing's parent company Associated Talking Pictures reported an overall deficit of £133,868: its chairman Stephen Courtauld mentioned in his report to shareholders that – due to a number of factors including unusually fine weather affecting box-office receipts and decreasing public expenditure on entertainment – 'even outstandingly successful films such as I have mentioned [*Passport to Pimlico, Whisky Galore!, Kind Hearts and Coronets*] did not mature to the full the revenue which the films themselves merited.'[47]

However, it was the Associated British Picture Corporation which provided the most striking evidence of the unprofitability of British films in the late 1940s. ABPC was the most economical of the major production groups: the average cost of the thirteen films for which it provided data – *While the Sun Shines, Temptation Harbour, Silver Darlings, Brighton Rock, My Brother Jonathan, Bond Street, Noose, The Guinea Pig, Queen of Spades, Silent Dust, For Them That Trespass, Man on the Run* and *Private Angelo* – was £164,536.[48] The most expensive of its films was *The Guinea Pig* (£252,418) and the least expensive was *Silver Darlings* (£94,731). What is striking about the ABPC schedule is that none of its films made a profit. Its biggest losses were recorded on *Queen of Spades* (-£214,822), *Private Angelo* (-£199,224), *The Guinea Pig* (-£130,594), *For Them That Trespass* (-£111,765) and *Bond Street* (-£104,018). But even ABPC's more modestly budgeted films such as *While the Sun Shines* (-£48,033), *Temptation Harbour* (-£61,148), *Silver Darlings* (-£72,895) and *Man on the Run* (-£74,142) – all costing under £135,000 – also lost money in the home market.

A difference between the ABPC data and the other production groups was that ABPC also included estimated figures for the net box-office receipts (after Entertainment Tax but before exhibitors' share had been deducted) of each film in the United Kingdom. This data provides even more compelling evidence of how the system of distribution and exhibition was weighted against producers. Three ABPC films returned net box-office receipts over £500,000 – *My Brother Jonathan* (£844,725), *Brighton Rock* (£586,595) and *The Guinea Pig* (£665,107) – and a fourth, *Noose* (£498,800), was very close to that amount. These films were all considered 'hits' by the trade press. However, not only were they loss-makers for their producers but in each case the producer's share was less than 20 per cent of the total box-office gross: 16.9 per cent for *My Brother Jonathan* (£142,813), 18.3 per cent for *Brighton Rock* (£94,902) and 16.9 per cent for *The Guinea Pig* (£121,824). The operation of break points in the amount returned by exhibitors to the distributor meant that producers' shares for the more successful films were a higher percentage of the total receipts than for the less successful films. For the three films where net box-office receipts were below £250,000 – *Silver Darlings* (£244,721), *Queen of Spades* (£226,096) and *Private Angelo* (£177,152) – the producer's share amounted to only 8.9 per cent, 7.8 per cent and 6.2 per cent of the total. It is therefore little wonder that ABPC's chairman Sir Philip Warter commented in 1949: 'Under present conditions, film production is a hazardous business and is only justified in the national interest, and by the necessity under the Cinematograph Films Act of ensuring a steady supply of British product.'[49]

What the evidence of costs and returns demonstrates overwhelmingly is that the entire business of film-making was structurally unprofitable: few films made a profit and those that did often represented a relatively modest return in relation to the investment. This naturally impacted upon the provision of finance for film-making. As a *Kine* editorial in February 1949 remarked: 'It is an axiom of commercial life that no enterprise which can be guaranteed to return profits to an investor need lack for capital. Conversely, any enterprise which entails expenditure which cannot be covered by eventual income finds capital impossible or at least very hard to maintain.'[50] The producers most affected by the shortage of finance were the independents who produced one film at a time: the major groups – whose operation allowed them to spread their risks across a portfolio of films and (in the case of Rank and ABPC) could offset their losses in production against their profits from exhibition – were in a better position to ride out the crisis, though even so their losses on production were heavy. This was the context in the late 1940s that prompted the government to take action in the form of two initiatives to assist the British production sector: the setting up of the National Film Finance Corporation (1948) to provide loans to British producers and the establishment of the British Film Production Fund (1950), which increased the amount of the box-office receipts returned to producers through the introduction of a levy on ticket sales. These two measures were the cornerstones of the Labour government's rescue plan for the film industry: each will now be considered in turn.

Notes

1. Sydney Box, *The Lion That Lost Its Way and Other Cautionary Tales of the Show Business Jungle*, ed. Andrew Spicer (Lanham, MA: Scarecrow Press, 2005), p. 117.
2. *Distribution and Exhibition of Films: Report of the Committee of Enquiry appointed by the President of the Board of Trade*, Cmd. 7837 (November 1949), p. 19 (40).
3. 'Hire Finance', *Kinematograph Weekly*, 14 December 1950, p. 11.
4. Political and Economic Planning, *The British Film Industry: A report on its history and present organisation, with special reference to the economic problems of British feature film production* (London: Political and Economic Planning, 1952), p. 281.
5. TNA BT 64/4511: Entertainment Tax: Joint Memorandum by Exhibitors and Producers, 7 December 1949.
6. Political and Economic Planning, *The British Film Industry*, pp. 170, 172.
7. TNA BT 64/95: J. Arthur Rank to Hugh Dalton, 'The Future of the British Film Production Industry', 1 July 1944. The memorandum was sent on behalf of the British Film Producers' Association (Rank was the BFPA's president at the time) rather than the Rank Organisation.
8. A. L. Carter, 'British Production', *Kinematograph Year Book 1944* (London: Kinematograph Publications, 1944), p. 268.
9. 'Medium Cost Quota Subjects Needed', *Kinematograph Weekly*, 3 January 1946, p. 7.
10. 'Long Shots', *Kinematograph Weekly*, 31 January 1946, p. 7.

11. 'CEA Grades 70 British Feature Films', *Kinematograph Weekly*, 17 March 1949, p. 9.
12. The films identified as being of 'middling quality' were: *Bonnie Prince Charlie* (British Lion), *London Belongs To Me* (Rank), *Saraband for Dead Lovers* (Ealing), *Broken Journey* (Gainsborough), *Once a Jolly Swagman* (Rank), *One Night With You* (Rank), *Esther Waters* (Rank), *Another Shore* (Ealing), *The Calendar* (Gainsborough), *Good Time Girl* (Rank), *Mr Perrin & Mr Traill* (Rank), *Quartet* (Gainsborough), *Woman Hater* (Rank), *The Weaker Sex* (Rank), *Sleeping Car to Trieste* (Rank), *Eureka Stockade* (Ealing), *Daybreak* (Tritan). *Bond Street* (World Screen Plays), *Blind Goddess* (Gainsborough), *Noose* (Edward Dryhurst), *It's Hard To Be Good* (Rank), *Look Before You Love* (Burnham), *The Small Voice* (Constellation), *My Sister and I* (Burnham), *A Warning to Wantons* (Aquilus), *My Brother's Keeper* (Gainsborough), *Counterblast* (British National), *Third Time Lucky* (Kenilworth), *William Comes to Town* (Diadem Films), *Uneasy Terms* (British National) and *Whispering City* (Quebec Productions).
13. The films listed in this group were: *Things Happen at Night* (Tudor), *Calling Paul Temple* (Butcher's Film Services), *The Story of Shirley Yorke* (Nettlefold), *Cup-Tie Honeymoon* (Mancunian), *Holidays With Pay* (Mancunian), *The Fool and the Princess* (Merton Park), *House of Darkness* (International), *Colonel Bogey* (Production Facilities), *A Song for Tomorrow* (Production Facilities), *Penny and the Parnell Case* (Production Facilities), *Trouble in the Air* (Production Facilities), *Fly Away, Peter* (Production Facilities), *Love in Waiting* (Production Facilities), *A Piece of Cake* (Production Facilities), *A Sister to Assist 'Er* (Brunton), *The Fatal Night* (Anglofilms), *The Monkey's Paw* (Kay Film Printing), *The Last Land* (Elstree Independents), *The Dark Road* (Marylebone), *The Clouded Crystal* (A. Grossman), *A Gunman Has Escaped* (Condor), *My Hands are Clay* (Dublin Films), *Date With A Dream* (Tempean), *Trinity House* (Ace Distributors), *It Happened in Soho* (F. C. Film Productions) and *Loco Number One* (E.F.D.).
14. *Report of the Working Party on Film Production Costs* (1949), p. 27.
15. 'Films cost too much, Rank tells Oxford students', *Kinematograph Weekly*, 14 February 1946, p. 32.
16. 'The Production Slump', *Kinematograph Weekly*, 17 February 1949, p. 6.
17. 'Rank Will Cut His 1950 Film Programme', *Kinematograph Weekly*, 31 March 1949, p. 12.
18. TNA BT 64/4515: 'Present State of the Film Industry', speech prepared for the President of the Board of Trade, March 1949.
19. *Report of the Working Party on Film Production Costs*, pp. 9 (18), 14 (32).
20. 'Minney and costs', *Kinematograph Weekly*, 6 February 1947, p. 20.
21. TNA BT 64/4490: J. Arthur Rank Organisation Ltd: Memorandum regarding information required by the Board of Trade regarding Film Production and Distribution, Schedule I.
22. TNA BT 64/4492: Associated British Picture Corporation Ltd: Production Department: Summary of production costs of *Queen of Spades*.
23. Ibid.: Associated British Picture Corporation Ltd: Production Department: Summary of production costs of *The Guinea Pig*.
24. 'The First Independent Frame-Made Feature Comes to the Screen', *Kinematograph Weekly*, 6 January 1949, p. 6.
25. Geoffrey Macnab, *J. Arthur Rank and the British Film Industry* (London: Routledge, 1993), pp. 122–31.
26. Oliver Blakeston and David Rawnsley, 'Design by Inference', *The Penguin Film Review*, 9 (May 1949), p. 34.

27. Macnab, *J. Arthur Rank and the British Film Industry*, pp. 129–30.
28. *Report of the Working Party on Film Production Costs*, p. 7 (11).
29. Ibid. p. 7 (12).
30. Ibid. p. 7 (11).
31. 'Bricks without Straw', *Kinematograph Weekly*, 1 December 1949, p. 4.
32. '70 Per Cent Asked for Solo Booking of *Spring in Park Lane*', *Kinematograph Weekly*, 17 February 1949, p. 22.
33. 'The *Real* Story of the Film Crisis', *Evening News*, 22 February 1949, p. 5.
34. TNA BT 64/4468: Association of Independent Producers, 'The Plant Report and the Independent Producer', n.d.
35. *Distribution and Exhibition of Films*, p. 18 (39).
36. Ibid. pp. 16–17 (35).
37. TNA BT 64/4466: Bernard Miles to Harold Wilson, 4 January 1950.
38. Ibid.: Sir Arthur Jarratt to A. G. White, 4 January 1950.
39. The chair of the Film Selection Committee was Lord Drogheda (chairman of the Cinematograph Films Council and Deputy Speaker of the House of Lords) and the four independent members were Rupert Somervell (Board of Trade), C. J. Geddes (General Secretary of the Union of Post Office Workers), Margaret Stewart (industrial correspondent of the *News Chronicle*) and the Hon. D. Bowes-Lyon (a banker and brother of Queen Elizabeth who was absent from the meeting due to illness). The three trade representatives – Sir Philip Warter, Mr Hamer and Mr Kent – did not vote. Three films were considered: *Torment, High Jinks in Society* and *Chance of a Lifetime*. The committee dismissed the other two films but resolved that *Chance of a Lifetime* was worthy of a circuit release.
40. Ibid.: Appendix to the Minutes: Discussion of the Independent Members before the third meeting of the Committee.
41. Vincent Porter, 'Feature Film and the Mediation of Historical Reality: *Chance of a Lifetime* – a case study', *Media History*, 5: 2 (1999), pp. 181–99.
42. TNA BT 64/4490: J. Arthur Rank Organisation Ltd; Memorandum regarding information required by the Board of Trade regarding Film Production and Distribution, Schedule III.
43. TNA BT 64/4493: British First Features Released Through British Lion Film Corporation Ltd During 30 Months to 30 June 1949.
44. TNA BT 64/4491: Ealing Studios Ltd: Untitled memorandum documenting production costs and revenues of films between 1947 and 1950.
45. Michael Balcon, *Michael Balcon presents . . . A Lifetime of Films* (London: Hutchinson, 1969), p. 154.
46. 'Balcon Charter for 1949: Calls for More Cuts in Costs and Union Streamlining', *Kinematograph Weekly*, 2 June 1949, p. 17.
47. 'Associated Talking Pictures Limited', *The Economist*, 24 December 1949, p. 1438.
48. TNA BT 64/4492: Associated British Pathé: UK Distribution: Analysis of contracts played to 1 April 1950.
49. 'ABP's Sir Philip writes off film losses', *Daily Herald*, 14 July 1949, p. 5.
50. 'Production Crisis', *Kinematograph Weekly*, 17 February 1949, p. 3.

CHAPTER 5

The National Film Finance Corporation

> The Government's decision to give Treasury support to independent film finance was spectacular in the extreme . . . If the Films Bank, for that is what it is, call it what one likes, preserves independent British pictures at a time when the really independent producer is being driven practically out of the market, then it will have wholly justified itself. (*Kinematograph Weekly*)[1]

The circumstances that brought about the creation of the National Film Finance Corporation (NFFC) were remarkable in many respects – not least of which was the speed and alacrity with which the government acted once it had decided upon a course of action. By mid-1948 the production crisis had become so acute that the Board of Trade, having previously opposed the idea of a state-funded film bank, made an extraordinary *volte face* and hurried through legislation to create just such a body. Initially, at least, Harold Wilson seems to have envisaged that private investment could be unlocked without the need for state aid. In March 1948 he told the Cinematograph Exhibitors' Association that 'he had now concluded talks with various banking houses in London, and was convinced that there was sufficient capital available to make sure that the British film production programme could go through as planned by producers at the moment'.[2] However, at some point during the spring or early summer of 1948 Wilson concluded that the only way to ensure the continuation of domestic film production was through some measure of state funding. In July he announced that a 'Government Film Corporation' would be set up for this purpose as soon as possible.[3]

On one level the decision to establish a state-funded film finance agency can be seen as a short-term response to the financing and production crisis of the late 1940s. In April 1948 the *Kine* predicted that there would be only 45 first features from British studios in the calendar year – a total wholly insufficient for exhibitors to meet their quota.[4] In early July a deputation from the British Film Producers' Association met Harold Wilson 'to acquaint him with the seriousness of conditions currently existing in British studios' and told him that 'there will shortly be no more studios to close down, so seriously is closing down outstripping putting up'.[5] The plight of independent producers was exemplified by the case of Pilgrim Pictures, which Filippo Del Giudice had set up after losing control of Two Cities Films to Rank. At this stage Pilgrim had made only one film (*The Guinea Pig*), but it was already experiencing difficulty in raising finance. W. G. Riley, a private investor, wrote what was in effect a begging letter to Wilson playing the national interest card: 'I did not go into Pilgrim initially, and support it with my capital, with any intention of making a living out of it, or adding further to my commercial headaches – I did it solely as a gesture, in the National interest.'[6]

It was also during the spring of 1948 that it became evident that the British Lion Film Corporation was severely compromised. Alexander Korda's ambitious production programme had sustained heavy losses and British Lion needed an immediate bail-out if it was to continue making films. In April 1948 Korda asked the Board of Trade for a loan of £1 million in order to allow British Lion to become 'the instrument for the production and distribution of films made by British independent producers . . . For future productions which will be greatly expanded a revolving credit will be opened up by a consortium of Banks to the amount of four or five million pounds.'[7] The first indication that the government was willing to consider mounting a rescue operation for British Lion is to be found in the record of a meeting between Wilson, Korda and Sir Arthur Jarratt on 13 April where Wilson 'explained something of our plans for British Lion and both were very favourably impressed. They agreed in principle to the reconstitution of the Board and Sir Alexander said that as the present Chairman was his nominee it would be perfectly simple to secure a change in that office.'[8] Korda evidently understood that the price of a bail-out would be that he personally should take more of a back seat. At this stage, however, Sir Wilfrid Eady at the Treasury said that he was 'disinclined' to see Korda relinquish control: 'In the first place if he is bought out somebody has to find that money . . . In the second place there is, I think, some advantage in having someone like Korda "knocking about the office".'[9]

In a wider political context the establishment of the NFFC was consistent with the Labour government's policy for economic reconstruction. There were precedents for the NFFC in both the Finance Corporation for Industry (FCI) and the Industrial and Commercial Finance Corporation (ICFC). The FCI had been set up in order to provide government loans for manufacturing industries: it was backed by the Bank of England and by a consortium of investment trusts and insurance companies. The role of the ICFC was to assist the growth of small and medium-sized businesses by providing investment for expansion: its capital was subscribed by the banking sector. The rationale behind these bodies was that there was a role for the state in industry that fell short of full nationalisation: they were intended to provide stimulus for growth that would allow industry to unlock further investment from the private sector. There was a suggestion that the FCI might extend its loans to the film industry: Nicholas Davenport suggested the idea of 'a new "film FCI", the insurance companies being the shareholders with, if possible, the Bank of England as co-shareholder'.[10] Davenport drew up a memorandum proposing that the Bank of England should set up 'a Film Credits Corporation – a sort of specialised Finance Corporation of Industry – and should direct joint stock banks to take up, say, 45% of its capital'. Its role would be to advance to 'approved film producers' the 25 per cent of the budget not covered by standard distribution guarantees and to provide 'medium-term credit' for established production groups in cases where they needed more credit than was acceptable to their bankers.[11]

In the event, the FCI decided that it did not want to get involved in the film industry, and there were also fundamental objections at both the Treasury and the Board of Trade to the idea of subsidising the major combines whom it was felt should be able to stand on their own feet. Nevertheless, Davenport's proposal did contribute to the growing tide of opinion that some form of government-backed support was necessary for the short-term survival of the industry.

What now seems most remarkable about the origin of the NFFC is that it was set up with such expediency. As there was no time to introduce the necessary legislation before Parliament's summer recess, an interim body, the National Film Finance Company (NFFCo.), was created in order 'to bridge the gap between now and the establishment of the Statutory Corporation'.[12] As a limited company, the NFFCo. did not require statutory authority and could be incorporated under the terms of the Companies Act of 1948. The company was duly incorporated in October 1948 with an overdraft of £2.5 million guaranteed by the Treasury.[13] Its interim chairman and managing director was James Lawrie, previously managing director of the ICFC. Lawrie was joined on the board of the new company by Nicholas Davenport, solicitor C. H. Scott, accountant S. J. Pears, formerly of the Ministry of Supply, and lawyer Richard Stopford, who specialised in international finance.[14] Davenport was the one member of the board with experience of the film industry: he relinquished his directorship of British Lion in order to join the NFFCo. because it seemed very likely that a substantial loan would be made to British Lion. Indeed, within a month of its establishment, the company confirmed that its first loans had been agreed: £1 million to British Lion and £20,000 to Exclusive Films.[15] The loan to British Lion was to all intents and purposes working capital rather than advances for specific films. Lawrie justified it on the grounds that it had been necessary to keep the company going: 'Without our help, British Lion would have found it difficult to carry out its programme of production. We have kept British Lion in operation to an extent it could not have operated without our money.'[16]

At the start the NFFCo. was empowered to lend only to distributors rather than direct to producers: the distributors would invest the money in production by making advances to producers secured against the box-office receipts. The rationale for this arrangement was that the Board of Trade did not want the NFFCo. or its statutory successor to be seen as in direct competition with private capital for the provision of production finance. Wilson stressed that 'this money is *not* being provided with the intention that any and every producer or would-be producer of films can obtain finance for any project that he likes to put forward'.[17] At this stage it was evidently felt that proper scrutiny of projects was best left in the hands of the distributors who would be handling the films in the marketplace: this decision drew criticism from independent producers who felt that it left too much power with distributors who were likely to be cautious in their choice of subjects at the expense of producers who were more willing to take commercial and artistic risks. Furthermore, it did nothing to address one of the key concerns of producers: that they were the last to share in box-office receipts. *Kine* argued that Wilson had ignored 'the basic cause of the present condition of British film-making . . . The inference that the promise of finance is coupled with an adequate return on a film when it reaches a kinema is fallacious unless a satisfactory remunerative outlet is assured.'[18]

In the meantime the Board of Trade concerned itself with preparing the legislation necessary to establish the NFFC on a statutory basis. The aim of the Cinematograph Film Production (Special Loans) Bill was 'to make provision for the lending of money to be employed in financing the production or distribution of cinematograph films, and to provide for the taking over by a national corporation established for the purpose aforesaid of [the] National Film Finance Company Limited'.[19] The NFFC would be established on a temporary basis for five years and would be able to draw upon advances from the Board of Trade to a maximum of £5 million which it would then use to make loans to support film production. The requirement that loans could be made only to distributors was relaxed in such cases 'where the producer can point to a satisfactory record of production; can demonstrate to the Corporation that the risk will be spread over a programme of pictures (i.e. will not be concentrated on one picture or one pair of pictures which may both of them be "flops"); and can get some finance or guarantees of completion from private backers or from renters.'[20] Wilson was at pains to stress that the NFFC was intended to supplement private finance and that 'the Corporation will be a lender of last resort':

> The facilities offered by the Corporation are not offered *in competition* with the facilities already available to the industry through existing channels, but are offered to *supplement* those other facilities where the normal facilities would otherwise be inadequate. Broadly speaking, this means that the Government still relies on the banks and other private financial institutions to provide the first-charge fixed-interest capital required for any given production (normally 75% of whatever minimum fixed amount has been guaranteed to the producer by the distributor as the producer's share of the eventual proceeds), but the Corporation will be empowered to help provide the remainder (the 'end money').[21]

In this way 'it is hoped and believed that film production, conducted on sound economic lines, will be recognised by the City as credit-worthy, and that film producers of standing and repute will be able thereafter to obtain their finance by normal methods from private investors'.[22] Evidence that officials were sensitive to the likely criticisms of the provision of government aid for film production from the Tory right can be found in a memorandum regarding the corporation's draft regulations: 'They deal with matters of pure formality and although they have to do with films, I venture to think that our most violent critics – even for instance the *Daily Express* – will find them unexceptionable.'[23]

In the event, the legislation to establish the NFFC had a relatively straightforward passage through Parliament: the bill passed without division through the committee stages and its readings in both Houses. The consensus was that it was 'a matter for regret' that the situation of the film industry had become so bad that the measure had become necessary, but there was a general acceptance of the need to establish the corporation. Some Conservative MPs did indeed raise the question of providing public money for the film industry, though their concern was more to do with protecting the government's investment than opposition to the scheme in principle. Oliver Lyttelton, the Opposition spokesman for trade, proposed an amendment during the committee stage 'to prevent advances against one or two films when in fact the commercial basis on which the production is put is a "goner", if I may use a vulgarism, before it starts': he cited Korda's *Bonnie Prince Charlie* (1948) as an example.[24] The Korda film became something of a whipping boy during the debate as it was the most recent case of an expensive super-production that had flopped at the box office. Nevertheless, it seems that the Opposition did not wish to be too obstructive over the bill: a Board of Trade memorandum records that 'Mr Lyttelton accepts our latest version of the so-called "Lyttelton amendment" and will give it "such qualified blessing as his hostile character allows"!'[25]

The NFFC was formally constituted in April 1949 and took over the assets – and perhaps more to the point the liabilities – of its predecessor. James Lawrie continued as managing director and the same board of directors remained except for Nicholas Davenport, who resigned at the start of the year in order to become chairman of a new production outfit.[26] However, Wilson appointed Lord Reith of Stonehaven as the NFFC's chairman at a salary of £3,500 per year. Reith had been the first Director General of the British Broadcasting Corporation between 1927 and 1938 and had served (briefly) as Minister of Information during the Second World War. He was known for his organisational skills as well as for his puritan outlook on matters cultural. Wilson felt 'that Reith will put his heart into this job, and I believe that he can make a very valuable contribution towards solving the problem of the industry'.[27] His appointment suggests that Wilson saw the role of chairman as being more wide-ranging than envisaged in the original terms of reference of the NFFC. He told Reith that 'the contribution for which I am looking from the Chairman of the Corporation is really twofold. In addition to presiding over the Board and fulfilling the normal functions of a Chairman, I want him from the vantage point which he occupies to give time and thought to the problems of the film industry, its structure, its economic base, its public responsibilities and so on.'[28] There was some suggestion that James Lawrie did not welcome Reith's appointment, as 'Mr Lawrie's conception of the Chairman as a person who is as part-time as the other Directors and is no more than *primus inter pares* among them ... will not be adequate for dealing with the responsibilities which I feel are likely to fall on the Corporation from now on, and will not work in terms of this particular leonine personality'.[29]

There were two immediate issues facing the newly constituted NFFC. One concerned the different classes of loan. In May 1949 Lawrie reported that 'we are at present principally engaged in making loans direct to producers and are only lending the front part of the end money – a sum which, though vital, is not in most cases large'.[30] On this basis he estimated that the corporation had sufficient funds 'to last quite a long time'. However, he predicted that if private investment was not readily forthcoming the corporation would begin to receive applications for 'front money', in which case its funds would be exhausted more quickly. The other issue was the loan to British Lion. It soon became apparent to all parties that British Lion needed a further cash injection if it was to continue its production activities. In April 1949 British Lion declared losses of £700,000 on film production for the previous financial year and announced that it would have to offset its future profits from distribution against the unrecouped costs of films.[31] And before the end of the year it emerged that British Lion was in even worse difficulty than the NFFC had known: it now estimated its losses at £1,389,000.[32] Privately, Reith acknowledged that 'British Lion continues to give us a good deal of concern. Most of their commitments were assumed before we came on the scene; we are not directly in charge; the situation generally is rather equivocal and difficult.'[33]

There could be no accusation that the NFFC was idle during its first year of operation. By the end of 1949 it had advanced a total of £3.5 million to 26 companies, with further loans of £699,000 approved in principle: the largest loan by far was £3 million for British Lion (of which £2,750,000 had been advanced) but there were also substantial sums for Romulus Films (£272,500), Plantagenet Films (£132,000) and Jay Lewis Productions (£110,500). Most other loans were between £20,000 and £50,000. In total the NFFC had invested in 38 first features and twelve second features.[34] Most loans were for 'end money', but there were two 'front money' loans for *Give Us This Day* (Plantagenet Films, 1949) and *Morning Departure* (Jay Lewis Productions, 1950). It supported the former, directed by the blacklisted American Edward Dmytryk, as it was 'a small picture for which discountable distribution guarantees are not easily obtained', while *Morning Departure*, a drama about the rescue of a disabled Royal Navy submarine, 'seemed to merit special help as the usual support was not available'.[35] Reith was keen to paint a positive picture of the corporation's achievements:

> We are sure that our operations have had at least two definite results: much more production than there otherwise would have been – about half of the films now in production are being financed by us; and, as to them, a much greater measure of control in the compiling of budgets, critical examination of items therein, care and supervision of expenditure after budget approval – than has been generally exercised in the industry – a fact which is being taken to heart by the industry.[36]

At the same time, however, Reith felt it necessary to add a caveat that it was difficult to know whether or not the NFFC had made good investments: 'There is perhaps no business in which it is more difficult to judge the prospects of commercial success; cinema revenue in general, and the revenue from a particular film, seem to obey no known or definable rules.'

In its early years the NFFC approved just under half of the applications it received for loans: this inevitably raises questions about the criteria for selection. The principle that the corporation should be the lender of last resort seems to have been interpreted loosely: in particular its support for low-budget second features that could more or less be guaranteed exhibition to fill quota might have been outside the original remit of the legislation. It also drew criticism for advancing £45,000 to a company called Parthian Productions to make a series of short films for sale to American television: the company was wound up four years later without repaying any of the loan.[37] There was one occasion when the NFFC considered withholding its support from a film on political grounds. In October 1949 Lawrie asked the Board of Trade to review a script entitled *The Fallow Land* 'as it occurs to me that there are certain matters touched on here which perhaps are affected by Government policy. It would be unfortunate if a film financed by us were perhaps taken in Cornwall as an indication that the Government was going to change its policy at some point!'[38] *The Fallow Land* had been submitted by Eclipse Film Productions and was adapted from a novel by H. E. Bates: it was a drama of the hardships of rural life in which Lawrie apparently detected some political inflection. However, the Board of Trade rebutted any suggestion of political censorship on the grounds 'that it would be wholly improper for us to make any attempt whatsoever to influence the attitude of the NFFC towards a production by reference to considerations of the kind to which this letter refers'.[39] In the event it made no difference: the NFFC approved the loan, but the film was never made.

The NFFC was particularly concerned to support independent producers as a counter to the dominance of the combines. This was demonstrated at the end of 1949 by the case of Anatole de Grunwald. De Grunwald – a Russian émigré whose films included *The Demi-Paradise*, *English Without Tears*, *Queen of Spades* and *The Winslow Boy* – had borrowed £25,000 from the NFFC to produce *Now, Barabbas* at Teddington Studios.[40] In November 1949 de Grunwald telephoned Harold Wilson, then on a mission to Washington to negotiate renewal of the Anglo-American Film Agreement, 'informing me that he had yesterday asked [the] National Film Finance Corporation to put in a receiver owing to his financial difficulties . . . He frankly admitted that he had no security to put up and secondly that there have been several administrative mistakes on his part; and I am not sure if he did not imply some misrepresentation of the facts to NFFC.'[41] Notwithstanding this 'misrepresentation', Wilson was concerned 'that a further shutting down may be the beginning of the end as far as film production is concerned'. Wilson's Permanent Under-Secretary replied to the effect that the NFFC was 'anxious to maintain de Grunwald and his Unit in a position to go on making films. They hope that the measures they propose to take will enable this to be done.'[42]

It was the NFFC's support for lower-budget supporting features during its early years that became a bone of contention for some of its critics. It had made loans to second-feature distributors Exclusive Films to support the production of six films and Mancunian Films for three.[43] On the one hand investing in second features was relatively low-risk in comparison to more expensive first features: it also meant that the NFFC could spread its resources more widely to support more films. And support for the smaller distributors was also a means of ensuring that the NFFC was not seen to be solely favouring British Lion.[44] The NFFC held up Exclusive Films as a success story, as 'their 1950/51 productions were financed without the Corporation. Exclusive repaid all loans – a fine small-scale example of the Corporation's main object – production stepped up and carried entirely by private finance.'[45] On the other hand, however, others were sceptical of the value of investing in routine genre films. These included Oliver Lyttelton:

> I confess to some amusement, as a Tory not untinged by nostalgic sentiments, to see that the taxpayers' money has been used to finance productions which are intended to titillate the public fancy under such titles as *Saints and Sinners*, *The Wonder Kid* – I wonder if that has any particular significance – *What a Carry On*, *School for Randle*, *Skimpy in the Navy*, *She Shall Have Murder*, *Happy Go Lucky*, *The Galloping Major*, *The Body Said No* and *Her Favourite Husband*.[46]

The corporation seems to have taken Lyttelton's comments – made in the course of a debate over the extension of its borrowing powers – to heart. Its first annual report acknowledged that some of the films it had supported were not 'of as high a quality as the Corporation would have wished' and intimated that it intended to become more selective in the films it supported: 'Though the Corporation is not promoter, arbiter of taste or censor, it cannot be indifferent to the content of films in which public money is being invested.'[47]

Yet the debate over the type of films which the NFFC should support was really a secondary issue: the crucial matter was whether it had succeeded in restoring stability to the production sector and confidence on the part of investors. And in this regard the jury was out. The film trade broadly welcomed the corporation's role in supporting British production. Peter Baker offered a balanced assessment for the *Kine*:

> There is little doubt that without the support of the Corporation, the British Lion studios would not be in full production to-day. Many of the smaller studios would have remained idle and thousands more technicians and craftsmen would be out of work. How successful the loans will be remains to be seen. But it may be queried whether the Corporation is pursuing the right policy by making so many loans for the making of less ambitious and second-feature productions. Certainly it is difficult to appreciate why it should support the making of shorts for American television![48]

However, there was another body of opinion that the NFFC had failed in its primary objective of putting the film production industry back onto a sound economic basis. An editorial in *The Financial Times* suggested that the corporation had been too concerned with supporting volume of production and that in so doing it had merely buttressed the existing financial structure of the industry rather than encouraging change:

> In the light of this sorry production story the activities of the National Film Finance Corporation have been deplorable. When the national film accent should be on quality, the Corporation's accent has been on quantity again – on getting employment back to the studios at any cost. When the crying need of British

studios was to devise a new technique of production which should reduce studio costs and raise artistic quality, the Corporation has been handing out public money for exactly the same production set-up which has proved uneconomic and unsound in the past.[49]

Film-maker John Boulting was also a critic, albeit for different reasons: 'The greater part of its five million pounds has now been expended and, apart from the alarmingly high incidence of unemployment, the low level of production and the increasing intervention of Hollywood interests, I fail to see any sign whatsoever of that return to confidence in financial circles anticipated by Harold Wilson at the time of the inception of the NFFC.'[50]

In fact, the problem of the NFFC exhausting its funds had arisen within months of its incorporation. By June 1949 the corporation had outstanding commitments of nearly £3.5 million: allowing for the likely non-recovery of some of its loans, it had only around £1 million of its original funds remaining and had yet to see a return on any of its investments. Lawrie advised the Board of Trade that 'if the banks are sticky – and from time to time there is some evidence of this – we might find that we are being driven to put up front money as well, and, if that were so, it would not take long to get rid of the £1,000,000'.[51] In July 1949 the Board of Trade asked for a further £5 million for the NFFC as the current statutory maximum would soon be exhausted. It argued that further loans would be necessary because 'there is still little or no evidence that City provisions of "equity" money will be forthcoming in the fairly near future on a scale commensurate with the industry's needs' and that an extension of the scheme would 'afford an opportunity to the industry of demonstrating to the City that, subject to proper safeguards, film production should be regarded as a sound field for investment'.[52] However, the Treasury pooh-poohed the application. 'It cannot be said that a case for further finance has been made', an internal Treasury briefing note averred, adding that the Board of Trade's memorandum 'is in effect a cry of despair':

> The case for providing more money rests on the argument that, without such money, production will be even less than it is, and that even if most of the money is lost, we shall be strengthening our position as against the Americans; we may directly save some dollars, and our hand will be strengthened when it comes to further discussions with them. The case against providing more money rests on the argument that without a shake-out the abuses in the industry will continue; that any new money will be lost; and that the crisis will only be postponed.[53]

The Treasury was evidently concerned that the NFFC might become a bottomless pit into which more public money would be sunk without any guarantee of a return on its investment. Another memorandum indicates that it expected 'an appreciable proportion' of the current loan 'will in fact be lost' and that 'no guarantee could be given that a similar proportion of any new £5 million would not also be lost'.[54] The showdown between the Treasury and the Board of Trade came at a meeting of the Cabinet Production Committee on 13 October 1949 when Wilson's request for further advances for the NFFC was declined: Sir Stafford Cripps decreed that it would 'be most inexpedient to introduce legislation to provide for an increase of £5 millions in the Government advances to the National Film Finance Corporation at a time when the internal financial situation rendered it necessary to make reductions in public expenditure and capital investment'.[55]

The fact was that the NFFC was caught between a Scylla of increasing demands on its resources from the film industry and the Charybdis of economic retrenchment on the part of government. On the one hand the private capital available for the film industry, rather than being freed up as had been hoped, was actually being reduced. In January 1950 Lawrie reported 'an important development in the realm of film finance' in so far as General Film Distributors were to reduce their distribution guarantees from 75 per cent of the budget to 70 per cent.[56] This was occasioned by the Rank Organisation's fiscal retrenchment following its heavy losses in 1949, but the consequence was that either the producer or the NFFC would be expected to find a further 5 per cent of the budget. Other distributors quickly followed suit. On the other hand the Treasury remained adamant 'that no promise should be held out of further large sums of Government money for the industry'. 'Some healthy signs are apparent among producers and exhibitors,' noted Sir Wilfrid Eady, 'but they have still got a long way to go before we should be justified in embarking further large sums of public money to them.'[57] It was agreed in April 1950 that a further advance of £1 million could be made to the NFFC, but it was stressed that this was 'strictly an interim measure designed to enable the Corporation to carry on until the Government can reach a decision about the general economic position of the film industry and its need for further financial assistance'.[58]

The NFFC was now feeling the pinch. It acknowledged that the additional £1 million was 'not a large sum in relation to the demands upon it'. In September 1950 it issued a press release to the effect that 'the Corporation is gradually becoming more selective concerning the quality of projects and the records of producers'.[59] One consequence was that it stopped loans to all distributors except British Lion: hence it ceased supporting small distributors which specialised in supporting features.[60] This decision was not popular with the trade: there was a hostile exchange of letters between James Lawrie and John Blakely of the Mancunian Film Corporation in which the latter vigorously denied the accusation that his company had failed to provide the NFFC with proper budgets and cost statements.[61]

Perhaps the NFFC's most important initiative, however, was to propose a new method of structuring film finance. This was what became known as the Group scheme. Its origin can be found in a proposal by Sir Wilfrid Eady to use some of the additional £1 million to create a new company dedicated to the production of low-budget films by new film-makers. 'What I have in mind is really a reversion to some of the experimental work done in the 30s,' Eady said, suggesting that the aim would be to 'get back some of the artistic excitement which was the motive power of the young men who went into the Empire Marketing Board, Crown Film

Unit, etc, and to get the same concept of the team spirit which was the remarkable part of that effort'.[62] By chance a similar proposal had been made at much the same time by John Grierson, regarded as the founding father of the British documentary movement and who had been the driving force behind the Empire Marketing Board Film Unit in the 1930s. Michael Balcon, who acted as an adviser to the NFFC, put Eady in touch with Grierson. 'I want to see whether we can introduce an entirely new level of production costs for a successful first feature,' Eady wrote in a personal letter to Grierson. 'On the assumption that a good first feature cannot count on more than £150,000 net box office receipts in the UK, we have to see whether, in fact, "box office" can be produced fairly regularly at a figure which will allow a profit to the production company.'[63] Eady proposed using £250,000 of the additional funding for the NFFC to set up a production group that would work collaboratively in the production of low-cost first features in the budget range of £60,000–£80,000.

The idea of providing finance for selected production groups was subsequently taken up and significantly expanded by Reith, who was the real architect of the Group scheme. Its rationale was that rather than making loans on a more or less *ad hoc* basis to individual producers, the NFFC should instead pool those resources by supporting groups of producers working together on a co-operative basis. Reith explained the reasoning behind the scheme was that after two years of making loans, the NFFC 'can now judge reasonably well which are the production companies that can be trusted with a loan from public funds without having any money of their own behind it'. He proposed the establishment of three groups, two of which would be attached to the major combines. One group would be based at Pinewood Studios and would produce first features for distribution by GFD. The second would be based at Elstree and its distribution would be handled by Associated British-Pathé. The third group – evidently inspired by the proposals from Eady and Grierson – would be 'drawn largely from producers trained in the documentary school, to produce low-cost first and second features'.[64] The NFFC would not cease to make loans for single pictures, but such loans would require producers to provide some of the end money themselves.

There was initially some resistance to Reith's proposal within government. Neither the Treasury nor the Board of Trade were happy about such a significant extension of the NFFC's powers. Eady – perhaps smarting from his baby having been adopted by others – was most adamant that 'I am not willing to recommend that the groups should be creatures of the NFFC' and for that reason opposed Lawrie sitting on any of the management boards.[65] However, the principal objection was that two of the groups would be aligned with the major combines. Eady felt this was a 'reactionary' step, and Wilson was concerned that it would reinforce the monopolistic tendencies within the industry that had been a matter of such concern only a few years before. Reith, however, defended his proposal:

> No NFFC money will go to the Rank Organisation or ABPC directly; no more indirectly than in the past . . . We maintain that a producer with a GFD guarantee

and producing at Pinewood is as independent as one with a British Lion guarantee producing at Shepperton.

We are not driving the producers to the big organisations. We are carrying out your orders not to replace bank finance but to supplement it. Banks only lend against guarantees from distributors strong enough to satisfy them; the best risks are the two big organisations. The independents must therefore look to them for support, whether we like it or not.[66]

In the event, a compromise was reached: Wilson accepted Reith's proposal on condition that the costs were met from the NFFC's existing resources. One of Wilson's last actions before leaving the Board of Trade in January 1951 was to formally approve the Group scheme.

The Group scheme was to comprise three production units. Group 'A' was to be formed in association with General Film Distributors and based at Pinewood Studios: its members were Anthony Asquith, Edward Baird, Betty Box, George Brown, Jeffrey Dell, Thorold Dickinson, Anthony Havelock-Allan, Ronald Neame, Sergei Nolbandov, Paul Soskin, Hugh Stewart and Julian Wintle. GFD would guarantee 70 per cent of production finance, with the NFFC providing the rest: producers were to receive an agreed 7 per cent of profits but would not be required to invest their own money in their films. Michael Balcon would be the chairman of the group — which later came to be known as British Film Makers — and its management company would include representatives of Pinewood (Earl St John) and the NFFC. Group 'B' — comprising Leslie Arliss, Aubrey Baring, Ivan Foxwell, Marcel Hellman, Walter Mycroft, Maxwell Setton, Victor Skutezky and Mario Zampi — would be based at Elstree Studios and distribute through Associated British-Pathé: it was constituted on similar lines to the Pinewood group but was 'smaller in scope'. Finally Group 'C' — or Group 3 as it became known — was to be set up under the direction of John Grierson and John Baxter with a remit to increase opportunities for new film-makers who otherwise struggled to find backing: it would be based at Beaconsfield Studios and backed by Associated British Film Distributors, with the greater part of the cost advanced by the NFFC.[67] The NFFC had approximately £1.2 million of its funds left: it proposed to allocate about £700,000 to the groups, with the rest continuing to be available for supporting single-film projects.[68]

The Group scheme represented a significant shift of policy for the NFFC: it had been set up to support independent producers but now it was going to allocate funds to producers associated with the two combines. There were some voices within the industry who felt that the whole scheme had been devised to benefit the Rank Organisation, or at the very least to prevent Rank from withdrawing from production following its recent losses. However, *Kine* editor A. L. Carter rejected this claim, and extended a cautious welcome to the scheme:

> In some quarters it is considered that the whole scheme is designed to give financial assistance to vertically integrated combines which should subsidise production on their own account. The fact is that both the Rank Organisation and ABPC are supporting a certain amount of production; but only as much as they can afford.

> The new NFFC scheme, suffering as it does from some disadvantages, is a compromise on the best business lines. The two new companies at GFD and ABPC will ensure to producers a distribution guarantee (and a good chance of a cinema release), they will be assured the services of the most efficient production plants in the industry and they will be given some continuity of production. The fact that the combines may benefit from this arrangement is no reason to condemn the scheme.[69]

Carter averred that the 'NFFC is spending the money it has left in a way that should promote the production of more films – only Communists within the industry want fewer films made, with the worse unemployment chaos which would follow'. Indeed, the Association of Cine Technicians did oppose the scheme, which it felt 'will not only cripple independent producers outside the scheme, but in time may end the independence of those inside it'.[70] Much the same point was made by Derrick de Marney of Concanen Films: 'If you are in one of the Group schemes, you are all right, but there are only three or four genuine independent producers left now and their position is becoming intolerable.'[71]

The institution of the Group scheme more or less accounted for the remaining balance of the NFFC's funds. In May 1951 the NFFC reported to the new President of the Board of Trade, Sir Hartley Shawcross, that 'we have reached the stage where our resources are in effect fully committed'.[72] At this point the NFFC had made loans totalling £5,446,495, with a further commitment of £268,917 under the Group scheme: it had also agreed in principle pre-production loans of £360,000 for eight films by British Film Makers and £95,000 for five films by Group 3. Outside the Group scheme its largest investment in a single picture was *The Magic Box* (1951). This film – a biopic of the forgotten British pioneer cinematographer William Friese-Greene – was the film industry's contribution to the Festival of Britain: it was produced by Festival Film Productions, a co-operative venture backed by Rank, ABPC, British Lion and Technicolor, with many of the key participants – including director John Boulting, cinematographer Jack Cardiff and star Robert Donat – either deferring their salaries or working for nominal fees. *The Magic Box* cost £300,000 including deferments: the NFFC advanced £100,000 'on a basis that two-fifths would be repaid before companies, who provided services on a co-operative basis, receive their payments from receipts. The remainder of the NFFC loan is to be paid *pari passu* with the other deferments.'[73] However, *The Magic Box* failed to recoup its costs despite being shown on all the major circuits: its box-office failure was blamed for turning what would otherwise have been a profit for the year of £87,495 for the NFFC into a loss of £45,851.[74] Its perceived anti-American bias – the film suggests that Friese-Greene invented a moving picture camera before Thomas Edison – prompted Terry Ramsaye, editor of the *Motion Picture Herald*, to accuse the NFFC of being 'the socialist big foot-in-the-door in the direction of nationalizing the industry for Britain'.[75] However, Ramsaye could not have been more wrong: at this point the NFFC had almost run out of funds and *The Magic Box* was one of the last films it would support to this degree.

At this point the future of the NFFC was far from certain. Reith had departed: he took up a new post as chairman of the Commonwealth Development Corporation at the invitation of Prime Minister Clement Attlee. It has been suggested that Reith was offered this role in order to remove him from the NFFC as his plans for reorganising the film industry were more radical than the government was willing to contemplate.[76] In July 1951 the government announced that no further public funding would be available for the corporation.[77] This was followed by the NFFC being censured by the Public Accounts Committee, which questioned 'the wisdom of not insisting on some share in the control of a company [British Lion] before lending it a large sum of public money'.[78] (In fact, the NFFC had insisted as a condition of its loan that City financier Harold Drayton should be appointed chairman of British Lion: Alexander Korda stood down as managing director to take the role of 'production advisor'. The Public Accounts Committee's concern was that the NFFC did not have either a shareholding in the company or a representative on the board of directors.)

It was at this point that the future of the NFFC became dependent upon the wider political situation. Shawcross was less of a supporter of the film industry than Harold Wilson had been: he evidently wanted to ease the Board of Trade out of its financial commitment to the NFFC. He suggested that 'it is necessary to bring home to the industry that it cannot sit back and rely indefinitely on Government finance but must take every opportunity to recover its contacts with the City and regain its independence of Government assistance'. At the same time, however, he added: 'I regard it as equally essential that the withdrawal of Government support through NFFC should be so arranged as to avoid any hiatus in production with a consequent drop in the present quota percentage which is generally recognised as representing the efficient level of employment for the present resources of the industry.' Accordingly he suggested the provision of a further £3 million for the NFFC while 'making it clear at the same time that this represents the final stage'.[79] Following 'considerable discussion' between Shawcross and Chancellor of the Exchequer Hugh Gaitskell, a further £2 million was agreed.[80]

However, the government's announcement in September 1951 that it was to call a snap general election 'has embarrassed the National Film Finance Corporation, which has been waiting for confirmation by Parliament of a loan of a further £2 million and which, in an effort to maintain a steady flow of production for the 1952–53 quota, is believed to have overspent its £6 million loan'.[81] Sir Frank Lee, the Permanent Secretary to the Board of Trade, suggested making 'an approach to the Opposition to see whether they would agree that a Bill to authorise the increase of the limit of advance by £2 million should have an early place in their legislative programme if they should be returned to power'.[82] Sir Wilfrid Eady duly sounded out Oliver Lyttelton on behalf of the Treasury: however, the response from the Conservative Party was they were 'not prepared to enter into any undertaking of the kind you mention before the Election'.[83] A note from Eady records: 'NFFC will play it long.'[84]

The election of a Conservative government on 25 October 1951 threw the whole future of the NFFC into question. It soon became clear that the new administration wanted to 'get out' of the film industry. A quick decision was needed whether the Conservatives would honour the promise of the additional £2 million. A handwritten note by R. A. Butler, the new Chancellor of the Exchequer, records: 'I shall agree to this only if it is an inescapable moral obligation. I am aware of the skill with which our contacts with the Film Industry have been handled & of past history, but can we not get out for under £2m? I <u>must have economy</u>.'[85] Eady informed James Lawrie that 'the economic climate has worsened against the NFFC's position': he reported that the incoming President of the Board of Trade, Peter Thorneycroft, said that he 'would very much hesitate' to invest more public money in film production and that to do so 'would be altogether an incongruous proposal'.[86] In the meantime, the trade press reported that several films were held up pending the government's decision.[87]

While it would seem that the new government would probably have liked nothing better than to abolish the NFFC – one of the easier targets left behind by its predecessor given that the Conservative manifesto had undertaken not to dismantle Labour's social reforms or to reverse its nationalisation of key industries – it was nevertheless mindful of the underlying problems of the industry. In the event the decision to keep the NFFC in being was influenced by several factors. The production industry was still in dire straits: there had been only 51 British first features in 1951 – nine fewer than the previous year – and both Denham and Teddington studios had closed during the year.[88] And there was still much evidence that the City was wary of investing in the film industry. Six weeks after the election the joint secretary of the Prudential Assurance Company – which had been sounded out about the possibility of investing in the NFFC – told the Treasury that 'it is only fair to mention that one or two of my Directors . . . expressed their concern about going back into film finance. My Chairman has asked me to mention that we should not regard it as an investment proposition, but rather as a gesture towards His Majesty's Government in helping to solve a financial problem.'[89]

This was the context in which the new government decided that the NFFC should in the event be allowed to borrow the additional £2 million. However, there was a caveat: that the money would come not from the Treasury but from 'other persons' than the government. Initially it seems to have been envisaged that either the Finance Corporation for Industry or the Industrial and Commercial Finance Corporation might lend to the NFFC.[90] *Kine* suggested that 'James Lawrie and his colleagues at the NFFC must begin to feel like the orphans nobody wants'.[91] In the event the NFFC's borrowing powers were extended to allow it to raise further funds from private investment.[92] Yet – in an oddly perverse sort of way – the Conservative government's decision to cut the NFFC free from dependency upon the public purse would create the conditions in which the life of the corporation could be extended. The NFFC did not immediately avail itself of the additional borrowing from the private sector. By the end of its third full year of operation the NFFC was finally starting to recover some of its investments and regarded the additional £2 million as a 'safety valve'.[93] In 1952 it made its first (albeit modest) operating profit: excepting its loan to British Lion – which it was already accepted was unlikely to be recovered – the NFFC made an annual profit of £10,891.[94] The corporation had invested in 78 films in the year: 25 of the loans had been repaid and five of the films had made a profit. *Kine* averred that 'some gratification is to be found in the news that the repayments expected in the future are likely to make it unnecessary for the Corporation to go to the banks for further loans'.[95] This would set the pattern for the following years whereby the NFFC would make a modest profit or loss each year. And there was already a sense that by the time its term was due to expire in 1954 the lifetime of the NFFC would be extended. In the event the organisation that had been created as a temporary measure to assist the production sector in picking itself up and moving towards the restoration of a sound economic base would survive far beyond its original five-year term and would become a permanent feature of the institutional and fiscal landscape of the British film industry.

Notes

1. 'Long Shots', *Kinematograph Weekly*, 29 July 1948, p. 4.
2. 'Wilson Predicts Finance for Production', *Kinematograph Weekly*, 11 March 1948, p. 3.
3. 'Film Bank Names May Not be Published Until Autumn', *Kinematograph Weekly*, 29 July 1948, p. 4.
4. 'The Truth About Production', *Kinematograph Weekly*, 8 April 1948, p. 4.
5. 'Close-Ups', *Kinematograph Weekly*, 1 July 1948, p. 5.
6. TNA BT 64/2366: W. G. Riley to Harold Wilson, 12 April 1948.
7. Ibid.: Nicholas Davenport to Harold Wilson, 16 April 1948.
8. Ibid.: Minute 4.36, 13 April 1948.
9. Ibid.: Sir Wilfrid Eady to R. G. Somervell, 19 April 1948.
10. Ibid.: Nicholas Davenport to Harold Wilson, 24 April 1948.
11. Ibid.: 'Film Credits Corporation: A Memorandum by Nicholas Davenport', 20 February 1948.
12. TNA BT 103/192: 'Instructions to Counsel: Film Finance Corporation', n.d.
13. 'Company to Administer Film Finance', *Kinematograph Weekly*, 16 September 1948, p. 3.
14. 'Film Finance', *The Economist*, 26 September 1948, p. 511.
15. 'British Lion Gets a Million Pounds Loan from the State', *Kinematograph Weekly*, 11 November 1948, p. 3.
16. 'Lawrie on Reasons for Br. Lion Loan', *Kinematograph Weekly*, 27 January 1949, p. 7.
17. TNA BT 103/192: 'Cinematograph Film Production (Special Loans) Bill – Notes on Clauses', p. 7.
18. 'What Wilson Overlooked', *Kinematograph Weekly*, 18 November 1948, p. 4.
19. TNA BT 103/192: 'Cinematograph Film Production (Special Loans) Bill – Financial Resolution', 27 November 1948.
20. Ibid.: 'Cinematograph Film Production (Special Loans) Bill – Notes on Clauses'.
21. Ibid.
22. Ibid.
23. Ibid.: A. G. White to Savage, 29 March 1949.
24. *Parliamentary Debates: House of Commons*, 5th Series, vol. 459, 8 December 1948, col. 426.
25. TNA BT 103/192: A. G. Whyte to R. G. Somervell, 4 February 1949.

26. 'Financing of Films: New Producing Group', *The Financial Times*, 21 January 1949, p. 1.
27. TNA BT 64/2443: Harold Wilson to Sir Stafford Cripps, 12 April 1949.
28. Ibid.: Wilson to Lord Reith, 8 April 1949.
29. Ibid.: Minute by the President of the Board of Trade, n.d.
30. Ibid.: James Lawrie to R. G. Somervell, 20 May 1949.
31. 'British Lion Film', *The Financial Times*, 4 April 1949, p. 1.
32. 'British Lion Film', *The Financial Times*, 9 December 1949, p. 4.
33. TNA BT 64/4476: Lord Reith to Wilson, 12 December 1949.
34. Ibid.: 'National Film Finance Corporation: Position of loans as at 31st December, 1949.'
35. *National Film Finance Corporation: Annual Report and Statement of Accounts for the year ending 31 March 1950*, Cmd. 7927 (April 1950), p. 8 (74).
36. TNA BT 64/4476: Lord Reith to Harold Wilson, 12 December 1949.
37. 'State Finance Lost £41,500 on TV Films', *Kinematograph Weekly*, 16 July 1953, p. 9.
38. TNA 64/4476: James Lawrie to R. G. Somervell, 3 October 1949.
39. Ibid.: A. G. White to Sir James Helmore, 7 October 1949.
40. 'De Grunwald Reopens Teddington – And Plans to Keep it Going', *Kinematograph Weekly*, 6 January 1949, p. 22.
41. TNA BT 64/4511: Harold Wilson to R. G. Somervell, 26 November 1949.
42. Ibid.: Somervell to Wilson, 29 November 1949.
43. The six films produced by Exclusive Films were *Meet Dr Morelle* (1949), *The Adventures of PC 49* (1949), *Celia* (1949), *Meet Simon Cherry* (1949), *The Man in Black* (1950) and *The Dark Light* (1951). The three films from Mancunian Films were *What a Carry On* (1949), *School for Randle* (1949) and *Over the Garden Wall* (1950).
44. 'Long Shots', *Kinematograph Weekly*, 5 May 1949, p. 4.
45. *National Film Finance Corporation: Annual Report and Statement of Accounts for the year ended 31 March 1951*, Cmd. 8193 (April 1951), p. 2 (13).
46. *Parliamentary Debates: House of Commons*, 5th Series, vol. 476, 29 June 1950, col. 2517.
47. *NFFC Annual Report 1950*, p. 2 (32), p. 5 (52).
48. Peter C. Baker, 'Focus on Revival', *Kinematograph Weekly*, 30 June 1949, p. 5.
49. 'Quality and Quantity', *The Financial Times*, 30 July 1949, p. 4.
50. 'Gross Waste a Thing of the Past', *Kinematograph Weekly*, 16 February 1950, p. 21.
51. TNA BT 64/4476: James Lawrie to R. G. Somervell, 20 May 1949.
52. TNA T 228/362: Draft memorandum for the Lord President's Committee: Cinematograph Film Production (Special Loans) Act Amendment Bill, July 1949.
53. Ibid.: P.C. (49) 111. Cinematograph Film Production (Special Loans) Act Amendment Bill.
54. Ibid.: I. de L. Radice to Armstrong, n.d.
55. Ibid.: Minutes of the Cabinet Production Committee PC (49) 23rd Meeting, 13 October 1949.
56. TNA BT 64/4476: James Lawrie to R. G. Somervell, 27 January 1950.
57. TNA T 228/362: Sir Wilfrid Eady to Armstrong, 29 March 1950.
58. TNA BT 64/4480: Cinematograph Films Production (Special Loans) Bill 1950: Brief on Memorandum to be considered by the Legislative Committee on Tuesday, 25 April.
59. TNA BT 64/4476: Press announcement: 'National Film Finance Corporation', 26 September 1950.
60. *NFFC: Annual Report 1951*, p. 2 (13).

61. 'Lawrie Explains Ban on Further Loans to Mancunian', *Kinematograph Weekly*, 29 March 1951, p. 20.
62. TNA T 228/273: Sir Wilfrid Eady to Mr Trend, 31 May 1950.
63. Ibid.: Eady to John Grierson, 2 October 1950.
64. TNA BT 64/4521: 'NFFC's Future Operations', 3 November 1950.
65. Ibid.: Eady to Calder, 22 December 1950.
66. Ibid.: Reith to Wilson, 15 December 1950.
67. 'James Lawrie Denies Finance Scheme Was Planned to Help Rank', *Kinematograph Weekly*, 1 February 1951, p. 34.
68. *NFFC: Annual Report 1951*, pp. 11–13 (Appendix C).
69. 'The Chance of A Million', *Kinematograph Weekly*, 1 February 1951, p. 4.
70. 'Group Scheme Flayed: "Lawrie Must Go"', *Kinematograph Weekly*, 19 April 1951, p. 9.
71. 'British Stars Not Good Enough for Distributors', *Kinematograph Weekly*, 4 October 1951, p. 28.
72. TNA T 228/362: R. J. Stopford to Sir Hartley Shawcross, 16 May 1951.
73. 'State Pays £250,000 for "Magic Box"', *Kinematograph Weekly*, 3 April 1952, p. 3.
74. 'Failure of *The Magic Box*', *The Times*, 29 April 1953, p. 3.
75. 'British Friese-Greene Eulogy-on-Film Called Romantic Fabrication', *Motion Picture Herald*, 9 June 1951, pp. 8–9.
76. Sue Harper and Vincent Porter, *British Cinema of the 1950s: The Decline of Deference* (Oxford: Oxford University Press, 2003), p. 19.
77. 'No More for Finance Corporation', *Kinematograph Weekly*, 5 July 1951, p. 4.
78. 'Public Accounts Committee Criticises NFFC', *Kinematograph Weekly*, 9 August 1951, p. 9.
79. TNA T 228/362: Sir Hartley Shawcross to Hugh Gaitskell, 23 July 1951.
80. Ibid.: Frank Lee to Sir Wilfrid Eady, 4 October 1951.
81. 'Industry Policy Reacts to General Election', *Kinematograph Weekly*, 27 September 1951, p. 3.
82. TNA T 228/362: Lee to Eady, 4 October 1951.
83. Ibid.: Oliver Lyttelton to Eady, 12 October 1951.
84. Ibid.: Eady to Shaw, 16 October 1951.
85. Ibid.: Handwritten note by 'R.A.B.' dated 3 November, on Treasury memo 'National Film Finance Corporation' (emphasis in original).
86. Ibid.: Eady to Lawrie, 1 December 1951.
87. 'NFFC Holds Up New Production Plans', *Kinematograph Weekly*, 29 November 1951, p. 3.
88. 'Nine Fewer British Pictures in First Year of "Levy"', *Kinematograph Weekly*, 6 December 1951, p. 3.
89. TNA T 228/362: C. W. A. Ray to Sir Frank Lee, 12 December 1951.
90. 'State Takes Risk of Private Loans to NFFC', *Kinematograph Weekly*, 28 February 1952, p. 7.
91. 'Long Shots', *Kinematograph Weekly*, 17 January 1952, p. 4.
92. 'New Money for Films?', *The Economist*, 1 March 1952, p. 550.
93. 'NFFC May Not Need That Extra £2m.', *Kinematograph Weekly*, 26 June 1952, p. 3.
94. *National Film Finance Corporation: Annual Report and Statement of Accounts for the year ending 31 March 1952*, Cmd. 8523 (April 1952), p. 4 (27).
95. 'A Heartening Record', *Kinematograph Weekly*, 1 May 1952, p. 4.

CHAPTER 6

The Eady Levy

> It is becoming quite clear that film production has not yet made very much progress at securing *from within the industry* the money to maintain production. Some progress has been made towards reduction in the cost of production but its average is still too high in relation to the standards which the industry will have to adopt. But even if the cost of production were brought down to what would be a reasonable average, having regard, among other things, to the maintenance of quality, the producers' share of box office receipts (after tax) is inadequate and, in my opinion, unfair. (Sir Wilfrid Eady)[1]

Despite its early teething troubles, the National Film Finance Corporation made an important contribution to supporting the British film production industry. It almost certainly saved the British Lion Film Corporation from collapse, and in providing part-finance for around half of all British feature films in its early years it secured the immediate future of the industry. However, it soon became apparent that the provision of end money loans was not sufficient in itself to solve the underlying economic problems of the British production sector. There still remained the question of the inadequate returns to producers from the box-office receipts of their films. The initiative to establish a production fund for British films raised through a levy on ticket sales was influenced by both political and economic considerations. Unlike the setting up of the NFFC, however, which had been achieved quickly and with relatively little difficulty, the process of establishing the British Film Production Fund – popularly known as the Eady levy after Second Secretary to the Treasury Sir Wilfrid Eady – involved protracted negotiations with all sections of the trade.[2] Like the NFFC, there are differing views of how effective the Eady levy actually was. Geoffrey Macnab suggests that it 'stands as one of the few practical interventions to benefit British cinema made by any government'.[3] However, Margaret Dickinson and Sarah Street offer a more qualified verdict in so far as 'if anything, the levy reinforced the existing trade structure. Producers received payments in proportion to the box office earnings of their films, so those who benefited most were those already favoured by the system of distribution and exhibition.'[4]

There were several contexts for the establishment of the production fund. One of these was the film industry's campaign for a reduction of the Entertainment Tax.[5] This had originally been introduced as a temporary measure during the First World War, when it was applied to 'any exhibition, performance, amusement, game or sport', but it remained in force after the war. In 1935 a reduced duty was introduced for live entertainments including theatre, music hall, ballet, circuses and travelling shows. At the same time the exemption limit at which the duty was not applicable was raised from tickets costing 2 *d.* to 6 *d.*: this made little difference to the cinema trade as most seats were above the exemption level. In 1940 Entertainment Tax took 16 per cent of the total box-office income of Britain's cinemas and the cinema industry accounted for around 70 per cent of the total revenue raised by the tax. The tax was increased three times between 1940 and 1943 without affecting cinema admissions, which rose every year during the war. The combined effect of raising the tax and increasing admissions meant that the amount contributed in Entertainment Tax by the cinema industry increased from £5.6 million in 1940 to £41.4 million in 1945. In 1946 the reduced rate was extended to include sport – football and cricket were the main beneficiaries – but cinemas continued to pay the higher rate. In 1948, for example, the tax on a cinema ticket priced at 1 *s.* 9 *d.* was 8½ *d.*, compared to 2 *d.* on a seat of the same price for sport or live entertainment. By 1950 the amount paid by the cinema industry in Entertainment Tax amounted to £37.2 million – a figure that represented 35 per cent of box-office receipts.[6]

The trade had many reasons to dislike the tax. For one thing there was a view that the film industry was treated unfairly in relation to live entertainments such as theatre and music hall. It was a bugbear for exhibitors who argued that it ate into their profits and left them unable to invest in the maintenance or improvement of their cinemas. And it was also blamed for the inadequate returns to producers: the tax was sliced off the top of the box office before exhibitors and distributors had taken their share, rather than being applied as a percentage of the exhibitors' or distributors' receipts. This eroded the amount left over for producers. In December 1949 the BFPA and CEA issued a joint memorandum arguing that some of the income raised through Entertainment Tax should be reinvested in the industry:

> So far as can be ascertained, with the exception of USA, Britain is unique in leaving its film production industry to struggle against the competition of imported films without any financial support. In every European country where there is a film production industry of any size, it is assisted by money derived from the equivalent of Entertainment Tax or by some similar arrangement. In other words, local production is encouraged by grants in addition to and apart from film hire. . . .
>
> An industry cannot flourish which is not reasonably secure in its own home market. The film production industry's present financial insecurity is mainly due to the intolerable burden of Entertainments Tax.[7]

This argument was also supported by the Plant Report: 'The case for a reduction in the burden of Entertainments Duty rests upon the evidence that the share of the box-office receipts left in the industry is not large enough to permit the exhibitors to pay British producers a sufficient return on the films they produce.'[8]

The joint memorandum on Entertainment Tax was a rare example of coordinated action by two of the main trade associations but even so it fell on deaf ears in Whitehall. Harold Wilson felt that 'the Entertainment Duty has to some extent been used as a scapegoat for what has been an unsuccessful policy' and suggested that the different trade associations had 'found this glorious new alibi under which the Government can be blamed for all their misfortunes'.[9] The Treasury, naturally enough, was disinclined to relinquish such a lucrative source of tax revenue. Sir Wilfrid Eady pooh-poohed the claim that exhibitors were impoverished as exhibition remained the one profitable sector of the film industry:

> The exhibitors are by no means in such a bad position. ABPC are likely to produce a balance sheet showing very substantial profits from exhibition; among the most notable box office successes they have had are a number of films produced by British Lion ... It seems probable that the Rank Organisation will produce only a very limited number of films, and that, in effect, it will trade as an exhibitor for a couple of years or so until it has put right its finances out of the profits of exhibition. Both ABPC and the Rank Organisation will be exhibiting an appreciable number of imported American films. The smaller circuits and a large number of smaller cinemas are not doing too badly, though some of the flea-pits will only be able to continue if they spend money on modernising their projection equipment.[10]

Eady felt that exhibitors 'seem to think they are entitled to live on the monetary standards they had in the boom years immediately after the war' and believed they were using the Entertainment Tax as a means of deflecting attention from other issues: 'The industry has wasted two precious years in asking the taxpayer to pay for the maintenance of false standards by remission of Entertainments Duty, rather than face up to the general problem of costs or to the possibility of passing on part of the additional costs to the customer ... Mr Rank has also wasted quite a lot of time talking about Entertainments Duty.'[11]

If there was little sympathy for the plight of exhibitors, however, the government was more favourably inclined towards addressing the problems faced by producers. The catalyst was the data on production costs and revenues provided by the four main production groups (Rank, British Lion, ABPC and Ealing Studios) early in 1950 which demonstrated that the large majority of British first features were loss-makers in the home market: in total only twelve films of the 72 films for which cost and revenue details were provided returned a profit to the producer. Moreover, the profits on the few successful films were often quite modest in relation to the cost of production, while even some of the profitable films, notably those from the Rank group, were dependent upon their overseas revenues for their profits. It was this evidence that seems to have persuaded the government of the need to alleviate the problem. By the spring of 1950 the idea of providing some form of 'special assistance' for the production sector was gaining traction in Whitehall. A Treasury memorandum of March 1950 suggested 'that there may be a case for some form of financial assistance to British film producers on the ground that even with the utmost care and economy the present level of production costs does not on average give the producer a chance to recoup his costs from sales in the home market'.[12] And in April 1950 Rupert Somervell of the Board of Trade wrote: 'If the Government decides on the basis of the producers' figures (when we get them) that some form of direct assistance to production is necessary, I am sure we should be under great pressure to produce a scheme quickly and, indeed, it is unlikely that any final decision will be taken except in the light of a definite scheme.'[13] Officials were careful to avoid the word 'subsidy', though it is clear that what was being proposed amounted to a subsidy in all but name. In May 1950 Sir Stafford Cripps intimated that he was prepared 'to help film production by a reduction in Entertainment Duty combined with the imposition of a special levy on exhibition from which payments should be made to British producers'.[14]

The Board of Trade investigated the subsidy schemes in place elsewhere, particularly in France and Italy. In France the film industry was regulated by the Centre National de Cinématographie, established in 1946. In 1948 a Temporary Assistance Law – also known as the *fonds d'aide* – was introduced. This levied two new taxes – one on ticket sales and another related to the length of films passed for exhibition per foot – in order to raise a fund which then distributed money to both producers and exhibitors according to a prescribed formula. For producers the subsidy was calculated as a percentage of the box-office receipts: 7 per cent of the gross domestic receipts arising from the first three years of exhibition in France and 15 per cent of the net overseas receipts. Exhibitors received a payment towards the costs of maintenance and repairs to their cinemas. The subsidy 'is applied exclusively to the creation of new films and to the exhibition of French films abroad'.[15] In Italy the Cinema Law of 1949 introduced a levy of 2.5 million lire (approximately £1,500) on every foreign film dubbed into Italian. The money raised in this way was paid into a special fund administered by the Sezione Autonoma del Credito Cinematografico and to be used exclusively for the financing of national film production. Italian producers would receive a subsidy of 10 per cent of their production costs, with an additional 8 per cent if their film was deemed to be of 'particular artistic value'.[16] Italy, like Britain, had a quota system and an entertainment tax: the latter was on a sliding scale ranging from 15 per cent on the cheapest seats to 50 per cent on the most expensive. Exhibitors were encouraged to show more Italian films than mandated by the quota by rebating 20 per cent of the entertainment tax on Italian films: American films were most popular at the box office but the number of Italian films nevertheless increased following the Cinema Law.[17]

In March 1950 the BFPA had put forward its own proposals for a scheme of financial assistance for British film production. It suggested that 12.5 per cent of the gross box-office receipts of every British first feature should be set aside in a consolidated fund and 'should become payable to the producer when he starts making another British film of not less than the same grade as the film in respect of which the balance of the Exchequer payment had been set aside'. It calculated – based on total box-office receipts of £106 million per year, of which a quarter was for British films – that a 12.5 per cent levy would raise £3,312,500. A further £552,500 would be raised for second features, with the levy set at one-sixth of the amount for first features. The BFPA averred that such a level of assistance (amounting to a round figure of nearly £4 million) compared favourably with the £9.5 million which British films earned for the Exchequer in Entertainment Tax.[18]

At the same time there is some evidence that the BFPA was hedging its bets by balancing its proposals for a subsidy against further support via the NFFC. Sir Henry French, the BFPA's chairman, told Somervell that 'there is widespread feeling in the industry that the Government may be impressed with the case which has been put forward against the present high level of Entertainment Tax from the point of view of British film production but they may decide that the easiest way of meeting this case will be to give a further sum of money to the Corporation'.[19]

Understandably the government was more inclined towards a scheme whereby the additional money for producers was provided by the industry itself (or rather by its patrons) than by the Treasury. At the same time it recognised that the main stumbling block to any such scheme was likely to be the cinema exhibitors, who would be opposed to any levy on ticket sales unless it was coupled to a reduction in Entertainment Tax. By the spring of 1950 cracks were appearing within the previous united front between the BFPA and the CEA. Following a bad-tempered meeting at the House of Commons attended by representatives of all sectors of the industry – in the course of which the exhibitor Sir Alexander King reportedly complained that 'the producers are only putting forward their own case' – French told Somervell: 'The whole tenor of the meeting was sympathetic to production and the need for maintaining a British production industry but there was very little sympathy expressed with the case for the exhibitor obtaining relief from taxation.'[20] One suggestion – 'provided everybody will play the game' – was that Entertainment Tax should be reduced for British films and in return exhibitors would return a higher percentage of box-office receipts to the distributor, 'which would put more money into the pocket of the British producer of a successful box office British film'.[21] However, Harold Wilson was sceptical that exhibitors would 'play the game' and instead suggested a statutory scheme:

> The President was of the view that even if the exhibitors would agree to give the producers their share under a voluntary scheme, they would never do so in practice, and his view is that this difficulty can only be got over by creating as its basis some sort of statutory levy, rather on the lines of the old cotton spindles levy, but of course for a totally different object.[22]

Eady – who previously had been opposed to a reduction of Entertainment Tax 'simply for the benefit of the exhibitors' – now suggested that such a prospect could be held out in return for their co-operation: 'I would hope we would be allowed to be in a position to say to the industry that if they are not prepared to play along very closely to these lines we can make no recommendation to the Chancellor on Entertainments Duty for this year.'[23] Throughout the discussions the civil servants concerned played a canny hand in exploiting the differences between the different trade interests: Eady and Somervell had both been involved in the negotiation of the Anglo-American Film Agreement and by now were very knowledgeable about the film industry. A Board of Trade paper in late June 1950 (unsigned but judging from the tone most probably written by Somervell) advised: 'Our general impression is that the various Associations can be led gently in the right direction. A good sheep dog does not get the sheep into the pen by barking at them or biting them, but by lying down and watching them with a hypnotic eye.'[24]

In the event it was a voluntary levy that was proposed: the reason for this seems to have been entirely pragmatic in so far as a voluntary scheme would be easier to include in the Finance Bill currently being prepared whereas the legislation required for a statutory scheme might have delayed its introduction by another year. Eady devised the formula that coupled a partial reduction in Entertainment Tax with the establishment of a levy on ticket sales. Entertainment Tax was removed on seats costing up to 7 *d.* and was reduced to a half-penny on seats between 7 *d.* and 1 *s.* 6 *d.*: it was estimated that this would save about £3 million a year for exhibitors. A levy of one penny was then to be introduced on seats of 1 *s.* 3 *d.* and above. A detailed comparison of box-office receipts with and without the levy was drawn up based on the available figures for the first six months of 1950. This estimated total gross box-office receipts for the year at £106.7 million, of which £37.8 million went to the Exchequer in Entertainment Tax, leaving net receipts of £68.9 million which were divided as follows: £44.2 million to the exhibitors, £6.2 million to the distributors and £18.5 million to the producers (£12.3 million to American producers and £6.2 million to British producers). Under what was already being referred to as the Eady scheme, the estimated total gross box-office receipts would be increased to £109.4 million (an additional £2.7 million) with a slightly lower return to the Exchequer due to removing Entertainment Tax on seats under 7 *d.* but increased net receipts of £71.9 million. Exhibitors and distributors would be left with a slightly increased amount of the net receipts, while producers would have £20.4 million. In total it was estimated that British producers would receive an additional £1.5 million.[25]

The initial response to the Eady plan from the trade was lukewarm at best. It was 'accepted under duress' by exhibitors who regarded it as simply one tax replacing another.[26] W. R. Fuller, the general secretary of the CEA, argued that while British renters might be persuaded to co-operate with the plan, 'they could not hope to get the Americans to help in working out a scheme for assisting British production'.[27] A joint memorandum by the BFPA, CEA and the Association of Specialised Film Makers stated that the three associations felt the proposals 'fall far below what is required to put the industry on a reasonably sound financial basis. As, however, they have been informed, in effect, that they must accept or reject them in the form set out in this letter, they have decided to accept them as an interim measure and will do their utmost to make them work to the best advantage of the Industry.'[28] But this outward show of unity disguised the fact that the producers welcomed the scheme in principle: the BFPA informed the government in August 1950 that it would 'proceed at once with the setting up of the British Film Production Fund Company and the Memorandum and Articles of Association were signed at the meeting by the Subscribers'.[29]

It had been left to the trade to decide how the fund should be allocated. A consensus quickly emerged that 'the bulk of the money in the Fund will go to support first features and other films required for ordinary cinema programmes, and allocations to individual films will in all probability be made on the basis of automatic formulae related in some way to box-office takings for screen time'.[30] The producers would be allowed to decide the respective allocations for first features, supporting features and short films. It was Eady's suggestion that 'it would be an act of policy to set aside say not more than 10 to 15 per cent of the Pool for the deliberate financial encouragement of certain types of production which the industry would like to see back on the screens, e.g. documentaries, children's films, etc.'[31] The British Film Production Fund was set up as a limited company in August 1950 in order to administer the levy. Its board of directors included three representatives of each of the four trade associations – BFPA, KRS, CEA and Association of Specialised Film Producers – with chartered accountant Sir Harold Barton appointed as chairman by the Board of Trade. Eady was not happy that the BFPA had not nominated any independent producers: 'It is thoroughly unsatisfactory that the BFPA should have chosen French, Baker and Jarratt as their representatives. French promised that he would do his best to secure an independent producer. Jarratt has no real understanding of the financial problems of production and in any case represents a distributing organisation.'[32] Nevertheless the BFPA's nominations were accepted in order not to delay the implementation of the scheme. Each quarter distributors would submit a statement of their earnings per film and a disbursement would be made from the fund calculated as a percentage of the distributors' gross receipts: initially this amount was set at 12.5 per cent for features, with the receipts for shorts (which generally earned very little) multiplied by 2.5 per cent to arrive at the figure on which the payment was made.

How far did the Eady levy actually go in alleviating the problems of the production sector? Early forecasts were optimistic. In November 1950 the Treasury claimed that 'during the first year of the scheme, box-office returns will be so good that British producers will get more than the £1,500,000 estimated by the Government'.[33] A month later, however, the *Kine* reported that '[it] now looks as though the final return to the fund will be more in the realm of £1,000,000 to £1,250,000 at the end of the year than the estimated £1,500,000'.[34] It turned out that the calculations of the amount the levy would raise had not taken into account the decline of cinema attendances: these fell from 1,480 million in the financial year 1948–9 to 1,212 million in 1950–1.[35] A proportion of the shortfall was also due to the fact that some exhibitors refused to comply with the scheme. These tended to be independent exhibitors: the major circuits complied as they were in effect putting money back into their own production and distribution arms. In the early years of the British Film Production Fund it was estimated that up to a third of independent exhibitors did not comply with the scheme.[36] After its first full year of operation the total collected by the levy stood at £1,093,647.[37]

It had been accepted from the outset that the operation of the levy might need to be reviewed in light of experience. It was soon apparent that even the optimistic estimate of a total subsidy of £1.5 million was insufficient to put the film production industry on a secure economic footing. A Treasury paper of February

1951 suggested that '[a] home revenue of about £10 million should be sufficient to provide for an annual programme of about 60 first feature films, and maintenance of production of second feature and short films at about the same level'.[38] To this end the Treasury recommended increasing the amount of the levy:

> If the levy were to produce another £2 million for the producers, they will have had their annual income increased by something like 50% as the result of the levies. This is probably all that they can reasonably expect to get out of net box office receipts, and on the present average cost of production it ought to yield them, on average, a profit from the UK screen + such 'foreign' revenues as the best films can secure.[39]

'One of the difficulties we shall experience in negotiations with the cinema industry about the new levy will be the attitude of the renters,' Eady cautioned. 'We are once again interfering with their contractual rights under the hire agreements.'[40]

The case for an increase in the levy was strengthened by evidence that even following its introduction there was still a significant gap between producers' costs and their receipts. A document in the Treasury archives recording the costs and revenues of 15 first features supported by the NFFC and released during the first six months of the levy's operation indicates that only six of them returned a producers' share in excess of the production cost:[41]

Film	Cost	Producers' share
Give Us This Day	£195,000	£80,000
The Interrupted Journey	£96,700	£107,000
The Romantic Age	£119,400	£30,000
Your Witness	£108,600	£90,000
Morning Departure	£127,500	£190,000
Double Confession	£88,000	£55,000
Shadow of the Eagle	£128,500	£55,000
Cairo Road	£108,000	£112,000
Waterfront	£121,200	£90,000
Tony Draws A Horse	£93,400	£80,000
The Woman With No Name	£116,500	£105,000
The Woman in Question	£111,800	£130,000
The Clouded Yellow	£152,800	£170,000
The Dark Man	£58,200	£90,000
Pandora and the Flying Dutchman	£308,800	£225,000

This was a better record than during the late 1940s when very few films had ever returned a profit to the producer, but it was still significantly less than Whitehall and the industry had hoped for when the levy was introduced. The most profitable film on the list by some distance was *Morning Departure*: otherwise even the successful films returned only modest profits. What the table reveals quite strikingly is that the overall increase in receipts for British films under the levy was not shared equally. It was always the more successful films – and therefore those least in need of subsidy – that benefited most from the levy.

However, the Treasury was initially unwilling to increase the rate of the levy without also procuring some benefit for itself. Hugh Gaitskell's Budget of April 1951 proposed an increase in Entertainment Tax of one penny on all seats between 6 *d.* and 9 *d.*, with further incremental increases on a sliding scale up to 5 *d.* on the most expensive seats. This was expected to raise another £10 million for the Exchequer but only £2.5 million for the levy.[42] The proposal was not welcomed by the trade and several months of intense negotiations followed until a compromise settlement was reached. In the event the tax on seats up to one shilling was reduced by a penny, while the levy on seats up to a shilling was set at a quarter of a penny and three-quarters of a penny on seats above a shilling. The cumulative effect of the changes to both the tax and the levy was that the cost of seats between 1 *s.* 3 *d.* and 2 *s.* 10 *d.* (the most popular price range) increased by threepence, while those costing more increased by fourpence. This was calculated to raise an additional £6.5 million for the Exchequer (as against £7.5 million in the original Budget) and to increase the amount for producers by an additional £2.3 million. Gaitskell acknowledged that the trade interests 'have certainly driven a hard bargain with us and we have had a lot of argument about it, but I think it is reasonably satisfactory in outcome'.[43] However, this was not a universal view. Charles Wilson, the Conservative MP for Torquay, felt that the revised arrangements – which raised less in taxation while providing an enhanced subsidy for a private industry – meant that the taxpayer 'came out of this very, very badly': 'I congratulate the cinema industry. I only wish that the ordinary people of the country whom I represent came off better out of this.'[44]

The revised Eady levy came into effect from 5 August 1951 and would remain in force for three years. It was estimated that the new levy would increase receipts for British producers by around £3.5 million annually. Eady told Sir Harold French:

> To the best of our judgement, and unless all costs go haywire, the additional income for British producers that will be secured within the next three years should be sufficient to ensure for an average film of reasonable quality at least its manufacturing costs from the box office.
>
> If this is broadly true, there is at least an opportunity for a very complete overhaul of the financing of production. It will obviously be imperative for any company working to a programme of films to put back into the business any surplus that it gets from the box office, so as to finance the inevitable gap between some costs of production and some box office receipts. We should hope that Rank, ABPC and others might now be willing to find more end money.[45]

An amendment to the administration of the fund was that a proportion should be set aside 'for the general encouragement and support of the British film industry'. This seems to have been regarded as a token gesture to alternative cinema. Eady commented: '[There] are some amusing odds and ends of avant-garde stuff being produced by the Left Wing boys. None of it looks very box office, but, of course, any self-respecting art ought to be able to afford a few inexpensive experimental eccentrics at the edge of the movement!'[46] In the event it was decided that the 'special fund' should be used to support the Children's Film Foundation, a unit set up to produce films for juvenile audiences under the supervision of Mary Field.

Political and Economic Planning calculated in 1952 that 'the augmented British Film Production Fund should at least place production within the reach of solvency'.[47] This was based on the assumption that box-office revenues remained constant and that average production costs would not too far exceed £150,000. Any change in the balance – whether falling revenues or increased costs – would naturally affect the profit margin. The Treasury seemed confident that production costs could be kept in check, though its apparent belief that there would be no further decline in cinema attendances is curious. The production interests (particularly the larger production groups) were mostly satisfied with the levy: it was the exhibitors who actively disliked it. The exhibitors 'are not satisfied with a scheme which, in their opinion, puts both the Exchequer and the producers on "Eady Street" and leaves them with the problems of severe rising costs and a patronage which has little spare money to spend on entertainment'.[48] The scheme had to some extent driven a wedge between the producers' and exhibitors' trade associations. The chairman of the CEA's Bristol and West of England branch, for example, referred to the BFPA as 'an ostrich with its head in the sands' and argued that its call for an extension of the levy was 'absolutely selfish and without regard for the position of the exhibitors today'.[49] The exhibitors disliked the levy because, as they saw it, they were now subsidising the production sector as well as the Exchequer. The CEA's outgoing president, Harry Mears, summed up his members' views when he remarked: 'The Production Fund has put many producers on easy street. For the integrated combines it must be a financial paradise.'[50] This is borne out by the payments from the levy's second full year of operation in 1951–2: the biggest payments were to General Film Distributors (£747,671), Associated British-Pathé (£331,864) and the British Lion Film Corporation (£380,189), whereas smaller distributors such as Butcher's Film Services (£45,373), Adelphi Films (£23,564) and Anglo-Amalgamated Film Distributors (£14,405), which mostly handled films by independent producers, received a much smaller share of the pot.[51] To this extent the evidence would seem to bear out Dickinson and Street's contention that the levy ultimately reinforced the existing economic structure of the film industry as those who benefited most were the major producer-distributors.

Sir Wilfrid Eady retired from the Treasury in 1952: he had regarded the levy that bore his name as a temporary measure of assistance for the film production industry. Yet within a few years 'Eady money' had become such an important feature of the financial landscape of the British film industry – it could add around 25–30 per cent to the box-office returns for a successful film – that producers were arguing for its retention. According to J. Arthur Rank in 1955: 'Our production programme, which is achieving a measure of success, would not have been possible without the aid of the fund . . . I regard it as a matter of major importance that the future of the fund be set up in such a way that its continuity will be assured, either by statutory or other means, which will at the same time eliminate many of the frictions between different sections of the industry which have unfortunately been created by its voluntary operation.'[52]

Notes

1. TNA BT 64/4512: 'Finance for Film Production', 9 June 1950 (emphasis in original).
2. However, Harold Wilson claimed that the scheme was his idea: 'I thought this one up while on holiday in Cornwall on a particular favourite walk of mine down to the beach, and succeeded in getting it through the Treasury . . . I was only too happy to father its title on the hard-working Treasury Official who turned my ideas into a detailed official scheme.' Quoted in Andrew Roth, *Sir Harold Wilson, Yorkshire Walter Mitty* (London: The Book Service, 1977), p. 120.
3. Geoffrey Macnab, *J. Arthur Rank and the British Film Industry* (London: Routledge, 1993), p. 197.
4. Margaret Dickinson and Sarah Street, *Cinema and State: The Film Industry and the British Government 1927–84* (London: British Film Institute, 1985), p. 226.
5. Strictly speaking it was a duty rather than a tax, but as the term 'Entertainment Tax' was used so widely I have stayed with that term except for quotations which refer to it as a duty.
6. Political and Economic Planning, *The British Film Industry: A report on its history and present organisation, with special reference to the economic problems of British feature film production* (London: Political and Economic Planning, 1952), pp. 124–7.
7. TNA BT 64/4511: *Entertainments Tax: Joint Memorandum by Exhibitors and Producers*, 7 December 1949.
8. *Distribution and Exhibition of Films: Report of the Committee of Enquiry appointed by the President of the Board of Trade*, Cmd. 7837 (November 1949), p. 29 (67).
9. *Parliamentary Debates: House of Commons*, 5th Series, vol. 470, 14 December 1949, col. 2794.
10. TNA BT 64/4511: Sir Wilfrid Eady to W. Armstrong, 9 June 1950.
11. Ibid.
12. Ibid.: V. I. Chapman to Armstrong, 31 March 1950.
13. Ibid.: R. G. Somervell to Sidney Golt, 27 April 1950.
14. Ibid.: Minute 266: 'Films – Entertainment Duty, etc', 6 May 1950.
15. Ibid.: 'Internal measures for protection of local film producers', n.d.
16. Ibid.: 'New cinema bill passed 26 July 1949', n.d.
17. Political and Economic Planning, *The British Film Industry*, pp. 171–2.
18. TNA BT 64/4511: Memorandum I: 'Outline of BFPA proposals for Financial Assistance to British Film Production', 9 March 1950.
19. Ibid.: Sir Henry French to Somervell, 3 April 1950.
20. Ibid.: French to Somervell, 19 May 1950.
21. TNA BT 64/4512: Willis to Somervell, 5 June 1950.
22. Ibid.: Somervell to Eady, 8 June 1950.
23. Ibid.: Eady to Armstrong, 9 June 1950.
24. Ibid.: 'Notes on the Memorandum of Agreement', 29 June 1950.
25. Ibid.: 'Eady Scheme: Annual rate based on stats, figures for January–June 1950.'
26. 'We Must Work the Eady Plan', *Kinematograph Weekly*, 27 July 1950, p. 4.

27. TNA BT 64/4512: Taylor to Eady, 16 June 1950.
28. Ibid.: J. Arthur Rank (BFPA), A. R. Watts (CEA) and Donald Carr (ASFM) to Eady, 22 June 1950.
29. Ibid.: Sir Henry French to Somervell, 23 August 1950.
30. Ibid.: 'Central Fund to Assist UK Film Production', n.d.
31. Ibid.: Eady to Somervell, 21 June 1950.
32. Ibid.: Eady to Somervell, 10 August 1950.
33. 'Producers Should Get More Than £1½ Million', *Kinematograph Weekly*, 5 October–9 November 1950, p. 3.
34. 'Long Shots', *Kinematograph Weekly*, 7 December 1950, p. 3.
35. '200 Million Attendances Lost in Two Years', *Kinematograph Weekly*, 13 September 1951, p. 6.
36. 'CEA "Powerless" Against Eady Levy Defaulters', *Kinematograph Weekly*, 14 February 1952, p. 3.
37. TNA T228/525: Sir Harold Barton to Rupert Somervell, 1 August 1951.
38. Ibid.: Sidney Golt, 'Note on Film Finance', 22 February 1951.
39. Ibid.: 'Film Finance', 5 February 1951.
40. Ibid.: Eady to Somervell, 29 March 1951.
41. TNA T 228/525: Untitled document listing costs and producers' shares of NFFC-funded films produced in 1950.
42. '£10m. More from Box-Office', *Kinematograph Weekly*, 12 April 1951, p. 3.
43. *Parliamentary Debates: House of Commons*, 5th Series, vol. 489, 2 July 1951, col. 1598.
44. Ibid. col. 1964.
45. Ibid.: Eady to French, 5 July 1951.
46. Ibid.
47. Political and Economic Planning, *The British Film Industry*, p. 130.
48. 'It all depends on the Public', *Kinematograph Weekly*, 28 June 1951, p. 4.
49. 'Producers' Levy Approach is Selfish – Rogers', *Kinematograph Weekly*, 23 July 1953, p. 10.
50. 'Eady – Matter of Life and Death', *Kinematograph Weekly*, 8 January 1953, p. 6.
51. 'Where Eady Money Goes', *Kinematograph Weekly*, 20 November 1952, p. 6.
52. 'Exchequer May Lose On It – Rank', *Kinematograph Weekly*, 22 September 1955, p. 6.

Part II

A Fragile Stability: 1951–1969

CHAPTER 7

The Road to Recovery

> It would be foolish to pretend that everything is now all right as far as British production is concerned. Far from it. But the recent period of retrenchment has given the industry the chance of putting a small core of production activity on to a more permanent economic basis. The National Film Finance Corporation and the Eady scheme were created to achieve just that. (*Kinematograph Weekly*)[1]

By the early 1950s there was a feeling in the British film industry that the worst of the crisis had passed and that the first green shoots of recovery could be glimpsed. In June 1950 *Kine* editor A. L. Carter intimated that 'we are likely to ignore the signs – small yet unmistakable – that our industry may possibly be emerging from the slough in which British producers have been floundering for one reason or another since the Dalton duties'.[2] At the end of a year in which 74 British features were made – 62 first features and 12 second features – the *Kine Year Book* noted the paradox that 'in a year when almost everyone in the industry (with some factual justification) has been metaphorically buying crepe for the funeral, British production has actually achieved a series of good quality films that have been successful'.[3] This verdict was confirmed by the *Kine*'s chief reviewer R. H. 'Josh' Billings, who reported that 'British films have done much better during recent months. I am thinking in particular of *The Blue Lamp*, *Odette*, *The Wooden Horse*, *Seven Days to Noon* and, of course, *Her Favourite Husband*.'[4] And in January 1951 the *Kine*'s City editor V. L. Burtt, reporting that share values across the industry as a whole had risen by £6 million over the last year, sounded an optimistic note about its prospects: 'There is a general feeling in the City that the industry is rebuilding on a much sounder foundation than hitherto. This, in time, will boost up patronage again, and thus complete the circle and the basis for a real revival.'[5]

To a large extent this impression of recovery is borne out by the statistical evidence. For one thing the number of feature films being produced was on an upward curve during the 1950s: there were 67 British features released in 1951, 79 in 1952, 86 in 1953, 93 in 1954, 82 in 1955, 81 in 1956 and 96 in 1957.[6] Furthermore, British films were earning more at the box office. In 1951 British feature films returned total gross distributors' receipts of £4.2 million (an average of £63,000 per picture) in the United Kingdom: the amount recovered by producers following deduction of renters' fees and expenses was £2,961,000.[7] In 1952 the gross receipts of British films in the United Kingdom were £5.7 million (£72,700 per picture average) and in 1953 they were £6.3 million (£73,460 per picture average).[8]

British films' share of the home box office increased from 27 per cent in 1951 to 32.5 per cent by 1954.[9] Against these figures must be set the fact that cinema attendances were declining slowly year on year: from 1,365,000 in 1951 to 1,102,000 in 1956. Even so, however, attendances remained above their pre-war levels, while an increase in ticket prices meant that box-office revenues were not affected: total box-office takings at Britain's 4,500-plus cinemas amounted to £108.3 million in 1951, £108.8 million in 1953 and £105.8 million in 1955.[10] The main reason the government was deaf to exhibitors' lobbying for a reduction in Entertainment Tax was that box-office revenues suggested an industry in a state of buoyant good health.

In British cinema historiography, the 1950s have generally been dismissed as a dull, stagnant period where British films were characterised by their conservatism in both subject matter and visual style. Lindsay Anderson, a polemical film critic for *Sequence* and *Sight & Sound* who would turn film-maker through his association with the Free Cinema movement, described British cinema as 'snobbish, anti-intelligent, emotionally inhibited, wilfully blind to the conditions and problems of the present, [and] dedicated to an out-of-date, exhausted national ideal'.[11] Raymond Durgnat, noting the preponderance of films about the Second World War, referred to 'doldrums-era movies about World War II': 'doldrums era' has since become something of a catch-all description for British cinema of the 1950s despite more sympathetic reassessments of the film culture of the period.[12] Regardless of the quality of the films, however, all the evidence points to British films being more consistently popular with audiences than at any time before or since. British films feature prominently, for example, in the *Kine*'s annual surveys of box-office hits. In 1950 British films claimed five of the top six positions: *The Blue Lamp*, *The Happiest Days of Your Life*, *The Wooden Horse*, *Treasure Island* and *Odette*.[13] Three of those films – *The Happiest Days of Your Life*, *The Wooden Horse* and *Odette* – had been supported by the National Film Finance Corporation. American films topped the box office in 1951, when *The Great Caruso* and *Samson and Delilah* beat *Laughter in Paradise* into third place, and in 1952, when *The Greatest Show on Earth* was the top box-office attraction, though Ealing's *Where No Vultures Fly* was second and other British films – *Ivanhoe*, *Angels One Five*, *Scrooge* and *The Sound Barrier* – were listed as 'big money-takers'.[14] Thereafter, British films topped the box office every year for the rest of the decade, with the exception of 1957: *A Queen is Crowned* in 1953, *Doctor in the House* in 1954, *The Dam Busters* in 1955, *Reach for the Sky* in 1956, *The Bridge on the River Kwai* in 1958 and *Carry On Nurse* in 1959.[15] *A Queen is Crowned* – a Technicolor documentary of the Coronation of Elizabeth II produced by Castleton Knight for the Rank Organisation – was an unusual and utterly exceptional film: otherwise the most successful British pictures were either comedies or war movies. In fact, the *Kine*'s annual surveys provide even more evidence that British films were consistently popular. In 1954, for instance, British films took all places in the top three (*Doctor in the House*, *Trouble in Store*, *The Belles of St Trinian's*), and in 1959 British films accounted for the top four places (*Carry On Nurse*, *I'm All Right Jack!*, *The Inn of the Sixth Happiness*, *Room at the Top*), while in addition *The Cruel Sea* came third in 1953,

Doctor at Sea was second in 1955, *Private's Progress* third in 1956, *Doctor at Large* and *The Battle of the River Plate* second and third in 1957, and *Dunkirk* third in 1958. Sue Harper and Vincent Porter marshal convincing evidence that the most successful British films were those which attracted the 'occasional' cinema-goers: those who did not attend the cinema out of habit but who made the effort to see particular films 'that made the difference between the audience for a run-of-the-mill film and one that was really popular'.[16]

The relative stability of the film industry in the early and mid-1950s may be attributed to a number of factors. The escalation of production costs that had got out of control in the mid-1940s had to a large extent been brought under control: certainly there were fewer of the expensive 'supers' that had been a feature of the previous half-decade. *Kine* credited the National Film Finance Corporation with helping to curb extravagance and suggested that it had instilled a much-needed sense of fiscal discipline upon producers:

> Another aspect of the NFFC's work has been to control production costs of films in which it has an interest, particularly the British Lion group. In this way it has helped producers to make pictures with greater economy than in the past. This is a service to the industry which cannot be ignored when the future of the NFFC comes up for review in Parliament later this year.[17]

This is confirmed by the statistical evidence. The NFFC's published reports demonstrate that for the first features it had supported, costs were being kept in check and fewer were going over budget. The average cost of high-end features (those costing over £175,000) had fallen from £231,596 in 1949–50 to £220,778 in 1951–2 and the average overcost had fallen from 17 per cent to 5 per cent. In the medium-budget range (between £125,000 and £175,000) the average cost had remained around £150,000 but overcosts had fallen from 21 per cent to 3 per cent, while in the lower-budget range (under £125,000) the average cost had fallen from £105,981 to £93,606 and the average overcost from 14 per cent to 2 per cent.[18]

There was a growing body of opinion in favour of extending the lending powers of the NFFC when its five-year statutory life came to an end in 1954. The arguments in favour of maintaining it rested on its record in supporting the independent production sector. In February 1950 it was estimated that 'the Corporation has been responsible for some 50 films completed, started or ready for starting; about half the productions currently being shot in British studios are being directly or indirectly financed by it.'[19] Even the Treasury had come round to the view that continuing uncertainty meant that 'some institution is desirable to operate in the same way as the Film Finance Corporation, not only as a stabilising factor but, by exercising some control of the level of production costs, to exert an influence towards maintenance of economic standards of production'.[20] At the same time, however, there were some criticisms of the NFFC. Its opponents focused on two issues: that the corporation had frittered away public money on unprofitable films and that it had failed to restore the confidence of private investors. Nicholas Davenport, who had been one of the directors of the original National

Film Finance Company, was a consistent critic. After nearly two years, Davenport felt that the NFFC had done little or nothing to change industry practices:

> For this I blame the National Film Finance Corporation, or rather the way it has been operated. There is always a danger, in the transition from a free to a controlled economy, of some industries falling between the two stools of private enterprise and nationalisation. The film industry fell heavily. If it had been left entirely to private enterprise, the inefficient and uneconomic production would have been shut down completely in 1949 except in those studios (such as ABPC) which can afford to produce a limited number of films at a loss . . . But the intervention of the NFFC had the effect of perpetuating the conventional set-up in the industry which had been losing money.[21]

Davenport suggested that the NFFC's loan to the British Lion Film Corporation was unlikely ever to be repaid and that the system of making loans 'has [not] done anything but bolster up the uneconomic lay-out in the industry, but keep alive some inefficient producers who should have gone out of business, but turn out many films which have no chance of making a profit in the home market, much less of being exported'. From a purely economic perspective it would be fair to say that the NFFC's record was not good. After three years of operation the NFFC had made total loans of £6,243,050 but only £1,114,816 had been repaid: its accumulated deficiency (including the loan to British Lion) amounted to £5,293,101.[22]

Ultimately the decision to extend the statutory life of the NFFC was also an admission of the failure to restore the confidence of investors in the film industry. As the corporation observed in its fifth annual report: 'Unfortunately, the hope that the need for assistance from Public Funds would only be temporary has not been fulfilled, since fresh private finance has not been forthcoming to any considerable extent.'[23] It could even be argued that the very existence of the NFFC militated against this: it had become the default provider of end money rather than (as originally envisaged) the lender of last resort. Richard Stopford, the investment banker who succeeded Lord Reith as chairman in 1951, argued that a decision on its future needed to be made in order to restore investors' confidence:

> The need of the industry now is for long-term capital. This must be faced, and the sooner the better. It is a common aim from all of us to secure as much of this capital as possible from outside sources. This depends on confidence; and the growth of confidence, both inside and outside the industry, is likely to be retarded rather than helped by a further two years of uncertainty as to HMG's intentions with regard to future financial organisation.[24]

Another factor influencing the decision over the future of the NFFC was the question of its outstanding loan to British Lion. This was partly a matter of the Treasury wanting to recover at least some of its £3 million; but it also represented a recognition of the fact that British Lion was the only real counterweight to the power of the two combines.

This was the context in which the Conservative government undertook to extend the life of the NFFC. In April 1952 Peter Thorneycroft, the President of the Board of Trade, tasked Sir Frank Lee, the Permanent Secretary, with reviewing all areas of film policy: the NFFC, Eady levy and Anglo-American Film Agreement. Lee concluded that there were three options for the future of the NFFC: that its lending powers should be allowed to lapse at the end of its present five-year term, leaving the corporation simply to collect what it was owed; that its powers should be extended for a further period 'with no fundamental change in the Corporation's present method of operation'; or to create a successor organisation to take over the role and assets of the NFFC – which it was recognised 'would be unattractive politically' due to the need for new legislation.[25] Nevertheless a number of ideas were considered for a potential successor. The Board of Trade drew up a plan to create a National Film Bank 'as a successor to the Film Finance Corporation': it suggested a working capital of £6 million consisting of £3 million ordinary shares – half would be held by the government and half by 'responsible City institutions' – and £3 million preference shares held by the public.[26] The proposal therefore envisaged the NFFC's successor becoming a private rather than a public corporation: this would satisfy the government's desire to 'get out' of the film industry without leaving it entirely unsupported. A similar proposal was put forward by the NFFC itself. Stopford suggested creating a National Film Investment Corporation: this would be something along the lines of the Industrial and Commercial Finance Corporation, with a capital of £5 million provided initially by government and later by private subscription.[27] It is clear that Stopford did not see a simple extension of the NFFC's powers as a long-term solution: the industry's need was for equity capital from the private sector.

In the event the decision on the NFFC's immediate future fell to Peter Thorneycroft, who chose the easiest option of extending its lending powers for another three years.[28] The Cinematograph Films Production (Special Loans) Act of 1954 extended the NFFC's life to April 1957: it also introduced a provision whereby the corporation could suspend interest payments and accept shares or debentures in a company in lieu of repayment of loans. The latter clause was inserted in order to allow it to restructure the British Lion Film Corporation. The debate over the passage of the bill indicates how the NFFC had become part of the landscape of the film industry. The Conservative Party now argued that the corporation had done much to restore confidence to the industry and that an extension of its powers was necessary to safeguard the industry's recovery. Some Labour MPs went further and argued that the corporation should become permanent. These included Harold Wilson, who 'had come to the conclusion that the Film Finance Corporation should be a permanent part of the finance of the film industry'.[29] The main dissenting voice in the debate was Labour MP Harold Lever. Referring back to the origin of the NFFC in the crisis of the late 1940s, Lever averred that 'the emergency has become something permanent'. He was also critical of the Conservative government's 'impertinence and effrontery to talk of the cultural value of the film industry' when one of its first actions upon taking office had been to disband the Crown Film Unit. Lever felt that if the film industry became dependent upon state aid it would become 'a pauper industry in which the most efficient producers will not make a claim on public funds, and the less efficient the producer the bigger claim on public funds'.[30] Lever argued that the best interests of the industry could be met by dismantling the monopoly of the major distributors and by a reduction in Entertainment Tax. However, his remained a lone dissenting voice: the Conservative government was no more interested than its Labour predecessor in dismantling the Rank/ABPC duopoly, while propping up the ailing British Lion was still seen as a more effective way of countering their dominant position.

Another factor in the industry's recovery was the Eady levy. Although the trade press seems to have reported every year that returns from the levy were likely to be lower than anticipated, the revenues were in fact remarkably stable during the early 1950s. In 1952, its first full year of operation, the levy raised £2.9 million. In 1953 it raised £2.7 million, and the same amount again in 1954. The NFFC felt that the introduction of the levy had helped to unlock more production finance, as it 'has reduced to small proportions the risks of distributors if they guarantee about 70 per cent of the production cost; and it has made it possible to invest end money with profit if it is spread over several pictures'.[31] As the number of British films was increasing during these years, however, the disbursements from the levy to individual producers were getting smaller. The paradox was summed up by the *Kine*: 'There are more British films, and a higher proportion of them is taking really good money at the box office . . . But there is a danger if, as a result of reduced benefit from the levy, many of these films are to finish up on the wrong side of the balance sheet.'[32] Nevertheless, the levy often made the difference between a profit and a loss. Even for a film considered a box-office failure such as *The Gift Horse* (1952), the Eady payment of £51,205 was worth an additional third on the distributor's receipts of £152,287 and ensured that it just broke even.[33] And for a successful film the 'Eady bonus' provided a significant boost to the box-office receipts. *Genevieve* (1953) – the romantic comedy produced and directed by Henry Cornelius for Sirius Film Productions backed by a distribution guarantee from the Rank Organisation at a modest cost of £124,658 – is a good example. By the end of 1953 its distributor's gross receipts of £176,829 in the United Kingdom meant a further Eady payment of £35,623: hence the levy added an additional 20 per cent to the receipts.[34]

The improving economic outlook of the industry in the early and mid-1950s was best demonstrated by the fortunes of the two major combines: Rank and ABPC. Indeed, the Rank Organisation's recovery from its massive losses in 1948–9 was nothing short of remarkable. In 1950 the Rank group as a whole was back in the black with trading profits of £1.8 million and it remained in profit for the rest of the decade: £3.7 million in 1951, £5.4 million in 1952, £5.7 million in 1953, £6.3 million in 1954, £7.4 million in 1955, £6.4 million in 1956, £5.8 million in 1957, £3 million in 1958 and £4 million in 1959.[35] In September 1951 Rank was able to pay a dividend to its shareholders for the first time in two years: this news prompted *Kine* to pronounce that the group's results 'prove beyond all doubt that the cynics were wrong when they prophesied the Rank *gotterdammerung*'.[36] The bulk of Rank's profits came from film exhibition in the United Kingdom: it sought to increase its overseas revenues by acquiring cinemas in Canada, Ireland and Jamaica, though profits from overseas exhibition never amounted to more than £600,000 in any year and were usually lower. Film production remained a loss-maker in the early 1950s, but between 1953 and 1957 even this area started to return profits between £300,000 and £900,000 before plunging back into the red at the end of the decade. Rank's return to profitability meant that the group was able to pay back over £11 million of its loans and overdrafts within five years: these were reduced from £16.2 million in 1949 to the much more manageable level of £5.1 million by 1954.[37]

Rank's recovery was achieved through a strategy of restructuring and retrenchment. In 1948–9 Rank closed its smaller studios – Shepherd's Bush, Islington and Highbury – in order to concentrate production at Denham and Pinewood as a 'big step towards economic production'.[38] In 1951 it also closed Denham (the last film to be shot there was Disney's *The Story of Robin Hood and His Merrie Men*) and concentrated all production at Pinewood.[39] For a short while in the early 1950s Rank was a partner in the NFFC's Group scheme: British Film Makers (BFM) was based at Pinewood from early 1951, with its nominal capital shared between General Film Distributors (40 per cent) and the NFFC (60 per cent). The filmmakers associated with BFM included Anthony Asquith, Edward Baird, Betty Box, Thorold Dickinson, Anthony Havelock-Allan, Ronald Neame, Peter de Savigny and Paul Soskin. GFD would provide distribution guarantees of 70 per cent, with the NFFC providing end money and producers working for a fixed fee. It is difficult to avoid the conclusion that Rank saw BFM as an easy source of end money that reduced its risks in offering distribution guarantees to independent producers. It is a moot point how independent BFM was within the Rank set-up. A note by the First Secretary to the Treasury in April 1952 records:

> [British Film Makers] was working as a scheme far better than might have been expected; things were going smoothly and without friction. But certainly it was very far from having developed any group consciousness; and at present it was no more than an arrangement for pooling finances. They did not see any likelihood for some time ahead of developments towards a corporate personality; but it was quite certain that if the Group was left with some strong outside partner apart from the Rank Organisation and the producers, the Group would become either the same kind of body as the Rank production organisation had been before with all its shortcomings and dangers, or would disintegrate.[40]

The NFFC advanced a total of £706,000 to BFM. The group produced fourteen films in 1951–2 – *Appointment With Venus*, *The Card*, *Top of the Form*, *The Importance of Being Earnest*, *Something Money Can't Buy*, *Hunted*, *The Long Memory*, *Meet Me Tonight*, *High Treason*, *Venetian Bird*, *It Started in Paradise*, *Made in Heaven*, *Desperate Moment* and

The Malta Story – before it was wound up at Rank's request after eighteen months. As £145,000 of the NFFC's advances was still outstanding in 1957, the group overall had lost money.[41]

For Rank, the Group scheme had been a temporary expedient until its own finances had recovered sufficiently to resume production under its own banner. Rank decided that its priority should be to produce around fifteen first features a year through a combination of direct financing and distribution guarantees: producers were expected to use Rank's studios and contract artistes. Until 1955 Rank also co-financed around half a dozen films a year from Ealing Studios, which released through GFD. With J. Arthur Rank himself taking more of a back seat as the decade went on, day-to-day control was left in the hands of John Davis and Pinewood studio manager Earl St John. Vincent Porter avers that Davis and St John 'were unimaginative and conservative in their attitude to film and appear to have had little feel for public taste'.[42] This view is confirmed by the memoirs of film-makers. Roy Baker, who directed seven films for Rank between 1954 and 1961, said that 'there was not enough imagination at the top and a reluctance to take risks, not only with money but with audience appeal as well'.[43] Davis was an accountant more interested in budgets and balance sheets than the art of cinema: most film-makers despised him. Lewis Gilbert described him as 'a monster whose employees lived in fear and trembling of him'.[44] Pat Jackson could not even bring himself to mention Davis by name and referred to him as 'the "éminence grise" . . . whose knowledge of cinema was nil, who had no experience, had never joined two pieces of film, let alone made one, had no knowledge of the craft and was therefore ideally endowed to have the power of life or death over the most promising story propositions and talent'.[45]

Yet it was due in large measure to Davis's conservatism in project selection and his strict control of budgets that Rank's film production and distribution arm returned to profit in the 1950s. Davis imposed an upper budget limit of £150,000 in order to ensure that films stood a reasonable chance of recovering their costs from the home market.[46] Rank's most successful films of the decade were comedies. *Genevieve* – the third most successful British film of 1953 – was the 'sleeper' of the decade. This film had come to Rank by chance as Ealing had turned it down on the grounds that director Henry Cornelius had left the studio.[47] It was reissued every year for the rest of the decade and was consistently successful: 'The older this British comedy gets,' reported Josh Billings, 'the more it takes, and whenever an exhibitor needs a tonic he inevitably utters a glad cry for *Genevieve*, the mightiest blues-chaser of all time.'[48] Rank also hit a rich box-office seam with its series based on Richard Gordon's 'Doctor' books: *Doctor in the House* (1954) – by the producer-director team of Betty Box and Ralph Thomas and with Rank's major box-office star Dirk Bogarde – was the first of a successful series that would extend into the 1960s.

By the mid-1950s Rank's recovery was secure enough that the organisation began to look again at more ambitious projects. In 1956 Davis lured Michael Powell and Emeric Pressburger back to the group by backing their production of *The Battle of the River Plate*: J. Arthur Rank Film Distributors loaned £257,000 towards the budget of £274,071.[49] Powell claimed that *The Battle of the River Plate* was 'our most successful film commercially'.[50] Powell's decision to decline the offer of a long-term contract from Davis (Pressburger was in favour) brought about the end of The Archers following their last film for Rank, *Ill Met By Moonlight* (1957).[51] At the beginning of 1957 Davis was confident enough to announce that Rank's future production programme would be on a 'massive scale'.[52] The formation the same year of Rank Film Distributors of America heralded another attempt to break into the US market. In 1958 Rank announced that it was reorienting its strategy towards fewer but bigger films: *Ferry to Hong Kong* – budgeted at £500,000 – 'will be the most expensive film ever made at Pinewood' and was expected to be 'just the first in a series of pictures in this price bracket'.[53] *Kine* felt that Rank 'has moved courageously and boldly' in responding to public taste at a time when the increasing popularity of television 'would create a demand for higher quality films and this in turn would mean that fewer films will be produced'.[54]

ABPC's recovery was less spectacular than Rank's, but by 1954 it had cleared all its loans and overdrafts and was also operating at a profit: in July that year the *Kine* reported that ABPC 'has not only wiped out bank overdrafts but is now also making profits – and believes it can continue to make profits – from British film production and distribution as well as exhibition'.[55] The NFFC-supported production group at Elstree Studios – including Leslie Arliss, Aubrey Baring, Ivan Foxwell, Marcel Hellman, Maxwell Setton and Mario Zampi – was set up on different lines to British Film Makers. It was smaller in scale and ABPC would provide its contribution (70 per cent) as a cash advance rather than a discountable distribution guarantee. There was no separate holding company for the group: this was at the insistence of ABPC's chairman Sir Philip Warter who claimed that it would not be compatible with the corporation's internal structure.[56] The NFFC did not seem inclined to contest the point. According to James Lawrie: 'This arrangement may, indeed, enable us to make our Elstree group rather more elastic than it was originally envisaged, and I think this is an advantage, since it is quite clear from the personalities involved that this group is never likely to co-operate in exactly the same way as the Pinewood group.'[57] However, the group would produce only five films over two years – *The Woman's Angle*, *So Little Time*, *Angels One Five*, *Father's Doing Fine* and *The Yellow Balloon* – before it was wound up in 1953. The NFFC advanced £213,750 in total.[58] Again the films overall recorded a loss: indeed, other than the successful *Angels One Five*, they were among ABPC's least successful films.[59]

Like Rank, ABPC's return to profitability was driven by its exhibition interests, but its distribution arm (Associated British-Pathé) also made solid if not spectacular profits throughout the decade: its most successful year was 1955 when total profits amounted to £200,036. What was unusual about ABPC was that the group's own films tended to return better box-office receipts than the American films (mostly MGM and Warner Bros.) that it also distributed. In 1952, for example, the first year that the combine made a profit on production as well as distribution, total distributor's receipts from four ABPC films (*Talk of a Million*, *Happy*

Go Lucky, Laughter in Paradise, Young Wives Tale) amounted to £730,466 compared to £659,690 for six MGM films and £700,064 for six Warner Bros. films. In 1955, its most successful year, two ABPC films (*The Dam Busters* and *Oh . . . Rosalinda!!*) grossed £540,464 compared to £721,445 for six MGM films and £598,279 for six Warner Bros. films.[60] Sir Philip Warter stressed the importance of the Eady levy to making film production a profitable undertaking: 'During the last few years the production position has improved. Subject to the Eady scheme continuing on its present basis production will not be a drag but a help to the group as a whole.'[61] Sir Wilfrid Eady – never short of an opinion on the personalities in the film industry – felt that ABPC 'are an uninspired Company generally, but they have taken hold of their financial position in the last three years, and Sir Philip Warter recognised that, as a result of that, and of the levy plan, he is under a public obligation to make a real effort once more on production programmes'.[62]

ABPC's biggest success of the decade by some distance was *The Dam Busters* (1955). The studio's director of production Robert Clark bought the rights to Paul Brickhill's book of the wartime raid on the Ruhr dams by Lancaster bombers of 617 Squadron and produced the film himself with Michael Anderson as director.[63] *The Dam Busters* was the leading box-office attraction of 1955: it earned a distributor's gross of £552,687 and was one of the most successful films of the decade. It seems to have been one of those films which drew occasional cinema-goers: it was evidently something of an 'event' picture though, unusually, its success on first release did not continue into reissues. Billings reported that it 'did not ring the bell at the second time of asking, but all the same its earnings as a re-issue were considerable and helped to lift it to the top of the tree'.[64] Other than *The Dam Busters* and *Angels One Five*, ABPC's most successful films were comedies or musicals: *The Dancing Years* (£221,840), *Laughter in Paradise* (£298,493), *Happy Go Lucky* (£314,794), *Happy Ever After* (£256,708) and *It's Great to be Young* (£215,310). The fact that light escapist fare proved more successful at the box office than more critically acclaimed social problem films such as *Yield to the Night* (£110,367) highlights the discrepancy between critical and popular taste that was also evident in the success of Rank's 'Doctor' and Norman Wisdom comedies.[65]

The situation of the smaller production units was more precarious than the combines: they were less able to sustain big losses on single pictures and they were dependent upon the major circuits for the exhibition of their films. The history of Ealing Studios in the 1950s is a case in point. Ealing was regarded as the most quintessentially British studio and won critical plaudits for its cycle of comedies in the late 1940s and early 1950s, including *Passport to Pimlico*, *Whisky Galore!*, *Kind Hearts and Coronets* and *The Lavender Hill Mob*. But this *succès d'estime* did not cross over to the box office. Ealing had few major hits in the 1950s and those were all early in the decade: its only films listed by the trade press as being among the leading attractions were *The Blue Lamp* (first in 1950), *Where No Vultures Fly* (second in 1952) and *The Cruel Sea* (third in 1953). While Ealing's parent company Associated Talking Pictures made modest operating profits – £12,128 in 1952, £7,017 in 1953, £10,234 in 1954 and £12,286 in 1955 – it was, however, running an accumulated deficit of £95,500. The problem was summarised by the Board of Trade in 1955: 'An annual profit of around £12,000 on such a risky enterprise as film production does not really allow any margin of safety – a very slight fall in the box office or one film which was a failure and they would be well in the red once again – obviously they could not carry on indefinitely on such an insecure basis.'[66]

Ealing's internal financial set-up was unusual. It was more or less bankrolled by its board of directors, who provided personal guarantees to the studio's bankers.[67] No dividend had been paid to shareholders since 1930. In the autumn of 1952 Ealing had extended its bank loan 'secured principally upon the guarantee of Mr Stephen Courtauld and, to a small extent, upon the personal guarantees of Sir Michael Balcon and Major [Reginald] Baker'.[68] When Courtauld gave notice of his intention to withdraw his guarantee, however, Ealing was left unable to extend its credit. This was the context in which Ealing was obliged to ask the NFFC for assistance. Hitherto the studio had not applied for any loans: now it requested a capital loan of £250,000 – subsequently increased to £500,000 – in order to be able to continue production. To some extent this might have seemed like a repetition of British Lion except that there was no suggestion of financial mismanagement in the case of Ealing, whose problems were due more to a run of bad luck in project selection. However, the application came at a difficult time for the NFFC as it was nearing the last year of its original loan-making powers and recognised that 'the Corporation would be open to criticism if it issued a whole series of large loans shortly before the end of its lending authority – and indeed it has been our policy, in the interest of getting the film industry to stand on its own feet, to insist that the Corporation should "taper off" the amount of its new lending in 1952–53'.[69] Nevertheless, as one Board of Trade official put it: 'We have always recognised that Ealing was in a special position and that a loan to them – even as a piece of working capital – should not be counted against the Corporation when assessing the scale of their operations during the last year or so of their loan-making powers.'[70]

In the event the NFFC's bailout of Ealing served only to postpone the end rather than to avert it. Ealing lost £178,000 on film production in 1953 and £107,800 in 1954. The Board of Trade noted that 'the company for the fourth year running has made a batch of "fair to middling" films and again has failed to produce a real winner with which to hit the jackpot'.[71] Ealing – concluding that it would be more economical to become a tenant producer rather than maintaining its own production facility – sold its studio to the BBC for £350,000: along with the sale of equipment which fetched £86,000, this was enough to pay off the capital loan from the NFFC, though there were still outstanding loans for films amounting to £237,115.[72] The Board of Trade predicted that 'the sale of the Ealing studio will be a sensation and will certainly provoke an outcry from the film trade press and (probably) from a good many other people concerned about the production of British films'.[73] When news of the sale – which unusually had not leaked – was announced, the *Daily Film Renter* remarked that it 'hit the Street like a blow in the face from Rocky Marciano'.[74] The *Kine* described the sale as 'a tragedy' and felt that it 'underlines, once again, the almost insurmountable problem for studio-owning production organisations of obtaining adequate returns, quick enough, to ensure a steady flow of product, and, at the same time, the maintenance of costly production facilities, and their continuous use on the most economic basis.'[75]

The sale of the studio coincided with Ealing severing its connection with Rank at the end of 1955: Balcon had become increasingly frustrated with John Davis's managerialism and his interference in project selection and budgeting.[76] Early in 1956 the renamed Ealing Films announced a new arrangement with Hollywood studio MGM whereby Ealing would produce between six and ten films at MGM's British studio at Borehamwood: MGM was to provide 80 per cent of the budget in return for worldwide distribution rights, with the profits shared equally between MGM and Ealing.[77] The Board of Trade felt that the agreement 'was well in line with the other contracts now being adopted by the large American companies in Hollywood and abroad. Having built up organisations capable of managing finance, studio and distribution facilities, they were prepared to engage on liberal terms production units capable of sustaining a production programme.'[78] The biggest of the Ealing/MGM productions was *Dunkirk* (1958), which cost around £365,000 and returned £730,000 from worldwide distribution after deduction of charges. The other five films – *Man in the Sky*, *The Shiralee*, *Barnacle Bill*, *Davy* and *Nowhere to Go* – were more modestly budgeted (the average cost was £189,000) but lost money overall.[79] MGM ended its deal after six films. Ealing made its last film in 1959 (*The Siege of Pinchgut*) in association with ABPC before it brought down the curtain on its production activities.[80]

It was a similar story for Group 3, the third of the NFFC's production groups. This was always intended to be different from the Rank and ABPC groups in so far as its aim was to provide both financial support and technical facilities for filmmakers who did not have a proven track record in the industry. As Lord Reith explained:

> The third company, 'C' [sic], will be different. The financial difficulties and risks of first feature films make it hard for the young and unknown producer. But his opportunities can be increased by production in an inexpensive studio and on location, of feature films of moderate cost. Some of the personnel will be those who have been trained in documentaries which have played an important part in British production. The executive leaders of the group will be Messrs John Grierson and John Baxter, but Sir Michael Balcon and a NFFC representative will be on the board of the Company.[81]

The appointment of Grierson and Baxter gave some indication of Group 3's likely production ethos. Grierson had been instrumental in setting up the Empire Marketing Board Film Unit and its successor the General Post Office Film Unit in the 1930s. He had headed the National Film Board of Canada during the Second World War and had been chief films officer of the Central Office of Information in the late 1940s. Grierson was regarded as the founder of the British documentary movement and so it is therefore no surprise that several of the directors who made their first features for Group 3, including John Eldridge and Philip Leacock, came from a documentary background. He was also an advocate of state-sponsored film production and was committed to an ideal of film-making as a progressive social practice. So, too, was John Baxter, an experienced director with a reputation for making low-cost films with a social purpose such as *Love on the Dole*, *The Shipbuilders* and *The Common Touch*. Baxter directed Group 3's first film, *Judgement Deferred*, which went on the floor at Beaconsfield Studios in June 1951.[82]

Group 3's films were to be financed jointly by Associated British Film Distributors, which provided a distribution guarantee of 50 per cent, and the NFFC, which advanced the rest of the budget and provided a guarantee of completion (a commitment to meet the excess if a film went over budget). Group 3 produced 22 films between 1952 and 1956.[83] The NFFC's total commitment to these films was £528,000: this amounted to an average of £24,000 per film.[84] It produced six films in its first year and seven in its second. Most of Group 3's films were in a vein of sub-Ealing comedy, though its most successful film was the documentary feature *The Conquest of Everest* (1953), fully funded by the NFFC, which returned a distributor's gross of £158,584 from a total of 318 cinema bookings.[85]

Grierson resigned as executive producer of Group 3 in October 1952: this left Baxter in effective control. Baxter reoriented the production strategy towards films which 'are quite definitely being aimed at the first feature market, through story, stars and production values'.[86] This coincided with a change of distributor from ABFD to British Lion 'in the hope that pairing with bigger films would increase returns'.[87] This move did not go down well with the British Film Producers' Association, which complained that Group 3 producing first features 'represents unfair competition'.[88] Group 3 had never been popular with other producers. There was a body of opinion within the BFPA – including its then-president Robert Clark and John Davis – which held that 'Group 3 Ltd was, in fact, a subsidiary of NFFC and that NFFC were, therefore, trading direct and they considered this was beyond its constitution'.[89] Even the *Kine*, which had extended a cautious welcome to the Group scheme, felt that Group 3 might have been a step too far: 'For all the sound arguments in favour of the project, James Lawrie may find it difficult to convince those critics, now out for his blood, that this is not a dangerous experiment which, apart from providing unfair competition for some independent producers, might dangerously bring the industry near to state control of an important section of film-making and distribution.'[90]

In the event, such fears would prove unfounded. For one thing Group 3 had never been a state-sponsored production unit in the manner of the GPO or Crown Film Unit: the NFFC's investment was in the form of loans rather than a grant. While it provided a larger proportion of the budget for Group 3's films, the lower cost of the films meant that the actual sums were generally no more than loans of 25–30 per cent to other producers. In fact, the NFFC lent more to Ealing (£689,512) than it did to Group 3.[91] And for another thing, none of the Group 3 films other than *The Conquest of Everest* had set the box office alight. In 1954 it announced that it was scaling back production from six films a year to two or three. *Kine* reported:

> The type of film that the NFFC directors seek is one that can be made on a budget of about £30,000, a quarter of the normal first feature. It has to have an individuality of approach that will put it out of the second feature class where it could not hope to recover that investment and it has to be a potential first or at least a strong co-feature . . . Not an easy task.[92]

By this time, however, the writing was on the wall for Group 3. A year later the NFFC's new managing director, David Kingsley, conceded that 'it is now apparent that the type of middle budget picture is not suited to the present pattern of exhibition'.[93] Group 3 was wound up in 1956 owing £226,279 to the NFFC: Beaconsfield Studios was sold to Sydney Box, who turned it over to low-budget feature and telefilm production. The last two Group 3 films – *John and Julie* and *The Love Match* – were released under the banner of Beaconsfield Films: the NFFC reported that they 'have done well commercially and the films show a profit'.[94]

The demise of the Group scheme meant that the NFFC had to find other ways of employing its limited resources. In the event, this was provided by the Cinematograph Films Act of 1957. This combined the three main aspects of government film policy – the quota, NFFC and Eady levy – into one piece of legislation for the first time: it extended the quota and the lending powers of the NFFC for another ten years and introduced a statutory levy that it was believed would raise 'at least £1 million more than they are currently receiving from the voluntary scheme'.[95] The extension of the quota – which had been widely expected within the industry – was a straightforward matter. The statutory levy was more problematic. From 1956 it had been the 'broad intention' of the government 'to convert the voluntary scheme into a statutory scheme without, at any rate in the first year or two, substantially varying it'.[96] The government favoured this approach as it was a way of providing assistance to producers from the industry itself rather than from public funds. At the same time it was evidently tiring of having to appease the different trade factions:

> [The] problem of finding a reasonable compromise between the varying and sometimes opposing interests of the film industry, and of seeking to protect and encourage film production without interfering too much in day to day business, means that almost any policy is likely to be criticised for some reason or other. I know that Peter Thorneycroft has long despaired of doing anything for this rather pampered industry which does not arouse a storm of criticism.[97]

The compromise reached was to replace the existing sliding scale with a single levy of 1½ d. on seats above 1 s. 9½ d., which it was estimated would yield £3.75 million a year: this was less than the producers – who estimated that a threepenny levy would have raised up to £8 million – had wanted.[98] In the event, exhibitors accepted the new levy as it 'allows a far greater degree of flexibility for the adjustment of seat prices than the old scale'.[99]

While extending the life of the NFFC for another ten years, the Cinematograph Films Act also made significant changes to its terms of reference that would fundamentally alter the way it operated in future. The government was determined that the NFFC 'should operate as profitably as possible': for this reason it removed the stipulation that the NFFC should make loans only to producers who 'are not for the time being in a position otherwise to obtain adequate financial facilities for the purpose or reasonable terms from an appropriate source'. The aim of the legislation was that 'the Corporation might be able to operate as a specialised commercial bank with the object of breaking even one year with another'.[100] It no doubt helped the passage of the bill that the NFFC had made operating profits in 1956 (£79,132) and 1957 (£84,727). The NFFC's new remit and the requirement to pay its own way was the context in which the corporation came to support popular British genre films in the late 1950s such as the 'Carry On' series and the Hammer horror films. However, it would seem that the NFFC did not entirely welcome the change to its remit. Its annual report for 1959 stated:

> The Corporation is therefore faced with a dilemma. If it were to adhere with absolute strictness to the duty to pay its way laid down in the Act of 1957, it would make only 'guaranteed loans' – i.e. secured loans which in most cases could be made equally well by a Bank. But the underlying purpose of the Corporation is to assist British film production by lending money which cannot be obtained through the ordinary banking system, and accordingly the Corporation must continue to make 'risk loans' – i.e. loans dependent for recovery on the commercial results of the film in question.[101]

The schedule of loans approved for the year included several social problem films that were not obvious box-office subjects, such as *Sapphire* (1959) and *Serious Charge* (1959). And in 1960 the corporation reported that 'two-thirds of the loans approved during the year were loans of "risk money"': these included *The Angry Silence*, *The Entertainer* and *Saturday Night and Sunday Morning* (all released in 1960).[102] Some of these films – notably *Sapphire* and *Saturday Night and Sunday Morning* – returned significant profits but might not have been made without the corporation's support.

A decade after its inception on a temporary basis, the NFFC had become a fixture of the British film industry. It had supported around a third of all British first features during the 1950s and in the process had backed some of the most successful films of the decade, including *The African Queen*, *Moulin Rouge*, *Genevieve*, *The Colditz Story*, *Private's Progress*, *The Baby and the Battleship*, *The Curse of Frankenstein*, *Dracula*, *Carry On Nurse* and *I'm All Right, Jack!*. The fact that it had also backed its share of loss-making films and that many of its loans had not been repaid was as much an indication of the uncertainty of commercial success in the industry as poor judgement on the corporation's part. However, it had never recovered any of the £3 million it had loaned to the British Lion Film Corporation. During the 1950s the histories of the NFFC and British Lion became inextricably linked: the next chapter will document this complex relationship.

Notes

1. 'Up Quality Street', *Kinematograph Weekly*, 6 December 1951, p. 4.
2. 'Heartening Progress', *Kinematograph Weekly*, 8 June 1950, p. 4.
3. 'British Production Survey', *Kinematograph Year Book 1951* (London: Odhams Press, 1951), p. 155.
4. 'Producers Maintain Output and Improve Quality', *Kinematograph Weekly*, 28 September 1950, p. 3.
5. 'Film Shares Up by Over £6 Million in Twelve Months', *Kinematograph Weekly*, 18 January 1951, p. 3.
6. Linda Wood (ed.), *British Film Industry: BFI Information Guide No. 1* (London: British Film Institute, 1980), Appendix A, unpaginated.
7. 'Producers Now Making Profits', *Kinematograph Weekly*, 28 August 1952, p. 3.
8. 'British Films Earning More', *Kinematograph Weekly*, 9 September 1954, p. 7.
9. 'British Films Take More at Box-Office', *Kinematograph Weekly*, 21 April 1955, p. 3.
10. Wood (ed.), *British Film Industry*, Appendix A.
11. Lindsay Anderson, 'Get Out and Push!', in Tom Maschler (ed.), *Declaration* (London: MacGibbon & Kee, 1957), p. 157.
12. Raymond Durgnat, *A Mirror for England: British Movies from Austerity to Affluence* (London: Faber & Faber, 1970), p. 140. More recent reassessments are provided by Sue Harper and Vincent Porter, *British Cinema of the 1950s: The Decline of Deference* (Oxford: Oxford University Press, 2003); Christine Geraghty, *British Cinema in the Fifties: Gender, Genre and the 'New Look'* (London: Routledge, 2000); and Ian MacKillop and Neil Sinyard (eds), *British Cinema in the 1950s: A Celebration* (Manchester: Manchester University Press, 2003).
13. 'Box-Office Winners of 1950', *Kinematograph Weekly*, 14 December 1950, p. 5.
14. 'Box-Office Winners of 1951', *Kinematograph Weekly*, 20 December 1951, p. 5; 'Box-Office Winners of 1952', *Kinematograph Weekly*, 18 December 1952, p. 9.
15. The results of the *Kine Weekly* and *Motion Picture Herald* box-office surveys are collated in Janet Thumim, 'The "popular", cash and culture in the postwar British cinema industry', *Screen*, 32: 3 (1991), pp. 245–71.
16. Harper and Porter, *British Cinema of the 1950s*, p. 247.
17. 'Long Shots', *Kinematograph Weekly*, 19 March 1953, p. 4.
18. *National Film Finance Corporation: Annual Report and Statement of Accounts for the year ending 31 March 1952*, Cmd. 8523 (April 1952), p. 11 (Appendix C).
19. 'To Lighten the Trade Burdens', *Kinematograph Weekly*, 2 February 1950, p. 6.
20. TNA BT 258/1946: Sidney Golt and A. T. K. Grant, 'Film Finance: Making Production Profitable', 22 February 1953.
21. 'Hire Finance', *Kinematograph Weekly*, 14 December 1950, p. 11.
22. Ibid.
23. *National Film Finance Corporation: Annual Report and Statement of Accounts for the year ending 31 March 1954*, Cmd. 9166 (June 1954), p. 11 (49).
24. TNA BT 258/1946: Richard Stopford to Sir Maurice Dean, 2 March 1953.
25. Ibid.: Richard Stopford, 'Future of the National Film Finance Corporation', n.d.
26. Ibid.: 'Film Finance: Making Production Profitable'.
27. Ibid.: Richard Stopford to Sir Maurice Dean, 2 March 1953.
28. Ibid.: Dean to Stopford, 14 May 1953.

29. *Parliamentary Debates: House of Commons*, 5th Series, vol. 521, 25 November 1953, col. 420.
30. Ibid. col. 419.
31. 'Long Shots', *Kinematograph Weekly*, 19 March 1953, p. 4.
32. 'Film-by-Film Drop in Eady Bonus', *Kinematograph Weekly*, 6 May 1954, p. 3.
33. FFA Realised Film Box 21: *The Gift Horse*: Independent Film Distributors Royalty Statement, 2 January 1954.
34. FFA Realised Film Box 56: *Genevieve*: General Film Distributors Royalty Statement, 31 December 1953.
35. Harper and Porter, *British Cinema of the 1950s*, p. 37.
36. 'Long Shots', *Kinematograph Weekly*, 6 September 1951, p. 4.
37. 'Mr Rank Tells the Triumphant Story', *Kinematograph Weekly*, 28 September 1954, p. 6.
38. 'Shepherd's Bush to Close Down', *Kinematograph Weekly*, 3 March 1949, p. 3.
39. 'Prime Minister is Told Denham Closing', *Kinematograph Weekly*, 26 July 1951, p. 3.
40. TNA BT 258/1945: Sidney Golt to R. G. Somervell, 28 April 1952.
41. TNA BT 15/340: David Kingsley to S. G. Knight, 20 March 1957.
42. Vincent Porter, 'Methodism versus the Market-Place: The Rank Organisation and British Cinema', in Robert Murphy (ed.), *The British Cinema Book* (London: British Film Institute, 1997), p. 128.
43. Roy Ward Baker, *The Director's Cut: A Memoir of 60 Years in Film and Television* (London: Reynolds & Hearn, 2000), pp. 115–16.
44. Lewis Gilbert, *All My Flashbacks* (London: Reynolds & Hearn, 2010), pp. 159–60.
45. Pat Jackson, *A Retake Please!: 'Night Mail' to 'Western Approaches'* (Liverpool: Liverpool University Press/Royal Naval Museum Publications, 1999), p. 306.
46. Geoffrey Macnab, *J. Arthur Rank and the British Film Industry* (London: Routledge, 1993), p. 199.
47. Michael Balcon, *Michael Balcon presents . . . A Lifetime of Films* (London: Hutchinson, 1969), p. 168.
48. 'British Films Set the Pace During 1954', *Kinematograph Weekly*, 16 December 1954, p. 8.
49. FFA Realised Film Box 156: *The Battle of the River Plate*: Agreement between Arcturus Productions and J. Arthur Rank Film Distributors, 20 September 1955.
50. Michael Powell, *Million Dollar Movie* (London: William Heinemann, 1992), p. 148.
51. Ibid. p. 350.
52. '"Massive Scale" of Rank Future Programme', *Kinematograph Weekly*, 10 January 1957, p. 7.
53. 'Big-Budget Picture for Pinewood', *Kinematograph Weekly*, 2 October 1958, p. 3.
54. 'Pattern', *Kinematograph Weekly*, 9 October 1958, p. 4.
55. 'Long Shots', *Kinematograph Weekly*, 8 July 1954, p. 4.
56. TNA BT 64/4522: Sir Philip Warter to Lord Reith, 30 January 1951.
57. Ibid.: James Lawrie to R. G. Somervell, 28 February 1951.
58. TNA BT 64/4521: Lawrie to Sir Wilfrid Eady, 5 January 1951.
59. Vincent Porter, 'The Robert Clark Account: Films released in Britain by Associated British Pictures, British Lion, MGM, and Warner Bros., 1946–1957', *Historical Journal of Film, Radio and Television*, 20: 4 (2000), pp. 472–3.
60. Ibid. pp. 494–6, 505–7.

61. 'Associated British Has £745,000 Surplus', *Kinematograph Weekly*, 8 July 1954, p. 7.
62. TNA T 228/273: Sir Wilfrid Eady, 'Film Finance Corporation', 2 August 1951.
63. John Ramsden, *The Dam Busters: A British Film Guide* (London: I. B. Tauris, 2003), p. 35.
64. 'Honours Were Divided in a Not-so-Golden Year', *Kinematograph Weekly*, 15 December 1955, p. 4.
65. Porter, 'The Robert Clark Account', pp. 475–6.
66. TNA BT 64/5067: D. J. Minchin to (Mrs) P. B. M. James, 1 December 1955.
67. 'Ealing Studio Record Brings New Finance', *Kinematograph Weekly*, 2 April 1953, p. 16.
68. TNA BT 64/5067: Robert Stopford to Sir Maurice Dean, 18 February 1953.
69. Ibid.: 'T. G. L.' to Dean, 13 December 1952.
70. Ibid.: Sidney Golt to Dean, 4 December 1952.
71. Ibid.: Minchin to James, 1 December 1955.
72. Ibid.
73. Ibid.: 'T. G. L'. to Glaves-Smith, 11 October 1954.
74. 'Ealing Studios Sold to BBC', *Daily Film Renter*, 20 October 1955, p. 1.
75. 'Long Shots', *Kinematograph Weekly*, 27 October 1955, p. 4.
76. Balcon, *A Lifetime of Films*, p. 184.
77. 'American Finance is Not Influencing Ealing Policy', *Kinematograph Weekly*, 22 November 1956, p. 21.
78. TNA BT 64/5067: 'Record of conversation' by P. B. M. James, 22 March 1956.
79. Harper and Porter, *British Cinema of the 1950s*, p. 71.
80. 'Balcon Deal', *Kinematograph Weekly*, 3 September 1959, p. 3.
81. TNA BT 64/4522: Lord Reith to Harold Wilson, 12 January 1951.
82. 'Group "Three" Starts Production', *Kinematograph Weekly*, 7 June 1951, p. 29.
83. The Group 3 films were *Judgement Deferred* (1952), *Brandy for the Parson* (1952), *Time Gentlemen, Please!* (1952), *You're Only Young Once* (1952), *The Brave Don't Cry* (1952), *Miss Robin Hood* (1952), *The Oracle* (1953), *Laxdale Hall* (1953), *Background* (1953), *The Conquest of Everest* (1953), *Devil on Horseback* (1954), *Conflict of Wings* (1954), *Man of Africa* (1954), *The Angel Who Pawned Her Harp* (1954), *The End of the Road* (1954), *Child's Play* (1954), *Make Me an Offer* (1954), *Orders Are Orders* (1955), *The Love Match* (1955), *John and Julie* (1955), *The Blue Peter* (1955) and *Double Cross* (1956).
84. Simon Popple, 'Group Three: A Lesson in State Intervention?', *Film History*, 8: 2 (1996), pp. 141–2.
85. Porter, 'The Robert Clark Account', p. 501.
86. 'Group 3 Moves Into First-Feature Market', *Kinematograph Weekly*, 30 July 1953, p. 23.
87. 'British Lion to Release Group 3 product', *Kinematograph Weekly*, 30 July 1953, p. 3.
88. 'Producers Will Debate NFFC's Group-3 Plan', *Kinematograph Weekly*, 3 September 1953, p. 3.
89. British Film Producers' Association Executive Committee Minutes: Minutes of a meeting of the Executive Council, 2 December 1953, minute 233.
90. 'Long Shots', *Kinematograph Weekly*, 20 August 1954, p. 4.
91. 'Here Are the NFFC Figures', *Kinematograph Weekly*, 3 June 1954, p. 8.
92. 'Long Shots', *Kinematograph Weekly*, 14 October 1954, p. 5.
93. 'Out of the Crisis', *Films and Filming*, 1: 11 (August 1955), p. 7.
94. *National Film Finance Corporation: Annual Report and Statement of Accounts for the year ending 31 March 1956*, Cmd. 9751 (May 1956), p. 2 (11).

95. TNA BT 258/664: Legislative Committee: Cinematograph Films Bill (1957) L (56) 53.
96. Ibid.: Minute No. 21 by R. C. Bryant, 21 September 1956.
97. Ibid.: F. d. Erroll to Lord Mancroft, 16 January 1957.
98. Ibid.: Briefing note by P. B. M. James, 1 February 1957.
99. 'Advantages', *Kinematograph Weekly*, 4 July 1957, p. 4.
100. TNA BT 258/664: Handwritten note with illegible signature, dated '18/4', on Minute No. 21 by R. C. Bryant, 21 September 1956.
101. *National Film Finance Corporation: Annual Report and Statement of Accounts for the year ending 31 March 1959*, Cmnd. 799 (July 1959), p. 1 (4).
102. *National Film Finance Corporation: Annual Report and Statement of Accounts for the year ending 31 March 1960*, Cmnd. 1096 (July 1960), p. 2 (4).

CHAPTER 8

The British Lion Film Corporation

> The 'City' has never been excited about a British film industry. All that Whitehall should realise is that when they destroy British Lion, they admit their failure to maintain a film industry in the UK. (Bank of England)[1]

The case of the British Lion Film Corporation merits special consideration in the history of film finance. In the late 1940s British Lion had been the principal beneficiary of the state loans for production available through the National Film Finance Corporation. In 1948–9 the NFFC loaned British Lion a total of £3 million to support its production programme.[2] What amounted in effect to a government bailout of British Lion had been an emergency measure to ensure that the company – the second-largest in Britain in terms of production output – was able to continue operating. However, the bailout had longer-term consequences: British Lion 'became a central player in debates about state control and cinematic creativity'.[3] Indeed, the histories of British Lion and the NFFC were so closely linked that it is difficult at times to separate them: British Lion owed its continued existence to the NFFC's support and had to determine its production strategy within a framework approved by the corporation, while the NFFC found that its overall policy was influenced to a very large extent by the state of affairs at British Lion at any given time. There were also conflicting pressures from official quarters. The Board of Trade was concerned that British Lion should operate as efficiently as possible in order to provide a viable alternative to the Rank/ABPC duopoly, while the Treasury's only interest was to reclaim as much of the £3 million as it could. It might even be argued that one of the reasons for the decision to extend the statutory life of the NFFC was down to the government holding out the hope that the British Lion loan might be repaid.

The argument always advanced by the NFFC to defend both its initial loan to British Lion and its ongoing support for the company was that British Lion was the major supporter of independent production: it provided an alternative source of distributor finance for those producers and directors who baulked against either the draconian managerialism of John Davis at the Rank Organisation or the budgetary parsimony of ABPC. A briefing note for the Cinematograph Films Production (Special Loans) Act Amendment Bill of 1950, which provided an additional £1 million for the NFFC, stated: 'It is not too much to say that without the support of the Finance Corporation, last year or this year would have seen the collapse of the British Lion Film Corporation – the company mainly responsible for the financing of the chief "independent" producers who prefer not to rely for their finance on the two vertically integrated combines.'4 The NFFC loan in effect underwrote British Lion's entire production programme. A schedule of approved loans in March 1950 included eight produced directly by British Lion Production Associates – *The Last Days of Dolwyn, Saints and Sinners, Seven Days to Noon, Gone to Earth, State Secret, My Daughter Joy, The Wooden Horse* and *The Wonder Kid* – and another twelve distributed by British Lion: *That Dangerous Age, Maytime in Mayfair, The Third Man, The Cure for Love, The Angel With the Trumpet, The Elusive Pimpernel, The Happiest Days of Your Life, Odette, Children of Chance, Interrupted Journey, Honeymoon Deferred* and *Maria Chapdelaine*.[5]

A condition of the NFFC loan was that Alexander Korda should stand down as the managing director of British Lion: Korda's extravagance and poor management were blamed for the company's losses. The role of managing director accordingly passed to Arthur Jarratt, with Korda assuming the mantle of 'production adviser'. At this point there were two distinct groups within British Lion. On the one hand there were the 'Korda producers' – Herbert Wilcox, Anatole de Grunwald, Carol Reed, Michael Powell and Emeric Pressburger, Frank Launder and Sidney Gilliat – who specialised in 'high-end quality films of an expensive kind, usually designed for the international market':

> These producers have in recent years produced films that have had great success in the international market and have contributed greatly to building up the high reputation of British films. I have therefore confirmed to the directors of the Corporation the desirability, in the national interest, during the critical period through which the industry is passing, of assisting this important unit to continue its operations.[6]

On the other hand there were the 'Jarratt producers' who were responsible for 'first features, and have obtained circuit bookings, but have for the most part been cheaper than those of the Korda producers'. This group included Rudolph Cartier, Ian Dalrymple, Anthony Havelock-Allan, Joseph Janni, Gene Markey and Gregory Ratoff. The Boulting brothers and David Lean were later recruits to the ranks of the Korda group.

There is some evidence to suggest that the NFFC did not know what a parlous state British Lion was in when it bailed out the company. NFFC board member and chartered accountant S. J. Pears was sceptical of the company's accounts showing a profit of £45,000 after tax in 1948: '[It] is possible to draw the conclusion that the company during the last 2½ years has in fact been making trading losses . . . It is also possible that it may have lost more than its share and capital reserves.'[7] In particular the NFFC felt that the value of films had been overestimated by as much as £1 million (it was common for film companies to include anticipated earnings from films on the balance sheet as assets: these were usually written off after two years). It soon became clear just how bad the balance sheet really was. In April 1949 British Lion estimated losses of £700,000 for the year: this total was later adjusted upwards to £1,388,797.[8] Its losses were incurred on film production and distribution: the British Lion Studio Company usually made a modest profit each year.

The NFFC's immediate response to the British Lion situation was to look to reduce costs and in particular to instil greater fiscal discipline in the budgeting of films. It installed Harold Drayton as chairman: Drayton was a City financier with various directorships who had become involved with British Lion when he guaranteed a loan of £250,000 from British Electric Traction to produce *The Courtneys of Curzon Street*. Herbert Wilcox described Drayton as '[a] very hard business-man but a man of compassion and inflexible principles, who understood the imponderables in our industry and the elements that could bring big results'.[9] Drayton was the NFFC's man: he was there to protect the corporation's interest. Even so, the NFFC conceded that the arrangement was far from ideal:

> Such control as the Corporation exercises over the costs of films produced by the British Lion group is indirect, as it is inherent in the financing of production through distributors. It is therefore less effective than elsewhere ... [The chairman] supplies progress reports and cost sheets for each film; but the degree of independence given to, or assumed by, some of the producers is such that full information, especially when units are on location, is not always provided.[10]

The corporation's admission that it had 'less effective' control provided ammunition for its critics, including Nicholas Davenport, one-time board member of both British Lion and the National Film Finance Company: 'It is an open secret that the Government originally intended British Lion to be its instrument in the servicing and financing of the leading independent producers ... The public will naturally want to know why the NFFC lent so much public money to British Lion and did not insist on getting the control it wanted.'[11]

British Lion was the second-largest distributor of British films in the early 1950s after the Rank Organisation. Between 1950 and 1953 British Lion released 77 British features: these included 33 produced under the umbrella of British Lion Production Associates and 15 on behalf of Independent Film Distributors. The average cost of films produced by British Lion and its associated companies was £261,200: this marked a significant reduction from the £323,700 average of films before 1950.[12] A Treasury paper noted (with approval) that 'the reduction [in cost] is substantial, and must be largely due to the Corporation's cost control'.[13] There was also something of an upturn in box-office returns. Most of British Lion's films were released on the ABC circuit. The records of the distributor Associated British-Pathé indicate that in 1949 eight British Lion films – *The Last Days of Dolwyn, Saints and Sinners, That Dangerous Age, Maytime in Mayfair, The Third Man, Interrupted Journey, The Cure for Love* and *The Angel With the Trumpet* – earned total distributor's receipts of £1,324,168 or an average per picture of £165,521. The two most successful films by some distance were Carol Reed's *The Third Man* (£277,549) and Herbert Wilcox's *Maytime in Mayfair* (£268,984).[14] At this time a distributor's gross over £250,000 was taken as the yardstick for a major hit. At the beginning of 1950 Drayton was able to report: 'In the last six months we have released a number of good films, and I am pleased to say they are making money . . . I am hopeful that the films we are now producing, and will produce in the future, will on balance not lose more money.'[15] This is confirmed by the quantitative evidence: in 1950 seven British Lion films – *The Happiest Days of Your Life*, *My Daughter Joy*, *State Secret*, *Odette*, *The Wooden Horse*, *Gone to Earth* and *The Elusive Pimpernel* – earned total receipts of £1,351,285 or an average of £193,041 per picture. The major box-office hits were *The Happiest Days of Your Life* (£278,502), *Odette* (£269,403) and *The Wooden Horse* (£266,545).[16]

The upturn in box-office revenues in the early 1950s was sufficient for *The Economist* to sound an optimistic note about the company's fortunes:

> Financial success in film-making is too clearly bound up with the quality and fortunes of individual films for any one company to reflect the industry's general prosperity – or more often adversity – very clearly. But British Lion Film Corporation, as one of the largest companies in the industry not directly linked with cinema ownership, may give some pointers. Its results this week would seem to confirm the outsider's impression that the internal economies carried out by producers, in conjunction with the external assistance that the Government has been providing in the past two years, are bringing the production side of the industry into a slightly better state of health.[17]

However, this optimism was not borne out by the statistical evidence. British Lion was still operating at a loss: even in 1950 it reported a net loss of £148,422. The Board of Trade estimated that British Lion's releases earned back on average 50–60 per cent of their costs in the home market: a domestic return of 70 per cent of the cost was deemed the minimum necessary to make a profit when overseas receipts were added. Furthermore, British Lion was also carrying an accumulated deficit due to its losses in the late 1940s and the interest accruing on its loan from the NFFC: 'It seems most unlikely that the films made before 1951 or 1952 will, in total, make a profit . . . If previous losses could be disregarded, and if British Lion were to continue to operate at their 1953 levels of costs and earnings (implying continued pressure to enforce economy), they might very well strike even; but there is little prospect of them making a sufficient profit to wipe out the burden of past losses.'[18]

Moreover, the upturn in revenues in 1950–1 was not sustained. In 1952 thirteen British Lion films returned distributor's receipts of £1,561,922, which represented an average of £130,160 per picture. *The African Queen* (£256,267) was the only major hit, and the average gross per film was down by nearly a third. Drayton told shareholders that 'we have been unable to maintain the high level of distribution earnings in recent years. This is partly due to the late delivery of some of our productions which prevented us from having the benefit of a full year's receipts in these accounts and also the box-office receipts from some of them did not come up to expectations.'[19] And in 1953 the total receipts for nine films amounted to £1,234,566 or an average per picture of £137,174: the most successful film was *The Sound Barrier* (£227,978). There were mixed fortunes for the 'Korda producers'.

Powell and Pressburger's films, for example, did moderate business at the box office, including *Gone to Earth* (£110,000), *The Elusive Pimpernel* (£133,353) and *The Tales of Hoffmann* (£105,035), while Herbert Wilcox scored with *Odette* but saw lesser returns for *The Lady With a Lamp* (£151,091), *Derby Day* (£150,010) and *Trent's Last Case* (£155,903).

The most successful of the new independent groups to emerge during the 1950s was Independent Film Distributors (IFD): this company had a close relationship with British Lion, which handled the physical distribution of its films while IFD provided the guarantees and finance.[20] John Woolf, the eldest son of veteran distributor C. M. Woolf, set up Romulus Films with his stepbrother James in 1950 to act as the production arm of IFD. The Woolfs sought to develop co-production arrangements with other independents: these included British producers such as Monja Danischewsky (*The Galloping Major*) and Daniel Angel (*Women of Twilight*), and the Americans Albert Lewin (*Pandora and the Flying Dutchman*) and Sam Spiegel (*The African Queen*). The Woolfs were adept at negotiating the fiscal and legal complexities of co-production arrangements. *The African Queen* (1951), for example, was a dual-budget picture for which Romulus provided the sterling budget covering the 'below-the-line' costs of shooting the film, while Sam Spiegel's Horizon Pictures raised dollar finance to cover the 'above-the-line' costs for the fees of director John Huston and stars Humphrey Bogart and Katharine Hepburn.[21] The NFFC contributed to the sterling budget. *Beat the Devil* (1953) was an even more complex international co-production with three budgets: an 'English budget' (£160,000) raised against a distribution guarantee from IFD in order to finance the making of the picture by Romulus Films, an 'Italian budget' (170 million lire) provided by Italian partners (Angelo Rizzoli and Robert Haggiag) for location shooting in Italy in return for Eastern hemisphere distribution rights outside those territories where IFD held the rights, and the 'Santana budget' (US $600,000) provided by Humphrey Bogart's production company Santana Pictures to cover the fees of Bogart, John Huston and Jennifer Jones (loaned from David O. Selznick) in return for Western hemisphere rights.[22] Most of the Woolfs' films were successful, particularly *The African Queen* and *Moulin Rouge* (£205,453). Their biggest loss-maker was the Graham Greene-scripted *The Stranger's Hand* (1954), a co-production with Milos Films of Rome for which IFD put up half the budget of £145,000 but which returned a distributor's gross of only £45,435.[23]

British Lion's continuing losses in the early 1950s made it look increasingly unlikely that it would be in a position to repay the NFFC loan. By 1953 the Board of Trade accepted that remedial action was necessary. The easiest intervention would be to put the company under new management. The Board of Trade was particularly concerned that British Lion lacked effective leadership: it felt that 'there was really no central direction of the whole organisation and that Mr Drayton had not proved to be the asset that had been hoped for but, on the contrary, was something of a drag on efficient reorganisation'.[24] The institution of a new management regime would be a condition of any restructuring of the company. 'It seems to me', wrote one Treasury official, 'that everything depends on finding the right chap to take control of British Lion . . . I do not know if any steps are being taken to find such a man, but that is what we must begin if we are to get anything going.'[25] The Bank of England was asked for its recommendation but was of little help: 'It is not easy to find a Chairman for a lame duck in a not too healthy industry.'[26]

Various options were discussed. The most drastic would have been to put British Lion into liquidation. This course of action was supported by John Davis, who 'had formed the definite opinion that the best interests of the industry would be served if British Lion were wound up without an attempt either to continue it or to provide a successor company . . . [The] present management was hopeless . . . Generally, he did not think that the departure of British Lion would greatly disturb the finances of the industry.'[27] Davis's attempt to undermine British Lion was no doubt motivated by wanting to further consolidate Rank's position in the industry. However, there was little support for this course of action in government circles. The Treasury initially rejected the appointment of an official receiver on the grounds that it would be 'a devastating check to confidence in the British film production industry; it would certainly represent a confession that Government policy in regard to the film industry had failed; and, if the appointment of a Receiver was followed by putting British Lion into liquidation, the Government might well find themselves with the responsibility of creating something to take its place, involving further expenditure.'[28] The NFFC put forward a plan that would see one-third of its loan to British Lion converted into equity in the company, with the rest converted into a long-term debenture investment.[29] However, the Treasury was also resistant to this proposal as even partial state ownership of a film company would be politically problematic: 'The unfair critic might say that this was a trial trip for the new socialisation policy?'[30] The Board of Trade therefore sought an 'outside opinion' from banker Sir John Keeling (chairman of the London and Yorkshire Trust) and City consultant Sir Richard Yeabsley: they recommended that the NFFC's loan should be extended for two years and the interest payments should be reduced in order to give British Lion 'one more try'.[31] R. A. Butler, the Chancellor of the Exchequer, agreed to the plan 'but he would emphasise the importance of improving the general direction of the affairs of British Lion; it should be given new teeth and a fresh set of whiskers'.[32]

However, no sooner had this plan been agreed than it was overtaken by events. British Lion had been trading at a loss for several years, but now it reported that it expected its loss for 1954 to amount to £350,000: the loss 'arises mainly on three recent films' – *The Story of Gilbert and Sullivan*, *The Heart of the Matter* and *The Beggar's Opera* – which were 'all well received by the critics' but had flopped commercially.[33] The fact that these films had been made by producers with good track records at the box office – Launder and Gilliat (*The Story of Gilbert and Sullivan*), Ian Dalrymple (*The Heart of the Matter*) and Herbert Wilcox (*The Beggar's Opera*) – again highlights the uncertainty of popular appeal in the film industry.[34] In April 1954 a Treasury memorandum noted that 'British Lion is in a bad way. It looks as if we shall have to take pretty drastic action.'[35] The higher than expected projected losses caused jitters in the City, to the extent that some of the lending banks were reluctant to accept British Lion's distribution guarantee. In May 1954 it was reported that 'the Bank of America have decided that they cannot discount the British Lion guarantee on [The] Colditz Story until either they can see British Lion's Balance Sheet or be given some information about the future of British Lion'.[36] This was clearly a matter of great concern, as the Bank of America was one of the three main lenders of front money to British producers. *The Colditz Story* was produced by Ivan Foxwell: when the bank pulled out the NFFC stepped in to rescue the film and loaned the whole of the £136,000 budget.[37] The idea of giving British Lion 'one more try' was now dead in the water: the NFFC accepted the inevitable and appointed an official receiver and manager of the corporation.[38]

The resulting audit made for grim reading. It found that in addition to the £3 million loan from the NFFC, British Lion owed a further £1.8 million to banks and other creditors.[39] The bank loans for eighteen films had not been repaid.[40] The company was in an impossible position: it was unable to repay the government loan but at the same time could not raise further capital from the banks. In October 1954 the Treasury accepted that 'all the £3 million is lost, except possibly for some £25,000'.[41] Sir John Keeling, newly installed as chairman of the NFFC, wrote to the Treasury to propose a radical restructuring of British Lion:

> It is, I regret to say, becoming increasingly apparent to me that we cannot re-establish a sound British Lion Group other than on a comprehensive basis . . . I have therefore become convinced that if the NFFC is to fulfil its task and the British Lion is to be commercially successful we must be prepared to give certain services to producers and to promote production. In fact in this regard we must follow the precedent set by the two vertical combines.[42]

The precedent Keeling had in mind was the provision of distribution guarantees rather than direct production. This was based on the suggestion that most of British Lion's losses in the early 1950s had arisen from its own in-house productions. In fact, this was not necessarily the case: Launder and Gilliat's *The Belles of St Trinian's* – the first of a cycle of films based on Ronald Searle's cartoons of unruly schoolgirls – was among the biggest hits of 1954.

The reorganisation involved the NFFC writing off losses of £2,969,000 to the old British Lion Film Corporation and underwriting the total share capital of £600,000 of the new British Lion Films, in which it effectively became the sole shareholder. It also provided £964,000 to pay off the outstanding creditors and bank loans, but there was no compensation for shareholders in the old corporation. The new company's directors were Sir John Keeling (chairman), Sir Arthur Jarratt, Sir Arnold Overton and David Kingsley (the new managing director of the NFFC). The new company 'will continue without interruption the distribution of current films and the servicing of outstanding contacts with exhibitors'.[43] There was some discussion as to whether the name of the company should be changed:

> The difficulty is to reconcile the very understandable wish of Ministers that the new company should have an entirely 'new look' with the need to utilise to the

full the goodwill of the old Company in order to recover as much of the NFFC loan as possible . . . I doubt, on reflection, whether there would be much to be gained by having a wholly new name for the new Company, since it might only lend point to critics who were inclined to say that this was the same set-up under a new name.[44]

The Economist, no longer so upbeat about British Lion's prospects, saw the nationalisation of the company as evidence of the failure of the government's film policy: 'It is only fair to say that the whole sorry venture is not an example of the film finance corporation's business judgement in backing British film production; the initial and continued support of British Lion has been a matter of Government policy, cost what it may.'[45]

The reconstituted British Lion initially fared somewhat better than its predecessor. The writing off of its debts meant that it was able to return to profit: it recorded profits of £231,738 in 1956 and £80,592 in 1957.[46] This was mostly on the back of several successful films – some already completed or in production before the restructuring – including *Hobson's Choice* (£206,579), *Geordie* (£218,384), *Private's Progress* (£310,870), *The Baby and the Battleship* (£258,845), *Sailor Beware!* (£221,779) and *Raising a Riot* (£231,148). It did particularly well with comedy: this was a genre that could be produced economically and with reasonable expectation of returning a profit in the home market. For example, *Private's Progress* (1956) – produced by Roy Boulting and directed by John Boulting for Charter Film Productions – was budgeted at £143,647. Even with an overcost of £17,420, *Private's Progress* earned distributor's receipts nearly twice the cost of production and was one of British Lion's most profitable films.[47]

Most of British Lion's films during this period followed the standard financing model of a discountable distribution guarantee (usually 70 per cent of the budget) with end money provided by the NFFC and producer deferments. The close link between British Lion and the NFFC was reinforced by the presence of NFFC managing director David Kingsley on the British Lion board. British Lion also strengthened its link with Independent Film Distributors when they merged their overseas distribution arms in 1955 to create Lion International Films.[48] IFD remained the most ambitious of the independent producer-distributors of the 1950s: the same year it announced an investment of £2 million in eight pictures.[49] John Woolf had a clear understanding of the fiscal landscape of the industry and a strategic outlook. In May 1956 he wrote to the completion guarantor Film Finances:

> The only thing I would suggest to you is that there are not so very many substantial independent production companies with whom you deal, and that for the future, if we are going to continue these arrangements with the NFFC, which I anticipate will be the case, you might consider making exceptional terms for us. I realise that generally speaking you need to apply standard rules, but in as fluctuating a business as ours, there seems to be no reason why preferential terms should not be given to reliable customers, in which category I flatter myself we fall.[50]

Film Finances did indeed agree 'an exceptional arrangement' with Woolf for their guarantee of completion for *Three Men in a Boat* (1956) – produced by Jack Clayton and directed by Ken Annakin for Romulus Films – whereby Woolf agreed to meet the first 10 per cent of any overcost but not to increase the budget of a film which Film Finances felt 'is seriously under-scheduled and under-budgeted'.[51] *Three Men in a Boat* exceeded its budget (£191,579) by 29 per cent: domestic receipts of £212,723 probably represented a loss, though it may have gone into profit from overseas distribution.[52]

For the most part British Lion was now focusing on the home market: the failure of the international strategy of the late 1940s cast a long shadow. However, it was prepared to back more expensive pictures where other parties were willing to share the risk. Herbert Wilcox's *King's Rhapsody* (1955) – the second of two musicals starring Errol Flynn and Anna Neagle – was budgeted at £380,216. British Lion provided a distribution guarantee of £125,000, and Wilcox raised the rest of the sterling budget (£227,680) through deferments and studio credits. The balance was provided by various American and Yugoslavian interests. Wilcox also secured an NFFC loan of £45,000 as 'a stop-gap precaution in lieu of selling distribution rights'. He told David Kingsley: 'I believe it is reasonably safe to assume that before the actual studio shooting of the picture commences early in the New Year, the entire budgeted cost of the picture will be covered by advances or guarantees.'[53] However, domestic receipts of only £90,884 meant that British Lion did not recover its advance.[54]

Wilcox's last major production was the ill-fated *Yangtse Incident* (1957). On the face of it, this should have had all the ingredients of a popular success: a factually based naval picture depicting the escape of frigate HMS *Amethyst* from China in 1949 with excellent production credentials including the star (Richard Todd) and director (Michael Anderson) of the highly successful *The Dam Busters*. The financing arrangements for the film were complex to say the least. The NFFC advanced £150,000 towards the budget of £259,980 against a distribution guarantee from British Lion, with the Distributors Corporation of America paying US $157,500 for the Western hemisphere rights and a further cash investment of $205,000 from the Lustowe Corporation of New York.[55] The production had the co-operation of the Royal Navy, including the loan of HMS *Amethyst* herself. *Yangtse Incident* went over budget by £30,000, but after a year on general release its distributor's gross was only £187,196: the producer's share (£147,263 including Eady levy) was barely enough to repay the NFFC loan.[56] The overseas receipts were negligible. Wilcox blamed its poor performance on its release being pushed back by British Lion, which meant that *Yangste Incident* lost out to *The Battle of the River Plate* at the box office: 'By October [1957], the edge and excitement had been stripped from our film and audience attendance fell far short of expectations. I have, at the time, still not recovered the cost of the film. So one year's work went for nothing – except glory.'[57]

It was in the late 1950s that the NFFC started to look for potential buyers for British Lion. In 1957 the NFFC had estimated the net value of British Lion at around £750,000: the Treasury confirmed that it 'would be quite content to see the Board of Trade out of British Lion for a sum of £750,000 and a First Mortgage Debenture of £34,000 in the Studio Company'.[58] In 1960 the chartered accountant appointed to evaluate the company's value observed that 'the price which NFFC will receive for their interests in British Lion is rather low when considered in relation to asset values and present earning capacity. However, the past results indicate clearly the highly speculative nature of the business.'[59] However, this was not a propitious time to put the company up for sale. Shepperton Studios had been forced to close temporarily in 1957: this was in order to repair a structural defect in the roof, but it meant that the British Lion Studio Company was expected to sustain an operating loss in 1957–8. And the decline of cinema attendances was starting to take its toll: British Lion's focus on the home market made it more vulnerable to the contraction of the exhibition sector. The Treasury accepted that 'conditions in the cinema industry have been becoming steadily more difficult and British Lion has inevitably been severely affected'.[60]

With no prospective buyers for British Lion, the NFFC decided that another change of its management structure was necessary. It eased out Jarratt and appointed David Kingsley as managing director: Kingsley stepped down from the NFFC. It also brought four of British Lion's most successful film-makers – Frank Launder, Sidney Gilliat, John and Roy Boulting – onto the board of directors. This was a bold move: it returned British Lion to the business of making films and gave leading independent producers a stake in the company. *Kine* felt that the shake-up of the management group 'to take in such active and successful film makers . . . is an important development with considerable potential'.[61] The company's capital was reconstituted: the £600,000 of shares owned by the NFFC were converted into 600,000 preferred shares (still held by the NFFC) and 180,000 deferred shares worth one shilling each and issued equally between the five directors. Each of the four producers received a salary of £7,500 a year, plus 2.5 per cent of profits of all British Lion films and an additional 10 per cent for their own films. However, the restructuring of British Lion had partially tied the NFFC's hands when it came to finding a buyer:

> It is clear that, in considering a sale of its interests, NFFC must have in mind the position of the Deferred Shareholders whose collaboration is so important for the successful continuance of the business to which NFFC attaches great importance. These shareholders, four of whom have been very successful film producers, are, I understand, by no means willing buyers of such a large undertaking.[62]

The argument that the restructuring of British Lion had been undertaken in order to facilitate its sale to the private sector is lent some credence by the fact that it was after the restructuring that the NFFC began to receive offers for the company. However, all proved to be problematic in one way or another. An offer of £500,000 from Herbert Wilcox was rejected as being too low: there were also doubts that Wilcox would be able to raise the capital.[63] An offer from

Associated-Rediffusion – one of the contractors holding a regional franchise in the Independent Television network – was ruled out on political grounds:

> Though it is settled policy that we should try to get out of British Lion if we can, and though we should be prepared to do some loss-cutting in the process, it seems to me that the proposed deal is decidedly dubious, both on financial and on presentational grounds. Members of the Opposition are following every detail of this business with very critical attention.[64]

Another bid of £700,000 by a consortium led by Irving Allen – an American producer based in Britain – was favoured by the Board of Trade but opposed by the British Lion management group. The Boultings and Launder and Gilliat were adamant that British Lion should remain under British ownership and told the NFFC they would 'make a hell of a stink if British Lion is sold to this buyer'.[65] Sir Frank Lee at the Board of Trade wrote: 'Frankly, we regret the attitude of the deferred shareholders and do not find them convincing . . . But the President's view is that from a political standpoint their attitude, assuming that it is maintained, must be decisive *against* the proposed transaction at this time.'[66]

The absence of a credible buyer meant that British Lion would continue under its new management. However, it took time for the new set-up to show results. In 1958 British Lion Films reported a loss of £337,114 and the British Lion Studio Company lost £200,323: the chairman's report suggested that the parent company's losses were 'mainly due to a provision of £210,000 (against nil) for losses under distribution guarantees on films not released at the financial year-end, and depreciation and director's remuneration'.[67] British Lion's situation also reflected wider conditions in the industry. The NFFC's annual report for 1959 observed that 'accompanying the drop in admissions there has been a substantial change in the public taste as a result of which the kind of films which in the past would probably have recovered their cost or made a reasonable profit now turn out to be commercial failures'.[68] British Lion made losses again in 1959 but these were rather less than the previous year: British Lion Films lost £134,301 and the British Lion Studio Company lost £23,725.[69]

After two years of the new management regime, however, it seemed that British Lion had turned the corner: British Lion Films (£126,771) and British Lion Studios (£8,379) both reported profits in 1960. The annual report attributed 'the improved trading to the release of a number of successful films, notably *I'm All Right, Jack*, and to the full effect of operating economies'.[70] It also earned an undisclosed sum from the BBC/National Telefilm Associates series *The Third Man* (1959), for which it licensed the rights to the title and the character of Harry Lime. The Boultings' *I'm All Right, Jack!* was the second film at the British box office in 1959: it was also one of the NFFC's most profitable films that – along with other British Lion releases including *Happy is the Bride*, *Dentist in the Chair*, *Expresso Bongo* and *Saturday Night and Sunday Morning* (distributed by British Lion for the independent group Bryanston Films) – contributed to the corporation's record profit of £323,952 in 1962.⁷¹ Early in 1961 British Lion merged its domestic distribution organisation with the British subsidiary of Columbia Pictures to create BLC Films: it was estimated that the new distributor would be responsible for handling between a quarter and a third of all British first features and 'will therefore be a force to be reckoned with by the two groups that control the British cinema industry'.⁷² As part of the tie-up Columbia also agreed to bring all its British production to Shepperton: the first was the war epic *The Guns of Navarone* (1961).

British Lion's new-found profitability was due not so much to a shift in the nature of its output – comedy continued to be the most successful genre – than to its economic costing methods that ensured films were still able to make a profit in the home market. Film Finances often felt that the budgets of British Lion films were unrealistically low: even so, they often came in under budget or with only a small overcost. *Expresso Bongo* (1959) – produced by Jon Penington and directed by Val Guest – was budgeted at £149,468. Film Finances' production consultant John Croydon was sceptical that it could be produced for that amount: 'I feel the papers disclose a desire to make this film within a given period to bring the budget to a pre-determined figure not exceeding £150,000 . . . I would go as far as to say that certain omissions and contradictions tend to show that the budget has been prepared by someone who has only a limited knowledge of film technique.'⁷³ Guest was, however, an efficient director: *Expresso Bongo* was completed with only a small overcost and proved to be a box-office hit.⁷⁴ Croydon felt that to complete *Dentist in the Chair* (1959) within its projected £97,935 budget was 'a Herculean task which will be well nigh outside the capabilities of any director that I could name'.⁷⁵ Nevertheless, Don Chaffey did just that: the low final cost (£86,033) ensured that the film earned a tidy profit.

All things considered, British Lion was in better shape by the start of the 1960s than it had been during the previous decade. The improvement in its fortunes came at the expense of turning its back on its international ambitions and focusing on supplying first features for the domestic market. Its operation and future prospects were summed up by *The Economist* in 1961:

> British Lion, through its film producer board members, makes about six films a year and another nine or ten through its associated companies . . . Film making is British Lion's only genuine hope of making large profits. So far it has had considerable successes (*I'm All Right, Jack* was one) and at the same time it has avoided any big disasters. But Shepperton with its overheads of £300,000 a year to cover, and the British Lion film distribution organisation, costing some £250,000 a year to keep going in this country alone, have to be kept profitable even though they are useful adjuncts to the film production core of the company's business . . . But neither studio nor other force are much use without films that make money. And, though British Lion has shown that some films can, production is still basically a gamble. The company will have to keep out of the red for a number of years before the Government's ultimate intention of selling it to private shareholders is likely to be achieved.⁷⁶

Notes

1. BEA C48/325: Handwritten note by 'I. L.' on memorandum by 'H. C. B. M.', 'British Lion', 18 May 1954.
2. The £3 million total in fact comprised several loans. An initial 'temporary loan' of £1.2 million (subsequently reduced to £1 million) was agreed by the National Film Finance Company based on the schedule of films planned as of 31 March 1948, with the proviso 'that a request for a further loan of £400,000 would be sympathetically considered at the end of October'. In April 1949 the National Film Finance Corporation confirmed a further loan of £1.6 million, bringing the total loaned to British Lion to £3 million. At 31 March 1950, British Lion had availed itself of £275,000 of the £3 million. *National Film Finance Corporation: Annual Report and Statement of Accounts for the year ending 31 March 1950*, Cmd. 7927 (April 1950), p. 1 (9–12), p. 15 (Appendix C).
3. Sue Harper and Vincent Porter, *British Cinema of the 1950s: The Decline of Deference* (Oxford: Oxford University Press, 2003), p. 93.
4. TNA T228/362: Draft of memorandum for the Lord President's Committee: Cinematograph Film Production (Special Loans) Act Amendment Bill.
5. 'Schedule of Loans by National Film Finance Corporation', *Kinematograph Weekly*, 20 April 1950, p. 32.
6. TNA BT 64/5156: James Lawrie to Harold Wilson, undated draft of letter.
7. Ibid.: S. J. Pears to Lawrie, 24 December 1948.
8. 'State Money Saves British Lion from Receivership', *Kinematograph Weekly*, 5 January 1950, p. 30.
9. Herbert Wilcox, *Twenty-Five Thousand Sunsets: The Autobiography of Herbert Wilcox* (New York: A. S. Barnes, 1969), p. 202.
10. *National Film Finance Corporation: Annual Report and Statement of Accounts for the year ending 31 March 1950*, Cmd. 7927 (April 1950), p. 10 (63–4).
11. 'The Taxpayer's Stake in Films', *The Financial Times*, 18 January 1951, p. 4.
12. BT 64/5094: British Lion Film Corporation Ltd: Production and Distribution of Films 1947–1953, memorandum compiled by R. Colgate, 17 December 1953.
13. TNA T228/362: National Film Finance Corporation: Operations from 1/10/48 to 30/11/50, 8 December 1950.
14. Vincent Porter, 'The Robert Clark Account: films released in Britain by Associated British Pictures, British Lion, MGM, and Warner Bros., 1946–1957', *Historical Journal of Film, Radio and Television*, 20: 4 (2000), pp. 469–511.
15. 'Chairman's Points', *The Financial Times*, 3 January 1950, p. 4.
16. Porter, 'The Robert Clark Account', p. 492.
17. 'Optimism of British Lion', *The Economist*, 15 September 1951, p. 650.
18. BT 64/5094: British Lion: Production and Distribution of Films 1947–1953.
19. 'British Lion Film Corporation', *The Financial Times*, 24 September 1952, p. 2.
20. 'Woolf has Independent Release Set-Up Inside British Lion', *Kinematograph Weekly*, 4 May 1950, p. 3.
21. FFA Realised Film Box 20: *The African Queen*: John Woolf to Film Finances, 17 April 1951, and Supplemental Agreement between Romulus Films and Horizon Pictures, 18 May 1951.
22. FFA Realised Film Box 70: *Beat the Devil*: First 'Unofficial' Production Budget, 10 February 1953; Agreement between Romulus Films and Film Finances, 16 February 1953; Film Finances to Santana Pictures, 16 February 1953.

23. FFA Realised Film Box 75: *The Stranger's Hand*: British Lion Films Revenue Statement, February 1957.
24. TNA BT 64/5093: Note by Sidney Golt, 20 October 1952.
25. TNA T224/23: A. T. K. Grant to Compton, 5 February 1954.
26. BEA C48/325: 'British Lion Film Corporation', 24 February 1954.
27. TNA T224/23: Compton to Sir Frank Lee, 11 May 1954.
28. Ibid.: Sir Maurice Dean to Glaves-Smith, 31 December 1953.
29. Ibid.: R. J. Stopford to Sir Maurice Dean, 7 August 1953.
30. Ibid.: Golt to F. E. Figgures, 22 August 1953.
31. TNA BT64/5094: Minute 9 by Sir Maurice Dean, 15 January 1954.
32. TNA T224/23: E. A. (54) 4th Meeting, 4 March 1954.
33. TNA BT 64/5095: Sir Arthur Jarratt to Peter Thorneycroft, 17 May 1954.
34. *The Story of Gilbert and Sullivan* earned distributor's receipts of £98,139, *The Heart of the Matter* £123,429. There is no entry for *The Beggar's Opera*. Porter, 'The Robert Clark Account', p. 501.
35. TNA T224/23: Grant to Figgures, 23 April 1954.
36. Ibid.: Note by Sir Maurice Dean, 7 May 1954.
37. *National Film Finance Corporation: Annual Report and Statement of Accounts for the year ending 31 March 1955*, Cmnd. 9464 (May 1955), p. 18.
38. 'British Lion: Receiver is Appointed', *Kinematograph Weekly*, 3 June 1954, p. 3.
39. TNA T224/34: R. Martin to A. T. K. Grant, 6 October 1954.
40. TNA BT 258/295: List of liabilities agreed between the British Lion Film Corporation and the Official Receiver, 17 November 1954. Appendix D of this document reveals that British Lion owed £260,660 to the National Provincial Bank in respect of loans for *The Belles of St Trinian's* (£74,730), *The Constant Husband* (£114,430), *An Inspector Calls* (£26,118), *Eight O'Clock Walk* (£23,790) and *The Devil Girl from Mars* (£21,592); £380,675 to Lloyds Bank in respect of loans for *The Man Between* (£61,629), *Hobson's Choice* (£64,818), *Front Page Story* (£26,996), *They Who Dare* (£67,073), *Bang! You're Dead* (£18,818) and £141,341 for six unspecified Group 3 films; and £179,934 to the Bank of America for *Malaga* (£90,956) and *The Green Scarf* (£88,978).
41. Ibid.: Grant to Compton, 7 October 1954.
42. Ibid.: Sir John Keeling to Sir Frank Lee, 4 October 1954.
43. 'Government's New Deal for British Lion', *Kinematograph Weekly*, 27 January 1955, p. 3.
44. TNA BT 258/294: Minute No. 1 by G. S. Knight, 18 June 1954.
45. 'Tamed Lion', *The Economist*, 29 January 1955, p. 384.
46. TNA BT 103/1233: W. H. Lawson (Binden, Hamlyn & Co.) to Sir Nutcombe Hume, 4 August 1960.
47. FFA Realised Film Box 150: *Private's Progress*: Consequential Loss Claim, 27 October 1955.
48. 'British Lion, Independent Films Pact', *Kinematograph Weekly*, 22 September 1955, p. 3.
49. '£5m. Invested in British Films', *Kinematograph Weekly*, 27 January 1955, p. 34.
50. FFA Realised Film Box 174: *Three Men in a Boat*: John Woolf to Robert Garrett, 22 May 1956.
51. Ibid.: Maurice Foster to Garrett, 26 April 1956.
52. Porter, 'The Robert Clark Account', p. 509.
53. FFA Realised Film Box 134: *King's Rhapsody*: Herbert Wilcox to David Kingsley, 18 November 1954.

54. Porter, 'The Robert Clark Account', p. 506.
55. FFA Realised Film Box 184: *Yangtse Incident*: Completion Guarantee Agreement between Everest Pictures and Film Finances, Distribution Agreement between Everest Pictures and Distribution Corporation of America, and Financing Agreement between Everest Pictures and Lustowe Corporation, 12 September 1956.
56. Ibid.: British Lion Films Revenue Statement, September 1958.
57. Wilcox, *Twenty-Five Thousand Sunsets*, p. 200.
58. TNA T224/35: A. T. K. Grant to Ogilvy-Webb, 11 October 1957.
59. TNA BT 103/1233: W. H. Lawson to Sir Nutcombe Hume, 4 August 1960.
60. TNA T224/35: E. V. Marchant, 'British Lion Films Limited', 4 September 1958.
61. 'Long Shots', *Kinematograph Weekly*, 27 February 1958, p. 4.
62. TNA BT 103/1233: Lawson to Hume, 4 August 1960.
63. TNA BT 279/86: G. S. Knight to Bryant, 11 December 1958.
64. Ibid.: E. V. Marchant to Sir Thomas Padmore, 16 September 1958.
65. Ibid.: R. L. Workman to B. P. Hypher, 6 March 1959.
66. TNA BT 279/86: Sir Frank Lee to Sir Nutcombe Hume, 2 March 1959.
67. 'A Difficult Year for British Lion', *Kinematograph Weekly*, 9 October 1958, p. 7.
68. *National Film Finance Corporation: Annual Report and Statement of Accounts for the year ending 31 March 1959*, Cmnd. 799 (July 1959), p. 1 (4).
69. BT 103/1233: Lawson to Hume, 4 August 1960.
70. 'British Lion Film Makes a Profit', *The Financial Times*, 9 August 1960, p. 9.
71. *National Film Finance Corporation: Annual Report and Statement of Accounts for the year ending 31 March 1962*, Cmnd. 1792 (July 1962), p. 1 (2).
72. 'More Power to the Independent Film', *The Economist*, 11 February 1961, p. 591.
73. FFA Realised Film Box 263: *Expresso Bongo*: John Croydon to Robert Garrett, 7 June 1959.
74. Ibid.: The final statement of distributor's receipts (31 July 1972) records a profit of £251,217 including television sale.
75. FFA Realised Film Box 277: *Dentist in the Chair*: John Croydon to Robert Garrett, 5 November 1958.
76. 'Lion not so Mangy', *The Economist*, 12 August 1961, p. 156.

CHAPTER 9

Film Finances and the British Film Industry

> The saving of the British production industry and the start of its climb back to a reasonable state of stability was the establishment of the National Film Finance Corporation. Its aid, which is concentrated on providing the all-important end money, has since been supplemented by the Film Production Fund, known as 'Eady Money' ... Neither of these two are, however, a complete passport to putting a film on the floor and – which is sometimes more difficult – delivering it to the distributor. There is necessary, also, a guarantee of completion. (Robert Garrett)[1]

The incorporation of a company called Film Finances Ltd in London in March 1950 seems to have passed unnoticed in the trade press at the time. This might be because the trade was preoccupied with other matters: the exhibitors' campaign to reduce Entertainment Tax and complaints from independent producers of unfair treatment by the National Film Finance Corporation. It might also be because Film Finances was to be a company that would operate very much behind the scenes rather than in the limelight. Its business was not making films or even investing in film production but rather the provision of guarantees of completion. A guarantee of completion was necessary for producers to be able to secure the 'front money' loans for their films. It provided security in the form of a guarantee to investors and lenders that in the event of it not being possible to complete a film within the agreed budget, the film would be delivered on schedule without them being called upon to advance further monies beyond the amount originally agreed. While the larger production groups could afford to absorb overcosts on the films they produced themselves, the new post-war landscape of independent production – in particular the proliferation of small production companies with only nominal capital who were dependent on bank loans secured against distribution guarantees – created the conditions for the emergence of specialist completion guarantors. Panton Film Guarantees, incorporated in January 1950, was the first such company, though details are sketchy and it does not seem to have remained in business for very long.[2] Film Finances, incorporated two months later, not only stayed the course but quickly became an essential cog in the new system of film financing that had emerged in Britain.[3]

Hitherto the provision of guarantees of completion had been on a somewhat *ad hoc* basis. The common practice was for a producer to ask either insurance companies or 'persons of substance' to guarantee the repayment of bank loans.

Robert Garrett, the founder and managing director of Film Finances, explained the process thus:

> In the past the guarantee of completion has generally been what might be termed an isolated operation – that is to say, that a producer went to his friends or business acquaintances of substance and got them to give a personal guarantee to his bankers. Many of these personal guarantees were called upon which proved detrimental to the business as the individual guarantor concerned was discouraged from giving further guarantees.[4]

Garrett's uncle, Edward Bowring-Skimming, had been one of the pioneers of the guarantee business in the 1930s when his firm C. T. Bowring & Co. had guaranteed a loan from Lloyds Bank to Korda's London Film Productions.[5] The guarantee business had expanded during the production boom of the mid-1930s but the instability of the post-war years meant that fewer individuals were willing to take the risks. In May 1950, for example, Major Arthur Sassoon, a member of Lloyds and one of the directors of Two Cities Films, was declared bankrupt after being unable to fulfil a guarantee of £200,000 on behalf of Two Cities to the Rank Organisation.[6] Where Film Finances differed from individual guarantors was that it was formed specifically for the business of providing guarantees 'with a view to continuity of operation on business lines, it being hoped that by covering a certain number of pictures in each year some sort of average on insurance lines, would be struck'.[7]

It is rare that an individual agency alone is responsible for significant developments in the film industry, but this would seem to have been the case with Film Finances. There is no question that the driving force behind the formation and direction of the company during its formative years was Robert Garrett. A former independent producer who had entered the film industry in the 1930s, Garrett made two features in collaboration with American producer Otto Klement, *A Woman Alone* (1936) and *The Amazing Quest of Mr Bliss* (1936), the latter starring Cary Grant, borrowing £48,000 from Barclays Bank before the industry slump of 1937 curtailed their plans for further production.[8] Following wartime service in the Royal Air Force, during which time he worked at the code-breaking centre at Bletchley Park, Garrett resumed his career as a producer in the late 1940s, forming Constellation Films in association with Anthony Havelock-Allan, and producing two films, *The Small Voice* (1948) and *The Interrupted Journey* (1949). It seems to have been the difficulties encountered in financing the latter – one of the first films supported by the NFFC – that persuaded Garrett of the need to rationalise the business of providing completion guarantees.

The blueprint for the business model of Film Finances is to be found in a set of notes by Garrett dated 3 August 1949 which suggest that 'subject to certain safeguards, the giving of film guarantees of completion is a good business risk offering reasonable profits for the guarantors'. The document lists the principal safeguards as follows:

1. That the producer should have a satisfactory record in the matter of delivering his pictures at or under their agreed budgets.

2. That the producer should be sufficiently able, administratively and technically, to ensure that all operations connected with the making of the film are under efficient control.
3. That the producer's integrity should be undoubted.
4. That the producer's budget should contain sufficient financial margin and his schedule sufficient time margin to allow for those reasonable but unforeseeable delays to which any film could be subject.
5. That the production should not be one in which unknown hazards are likely to be encountered.
6. That where possible the producer himself should bear part of the risk of any over-cost.
7. That the guarantors should have at their disposal an efficient organisation both to examine a proposition initially and to keep in touch with its progress at all stages of production.
8. That as a last resort the guarantors have the necessary power to take over the production themselves.[9]

The plan was to launch the company with an initial capital of £200,000 and to guarantee 8–10 films a year: with this capital it was expected that the company could 'write' up to four films at any one time. The fee for providing the guarantee would be 4 per cent of the budget: it was estimated that on average one film in every five might exceed its budget and that an average overcost would be in the region of 10 per cent of the budget. Garrett believed that the risk of excessive overcosts could be minimised provided that the guarantor paid due diligence to the vetting of each proposition and to the subsequent 'policing' of productions on the studio floor. To this end the staff required for the company 'would be small but would have to be of high quality and experience'. This was to be what differentiated Film Finances from other guarantors who too often had insufficient knowledge and experience of the actual business of making films. The company would reinsure its risks by paying a premium for cover of up to £1,250 a day to cover the overcosts of any film which ran over schedule up to a maximum of ten days. In the event of the guarantee being called upon, the company would recoup its advances from the box-office receipts after the repayment of loans to the principal investors but before the producer received their share. This would provide an incentive for producers not to exceed budget, and to absorb small overcosts within their own resources.

This was in many respects an innovative business model. Film Finances would look to build up a 'book' of clients who would help to sustain and develop the business. It would later introduce the idea of a 'no-claim bonus': that in the event of there being no call upon the guarantee, the producer would be entitled to a remittance of a proportion of the fee if there was also no call upon their next film. The safeguard that 'the producer's integrity should be undoubted' offers an insight into Garrett's mindset: in its early years Film Finances would operate very much along gentlemen's club rules in which personal relationships and contacts often determined whether a particular film would be guaranteed. Another aspect in which Film Finances differed from private guarantors was that it expected to have to step in when films ran into difficulty. Garrett later explained that when Film Finances was founded 'there was a certain amount of feeling that a guarantor of completion must of necessity have only one interest – to avoid being called upon'. 'We believe we have succeeded in disproving that,' he went on, 'and in proving that we have a common interest with producers in that it is just as much in our interest as in theirs that pictures should be successful.'[10]

Garrett was at pains to explain that Film Finances did not offer a blank cheque for wayward producers who exceeded their budgets: a condition of the guarantee was that the film should be shot according to the script and budget approved by Film Finances and that the guarantor should be notified if the producer intended on making any significant changes to the script or 'improvements' to the film once it had started shooting. Garrett explained the company's philosophy in a letter to James Lawrie at the NFFC:

> We have quite clearly no right to compel a Producer to do anything which might prejudice his distribution contract. In fact so long as he is doing his best and sticking to the original script and has introduced no major innovations, we have, as I see it, no rights against him nor can we complain if he must make retakes ... It is, however, when the Producer belatedly discovers that, from the artistic or box-office point of view, he thinks he can improve his film by adding new scenes or by completely re-writing scenes already shot or by introducing, say, an unbudgeted-for player or a large crowd into his plan, that, in my view, the guarantor must be offered proper protection against the Producer who is in fact drastically altering the basis on which the original contract was made.[11]

The 'protection' which Garrett mentions was the condition of the guarantee that allowed Film Finances to take over the production if it felt costs were escalating beyond the budgeted figure or if the producer had departed significantly from the scope and ambition of the film as it had originally been proposed. This eventuality was regarded very much as a last resort. And, Garrett added, the producer 'is free to finance such "additional expenditure" out of his own pocket, or possibly, if he can sell the distributor the idea, out of the latter's pocket'.

Film Finances was incorporated in March 1950 with capital of £150,000 raised from the issue of ordinary shares at £1 each. The Treasury's Capital Issues Committee was initially hesitant to approve the share issue 'because it was felt that the purpose of the application could be achieved without the formation of a Limited Company or an issue of securities' – another indication of how Film Finances differed from the existing model of completion guarantees – but as the application was supported by the Board of Trade and the NFFC it was agreed on the basis that 'anything which strengthens the production of film in this country becomes a dollar saver and so fully justifies itself in terms of the instructions to the Capital Issues Committee'.[12] There were three directors – William Cullen (chairman), Robert Garrett (managing director) and Peter Hope – and 15 shareholders including the directors and their friends and business associates.

Cullen and Hope brought expertise of the financial markets – the former was a chartered accountant, the latter an insurance broker from the firm Tufnell, Satterthwaite & Co., which would underwrite Film Finances' guarantees – to complement Garrett's knowledge of film production. It would seem that for a while Garrett continued to harbour ambitions to produce films.[13] Indeed, one of the early propositions submitted to Film Finances was *The World is Ours*, to be produced by Garrett and Anthony Havelock-Allan.[14]

Garrett explained how Film Finances went about its business in an article for the trade press published after the company had been operating for two and a half years:

> The basis of our operation is a thorough investigation of the original script, budget and schedule, with a view to seeing that the last two are adequate for the first; and account is also taken of the principal personalities involved. This latter point does not mean that we express preferences for or against any individuals, but that we do consider, for instance, the length of a shooting schedule in relation to the usual speed of working of a director or lighting cameraman, and the problems they will have to encounter ... After having undertaken a guarantee of completion, it is the company's object so far as possible not to interfere with the film. It does, however, maintain both by means of progress reports and visits to the studios its contact with all productions under guarantee, and its agreement with the production company provides for some measure of control if matters appear to be getting out of hand. However, this again it endeavours to avoid.[15]

The task of assessing propositions submitted for guarantees was entrusted to John Croydon, regarded as 'one of the most experienced production executives in the British film industry'.[16] Croydon had started out as a production accountant for British Lion when it was set up by Edgar Wallace and had subsequently worked for the Gaumont-British Picture Corporation in the 1930s and for Ealing Studios during the Second World War as a production manager and associate producer. In the late 1940s he had been in charge of Rank's second feature unit at Highbury: his wide-ranging first-hand knowledge of the film industry meant that Croydon was ideally placed to assess the viability of budgets and schedules.

The first project which Film Finances guaranteed was Anthony Asquith's *The Woman in Question* (1950). The financing arrangements of this film were fairly representative of the independent production sector in the early 1950s. The film's budget of £129,986 came from two main sources – a bank loan of £91,000 secured against a distribution guarantee from General Film Distributors and an advance of £26,500 from the NFFC – with the balance made up by salary deferments by Asquith and producer Teddy Baird. Asquith's Javelin Films had initially approached the National Provincial Bank for the production loan, but the bank would not accept Film Finances' guarantee unless it was 'unlimited in amount and ... supported collaterally by cash or approved banking cover to the extent of £25,000 as a minimum'.[17] It would seem therefore that the bank was concerned that Film Finances did not have sufficient capital if the film went significantly over budget: indeed, it would take several years for the National Provincial to accept Film Finances' guarantees. Lloyds Bank proved more amenable and a letter of agreement between Film Finances and the bank was duly signed, whereby Film Finances undertook to procure the delivery of the film by the producer and would 'provide such monies as are necessary to defray the cost of such completion'.[18] The NFFC insisted on inserting a provision in the agreement that Film Finances should be required to obtain the NFFC's consent before exercising its right to take over the production of the film.[19] To this extent *The Woman in Question* was something of a test case not only for the new mechanism of providing completion guarantees but also for the relationship between Film Finances on the one hand and the bank and the NFFC on the other. In the event *The Woman in Question* was completed on schedule and within budget, so there was no call upon the guarantee. A crime melodrama shot mostly in the studio, it presented little in the way of production hazard, while the director 'Puffin' Asquith was an experienced film-maker who represented precisely the sort of personal integrity that Film Finances valued in their clients.

The Woman in Question was fairly typical of the films that Film Finances guaranteed during its first year. These were mostly British studio features – including *One Wild Oat*, *South African Story*, *Mrs Christopher*, *The Galloping Major*, *Tom Brown's Schooldays*, *No Resting Place*, *The Browning Version*, *Night Without Stars*, *White Corridors* and *Scrooge* – most of which were financed by bank loans secured against distribution guarantees with the NFFC providing the end money. An internal memorandum of July 1950 records that 'so far we have had a very easy (and lucky) time – although *Mrs Christopher* is about to give us at any rate some cause for uneasiness ... [The] other propositions have been so well within budget and schedule as to scarcely give us cause to do anything other than take a glance at the progress reports from time to time.'[20] The first problematic film was *Another Man's Poison* (1951). This was produced by Daniel Angel with an American star (Bette Davis) and director (Irving Rapper) and a budget of £93,844 raised through a loan from the Bank of America (£65,691) secured against a distribution guarantee from Eros Films with the balance provided by an advance from New World Pictures (£26,153) and producer deferment. John Croydon approved the proposition as Angel 'is not a man to allow a production to run away, as he has already demonstrated by his previous films' and the schedule 'in the hands of a Hollywood director, whose last two films have been shot in short schedule, should present little or no difficulty'.[21] However, the studio shooting proceeded slowly, and the film overran its schedule by 15 days. Angel blamed the director: 'It can now be concluded that Irving Rapper is the most incompetent Director that has ever reached these shores ... Here is a man who for years has been carried by various departments at Warner Bros and who merely directs a film as a stage director without any idea at all where to place the camera.'[22] Croydon, however, believed that Angel had failed to control the production adequately: 'I still maintain there was nothing to stop this film being made on schedule and budget were the producer capable of controlling his director, cameraman and star ... Angel has allowed an American Director, an Oscar Cameraman

[Robert Krasker] and a Hollywood star to run away with this production.'[23] Film Finances advanced a total of £12,405 towards completion of the film. When it became clear that there was little chance of recovering its advances, it sold its recovery rights in *Another Man's Poison* to a third party for £10,000.[24]

From the outset Film Finances sought to work with other interested parties in the field of film finance. It quickly established a co-operative working relationship with the NFFC: Garrett often lunched with James Lawrie and the two men sought to settle any problems and agree matters of practice. It was Lawrie, for example, who suggested the idea of a 'no-claim bonus' for producers who did not call upon the guarantee as he was concerned that the fee of 4 per cent of the budget would be too expensive for some independent producers.[25] Evidence that Lawrie saw the fledgling Film Finances as an important player in the industry can be seen in the fact that he sounded Garrett out about the possibility of placing all the guarantees for the Group scheme with the company – albeit on the condition that Film Finances relinquished its rights of take-over which Lawrie wanted to entrust to the studio management teams.[26] This put Garrett in a difficult position as he did not want to turn away business but at the same time he was not willing to give up the take-over clause which provided Film Finances with their most effective sanction against inefficient producers:

> This comes unfortunately at a time when we were just beginning to feel our feet and were seeking ways and means to reduce our charges . . . It seems unfortunate that we should at this point have to quite seriously consider abandoning the business and thereby doing a dis-service to outside first feature producers who are beginning to come to us, for reasons not of any objection on grounds of costs, but on the principle of control. We have the feeling that the getting together of our shareholders, our pioneering in a field that most reputable finance regarded as insane and efforts to do what you wanted, i.e. guarantee as many films as possible, may have all been in vain – and that the only consolation will be that our shareholders have a quick return.[27]

Garrett was evidently concerned that Film Finances would lose clients if it was denied business from the groups. His implicit threat that the company might have to cease providing guarantees if it lost the business was in all likelihood a bluff. Nevertheless, it was a successful bluff: in the event, Film Finances would provide guarantees to films produced under the aegis of the Group scheme on its usual terms and without relinquishing its control.

The *contretemp* over the Group scheme was a rare blip in an otherwise harmonious relationship between Film Finances and the NFFC. The NFFC, for its part, appreciated the discipline that Film Finances brought to the preparation of budgets and schedules. Following one of their regular lunches in November 1951, Lawrie wrote to Garrett:

> This seems a convenient opportunity for me to tell you how impressed we are with the way in which Film Finances does its scrutiny of budgets, schedules, etc, before

giving guarantees. I hope this doesn't sound patronising; it certainly isn't meant to be; it's just that I feel it is about time somebody from this office told you of our view that your company is making a very important contribution to the production of the films with which it is concerned.[28]

On another occasion Garrett intervened to head off a potential problem when some producers complained that the NFFC and Film Finances seemed to have conflicting priorities. On the one hand the NFFC was concerned to keep costs down: this meant that it sometimes required producers to reduce their budgets in order to secure its investment. On the other hand Film Finances felt that films were too often under-budgeted: sometimes it required producers to increase their contingency allowance – that part of the budget set aside to meet unexpected costs – as a condition of providing the guarantee. Garrett therefore suggested to Lawrie that 'if our respective cost departments could get together, and if we could have the budgets of these pictures which are coming to us at the same time as yourselves, we should each have an early opportunity of learning the other's point of view, and so avoid the possibility of later alterations which are as embarrassing to us as they may be troublesome to you'.[29]

After two years of operation for Film Finances, Garrett was able to report to his board that 'the past year has seen us take up a satisfactory position in the eyes of the industry'. Other than National Provincial, the main lending banks had 'definitely indicated to many of their customers that they would prefer a Guarantee of Completion to be got from us rather than from any other organisation or provided by a private individual'. Initially Film Finances had been involved with what Garrett described as 'films in the somewhat routine middle priced first feature studio picture class (£100,000 to £150,000)', but in its second year its business had grown to include bigger pictures up to £200,000. 'We have also had to do with films having fairly lengthy locations in Ceylon, North Africa, Spain and France,' Garrett reported, 'and have under consideration films to be made wholly in Austria and Germany.'[30] At this point Film Finances had guaranteed around 30 films and had been forced to claim on its consequential loss insurance only four times: for *Never Take No For An Answer*, *Another Man's Poison*, *High Treason* and *The Gift Horse*.[31] Garrett's hunch that the provision of completion guarantees would offer 'reasonable profits for the guarantors' is borne out by the company's accounts which show that in its first year it made a net profit of £8,104 and in its second year £12,879.[32]

The first major international production that Film Finances guaranteed was *The African Queen* (1951). This was an Anglo-American co-production between Sam Spiegel's Horizon Pictures, which provided the services of director John Huston and stars Humphrey Bogart and Katharine Hepburn, and John and James Woolf's Romulus Films. Film Finances' role in *The African Queen* was somewhat unusual in that it was asked to provide a guarantee for the American investment but not for the British end: at this stage the company's policy in respect of dual-budget films had yet to take firm shape. In April 1951 Woolf wrote to Garrett: 'The Horizon people have asked me to tell you that they would now like to avail themselves of the Delivery Guarantee for AFRICAN QUEEN as discussed and that they are prepared to pay in dollars the fee for which you have asked.' (Film Finances had offered to guarantee up to US $250,000 for a premium of $10,000 to guarantee delivery to the American distributor.) An unusual condition of the guarantee was that 'it can be conditional upon the provision of the American facilities upon which you were insisting, and that it becomes unconditional upon completion of the principle [sic] photography which includes the performance of the American Artistes'.[33] This condition was insisted upon because there was some uncertainty whether Katharine Hepburn would co-star in the film until shortly before shooting commenced. Garrett was not impressed when Spiegel's investors, Walter Heller & Co., wanted Film Finances to provide their guarantee without Hepburn having signed a contract. He told Peter Hope: 'My own view is that this is an attempt at a last-minute stick-up by Heller and his legal advisers and that any signs of weakness or giving way on our side would result in us having to do the same thing on future contracts ... I think we should stand firm on this particular point and prefer to lose the business if this is not conceded.'[34]

The African Queen was by some measure the riskiest proposition that Film Finances had yet guaranteed. It involved extensive overseas locations in difficult conditions in the Belgian Congo and Uganda. The unit was plagued by all manner of problems including heat, bad weather and dysentery.[35] The main unit was on location for 56 days – a very long location shooting period by contemporary standards – followed by studio scenes at Isleworth. Yet, despite all the difficulties, *The African Queen* was completed on schedule and without any call on the guarantee. Garrett was not happy when it emerged after the film had been completed – and when Film Finances' no claim bonus had been returned to the Woolfs – that Spiegel had left an unpaid legal bill which the Woolfs picked up. 'This is a matter of principle,' Garrett wrote to John Woolf, 'and I do not really see why Sam Spiegel should, by virtue of the guarantee given by yourselves, be allowed to get away with his indebtedness.'[36]

Film Finances may have been lucky not to have been called upon in the case of *The African Queen*: location pictures – especially those involving overseas locations – were among the most hazardous productions from a guarantor's point of view. The first occasion on which the company came close to getting its fingers seriously burned – and the first time it had to exercise its legal right to take over a production – came with *The Gift Horse* (1952). This was produced by Jay Lewis Productions, who had recently made the successful *Morning Departure*, and was another naval subject centring on the actions of an old destroyer 'gifted' to the Royal Navy from the United States in 1940 culminating in a St Nazaire-type raid on the French coast. *The Gift Horse* was budgeted at £155,000 and was financed on a standard basis of 70 per cent bank loan (Lloyds) against a distribution guarantee from Independent Film Distributors with the end money provided by the NFFC. John Croydon, who had experience of producing naval pictures such as *Ships With Wings* and *San Demetrio, London* at Ealing during the war, felt that 'the whole thing ... is quite ludicrous and impractical'.[37] The script was 'of abnormal length' and full of production hazards arising from the many action sequences, while the budget was wholly inadequate to the subject. 'I do not say it will happen,' Croydon warned, 'but, if the production did get out of hand, it could cost well over the £200,000 mark, and there would be little the Producer, the NFFC or ourselves could do about it.'[38] Film Finances declined to guarantee the film on its original budget, but Garrett indicated that they would be able to do so if the budget were increased to £180,000 and the length of the script was significantly reduced.[39] On this occasion there seems to have been an unusual degree of equivocation at Film Finances about guaranteeing the film. Garrett told the NFFC that 'we are still somewhat unhappy about this proposition in its present form'.[40] But – and this is a revealing insight into the way that Film Finances operated – the company seems to have felt that after negotiating with the producer for so long it was morally obliged to accept the risk. A letter from Croydon to Garrett is revealing in this regard: 'Whatever happens, I am certain the Guarantee will be called upon, but I suppose we now have to support the film. I would still like to reject it, but at least, we must have safeguards that will enable us to keep the overages to a minimum.'[41]

Film Finances issued its letter of intent – an agreement in principle to guarantee the film subject to approval of contracts and the required undertakings from the producer and director that the budget and film stock allocation were regarded as sufficient – on 27 August 1951: the revised budget was £167,272, of which £51,582 was put up by the NFFC.[42] But the production immediately began to go wrong. Lewis had wanted to cast American actor Robert Stack in the role of the destroyer's second-in-command, but Stack was denied a work permit by the Ministry of Labour.[43] This necessitated rewriting the script to facilitate the casting of a British actor (Richard Attenborough). The production was further hampered by a falling-out on set between Lewis and director Compton Bennett which came to a crisis point in mid-September with the two men refusing to work with each other. Lewis's version – as told to the press – was that 'the picture was getting out of hand on time on the floor and I did not approve of what was being shot on the floor; and the director complained that I interfered with his work on the floor'.[44] Garrett initially felt that 'we must take the side of the producer who has fathered this particular film . . . While I am not happy with the way in which the film has been handled to date by Jay Lewis, I believe in his sincerity.'[45] With some reservations, Garrett supported the idea that Lewis should take over direction of the film. However, at a meeting with the distributor and the NFFC, it was agreed that Lewis should step down as producer, leaving Compton Bennett 'to all intents and purposes . . . in sole artistic control of the picture'.[46] At this point Film Finances exercised its right – with the agreement of the NFFC – to take over the production. This clause of the guarantee had never come into force before and so Film Finances was entering uncharted waters. It appointed George Pitcher to manage the day-to-day production of the film while assuring the parties concerned that his role 'would be limited to the general one of shooting the present script under the artistic control of Compton Bennett and so far as is reasonably possible in accordance with the present schedule'.[47] As the original producer had to all intents and purposes been fired, an '*ad hoc* company' was set up under the name of Molton Films which by mutual agreement acquired all the rights in the film previously held by Jay Lewis Productions.[48]

Croydon's prediction that the guarantee would be called upon proved correct: *The Gift Horse* exceeded its budget by £42,500 (an overcost of 24 per cent) and the charges to complete it fell on Film Finances. There were various reasons for the very large overage, including underestimating the costs of various budget items, especially sets and models, and greater than expected charges from the Admiralty for the provision of technical services and the berthing of a destroyer.[49] Film Finances also felt that the production accountant 'did not have the necessary experience to cope with the situation that had arisen'.[50] Film Finances was able to recover some of its losses when Independent Film Distributors agreed to purchase Film Finances' recovery rights in return for a cash payment of £29,000.[51] The fact that Film Finances was willing to sell these rights at a loss indicates that the company did not expect to recover its advances. In the event the distributor received domestic receipts of £152,287 for *The Gift Horse* and a further payment of £51,205 from the Eady levy: this ensured that the bank loan and (eventually) the NFFC loan were repaid.[52]

Film Finances' business model allowed that a certain number of films would need to call upon the guarantee: *The Gift Horse* was an extreme case of how a film could go wrong. The company's other biggest commitment in its early years came with *Moulin Rouge* (1952). A lavish Technicolor biopic of Toulouse-Lautrec, *Moulin Rouge* was another dual-budget picture along the lines of *The African Queen*. John Woolf initially asked Film Finances to guarantee the dollar budget (US $160,000 covering director John Huston and stars José Ferrer and Zsa Zsa Gabor) and part of the sterling budget (£250,000), guaranteeing the remainder himself against the profits of *The African Queen*.[53] However, Film Finances was not happy with this arrangement, and in the event Woolf agreed that 'we would be better off to accept your usual form of guarantee, remitting the full premium to you'.[54] John Croydon felt that *Moulin Rouge* was 'the biggest and most difficult production we have yet had presented to us', but he was persuaded that the film was 'served by a group of men whose technical ability and integrity is of the highest'. His report on the proposition was complimentary about producer Joseph Somlo ('a man who has a great deal of experience'), associate producer Jack Clayton ('a man whom we know works not only in the interests of the producer, but in ours as well'), director of photography Oswald Morris ('a man whom we know from experience is capable of working very quickly, and at the same time obtaining quality which satisfies his producers') and art director Paul Sheriff ('a man who is capable of adapting himself and his designs to any form of Budget one likes to give to him'). 'I do not think we quarrel with the fact that John Huston is an economic director,' Croydon added – ironically given what was to transpire. 'I believe we can also accept that on "African Queen" the amount of film stock used was remarkably low.' His major concern was that the budget, while already high, would not be sufficient. He recommended that the sterling budget should be increased to £300,000, including a larger contingency allowance than the unrealistically low £5,000 suggested in the original papers.[55] In return for the producer increasing the contingency, Film Finances reduced its fee for providing the guarantee.[56]

Moulin Rouge was problematic from the outset. Whether the problems were due more to the scale of the project or to the personalities involved is a moot point, though Film Finances quickly came round to the view that the blame lay squarely at John Huston's door. When he saw the weekly cost reports from the location shooting, Garrett was concerned that 'Huston appears to have exhausted the whole of this additional contingency in the four weeks in which he has been in Paris'.[57] The production reports revealed evidence of new scenes being written and others shot on a more ambitious scale than indicated in the script. These were the sort of 'improvements' that Film Finances disliked, as they had not been agreed with the guarantor. In this regard *Moulin Rouge* seems to have been an instance of a director's artistic ambition exceeding his budgetary discipline. This, at least, was the view that Garrett formed. Noting the 'enormous overcost' of nearly 50 per cent, he told Woolf: 'I can only feel that not only is Huston out of control but that he has lost all sense of responsibility.'[58] Garrett had resisted the last resort of taking over the film, as he told Woolf, 'in case it might cause you any embarrassment. On the other hand it is quite clear that Huston has now let you in for a very much larger overcost than you ever thought possible and something must be done to contain this overcost.'[59] Ever the diplomat, there was an almost apologetic tone to Garrett's letters, which made it clear that he held the errant director rather than the producer responsible for the escalating costs:

> I know you must be beginning to regard me as a great nuisance who probably, in view of your undertakings to be responsible for the overcost, should not bother you about the progress of this picture. I think we are all agreed however that it is absolutely essential that shooting finishes on the picture on the 10th [October]. Yet as I understand it, Huston continues to do nothing towards assisting this aim. He has still what is anticipated to be a difficult scene to deal with and yet I believe he has insisted on retakes and to make matters worse, apparently decided on Sunday morning, of all days, not to work but to re-write the script. If my information is correct on this it seems that Huston remains as irresponsible as ever and that you will find yourself as you get near to 10th October with the fact that you will need extra days and that Huston will continue to assure everybody that all of this is to the ultimate financial good of the film.[60]

In the event Woolf was able to curtail Huston's excesses only by the drastic expedient of striking the sets. *Moulin Rouge* exceeded its budget by a massive £105,350: Film Finances advanced a total of £49,100 towards its completion, with the remainder paid by Woolf. Whatever his views of John Huston, Garrett felt that 'Woolf appears however to have a strict moral sense of his obligation and to be prepared to do everything possible.'[61]

Moulin Rouge highlighted a flaw in Film Finances' business model. It was not just the extent of the overcosts on *Moulin Rouge* that worried Garrett but the fact that it came so soon on the heels of *The Gift Horse*. In September 1952, when the overage on *Moulin Rouge* was estimated at around £65,000, an internal memorandum reveals that Film Finances was holding a balance of just £62,000 in its operating account. Garrett confided in Peter Hope that 'if we were called upon to put up £65,000 even if we were guaranteed it in quite reasonably spaced instalments over the next 12 months, the situation would not be so happy'.[62] This helps to explain why Film Finances had been willing to sell its recovery rights in *The Gift Horse* at a loss. An additional note in the files is revealing in this regard: 'Anxious not only protect financial credit but professional reputation.'[63] Garrett attached a great deal of importance to the company's reputation: this explains why he always regarded the issue of a letter of intent as being morally binding. In the event, Film Finances was able to recoup its advances on *Moulin Rouge*, which turned out to be a considerable success. The distributor's records indicate that by 1954 it was in profit by £18,886: Film Finances ranked behind the principal investors but ahead of the producers in recouping its share.[64]

It will be clear that the success of Film Finances' business model depended largely on two factors: its assessment of the risks of the proposition and its monitoring of the production process once the film was underway. The first stage was entrusted to John Croydon, who scrutinised budgets and schedules in forensic detail and advised whether they were adequate for the script. Croydon's reports reveal that he attached much weight to the previous records of the film-makers involved. For example, he approved *The Beachcomber* (1954) – despite the considerable production hazards represented by six weeks of location shooting in Ceylon and a star (Robert Newton) known for his alcoholism – on the past records of producer William MacQuitty and director Muriel Box: 'From our previous experience of this Producer and Director, I think we are running on pretty safe ground. There is, in this case, as always, a desire to shoot within budget, and it seems to me to be a perfectly safe proposition.'[65] *The Smallest Show on Earth* (1957) was the first proposition from the producer-director team of Michael Relph and Basil Dearden but Croydon was confident that 'we know they are experienced, competent and conscientious film-makers and I feel quite sure that they will take their new responsibilities to us as Guarantors of Completion very seriously. In fact, I would go as far as to say that they are two men upon whom we can rely with some degree of confidence.'[66] In contrast, Croydon was dismissive of the abilities of E. M. Smedley-Aston. When he saw the papers for *The Extra Day* (1956) he wrote: '[It] amazes me that British Lion should trust the first picture of a new Director to a man like Smedley-Aston. It certainly does not give [William] Fairchild much of a chance so far as his production and finance is concerned, as even if either were to go wrong I do not consider Smedley-Aston capable of either realising it or, if he did, correcting it.'[67] And he advised against guaranteeing the risky location picture *The Hellions* in 1961: 'Harold Huth isn't the best organiser in the world, and if things are in a muddle, he tends to let them slide, hoping more often than not against hope, that in some miraculous fashion they will right themselves. If Ken Annakin is the Director, then Huth will never, never control him.'[68]

Film Finances could not afford to decline all risky propositions, but on the occasions where it had concerns about the film-makers' record it exercised particularly close scrutiny. In 1954, for example, Michael Powell and Emeric Pressburger asked for a completion guarantee for their film of the Johann Strauss operetta *Die Fledermaus*. This was the first occasion on which the famed duo had dealt with Film Finances: *Die Fledermaus* – which would eventually be titled *Oh . . . Rosalinda!!* – was to be distributed by ABPC rather than by British Lion, which had backed their recent films. Powell's initial approach to Garrett was casual to the point of contempt: 'We hope you enjoy reading the Script. Everyone else has . . . We hope you know the music of "Die Fledermaus", because the Score will be one of the glories of the film.'[69] Croydon could not conceal his irritation: 'I take it that Powell phrases his letter in his own inimicable [*sic*] childish fashion as he probably thinks that our knowledge of film production is nil, and feels that he should mount the lecture platform for our benefit.' He felt that Powell's draft budget of £268,368 was in 'the realms of fantasy' and cautioned that 'if we enter into this Guarantee of Completion we should have egotistical, unpractical and intolerable clients'.[70] Nevertheless, Film Finances did undertake the guarantee, though only after sending Maurice Foster to work on the budget, which was revised upwards to £281,865, with Powell. Croydon felt that the revised budget and schedule 'are certainly realistic, and do not in any way indulge in the blunders, indicative of lack of knowledge, which was prevalent in the first set of papers I considered'.[71] Powell, for his part, seems to have been chastened by Film Finances' scrutiny of the budget and schedule. He wrote appreciatively to Garrett:

> We would like to say how much we admire the thorough methods of your representatives, their sympathetic approach to technical problems, their wide knowledge of the film-business, and their personal interest in quality and personality. In the past we have often found that a so-called 'realistic approach' to schedule and budget was depressing and deadening to the creators of the film: your representatives' methods, on the contrary, stimulate and encourage us.[72]

On this occasion the attention to detail and budgetary discipline which Film Finances brought to the project paid dividends, as *Oh . . . Rosalinda!!* came in £19,560 under budget.

A similar story emerges from Film Finances' involvement with Alexander Korda in the mid-1950s. Korda had been eased out of British Lion when the NFFC assumed control of the corporation in 1954: his response was to announce his own programme – including *A Kid for Two Farthings*, *Richard III*, *Summertime* and a remake of *The Four Feathers* – under the banner of London Film Productions.[73] Korda had a well-deserved reputation for profligacy and Film Finances was naturally cautious in dealing with him. The decision to guarantee *A Kid for Two Farthings* (1955) seems to have been based on faith in the director Carol Reed rather than Korda. Croydon disliked the treatment ('[The] document I have read is not a script. I could describe it as a draft for a novel, but where its application to cinema comes in, I fail to see') and complained that 'these papers bring very clearly into the open the sort of difficulty we are to encounter when we are asked to guarantee completion of London Film pictures'. Nevertheless, he recommended the guarantee 'provided you can be satisfied with Sir Carol Reed's assurances on the schedule period'.[74] Film Finances halved their fee in return for Korda providing a personal guarantee for the first overcost up to 10 per cent of the budget.[75] *A Kid for Two Farthings* came in close to its budget of £197,889.

Laurence Olivier's production of *Richard III* (1955) for London Films – the third of Olivier's cycle of expensively mounted Shakespearean films following *Henry V* and *Hamlet* – was the most expensive project that Film Finances guaranteed during the 1950s. Its budget was £443,209 with a sixteen-week schedule including locations in Spain and it was to be shot in VistaVision and Technicolor. Croydon weighed up the pros and cons of the proposition:

> This is one of the group of big films which hitherto we have not been asked to consider for a Guarantee of Completion. This is, I believe, the biggest budget we have yet had to consider, and it is difficult to assess the hazards . . . In the case of these very high budget figures, it seems to me that we place ourselves in the hands of the Producer and/or Director. In this case, let us face it, in the hands of Sir Laurence Olivier. It is not so much a question of Olivier obeying the restrictions he has imposed upon himself but that he should not ignore his budget in obtaining the degree of perfection towards which I am sure he will aim. Even *Richard III* should be made within a budget of half a million pounds. We know, however, that these films have, in the past, cost a great deal more.[76]

The decision to guarantee the film was based on the fact that the budget 'is very well laid out and has had a great deal of time and thought spent upon it'. Even so, Film Finances protected themselves against the risk by requiring the producer to provide the first £45,000 of any overcost, in return for which Film Finances agreed to remit half their fee if there was no call upon the guarantee.[77] Korda again agreed to cover the £45,000 on the explicit understanding that Film Finances would not exercise their take-over rights unless the film did go over budget by that amount or over schedule by three weeks.[78] An extra degree of security was provided in so far as Korda had cross-collateralised *Richard III* against *A Kid for Two Farthings* and *Storm Over the Nile*.[79] *Richard III* was completed without difficulty: there was a small overcost (£8,848), well within the £45,000 margin. Indeed, there was no call upon the guarantees for any of the London Films projects, suggesting that the guarantor's role in scrutinising budgets and schedules had instilled some fiscal discipline even upon Alexander Korda.[80]

By this time Film Finances had established itself not only as the leading provider of completion guarantees but also as an integral element of the landscape of independent film production in Britain. As it marked its tenth anniversary in the business in 1960, Film Finances had guaranteed nearly 300 films and had built up a client base including most of the major British independent producers and several of the Hollywood studios who were backing films in Britain, including United Artists, Columbia and MGM. In putting the business of providing guarantees of completion on a professional basis, Film Finances had not only supported the successful production of British films but had also made an important contribution to the recovery and stability of the industry as a whole.

Notes

1. 'This Guarantee Means Delivery', *Kinematograph Weekly*, 18 December 1952, p. 23.
2. Political and Economic Planning, *The British Film Industry: A report on its history and present organisation, with special reference to the economic problems of British film production* (London: Political and Economic Planning, 1952), p. 254.
3. Charles Drazin, 'Film Finances: The First Years', *Historical Journal of Film, Radio and Television*, 34: 1 (2014), pp. 2–22.
4. 'This Guarantee Means Delivery', p. 23
5. Drazin, 'Film Finances: The First Years', p. 4.
6. '£200,000 Film Guarantor's Failure', *Kinematograph Weekly*, 11 May 1950, p. 6.
7. 'This Guarantee Means Delivery', p. 23.
8. Barclays Group Archives 140/79: Advance Registers 1934–35: 28 August 1935. The loan to Garrett-Klement Pictures was guaranteed by the London Assurance Company.
9. FFA General Correspondence Box 100: 'Notes on proposed scheme to set up a company for the purpose of giving guarantees of completion to selected film producers', 3 August 1949.
10. 'This Guarantee Means Delivery', p. 23.
11. FFA General Correspondence Box 100: Robert Garrett to James Lawrie, 25 October 1950.
12. TNA T266/77: Capital Issues Committee Meeting of 19 December 1951: Film Finances Ltd. (The minute is a factual record of the incorporation of the company which records that consent to the share issue – originally for 160,000 ordinary shares – was given on 10 January 1950. This was subsequently altered to 150,000 ordinary shares, which were issued on 29 March 1950.)
13. 'Garrett production plans', *Kinematograph Weekly*, 31 January 1952, p. 5.
14. FFA Minute Book M.104: Minutes of the seventh meeting of Film Finances Ltd, 19 July 1950.
15. 'This Guarantee Means Delivery', p. 23.
16. Drazin, 'Film Finances: The First Years', p. 7.
17. FFA Realised Film Box 1: *The Woman in Question*: J. D. Chittleborough (Manager, National Provincial Bank, Piccadilly branch) to J. D. Saunders (Barker, Todman & Co.), 29 March 1950.
18. Ibid.: Letter of Agreement between Film Finances and Lloyds Bank, 25 April 1950.
19. Ibid.: Allen & Overy (solicitors) to William Cullen, 21 April 1950.
20. FFA General Correspondence Box 34: Robert Garrett to Cullen, 10 July 1950.
21. FFA Realised Film Box 16: *Another Man's Poison*: John Croydon to Garrett, 9 March 1951.
22. Ibid.: Daniel Angel to Garrett, 22 May 1951.
23. Ibid.: Croydon to Garrett, 21 May 1951.
24. Ibid.: Agreement between Film Finances and Gascoigne, St George & Hope, 23 February 1952.

25. FFA General Correspondence Box 100: James Lawrie to Robert Garrett, 18 September 1950.
26. Ibid.: Garrett to Peter Hope, 25 October 1950.
27. Ibid.: Garrett to Lawrie, 1 November 1950.
28. Ibid.: Lawrie to Garrett, 16 November 1951.
29. Ibid.: Garrett to Lawrie, 14 August 1952.
30. FFA General Correspondence Box 34: Garrett to W. B. Cullen, 7 July 1952.
31. Ibid.
32. Ibid.: Film Finances Ltd: Profit and Loss and Appreciation Account for the Year Ended 23 February 1952. In its second year Film Finances had net income of £52,495 while its outgoings amounted to £21,697 for claims under guarantees, £14,945 in premiums for consequential loss policies on the films it guaranteed, £2,408 in remuneration for directors, £105 in auditors' fees and £461 for 'furniture and motor car repairs' (Garrett was, by all accounts, a notoriously poor driver).
33. FFA Realised Film Box 20: *The African Queen*: John Woolf to Robert Garrett, 16 April 1951.
34. Ibid.: Garrett to Peter Hope, 5 April 1951.
35. The many travails of the production are recalled in Katharine Hepburn's memoir, *The Making of 'The African Queen': or How I Went to Africa with Bogart, Bacall and Huston and Almost Lost My Mind* (New York: Alfred A. Knopf, 1987).
36. FFA Realised Film Box 20: Robert Garrett to John Woolf, 26 March 1953.
37. FFA Realised Film Box 21: *The Gift Horse*: John Croydon to Garrett, 27 June 1951.
38. Ibid.: Croydon to Garrett, n.d.
39. Ibid.: Garrett to W. H. V. Able, 9 July 1951.
40. Ibid.: Garrett to J. Smuts, 23 August 1951.
41. Ibid.: Croydon to Garrett, 12 August 1951.
42. Ibid.: Susan Durnford to Anthony Overy, 27 August 1951.
43. 'US Actor Must Not Work Here', *Kinematograph Weekly*, 6 September 1951, p. 7.
44. 'Jay Lewis Leaves "The Gift Horse"', *Kinematograph Weekly*, 20 September 1951, p. 7.
45. FFA Realised Film Box 21: Garrett to James Lawrie, 13 September 1951.
46. Ibid.: Garrett to Lawrie, 15 September 1951.
47. Ibid.
48. Ibid.: Draft agreement between Jay Lewis Productions and Molton Films regarding the production of *The Gift Horse*, n.d.
49. Ibid.: Garrett to Board of Trade (Department of the Official Receivers), 4 February 1954.
50. Ibid.: Memo headed 'The Gift Horse – Overcosts', 11 February 1952.
51. Ibid.: Garrett to G. T. Sammons, 10 September 1952.
52. Ibid.: Independent Film Distributors Royalty Statement, 2 January 1954.
53. FFA Realised Film Box 42: *Moulin Rouge*: Robert Garrett to Peter Hope, 5 February 1952.
54. Ibid.: John Woolf to Garrett, 21 February 1952.
55. Ibid.: Croydon to Garrett, 16 May 1952.
56. Ibid.: Garrett to Woolf, 19 May 1952.
57. Ibid.: Garrett to Woolf, 16 July 1952.
58. Ibid.: Garrett to Woolf, 19 September 1952.
59. Ibid.: Garrett to Woolf, 23 September 1952.

60. Ibid.: Garrett to Woolf, 30 September 1952.
61. Ibid.: 'Note – "Moulin Rouge"', 24 September 1952.
62. Ibid.: Garrett to Hope, 17 September 1952.
63. Ibid.: 'Note – "Moulin Rouge"', 18 September 1952.
64. Ibid.: Independent Film Distributors Royalty Statement, 27 March 1954. The UK distributor's gross receipts were £177,848 and the overseas gross receipts £189,895. The film was tipped into profit by an Eady payment of £55,499.
65. FFA Realised Film Box 95: *The Beachcomber*: John Croydon to Robert Garrett, 14 October 1953.
66. FFA Realised Film Box 183: *The Smallest Show on Earth*: Croydon to Garrett, 9 July 1956.
67. FFA Realised Film Box 147: *The Extra Day*: Croydon to Garrett, 29 June 1955.
68. FFA General Correspondence Box 76: Croydon to Garrett, 15 January 1961.
69. FFA Realised Film Box 135: *Oh . . . Rosalinda!!*: Michael Powell to Garrett, 31 July 1954.
70. Ibid.: Croydon to Garrett, 16 August 1954.
71. Ibid.: Croydon to Garrett, 20 September 1954.
72. Ibid.: Michael Powell to Film Finances, 27 September 1954.
73. '£5m. Invested in British Films', *Kinematograph Weekly*, 27 January 1955, p. 34.
74. FFA Realised Film Box 120: *A Kid for Two Farthings*: Croydon to Garrett, 7 July 1954.
75. Ibid.: Garrett to Maurice Foster, n.d.
76. FFA Realised Film Box 127: *Richard III*: Croydon to Garrett, 12 August 1954.
77. Ibid.: Maurice Foster to Big Ben Films, 1 September 1954.
78. Ibid.: Garrett to Sir Alexander Korda, 30 September 1954.
79. Ibid.: Allen & Overy to Film Finances, 16 September 1954.
80. Ibid.: Foster to C. F. Turner, 16 January 1957.

CHAPTER 10

Rise of the Runaways

> [The] production industry in this country has never been in a more healthy, active state, nor on such a sound basis. Of significance is the participation on an increasing scale of American interests. More than a third of the films now in production are wholly financed by American money or have been made possible by American backing. (*Kinematograph Weekly*)[1]

There had been an American presence in the British cinema industry since before the First World War: Essanay and Vitagraph were the first US film manufacturing companies to open offices in Britain in 1912. They were followed within a few years by the Fox Film Company (1916) and Famous-Lasky Film Service (1919). By the end of the 1920s six of the eight US majors – Paramount, Fox, MGM, Universal, Warner Bros. and United Artists – had British distribution arms and were responsible for around half of the total films offered for rental.[2] It was in the 1930s that Hollywood began to invest in the British production sector as American companies would finance British films in order to meet their quota obligations under the Cinematograph Films Act of 1927. This was the context for the emergence of the notorious 'quota quickies' whereby, as Political and Economic Planning put it, 'the American renters gradually became "sponsors" of a series of cheap films which had little or no entertainment value even for the meanest taste'. 'By financing these "quota quickies", which gave employment but no prestige to the British industry,' it added, 'the foreign renters fulfilled their quota obligations without impairing the competitive advantage of their own product.'[3] In fact, by no means all American-sponsored quota films were necessarily the cheap and shoddy affairs implied by the derogatory label of 'quota quickies'. Warner Bros. established a permanent production facility at Teddington Studios in 1931 and Twentieth Century–Fox did likewise at Wembley in 1935.[4] MGM proved the most ambitious of the Hollywood studios when it opened its British subsidiary at Denham Studios in 1937 in order to produce first-class 'A' features that would be shown on equal terms in the United States: it produced *A Yank at Oxford*, *The Citadel* and *Goodbye Mr Chips* until the studio's British operation was interrupted by the outbreak of the Second World War.[5] The wartime currency controls imposed by the Treasury meant that American companies held blocked or 'frozen' funds in Britain which they could invest in British production. Hollywood studios produced a number of wartime British films, including *The Prime Minister* (Warner Bros.), *Dangerous Moonlight* (RKO), *Kipps* (Fox), *The Young Mr Pitt* (Fox) and *The Adventures of Tartu* (MGM). American investment in British production declined in the late 1940s – the abolition of renters' quota in 1948 meant that US distributors in Britain no longer needed to offer British-made films – but revived again in the early 1950s and grew significantly thereafter, to the extent that by the middle of the decade around a third of British first features were either partly or wholly financed by American money. This development inevitably had important consequences for the political economy of the British film industry.

The contexts for the growth of so-called 'runaway' productions – American films shot overseas – are to be found in the economic conditions of both the American and British film industries. By the early 1950s the US film industry was undergoing a period of transition: it was losing audiences to television, revenues were falling, and the studios were seeking to cut overheads by abandoning long-term contracts for artistes and personnel. A consequence of the Paramount Decree of 1948 – the US Supreme Court ruling that the major studios should separate their exhibition holdings from their production and distribution interests – meant that the majors focused on their role as distributors and turned more to independent producers to supply their product. Moving production overseas was advantageous in several respects. Studio rentals and labour costs were cheaper in Europe, and the Hollywood studios could benefit from subsidies offered to encourage inward investment in European film industries. There was also the consideration that by the 1950s overseas markets accounted for around 50 per cent of Hollywood's revenues: outside America the cinema-going habit had yet to be eroded as significantly by television. The largest proportion of foreign revenue came from Europe, and the biggest national market by some distance was Britain. In 1951, for example, there were a total 1,365,000 cinema admissions in Britain compared to 706 million in Italy, 555 million in West Germany, 372 million in France and 315 million in Spain.[6] It is perhaps no coincidence that Britain became the leading location for US runaway production. Between 1949 and 1957 there were a total of 109 American-financed films made in Britain compared to 30 in Italy, 29 in Mexico, 24 in France, 17 in West Germany and 12 in Spain.[7] In one sense, therefore, the rise of American-financed production in Britain can be seen as a process whereby the US film industry oriented itself towards its biggest overseas market. It is certainly no coincidence that many of the Hollywood runaways in Britain in the early 1950s were on British subjects, particularly historical and costume films: *Treasure Island, The Mudlark, Captain Horatio Hornblower, RN, Ivanhoe, The Master of Ballantrae, The Story of Robin Hood and His Merrie Men, Knights of the Round Table, Beau Brummell* and *The Adventures of Quentin Durward* were all shot in Britain between 1949 and 1955.

The immediate incentive for Hollywood to invest in the British production sector was that it was a means of using blocked sterling. The framework for this was provided by the Anglo-American Film Agreement of 1948. The basic provisions of this agreement – revised in 1950 and renewed in 1952 and 1956 – remained in place throughout the 1950s. American companies were allowed to repatriate a maximum of US $17 million of their earnings from film distribution in the United

Kingdom per year: the rest was 'frozen' in Britain but could be used for various purposes including film production, investment in studios and purchase of story rights. The definition of a British film under the agreement was the same as the Cinematograph Films Act of 1948: it had to be produced by a British-registered company, shot in a studio in Britain or one of the British Dominions (later extended to include the whole of the British Commonwealth) and have the majority of the labour costs paid to British workers. The provision for labour allowed either 80 per cent of the total cost excluding one individual to be paid to British subjects or 75 per cent of the total cost excluding two people, of whom one had to be an actor. The legislation was evidently drafted to encourage inward investment in the British production sector: the Board of Trade indicated that it 'would like to see ten to twenty films a year produced here by American companies out of a total UK production of fifty to eighty films'.[8]

It is difficult to arrive at a precise figure for the total amount of blocked sterling that American interests held in Britain at this time. In 1948 it was estimated that American films had earned £17 million from the British market in the previous year: under the terms of the Anglo-American Film Agreement a little over £4 million of this was remitted, which left an amount in the region of £13 million in blocked sterling.[9] The devaluation of sterling in 1949 meant that the value of the blocked currency was reduced, while the decline in cinema-going and consequent fall in revenues further eroded the total sum. Nevertheless, the British market was still worth around £13 million to Hollywood in 1950, of which – following a revision to the agreement which allowed American companies to remit an additional amount calculated as a proportion of the amount they had spent on making films in Britain – around £7 million remained in Britain.[10] It would seem that much of this money was indeed invested in British production. Board of Trade figures indicate that during the first two years of the agreement the US majors had invested a total of £5,429,779 of their frozen sterling in British production activities.[11] Indeed, the Hollywood spending spree in Britain was such that it was estimated US companies would have exhausted most of their frozen funds by September 1951.[12]

Walt Disney's *Treasure Island* (1950) provides a good early example of how the Hollywood studios invested in British production in order to use their blocked currency. This was a Technicolor family adventure film with an American director (Byron Haskin) and star (child actor Bobby Driscoll) but an otherwise British cast and crew. It would seem that Disney – a studio without its own distribution arm which at this time released its films through RKO – embarked upon the film principally in order to spend its blocked sterling before the currency regulations changed: the company reported that 'all its frozen funds had been used to make *Treasure Island* with the additional monies needed to complete the picture being furnished by RKO from its impounded sterling'.[13] *Treasure Island* was a popular success, especially in Britain, and prompted Disney to produce two further British costume adventure subjects: *The Story of Robin Hood and His Merrie Men* (1952) and *Rob Roy, the Highland Rogue* (1953). The fact that the definition of a British film extended to films shot overseas in the British Commonwealth also enabled RKO to use blocked sterling to send a British unit to British East Africa for *Tarzan's Peril* (1951), which therefore became the first Tarzan picture actually to be shot in Africa.[14]

However, the fact that runaway production continued – indeed, it increased in scale – after the studios had used up their blocked sterling suggests that this was not the only factor that influenced American investment in the British film industry. F. W. Allport, the European manager of the Motion Picture Export Association, reported that by 1956 blocked sterling accounted for only half of the estimated total of £6 million invested by the Hollywood majors in British production.[15] The cheaper production costs in Britain were undoubtedly a factor. Another major incentive was the introduction of the British Film Production Fund. The rules for payments from the levy meant that runaway productions were eligible for Eady money provided they met the official criteria of British films: moreover, the fact that American runaways were often among the most popular films meant that they would receive more Eady money in relation to their box-office receipts. According to the statistics published by the Board of Trade, the five American studios most active in Britain – MGM, Warner Bros., Twentieth Century–Fox, Columbia and United Artists – received a total of £737,000 from the British Film Production Fund between 1951 and 1953: this amounted to 13.8 per cent of the total paid back to producers.[16] The Motion Picture Export Association estimated that Eady money added 40 per cent to the distributor's receipts of a British-made film.[17] The fact that American runaways were eligible for the levy was a cause of some controversy in Britain. Sir Henry French, President of the British Film Producers' Association, complained that:

> In no other country, as far as I am aware, is there anything comparable with what has happened in Britain with regard to the production levy. This was established to ensure the survival of British films, but has in practice encouraged the production of films in this country by quasi-American companies and thus reduced the proportion of the levy which is available for films made by British producers.[18]

The situation was compounded by the fact that American distributors were usually prepared to offer distribution guarantees of 100 per cent of the budget compared to the 70 per cent offered by British distributors: French felt that producers with an American guarantee were therefore at a competitive advantage over wholly British-financed films as they ran less risk of losing their own capital and were more or less assured an American release.

The presence of American interests in the British film production industry divided opinions beyond the fact of their being able to draw money from the Eady levy. On the one hand it was argued that American investment was a sign of confidence in the British industry and had played an important role in supporting its recovery since the crisis of the late 1940s. On the other hand there was a view in some quarters that the American presence was becoming too dominant and might prove detrimental to the long-term sustainability of an indigenous production industry. A *Kine* editorial in 1956 – prompted by Twentieth Century–Fox's announcement of a new programme of British films – weighed up the pros and cons:

> The company's decision reflects a strong confidence in the future of the business and the growing realisation that there are distinct advantages to making films in this country. This increasing American participation in British production is to be welcomed because it brings hard currency to the country and makes a substantial contribution to the establishment of a prosperous production side of the industry.
>
> But, on the other hand, it is important to this country that it should have a strong and flourishing production industry backed largely by British resources, financial and artistic. The increasing support for British production by American interests is creating divided loyalties and this can be extremely detrimental to the progressive development of British interests.[19]

The argument – never to be resolved – hinged around the relationship between commerce and culture. Those who supported US interests in Britain – including, naturally enough, the Americans themselves – made their case on economic grounds: that US investment helped to sustain the British production industry as a going concern. Those resistant to the American presence argued that the growth of US influence led inevitably to the Americanisation of film content and therefore threatened the very existence of an indigenous national cinema.

The operation of runaway production in practice during the 1950s followed a number of different strategies. One model – particularly favoured by Hollywood independents who were not tied to a particular studio – was to enter into a co-production arrangement with a British partner. There were clear mutual advantages to such arrangements: the economic risks were shared – an especially important consideration for independent producers – while the chances of a circuit release on both sides of the Atlantic were significantly increased. The American producer Josef Shaftel explained the benefits of co-production for both partners:

> Shaftel says he is convinced that the only possible future for the independent producer here and in Hollywood lies in this type of Anglo-American production. The British producer is assured of a US circuit distribution and benefits by the use of American stars who can be paid in dollars by the American half of the set-up: the American producer gets production values in this country which would cost far more in Hollywood.[20]

British producer Raymond Stross made several co-productions during the 1950s. For *Star of India* (1954) – a swashbuckler with an American star (Cornel Wilde) and director (Arthur Lubin) featuring locations in Italy – United Artists was the US distributor and Eros Films the UK distributor. Wilde had personally financed the preparation of the script and had a stake in the film. Eros's distribution guarantee covered 70 per cent of the sterling budget (£111,135), with the balance in the form of a further cash advance (£10,500) and producer deferments, while an Italian partner (Titanus Films) advanced 47.5 million lire to cover location shooting in Italy.[21] There was some doubt whether *Star of India* would qualify for British quota due to the qualifying labour costs, though in the event it was registered as a British film.[22] Stross's *A Terrible Beauty* (1960) was an Anglo-US co-production with Robert Mitchum's production company DRM, with a budget of US $650,000 raised through a distribution guarantee from United Artists. It was produced at Ardmore Studios in Ireland (and therefore qualified for British quota) with an American director (Tay Garnett): the percentage of British labour costs was increased by Mitchum deferring his fee of $220,000, which was therefore not included in the budget.[23] Stross completed the film on budget and schedule, but United Artists insisted that 'substantial re-editing must be carried out' before releasing it.[24]

Another strategy was for Hollywood studios to produce directly through their own British subsidiaries: an advantage of this model was that they were better able to assert their control over the production process. In the early 1950s Warner Bros. and MGM were the most ambitious of the Hollywood studios in their British production activity. In 1950 Warner Bros. signalled its intention to shift to only top-class product for its British films when it closed Teddington Studios: 'Teddington is good for anything up to £250,000 but we are going into really big projects like *Hornblower* last year, and, perhaps, *The Master of Ballantrae* next year'.[25] Warner had wanted to make a film of C. S. Forester's Hornblower stories since 1940 when it had applied to the British government for remission of blocked sterling in order to produce the film in Hollywood as a pro-British propaganda piece: the proposal was supported by the Foreign Office but blocked by the Treasury.[26] It was another decade before Warner produced *Captain Horatio Hornblower, RN* (1950) in Britain: it was shot at Elstree Studios with an American director (Raoul Walsh) and two American stars (Gregory Peck and Virginia Mayo) and a mostly British supporting cast and technical crew. The total cost of the film was US $2.4 million: $1.4 million (approximately £500,000) came from blocked sterling, including Peck's salary of $250,000 which was paid to David O. Selznick's Vanguard Productions which held his contract. The investment paid off for Warner: *Captain Horatio Hornblower, RN* earned worldwide rentals of $5.3 million and was the studio's most successful film of 1951.[27] Its success persuaded Warner to go ahead with other British-made swashbuckling subjects such as *The Crimson Pirate* (1952) and *The Master of Ballantrae* (1953): these also both had American stars (Burt Lancaster, Errol Flynn) and directors (Robert Siodmak, William Keighley).

MGM was the other studio which sponsored production of high-end A-class features in Britain in the early 1950s. In 1948 it bought the former Amalgamated Studios site at Borehamwood and spent £1 million refurbishing and modernising the studio.[28] Its first British production was *The Miniver Story* (1950), but it was *Ivanhoe* (1952) that really signalled the studio's intention to produce British films for the international market. A studio press release declared that *Ivanhoe* 'ushers in a new era of production in Great Britain which is designed to bring the company's top stars and technicians to this country for a programme of pictures on the biggest scale'.[29] For *Ivanhoe*, MGM brought over an American director (Richard Thorpe) and star (Robert Taylor), though like *Captain Horatio Hornblower, RN* the rest of the crew and cast (including Hollywood-based co-stars Elizabeth Taylor and George Sanders) were British. *Ivanhoe* was an expensive production (US $3.8 million), but it proved a winner at the box office: it grossed $10.9 million worldwide and returned a profit of $2.6 million.[30] MGM followed *Ivanhoe* with another two swashbuckling epics, both again starring Robert Taylor and directed by Richard Thorpe: *Knights of the Round Table* (1953) was another success if not quite on the scale of *Ivanhoe* – it cost $2.6 million and returned a profit of $1.7 million – though the third of the triptych, *The Adventures of Quentin Durward* (1955), recorded a loss of $1.2 million against a production cost of $2.4 million. MGM produced fourteen British films between 1950 and 1958 – the others were *Calling Bulldog Drummond*, *Conspirator*, *The Hour of 13*, *Never Let Me Go*, *Seagulls Over Sorrento*, *Beau Brummell*, *Bhowani Junction*, *The Barretts of Wimpole Street*, *Invitation to the Dance* and *I Accuse!* – at a total cost of US $32 million (£11.5 million).[31]

As the decade went on, however, the trend of runaway production in Britain mirrored the changes in the US film industry as a whole. In particular there was a shift away from the model of in-house studio production and an increasing reliance on independent producers: this allowed the studios to reduce the overheads incurred by maintaining permanent production facilities and staff. The case of Twentieth Century-Fox exemplified this process. In 1953 Fox announced that it was closing its British studio at Wembley – where recent films had been mostly medium-budget fare such as *Night and the City* (1950), *The Mudlark* (1950) and *Sailor of the King* (1953) – as part of its strategy to reorient production around CinemaScope pictures.[32] It was a full three years before the studio resumed its British production activities: in 1956 it announced that it planned to back between eight and ten films a year from independent producers.[33] The first film under this new strategy was the war film *The Man Who Never Was* (1956): this was a dual-budget picture in which the dollar budget ($280,400) covered the fees of producer André Hakim and stars Clifton Webb and Gloria Graham, while the sterling budget (increased to £227,000 following consultation with completion guarantor Film Finances) covered the shooting costs and production unit salaries (including Ronald Neame, who was paid 'the extraordinarily high fee of £20,000' to direct).[34] Neame averred that he was essentially a director for hire and that the key creative decisions were made by the studio: 'That was purely 20th Century-Fox. Darryl Zanuck's son-in-law André Hakim came over to produce a film and he brought this story . . . I was what is laughingly known as a "hot" director at that time, and André asked me if I would direct it.'[35]

The Hollywood studio that most fully embraced runaway production during the 1950s was Columbia Pictures. Hitherto Columbia had not been a major player in the British film industry: it had been active as a distributor since 1929 but until the early 1950s it had handled fewer British films than the other American renting companies. However, in 1952 it began what would turn out to be a highly productive – and profitable – relationship with Warwick Film Productions. Warwick was a British-based production company set up by the Americans Irving Allen and Albert R. 'Cubby' Broccoli. Its first film, *The Red Beret* (1953), a Technicolor adaptation of Hilary St George Sanders's book about the Parachute Regiment, was initially to have been backed by RKO.[36] Columbia picked it up when Howard Hughes, the unpredictable owner of RKO, changed his mind about the film.[37] *The Red Beret* was a dual-budget picture in which the producers' fees and salary of American star Alan Ladd were charged to the dollar budget while other artistes, the director (Terence Young) and direct costs were included in the sterling budget. Its completion was guaranteed by Film Finances, whose managing-director Robert Garrett explained how the completion guarantee for dual-budget pictures worked in a letter to the head of Columbia's British division:

> When Anglo-American financial co-operation is involved and, say, the American financial interests are paying for certain services such as stars, directors, story rights etc, we are prepared to extend our guarantee to them inasmuch as we will undertake to deliver to them the picture in which they are interested by a reasonable date or failing that, they may call upon us to repay to them any dollars expended by themselves up to an agreed maximum.
>
> I mention this to you because your company may have in mind the making of pictures here by an independent producer, financing locally in the usual way but relying in some respects upon your American parent company for the provision of American stars, etc. In such a case we would expect each party to take its share and we would be prepared to issue a Guarantee of Completion to the English prime financier and a Guarantee of Delivery or Repayment to your parent company or its bankers.[38]

This was indeed the model that Columbia would adopt not only for the films it backed from Warwick but also for its other British productions during the 1950s.

The Red Beret was a problematic but ultimately successful venture. Film Finances' production consultant John Croydon felt that the sterling budget of £175,000 was too low and that in his estimation 'it belongs to the £200,000 plus class'.[39] Film Finances had some reservations about guaranteeing the film but at the same time recognised that this was an opportunity to expand its business: in the event its guarantee was conditional upon the producers providing an additional contingency of £10,000. Garrett told Irving Allen that Film Finances would usually expect the cost of the guarantee to be shared between the dollar and sterling budgets but made an exception in this case as the financing had been arranged before Warwick applied for a completion guarantee. 'I mention this,' Garrett wrote, 'because I hope we shall do business in the future and because your financial arrangements may on another occasion be different from those prevailing on *The Red Beret*.'[40] This was the first occasion on which Film Finances had dealt with Columbia and the studio evidently did not like some of the conditions of the guarantee. One clause that it objected to was the guarantor's right to take over the production in the event of it running into difficulties.[41] On this point, however, Garrett stood firm: 'I feel that an important question of principle is involved here and that we would probably be prepared to abandon the giving of the Guarantee of Completion rather than having it altered to suit Columbia.'[42]

The Red Beret established the template for most of Warwick's films for Columbia: it specialised in action-adventure films, usually in colour, featuring extensive locations and an American star who – unlike some of the Anglo-American co-productions of the 1950s – was generally of the top rank: Alan Ladd, Richard Widmark, Robert Mitchum, Victor Mature. Unlike most independent production units, which operated on a single-picture basis, Warwick was geared towards a programme of films. It also reduced the risks on individual pictures through cross-collateralisation: the production costs of one film could be offset against the profits of another. Its first three films with Alan Ladd – *The Red Beret, Hell Below Zero* (1954) and *The Black Knight* (1954) – were designated 'Unit One' films, while *Prize of Gold* (1955), *The Cockleshell Heroes* (1955) and *Safari* (1956) were 'Unit Two' films.[43] Allen and Broccoli maintained that as independent producers they were best placed to make the sort of films that accorded with the tastes of cinema-goers: 'The public is becoming more and more discriminating, demanding better entertainment, and the studios – and distributors – are realising that a wholesale, conveyor belt line-up cannot satisfy that demand.'[44] Evidence that their production philosophy was successful can be seen in so far as their films regularly featured in the top ten box-office listings. As Josh Billings noted in the *Kine*: 'No doubt about it, Warwick Films ... certainly know the shortest cut to the box office. So far, all their runners have been winners.'[45]

Warwick was by some measure the most successful producer of American runaways during the 1950s. Yet behind the scenes there were often problems. In particular Warwick had a reputation for shoddy preparation and unrealistic budgeting. Film Finances guaranteed nine of Warwick's eighteen pictures for Columbia: their commercial success meant that Film Finances was generally in a good recovery position if the guarantee was called upon – as it often was. A recurring theme of John Croydon's reports was that Warwick's paperwork was rushed and betrayed a lack of attention to detail, while the films themselves were almost always under-scheduled and under-budgeted. Hence guarantees were usually provided with conditions attached. When Croydon saw the papers for *Hell Below Zero*, for example, he reported that 'this film is ridiculously under-scheduled, and upon the present script, schedule and budget, as delivered to us, we should not contemplate this Guarantee under any circumstances'.[46] Warwick estimated the sterling budget at £201,046, but Croydon felt that it was more likely to cost between £250,000 and £275,000. Film Finances guaranteed the film when Columbia agreed to raise the budget to £211,000 and in the knowledge that they would be protected by cross-collateralisation against *The Red Beret*.[47] In the event *Hell Below Zero*, which involved location shooting at sea in difficult conditions in the South Atlantic, exceeded its budget by £36,512. There was no call upon the guarantee, however, as Columbia picked up the overcost in order to secure a no claim-bonus for *The Black Knight*.[48] Once again Croydon disliked the proposition ('There is nothing that I like about these papers, and I cannot give it any form of recommendation as it stands') and felt that it was seriously under-budgeted: 'It is my opinion that the cost of this film will be much nearer £350,000 than the combined total of £237,144.'[49] On this occasion Film Finances initially declined to guarantee the film, but agreed to reconsider on the basis of revised costings from the budgeting department at Pinewood Studios.[50] *The Black Knight* was guaranteed at a budget of £297,728 though with the caveat that Warwick's share of the profits from *The Red Beret* and *Hell Below Zero* were offered as security for any advances.[51] Yet again the film quickly exhausted its contingencies and ran over budget: on this occasion Irving Allen persuaded Columbia to buy out Film Finances from their guarantee.[52]

This set the tone for Film Finances' relationship with Warwick Films. John Croydon wanted nothing more to do with the producer. When he saw the budget and schedule for *A Prize of Gold*, for example, he told Garrett: 'I can safely say that we have now had too much of this Unit, and I do not want to be "persuaded" into the acceptance of any more of their papers, whether original or amended.'[53] As it happened *A Prize of Gold*, directed by the American Mark Robson, was completed with a modest overcost which was absorbed by the contingency.[54] Croydon was dismissive in the extreme of *The Gamma People* (1956), a low-budget (£71,177) science-fiction affair with a schedule of six weeks: 'These papers are a complete reversion to the sort of thing we have had from Warwick in their early days, only they are worse, and I think it would be simply ludicrous for us to even contemplate having any dealings with Warwick over this project in its present state.'[55] Film Finances agreed to provide a guarantee 'largely because we do not wish to endanger the film at the last minute and because we must from past experience have certain faith in John Gilling'.[56] And as for the melodrama *Safari* (1956) shot on location in Kenya: 'I am afraid that I get a sense of the same old Warwick fault in regard to scheduling and budgeting from these papers . . . The whole thing leaves me with a very uneasy feeling, as the project is so loosely scripted that I find it quite impossible to express any definite opinion about it.'[57] Film Finances agreed to guarantee the film only when the budget was increased from £192,869 to £274,372 with Columbia responsible for the first overcost up to £23,246.[58] *Safari* – predictably as far as Croydon was concerned – overran its schedule and exceeded its budget by £37,735.[59]

The fact that Film Finances continued to offer guarantees for Warwick's films despite all the problems – especially with the temperamental Irving Allen – suggests that Garrett saw his relationship with the studio as more important than that with the producer. In a personal letter to Columbia vice-president Leo Jaffe in New York, Garrett wrote: 'It seems unfortunate that the only times when Columbia and ourselves are involved in even the slightest form of disagreement, it is when Warwick are concerned.'[60] In fact this was not strictly correct. Film Finances had also guaranteed *Father Brown* (1954) – produced by Vivien Cox and directed by Robert Hamer for Facett Productions with a 75 per cent distribution guarantee from Columbia – and were not impressed when Columbia decided they wanted to shoot additional scenes but proposed to recoup the costs from the film's receipts before any sum advanced by the guarantor. Garrett considered this suggestion 'inequitable . . . It is quite clearly wrong that a distributor should be free to alter the size of the budget at will and thereby push us back further just so as to protect his own initial investment.'⁶¹ In the event *Father Brown* was completed without any call on the guarantee. There was also a dispute over legal expenses for *The Key* (1958), produced by Carl Foreman's Open Road Productions and directed by Carol Reed for Columbia. The studio queried the charges raised by Film Finances' solicitors. Garrett explained to William Graf of Columbia's London office: 'In many cases . . . our solicitors have to spend a considerable time asking for amendments which do not spring from any new wishes on our part but from well-established standard requirements or, as is more frequently the case, approving amendments to the distribution and other guarantees which are called for by the producer or his distributor.'⁶²

However, it was MGM which proved the most problematic of the Hollywood studios during the 1950s. In the late 1950s MGM decided to switch from producing through its British subsidiary to financing independent producers: this brought the studio into contact with Film Finances for the first time as completion guarantees were needed for such films. *Action of the Tiger* (1957) – a Cold War action-adventure in the mould of the Warwick films – was produced by Kenneth Harper's Claridge Film Productions, with MGM loaning US $750,000 and Harper providing an additional $100,000.⁶³ The start of filming was delayed when MGM failed to advance its contribution to the production account until the contract for the guarantee was signed and sealed – usually Film Finances' letter of intent was accepted by investors – and it later emerged that there was a shortfall in MGM's contribution, which Film Finances calculated was $115,583 short of its commitment.⁶⁴ This was problematic because Harper was not able to pay all his bills: 'We understand that Claridge are finding themselves in a somewhat embarrassing position as due to the withholding of the finance they are unable to meet some very heavy outstanding obligations, including of course the Studio account which has now reached something like £22,000.'⁶⁵ Film Finances was forced to issue writs against the producers over the withdrawal of funds from the production account to cover a number of unbudgeted items. Garrett wrote to MGM vice-president Saul Rittenberg:

> I regret, after due consideration, that my company has decided that there is only one way in which we can obtain satisfaction from Mr Lipsky and his clients and that is through legal action. The matter is not just simply a question of whether Van Johnson can be paid extra expenses, nor is it just a question of a few additional expenses such as Mr Blau's trip to Europe, which by themselves we could easily afford to overlook, but it is in fact an accumulation of matters which have forced us to take this action.⁶⁶

Film Finances advanced a total of £40,668 towards completion of the film – including post-production costs when it was decided that three of the actors would need to be redubbed – which it never recovered as it soon became apparent that *Action of the Tiger* 'has done exceptionally bad business in the States and poor business over here'.⁶⁷

The production of *tom thumb* (1958) was problematic for different reasons. This was produced by fantasy specialist George Pal at MGM's Borehamwood Studios.

Film Finances had no experience of such special effects-heavy films and was at something of a loss to know what to make of it: even John Croydon was unable to assess the validity of the budget and simply suggested 'that it must be protected by an enormous contingency'.[68] Film Finances proposed that instead of accepting the schedule as it stood, the progress of the film should be reviewed after two weeks and that if it was behind at that stage then the schedule should be extended and the budget increased proportionately.[69] Film Finances agreed the sterling budget of £179,574 subject to amendment 'to take account of legal and other costs incurred from independent production'.[70] One of the issues that affected the budgeting of the film was that MGM British Studios was charging rentals and facilities on the terms it would for an outside producer when in fact Pal was really more of an 'in house' independent who had a long-term association with MGM in Hollywood. After two weeks on the floor Film Finances estimated that the film was three and a half days behind schedule: Pal responded by increasing the budget to £194,027 and then trying to get out of the guarantee on the grounds that 'we were getting a fee for nothing, since he now felt pretty sure that he would not go over schedule by as much as we were suggesting'.[71] Again Garrett had to write to Saul Rittenberg:

> I am afraid that these post-factum arrangements, however good and fair they may appear at the time, have their disadvantages which only become obvious when they have to be brought into effect. The original conditions under which the arrangements were made tend to be forgotten by the protagonists and one finds a note of 'What does one need a guarantee for, at any rate?' creeping in. This is particularly so in this case as unfortunately the adjustment of schedule called for is far below the absolute ceiling and the picture has to date more or less continued at the rate of progress which was set in the first two weeks.[72]

It was not unusual at this time for Film Finances to find that some producers, especially American producers, did not fully understand the purpose of the completion guarantee and would attempt to renegotiate it if they thought it would not be called upon. In the event the final sterling cost of *tom thumb* was £235,415 of which Film Finances advanced £34,466.[73]

By the late 1950s the ecology of runaway productions was changing. It was becoming increasingly apparent that the routine bread-and-butter films which for so long had been the cornerstone of studio production were no longer profitable. Therefore the strategy embraced by the majors was to concentrate on fewer but bigger films in the view – generally supported by the evidence it has to be said – that it was the bigger films that returned the biggest profits. Columbia Pictures was the industry leader in this regard. In the late 1950s and early 1960s it financed three British-made war epics – *The Bridge on the River Kwai*, *The Guns of Navarone* and *Lawrence of Arabia* – that all qualified for British quota but were essentially international pictures. All three were big commercial and critical successes. *The Bridge on the River Kwai* (1957), adapted from Pierre Boulle's novel about British prisoners-of-war in the Far East, was produced by Sam Spiegel and directed by David Lean: it qualified as a British film because Spiegel's Horizon Pictures was registered in Britain and it was shot on location in Ceylon (British Commonwealth) with one American star (William Holden) and an otherwise largely British cast (Alec Guinness, Jack Hawkins, James Donald) and production crew. According to the trade press, *The Bridge on the River Kwai* cost around £1 million: at the time this was a very large budget for a British picture even with a Hollywood studio behind it. It was the biggest attraction at the British box office in 1958.[74] *The Bridge on the River Kwai* was the first genuine British box-office blockbuster: at a time when cinema attendances were declining and revenues falling, it demonstrated that there was still a large audience for major 'event' pictures. As *Kine* studio correspondent Bill Edwards said: 'I shall call 1958 the Year of the Kwai. The year when this British picture proved, contrary to popular belief, that there were still picture-goers left in the country.'[75]

The Bridge on the River Kwai was also a major success in America, where its rentals of US $17,195,000 made it the biggest-grossing British film since *The Red Shoes*.[76] Overall the 1950s had been a lean period for British films in the United States: the horror films of Hammer Film Productions – mostly backed by US distributors – had built up something of a cult following, but other British-made war subjects fared poorly at the American box office.[77] Columbia did not emphasise the Britishness of *The Bridge in the River Kwai* in promoting it in America.[78] It won Academy Awards for Best Picture, Best Director, Best Actor (Alec Guinness) and Best Screenplay (awarded to Pierre Boulle, who was credited for the screenplay by blacklisted Americans Carl Foreman and Michael Wilson).

Carl Foreman, originally denied a script-writing credit for *The Bridge on the River Kwai*, acted as both producer and writer of *The Guns of Navarone* (1961), adapted from the best-selling novel by Alistair MacLean. Foreman spent several years setting up this film through his British-based company Open Road Productions: it was first announced in the trade press in 1958 when Columbia's Mike Francovich declared that it would have a budget of £2 million and would be 'the biggest project the company have ever had'.[79] Shepperton Studios similarly described it as 'the most important and ambitious British picture ever undertaken'.[80] *The Guns of Navarone* was to have been written by Eric Ambler and directed by Alexander Mackendrick: J. Lee Thompson was a late replacement as director shortly before the film started shooting in spring 1960.[81] It had a similar production ecology to *The Bridge on the River Kwai*: a British-based American producer, British director and Anglo-American cast (Gregory Peck, David Niven, Anthony Quinn, Anthony Quayle, Stanley Baker), shot on location in Rhodes with the studio sequences at Shepperton. *The Guns of Navarone* was released in May 1961: after three months the net receipts from its roadshow release at 40 cinemas in Britain had reached £500,000 and it had taken over £1 million in 15 cities in the United States.[82] It was the leading 'hard ticket blockbuster' in Britain in 1961, and repeated the feat in 1962 as 'best combined "hard ticket" and general release'.[83] It earned US $13 million rentals in America.[84] Steve Chibnall contends that *The Guns of Navarone* 'had certainly broken the mould of British film making. It proved that British production with American backing could offer more than cosy comedies and modest thrillers.'[85]

Lawrence of Arabia (1962) was the fullest expression of the Anglo-American epic cinema heralded by *The Bridge on the River Kwai* and *The Guns of Navarone*. It again won Academy Awards for Best Picture and Best Director (David Lean) and earned US rentals of $15 million. *Lawrence of Arabia* had a long gestation. Columbia had first expressed an interest in the subject in the early 1950s when it had sounded out the Foreign Office whether there would be any political objection.[86] In the late 1950s the story of the enigmatic soldier-scholar T. E. Lawrence became the subject of a bidding war between British and American producers. Herbert Wilcox paid £100,000 for the screen rights to Terence Rattigan's play *Ross* – based on Lawrence's career after the First World War – which also included a script for *Lawrence of Arabia* written by Rattigan. However, Wilcox was outmanoeuvred by Sam Spiegel, who announced a film of *Lawrence of Arabia* to be directed by David Lean for Columbia.[87] It was an indication of the shifting political economy of the film industry that it was the American-backed film that went ahead. Wilcox reflected ruefully: 'I should have gone ahead and made *Ross*, defying Spiegel . . . However, the City wanted no part of litigation, and so I had to let the whole subject drop since no distributor would finance me with an injunction hanging over my head. Not a penny of the £100,000 did I recover.'[88]

Lawrence of Arabia was 'the most expensive production undertaken by Columbia to date and is expected to cost between £3.5 million and £4.5 million'.[89] It took over a year to shoot on locations in Jordan, Spain and Morocco and its eventual production cost amounted to £4.6 million.[90] Billings averred that '*Lawrence of Arabia* clearly establishes Columbia as the top producer of mammoth British films. The world is its oyster.'[91] There was in fact some question over the 'British' status of *Lawrence of Arabia*. The Board of Trade undertook a close investigation of its production and labour costs. *Lawrence of Arabia* demonstrates the highly complex production ecology of runaway productions. Columbia was the 'prime mover' which put up the money, with 'the usual foreign "middle" company' (in this case Swiss-registered Kwai AG) acting 'as general go-between between Columbia and the British company (Horizon) who made the arrangements for making the film'.[92] The only scenes in the 220-minute film actually shot in Britain were Lawrence's death and memorial service: less than a minute of footage shot at Shepperton was sufficient to satisfy the regulation about using a British studio. The Board of Trade felt that the salaries of Spiegel (£206,726) – who could be included in the costs of British personnel as he was a long-term resident – and Lean (£200,685) had been 'inflated' in order to raise the percentage of British labour costs above the minimum of 75 per cent. (It was noted that Spiegel had been paid £32,068 and Lean £58,894 for *The Bridge on the River Kwai*, though it was accepted that *Lawrence of Arabia* 'is, of course, a far greater production'). Quota regulations for labour costs might help to explain why the fees of British actors Peter O'Toole (£43,646) and Alec Guinness (£89,286) were significantly higher than those for Omar Sharif (£9,545), Arthur Kennedy (£8,928), Claude Rains (£7,143) and José Ferrer (£3,571). Anthony Quinn – who was paid £89,285 (US $250,000) – was the discountable foreign artiste. The Board of Trade concluded that 'there is no doubt that this film is essentially British in the light of the rather wide interpretation which . . . we allow to American-sponsored films'.[93]

It therefore took some fancy footwork by Spiegel to ensure that *Lawrence of Arabia* met the legal criteria of a British film. Jonathan Stubbs has suggested, furthermore, that the British quota requirements cast light on the controversy surrounding the screen-writing credit for *Lawrence of Arabia*. It has since been conclusively established that the early drafts of the script were by American screenwriter Michael Wilson: however his treatments were rejected and the final screenplay was credited to British playwright Robert Bolt. It has generally been maintained that Wilson was not credited for *Lawrence of Arabia* as he had been blacklisted by the House UnAmerican Activities Committee.[94] However, the fact that Wilson was not credited meant that his salary of US $200,000 (£72,000) did not have to be entered in the paperwork submitted to the Board of Trade, which might have tipped the overall costs for non-British personnel above 25 per cent. In this context, Stubbs argues, '[the] problem was not that Wilson was "unAmerican", it seems, but simply that he was American.'[95] There was evidently a lot more to the matter of being a British film than just being made in Britain.

Notes

1. 'Long Shots', *Kinematograph Weekly*, 19 April 1956, p. 4.
2. Rachael Low, *The History of the British Film 1918–1929* (London: George Allen & Unwin, 1971), p. 75.
3. Political and Economic Planning, *The British Film Industry: A report on its history and present organisation, with special reference to the economic problems of British feature film production* (London: Political and Economic Planning, 1952), p. 50.
4. On American production of quota films in Britain in the 1930s, see Rachael Low, *The History of the British Film 1929–1939: Film Making in 1930s Britain* (London: George Allen & Unwin, 1985), pp. 186–97, 259–70. See also Steve Chibnall, 'Hollywood on Thames: The British productions of Warner Bros.-First National, 1931–1945', *Historical Journal of Film, Radio and Television*, 30: 4 (2019), pp. 687–724.
5. H. Mark Glancy, 'Hollywood and Britain: MGM and the British "Quota" Legislation', in Jeffrey Richards (ed.), *The Unknown 1930s: An Alternative History of the British Cinema, 1929–1939* (London: I. B. Tauris, 1998), pp. 57–72.
6. Ginette Vincendeau (ed.), *The Encyclopedia of European Cinema* (London: Cassell, 1995), p. 466.
7. Irving Bernstein, *Hollywood at the Crossroads: An economic study of the motion picture industry* (Los Angeles: Hollywood Association of Film Labor, 1957), pp. 54–5.
8. BEA EC 5/263: E. C. Kahn to Rowe-Dutton, 9 February 1948.
9. Political and Economic Planning, *The British Film Industry*, p. 157.
10. Ibid.
11. Ibid, p. 160.
12. 'All "Frozen" Sterling Gone By Sept – BofT', *Kinematograph Weekly*, 19 April 1951, p. 3.
13. 'US Finds Way of Using Frozen Dollars, Says Johnston', *Kinematograph Weekly*, 19 January 1950, p. 10.

14. 'RKO-Radio Will Use British Unit for "Tarzan" in Africa', *Kinematograph Weekly*, 4 May 1950, p. 33.
15. 'Anglo-American Partnership', *The Financial Times*, 23 September 1957, p. 3.
16. 'The What and Where of Eady', *Kinematograph Weekly*, 30 December 1954, p. 6.
17. 'Future Prospects of British Pic Prod. Remains Wrapped Up in Eady Bonus', *Variety*, 7 January 1953, p. 191.
18. 'Government Should Consider Its Policy', *Kinematograph Weekly*, 5 September 1957, p. 5.
19. 'Investment', *Kinematograph Weekly*, 30 August 1956, p. 4.
20. 'Anglo-American Project', *Kinematograph Weekly*, 3 April 1952, p. 22.
21. FFA Realised Film Box 83: *Star of India*: John Croydon to Robert Garrett, 18 May 1953.
22. Ibid.: Garrett to A. J. Rossetti, 12 May 1953.
23. FFA Realised Film Box 265: *A Terrible Beauty*: Maurice Foster to Robert Garrett, 1 April 1959.
24. Ibid.: Victor Lyndon to Foster, 25 November 1959.
25. 'Teddington Goes Dark', *Kinematograph Weekly*, 16 November 1950, p. 28.
26. H. Mark Glancy, *When Hollywood loved Britain: The Hollywood 'British' film, 1939–45* (Manchester: Manchester University Press, 1999), p. 105.
27. Jonathan Stubbs, '"Blocked" Currency, Runaway Production in Britain and *Captain Horatio Hornblower* (1951)', *Historical Journal of Film, Radio and Television*, 28: 3 (2008), pp. 335–51.
28. Sue Harper and Vincent Porter, *British Cinema of the 1950s: The Decline of Deference* (Oxford: Oxford University Press, 2003), p. 117.
29. 'MGM-British Opens New Era in Production', *Kinematograph Weekly*, 12 June 1952, p. 18.
30. Harper and Porter, *British Cinema of the 1950s*, p. 119.
31. Ibid.
32. '20th Fox – No British Productions', *Kinematograph Weekly*, 23 July 1953, p. 7.
33. 'Fox to Restart British Production', *Kinematograph Weekly*, 31 May 1956, p. 3.
34. FFA Realised Film Box 46: *The Man Who Never Was*: John Croydon to Robert Garrett, 5 May 1955.
35. Brian McFarlane (ed.), *An Autobiography of British Cinema* (London: Methuen, 1997), p. 433.
36. FFA Realised Film Box 49: *The Red Beret*: Terence Young to John Croydon, 14 May 1952.
37. Albert R. Broccoli, with Donald Zec, *When the Snow Melts: The Autobiography of Cubby Broccoli* (London: Boxtree, 1998), pp. 103–5.
38. FFA Realised Film Box 49: Robert Garrett to Leslie E. Thompson, 27 June 1952.
39. Ibid.: John Croydon to Robert Garrett, 4 July 1952.
40. Ibid.: Garrett to Allen, 18 June 1952.
41. Ibid.: Memo from Maurice Foster: 'The Red Beret', 23 July 1952.
42. Ibid.: Garrett to J. Hughes, 6 August 1952. A compromise agreement was reached whereby in the event of the need to replace the producer, Columbia would nominate someone and if the nominee were unacceptable to Film Finances the guarantor would then suggest two others and the studio would pick one of them.
43. FFA Realised Film Box 151: *Safari*: Messrs Allen & Overy to Film Finances Ltd, 30 September 1955.

44. 'It's Independents' Day', *Kinematograph Weekly*, 15 December 1955, p. 79.
45. 'On Release', *Kinematograph Weekly*, 9 February 1956, p. 7.
46. FFA Realised Film Box 66: *Hell Below Zero*: Croydon to Garrett, 17 November 1952.
47. Ibid.: Garrett to Warwick Pictures, 20 November 1952.
48. FFA Realised Film Box 87: *The Black Knight*: Note – 'Meeting with Berkowitz and Graf', 3 June 1953.
49. Ibid.: Croydon to Garrett, 7 September 1953.
50. Ibid.: Maurice Foster to Warwick Film Productions, 1 September 1953.
51. Ibid.: Garrett to Warwick Film Productions, 21 September 1953.
52. Ibid.: Allen to Garrett, 15 December 1953.
53. FFA Realised Film Box 118: *Prize of Gold*: Croydon to Garrett, 20 May 1954.
54. Ibid.: John H. Smith to Maurice Foster, 23 December 1954.
55. FFA Realised Film Box 148: *The Gamma People*: Croydon to Garrett, 14 July 1955.
56. Ibid.: Garrett to William Graf, 19 July 1955.
57. FFA Realised Film Box 151: Croydon to Garrett, 17 July 1955.
58. Ibid.: William Graf to Film Finances, 5 September 1955.
59. Ibid.: M. J. Frankovich to Film Finances, 19 January 1956.
60. FFA Realised Film Box 118: Garrett to Leo Jaffe, 22 September 1954.
61. FFA Realised Film Box 89: *Father Brown*: Note by Robert Garrett, 'Father Brown', 28 August 1953.
62. FFA Realised Film Box 223: *The Key*: Garrett to William Graf, 3 April 1958.
63. FFA Realised Film Box 192: *Action of the Tiger*: B. H. Lewis to Maurice Foster, 13 September 1956.
64. Ibid.: Robert Garrett to Saul Rittenberg, 1 February 1957.
65. Ibid.
66. Ibid.: Garrett to Rittenberg, 7 May 1957.
67. Ibid.: Maurice Foster to Garrett, 13 March 1958.
68. FFA Realised Film Box 231: *tom thumb*: John Croydon to Robert Garrett, 24 July 1957.
69. Ibid.: Garrett to Matthew Raymond, 9 August 1957.
70. Ibid.: Garrett to Galaxy Films, 15 September 1957.
71. Ibid.: Maurice Foster to Garrett, 17 December 1957.
72. Ibid.: Garrett to Saul Rittenberg, 2 January 1958.
73. Ibid.: Maurice Foster to Murray Silverstein, 24 March 1960.
74. 'British Still Best In Exciting But Frustrating Year', *Kinematograph Weekly*, 18 December 1958, pp. 6–7.
75. 'Heartening Signs Abroad', *Kinematograph Weekly*, 18 December 1958, p. 85.
76. 'All-Time Boxoffice Champs', *Variety*, 7 January 1970, p. 25.
77. Sarah Street, *Transatlantic Crossings: British Feature Films in the United States* (London: Continuum, 2001), pp. 159–64.
78. 'Billings Is Right: Sell These Films as British', *Kinematograph Weekly*, 22 January 1959, p. 6.
79. 'Long Shots', *Kinematograph Weekly*, 2 October 1958, p. 4.
80. 'Shepperton Studios are proud to announce . . .', *Kinematograph Weekly*, 26 November 1959, p. 2.
81. 'Lee-Thompson will direct "Navarone"', *Kinematograph Weekly*, 17 March 1960, p. 6.
82. '"Guns" Set to Beat "Kwai"', *Kinematograph Weekly*, 24 August 1961, p. 3.

83. 'Three British films head the general releases', *Kinematograph Weekly*, 13 December 1962, pp. 6–7.
84. 'All-Time Boxoffice Champs', p. 25.
85. Steve Chibnall, *J. Lee Thompson* (Manchester: Manchester University Press, 2000), pp. 262–3.
86. TNA FO 371/91254: H. A. Dudgeon, 'A film on "Lawrence of Arabia"', 14 November 1951.
87. 'Spiegel-Lean Team for "Lawrence of Arabia"', *Variety*, 5 August 1959, p. 5.
88. Herbert Wilcox, *Twenty-Five Thousand Sunsets: The Autobiography of Herbert Wilcox* (New York: A. S. Barnes, 1969), p. 205.
89. 'Columbia is going ahead in Europe', *Kinematograph Weekly*, 1 June 1961, p. 3.
90. 'Cost of "Lawrence"', *Kinematograph Weekly*, 3 January 1963, p. 4.
91. 'Your Films', *Kinematograph Weekly*, 3 January 1963, p. 9.
92. TNA BT 64/5208: Minute No. 2 by W. C. F. Sowter, 8 April 1963.
93. Ibid.
94. John Hodson, '"Who Wrote *Lawrence of Arabia*?": Sam Spiegel and David Lean's Denial of Credit to a Blacklisted Writer', *Cineaste*, 20: 4 (1994), pp. 12–18.
95. Jonathan Stubbs, 'The Eady Levy – A Runaway Bribe? Hollywood Production and British Subsidy in the Early 1960s', *Journal of British Cinema and Television*, 6: 1 (2009), p. 11.

CHAPTER 11

New Waves, New Crises

> The year ended 31st March 1958 was one of increasing anxiety for the British film production industry. In particular, the serious decline which occurred in box office receipts and cinema admissions has materially affected the earnings of films shown in the United Kingdom. The fact that some films have suffered very much more than others and that certain films still fill the cinemas shows that the public, which is today presented with so many alternative attractions, has become much more discriminating about films than it has ever been in the past. (National Film Finance Corporation)[1]

Following the relative stability of the early and mid-1950s, the later years of the decade saw the British film industry experience another one of its frequent periods of crisis. This time the problem revolved around one issue: the severe – and rapid – erosion of the cinema audience. Although cinema attendances had been declining year on year since the high point of 1946, the rate of decline had been shallow, and until 1956, when ticket sales totalled 1,102,000, annual admissions had remained above the levels of the 1930s, when cinema-going had been 'the essential social habit of the age'. However, over the next four years the decline became precipitous: admissions fell to 915 million in 1957, 754 million in 1958, 581 million in 1959 and 501 million in 1960.[2] Within the space of four years, therefore, half the cinema-going audience in Britain had disappeared. It should be borne in mind that the film industry experienced this decline as a series of year-on-year shocks rather than necessarily seeing it as the pattern that becomes evident in hindsight. In 1956, for example, *Kine* editor William G. Altria reported that the 1,181,000 admissions for the previous year had been the lowest since 1940: 'Once again the statistics ... underlie the sharply deteriorating position of the industry – a state of affairs that is largely the outcome of unreasonable taxation, and which is aggravated by the state-aided competition of television which does not bear similar imposts.'[3] The following year it was reported that admissions were at their lowest since 1941, and the next year they were the 'lowest on record'.[4] The sharp decline in cinema attendances inevitably impacted upon box-office receipts, which over the same period fell from £104 million in 1956 to £63.4 million in 1960.[5] Another consequence of declining attendances was the accelerating rate of cinema closures. In 1956 there were 4,391 cinemas in the United Kingdom – only around a few hundred fewer than at the height of cinema-going in the 1940s – but nearly a third of those (1,357) had closed by 1960.[6] It tended to be the smaller houses and independent cinemas that were most likely to close – the sort of 'Bijou kinema' evoked so nostalgically in Basil Dearden's *The Smallest Show on Earth* (1957): a consequence of this process therefore was that the stranglehold of the major circuits was strengthened as it was their smaller competitors who were more severely affected.

While historians now argue that the reasons for the decline in cinema-going were complex and were related to changing social behaviour and patterns of consumption, at the time the film trade identified two causes: the rise of television and the continued imposition of Entertainment Tax.[7] Whether or not there was a direct causal relationship, there was certainly a very close correlation between declining cinema attendances and increasing television ownership. In 1955, for example, the year in which commercial broadcasting was introduced to Britain through the Independent Television network, 4.5 million combined television and radio licences were sold: this figure rose to 8 million in 1958 and 10.5 million by 1960.[8] In 1962 the economist John Spraos published a study entitled *The Decline of the Cinema* in which he concluded that television was 'the initiating and the main cause of the cinema's decline'.[9] Spraos analysed the relationship between the number of households with television and annual cinema admissions, and identified a correlation between the growth of television ownership and the rate of decline of cinema-going: he calculated that in 1951 only 3.5 cinema admissions were lost for each household with television, but this figure had risen to 36.4 admissions lost by 1955 and 134.6 admissions lost in 1958.[10] Furthermore, it was working-class households which accounted for the most rapid growth of television ownership between 1955 and 1960: this group also happened to be the most frequent cinema-goers.[11]

Evidence that the film industry regarded television as a major threat is to be found in the establishment of the Film Industry Defence Organisation (FIDO) in 1958. This was a rare instance of collaboration between the main trade associations – otherwise still at loggerheads over the Eady levy – and was intended to prevent the sale of British films to television. FIDO raised a fund through a voluntary levy on exhibitors (ironically given their opposition to the statutory levy) which was then used to purchase a covenant in any film that might otherwise have been sold to television. It also threatened, controversially, to boycott producers and distributors who sold their films to television. Formally established in August 1958, after one year FIDO had spent a total of £48,540 in acquiring the covenants to 57 British features.[12] 'Less tangible, but of vital importance to the industry,' *Kine* reported, 'is the claim that FIDO has had the effect of holding back the offer of many thousands of films to television.'[13] In the long term, however, FIDO was doomed to failure. Some producers – including Ealing Studios and Daniel Angel – were opposed to the scheme from the start.[14] The first major block sale of British films to television had been agreed shortly before the organisation was set up, when Ealing's parent company Associated Talking Pictures sold 95 features to the BBC for £40,000. FIDO was obliged to accept this as a *fait accompli*.[15] The organisation was weakened when the Kinematograph Renters' Society – itself facing the threat of a counter-boycott from suppliers of American films – withdrew in 1959. FIDO was dealt a further blow early in 1960 when the television company Associated-Rediffusion bought the entire share capital of Independent Film Distributors and with it the rights to 55 post-war British feature films.[16] It was already becoming apparent that the covenants offered by FIDO did not match the amounts that television was able to offer. In 1962 FIDO's funds were nearly exhausted and 'indicated that it was unlikely that FIDO would be able to treat for "backlogs" from the major companies'.[17] In 1964 an agreement was reached with the Cinematograph Exhibitors' Association whereby films over five years old could be sold to television. FIDO was wound up in 1965 when it agreed that producers could buy back covenants at the original price.[18]

Another industry-wide campaign in the late 1950s was more successful. The decline of box-office revenues lent weight to the calls for abolition of the hated Entertainment Tax. In 1955 an All-Industry Tax Committee (AITC) was set up in order to lobby more effectively for relief from the tax. While the trade received assurances from successive Chancellors of the Exchequer that the film industry would receive sympathetic consideration, it was not until April 1957 that Peter Thorneycroft announced a reduction in Entertainment Tax equivalent to £6.5 million per year – regarded as wholly insufficient in the view of the trade.[19] There was better news in 1958 when the exemption limit for the tax was raised from seats costing under 11*d.* to 1*s.* 6*d*: this amounted to an overall reduction of nearly 50 per cent.[20] By this time the decline of audiences and diminishing box-office receipts had become so acute that the AITC shifted its emphasis from lobbying for a reduction of the tax to complete abolition. In 1959 it was widely expected that the tax would be further reduced or even abolished entirely: Derrick Heathcoat-Amory's decision to leave it untouched 'has given the industry a staggering blow, to put it mildly'.[21] It was not until the Budget of April 1960 that the Cinema Tax – as it was now being called by the trade – was finally abolished and that '[at] long, long last the industry is totally relieved of a burden imposed as a "temporary" wartime expedient – during World War I'.[22]

As welcome as it was to the cinema trade, though, the abolition of Entertainment Tax provided scant relief for an industry that seemed helpless to prevent the haemorrhaging of cinema audiences. The major corporations were evidently feeling the pinch. In 1956 ABPC announced that its trading profits had fallen by almost a third from the previous year, from £2.9 million to £2 million.[23] And in 1958 the Rank Organisation announced that its profits had dropped by £2.7 million and that it had lost £850,000 on film production.[24] The response of the two combines, as it had been a decade earlier, was a strategy of retrenchment and reorganisation. In particular they sought to concentrate on their still-profitable exhibition interests and to reduce their production activities. In 1958 Rank announced a programme of 'rationalisation': the Odeon and Gaumont circuits – which hitherto had operated more or less independently from one another – were merged into one. This news was not welcomed by independent producers who 'are deeply concerned at the loss of the ready-made Gaumont release, as an alternative to the Odeon and ABC releases, which already has had the effect of hardening the attitude toward the backing of projects – notably in the case of the National Film

Finance Corporation'.[25] It was reported that some independent productions had been abandoned as producers were unable to obtain finance as a consequence of the rationalisation plan.[26] Following the Odeon-Gaumont merger, there was an attempt to create a 'third circuit' by amalgamating three smaller circuits (Granada, Essoldo and Shipman-King) with some of the cinemas sold off by Rank and ABC.[27] The National Circuit, as it became known, comprised around 400 cinemas. It was welcomed by independent producers, but it was never able to compete on equal terms with Rank and ABC, which naturally privileged their own films and had first call on films from the major American distributors. The National Circuit lasted for barely two years: its weakness from the outset had been 'the insufficiency of product of top box-office calibre'.[28]

The crisis of the late 1950s also forced the majors into rethinking their production strategies. There was increasing evidence by this time that it was the bigger films that generated the biggest profits. In December 1958 the *Kine* noted that 'the echo of the US situation is to be found in Britain, where the pattern of production in the immediate future is expected to result in fewer, but more important pictures'.[29] The success of Columbia's *The Bridge on the River Kwai* (*Kine* studio correspondent Bill Edwards described 1958 as 'the Year of the Kwai') confirmed this impression. The Rank Organisation announced that it was dropping its contract producers and directors to reduce overheads and that it 'would make fewer but larger pictures' costing around £500,000 each.[30] Its programme for 1959 included four regular A-pictures – *The 39 Steps* (a remake of Alfred Hitchcock's classic of 1935), *Whirlpool*, *Sapphire* and *Tiger Bay* – and three that it called 'blockbusters': *Ferry to Hong Kong*, *The Bolshoi Ballet* and *North West Frontier*.[31] Unfortunately, however, this coincided with the closing down of Rank Film Distributors of America, which had been operating at a loss for the last two years.[32] Although Rank had two films in the British top ten in 1959 – *North West Frontier* and *The 39 Steps* – it was faced again with the perennial problem that the British market was insufficient to secure a profitable return for more expensive films.[33]

The independent producers were even more adversely affected than the combines, which at least had their exhibition interests to balance their losses on production. A particular problem for the independents was that production costs were increasing at the same time as receipts were shrinking due to diminishing box-office revenues. There is much anecdotal evidence of inflation in production costs in the later 1950s. In 1957, for example, when Frank Launder and Sidney Gilliat were preparing *Blue Murder at St Trinian's*, the first sequel to their hit comedy *The Belles of St Trinian's*, 'they estimated that it would cost more or less the same, but during the four years since "The Belles" costs have risen by an estimated 25 per cent'.[34] Ivan Foxwell, producer of *The Colditz Story*, confirmed this and highlighted the problem for films budgeted for the domestic market:

> *The Colditz Story* in 1955 was budgeted and cost £136,000. I limited it to this cost because the story was obviously better suited to the United Kingdom and Commonwealth countries and had English stars. Today that film could not be

made for less than £175,000. This means in effect that it would be quite an unreasonable proposition to make *The Colditz Story* today since the domestic market cannot possibly justify the expenditure of such a sum.[35]

This anecdotal evidence was confirmed by the NFFC, which in its annual report for 1957 observed: 'The increase in the production costs of major films compared with two years ago is most noticeable.' The main cause, it suggested, 'has been the increase in fees and remuneration payable to personnel – producers, directors, artists, writers, technicians and craft labour'.[36] *The Financial Times* published a breakdown of the costs of the Boultings' *Lucky Jim* (1957), whose budget of £164,980 was 'about the average for a first feature independent British film': the costs were itemised as production unit salaries (£25,329), artistes (£23,404), sets and models (£28,301), studio rentals and facilities (£27,565), story and script (£10,150), film stock and laboratory fees (£6,660), miscellaneous items (£20,736), and interest, financial and legal charges (£22,835).[37] The Film Finances Archive reveals that *Lucky Jim* exceeded its budget by £7,310, an overcost of 4.3 per cent.[38]

Even so, some producers were still able to budget economically in order to ensure their films returned a profit from the home market. *Carry On Sergeant* (1958) – the first in what would become a long-running series of ensemble comedies, all of which were produced by Peter Rogers and directed by Gerald Thomas – was produced under conditions of strict budgetary economy. Rogers insisted 'that here was an opportunity for everybody concerned to see that pictures can be produced on a low budget'.[39] The NFFC agreed to loan half the budget on condition that the total cost did not exceed £80,000: Anglo-Amalgamated Film Distributors provided the other half as a distribution advance.[40] In the event, *Carry On Sergeant* cost only £68,714.[41] It scored at the box office – assisted to some extent by being released during an unusually wet summer – and became 'the surprise smash hit of the year'.[42] Rogers saw the potential of the 'Carry On' formula and was quick to capitalise: *Carry On Nurse* and *Carry On Teacher* followed inside the next twelve months. *Carry On Nurse* proved that the success of *Carry On Sergeant* was no fluke: it topped the British box office for 1959.[43] Rogers was a highly economical producer who budgeted his films carefully and exercised strict control over costs. He wrote to Anglo-Amalgamated's Stuart Levy during the preparation of *Carry on Nurse*: 'The fact that the *final* budget of "Sergeant" was £71,426 was a result of the management of the film and should not, I feel, be held as a yard stick for "Nurse". I cannot *guarantee* to come in under budget but I shall do my best – as usual.'[44] The final cost of *Carry On Nurse* (£73,680) was again under budget (£82,461).[45]

The changing industrial and cultural landscape of British cinema at the end of the 1950s was best exemplified by the emergence of new independent production groups. The idea of independent producers working together on a collaborative basis was not new: the Group scheme of the early 1950s had been one such initiative and the inclusion of independent producers in the management of British Lion Films from 1958 was another. But the two new production groups formed in 1959 – Bryanston Films and Allied Film Makers – were different from previous initiatives in several important respects. They were set up as co-operative ventures where members would share in the profits. *Kine* felt that the emergence of such groups 'was the inevitable outcome of a long-smouldering feeling among producers that they could make far better pictures – and possibly far better money – without the interference of the major companies'.[46] Bryanston was set up in April 1959: it comprised 'sixteen leading independent producers' – Aubrey Baring, George Brown, Monja Danischewsky, David Dent, Basil Dearden and Michael Relph, Charles Frend and Norman Priggen, Colin Lesslie and Ronald Neame, John Bryan and Albert Fennell, and Julian Wintle and Leslie Parkin, with Sir Michael Balcon as its chairman and Maxwell Setton as its managing director – backed by Lloyds Bank through a loan of £1 million.[47] Wintle and Parkin would leave the group after a few months when they signed a production and distribution deal with Anglo-Amalgamated.[48]

Michael Balcon explained the company's philosophy thus:

> The strength of the idea lay in that as a co-operative of reputable film-makers we were able to facilitate the financing of productions more easily than if the members had been operating as individuals. The financial method was that known as 'revolving credit' with the bank. This meant that if we put up, say, £200,000 for a production our credit was good for three times that amount, the bank recovering its money from the first proceeds of the film and the credit or loan continuing – or revolving – accordingly. When a subject was approved we gave the producers a guarantee of seventy per cent of the budget and the producers found the balance from private sources and/or the NFFC.[49]

Bryanston's bank credit allowed it to plan a programme of films rather than subsisting one film at a time: over the next five years it supported eighteen first features and another dozen second features.[50] A sub-committee was set up to scrutinise propositions: a majority of two-thirds was required to accept any project, but all members of the co-operative would share in the profits. Bryanston's role was to raise the finance and provide distribution guarantees, while the 'physical distribution and selling' of the films would be handled by British Lion for a commission of 17.5 per cent on home distribution and 12.5 per cent overseas.[51]

Bryanston's first film was an adaptation of James Thurber's novel *The Catbird Seat* produced by Monja Danischewsky and directed by Charles Crichton: the title was changed to *The Battle of the Sexes* (1960) during production. The NFFC refused to advance end money unless the budget (£135,176) was reduced by £40,000: Danischewsky declined as he felt 'I had a comedy with great international potential'. In the event, the film was only possible due to a £20,000 advance from the American distributor and star Peter Sellers agreeing 'to put half his fee back into the production on a speculative basis'.[52] Film Finances agreed to guarantee the film with an 'exceptional and without precedent' concession of accepting that the producer and star deferments would rank for recovery ahead of the guarantor on the grounds that the agreements had already been made.[53] *The Battle of the Sexes* was a modest commercial success, earning Bryanston a profit of £10,894.[54]

Bryanston's second film was Aubrey Baring's aviation drama *Cone of Silence* (1960). John Croydon's assessment was that it was under-budgeted: 'It is obvious that £132,149 is insufficient money to produce a film of the calibre expected. In my opinion, this script, adequately scheduled, would require a minimum of £175,000 budget figure before it could be reasonably considered.'[55] Film Finances agreed to a revised budget of £137,314 largely on the grounds that the director Charles Frend 'is a man of considerable experience'.[56] In the event, there was no call upon the guarantee. However, it was not a box-office success: Bryanston lost £32,458.

Allied Film Makers, which followed in November 1959, was described as 'a compact version of Bryanston with the important exception that its membership is extended to top working actors'.[57] Its members were Basil Dearden and Michael Relph (who were also members of Bryanston), Richard Attenborough and Bryan Forbes, director Guy Green and actor Jack Hawkins. Attenborough and Forbes had also produced *The Angry Silence* (1960) for their own company Beaver Films: *The Angry Silence* is sometimes described as an AFM production though in fact it had been made independently of the group. Each of the members put up £5,000 of their own money, while the National Provincial Bank provided a revolving credit secured against distribution guarantees from the Rank Organisation. Following the first AFM film, *The League of Gentlemen*, Rank would also provide 10 per cent of the production finance or half the end money. Bryan Forbes explained how the group worked in practice:

> We had internal autonomy as to choice of subjects, and since we were such a small board we agreed that voting should be unanimous. Once the vote to give approval on script and budget had been cast, then the individuals or partnerships actually making the films had total artistic control. The finished product was then distributed by the Rank Organisation at a fee of 27½ per cent, 2½ per cent of which was returned to Allied Film Makers. We also retained varying proportions of the profits of each film.[58]

The way that Forbes describes it makes Allied sound like a smaller-scale version of Rank's Independent Producers of the mid-1940s, in the sense that the film-makers chose their subjects and retained artistic control over the films: the key differences were that the films were on a less ambitious scale and Rank was not directly financing them.

Allied's first venture was *The League of Gentlemen* (1960), a comedy-drama about a group of cashiered army officers who turn their military skills to the task of bank robbery. It brought together most members of the group with the exception of Guy Green: Forbes wrote the screenplay, Dearden directed, Relph produced, and Hawkins, Attenborough and Forbes all played members of the gang. *The League of Gentlemen* was budgeted at £175,434, of which £122,804 (70 per cent) was loaned by the National Provincial Bank, with £22,500 from the NFFC and the balance from deferments. The NFFC cited *The League of Gentlemen* – alongside *The Angry Silence* – as an example of how deferments helped to reduce production costs: '[There] have been a few cases where individual fees have been substantially reduced or deferred – e.g. *The Angry Silence* where writers, producers, director and star artistes worked for nominal fees only and relied upon profits, and *The League of Gentlemen* where they deferred a large proportion of their fees.'[59] *The League of Gentlemen* includes an ironic reference to the financing of AFM when Colonel Hyde (Hawkins) reveals his plan to rob an unnamed bank and Major Race (Nigel Patrick) remarks: 'I do hope he hasn't got the National Provincial in mind. They're being awfully decent to me at the moment.' (In the first draft of the script the reference is to Barclays: it was changed to the National Provincial in the shooting script.[60]) *The League of Gentlemen* was completed for a final cost of £179,602. Film Finances offered Dearden and Relph an exceptional 'special rebate' of £1,000 – despite the fact that they were not entitled to a no-claim bonus, having called upon the guarantee for their previous film – 'in appreciation of the very fine way in which the production was carried out'.[61] Relph thanked Film Finances for the 'enormously generous gesture' while adding apologetically that 'the Rank Organisation, who are putting up the end money on our next production *Man in the Moon*, are also doing the completion guarantee'.[62]

The League of Gentlemen received generally good notices and appears to have been a solid box-office success.[63] However, the rest of Allied's programme produced mixed results. Dearden and Relph were responsible for the comedy *Man in the Moon* (1960) and the social problem films *Victim* (1961) and *Life for Ruth* (1962), while Attenborough and Forbes produced the drama *Whistle Down the Wind* (1961) and the psychological thriller *Séance on a Wet Afternoon* (1964). Hawkins did not make another film for Allied after *The League of Gentlemen*, while Green, originally slated to direct *Whistle Down the Wind* until he withdrew to direct another film, never made a film for the group. Sources are contradictory regarding the box-office performance of individual films, though it seems to be generally agreed that *The League of Gentlemen*, *Victim* and *Whistle Down the Wind* were successful while the others failed to recoup their costs. According to Allied's company secretary Leslie Baker: 'The total negative cost of the seven [*sic*] AFM films made for Rank was £1,042,157, the distributor's gross was £1,820,940 giving them a gross profit of £778,783. But the producers of the films still had to carry a loss of £142,934.'[64]

It was the combination of all these factors – the declining cinema audience, the retreat of the major combines from film production, and the creation of new production groups – that helped to create the circumstances for the emergence of a 'new cinema' in Britain at the end of the 1950s. The British new wave, as it came to be known, was a cycle of films between 1959 and 1963 of which the key titles were *Look Back in Anger*, *Room at the Top*, *The Entertainer*, *Saturday Night and Sunday Morning*, *A Taste of Honey*, *A Kind of Loving*, *The Loneliness of the Long Distance Runner*, *Billy Liar* and *This Sporting Life*.[65] These films all shared several common characteristics: their source material in the novels and plays of the 'northern realists', their narrative focus on the working classes, their frank representation of social and sexual mores, and their stark black-and-white cinematography. Most of the new wave films were 'X' certificate fare: they sought to draw adult audiences into cinemas by providing the sort of subject matter that television could not. And most of them were made by film-makers new to the industry: Tony Richardson, Karel Reisz, John Schlesinger, Lindsay Anderson. Film Finances provided completion guarantees for six of the major new wave films – *Room at the Top*, *The Entertainer*, *Saturday Night and Sunday Morning*, *A Taste of Honey*, *A Kind of Loving* and *Billy Liar* – and its archive provides a rich source of material about the political and cultural economies of production.[66]

Room at the Top (1959) – an adaptation of John Braine's novel directed by Jack Clayton and produced by John Woolf for Remus Films backed by a distribution guarantee from British Lion – was the first new wave box-office success: it was also something of an odd-one-out in so far that it was produced not by one of the new groups but by an established producer who was very much part of the commercial mainstream of British cinema. *Room at the Top* was budgeted at £227,779, of which the most expensive individual items were the salaries of stars Simone Signoret (£17,857) and Laurence Harvey (£10,000). The financing followed the standard model of 70 per cent bank loan (Lloyds) with the NFFC providing the end money, and deferments totalling £13,400. The main concern for Film Finances was the combination of a previously untried director (Clayton had directed two shorts in the previous fifteen years) and a schedule that included four weeks on location in Bradford:

> While we know Jack Clayton will do his best, we feel the present location schedule is an extremely difficult one. In addition to that there is no weather allowance. For that reason we feel another week's location should be provided for before the proposition could be considered to be normal. As you will probably not wish to alter the budget at this stage, we are prepared to accept an undertaking to provide it if necessary. I would not be frank, however, if I did not tell you that I think you will be very lucky indeed if this is not ultimately needed.[67]

In the event, an additional contingency of £3,975 was added to the budget to cover a further week of location shooting if necessary. An unusual condition of the guarantee was that Film Finances required the producer to indemnify them against any claim in the event of the delivery of the film being delayed due to intervention by the censors: Woolf had told Garrett that the script had not been submitted to the BBFC for approval before shooting. 'I agree that from the producer's point of view you are absolutely correct in not offering it to the censor at this point and that you will probably be able to get away with most of it as a fait accompli,' Garrett added. 'However, from our point of view I must ask for protection.'[68] In the event, *Room at the Top* came in slightly over budget but without any call on the guarantee.

The Entertainer (1960) – produced by Harry Saltzman and directed by Tony Richardson for Woodfall Films – was more representative of the production ecologies of new wave cinema. Woodfall was a partnership between Saltzman, Richardson and playwright John Osborne. Their first film had been *Look Back in Anger* (1959) – Richardson had directed the play to great acclaim at the Royal Court Theatre in 1956 – for ABPC. While the film drew good notices from the critics, it did little business at the box office. Woodfall therefore experienced some difficulty in putting together the finance for *The Entertainer*, an adaptation of Osborne's play which Richardson had directed at the Royal Court in 1957 with Laurence Olivier reprising his stage role as washed-up music-hall star Archie Rice. Unable to attract a major studio, even with Olivier's name attached, Woodfall turned to Bryanston. The budget for *The Entertainer* came from a loan from the NFFC (£56,500) and two separate loans from Lloyds Bank: one for £75,000 against a distribution guarantee from Bryanston and another for £56,000 against a guarantee from an independent American distributor (Continental Film Distributors).[69] Even so, Woodfall was only able to budget the film through substantial deferments, including Olivier (who deferred two-thirds of his £30,000 fee), Saltzman and Richardson (who each deferred £5,000 of their producer's and director's fees of £11,500 and £10,000 respectively). For once, John Croydon was satisfied with the budget and schedule: 'It seems to be a very practical job and outlines the production hazards quite well . . . I do not doubt that we shall be able to enter into this proposition with pretty easy minds.'[70] The budget for *The Entertainer* was fixed at £192,928.[71]

It soon became apparent that *The Entertainer* would exceed its schedule and budget. Croydon, who was acting as associate producer, reported that the location 'was shockingly unprepared, largely because Harry refused to have a location manager. That's what I've been doing!'[72] Saltzman had to commit money from his own pocket to cover the additional expense: Croydon estimated that 'Harry's own liability (outside the Guarantee) must be in the region of £10,000 plus his deferment'.[73] Saltzman had to ask Bryanston for an additional £6,000: they initially refused but then agreed to provide £4,000 provided the other partners would increase their investments pro rata. In the event, Film Finances – somewhat unusually – loaned Saltzman £1,500 separate to their completion guarantee secured against Woodfall's rights in *Saturday Night and Sunday Morning* and *A Taste of Honey*.[74]

Film Finances had previous experience of Saltzman's poor accounting practices: the final accounts of *The Entertainer* were not forthcoming until September 1960 – by which time the film had opened to mixed reviews and lukewarm box office – and indicated that it had come over budget at a final cost of £205,129. Additional legal costs had been incurred after the principal photography and there was an issue with the insurance for a knee injury to Olivier. Most of the location scenes had to be redubbed as the dialogue was inaudible due to the noise of Morecambe's seagulls. An audit of the production account concluded that the producers were responsible for £5,638 of the overage, leaving Film Finances to advance £3,604.[75] The film failed to recoup its production cost: by 1965 its receipts amounted to only £57,353 plus £22,582 from the Eady levy and £6,000 from its sale to television.[76]

The problematic experience of *The Entertainer* meant that Film Finances gave much closer scrutiny to Woodfall's next film, *Saturday Night and Sunday Morning* (1960), before agreeing to provide a guarantee. *Saturday Night and Sunday Morning*, adapted from his own novel by Alan Sillitoe, was to be directed by Karel Reisz with Richardson as co-producer. John Croydon reckoned that the budget of £114,980 was 'very, very tight'.[77] With no Olivier on board, the cost of artistes was kept to just £8,000 – Albert Finney receiving £2,000 for his starring role as Arthur Seaton – while Saltzman and Richardson took lower producers' fees of £3,050 each. A major saving was made in the script, for which Sillitoe was paid just £7,250 with no separate fee for rights. The production finance was again provided by loans from Lloyds Bank (£81,820) and the NFFC (£28,000), with the balance through a deferment from Twickenham Studios in return for a share of the profits.[78] When the project was submitted to Film Finances, Croydon evidently did not like the script ('It seems unnecessarily sordid and makes out the "hero" to be an amoral parasite, with little or nothing to recommend him'), but his main concerns, as for *Room at the Top*, were the extent of location shooting and the fact that Reisz was an untried director: 'We are dealing with a new director, a completely unknown quantity so far as feature films are concerned, though he has a good reputation in the documentary business . . . I am sure the question of his ability to handle actors will be watched carefully by all concerned during the first few days of the production.'[79]

Croydon's view of Reisz improved over the course of several pre-production meetings. After seeing the schedule and cross-plot, Croydon remarked that 'quite obviously Karel Reiss [*sic*] is a man who understands the technique of film production very thoroughly, and – as a first effort at feature film making – I think one must accept his theory that certain things can be done in a certain way within a given time'. Nevertheless, he was still concerned that 'the location work is very full, and allows no margin for weather delay, and the building schedule is a very, very onerous one'.[80] However, Croydon was mollified when it was suggested that Tony Richardson, whose abilities he respected, would take charge of a second unit. But he reiterated his original point about Reisz: 'I would not consider it beyond the capabilities of say Val Guest – it might be simple to him – but for a man, shall we say bred and born in the documentary world, where perfectionism is, despite limited budgets and enforced speed of production, an axiom, I wonder how he [is] going to fare with this?'[81] In the event, *Saturday Night and Sunday Morning* overran its location schedule by two days but completed its studio scenes on time. Film Finances advanced £3,600 towards the completion, with the film finally costing £120,604.[82] This was a relatively small overcost, especially in relation to *The Entertainer*, and represented a personal triumph for Reisz, who had shown he was capable of directing a feature film on a tight budget.

Saturday Night and Sunday Morning proved to be a major critical and commercial success. After three years it had earned gross distributor's receipts of £399,753 in the United Kingdom and a further £166,511 from the Eady levy. After deducting the cost of production (eventually revised downwards to £116,848 following audit) and Bryanston's distribution fee (£104,871) and expenses (£39,891), this still left a producer's share of over £300,000 in the home market alone. Revenues from foreign territories brought the net profits to £503,380.[83] The profits were divided 65 per cent between Bryanston, the NFFC and Twickenham Studios, with the remaining 35 per cent shared by members of the production group on a complex pro rata agreement. The one individual who seems not to have benefited financially from *Saturday Night and Sunday Morning* was Harry Saltzman, whose share of the profits was paid to ABPC, presumably to pay off its losses on *Look Back in Anger*.[84]

Tony Richardson was back in the director's chair for *A Taste of Honey* (1961), based on the play by Shelagh Delaney first performed at the Theatre Royal, Stratford, in May 1958. On this occasion the NFFC was not involved: the budget of £120,940 was provided through a loan from Lloyds Bank (£84,000) secured against Bryanston's distribution guarantee and an advance of £36,000 from Continental Film Distributors with the remainder as a producer's deferment. Croydon felt that 'this proposition follows the lines one might expect from Tony Richardson' in so far as the script and method of production 'defies convention', but he was persuaded 'that Richardson is a hard worker with a basic sense of responsibility ... I think one has to remember that he comes from a Lancashire family where a spade is called a spade and is an instrument with which to dig!'[85] *A Taste of Honey* was shot entirely on location (hence there were no studio overheads) and Croydon's estimation of Richardson's abilities was proved correct on this occasion when it came in on budget and schedule. Although it was not a box-office hit on the scale of *Saturday Night and Sunday Morning*, *A Taste of Honey* was a critical success and won the Best British Film award from the British Film Academy.[86]

Anglo-Amalgamated Film Distributors was the other major supporter of British new wave cinema: this has been seen as its move towards greater cultural respectability than it enjoyed with the 'Carry On' series. It provided distribution advances for Vic Films for *A Kind of Loving* and *Billy Liar*. These had higher budgets than the Woodfall productions (*The Entertainer* excepted), but producer Joseph Janni – who had come to Britain from Italy in 1939 and had enjoyed a successful career as an independent producer during the 1950s – was able to provide more of the cost from his own resources. *A Kind of Loving* (1962), adapted by Willis Hall and Keith Waterhouse from the novel by Stan Barstow, was budgeted at £148,000, of which the distributor advanced just under half (£70,000, borrowed from the National Provincial Bank) with Janni providing the balance in cash and by deferring his entire fee. Croydon admitted to 'mixed feelings' over the proposition. He recognised that it had 'a first class producing team, which has been associated with Janni on many occasions and for sustained periods', but had doubts about first-time feature director John Schlesinger: 'I know nothing about Schlesinger, but I cannot imagine him being a Tony Richardson, from whose work over the past few years, I imagine this project stems.'[87] An important factor in offering the guarantee was that Film Finances had faith in associate producer Jack Hanbury, 'who is a very reliable man and who has full control of the film'.[88] In the event, *A Kind of Loving* came in slightly under budget at £145,820.[89] Following recovery of the distribution advance, fees and Janni's deferment, the proceeds were divided 66 per cent to the distributor, 30.6 per cent to the producer and 3.4 per cent to Stan Barstow.[90]

Billy Liar (1963), again directed by John Schlesinger and adapted by Hall and Waterhouse from their own play first performed at the Cambridge Theatre, London, in September 1960, was originally budgeted at £198,706, with Janni again deferring his whole fee. Croydon had reservations about the project on the grounds that it included 'much more production hazard than was the case with *A Kind of Loving*, and to that end I feel that we must be much more severe in our attitude toward the proposition than we might have been otherwise'.[91] Film Finances guaranteed *Billy Liar* subject to increasing the budget to £209,000.[92] *Billy Liar* overran its schedule and exceeded its budget by £27,995 but this was not the producer's fault: it was due to the need to replace one of the key parts when the actress playing the role of Liz (Topsy Jane) suffered a nervous breakdown and was replaced by Julie Christie late in the shooting period. This was covered by the producers' insurance and there was no call upon the guarantee. Indeed, Janni was able to claim his rebate on the fee, having made no call upon the guarantee for either *Billy Liar* or *A Kind of Loving*.[93]

The British new wave demonstrated that in the right circumstances independent film production could still be profitable. But market conditions in the film industry rarely remain stable for very long, and by the early 1960s there was already a sense that the environment was changing. *This Sporting Life* (1963) – produced by Karel Reisz and directed by Lindsay Anderson for Independent Artists – was the last of the recognised new wave films. It had a different production ecology in so far as its budget (£197,381) was raised partly from a loan from Lloyds Bank (£145,506) secured against a guarantee from Rank Film Distributors and partly through a further advance from Rank (£51,875) secured through cross-collateralisation against other Independent Artists films (*The Fast Lady* and *Waltz of the Toreadors*).[94] Rank had hitherto been resistant to 'X'-certificate films: its decision to back *This Sporting Life*, which included outbidding Woodfall for the screen rights to David Storey's novel, might suggest that the organisation wanted to 'get in' on the new wave.[95] However, the film met with a mixed reception from critics and did not score at the box office. John Davis drew the lesson that the new wave had run its course. At the end of 1963 he told the Rank Theatre Division's Annual Showmanship Luncheon: 'I do feel that independent producers should take note of public demand and make films of entertainment value. The public has clearly shown that it does not want the dreary kitchen sink dramas.'[96] Davis had never approved of the 'kitchen sink' films and a suspicion has always persisted that the failure of *This Sporting Life* was due as much to Odeon's reluctance to book it as to the quality of the film itself. After thirteen years, *This Sporting Life* had earned a distributor's gross of only £92,612 in the United Kingdom (including £33,629 from the Eady levy) and £128,599 from overseas.[97]

The end of the British new wave also marked the eclipse of Bryanston Films. Bryanston had backed two dozen British films in the early 1960s, but its only outstanding success had been *Saturday Night and Sunday Morning*. Even within the short period in which Bryanston had been operating, the industrial landscape had changed: the bread-and-butter British studio feature was in decline. In March 1962 Bryanston signalled a change of strategy when it announced that it would produce three bigger films at a cost of around £300,000 each in association with US distributor Seven Arts: *Sammy Going South*, *The Small World of Sammy Lee* and *Tom Jones*.[98] In the event, only two of those pictures – *Sammy Going South* and *The Small World of Sammy Lee* – were released under the Bryanston-Seven Arts banner: both were loss-makers.[99] Bryanston's fate was sealed when it lost *Tom Jones* to United Artists when the budget escalated to over £400,000. *Tom Jones* went on to become one of the most successful British films of all time, returning an estimated profit of £3.5 million from worldwide release. Michael Balcon admitted after the fact that its decision to pass up *Tom Jones* spelled the end for Bryanston: 'I can only say that if I had the courage to pawn everything I had and risk it on *Tom Jones* it would have been a wise decision . . . No doubt *Tom Jones* is engraved on my heart.'[100]

Notes

1. *National Film Finance Corporation: Annual Report and Statement of Accounts for the year ended 31 March 1958*, Cmnd. 448 (June 1958), p. 1 (1).
2. Linda Wood, *British Film Industry: BFI Information Guide No. 1* (London: British Film Institute, 1980), Appendix A (unpaginated).
3. 'A Sorry State', *Kinematograph Weekly*, 17 May 1956, p. 4.
4. 'Attendance Decline Rate is Maintained', *Kinematograph Weekly*, 18 April 1957, p. 3; 'Admissions in 1957 Lowest on Record', *Kinematograph Weekly: Studio Review*, 27 March 1958, p. iii.
5. Wood, *British Film Industry*, Appendix A.
6. Ibid.
7. See John Hill, *Sex, Class and Realism: British Cinema 1956–63* (London: British Film Institute, 1986), pp. 35–52; David Docherty, David Morrison and Michael Tracey, *The Last Picture Show? Britain's Changing Film Audience* (London: British Film Institute, 1987), pp. 14–32; and Sue Harper and Vincent Porter, *British Cinema of the 1950s: The Decline of Deference* (Oxford: Oxford University Press, 2003), pp. 243–64.
8. Asa Briggs, *The History of Broadcasting in the United Kingdom Volume V: Competition 1955–1974* (Oxford: Oxford University Press, 1995), p. 1005.
9. John Spraos, *The Decline of the Cinema: An Economist's Report* (London: George Allen & Unwin, 1962), p. 166.
10. Ibid. p. 37.
11. Ibid. p. 38.
12. 'FIDO claims it has saved industry from catastrophe', *Kinematograph Weekly*, 3 September 1959, p. 6.
13. 'The Strength of FIDO', *Kinematograph Weekly*, 3 September 1959, p. 3.
14. 'FIDO All Set to Start', *Kinematograph Weekly*, 24 July 1958, p. 3.
15. British Film Producers' Association Executive Council Minute Book 1957–59: Minutes of a Special Meeting of the Executive Council, 9 October 1958, minute 724 and Annex A.
16. 'A-R breaks through FIDO banner', *Kinematograph Weekly*, 7 January 1960, p. 3.
17. BFPA Executive Council Minute Book 1961–64: Minutes of a meeting of the Executive Council, 4 April 1962, minute 182.
18. BFPA Executive Council Minute Book 1964–66: Minutes of a Special Meeting of the Executive Council, 5 March 1965, minute 192.
19. 'Budget: Less Than a Third of Industry's Needs', *Kinematograph Weekly*, 11 April 1957, p. 3.
20. 'Chancellor Rejects Abolition, But "Helps Small Man"', *Kinematograph Weekly*, 17 April 1958, p. 3.

21. 'Staggering', *Kinematograph Weekly*, 9 April 1958, p. 4.
22. 'At Last!', *Kinematograph Weekly*, 7 April 1960, p. 3.
23. 'ABPC Trading Profit Drops Sharply', *Kinematograph Weekly*, 5 July 1956, p. 6.
24. 'Rank Group Profit Is Down By £2.7 Million', *Kinematograph Weekly*, 4 September 1958, p. 3.
25. 'Pattern Emerging', *Kinematograph Weekly*, 18 December 1958, p. 3.
26. 'Rationalisation Hampering Film Finance', *Kinematograph Weekly*, 13 November 1958, p. 7.
27. 'Third Circuit of 400 Cinemas Agreed by 5 Groups', *Kinematograph Weekly*, 27 November 1958, p. 3.
28. 'A National Problem', *Kinematograph Weekly*, 13 April 1961, p. 4.
29. 'Pattern Emerging', p. 3.
30. 'Heartening Signs Ahead', *Kinematograph Weekly*, 18 December 1958, p. 85.
31. 'Rank Sticks to the Big Film Formula', *Kinematograph Weekly*, 26 February 1959, p. 16.
32. 'Rank Film Distributors of America Is Closing Down', *Kinematograph Weekly*, 19 March 1959, p. 3.
33. 'British films are way ahead at the box office', *Kinematograph Weekly*, 17 December 1959, pp. 6–7.
34. 'St Trinian's Sequel Mixes Comedy and Sex', *Kinematograph Weekly*, 25 April 1957, p. 29.
35. 'Rising Costs Demand Quality', *Kinematograph Weekly: Studio Review*, 12 December 1957, p. 83.
36. *National Film Finance Corporation: Annual Report and Statement of Accounts for the year ended 31 March 1957*, Cmnd. 176 (May 1957), p. 6 (25).
37. 'How to Make a Film', *The Financial Times*, 15 July 1957, p. 6.
38. FFA Financial Correspondence Box 24: List of Films Over Budget, 23 January 1957.
39. BFI Thomas GT 26/14: Minutes of pre-production meeting for *Carry On Sergeant* at Pinewood Studios, 20 March 1958.
40. Ibid.: Contract between Anglo-Amalgamated Film Distributors, Sydney Box and the National Film Finance Corporation, 31 March 1958.
41. BFI Thomas GT/26/10: P. H. Grislingham to Anglo-Amalgamated Film Distributors, 7 January 1959.
42. 'Anglo Provides Surprise Smash Hit of Year', *Kinematograph Weekly*, 18 December 1958, p. 7.
43. 'British films are way ahead at the box office', *Kinematograph Weekly*, 17 December 1959, p. 6.
44. BFI Thomas GT/23/6: Peter Rogers to Stuart Levy, 1 October 1958.
45. Ibid.: Pawley & Malya (chartered accountants) to Peter Rogers, 9 October 1959.
46. 'A Significant Year', *Kinematograph Weekly*, 17 December 1959, p. 99.
47. 'Independents Set Up New Outlet', *Kinematograph Weekly*, 16 April 1959, p. 3.
48. 'Long Shots', *Kinematograph Weekly*, 22 October 1959, p. 4.
49. Michael Balcon, *Michael Balcon presents . . . A Lifetime of Films* (London: Hutchinson, 1969), p. 195.
50. The first features produced under the Bryanston label were *The Battle of the Sexes* (1959), *Cone of Silence* (1960), *The Entertainer* (1960), *Light Up the Sky* (1960), *Saturday Night and Sunday Morning* (1960), *The Boy Who Stole a Million* (1961), *Double Bunk* (1961), *Spare the Rod* (1961), *A Taste of Honey* (1961), *Two and Two Make Six* (1962), *The Quare*

Fellow (1962), *A Prize of Arms* (1962), *The Loneliness of the Long Distance Runner* (1962), *A Place to Go* (1963), *The Girl in the Headlines* (1963), *Ladies Who Do* (1963), *Sammy Going South* (1963) and *The Small World of Sammy Lee* (1963). The supporting features were *The Big Day* (1960), *Linda* (1960), *Dangerous Afternoon* (1961), *The Impersonator* (1961), *The Wind of Change* (1961), *Dilemma* (1962), *Lunch Hour* (1962), *Don't Talk to Strange Men* (1962), *Strongroom* (1962), *Calculated Risk* (1963) and *A Matter of Choice* (1963).

51. Duncan Petrie, 'Bryanston Films: An experiment in co-operative independent film production and distribution', *Historical Journal of Film, Radio and Television*, 38: 1 (2018), pp. 95–115.
52. 'Production', *Kinematograph Weekly*, 20 August 1959, p. 13.
53. FFA Realised Film Box 262: *Battle of the Sexes*: Maurice Foster to Monja Danischewsky, 7 July 1959.
54. Petrie, 'Bryanston Films', p. 102.
55. FFA Realised Film Box 282: *Cone of Silence*: John Croydon to Robert Garrett, 19 October 1959.
56. Ibid.: 'Cone of Silence' – Note for file, 2 October 1959.
57. 'New Film Group', *Kinematograph Weekly*, 5 November 1959, p. 3.
58. Bryan Forbes, *Notes for a Life* (London: Collins, 1974), pp. 291–2.
59. *National Film Finance Corporation: Annual Report and Statement of Accounts for the year ended 31 March 1960*, Cmnd. 1096 (July 1960), p. 3 (7).
60. FFA Realised Film Box 283: *The League of Gentlemen:* Screenplay dated 3 September 1959 and Final Shooting Script dated 2 November 1959.
61. Ibid.: Maurice Foster to Basil Dearden and Michael Relph, 8 April 1960.
62. Ibid.: Relph to Garrett, 15 April 1960.
63. Sally Dux, 'Allied Film Makers: Crime, Comedy and Social Concern', *Journal of British Cinema and Television*, 9: 2 (2012), pp. 202–3.
64. Quoted in Alexander Walker, *Hollywood, England: The British Film Industry in the Sixties* (London: Michael Joseph, 1974), p. 248.
65. See Hill, *Sex, Class and Realism*, pp. 53–66; Roger Manvell, *New Cinema in Britain* (London: Studio Vista, 1969); Arthur Marwick, '*Room at the Top* (1959), *Saturday Night and Sunday Morning* (1960) and the "Cultural Revolution" in Britain', *Journal of Contemporary History*, 19: 1 (1984), pp. 147–52; and Robert Murphy, *Sixties British Cinema* (London: British Film Institute, 1992), pp. 10–33.
66. Sarah Street, 'Film Finances and the British New Wave', *Historical Journal of Film, Radio and Television*, 34: 1 (2014), pp. 23–42.
67. FFA Realised Film Box 245: *Room at the Top*: Robert Garrett to John Woolf, 29 May 1958.
68. Ibid.
69. FFA Realised Film Box 276: *The Entertainer*: Bernard Lewis to Maurice Foster, 6 August 1960. The NFFC loan was later increased to £58,500, the loan against the Bryanston guarantee to £76,000 and the loan against Continental Film Distributors to £58,500.
70. Ibid.: John Croydon to Robert Garrett, 6 August 1959.
71. Ibid.: Maurice Foster to Holly Productions, 2 September 1959.
72. Ibid.: Croydon to Foster, 25 September 1959.
73. Ibid.: Croydon to Foster, 1 October 1959.
74. Ibid.: Agreement between Film Finances and Harry Saltzman, 18 November 1959.

75. Ibid.: Bernard Smith to Tufnell, Satterthwaite & Co., 21 October 1960.
76. Ibid.: Bryanston Films; Revenue Statement No. 57 to 31 October 1965.
77. FFA Realised Film Box 289: *Saturday Night and Sunday Morning*: John Croydon to Robert Garrett, 4 February 1960.
78. Ibid.: G. C. Wheatley to Edward Dryhurst Productions, 20 June 1961.
79. Ibid.: Croydon to Garrett, 6 November 1959.
80. Ibid.: Croydon to Garrett, 23 November 1959.
81. Ibid.: Croydon to Garrett, 4 February 1960.
82. Ibid.: Bernard Smith to Tufnell, Satterthwaite & Co., 21 October 1960.
83. Ibid.: Bryanston Films: Revenue Statement No. 48 to 30 November 1964.
84. Ibid.: Saltzman to Bryanston Films, 17 April 1961.
85. FFA Realised Film Box 310: *A Taste of Honey*: John Croydon to Robert Garrett, 30 May 1960.
86. 'Family fare triumphs at box office', *Kinematograph Weekly*, 14 December 1961, p. 7.
87. FFA Realised Film Box 324: *A Kind of Loving*: John Croydon to Robert Garrett, 14 October 1961.
88. Ibid.: Bernard Smith to Tufnell, Satterthwaite & Co., 14 November 1961.
89. Ibid.: Statement of Production Cost, 3 June 1962.
90. Ibid.: Bernard Lewis to Garrett, 16 October 1961.
91. FFA Realised Film Box 355: *Billy Liar*: John Croydon to Robert Garrett, 6 October 1962.
92. Ibid.: Garrett to Vic Films, 12 October 1962.
93. Ibid.: Bernard Smith to Vic Films, 31 October 1963.
94. BFI Reisz KRE 1/5/9: Rank Film Distributors Ltd: *This Sporting Life*, 29 June 1979.
95. Anthony Aldgate, 'Defining the Parameters of "Quality" Cinema for "the Permissive Society": The British Board of Film Censors and *This Sporting Life*', in Anthony Aldgate, James Chapman and Arthur Marwick (eds), *Windows on the Sixties: Exploring Key Texts of Media and Culture* (London: I. B. Tauris, 2000), p. 21.
96. 'Davis Puts the Crisis in Perspective', *Kinematograph Weekly*, 19 December 1963, p. 123.
97. BFI Reisz KRE 1/5/9: Rank Organisation UK Film Distribution Division: *This Sporting Life*, 7 May 1976.
98. 'Bryanston deals', *Kinematograph Weekly*, 29 March 1962, p. 3.
99. Petrie, 'Bryanston Films', p. 107.
100. Balcon, *A Lifetime of Films*, p. 198.

CHAPTER 12

Hollywood, UK

> Although the British Film Industry appears to have a new lease of life, it is mainly with the American Corporations. Independent production is still fairly dormant, and therefore we are still not in a position to expand our operations any further than outside Europe. (Film Finances)[1]

From a cultural point of view, the 1960s was an exciting decade for British cinema. The sixties were characterised by a vibrant, popular film culture that was both more progressive and more diverse than the 'doldrums era' of the previous decade. Not for the first or the last time, a period of economic and structural instability created the conditions in which cultural creativity could flourish. It was in the early 1960s that the British new wave flowered with films such as *Saturday Night and Sunday Morning*, *A Taste of Honey*, *A Kind of Loving*, *The Loneliness of the Long Distance Runner*, *Billy Liar* and *This Sporting Life*, and that new British stars including Albert Finney, Tom Courtenay, Peter O'Toole, Richard Harris, Rita Tushingham and Julie Christie announced their arrival on the scene. It was in Britain that the exiled American director Joseph Losey and the voluntary émigré Stanley Kubrick made their most acclaimed films, while European *auteur* directors including Michelangelo Antonioni, François Truffaut and Roman Polanski were also drawn by the culture of 'Swinging London'. British cinema experienced a hitherto unprecedented degree of critical and commercial success: no fewer than four British films – *Lawrence of Arabia*, *Tom Jones*, *A Man for All Seasons* and *Oliver!* – won the Academy Award for Best Picture, while another three – *The Knack*, *Blow-Up* and *if . . .* – all won the prestigious Palme d'Or at the Cannes Film Festival. And in 1962 a fantastical secret agent thriller called *Dr No* marked the beginning of what would become the most commercially successful film series in the history of British cinema. Even with the caveat that, as ever, there was a hinterland of lesser films beneath the classics – the sixties were also the decade of such turkeys as *Gonks Go Beat* and *The Bobo* – there is nevertheless much substance to Robert Murphy's claim that 'the 1960s saw a greater number of significant and exciting films made in Britain than at any time before or since'.[2]

British films (or at least some British films) continued to be very successful at the box office in the 1960s. In 1960 the three most successful general releases were all British films – *Doctor in Love*, *Sink the Bismarck!* and *Carry On Constable* – and represented the preference for comedy and war pictures that had characterised the previous decade.[3] The top three general releases of 1961, however, were a more diverse group: a British-made Disney family adventure (*Swiss Family Robinson*), a Hollywood Western (*The Magnificent Seven*) and a British new wave drama (*Saturday Night and Sunday Morning*).[4] From the early 1960s the *Kine*'s annual surveys of the box office differentiated between general releases and what it called 'hard-ticket specials' – big films shown for longer runs at selected cinemas at higher prices: these included *The Guns of Navarone*, *The Longest Day*, *Lawrence of Arabia*, *How the West Was Won*, *Cleopatra*, *The Fall of the Roman Empire*, *My Fair Lady*, *The Sound of Music*, *Doctor Zhivago* and *Oliver!* Among the general releases the James Bond films were the box-office sensation of the decade. *Dr No* – which *Kine* described as 'a bizarre comedy melodrama' – was second-placed in 1962 behind the Cliff Richard musical *The Young Ones* (released several months before *Dr No*) and thereafter a new Bond picture invariably headed the general releases: *From Russia With Love* in 1963, *Goldfinger* in 1964, *Thunderball* in 1966 and *You Only Live Twice* in 1967.[5] The other popular cycle was the 'Carry On' series: *Carry On Constable* in 1960, *Carry On Cruising* in 1962, *Carry On Cleo* in 1964 and *Carry On Doctor* in 1968 were all in the top ten. In 1969 there were two 'Carry Ons' in the top ten: *Carry On Camping* and *Carry On Up the Khyber*. Other successful British films included *Summer Holiday* (second in 1963), *Tom Jones* (fourth in 1963), the Beatles films *A Hard Day's Night* (second in 1964) and *Help!* (second in 1965), *Alfie* (second in 1966), *Born Free* (third in 1966), *The Family Way* (fourth in 1967), *Up the Junction* (second in 1968), *Poor Cow* (fifth in 1968) and *Till Death Us Do Part* (first in 1969). *Oliver!* was the leading 'special presentation' of 1969. The most successful years for British films were 1964, when the top five general releases were British; 1966, when British films accounted for six of the top eight; and 1969, when six British films were again among the top ten general releases.[6] The varied nature of the successful British pictures – comedy, pop musical, social realism, costume drama and spy thriller – demonstrates the diversity of British film culture during the decade; but it also reveals the volatility of popular taste which, other than the Bond and 'Carry On' films, was rather more difficult to predict than in the 1950s.

However, the success of British films at the box office needs to be qualified in several respects. For one thing, an increasing number of British films were either wholly or partly financed by American money. The 'runaway' trend that had emerged during the previous decade became more dominant than ever in the 1960s. From 1964 the *Kine* began to note which of the top British box-office attractions were backed by American money. Of the six British films in the top ten in 1964, for example, two were wholly British-financed (*A Stitch in Time*, *Wonderful Life*) and four were American-financed (*Goldfinger*, *A Hard Day's Night*, *Zulu*, *633 Squadron*).[7] In 1966 there were again two British-financed films in the top general releases (*The Early Bird*, *The Great St Trinian's Train Robbery*), with four American-financed productions (*Thunderball*, *Alfie*, *Born Free*, *Those Magnificent Men in Their Flying Machines*) and three Hollywood-backed British films among the 'special presentations' (*Those Magnificent Men in Their Flying Machines* – which was included in both categories – *Khartoum* and *The Blue Max*).[8] All the Academy Award-winning British films and British Palme d'Or winners were financed by Hollywood. The increasing level of US investment in British cinema was noted at the time. John Terry, managing director of the National Film Finance Corporation, remarked at the end of 1964: 'Not only do over half of all the films for which the British public pays some £60 million a year originate in the United States, but over half of the films which are British in a statutory sense are now being made through the initiative, enterprise and finances of American companies operating in Britain.'[9]

The statistical record provides even more compelling evidence of the extent of the US presence in British production. From 1963 the NFFC reported on the number of British films that were funded in part or in whole by American interests. In 1963, for example, 23 of the 50 British first or co-features exhibited by the two major cinema circuits were American-financed: this amounted to 46 per cent of the total. The percentage of American-backed films rose to 64 per cent in 1965 (31 of 48 films), 72 per cent in 1967 (36 of 50 films) and reached a high of 88 per cent in 1968 (43 of 49 films).[10] This trend is confirmed by other sources. In 1965 the Board of Trade's Working Group on the Film Industry observed that 'there has been a considerable increase in the amount of money which US film organisations, with subsidiary companies in the United Kingdom, are investing in British film production'.[11] And in February 1966 a survey of current production by the *Kine* established that nine of the twelve films currently shooting in British studios were either wholly or partly American-financed (*Fahrenheit 451*, *A Countess from Hong Kong*, *Deadlier Than the Male*, *The Deadly Affair*, *Casino Royale*, *2001: A Space Odyssey*, *The Fearless Vampire Killers*, *Kaleidoscope* and *Prehistoric Women*) and only three were wholly British-financed (*Carry On Screaming*, *Brides of Fu Manchu* and *Daleks Invasion Earth: 2150 AD*).[12]

The American company most closely associated with 'Hollywood UK' in the 1960s was United Artists (UA). UA was different from the other Hollywood majors in that it was a financer-distributor without its own studio facilities: it had always relied upon independent producers for its product and was therefore particularly open to the production arrangements adopted for runaways. Film Finances had guaranteed several films for United Artists in the 1950s, but an internal memorandum records that they found it 'a very impersonal distribution company and although we have given them a number of guarantees, we have had hardly any contact with them'.[13] This changed following the appointment of George H. Ornstein as the head of UA's London office in 1961. Alexander Walker contends that Ornstein – whose background was as a film salesman in Latin America and Europe – 'knew the world sales markets at a level and with a detail certainly not shared by any British film executives, and by hardly any other American production chief in London at that date. By temperament, he was able to talk the artists' language as well as the financiers', and he was ready to go out and bat for a project.'[14] UA was popular with independent film-makers because it offered more generous terms than other studios – usually a fifty-fifty share of profits following deduction of distribution fees and expenses and the production cost – and was less interventionist.[15] Its British films in the early 1960s were conventional subjects such as the military drama *Tunes of Glory* (1960) and the naval war picture *The Valiant* (1962).

However, it was the success of the James Bond films that really put UA on the map. *Dr No* was produced for a final cost of £392,022: after eighteen months on general release it had returned a producer's share of over US $2.8 million from international distribution.[16] This was enough for UA – against the received wisdom that sequels were usually subject to the law of diminishing returns – to agree to increased budgets of £700,000 for *From Russia With Love*, £1 million for *Goldfinger* and £1.5 million for *Thunderball*: the films' profits increased in line with their budgets.[17] UA's other successful British films included *Tom Jones, 633 Squadron, A Shot in the Dark, A Hard Day's Night* and *Help!*. At the end of 1965 *Kine* reported that 'United Artists has had another great year and there seems no end to its marvellous run of successes. There is no doubt that UA has had the greatest number of successes on release – despite the fact that it did not have the benefit of a new James Bond picture this year.'[18]

It was *Tom Jones* (1963) which – perhaps to a greater extent even than the James Bond films – best exemplified the 'Hollywood UK' trend. Woodfall Films had hitherto been associated with the British new wave – *Look Back in Anger, The Entertainer, Saturday Night and Sunday Morning, A Taste of Honey* and *The Loneliness of the Long Distance Runner* – but *Tom Jones* marked a transition from modestly budgeted social realist films to a more flamboyant (and expensive) costume drama. Woodfall took the project to United Artists when Bryanston backed out after the estimated budget rose above £300,000. *Tom Jones* was budgeted at £412,374 when it was submitted to Film Finances for a guarantee of completion. John Croydon – who described the script as 'a rather ponderous restoration comedy' – felt that 'this is a most hazardous production' and had a long list of specific points including the problematic animal sequences and under-budgeting in relation to location and wardrobe. He was also concerned about Richardson's unorthodox working methods, given the scope of the film: 'One might think that, with the aid of his doctor, the pills prescribed and the particular form of unusual alcohol which he enjoys at the moment, that Richardson himself can sustain the effort for the period, but one wonders if the production team are prepared to go to such lengths and sustain the needed effort?'[19] Nevertheless, Film Finances agreed to guarantee *Tom Jones* despite their reservations – an indication of the importance of the long-term relationship with both producer and studio – though on condition that the contingency was increased from the 'ludicrously low' amount of £28,000 to £45,000.[20]

Almost immediately Film Finances had reason to regret their decision. It soon became apparent that Richardson was paying no heed to either budget or schedule: he ignored the injunction to 'cast to budget' and one of his first acts was to hire a helicopter (not included in the budget) to film aerial shots of the hunt sequence. In August 1962 Robert Garrett wrote to George Ornstein to express his concern about the escalating costs:

> We have hitherto found Woodfall a most business like concern and Tony Richardson one of those directors who knows what he is doing and what he can do. He is also a director who is capable, like most really good directors, of compromising when

needs be. I am wondering, and I hope I am wrong in this, if there might not be a slight tendency on this occasion, now they are connected with a big company operating on the scale that UA do rather than with a minor British company such as Bryanston, that they may be getting the sort of feeling (which you and I have noticed among certain other producers), that cost does not matter any more.[21]

Tom Jones would eventually cause a *caesura* in the relationship between Film Finances on the one hand and Woodfall Films and United Artists on the other. Film Finances believed that Woodfall had hidden the true extent of the overcost – which after ten weeks was estimated at around £45,000 – and felt that much of it arose from 'improvements' to the film 'which they have deliberately undertaken for which they have had in general United Artists' blessing'.[22] On 2 October Film Finances informed Woodfall and UA that 'we have decided to exercise our right to take over the production'.[23] Woodfall's solicitors demanded payment of the full overcost and accused Film Finances of withholding funds in a punitive manner.[24] Garrett stuck to his position that Film Finances was not liable for additional expenditure incurred by the producers without consulting the guarantor. The correspondence became increasingly acrimonious until the two parties agreed to sign a Deed of Variation which amended the original guarantee agreement: Film Finances agreed to pay Woodfall its no-claim bonus in return for Woodfall indemnifying the guarantor against any further costs and liabilities arising from the film.[25] *Tom Jones* would be the last time that Film Finances provided a guarantee for Woodfall Films, but it had also soured relations with United Artists. An internal memorandum reveals that Garrett was not happy that UA had sided with Richardson and had apparently allowed him wilfully to exceed his budget: 'United Artists appear, presumably for political reasons to keep Tony Richardson happy, to have taken what we consider a short-sided [*sic*] view and supported the production company in insisting contrary to what it had earlier said, that the entire responsibility for the overcost should be ours.' 'This may be politic as far as United Artists is concerned,' he concluded, 'but as I have already pointed out the production company in this case was perfectly capable of taking care of a great part of the overcosts which it had brought about.'[26]

Hollywood's increasing investment in the British production sector in the 1960s has inevitably provoked debate over the extent to which British cinema genuinely was British any longer. The issue was debated in Parliament on several occasions. Labour MP Roy Wilson, minister of state at the Board of Trade, argued that it was the cultural investment rather than the source of the finance that mattered when he told the House of Commons, 'the fact is that the Americans financed *Lawrence of Arabia, Becket, Tom Jones, The Knack, Alfie, Born Free, A Hard Day's Night* and *Help!*. These are all obviously British in origin and illustrate a blossoming rather than a smothering of British ideas and talent on the screen.'[27] However, Lord Willis (former Ealing and BBC scriptwriter Ted Willis) disagreed: 'It might be considered that these films help our image abroad. I am afraid that even this is not as much as we would hope. These films fly the Union Jack for quota purposes over here, but the moment they leave our territorial waters the British flag is hauled down and the Stars and Stripes is run up in its place.'[28] He cited the case of *Lawrence of Arabia*, which drew money from the Eady levy as a British quota film but was submitted as an American film to the Acapulco Film Festival in 1963. (The Board of Trade accepted the explanation of distributor Columbia Pictures that this had been a mistake by the festival organisers due to confusion over the licence to import a print from the United States.[29]) On balance, however, the consensus seems to have been that it was cultural rather than economic capital that mattered. Looking back on the period in his book *Hollywood, England*, Alexander Walker averred: 'The nationality of a film industry, considered in its narrowest definition, does not really matter . . . Thus xenophobia should not make us condemn the American investment in our films throughout the 1960s – though it certainly encouraged us in the vice of remittance men everywhere, which is "dependence".' 'The positive aspect', he suggested, 'is that American confidence lent the British industry drive and impetus and gave its film-makers a far wider creative horizon than anyone thought available in the previous decade.'[30]

Other caveats need to be lodged about the popularity of British films in the 1960s. It remained the case that for every film that scored at the box office there were several that failed. The most generous estimate suggests that around 40 per cent of British films returned a profit to the producer, while 30 per cent broke even and 30 per cent made a loss: John Davis, however, suggested in 1966 that eight out of ten British films lost money.[31] The British Film Producers' Association estimated in 1965 that the average producer's share of a British first feature was £54,000, and that as 85 per cent of the films produced by its members over the last three years had cost over £100,000, it was 'therefore inescapable that a substantial majority of British first features fail to recover their costs from their UK distribution'.[32] However, the most successful films evidently did very well indeed. United Artists was on a particularly hot streak in the early 1960s. *Goldfinger* broke the house record at the Odeon, Leicester Square, where it grossed £81,000 over a six-week period (the previous record of £52,000 was held by *From Russia With Love*) and UA 'expected the total box office take in the UK to come out eventually at something over £2 million . . . [The] distributors' gross for the country as a whole would probably be as high as £1 million.' The Bond film returned a higher-than-usual distributor's gross because as well as the circuit release 'every independent [exhibitor] who could get hold of it would play it' and the distributor was therefore able to demand a higher percentage of the box-office receipts.[33] Further evidence that the big pictures could return handsome profits was provided by the head of United Artists' British distribution subsidiary Monty Morton:

> So far as exports were concerned Mr Morton took *Tom Jones* as his main example. He estimated that the distributor's gross on this throughout the world would probably be about £7 million. After deducting advertising expenses of say 10% and an average distributor's commission of say 35% and print costs, etc, that would leave about £3.5 million as the producer's share. Under the contract after the cost of the

film (some £480,000) had been paid off, the profits (some £3 million) were divided equally between United Artists who put up 100% of the finance, and Woodfall Productions (Tony Richardson and John Osborne) who inspired, wrote, produced and directed the film.[34]

United Artists scored another major hit with *A Hard Day's Night*, which grossed £711,000 on its London release and 'is overtaking the outstandingly successful *Tom Jones* and is hard on the heels of the record-breaking *From Russia With Love*'.[35] These were all exceptional cases, of course: UA expected that the 'normal return for a successful film would be £90,000 or so'. On balance the company felt that 'film production was still a paying activity'.

At the same time, however, film production costs continued to rise during the 1960s. In 1963 F. L. Thomas, managing director of the British division of Rank Film Distributors, told the *Kine*: 'Today, the cost of "an averagely good, well-polished, well-starred picture" was £200,000–£250,000, though there was the occasional "sleeper" made for £80,000–£100,000. For a truly international picture one had to think in terms of upwards of £500,000.'[36] John Davis suggested that 'a realistic budget for a totally British production is from £250,000 to £400,000'.[37] Even an economical producer such as Hammer Film Productions was affected by rising costs. In 1964 managing director James Carreras said that while in the late 1950s Hammer could produce a first feature for £80,000 and make a profit in the home market, the cost had now doubled while the return remained the same.[38] Hammer – best known for a cycle of Gothic horror films beginning with *The Curse of Frankenstein* in 1957 – was one of the most successful British producers of the decade: Carreras claimed that it was 'the only truly British independent production organisation remaining'.[39] In 1968 it was presented with the Queen's Award to Industry 'in recognition of export achievements'.[40] The company's accounts submitted in support of its application reveal the increasing importance of overseas revenues. In 1965 Hammer had received total payments from film distribution of £1,031,836, of which 47 per cent (£488,605) was from overseas distribution: the value of foreign earnings rose to 74 per cent in 1966 (£966,903 of a total of £1,338,478) and 82 per cent in 1967 (£1,257,289 of the total of £1,540,747).[41]

There was evidently much variation in budgets and costs. Nevertheless, the Film Finances Archive reveals some patterns and trends. The most evident of these is that films backed by American studios generally had significantly more luxurious budgets than wholly British-financed films. In the early 1960s, for example, even the more expensive British-financed independent productions, such as *The Entertainer* (£205,129), *The Day the Earth Caught Fire* (£213,581) and *The Wrong Arm of the Law* (£233,570), cost less than American-backed films such as *Tunes of Glory* (£267,731), *The Valiant* (£245,439) and *Dr No* (£392,022), while at the lower end of the budget range the most economical British films, such as *Peeping Tom* (£133,394), *Saturday Night and Sunday Morning* (£116,848) and *A Taste of Honey* (£120,329), cost significantly less. While it has to be borne in mind that American companies tended towards the more expensive location and action pictures, it was not just production values that affected costs. Anatole de Grunwald's production of *The VIPs* (1963) for MGM, for example, was an ensemble drama budgeted at a staggering £982,142 and finally costing £1,071,314: the inflated cost was due largely to the fees and expenses paid to Elizabeth Taylor and Richard Burton, whose joint remuneration of £530,000 accounted for 54 per cent of the budget and 78 per cent of the total cast budget of £683,038.[42]

There is much evidence of the escalating costs of American runaways during the 1960s. *Zulu* (1964) – produced by director Cy Endfield and star Stanley Baker and backed by Paramount and Joseph E. Levine's Embassy Pictures, which shared the distribution rights – was budgeted at £666,554.[43] Film Finances was cautious about guaranteeing the film: Garrett confided 'that we were very far from keen on undertaking anything of this sort' on account of its size and extensive location shooting.[44] *Zulu* was far from a happy production – Endfield was no diplomat and upset members of the unit on location in South Africa – but in the end it was completed under budget. (The press book for *Zulu* claimed that it cost US $3.5 million – double the actual cost – though this was probably a case of Joseph Levine wanting to make the film appear even bigger than it was: the inflated figure might also have included the promotional costs.) Twentieth Century–Fox co-financed Ivan Foxwell's production of *The Quiller Memorandum* (1966) with the Rank Organisation. The budget was £956,339: the most expensive items were story and script (Harold Pinter was paid £17,500 plus 1 per cent of the profits for adapting Adam Hall's novel) and artistes (Alec Guinness receiving £89,286 – equivalent to US $250,000 – for what amounted to a glorified cameo as the spymaster Pohl). John Croydon noted that the film 'is obviously expected to be a top quality job . . . Obviously big risks apply to a film of this magnitude; the distributors, especially perhaps the Americans, will want the best possible film and usually this is achieved without much reference to the cost.'[45] However, Croydon had faith in director Michael Anderson, who had made *The Dam Busters*, *Around the World in 80 Days* and *Operation Crossbow*. Anderson justified this confidence: *The Quiller Memorandum* came in £43,602 under budget.[46]

For British independent producers not attached to one of the majors, however, there was no such largesse. In the early 1960s most independent producers were 'geared to production budgets of about £150,000'.[47] The British films of Joseph Losey are a good case in point. *The Servant* (1963) – the first of Losey's critically acclaimed collaborations with playwright Harold Pinter – was initially budgeted at £162,160, of which the NFFC advanced £33,017 with the balance secured against a guarantee from Elstree Distributors.[48] The budget was reduced to £141,725 through deferments by Losey, Pinter, co-producer Norman Priggen and star Dirk Bogarde.[49] Losey agreed not to draw half his director's fee of £10,000 'until such time as the picture is considered "safe"'.[50] *The Servant* was completed for a small overcost. John Croydon's assessment of *King and Country* (1964) – Losey's film of John Wilson's play *Hamp* about the injustice of military executions during the First World War – indicates that he did not think it a very commercial prospect: 'It is in the hands of very professional people, who obviously intend to set out to accomplish a purpose, i.e. a subject of some social significance, the entertainment value of which I personally question, for a low budget, but containing star names for box-office attraction.'[51] Even with a low budget (£82,728) there were problems in raising the finance. Producer Daniel Angel revealed: 'The NFFC are not in and . . . we are not borrowing any money from the bank.'[52] Losey would enjoy significantly larger budgets when he made films for American studios: these included *Modesty Blaise* (1966) for Fox (£1.2 million) and *Boom!* (1968) for Universal (£1.5 million). Whether the films themselves were any better in quality is another matter entirely.

The demise of Bryanston Films left Anglo-Amalgamated Film Distributors as the leading independent British distributor of the early and mid-1960s. Anglo had sponsored the 'Carry On' films since 1958 and produced a series of Edgar Wallace thrillers at Merton Park Studios between 1960 and 1964, but it had loftier ambitions. In 1965 Anglo-Amalgamated announced an investment of £3 million in ten pictures: managing director Nat Cohen claimed that 'without a doubt we will be the largest British production firm in 1965'.[53] Its biggest critical success was *Darling* (1965), producer Joseph Janni and director John Schlesinger's third collaboration following *A Kind of Loving* and *Billy Liar*. *Darling* was initially budgeted at £353,949: this was reduced to £331,000 by deferments. Laurence Harvey was offered 10 per cent of the distributor's gross receipts from the Western hemisphere instead of taking a deferment.[54] Bad weather on the Italian location meant that the film exceeded its schedule by thirteen days and its budget by £37,000.[55] Film Finances felt that 'it would appear from the weekly Cost Statements that a good deal of money is being spent on "improving" the film'.[56]

Darling was always likely to be too expensive to recoup its costs from the British market, though it had been produced without an international distribution deal. In the event, it was picked up by Joseph E. Levine's Embassy Pictures, which paid an advance of US $1 million for distribution rights outside the United Kingdom.[57] After a year Embassy reported distributor's gross receipts of $2,287,681, but a dispute arose over the payment of Laurence Harvey's percentage.[58] Robert Garrett also suspected that Embassy had over-stated its publicity expenditure and expenses.[59] Janni was not happy with the terms on which Anglo had sold the international distribution rights. He wrote to Cohen:

> The very last time we lunched together you said to me that I should make films with you instead of the Americans and that by so doing, I would most probably be financially better off . . . It is obvious that when it was agreed you should receive a commission of 15%, the intention was that you should receive each commission for the work of selling the film all over the world. You have made one sale to Levine and entrusted him with selling the film in various countries. Why should I now pay a commission to Joe Levine for selling the film and then again 15% to you, not for selling the film but just for collecting the money?[60]

Levine was entitled to 30 per cent of the distributor's gross receipts in the United States and 10 per cent on other foreign sales. In the event, the producer's share from *Darling* amounted to £354,104: £123,780 from the United Kingdom (including the Eady payment) and £230,324 from overseas. Following repayment of advances from Anglo-Amalgamated, the NFFC and Film Finances, Janni was left with £3,944 to share with Anglo, Schlesinger, writer Frederick Raphael and star Dirk Bogarde, who had all deferred part of their fees.[61]

The major combines were now focusing on their role as distributors and exhibitors. Following a hiccup in the late 1950s, the Rank Organisation recorded a consolidated profit of £4 million in 1960. This included a profit of £217,000 on film production and distribution compared to a loss of £875,000 the previous year. Lord Rank told shareholders: 'The whole pattern of our film production has been modified to meet the changed conditions in the industry, and I am pleased to be able to report that the steps taken have justified our expectations.'[62] Rank's profits continued on an upward curve: the group reported trading profits of £11.2 million in 1963, £16.9 million in 1964 and £23.5 million in 1965. However, the proportion of Rank's profits that came from its film production and distribution activities was declining. Since the 1950s the Rank Organisation had diversified into other leisure and entertainment markets including bowling alleys and bingo halls. And in 1956 it had bought the overseas manufacturing and marketing rights for the 'rectograph' photocopying process patented in the United States by the Haloid Company.[63] By the mid-1960s over 50 per cent of Rank's profits came from outside the film industry: its Rank Xerox subsidiary was the most successful branch of the business. John Davis reported: 'I am encouraged by the improving earnings from our largely unfructified capital expenditure on activities which are designed to attract leisure money, as well as by the splendid progress of Rank Xerox.'[64]

Rank's most consistently successful films during the 1960s were the 'Carry On' films, which the corporation took over from Anglo-Amalgamated in 1965. Even so, it is evident that the financial margins were tight for films produced essentially for the home market. John Davis was impressed by *Don't Lose Your Head* (1966) – the first two films for Rank dropped the 'Carry On' prefix – and told producer Peter Rogers that 'you put in some pretty good production values at a viable figure'.[65] *Don't Lose Your Head* was budgeted at £249,538 but Rogers brought it in significantly under budget at £215,152.[66] However, there was evidently pressure on Rogers to keep costs down. Rank rejected Rogers's original budget of £228,512 for *Carry On Up the Khyber* (1968): 'Frankly the Board will not accept this figure on the score that it is uneconomic and cannot help but show a loss situation. The maximum we are prepared to put up is £200,000.'[67] In the event, Rogers provided a personal guarantee to cover the additional expenditure in return for a share of the profits: the final cost of *Carry On Up the Khyber* was £235,637.[68] Rank's accountants also questioned the budget of £208,354 for *Carry On Camping* (1969). This prompted an extraordinary response from Rogers which made clear his growing frustration with Rank's *modus operandi*:

> Now, in spite of the increased costs of so many facets of film production, you will see from the enclosed breakdown of comparative figures that I am, by my own

peculiar method of production, devising a means of presenting each subject more economically than the last – this in spite of the fact that I am neither a magician nor a mathematician nor a company secretary nor one in a position to impose charges for imagined increases of otherwise normal facilities. I am a writer first and a producer second.[69]

Rogers must have felt vindicated when *Carry On Up the Khyber* and *Carry On Camping* both featured in the top ten films of 1969, but nevertheless Rank's parsimony demonstrates the tight margins involved in the production of films for the home market.

However, as the decade went on Rank's strategy was to focus on fewer but bigger films: it produced fewer films in-house – exemplified by the 'Doctor' and Norman Wisdom comedies – and instead offered distribution guarantees and facilities for independent producers. Rank would continue to finance around ten British pictures a year, but would also look to make deals with international partners, which often involved providing distribution guarantees for different hemispheres.[70] A fairly representative example would be *The Ipcress File* (1965) – produced by Harry Saltzman and directed by Sidney J. Furie – with a budget of £309,261 raised through a loan from the Bank of America secured against distribution guarantees from Rank for the Eastern hemisphere and Universal Pictures for the Western hemisphere.[71] The more expensive end of the budget range was exemplified by *The Heroes of Telemark* (1965), a war picture in the tradition of *The Guns of Navarone* produced by Benjamin S. Fisz costing a reported £2 million. 'Never before have we linked up with an American company on a film venture on this really big scale,' said John Davis.[72] On this occasion the distribution was split between Rank and Columbia. In contrast, Rank advanced the full budget of £1,056,211 for *The Long Duel* (1967) – a Northwest Frontier adventure developed by Sydney Box and produced by director Ken Annakin following Box's retirement – with Paramount taking a negative pick-up for US distribution.[73]

The Associated British Picture Corporation remained the less adventurous of the two vertically integrated combines. It started the decade by announcing an investment of £2 million in eleven films: the programme was trumpeted as the 'biggest ever produced by ABPC', though the inclusion of several parochial comedies – including vehicles for Charlie Drake (*Petticoat Pirates*) and Tony Hancock (*The Rebel*) – would suggest that its ambitions were limited to the domestic market.[74] In 1962 ABPC announced overall trading profits of £5.8 million: these included £3.2 million from television and £2.6 million from film production, distribution and exhibition. The corporation bought a 50 per cent stake in Anglo-Amalgamated Film Distributors and set up Elstree Distributors in association with the Rank Organisation in order 'to enlarge the supply of British films for the cinemas': the first film to be produced under this arrangement was *The Young Ones* (1962).[75] The Cliff Richard musicals of the early 1960s – *The Young Ones*, *Summer Holiday* and *Wonderful Life* – were ABPC's major hits of the decade. However, the corporation's profits from film production and distribution were declining: ABPC was more exposed to the decline of cinema-going than Rank due to its focus on the domestic market.[76]

By the end of the decade ABPC was an ailing giant that had all but ceased active film production. This made it a ripe target for takeover. The context for the acquisition of ABPC by EMI (Electric and Musical Industries) was similar to what was happening in the US film industry in the late 1960s, where most of the major studios were bought by large corporations whose interests were not solely in the film industry. EMI's business was in music-recording and electrical equipment: in that sense its move into the film industry was an extension of its existing show business interests. It had bought Leslie Grade and Bernard Delfont's talent agency in 1967, and the Shipman-King cinema circuit. ABPC had substantial capital interests in the film industry – including 270 cinemas, a major studio facility (Elstree), a 50 per cent stake in Anglo-Amalgamated Film Distributors and a 50 per cent stake in Thames Television – but it had lost direction. In February 1968 EMI bought the 25 per cent stake in ABPC owned by Warner-Seven Arts for £9.5 million and declared that it intended to make an offer for the rest of the company.[77] Early in 1969 ABPC's board rejected an offer of £34 million from EMI on the grounds that it undervalued the company: ABPC also fought the takeover by proposing to increase its own share capital by £5 million by creating 20 million additional shares.[78] When ABPC rejected an increased offer a few weeks later it prompted a short but fierce hostile takeover which ended with EMI owning 50.3 per cent of ABPC shares.[79]

It soon became apparent that EMI had ambitious plans to restart ABPC's production programme. In April 1969 Bryan Forbes was appointed head of production for EMI-Elstree Films and managing director of Elstree Studios. Bernard Delfont, who became the new chief executive of ABPC, declared that 'it is the intention for Elstree Studios to produce a steady stream of major films aimed at the international market'.[80] Forbes, an actor turned writer turned director and producer, had extensive experience of the production side of the British film industry: he had set up Beaver Films with Richard Attenborough, had been involved in the co-operative venture Allied Film Makers in the early 1960s, and had directed several British features including *Whistle Down the Wind*, *The L-Shaped Room* and *The Wrong Box*. In August 1969 Forbes announced a programme of fifteen films which he averred amounted to 'the most ambitious attempt to revitalise the British film industry in twenty years'.[81]

British Lion Films remained the major supporter of British independent production in the 1960s. Following the travails of the previous decade, British Lion returned to profit in the early 1960s. In 1961 it announced trading profits of £755,952 for the previous financial year, including a profit of £200,087 on production and distribution arising largely from the success of *The Pure Hell of St Trinian's*, *Two-Way Stretch* and *Saturday Night and Sunday Morning*. Managing director David Kingsley explained: 'We have made it our policy to stimulate and sustain the film that is different . . . I feel that the successful film can do better today in this country than ever before and the successful British film can do better abroad than ever before.'⁸² British Lion's profits increased again in 1962 and it was able to pay a dividend on the government-held preference shares for the first time.⁸³ With British Lion returning to profit, the NFFC was finally in a position to sell its interest in the company. In late 1963 the NFFC exercised its right to buy back the share capital of British Lion Films held by the five independent directors (Kingsley, Frank Launder, Sidney Gilliat, John and Roy Boulting).⁸⁴ At the end of November the directors were offered an opportunity to buy the company themselves, but the short deadline (31 December) meant they were unable to raise the capital of £1.5 million in time.⁸⁵ They argued that it would be preferable to maintain government ownership of British Lion in order for it to provide an effective counter to the Rank/ABPC duopoly. Kingsley told NFFC chairman Sir Nutcombe Hume that the government's support for British Lion 'is a factor of enormous psychological importance, and in our view the company's ability to bargain with the major combines is greatly assisted by everybody's awareness that the British taxpayer is present, if invisible, at the negotiating table'.⁸⁶

At the end of 1963 the NFFC issued a prospectus offering British Lion for sale for a price of £1.6 million: the corporation was to maintain one voting share which would give it a veto over any future decision to sell the company – a safeguard against the possibility that the Shepperton Studios site might be sold for property development. In the event, the Board of Trade received three bids for British Lion: from consortiums headed by Sydney Box and Michael Balcon and from the Freedom Group which held interests in publishing. A fourth bid by Sir John Woolf was withdrawn on the grounds that the NFFC's nominal £1 shareholding meant that the government 'would remain in virtual permanent control of the company thereby depriving the investors and management of powers normally reserved to them in any commercial undertaking'.⁸⁷ The Box group had emerged as an early favourite and seems to have been supported by the NFFC. The group – which also included Lord Willis, William MacQuitty, Michael Bromhead and Victor Hoare – was backed by the Standard Industrial Trust. It proposed to operate British Lion as an independent distributor supporting eight to twelve films a year, of which half would be 'prestige' pictures costing around £500,000. However, their cash offer of £1.3 million was short of the offer price and the bid was posited on the NFFC maintaining a preferred shareholding of £300,000. Box's offer was therefore deemed unacceptable.⁸⁸ It may also have been undermined when the chairman of the Standard Industrial Trust told the NFFC that he had advised Box not to proceed with the offer on the grounds – similar to Woolf's – 'that the conditions attaching to the sale ... are too restrictive to make it a suitable proposition to which to invite members of the public to subscribe, and to give the directors a reasonable degree of commercial and financial discretion in running the business'.⁸⁹ The Freedom Group, led by Edward Martell, offered £1.6 million which it proposed to raise from around 100,000 small investors, with no individual owning more than 7.5 per cent of the company: this was the model on which it had recently acquired the games manufacturer Waddington's and the *New Daily* newspaper.⁹⁰ While the Freedom Group's bid, unlike Box's, met the terms of the sale, the NFFC did not favour it on the grounds that the group 'have not the necessary film knowledge behind them' and 'would be bound to run into great difficulties with the militant film trade unions'.[91]

This left Michael Balcon's group. This comprised Balcon, the American distributor Walter Reade, who had been involved with some of Bryanston's films, Neme Enterprises (the management company of Beatles manager Brian Epstein) and eight other partners who would work as semi-autonomous producers within the new British Lion: Tony Richardson and John Osborne, Joseph Janni and John Schlesinger, Frank Launder and Sidney Gilliat and John and Roy Boulting. The group offered £1.6 million, of which £800,000 was put up by the partners themselves, £700,000 was in the form of a loan by Hambros Bank and £100,000 would be raised through a share issue.[92] The Board of Trade preferred Balcon's bid, which it felt would be 'a highly satisfactory outcome. He has succeeded in attracting to his group some of the most successful and lively talent in the film producing world ... The strength of the supporting cast is such as to outweigh any doubts one might have about Sir Michael Balcon personally.'[93] An important factor was that the group 'will have the advantage of the proven managerial skill of Mr Kingsley, the Boulting Brothers, and Messrs Launder and Gilliat, but the extreme approach of these men to the big circuits will be tempered by the presence of the other members of the Group'.[94] Accordingly it was the Balcon group's bid that was recommended by the Board of Trade, which was 'satisfied that this Group would run the business well in the best interests of independent film production and at the same time remain reasonably, while not over belligerently, independent'.[95]

The new management group assumed control of British Lion in April 1964: the board comprised Balcon (chairman), David Kingsley (vice-chairman), Sir Lionel Heald, Baroness Wootton and a representative of Hambros Bank. Balcon sought to reassure the trade that the new management 'regard the functions we have now undertaken as a public trust to ensure that the British film industry remains open to the independent producer of talent, imagination and quality'.[96] However, two of the production groups never made any films for British Lion: Richardson and Osborne were too busy with Woodfall, while Janni and Schlesinger were committed to Anglo-Amalgamated for *Darling*. The successful 'in-house' films were made by British Lion's old guard Launder and Gilliat (*The Great St Trinian's Train Robbery*, 1966) and the Boultings (*The Family Way*, 1966). Overall the new British Lion would prove rather less successful than the previous regime. In 1965 its net profits were down by 33 per cent on the previous year from £230,384 to £153,440.[97] It was reported that projects from independent producers submitted to British Lion 'have been few and generally below the required standard in the present conditions in the market'. Balcon suggested that the problem arose 'largely from the ability of American controlled companies with long established distribution facilities throughout the world to attract the proven talent with offers of large scale finance and terms with which we have not deemed it prudent to compete'.[98]

British Lion's inability to compete with American budgets was exemplified by the case of *Modesty Blaise*. In June 1964 it was announced that 'a lavish, spectacular production of *Modesty Blaise* will be the first major production from the new British Lion film company'.⁹⁹ In February 1965 *Modesty Blaise* was included in British Lion's production programme at a budget of £600,000.¹⁰⁰ At this stage the film – based on the *Evening Standard* comic strip written by Peter O'Donnell chronicling the adventures of a glamorous female adventurer – was to have been produced by Joseph Janni and directed by Sidney Gilliat. In the event, however, British Lion lost the project, which Janni took to Twentieth Century–Fox and was directed by Joseph Losey with a budget of £1.2 million.¹⁰¹ For Balcon it must have seemed like *Tom Jones* all over again as an American studio with deeper pockets poached the film from the smaller British company. As it happened, British Lion might not have regretted losing *Modesty Blaise* too much: Losey's film – starring a miscast Italian art-house darling Monica Vitti and Dirk Bogarde as a decidedly camp villain – was a glossy but shallow extravaganza that failed to recover its cost despite some favourable notices. But the episode was symptomatic of wider problems in the industry. Early in 1966 British Lion announced that it was reducing output 'as a matter of commercial prudence'.¹⁰² Balcon stood down as chairman later in the year and immediately launched a bid to buy British Lion in association with Walter Reade: the offer was rejected by the board of directors.

By the mid-1960s there was a sense in which there were really two film industries in Britain. On the one hand there was a domestic British cinema exemplified by films such as the Cliff Richard musicals and the 'Carry On' comedies: these films were budgeted in the expectation of returning a (small) profit from the domestic market. On the other hand there was an international British cinema backed by American money and exemplified by the James Bond series and expensively produced historical and costume pictures such as *Tom Jones*, *Zulu*, *Khartoum* and *A Man for All Seasons*. The ascendancy of 'Hollywood UK' gave rise to concerns about the future of wholly British-financed production and what that might entail for an indigenous national cinema. In particular, the role of the NFFC came under renewed scrutiny. At the same time the increasing dependence on American finance – by the later years of the decade it was estimated that over 80 per cent of British films were backed by US dollars – left a metaphorical sword of Damocles hanging over the head of the British film industry. What would happen if the Americans were to pack up and go home?

Notes

1. FFA General Correspondence Box 21: Bernard Smith to Albert E. Marten, 1 March 1965.
2. Robert Murphy, *Sixties British Cinema* (London: British Film Institute, 1992), p. 278.
3. 'It's Britain 1, 2, 3 again in the 1960 box-office stakes', *Kinematograph Weekly*, 15 December 1960, pp. 8–9.
4. 'Family fare triumphs at box office', *Kinematograph Weekly*, 14 December 1961, pp. 6–7.
5. 'Three British films head the general releases', *Kinematograph Weekly*, 13 December 1962, p. 6.

6. Richard Farmer, Laura Mayne, Duncan Petrie and Melanie Williams, *Transformation and Tradition in 1960s British Cinema* (Edinburgh: Edinburgh University Press, 2019), pp. 354–62.
7. 'British Films Romp Home – Fill First Five Places', *Kinematograph Weekly*, 17 December 1964, pp. 6–7.
8. 'Britain dominates top ten releases', *Kinematograph Weekly*, 17 December 1966, pp. 6–7.
9. 'Where have all the young men gone?', *Kinematograph Weekly*, 17 December 1964, p. 10.
10. *National Film Finance Corporation: Annual Report and Statement of Accounts for the year ended 31 March 1969*, Cmnd. 4094 (June 1969), p. 4 (13).
11. TNA BT 258/2038: 'Film Finance Review: Need for continuing Government assistance', July 1965, p. 5 (19).
12. 'US finance is behind nine new productions', *Kinematograph Weekly*, 17 February 1966, p. 13.
13. FFA General Correspondence Box 31: 'Outstanding American Business', 12 July 1960.
14. Alexander Walker, *Hollywood, England: The British Film Industry in the Sixties* (London: Michael Joseph, 1974), p. 137.
15. 'The film industry's quest for funds', *The Financial Times*, 22 December 1969, p. 23.
16. FFA Realised Film Box 328: *Dr No*: United Artists – Distribution statement to 29 February 1964.
17. 'Eon Budgets', *Kinematograph Weekly*, 11 February 1965, p. 11.
18. 'Musicals make it a great year', *Kinematograph Weekly*, 16 December 1965, pp. 6–7.
19. FFA Realised Film Box 346: *Tom Jones*: John Croydon to Robert Garrett, 28 May 1962.
20. Ibid.: Garrett to Woodfall Film Productions.
21. Ibid.: Garrett to George. H. Ornstein, 9 August 1962.
22. Ibid.: Memorandum – 'Tom Jones', 27 September 1962.
23. Ibid.: Bernard Smith to Woodfall Film Productions, 2 October 1962.
24. Ibid.: Oscar A. Beuselinck to Film Finances, 16 October 1962.
25. Ibid.: Deed of Variation between Woodfall Film Productions and Film Finances, 22 February 1963.
26. FFA General Correspondence Box 31: Memorandum – 'United Artists', 23 January 1963.
27. *Parliamentary Debates: House of Commons*, 5th Series, vol. 734, 21 October 1966, col. 608.
28. *Parliamentary Debates: House of Lords*, 5th Series, vol. 272, 2 February 1966, col. 374.
29. TNA BT 64/5208: Minute No. 12 by D. E. F. Canter, 12 December 1963.
30. Walker, *Hollywood, England*, p. 462.
31. 'Film Finance' (Letters to the Editor), *The Financial Times*, 4 January 1966, p. 10.
32. British Film Producers' Association Executive Council Minute Book 1964–1966: Annex B to BFPA Statement to the Monopolies Commission, 11 February 1965.
33. TNA BT 258/2036: R. B. Tippetts, 'Profitability of Film Production', 2 November 1964.
34. Ibid.
35. 'Long Shots', *Kinematograph Weekly*, 30 July 1964, p. 4.
36. 'Greater flexibility in booking is needed says F. L. Thomas', *Kinematograph Weekly*, 30 May 1963, p. 95.
37. 'Long Shots', *Kinematograph Weekly*, 3 October 1963, p. 4.

38. 'Long Shots', *Kinematograph Weekly*, 3 September 1964, p. 4.
39. 'Hammer sets an eight picture programme', *Kinematograph Weekly*, 28 March 1963, p. 3.
40. TNA BT 316/59: C. R. Walker to James Carreras, 10 April 1968.
41. Ibid.: Memorandum supporting claim for The Queen's Award to Industry, 1 October 1967.
42. FFA Realised Film Box 356: *The VIPs*: Production Budget, n.d.
43. FFA Realised Film Box 366: *Zulu*: Diamond Films: Final Production Budget, based on Final Shooting Script of 25 February 1963.
44. Ibid.: Robert Garrett to Peter Hope, 7 November 1962.
45. FFA Realised Film Box 410: *The Quiller Memorandum*: John Croydon to Robert Garrett, 23 March 1966.
46. Ibid.: Ivan Foxwell to Bernard Smith, 25 November 1966.
47. 'Long Shots', *Kinematograph Weekly*, 3 October 1963, p. 4.
48. FFA Realised Film Box 360: *The Servant*: Ron Aiken to Bernard Smith, 3 January 1963.
49. Ibid.: Memorandum of agreement between Film Finances and Springbok Films, 1 February 1963.
50. Ibid.: Robert Garrett to Joseph Losey, 14 December 1962.
51. FFA Realised Film Box 380: *King and Country*: John Croydon to Robert Garrett, 25 April 1965.
52. Ibid.: Daniel M. Angel to Bernard Smith, 29 April 1964.
53. 'Anglo: "The largest British production firm in 1965"', *Kinematograph Weekly*, 21 January 1965, p. 19.
54. FFA Realised Film Box 390: *Darling*: 'J.C.G.C.' to Bernard Smith, 10 September 1964.
55. Ibid.: Smith to Tom Gauge, 29 January 1965.
56. Ibid.: Robert Garrett to Joseph Janni, 7 April 1965.
57. 'Million dollar advance for Anglo's "Darling"', *Kinematograph Weekly*, 25 February 1965, p. 3.
58. FFA Realised Film Box 390: S. Norton to Film Finances, 5 October 1966.
59. Ibid.: Garrett to Janni, 20 October 1966.
60. Ibid.: Janni to Nat Cohen, 3 June 1966.
61. Ibid.: Anglo-Amalgamated Film Distributors Statement of Accounts to 31 July 1966.
62. 'Lord Rank is optimistic about profits from film interests', *Kinematograph Weekly*, 22 September 1960, p. 7.
63. Geoffrey Macnab, *J. Arthur Rank and the British Film Industry* (London: Routledge, 1993), p. 227.
64. 'Rank profits up by £6½ million', *Kinematograph Weekly*, 9 September 1965, p. 3.
65. BFI Thomas GT/14/9: F. L. Thomas to Peter Rogers, 20 December 1966.
66. Ibid.: Peat, Marwick, Mitchell & Co. to Rogers, 4 August 1967.
67. BFI Thomas GT/30/7: Thomas to Rogers, 11 March 1968.
68. BFI Thomas GT/30/6: Peat, Marwick, Mitchell & Co. to Rogers, 28 July 1969.
69. BFI Thomas GT/6/7: Rogers to Graham Dawson, 23 September 1968.
70. 'Seven co-productions in Rank's 1966–67 budget', *Kinematograph Weekly*, 24 March 1966, p. 3.
71. FFA Realised Film Box 389: *The Ipcress File*: Agreement entered into in New York as of October 15th, 1964, by and between Steven S.A. and Universal Pictures.
72. 'Co-production – key to future success', *Kinematograph Weekly*, 9 September 1965, p. 7.

73. FFA Realised Film Box 423: *The Long Duel*: Agreement between Rank Organisation Film Production and Film Finances, 8 November 1966.
74. 'ABPC launches a record production programme', *Kinematograph Weekly*, 13 April 1961, p. 3.
75. 'Whatever the future holds ABPC is ready – Warter', *Kinematograph Weekly*, 26 July 1962, p. 6.
76. 'ABPC's Trading Profits Down By £1 Million', *Kinematograph Weekly*, 11 July 1963, p. 3.
77. 'EMI to buy Warner Bros.-Seven Arts' 25 p.c. stake in ABPC', *Kinematograph Weekly*, 3 February 1968, p. 3.
78. 'ABPC gives five-point answer to EMI offer', *Kinematograph Weekly*, 4 January 1969, p. 3.
79. 'EMI Wins ABPC', *Kinematograph Weekly*, 1 February 1969, p. 3.
80. 'Bryan Forbes to head ABPC production', *The Financial Times*, 9 April 1969, p. 32.
81. 'ABP – 15 British features for world market', *Kinematograph Weekly*, 16 August 1969, p. 3.
82. 'British Lion makes "landmark" profit of £755,952', *Kinematograph Weekly*, 17 August 1961, p. 7.
83. 'British Lion Profit Soars to £310,162', *Kinematograph Weekly*, 5 July 1962, p. 3.
84. 'British Lion Bought Out by the NFFC', *Kinematograph Weekly*, 26 December 1963, p. 3.
85. 'Carving up the Lion', *The Observer*, 29 December 1963, p. 20.
86. 'Kingsley's Letter to Hume', *Kinematograph Weekly*, 9 January 1964, p. 21.
87. TNA BT 64/5285: John Woolf to John Terry, 2 March 1964.
88. TNA BT 279/88: J. Leckie to Carey, 13 March 1964.
89. TNA BT 64/5285: A. F. de Breyne to Sir Nutcombe Hume, 24 February 1964.
90. Ibid.: Edward Martell to John Terry, 10 March 1964.
91. Ibid.: Minute by R. B. Tippets, 2 March 1964.
92. Ibid.: Goodman, Derrick & Co. to NFFC, 11 March 1964.
93. Ibid.: Minute by J. Leckie, 13 March 1964.
94. Ibid.: Minute by R. B. Tippets, 12 March 1964.
95. Ibid.: Draft minute from the President of the Board of Trade to the Prime Minister, March 1964.
96. 'British Lion Profit Down', *Kinematograph Weekly*, 9 July 1964, p. 3.
97. 'Sharp setback for British Lion Films', *The Guardian*, 6 August 1965, p. 4.
98. 'British Lion: Few approaches from independents', *Kinematograph Weekly*, 19 August 1965, p. 3.
99. 'First major film from new British Lion', *Kinematograph Weekly*, 18 June 1964, p. 3.
100. 'Lion's roar: £2 million on a dozen features', *Kinematograph Weekly*, 18 February 1965, p. 3.
101. 'Moral Modesty', *Kinematograph Weekly*, 15 July 1965, p. 17.
102. 'British Lion To Cut Film Outputs', *The Financial Times*, 11 February 1966, p. 9.

CHAPTER 13

Backing British

> We were on the edge of establishing a commercially viable British film industry, but that objective has slipped out of our reach. Unless action is taken quickly, native British production will virtually disappear. (David Kingsley)[1]

The increasing American presence in the British production sector and the decline of wholly British-financed production had far-reaching consequences for the film industry. It is a moot point, perhaps, whether there ever really was the 'commercially viable British film industry' that David Kingsley thought was about to emerge in the early 1960s or whether this was just a chimera. The success of British-financed films such as *I'm All Right, Jack*, *Carry On Nurse* and *Saturday Night and Sunday Morning* – all listed as major profit-makers by the National Film Finance Corporation at the turn of the decade – disguised the fact that most British films lost money. As the NFFC noted in its annual report for 1962: 'The Corporation's profit for the year does not mean that British films are generally profitable, even with the aid of the levy. A few very successful films attract an exceptional amount of levy but many others saw a substantial loss.'[2] And British independent producers continued to experience difficulty in securing distribution guarantees – and therefore finance – for their films. Hal Chester, producer of the popular comedy *School for Scoundrels* (1960), for example, told the *Kine*: 'You know how many times *School for Scoundrels* was turned down? Four times, that's how many. It took years to get that property off the ground.'[3]

The decline of cinema admissions and the consequent contraction of the exhibition sector inevitably impacted upon the industry. The casualties in the early 1960s tended to be producers and distributors of supporting features, a mode of low-budget film-making that had now become an uneconomic anachronism.[4] In January 1961, for example, Sapphire Films, which had produced *The Adventures of Robin Hood* and other telefilm series in the 1950s, went into receivership, and Walton Studios closed.[5] Sapphire's Hannah Weinstein had ventured into low-budget feature production with the horror film *City of the Dead* (1960) in association with Max Rosenberg: it was a cheap affair (£44,965) but returned a distributor's gross of only £30,027.[6] In June 1961 Eros Films, an independent distributor founded by the Hyams brothers, which throughout the 1950s had existed on mostly co-feature fare, went out of business owing £271,228 to the National Provincial Bank.[7] And Edward and Harry Danziger, enterprising Americans who since 1956 had produced around a dozen second features a year, and several telefilm series, announced that they were closing their production facility New Elstree Studios on the grounds that 'being an independent producer with a studio doesn't pay any more'. *Kine* saw this as 'another manifestation of the economic ills that beset production, particularly in the area of the making of supporting features and programme material for television . . . [It] is abundantly evident that the possible rewards for their kind of enterprise are not commensurate with the financial risks involved.'[8]

It was not just the second-feature producers who were affected. The early success of Bryanston prompted other independent distributors to enter the medium-budget first feature market in the early 1960s. *Kine* suggested that the arrival of companies such as Britannia, Albion, Pax, Garrick, Wessex and Nova – all of which operated as satellites of British Lion Films – represented 'the new thinking in production . . . Assuming control of financing and marketing, it gives freer rein to creative enterprise and furthermore provides opportunities for the injection of new talent into the business.'[9] However, none of these newcomers lasted very long. Pax Films, for example, was formed early in 1961 as a collaborative venture between Bryanston and Stephen Pallos. The Austrian-born Pallos had experience of setting up international distribution arrangements and it was intended that Pax would produce one or two 'very big' films a year in association with overseas partners.[10] Its first film was Val Guest's apocalyptic drama *The Day the Earth Caught Fire* (1962). John Croydon, assessing the proposition for Film Finances, disliked the papers:

> It is quite obvious that the budget has been prepared on a preconceived price and in effect it bears no relationship whatsoever to the other documents . . . I think we know enough about Stephen Pallos to realise that if he has said that Val Guest can have between £180,000 and £185,000 for the purpose of shooting this story, then that is the limit and I am quite sure that it could not be shot for this sum of money, even under the circumstances indicated in this schedule, even if one could accept the schedule in relation to the script![11]

Croydon felt that on the evidence of this and other recent propositions – he mentioned *The Valiant*, *The Hellions* and *The Hair of the Dog* – 'I have very definite reasons for thinking that the industry generally might be trying to make monkeys of us by simply pushing in our direction any proposition which does not follow the conventions or which . . . shows a degree of impossibility even to the most obtuse financier.' Film Finances did agree to guarantee *The Day the Earth Caught Fire* but only when the budget was increased to £190,818, which was provided by deferments.[12] The film went £22,763 over budget, though there was no claim on the guarantee as the overage was partly compensated by an insurance claim and the National Provincial Bank advanced £3,000 over its original loan of £133,573. *The Day the Earth Caught Fire* was listed as a 'money maker' by the trade press. Nevertheless, it took a decade for the film to show a profit: by 1973 its total distributors' receipts were £227,540, which amounted to an overall profit of £22,258 shared between Pax Films (30 per cent), the NFFC (33.75 per cent), Val Guest (7.5 per cent) and Melina Productions (25.25 per cent).[13]

The case of Garrick Film Distributors provides an object lesson in the problems of the independent sector of the British film industry in the early 1960s. Its partners were David Brown, Louis Ellman, Robert Garrett, Raymond Stross and John Sutro.[14] The intention was that Stross would produce at Ardmore Studios in Ireland, in which Ellman had an interest. Sutro brought his expertise in distribution, and Film Finances would provide its guarantees of completion. In April 1962 Garrick announced a four-picture co-production deal between Stross and German producer Artur Brauer.[15] In the event, Garrick would sponsor three films in 1962 – *The Very Edge*, *The Brain* and *The Leather Boys* – for which the National Provincial Bank loaned a total of £223,870 against its distribution guarantees.[16] *The Very Edge* (a psychological thriller) and *The Brain* (horror) were fairly run-of-the-mill fare, but Stross evidently saw *The Leather Boys* – best described as a British version of *The Wild One* with Dudley Sutton in place of Marlon Brando – in the mould of the new wave films:

> Although this production is completely original within its own sphere, it follows the trend of *Saturday Night and Sunday Morning*, *A Taste of Honey* and *A Kind of Loving*. These three pictures as you know between them will make well over a million pounds profit, of this there can be no argument. Mr Furie's last picture was *The Young Ones*, again one of the most successful pictures ever made in England, and since then he has completed *The Boys*, which I believe had a budget of approximately £110,000 and came in at £92,000.[17]

However, Garrett and the other partners were sceptical. Stross told Garrett: 'With every respect in the world to both yourself and John, I believe that "you are not with it"! . . . Forgive me if I am outspoken but I have no alternative to be "with it" for the industry needs winners and I reiterate the world is crying out for teenage stories.'[18] *The Leather Boys* was finally agreed at a budget of £106,000 including 25 per cent from the NFFC with the balance coming from deferments by Stross and Sidney J. Furie. Yet Garrett's instinct proved correct: the new wave had largely run its course by this time, and no one was interested in *The Leather Boys*. It was completed early in 1963 but sat on the shelf for over a year before it had a low-profile release on the ABC circuit. Stross was furious: 'Not only do the circuits seem quite incapable of keeping their word, but it seems that they are completely contemptuous of their undertakings to British Lion.'[19] In the meantime, the other two films had not lived up to expectations at the box office. Garrick estimated 'that [*The*] *Very Edge* will not recover its guarantee, that we may get out of *The Brain* if we take our percentages into account, but that the company now stands or falls by the results on [*The*] *Leather Boys*'.[20] The end for Garrick was signalled when the National Provincial Bank decided that it would not advance any more loans against Garrick's distribution guarantees until it had recovered its loans from the first three films: the company remained in being for another decade but had to all intents and purposes ceased to be an active player in the industry by 1963.

The precarious state of independent production inevitably gave rise to talk of yet another crisis for the British film industry. This duly arose over the winter of 1963–4. At the end of November 1963 there were only ten feature films and two telefilm series shooting in British studios compared to fourteen features and three telefilm series at the end of August: these numbers were also lower than at the same time in 1962. *Kine*'s studio correspondent Derek Todd believed that the declining level of production was more than the traditional seasonal fluctuation: 'The crisis could reach a peak next month when the usual seasonal decline will coincide with the current production contraction: as far as can be seen, only two new films are scheduled to start and some of those now shooting will have finished.'[21] The impending crisis was serious enough to warrant a debate in Parliament, where Labour MP Eirene White diagnosed deep-rooted structural problems in the industry as the cause:

> The immediate cause of the difficulties with which the industry is confronted and of the ill-feeling which, I am afraid, has been aroused, was the assertion by a number of independent film producers that their films have been held up, that they have not been booked by the circuits and that, consequently, money invested in them is tied up and has not become available for ploughing back into future production. This has led, it is claimed, to the situation in which, for example, at Shepperton Studios there is no film on the floor and none in prospect for at least this month, while another studio is closed completely. The independent producers concerned say that they are quite unable to make any plans for the future or obtain any finance for fresh production.[22]

The debate touched on a number of issues including the role of the National Film Finance Corporation and the position of British Lion Films. But the main issue was that independent producers were unfairly treated by the two major cinema circuits: this was precisely the point that Raymond Stross had made when complaining about ABC's handling of *The Leather Boys*. John Davis – who probably had more influence over production and exhibition than any other single individual in the British film industry – rebutted this charge: he averred that the 'atmosphere of crisis . . . has been brought about by some people who deliberately started a campaign attacking the two major organisations which have done so much for British film production since the war' and suggested 'that heavy production losses are going to be made by the backers of some of the films which were put into production a year or more ago'.[23]

Alexander Walker contends that the crisis of 1963–4 'dealt a blow to the confidence of independent British film-makers from which they never recovered'.[24] It had been a crisis of exhibition as much as one of production, but the consequence was that many independent producers found themselves unable to reinvest. Indeed, in some circumstances it was now more difficult to mount a low-budget production than a more expensive one. The example of *He Who Rides A Tiger* (1965) is a case in point. This was a low-budget (£47,479) crime drama produced by David Newman and directed by Charles Crichton. The budget seems to have been provided through a combination of private investors, studio and other trade credits and deferments. However, the film got into difficulty during production when Newman had to pay off sundry creditors and when it emerged that the cast and crew were owed back pay. Newman applied to the NFFC for a bailout loan to complete the film: this was initially refused on the grounds that Newman had not been able to finalise a guarantee of completion before starting production.[25] Newman asked Film Finances for 'further remuneration' but was rebuffed by Garrett: 'While we have every sympathy for your present position, we feel that in view of the overcost and the fact that no such provision was made when the original re-budgeting was being done that we cannot agree to it.'[26] Newman was finally able to meet the conditions for the NFFC loan (£5,000), and Film Finances advanced a further £1,850 towards what it considered were legitimate overcosts. The film was completed, but at a final cost of £76,093 it was significantly over budget and Newman was left having to find this himself: David Newman Films went into liquidation shortly thereafter.

By the middle of the decade the decline of wholly British-financed production had brought the role of the National Film Finance Corporation under renewed scrutiny. In 1960 the NFFC had made loans totalling over £1.5 million towards 67 films (including 46 features) but thereafter it began gradually to reduce the number and amount of loans. The corporation made modest operating profits in 1961 (£18,441) and 1962 (£49,564) but in 1963 it recorded a loss of £219,867, which it attributed to a decrease in its share of the profits from successful films.[27] An immediate consequence of the large loss it sustained in 1963 was that the NFFC had to scale back on the number of films it supported. In 1964, for example, it supported eighteen features, half the total of the previous year, while in 1965 it supported only twelve. Managing director John Terry recognised that the decline of low-budget film-making and the increasing number of British films backed by American money necessitated a change of policy for the corporation. In July 1964 he told the trade that 'we shall have to take the changed market into account in the future . . . We are trying to work out a scheme whereby we can participate more generally in production – in projects which are obviously going to be successful like The Beatles film [*A Hard Day's Night*] – and not only in the more chancy films as we have often tended to do in the past.'[28] Some voices were starting to argue that the influx of US investment made the NFFC redundant. As *The Economist* noted in 1966: 'If enough money is coming from elsewhere to support the industry in Britain there may be no function for the NFFC to serve in its present form . . . The NFFC has served its purpose; there is no reason to beef it up to compete as a financing body in a freely supplied market. There is a strong argument for turning its attention elsewhere altogether.'[29]

In June 1964 the Board of Trade set up a Working Group on the Film Industry to consider the future of the NFFC: the review was occasioned by the sale of British Lion, which meant that the corporation no longer had a direct stake in the company. The Working Group's membership was entirely comprised of civil servants – four from the Board of Trade including its chairman (C. M. P. Brown) and one from the Treasury (Leo Pliatzky) – with John Terry invited to attend meetings. Terry was invited to outline his views on the future of the industry and the NFFC's role in supporting it. His view was that the NFFC's future hinged on its role in discovering new talent rather than in supporting production *per se*:

> If NFFC support were withdrawn, the necessary number of British films would probably still be made, but British production would become very largely dependent on US finance. If the Government did not consider this to be a bad thing, then there would be no role for the Corporation except to bring forward new talent . . . While the Americans were showing more interest in up-and-coming producers, directors, etc, they were not good at unearthing new talent. Many of the leading young producers and directors of the present day might never have been given an opportunity but for the Corporation. Unfortunately the Corporation had lost these people to the Americans once they became established.[30]

Although Terry did not mention any specific individuals, examples of film-makers who had been 'lost' to the Americans would include the likes of Michael Winner and Richard Lester. Winner, whose breakthrough came with a low-budget naturist film, *Some Like It Cool* (1961), made several films for British distributors in the early 1960s such as *West 11* (Associated British-Pathé, 1963) and *The System* (Bryanston, 1964), but increasingly gravitated towards the Americans: *The Cool Mikado* (Columbia, 1963), *You Must Be Joking!* (Columbia, 1965) and *The Jokers* (Universal, 1967). Lester was himself an American who had lived in Britain since the mid-1950s: his first feature was the musical comedy *It's Trad, Dad!* (1962) – one of the first productions by Amicus Films – though his breakthrough came with the Beatles films *A Hard Day's Night* and *Help!* for United Artists.

As part of the inquiry, the NFFC was asked to provide representative examples of successful and unsuccessful films released in 1963: these were *Ladies Who Do* (Bryanston) and *The World Ten Times Over* (ABPC). Terry explained that '*Ladies Who Do* is not likely to be a profitable film, but it is described as a comparative success because the distributor has told us that it is likely to recover its cost in due course. *The World Ten Times Over*, however, which is described as a comparative failure, is unlikely to recover more than the front money investments provided by ABPC and NFFC.'[31] For *Ladies Who Do*, the NFFC loaned £27,099 towards the total cost of £116,997: after eighteen months the distributor's receipts amounted to £83,223. A minute by the Working Group's secretary caustically remarked: 'It is noteworthy that the NFFC have to put up a failure like *Ladies Who Do* as a comparative success!'[32] For *The World Ten Times Over*, the NFFC advanced £38,410 towards the final cost of £110,036 but the distributor's receipts were only £36,519.

The Working Group reported in July 1965: it 'came to the conclusion that circumstances which had originally justified the provision of Government money for film production had now completely changed and that . . . there is no economic case for maintaining this facility in order to secure a reasonable level of film production'.[33] Accordingly it recommended that the NFFC's loan-making powers should be allowed to lapse upon the expiry of its statutory authority in 1967. A wide range of factors identified in the Working Group's report all pointed to this conclusion. On the broadest level it was felt that the conditions in the film industry had changed in a number of significant ways since the establishment of the NFFC in 1948 and that 'many of the considerations ... which helped to justify the creation of the NFFC no longer have the same importance'. The decline of the cinema-going audience meant there was less need to support British films just to fill cinemas; the cinema was no longer regarded as such an important medium of national projection as it had been a generation earlier, especially given the rise of television; there was no longer such an acute shortage of capital due to increasing levels of US investment in British production; and British film exports had grown to the extent that overseas receipts were now worth around £3.5 million more than payments out (those receipts were due in large measure to the international success of American-financed films such as *Tom Jones* and the Bond pictures). The Working Group noted that the NFFC was already reducing its investment: total loans which had amounted to £1,034,000 in 1962 and £1,688,000 in 1963 had fallen to £473,000 in 1964 and £462,000 in 1965. It concluded that the existing sources of finance were sufficient to meet the needs of the industry:

> The present volume of American financing of British film production, initiated by the half dozen major US distribution companies, taken together with the activities of Rank and ABPC seems to us to provide any genuinely talented British independent producer with a reasonably wide choice of sources of finance ... To the extent that the NFFC were retained in being to finance projects which were not acceptable to these major concerns, the Corporation would be bound to operate at a loss. We do not consider therefore that there is, in present circumstances, any logical and compelling anti-monopoly reason for keeping the NFFC in being.[34]

More specifically, the report suggested that the changing pattern of finance and exhibition had seen a shift towards bigger films deemed more likely to return a profit – the sort of films that would generally attract US backing – at the expense of smaller films which tended not to be profitable but were the sort of films the NFFC had supported in recent years. The report surmised that 'their role of providing mainly "end-money" for films which other groups have declined to finance is one in which they are virtually bound to lose money'.[35]

All the arguments therefore seemed to point towards discontinuing the NFFC when its statutory life ended in two years' time. In the event, however, the report was shelved and the corporation was reprieved. The official records do not reveal the reason. One likely context was that there had been a change of government since the Working Group was appointed: the Labour Party was elected on a narrow majority in October 1964 – another general election in April 1966 would see its majority increased – and the new Prime Minister was none other than the 'father' of the NFFC. As President of the Board of Trade in the late 1940s, Harold Wilson had been responsible for establishing the NFFC. He had also argued that it should be put onto a permanent footing while in Opposition during the 1950s. The NFFC had to a large extent been Wilson's baby: it is therefore entirely plausible that the NFFC may have been saved through prime ministerial intervention. It was also the case that the Working Party was not unanimous. Its secretary R. B. Tippetts seems to have exerted a stronger influence than some of its members. Before publication of the report, Tippetts said: 'I am urging that the NFFC should be continued in being substantially with its present powers and resources until its long-term future can be finally decided along with that of the quota, levy, etc, in 1968/69 or thereabouts.'[36] In the event, this was the course of action adopted by Douglas Jay, the new President of the Board of Trade, who announced in February 1966 that decisions on the future of the NFFC, Eady levy and quota would be deferred until 1970.[37]

Another factor that may have saved the NFFC in 1965 was that it could demonstrate that it was adjusting its policy in response to changing economic conditions in the industry. In September 1964 Terry announced that the NFFC would use £500,000 of the cash injection it had received from the sale of British Lion to back a range of films from one of the major production groups if the producer would match the amount.[38] The idea was to provide a 'backing fund' in order 'to act as security for one of [the] joint stock banks to provide a "front fund"'.[39] This was intended to facilitate the NFFC's move into the higher-budget range of films that hitherto had been the preserve of the American studios. Terry entered into negotiations with several groups, including British Lion and the Rank Organisation. Early in 1965 the NFFC announced that it had agreed to set up a backing fund of £2.5 million in association with Rank: each party would put up £500,000, with the National Provincial Bank providing an additional £1.5 million. Terry explained how the fund would work: 'The finance will be made available to meet up to 100 per cent of the budget finance for selected films, i.e. the entire budget finance less any producers' investments and/or foreign investments. The scheme is thus designed to provide the whole of the finance required by an independent producer from a single source.'[40] The provision of full financing as opposed to the standard 70 per cent distribution guarantee was obviously seen as necessary to match the American companies who usually offered guarantees for 100 per cent of the budget. The films would be shot at Pinewood 'on standard terms'. *Kine* suggested that the NFFC/Rank scheme 'should go some way to dispel the despondency of British producers who are worried about the growing dominance of American backing of British production'.[41]

On the face of it, the NFFC/Rank joint financing initiative bore certain similarities to the Group scheme of the early 1950s. But there were also some important differences. One was that the NFFC and Rank were equal partners, each contributing half the backing fund: this differed from the previous collaboration between the two parties in British Film Makers where Rank had offered 70 per cent guarantees and the NFFC had put up the end money. As the investment was shared, the recoupment would be on a *pari passu* basis: this reduced the NFFC's risks as it would no longer rank behind other investors. Another difference from the Group scheme was that the management of the joint financing scheme – including the final decision on the choice of films – would rest with the NFFC. This was important as it provided the NFFC with a response to the likely criticism – also made of the Group scheme some fifteen years earlier – that it would in effect be subsidising one of the major combines at the expense of independent producers. In the NFFC's annual report for 1965, Terry was at pains to emphasise that 'there can be no suggestion that NFFC would be providing finance to the Rank Organisation. On the contrary the Rank Organisation would be providing £500,000 for the benefit of films to be made by independent producers selected by the NFFC.'[42]

The NFFC received around 80 applications for the scheme: the first project accepted in May 1965 was *Passage of Love* – later retitled *I Was Happy Here* (1966) – from a new producer (Roy Millichip) and director (Desmond Davis).[43] John Croydon, assessing the proposition for a completion guarantee, was sceptical about the director's approach: 'Having read recently an article in which Davis set out his opinions and methods of Direction, I must say that I find the article a little difficult to reconcile to the idea of working to a fixed schedule!'[44] In the event, the film – a bittersweet drama about a married Irishwoman rekindling a romance with an old boyfriend – was completed on schedule and slightly under its budget of £169,200. The second project was announced in September 1965: *The Sandwich Man* (1966) – described as 'a comedy for our time' – was produced by Peter Newbrook and directed by Rupert Hart-Davis for Titan International Pictures.[45] Croydon felt the script was 'badly put together' and was concerned that the all-location picture 'is under-scheduled . . . by between three and four weeks. I get the impression that no-one on the unit has any appreciation of the trials and tribulations they will encounter in shooting a picture of this nature.'[46] Film Finances insisted that the budget should be increased from £214,188 to £250,253 as it expected time to be lost to weather during the autumn shooting period. Croydon's assessment proved over-cautious as the film was completed close to the original budget figure at £214,452. The third NFFC/Rank film was Michael Powell's *They're A Weird Mob* (1966), another all-location picture, shot in Australia. NFFC/Rank advanced £166,925 towards the budget of £234,925, with the balance from the Australian distributor Greater Union. This time Croydon was satisfied with the proposition 'provided Powell is prepared to tackle the film in the way he did *Peeping Tom*'.[47]

Maroc 7 (1967) – produced by John Gale and directed by Gerry O'Hara for Cyclone Films – was the most problematic of the NFFC/Rank films. This was a 'caper' movie of a sort popular at the time, with an international cast (Gene Barry, Elsa Martinelli, Cyd Charisse, Leslie Phillips) and locations in Morocco. Rank and Paramount shared the distribution, and the final budget was £319,000. Croydon initially had reservations about the length of the script: he felt it 'is full of hazard and is based throughout on minimal schedule and budget where the slightest deviation will undoubtedly affect the final result'.[48] The usual problems associated with location pictures – late charter planes, difficulties with local contractors, injuries to the cast – were compounded by an entirely unforeseen eventuality when the unit was required to find alternative accommodation due to a state visit to Morocco by the King of Saudi Arabia.[49] *Maroc 7* was soon in serious difficulties, and Film

Finances exercised its right to take over the production.⁵⁰ Gale and Phillips, who had a stake in the production company, pleaded their case with Film Finances:

> As I am sure you are aware, we are a small company and this has been our first big venture. Together with [executive producer] Martin Schute we had to work extremely hard to make this film and our objective has always been to finish the film as quickly as possible commensurate with the quality necessary for a big scale international motion picture... Now that we are moving into the last few weeks of completion there is still a considerable amount of work to do and we are now told that you are refusing to pay us the money that we are not only due, but need very badly to complete and survive.⁵¹

Film Finances maintained that the producers had not provided accurate cost reports and had left behind a 'large number' of unpaid bills in Morocco. In total Film Finances advanced £61,137 towards completion of the film, which had a final certified cost of £399,835.⁵²

By this time there were doubts about the future of the NFFC/Rank scheme. In its annual report for 1967 the NFFC tried to put a positive spin on the results of the films:

> *Romeo and Juliet* has been widely acclaimed as an artistic success and the commercial results are promising. *They're a Weird Mob*, though it has not done well in the rest of the world, has been a record-breaking success in Australia. Paramount Pictures Corporation, which will distribute *Maroc Seven* in the Western Hemisphere, has made a payment on account of revenues equal to half the cash cost of production. Losses are feared on *The Sandwich Man*, despite its star-studded cast, and *I Was Happy Here*, despite international awards and almost universal praise from the critics.⁵³

Romeo and Juliet (1966) was a film of the famous Royal Ballet production starring Rudolf Nureyev and Margot Fonteyn, produced and directed by Paul Czinner. However, other assessments of the qualities of the films were rather more jaundiced than the NFFC. Writing in *Films and Filming* early in 1967, Robin Bean declared: 'The saddest event of the year was the failure of the joint NFFC/Rank financing scheme to "encourage independent production" . . . Artistically, the majority of their productions were highly questionable and gave the appearance of being projects where the producers had been unable to raise money from commercial sources.'⁵⁴ *Two Weeks in September* (1967) – an Anglo-French co-production starring Brigitte Bardot as a French fashion model in 'Swinging London' – was the last film produced under the scheme before it was terminated by mutual consent.

Economically the scheme was a failure. The NFFC had advanced a total of £601,464 towards the scheme over three years – most of the investment came in 1966 (£272,926) and 1967 (£325,010) – but recouped just £268,004.⁵⁵ Terry reported healthy overseas receipts for *They're A Weird Mob* (£207,821) and *Maroc 7* (£214,494), but returns from the other films were disappointing.⁵⁶ In his report for shareholders in 1967, John Davis announced: 'Whilst our arrangements with the

National Film Finance Corporation . . . have worked smoothly and harmoniously, I am sorry to say that we have had to provide in excess of £200,000 against anticipated losses.'[57] The fact of being produced under the scheme did not guarantee a wide circuit release: *I Was Happy Here* sat on the shelf for some time, while *The Sandwich Man* and *They're A Weird Mob* were released only as co-features on the Odeon circuit.

The NFFC/Rank joint financing scheme had been a worthwhile initiative to make the best use of the NFFC's limited resources in supporting British production. If it demonstrated anything, it was that John Terry and his colleagues were no more adept at picking winners than anyone else in the industry.[58] Ironically, the NFFC had more success with films it supported outside the scheme. Its most profitable films in the mid-1960s were *The Family Way*, *Poor Cow* and *Ulysses*.[59] *The Family Way* (1966) – produced by John Boulting and directed by Roy Boulting for British Lion – was fourth at the British box office in 1967. The NFFC had loaned £190,499 towards the budget of £460,641: the film was reported to have returned distributor's receipts of over £500,000.[60] *Poor Cow* (1967) – the first feature directed by Ken Loach, for Joseph Janni's Vic Films – was jointly financed by the NFFC and Anglo-Amalgamated Film Distributors with a budget of £242,607.[61] The NFFC considered it 'the outstanding success of the year . . . The film has done very well in the United Kingdom and was sold for the Western Hemisphere for a substantial sum of revenue.'[62] *Ulysses* (1967) – produced and directed by Joseph Strick for British Lion – was a troubled production from the start. The NFFC advanced £57,041 towards the original budget of £183,036.[63] This was increased to £222,269 following consultation with Film Finances: Lloyds Bank would not accept the completion guarantee offered by City Shares Trust.[64] Nevertheless, at the end of 1967 executive producer Walter Reade was able to point to 'the very successful release of *Ulysses* in many important places throughout the world'.[65]

Yet these successes were exceptions to the rule: most of the films supported by the NFFC in the late 1960s were loss-makers. The corporation was investing more per picture but it was supporting fewer films. It was affected by the increasing production costs across the industry: the average cost of the features supported by the NFFC increased from £125,287 in 1965 to £179,081 in 1966 and £259,964 in 1967.[66] Rising costs meant that the NFFC's resources were no longer sufficient to support even around twelve to fifteen films a year. In 1965 the corporation decided to avail itself of more of the additional £2 million that it was entitled to borrow from non-government sources under the Cinematograph Film Production (Special Loans) Act of 1952: to this end it negotiated an overdraft of £750,000 with Lloyds Bank.[67] Even so, the NFFC was obliged temporarily to suspend making loans in October 1966 when it realised that its loss for the year was going to be larger than expected: it lost £369,699 (largely on the films produced through the joint financing scheme).[68] It resumed making loans in August 1967 but on a reduced scale.[69] In 1967 it loaned £936,161 towards fifteen films (twelve features), in 1968 it loaned £258,851 for nine films (six features) and in 1969 it loaned £778,208 towards eight films (six features).[70]

At the start of the 1960s the NFFC had been an important supporter of the British new wave and was still involved with around a third of all British features. But by the decade's end it had become a marginal presence that was able to support only a handful of films a year. The corporation was caught in a paradox. On the one hand the commercially successful British films – which tended to be those produced with American finance – had no need for the NFFC's support. On the other hand the films that most needed its support were the riskier propositions that often turned out to be loss-makers. And the changing economic conditions in the film industry – the combination of increasing production costs and a contracting domestic market – meant that the NFFC's limited resources were stretched to the limit. There was a potential lifeline: that in the event of the large-scale withdrawal of American finance – a possibility that was becoming the subject of increasing speculation by the end of the decade – there would still be a role for the NFFC in the provision of risk capital for British film production. The dilemma facing the NFFC was summed up in a report by the Industrial Reorganisation Corporation – a body set up by the Labour government to promote competitiveness in industry – in January 1969: 'The worth of a revitalised Corporation, however, would appear should the American companies withdraw a large part of their finance from British productions. It must, however, be appreciated that the funds which would be required to maintain British film production at an economic level in the face of a major American withdrawal would almost certainly be considerably greater than the Corporation has ever had available in the past.'[71]

Notes

1. 'Will British Lion Ever Roar Again?', *The Observer*, 11 December 1966, p. 7.
2. *National Film Finance Corporation: Annual Report and Statement of Accounts for the year ended 31 March 1962*, Cmnd. 1793 (July 1962), p. 4 (14).
3. 'Production', *Kinematograph Weekly*, 14 July 1960, p. 25.
4. Laura Mayne, 'Whatever happened to the British "B" movie? Micro-budget filmmaking and the death of the one-hour supporting feature in the early 1960s', *Historical Journal of Film, Radio and Television*, 37: 3 (2017), pp. 559–76.
5. 'Walton Closes: Receiver takes over', *Kinematograph Weekly*, 19 January 1961, p. 3.
6. FFA Realised Film Box 278: *City of the Dead*: Britannia Film Distributors Royalty Statement to 28 February 1963.
7. 'Eros in liquidation with deficiency of £433,608', *Kinematograph Weekly*, 8 June 1961, p. 6.
8. 'A Question of Economics', *KInematograph Weekly*, 7 December 1961, p. 4.
9. 'Vitality in Production', *Kinematograph Weekly*, 14 November 1961, p. 4.
10. 'Sir Michael Balcon heads new production company', *Kinematograph Weekly*, 12 January 1961, p. 3.
11. FFA Realised Film Box 312: *The Day the Earth Caught Fire*: John Croydon to Robert Garrett, 6 March 1961.
12. Ibid.: Garrett to Melina Productions, 11 April 1961.
13. Ibid.: Pax Films: Royalty Statement to 30 April 1973.

14. 'More Groups Sign With British Lion', *Kinematograph Weekly*, 28 September 1961, p. 3.
15. 'Production', *Kinematograph Weekly*, 26 April 1962, p. 19.
16. FFA General Correspondence Box 30: Garrick Film Distributors Ltd: Estimate of revenues (undated).
17. FFA Realised Film Box 353: *The Leather Boys*: Raymond Stross to Robert Garrett, 18 June 1962.
18. Ibid.: Stross to Garrett, 3 August 1962.
19. Ibid.: Stross to Victor Hoare, 18 November 1963.
20. FFA General Correspondence Box 30: William Croft to Garrett, 28 October 1963.
21. 'Production Crisis: The Peak May Be Reached Next Month', *Kinematograph Weekly*, 28 November 1963, p. 27.
22. *Parliamentary Debates: House of Commons*, 5th Series, vol. 686, 20 December 1963, col. 668.
23. 'Davis Puts the Crisis in Perspective', *Kinematograph Weekly*, 19 December 1963, p. 123.
24. Alexander Walker, *Hollywood, England: The British Film Industry in the Sixties* (London: Michael Joseph, 1974), p. 456.
25. 'NFFC backs down from "Tiger"', *Kinematograph Weekly*, 8 April 1965, p. 6.
26. FFA Realised Film Box 396: *He Who Rides A Tiger*: Robert Garrett to David Newman, 7 July 1965.
27. *National Film Finance Corporation: Annual Report and Statement of Accounts for the year ended 31 March 1963*, Cmnd. 2079 (July 1963), p. 1 (1).
28. 'NFFC Changes Policy on Future Lending', *Kinematograph Weekly*, 23 July 1964, p. 3.
29. 'Crowded out', *The Economist*, 6 August 1966, p. 577.
30. TNA BT 258/2036: Board of Trade: Film Finance Review: Minutes of Fourth Meeting of the Working Group, 10 February 1965.
31. TNA BT 248/2036: John Terry to R. B. Tippetts, 25 March 1965.
32. Ibid.: Tippetts to Ord Johnstone, 26 March 1965.
33. TNA BT 258/2038: Minute by C. M. P. Brown, 28 July 1965.
34. Ibid.: 'Film Finance Review', July 1965, p. 13 (43).
35. Ibid. pp. 8–9 (31).
36. Ibid.: Tippetts, 'National Film Finance Corporation', 19 March 1965.
37. Ibid.: 'Film Industry Review', Paper No. 3.
38. 'NFFC Has New Finance Plan To Boost Production', *Kinematograph Weekly*, 17 September 1964, p. 6.
39. 'NFFC Embraces More Groups in Finance Discussions', *Kinematograph Weekly*, 24 September 1964, p. 3.
40. 'NFFC and Rank set up a £1 million fund to back independent production', *Kinematograph Weekly*, 21 January 1965, p. 3.
41. 'Long Shots', *Kinematograph Weekly*, 21 January 1965, p. 3.
42. *National Film Finance Corporation: Annual Report and Statement of Accounts for the year ended 31 March 1965*, Cmnd. 2770 (September 1965), p. 5.
43. 'First NFFC-Rank Film Set', *Kinematograph Weekly*, 27 May 1965, p. 3.
44. FFA Realised Film Box 397: *Passage of Love (I Was Happy Here)*: John Croydon to Robert Garrett, 31 May 1965.
45. 'Rank-NFFC scheme: second film is "Sandwich Man"', *Kinematograph Weekly*, 2 September 1965, p. 3.
46. FFA Realised Film Box 401: *The Sandwich Man*: Croydon to Garrett, 15 August 1965.

47. FFA Realised Film Box 403: *They're A Weird Mob*: Croydon to Garrett, 19 September 1965.
48. FFA Realised Film Box 418: *Maroc 7*: Croydon to Garrett, 26 June 1966.
49. Ibid.: Martin C. Schute to Douglas Gosling, 18 July 1966.
50. Ibid.: Robert Garrett to John Dale, 22 August 1966.
51. Ibid.: John Gale and Leslie Phillips to Garrett, 25 October 1966.
52. Ibid.: Garrett to Messrs Peat, Marwick, Mitchell & Co., 19 June 1967.
53. *National Film Finance Corporation: Annual Report and Statement of Accounts for the year ending March 31, 1967*, Cmnd. 3418 (October 1967), pp. 1–2 (5).
54. 'Trapped in a Sandwich', *Films and Filming*, 12: 4 (January 1967), p. 60.
55. *NFFC Annual Report 1967*, p.1 (6).
56. TNA BT 279/283: John Terry to Board of Trade, 14 December 1967.
57. TNA BT 258/2040: Annual Accounts of the Rank Organisation, 1967.
58. Duncan Petrie, 'Resisting Hollywood Dominance in Sixties British Cinema: the NFFC/Rank Joint Financing Initiative', *Historical Journal of Film, Radio and Television*, 36: 4 (2016), p. 563.
59. *National Film Finance Corporation: Annual Report and Statement of Accounts for the year ended 31 March 1969*, Cmnd. 4094 (June 1969), p. 1 (3).
60. TNA BT 279/283: 'Review of Film Support Policy and Legislation', 14 December 1967.
61. FFA Realised Film Box 431: *Poor Cow*: Robert Garrett to Joseph Janni, 10 April 1967.
62. *National Film Finance Corporation: Annual Report and Statement of Accounts for the year ended 31 March 1968*, Cmnd. 3716 (July 1968), p. 2 (7).
63. FFA Realised Film Box 417: *Ulysses*: Production Budget, n.d. The original total budget figure of £181,256 has been crossed out and £183,036 added in pencil.
64. Ibid.: Garrett to C. Collins (Lloyds Bank), draft, n.d.
65. Ibid.: Walter Reade Jr to Garrett, 11 December 1967.
66. *NFFC Annual Report 1968*, p. 13 (12).
67. TNA T 244/2035 includes extensive correspondence between John Terry and the Cox's and King's branch of Lloyds Bank in the mid/late 1960s.
68. *NFFC Annual Report 1967*, p. 3 (11).
69. 'NFFC to resume loans – on limited scale', *Kinematograph Weekly*, 12 August 1967, p. 3.
70. *NFFC Annual Report 1969*, p. 2 (7).
71. TNA T 224/1832: Industrial Reorganisation Corporation: Report on the National Film Finance Corporation, January 1969.

CHAPTER 14

Decline and Fall

> At the moment the Americans are here, occupying our studios and bringing work to our technicians and to our other film-makers; but there is no guarantee whatsoever that they will stay. If, for economic or political reasons, they were to pull out of production here, the British film industry could collapse in a month. (Lord Willis)[1]

The end of the 1960s saw the onset of yet another crisis for the British film industry. For some years, American finance had accounted for a majority of British films: this had provided an important stimulus for the domestic production sector but also gave rise to concerns that the industry had become too dependent upon American money. In 1966 the National Film Finance Corporation's annual report echoed Lord Willis of Chislehurst in highlighting the potentially disastrous consequences for the British production sector if the flow of dollars suddenly dried up: 'It can be argued that there is no assurance that the US distributors will continue to finance British films on the present large scale, or at all, and if for any reason "runaway" production were to return to Hollywood, or to go elsewhere, British film production would be so gravely weakened that its survival might be in peril.'[2] In 1969 the sword of Damocles that had been hanging over the head of the British film industry fell as the major Hollywood studios significantly – and more to the point, suddenly – cut back their investment in British production. Some estimates suggest that total US investment in British films fell by two-thirds between 1968 and 1970. Two questions that need to be asked are why British film production had become so dependent upon American money and what the reasons were for the withdrawal of that investment at the end of the decade.

There were both cultural and economic contexts for the increasing level of American investment in British production. On one level British cinema became – at least for a brief period in the mid-1960s – a site of great cultural vitality and innovation. The phenomenon of 'Swinging London' – as much of a culturally created myth as a real social movement – was credited with drawing film-makers such as Otto Preminger (*Bunny Lake is Missing*, 1965), François Truffaut (*Fahrenheit 451*, 1966) and Michelangelo Antonioni (*Blow-Up*, 1966) to Britain.[3] Stanley Kubrick came to Britain to make *Lolita* in 1962 and remained for the rest of his career. In 1966 Penelope Houston, the editor of *Sight & Sound*, recognised the importance of Hollywood studios in supporting these and other film-makers: 'MGM money backs Kubrick and Antonioni; MCA backs Universal; Fox money backs Losey. British crews make the pictures, which means that they qualify for quota and Eady money here.'[4] British film-makers also benefited from US investment, including Lewis Gilbert (*Alfie*, 1966), Michael Winner (*The Jokers*, 1967), John Schlesinger (*Far From the Madding Crowd*, 1967), Karel Reisz (*Isadora*, 1968) and Lindsay Anderson (*if . . .*, 1968). David Robinson argued that Hollywood was attracted by the creativity of British film-makers:

> For a time all went well. Not all the films were bad, and there were enough commercial successes – the Beatles films, *Darling, Georgy Girl, Blow-Up* – to convince producers in the States that here was a goldmine, an endless supply of free talent and new ideas. Perhaps at no time in the remembered history of the cinema had the money-men been as receptive to new people and new ideas. It was a brief Utopia.[5]

There was a particular vogue in the late 1960s for what might be described as vanity projects by British actors who believed they were capable directors, notably Albert Finney (*Charlie Bubbles*, 1967) and Anthony Newley (*Can Heironymous Merkin Ever Forget Mercy Humppe and Find True Happiness?*, 1968). John Croydon's assessment of *Charlie Bubbles* for a completion guarantee was incredulous: 'I don't know what all this is about!! . . . It does not "start", it has no "middle" and also does nothing. To that end I suppose it is "modern", but I think does not belong to the medium of cinema . . . This film is obviously going to be a "Finney Special".'[6] However, Universal Pictures – which backed both *Charlie Bubbles* and *Heironymous Merkin* – was evidently willing to invest in 'artistic' projects. According to Jay Kantner, Universal's head of European production: 'I saw *Charlie Bubbles* as a minority film, but thought that it could be realistically budgeted as such.'[7]

Yet underlying the 'Hollywood UK' trend was hard-headed economic reality. Britain was an economical production base: studio rents and labour costs were lower than in America for a comparable level of technical and professional quality. Some estimates suggest that three regular features could be made in Britain for the same cost as two in Hollywood.[8] And the devaluation of sterling in November 1967 meant that Hollywood's dollars went further: every £1 million invested in British production by American interests cost them only $2.4 million instead of $2.8 million.[9] The high point of US investment in the British production sector was in 1967, when Hollywood spent £33.4 million on British production.[10] Hollywood no longer had frozen revenues in Britain: the major studios chose to reinvest their income from the British market in local production. According to industry analyst Chris Muson in his independently published study *The Marketing of Motion Pictures* in 1969: 'The financing of most British production by American companies is accomplished by a revolving system. Rental income earned by distribution subsidiaries of American companies are passed to the production companies and used to finance further production.'[11]

Another significant factor in attracting US investment was the availability of subsidy from the Eady levy. American distributors often made it a condition of financing British films that they should be eligible for the levy. The distribution agreement for the Bond pictures, for example, stipulated that each film was 'to be capable of being duly registered as a British film and as an Exhibitors' Quota film and of participating in the British Film Production Fund as an eligible film'.[12] And the contract for Stanley Kubrick's *2001: A Space Odyssey* (1968) – shot at Borehamwood and Shepperton over a period of eighteen months for MGM at an estimated cost of £4.3 million – stipulated that it 'shall qualify as a British film and be eligible for participation in the Fund operated by the British Film Fund Agency'.[13] However, Jay Kantner added an important caveat that Eady eligibility was only a consideration if there was deemed to be a significant market in Britain: 'There are a few films where it would be a factor in planning. Essentially films are made where they need to be made . . . It would depend very much on my judgement of the likely British market for the film.'[14]

There were differing opinions about the benefits of the increasing level of American investment. On the one hand it was seen as a sign of the creative vitality of British cinema that Hollywood should want to invest in British films. In his survey of British production activity in 1967, for example, *Kine*'s studio correspondent Derek Todd argued that American investment had cultural as well as economic benefits for British cinema: 'And, indeed, many British film makers will tell you they get more creative freedom from the Americans than they ever did from their own countrymen: with their own massive home market and entry into the world cinemas, the Americans can afford to take risks.'[15] And for British studios, US runaways were an important source of income and employment. Sidney Gilliat indicated that Shepperton Studios' record profit of £199,544 in 1967 was due in large measure to 'the continuance of the supply of high-budget pictures for which the larger stages at Shepperton are particularly suitable'.[16] Among the runaways shot at Shepperton in the late 1960s were Charles K. Feldman's extravagant Bond spoof *Casino Royale* and Columbia's lavish musical *Oliver!*. As Antony Thorncroft wrote in an article for *The Financial Times*:

> The inescapable fact is that only American companies have the financial resources to invest in blockbusters. British film makers, with tight budgets, dare not put all their money into one film. That is why Paramount put up the £1 m.-plus for *Half a Sixpence*, Columbia the £1.5 m. for *Oliver!*, United Artists even more for [*The*] *Charge of the Light Brigade*, and why Anglo-Amalgamated, in which ABC has a substantial interest, was forced to co-operate with MGM when planning its most costly venture, the £1.5 m. *Far from the Madding Crowd* . . . To spend £350,000 on one set, as Columbia [*sic* - actually United Artists] did for the volcano sequence in *You Only Live Twice* (exceeding in the process the total cost of the first Bond picture), needs the international outlook, and the ability to wait years for your return – neither qualities can exist in the UK.[17]

The Board of Trade confirmed this assessment and pointed out that the American companies could afford to support full production programmes in the expectation that the profits of the successful films would cancel out the loss-makers: 'Only the US "majors" have the necessary financial resources to stand a run of perhaps five or six failures, each costing £½m or more before the financial winner comes along and more than recoups the losses on the whole series.'[18] The greater financial resources of the American studios arose from their worldwide distribution organisations and their large domestic market. In contrast, the Rank Organisation was the only British group with an international distribution set-up, and even then the closure of Rank Film Distributors of America meant that it had no guaranteed access to the American market without a co-production and distribution arrangement with one of the majors.

On the other hand there were concerns that the increasing dependence upon American finance exposed the British film industry to significant risks. For independent producer Stephen Pallos those risks included rising production costs and the possibility that American interests might find more advantageous conditions elsewhere. His prognosis was a gloomy one: 'If this occurred it would mean a collapse of British film production, because outside of American investment only a small amount of money would be available for British film production today.'[19] In 1969 the NFFC cautioned that 'considerable economic opportunities are being lost to the United Kingdom through the lack of strong sources of British finance for British films'.[20] And John Boulting averred that 'British production has developed, under the influence of American finance, in economic terms that have increasingly made less and less sense. And what I don't think you can do is to carry on paying more and more for talents and skills and so forth in the face of an overall market that continues to contract.'[21] It was not just that British distributors were unable to match the largesse of the Americans and so lost certain projects to them – *Tom Jones* and *Modesty Blaise* were two high-profile examples – but also that the higher costs of American-backed runaways contributed to inflationary pressure across the production sector as a whole. Alexander Walker described the escalating costs of the late 1960s as 'the production escalator . . . which dragged films up to and past the floor where their makers should have prudently called a halt or got off'.[22]

The Film Finances Archive provides evidence of the higher costs of American-backed films. Universal, for example, which had become the leading American sponsor of British production in the later 1960s, backed *The Jokers* (£228,725), *Charlie Bubbles* (£324,151), *Can Heironymous Merkin Ever Forget Mercy Humppe and Find True Happiness?* (£443,500), *Pretty Polly* (£589,434), *Boom!* (£1,531,324) and *Isadora* (£1,283,942).[23] There were various reasons for the increasing costs beyond the effects of inflation. For *Boom!* (1967) – which despite its excessive cost was actually efficiently directed by Joseph Losey – it was due to the salaries paid to Elizabeth Taylor and Richard Burton which amounted to £769,000 (50.2 per cent of the total budget for the film). For *Isadora* (1968) – Karel Reisz's biopic of dancer Isadora Duncan starring Vanessa Redgrave – it was due to the scale of a film intended for a prestigious roadshow release. The film incurred significant overcosts due to 'improvements' which Reisz blamed on the studio. At the end of what had been a difficult production, Reisz wrote to Film Finances: 'This may not be the time or place to speak of our little histoire . . . Enough to say perhaps that my lords and masters decided, at a certain point, that they wanted a bigger, more ambitious film: I confess, I concurred.'[24]

Film Finances was rightly wary when offering guarantees for American runaways. It had incurred heavy losses on Universal's *Lancelot and Guinevere* (1963) – produced and directed by star Cornel Wilde – which exceeded its original budget (£494,746) by some 40 per cent: the final audited cost of the production was £690,971.²⁵ The high overcost arose from overrunning on location in Yugoslavia – the unit had to return to complete several key sequences after the studio period – and the incompetence of the accounting department, which miscalculated the exchange rate. Film Finances advanced over £100,000 towards its completion: Wilde – having taken some of the overcost himself – assigned half the producer's share to the guarantor, though the film never recovered its cost.²⁶ Film Finances baulked at the budget of Paramount's *The Amorous Adventures of Moll Flanders* (1965), which at £911,393 was over twice that of *Tom Jones*, telling the studio 'that were we to do anything of this sort it would be important psychologically with regard to the producer, and in order to make it possible for us to keep control of things and if needs be play the heavy, that any private arrangement between Paramount and ourselves in respect of finance, should not be known to the producer'.²⁷ In the event, a combination of the experience of *Tom Jones* and a notoriously spendthrift director in Terence Young seems to have persuaded Film Finances against offering a guarantee on this occasion.

It was not just the increasing costs of American runaways that presented a problem. Film Finances tended to find that American studios were more *laissez-faire* when it came to controlling production costs and had a tendency to indulge temperamental stars and directors. A good case in point was *The Bobo* (1967). This film – a star vehicle for Peter Sellers – was produced by Jerry Gershwin and Elliott Kastner for Warner Bros. with a budget of £985,061. Sellers was originally to have directed the film, but relinquished the role to Robert Parrish before production commenced. Film Finances was concerned about Sellers's reputation and wanted to ensure there was sufficient protection against his wayward behaviour: '[When] dealing with an artiste, who in this case is quite frankly unpredictable and is also so to speak the whole picture, it seems incredible that the Producers should have entered into a contract with him which only covers the shooting period and then agree to pay him pro rata overage in cash'.²⁸ Its guarantee included a 'special franchise' whereby any overage payments owed to Sellers would be borne by the studio and not charged to the budget.²⁹ At some point during the course of filming, however, Sellers took over directing the film and fell behind schedule due to making 'improvements' including an unusually large number of retakes:

> It would be interesting to know if and when Warners agreed to Peter Sellers co-directing the picture – the effect of which has been to cost them a considerable amount of money. We never had any direct intimation with regard to this and we would certainly have had views on its advisability. The first indications we had were from a friend of the Editor, who said to us that the latter told him that he now had two directors . . . There can be very little doubt that Peter Sellers's subsequent intervention in direction of the picture has caused all the trouble.³⁰

Film Finances exercised their right to take over the production and insisted 'that he [Sellers] should revert to the position for which he was originally engaged, i.e. as an actor'.[31] As the film went into post-production, Kastner's production manager estimated a finishing date of 7 April ('If Peter Sellers is excluded from cutting') or 21 April ('If Peter Sellers remains in the cutting room').[32] The final overcost on *The Bobo* amounted to US $550,000: Film Finances – maintaining that $145,000 of the additional expenditure was not their responsibility – blamed the overcost on 'what seems to us to have been an extravagant and irresponsible approach to the picture. This may have been the Producer's ultimate responsibility, but we feel sure that Warners cannot help but to have been fully aware of it.'[33]

Lock Up Your Daughters (1969) was another example of a runaway that ran away. This film – produced by David Deutsch and directed by Peter Coe for Columbia – was yet another attempt to make another *Tom Jones*. Film Finances initially felt that the project 'contains many favourable aspects' and agreed to the budget – a relatively modest £543,558 – 'subject to any adjustment which may become necessary after the reconnaissance in Ireland and any repercussions from the recent currency devaluation'.[34] However, following a visit to the location, John Croydon reported that there were logistical problems which 'can only be solved by the expenditure of what could prove to be large sums of money; that the budget is short by the cost of renting local stores, workshops and offices; could run into financial problems on the question of local labour and could easily encounter local resistance once the subject matter becomes public property.'[35] Columbia then informed Film Finances that 'we have agreed with Domino Productions Limited that some of the parts cast for this picture will be played by more important artists than originally envisaged, and we have also agreed that a further £2,000 should be paid for script revisions. Apart from these items, however, we are looking to you for the Guarantee on the basis of the original budget.'[36] Garrett was having none of it: he felt that Columbia 'are up to their usual tricks, and are trying to use David to put them over'.[37] The budget was revised upwards to £755,423. Croydon intimated that it was going to be a difficult production, though he had some faith in the producer and director:

> I do not think this is going to be an easy film. Its success so far as we are concerned depends entirely on the abilities of the director and producer to limit themselves to what they have to spend. I think, though, that Coe is sufficiently professional not to over-reach himself and Deutsch is a producer who does not want to over-run, especially as I have a feeling that he believes his film to be riding on the edge of its commercial potential.[38]

However, the film was soon running over schedule and budget. Croydon felt that Coe 'has an incorrect approach to his shooting' and 'must learn to restrict the amount of "business" he is injecting into the scenes, which is causing his screen time to rise disproportionately to the amount of dialogue'.[39] Film Finances were not happy when they learned that the role of Lord Foppington had been expanded to justify the casting of Christopher Plummer. Hugh Griffith, originally cast as

Mr Justice Squeezum, walked off the set in protest at the diminution of his role. Garrett, noting the increasing overcost, wrote to Deutsch: 'A picture only three days over schedule, but £64,000 into its contingency suggests that something has gone very badly wrong somewhere. It also still looks as though the picture is running well over length and must be further tailored.'[40] In the event, the cost of *Lock Up Your Daughters* escalated to £878,986, with Film Finances advancing £52,060 towards its completion.[41]

And these were not even the most expensive runaway productions. Film Finances did not touch the very high-end budgets. It passed on Elliott Kastner's production of *Where Eagles Dare* (1968) for MGM – budgeted at US $4.5 million – on the grounds that 'the budget above and below the line would seem to possibly come out beyond what we consider our normal price range'.[42] The fact that Kastner had nominally been in charge of *The Bobo* may also have been a factor. It was a similar case with the war epic *Battle of Britain* (1969), which Harry Saltzman and Benjamin S. Fisz brought to Film Finances in 1966. 'This proposition,' Garrett noted, 'by virtue of its size, its budget, its nature and the personalities involved is we feel somewhat out of our class.'[43] *Battle of Britain* was originally to have been a co-production between Rank and Paramount.[44] However, Rank was unable to agree terms for its percentage from overseas distribution and withdrew from the project. In the event, *Battle of Britain* was financed by United Artists, which provided a guarantee of US $10 million which Saltzman and Fisz discounted with the Bank of America and a further cash advance of $3,225,000.[45] The Ministry of Defence was left chasing the producers for an unpaid charge of £35,061 for the provision of technical facilities for the film.[46]

The American studios were now facing up to the same problem that had affected British producers for two decades: that the combination of rising budgets and a contracting market meant that the likelihood of recovering their costs from the British market alone was significantly reduced except in the case of an outstanding box-office success. Furthermore, by the late 1960s it was becoming increasingly apparent that the 'Hollywood UK' boom had run its course. Most of the exceptionally successful films – such as *Tom Jones* and *A Hard Day's Night* – had been made during the first half of the decade. But there were fewer major runaway hits after 1965. The annual production cycle of the Bond pictures became less regular after *Thunderball* (1965). By the end of the decade the cultural moment of 'Swinging London' had passed and the spy craze had fizzled out. The fate of American runaways, in commercial terms, now depended more on their performance at the US box office.

The failure of a slew of top-budget runaways in the late 1960s – the two exceptions were MGM's *2001: A Space Odyssey* and Columbia's *Oliver!* – was undoubtedly a major factor in the decision by the Hollywood majors to cut back their British production activity. But it was not the only reason. At the same time the US film industry was facing severe difficulties at home. Cinema attendances had fallen to a quarter of their mid-1940s peak: in 1968 they fell below 20 million a week for the first time since records began.[47] For much of the 1960s Hollywood had clung stubbornly to the idea that the traditional family audience still existed – a perception apparently reinforced by the spectacular success of *The Sound of Music* (1965) – and it was only from 1967 that films such as *The Graduate*, *Bonnie and Clyde*, *Butch Cassidy and the Sundance Kid*, *Midnight Cowboy* and *Easy Rider* revealed the extent to which the cinema-going demographic had shifted towards a younger audience. These films also demonstrated – against the prevailing industry lore – that low-cost films could make big profits. *The Graduate* cost US $2.5 million and earned $40 million in rentals; *Easy Rider* cost a mere $375,000 and earned $50 million in rentals.[48] *Kine* editor Bill Altria observed in 1969: 'In America there is growing resistance to the backing of astronomical budgets and high cost talents, a trend given impetus by a number of costly failures and the success of many relatively low-cost features produced by new young talents.'[49]

The combination of declining audiences and diminishing revenues left the studios in a weakened position. This created the conditions for structural reorganisation within the industry that saw most of the studios bought by giant conglomerates whose primary interests were not necessarily in the movie business. Universal had been owned by MCA (the Music Corporation of America) since 1962. In 1966 Paramount was taken over by the mining giant Gulf + Western; United Artists was acquired by the Transamerica Corporation in 1967; Warner Bros.-Seven Arts was taken over by Kinney National Services in 1969; and in the same year property tycoon Kirk Kerkorian bought a controlling interest in MGM's parent company Loew's Incorporated. David A. Cook explains the interest of these corporations in so far as, despite their current difficulties, the studios 'represented good investments, since their shares were temporarily under-valued and they owned huge tracts of real estate in one of the nation's most lucrative markets'.[50] However, the studios' new owners tended not to subscribe to the philosophy of the old studio heads that it was necessary to spend money in order to make money: their outlook was to reduce what they saw as unnecessary costs. And in this context the strategy of producing overseas – where the geographical distance meant that it was less easy for the New York offices to exercise control – came under scrutiny. When George Ornstein stood down as Paramount's vice-president in charge of foreign production in 1969, his successor James Tofosky was sacked after only one week and not replaced.[51] It was the same later in the year when there was no immediate replacement for United Artists' British managing director Kenneth Winckles.[52]

And by the end of the decade Hollywood was facing its own crisis. The studios were facing heavy losses following over-investment in expensive projects that fell a long way short of expectations. In 1969 MGM lost $35 million on film production: its success with *2001: A Space Odyssey* was offset by the failures of the British-made runaways *Goodbye, Mr Chips* (a musical remake of the 1939 film which was severely cut for its US release) and *Alfred the Great* (a would-be 'youth epic' of which 'a wit said omitting the burning of the cakes hadn't stopped the film-makers burning their fingers').[53] United Artists lost $45 million, including an investment of $40 million in three expensive British films – *Chitty Chitty Bang Bang* ($15 million), *The Charge* of the *Light Brigade* ($12 million) and *Battle of Britain* ($13 million) – which between them returned less than $10 million in America.[54] Twentieth Century–Fox's disasters were all home-made: it lost $28 million on *Doctor Dolittle*, *Hello, Dolly!* and *Star!* in vain attempts to repeat the success of *The Sound of Music*.[55] Universal and Warner Bros. were less severely affected: both had moved into television production where international sales were lucrative enough to offset losses on film production. Columbia was probably in the best position of any of the majors at the end of the decade. Its British films had enjoyed critical acclaim (*A Man for All Seasons*) and popular success (*Oliver!*), but it also scored with the musical *Funny Girl* and reaped the benefits of distributing *Easy Rider*.[56]

It was in 1969 that the 'Hollywood UK' bubble finally burst. For three years the British production industry had been ignoring the warning signs. And throughout the first half of 1969 there was still a sense of denial on the part of some trade commentators. In February, for example, the *Kine* suggested that talk of the withdrawal of US finance was unduly pessimistic and pointed to the fact that 'current production is at the same level as this time last year . . . The fluidity of the American investment situation prompts caution in predicting the prospects for 1969, but an extremely pessimistic view is not justified, especially if it is generated from within the industry.'[57] It pointed out that the twelve films currently shooting in British studios was the same number as the same time the previous year and included several big American-backed pictures, including Columbia's *Cromwell* at Shepperton and United Artists' *The Private Life of Sherlock Holmes* at Pinewood. However, Shepperton's managing director Sidney Gilliat predicted difficult times ahead:

> We can see the dip coming and it is quite possible that there will be some recession this year. We don't envisage any mass exodus of the American companies, but more of an orderly readjustment. If the position worsens, it will be very bad and British investment will not be able to bridge that gap.[58]

In May Universal decided to postpone production of its planned film of *Mary Stuart* – a British historical subject in the tradition of *A Man for All Seasons* and *Anne of the Thousand Days* – on account of budgeting and scheduling difficulties.[59] It also never went ahead with a film of *Biggles* – based on the popular juvenile adventure stories of W. E. Johns – which had been approved in principle at a budget of over £1 million.[60] As late as August *The Economist* was suggesting that the large-scale withdrawal of American finance 'looks unlikely now'.[61] But a few months later the news that MGM – the one remaining Hollywood company to own its own British production facility – was pulling out of the production of Fred Zinnemann's £4 million film of *Man's Fate* at Borehamwood was taken as a sign that 'British film making is entering a period of major crisis'.[62] MGM explained its decision on the grounds of 'not being involved in high budget production'.[63] The film's Italian producer Carlo Ponti tried to restart it as a co-production with Dimitri de Grunwald's London Screenplays, to no avail.[64] In November Clifford Barclay, President of the

Film Production Association, reported following a visit to Hollywood 'a widespread view that production will slow down until the middle of next year, by which time some revival may occur if the decision is taken to increase the stock of films to feed the distribution organisations which are extremely costly to maintain'.[65] Even the ever-optimistic Bill Altria was forced to accept the reality of the crisis when the studios announced much-reduced production plans for 1970: 'The situation is more serious than the previous "crisis" in recent years . . . It is directly attributable to the upheaval among the US majors; the retrenchment of Universal, Paramount and 20th Century–Fox; and the hiatus resulting from the changes in control of MGM and Warner Bros.'[66]

The impact of the withdrawal of American finance on the British production sector was both sudden and severe. In 1968 the British subsidiaries of US film companies had pumped a total of £31.3 million into the production of British films: this fell to £20.9 million in 1969 and £12.8 million in 1970.[67] Such a precipitous fall in investment necessitated retrenchment: fewer films were produced and budgets were cut. MGM, for example, said that it would 'probably not finance pictures costing more than £200,000'.[68] Columbia Pictures – significantly one of the two majors (the other was Fox) not to have been taken over by a conglomerate in the late 1960s – was the only studio that announced it was stepping up British production for 1970–1.[69] But other studios – including Paramount, Universal, Fox and Warner Bros. – announced no British productions for 1970.[70] Hollywood's economic retrenchment affected the British industry in several ways. For British producers it meant they had to look to other sources of finance than American studios: this would pave the way for the entry of new players in the field of film finance in the early 1970s. And British studios, which had been full to capacity at the height of the runaway boom, now had to face up to the prospects of empty stages and laying off personnel.

As the 1960s drew to a close, therefore, the British film industry was entering another one of its frequent periods of crisis. It was a crisis both deeper and more severe than at any time since the late 1940s. But there were differing assessments of the reasons for the crisis, in particular the extent to which the withdrawal of American finance was a symptom or a cause of the industry's difficulties. James Clark, the editor of *Midnight Cowboy* (an American film made by British director John Schlesinger), blamed the industry's dependence on Hollywood for its woes: 'The British cinema has been whoring long enough, living off immoral dollar earnings. It has taken an American recession to bring us finally to our senses . . . It is clear that the industry, as an organised whole, barely exists.'[71] The film-maker and film historian Kevin Brownlow, however, believed that the industry's problems were due more to underlying structural factors: 'The crisis is not the result of a sudden withdrawal of American finance. It is the end result of a process which has been steadily exacting its toll since the end of the war.'[72] In truth there is something to both these arguments. There is no doubt that the drastic reduction in American finance in 1969–70 came as a severe shock; but it was a crisis that could have been foreseen, and that some had indeed predicted.

There were different prognoses for the immediate future of the British film industry. A relatively upbeat note was sounded by *The Times*: 'Altogether, at both the exhibition and production end, a more athletic industry seems to be shaping up. Add more home finance, and the longed-for artistic revival may be with us.'[73] There was a view that British producers who had been squeezed out of the market by their inability to match the budgets offered by the Hollywood studios now had an opportunity to rebuild the domestic production industry. And the reduction in American finance strengthened the case for the retention of the National Film Finance Corporation. But the *Kine* – which had borne witness to the recurrent crises of the film industry for over half a century – was rather less sanguine: 'The decade of the 60s draws to a close with the industry in a state of crisis . . . In simple terms, it is a crisis of economics. Although attendances have declined, industry income has been maintained at a fairly stable level by admission price increases. But against this the cost of film production has increased many times.'[74]

Notes

1. *Parliamentary Debates: House of Lords*, 5th Series, vol. 272, 2 February 1966, cols 374–5.
2. *National Film Finance Corporation: Annual Report and Statement of Accounts for the year ended 31 March 1966*, Cmnd. 3066 (August 1966), p. 6 (27).
3. 'What is Luring the World's Film Makers to London?', *The Financial Times*, 10 May 1966, p. 16.
4. Penelope Houston, 'England, Their England', *Sight & Sound*, 35: 2 (Spring 1966), p. 55.
5. David Robinson, 'Case Histories of the Next Renaissance', *Sight & Sound*, 38: 1 (Winter 1968–9), p. 36.
6. FFA Realised Film Box 422: *Charlie Bubbles*: Handwritten notes by John Croydon, n.d.
7. Quoted in John Russell Taylor, 'Backing Britain', *Sight & Sound*, 38: 3 (Summer 1969), p. 114.
8. 'Hollywood and the Runaway Productions', *The Times*, 11 July 1962, p. 13.
9. 'US investment will benefit from devaluation – but . . .', *Kinematograph Weekly*, 25 November 1967, p. 3.
10. 'US film-makers in Britain may start a dollar drain', *The Times*, 10 February 1969, p. 21.
11. Quoted in Paul Monaco, *The Sixties: History of the American Cinema 1960–1969* (Berkeley: University of California Press, 2001), p. 14.
12. FFA Realised Film Box 328: *Dr No*: Distribution Agreement between Danjaq SA and United Artists Corporation, 10 April 1962.
13. Stanley Kubrick Archive, University of the Arts SK/12/2/5: Letter of agreement between MGM and Polaris Productions, 22 May 1965.
14. Quoted in Taylor, 'Backing Britain', p. 115.
15. '1968 – boom year for the magnificent seven', *Kinematograph Weekly*, 16 December 1967, p. 140.
16. 'Clear improvement in British Lion profit', *Kinematograph Weekly*, 22 July 1967, p. 5.
17. 'Film studios enjoy a boom – thanks to American money', *The Financial Times*, 21 September 1967, p. 16.
18. TNA BT 258/2038: 'Film Finance Review', p. 7 (23).
19. 'If American finance stops . . .', *Kinematograph Weekly*, 3 August 1968, p. 9.

20. *National Film Finance Corporation: Annual Report and Statement of Accounts for the year ended 31 March 1969*, Cmnd. 4094 (June 1969), p. 4 (15).
21. 'The Stable Door after the (US) force has gone', *Kinematograph Weekly*, 6 December 1969, p. 5.
22. Alexander Walker, *Hollywood, England: The British Film Industry in the Sixties* (London: Michael Joseph, 1974), p. 443.
23. Llewella Chapman, '"They wanted a bigger, more ambitious film": Film Finances and the American "runaways" that ran away', *Journal of British Cinema and Television*, 18: 2 (2021), p. 189.
24. FFA Realised Film Box 438: *Isadora*: Karel Reisz to Robert Garrett, n.d.
25. FFA Realised Film Box 339: *Lancelot and Guinevere*: Certified final cost of production (Nyman Libson, Paul & Co.), 31 July 1963.
26. Ibid.: Universal Pictures' statement of revenues re: *Sword of Lancelot* to 27 September 1980. By this time the 'total accountable gross' amounted to US $2,592,827.
27. Ibid.: Robert Garrett to Howard Harrison, 26 August 1964.
28. FFA Realised Film Box 421: *The Bobo*: Robert Garrett to Gerry Blattner, 10 October 1966.
29. Ibid.: Garrett to Gina Productions Inc., 5 October 1966.
30. Ibid.: Garrett to Blattner, 26 January 1967.
31. Ibid.: Garrett to Elliott Kastner, 25 January 1967.
32. Ibid.: Denis Holt to Garrett, 6 February 1967.
33. Ibid.: 'RSA' to Garrett, 9 October 1969.
34. FFA Realised Film Box 447: *Lock Up Your Daughters*: John Croydon to Robert Garrett, 4 October 1967; Garrett to Domino Productions, 22 November 1967.
35. Ibid.: Croydon to Garrett, 1 December 1967.
36. Ibid.: R. E. Atkinson to Film Finances, 25 January 1968.
37. Ibid.: Garrett to Bernard Smith, 12 February 1968.
38. Ibid.: Croydon to Garrett, 23 February 1968.
39. Ibid.: Croydon to Garrett, 8 March 1968.
40. Ibid.: Garrett to David Deutsch, 18 April 1968.
41. Ibid.: W. R. Cullen to Messrs Wood, King & Co., 24 February 1983.
42. FFA General Correspondence Box 43: Robert Garrett to Denis Holt, 25 January 1967.
43. Ibid.: Note – 'Battle of Britain', 9 September 1966.
44. 'Rank plans to spend £4M on new films', *The Guardian*, 18 March 1966, p. 16.
45. TNA TS 66/17: Messrs Harbottle & Lewis to W. H. Godwin (Treasury solicitor), 27 October 1970.
46. Ibid.: A. D. Osborne to Messrs Hooton and Charlton, 15 September 1970.
47. Monaco, *The Sixties*, p. 40.
48. Ibid. p. 187.
49. 'Uncertainties in the Hollywood scene', *Kinematograph Weekly*, 13 September 1969, p. 4.
50. David A. Cook, *Lost Illusions: American Cinema in the Shadow of Watergate and Vietnam, 1970–1979* (Berkeley: University of California Press, 2000), p. 16.
51. 'Ornstein's new role with Paramount', *Kinematograph Weekly*, 15 February 1969, p. 3.
52. 'No name yet for UA top job in Britain', *Kinematograph Weekly*, 13 September 1969, p. 3.
53. Walker, *Hollywood, England*, p. 443.
54. Cook, *Lost Illusions*, p. 496.
55. Monaco, *The Sixties*, p. 37.

56. Ibid.
57. 'No justification for extreme pessimism', *Kinematograph Weekly*, 15 February 1969, p. 4.
58. 'US film-makers in Britain may start a dollar drain', *The Times*, 10 February 1969, p. 21.
59. FFA General Correspondence Box 76: Sanford Lieberson to Robert Garrett, 6 May 1969.
60. Ibid.: Robert Garrett to Universal Pictures, 4 November 1968. Film Finances had agreed in principle to guarantee the film at a budget of £1,152,969.
61. 'The Bank of Soho Square', *The Economist*, 2 August 1969, p. 56.
62. 'Film-making crisis: MGM ready to quit Boreham Wood', *The Financial Times*, 21 November 1969.
63. 'MGM Pulls Out of £4m Zinnemann Film', *Today's Cinema*, 24 November 1969, p. 3.
64. FFA General Correspondence Box 76: Robert Garrett to Bernard Smith, 28 November 1969.
65. 'Barclay Warns: A Major Crisis Developing', *Kinematograph Weekly*, 29 November 1969, p. 3.
66. 'The production crisis and the trends', *Kinematograph Weekly*, 8 November 1969, p. 4.
67. Margaret Dickinson and Sarah Street, *Cinema and State: The Film Industry and the British Government 1927–84* (London: British Film Institute, 1985), p. 240.
68. 'The film industry's quest for funds', *The Financial Times*, 22 December 1969, p. 23.
69. 'Columbia to step up European production activity', *Kinematograph Weekly*, 1 November 1969, p. 3.
70. 'British Investment Helping to Fill the Gap', *Kinematograph Weekly*, 20 December 1969, p. 138.
71. 'The Crisis We Deserve', *Sight & Sound*, 39: 4 (1970), p. 176.
72. Ibid.
73. 'The money flows into British films', *The Times*, 16 June 1969, p. 23.
74. '1970 – A Year for Change', *Kinematograph Weekly*, 20 December 1969, p. 3.

Part III

Crises and Contraction: 1970–1985

CHAPTER 15

Restructuring the Film Industry

> The British film industry entered 1971, if not in a state of actual crisis, at least in a kind of frenzied anxiety about the future which permeated all levels of the industry. Production during 1970 was not in fact substantially reduced, contrary to gloomy forecasts last summer, but fewer films were making money and there is something more manic than ever in the search for the correct box-office formula. (David Pirie)[1]

At the start of the 1970s the British film industry was faced with a crisis more acute than at any time since the end of the Second World War. A perfect storm of factors – the failure of a number of expensive films in the late 1960s, the withdrawal of large amounts of American capital, the continuing contraction of the market, and a deteriorating economic outlook for the country as a whole – combined to create especially challenging conditions for the film business. The statistics paint a grim picture. The market for films contracted severely during the 1970s. Annual cinema attendances fell from 193 million in 1970 to 103 million in 1977, and while the closure of cinemas abated, the total seating capacity of Britain's cinemas fell by around half from 1,446,000 in 1970 to 738,000 by 1978.[2] A particular feature of the 1970s was the conversion of some larger cinemas into multiples of two or three screens: this was meant to offer more choice for audiences and to provide a space for alternative films, though in practice it only further strengthened the position of the two major circuits who owned the larger cinemas best suited to conversion and who consequently controlled more screens. The exhibition industry attempted to compensate for declining admissions by increasing ticket prices: this had worked in the past but there came a point at which it became counterproductive. As *The Financial Times* remarked in 1971: 'The argument currently raging in the film business is whether or not the rising prices are responsible for the declining audience. In the past two years, cinema admission prices have risen twice as fast as the cost of living.'[3]

To read the trade press in 1970–1 reveals a narrative of crisis and uncertainty: studio closures, rumours of studio closures, the laying off of studio workers and the cancellation of film projects through lack of finance. MGM – the last Hollywood company to maintain its own British production facility – closed Borehamwood Studios in April 1970: the news had been expected for some months but it was greeted with much despondency by the trades unions, who described the closure as 'another example of the general incompetence of the management of the

British film industry for the past 40 years'.[4] In July it was reported that the 'substantial reduction in American-sponsored British films resulted in the cancellation of a number of important and valuable bookings' at Shepperton.[5] In September Hammer Film Productions announced that it was selling Bray Studios: it had not shot a film there since 1966.[6] In the same month it was reported that there were only six feature films shooting in British studios.[7] And in February 1971 it was reported that the crisis was also affecting the television industry as the costs of telefilm production were increasing but the price paid by networks had remained the same: there were only two telefilm series currently in production.[8] The contraction of the industry even impacted upon the film trade press: the two surviving trade papers, *Kine Weekly* and *Today's Cinema*, merged in September 1971. An editorial in the latter blamed the fall in advertising revenues and concluded that 'the film industry in this country can support and sustain only one film paper'.[9]

Allied to the shrinking market and contracting production sector was the diminishing supply of capital. Hollywood's economic retrenchment inevitably impacted upon the British film industry. The American presence did not disappear entirely from British cinema – United Artists and Columbia continued to support British film-making during the early 1970s – but there was a safety-first strategy focusing on tried-and-trusted formulas. United Artists, for example, continued to sponsor the James Bond films, which showed no sign of losing their appeal at the British (and international) box office: *Diamonds Are Forever* topped the box office in 1972, *Live and Let Die* in 1973, *The Spy Who Loved Me* in 1977 and *Moonraker* in 1979, while *The Man With the Golden Gun* was third in 1975.[10] However, American investment in the British production sector fell sharply during the early 1970s. The National Film Finance Corporation calculated that US investment had fallen from £15.5 million in 1970 to £4.8 million in 1973 and £3.3 million in 1974.[11] This was only one-tenth of the amount of US investment at the height of the 'Hollywood UK' boom of the 1960s. And the reduction in American finance reflected a drop in production investment across the board. In July 1972 *CinemaTV Today* reported that total investment in production during the first six months of the year had halved since the previous year: a total of £16.4 million had been invested in 46 British films compared to £31.2 million in 49 British films over the same period in 1971.[12] According to a report by the Cinematograph Films Council:

> In the summer of 1973 it became apparent that the serious drop in finance available for film production was such that the production side of the UK film industry was likely to experience a serious run-down in the scale of its activities and that this in turn would have a detrimental effect on the industry as a whole, exhibitors as well as production . . . It is necessary for British producers to look elsewhere, which means mainly to domestic sources, for any further finance. Insufficient funds are available from these sources to maintain production at anything like present levels.[13]

The volume of British production had actually increased in the early 1970s. From around 70 films a year for most of the 1960s, the number of British films rose to between 80 and 90 a year in the early 1970s. However, many of these were relatively cheaply made films for the home market. *Kine*'s Rod Cooper reported that the increase in production in 1970 'is explained by the generally lower budgets, [and] shorter schedules of this year's films'.[14] In particular, low-budget television spin-offs and 'X'-certificate sex comedies proliferated in the early 1970s. However, production declined sharply after 1974: the number of British features fell from 64 in 1976 to 50 in 1978 and only 40 in 1979. Alexander Walker contends that the mid-1970s 'were the lowest, the most shameful nadir of film industry fortunes'.[15]

Against this background British films were still able to hold their own at the domestic box office in the early 1970s. In 1970, for example, *Battle of Britain* was the leading box-office attraction 'on the strength of its initial performance as a special presentation at the end of last year and during this year and its subsequent in-depth exposure on wave release which started in September'.[16] Otherwise there were five British films in the top ten general releases (*On Her Majesty's Secret Service, Where Eagles Dare, Women in Love, Carry On Up the Jungle, Every Home Should Have One*) and four in the 'special presentations' category (*Oliver!, Cromwell, Anne of the Thousand Days, The Lion in Winter*). Broadly speaking these were residual genres: war films, historical pictures and the sixth James Bond adventure. *Oliver!* had run for 90 consecutive weeks in the West End of London, during which time it had recorded 1,115,000 admissions and had taken over £830,000 at the box office.[17] In 1971 there were nine British films in the top twenty including two popular family films (*The Railway Children, The Tales of Beatrix Potter*) and one action thriller (*When Eight Bells Toll*), but newly emergent genres were represented by sex comedy (*Percy*) and no fewer than three spin-offs from television sitcoms: *On the Buses, Up Pompeii* and *Dad's Army*. Other than the Bond movies, however, no British film topped the annual box office after 1970. And as the number of British films declined, American films regained their overall ascendancy. There were only four British films in the top twenty in 1974 (*Don't Look Now, Confessions of a Window Cleaner, Stardust, Gold*) and five in 1975 (*The Man With the Golden Gun, Murder on the Orient Express, Tommy, The Land That Time Forgot, Monty Python and the Holy Grail*). In 1974 the total distributors' receipts for all British films in the home market were £6.5 million, compared to £18.4 million for foreign (mostly American) films.[18] With the 'Carry On' series waning in popularity – *Carry On Up the Jungle* was the last to feature in the top twenty in 1970 – the only other British films to be consistently successful were the revived 'Pink Panther' series starring Peter Sellers as the hapless Inspector Clouseau: *The Return of the Pink Panther* was fourth in 1975, *The Pink Panther Strikes Again* fourth in 1977 and *Revenge of the Pink Panther* fifth in 1978. The trend as the decade went on followed what had happened in the United States as a small number of highly successful films broke box-office records. The 'New Hollywood' blockbusters that had recalibrated box-office expectations in the mid-1970s also scored in Britain: *Jaws* grossed £500,000 inside two weeks and *Star Wars* was the leading attraction in the 'Year of the Blockbuster' in 1978, which in Britain also included *Grease* and *Saturday Night Fever*.[19]

However, the successful British films were exceptional. In 1974 the NFFC reported that 'the inflation of production costs and the contraction of the home market mean that British films, even if they reach the audiences for which they are intended, are overall likely to incur losses in direct financial terms'.[20] The Stock Market crash of 1973–4 was compounded by a secondary banking crisis when the Bank of England had to bail out lending banks to the tune of £100 million following the collapse of the housing market: one of the consequences was increasing interest rates which impacted particularly severely on the film industry as loans for film production were charged at a higher rate due to the inherently risky nature of the business.[21] The difficulty of raising finance prompted producers to find new ways of packaging their films. For *Universal Soldier* (1971) – a mercenary drama starring former James Bond George Lazenby and the last film directed by Cy Endfield – half the budget of £300,000 came from bank loans, with the rest realised through deferments by the cast and crew. According to producer Frederick J. Schwartz: 'With the film industry in the state it is, financially, this is the only sane way to make a picture. We are all involved in a group project, and directly concerned in making the film a success.'[22] However, *Universal Soldier* was a box-office flop and none of the deferments were recouped.

The contraction of the market necessitated retrenchment in production expenditure. The British Film Producers' Association reported in 1971 that over the last year film-makers had shown an 'increasingly realistic appreciation of present economic conditions by cutting their budgets and constantly examining their working patterns to eliminate waste'.[23] The NFFC also provided evidence of cost reduction: it supported eight feature films in 1970–1 with an average budget of £133,936, compared to eight in 1969–70 with an average budget of £322,921.[24] And in 1971 *The Financial Times* reported that it 'is a rare British picture to-day that costs more than £500,000. It is hardly a secret that the accountants have been getting to grips with film production costs.'[25] Tony Tenser, who founded Tigon Film Productions in the late 1960s, adhered to a low-cost, low-risk philosophy: 'We will make commercial films with commercial budgets . . . I have always tried to make films not looking for big profit but to bring a reasonable return on the capital invested in the film. Therefore most of our films break into the profit area.'[26] In 1971 Tigon announced four films – *Doomwatch*, *For the Love of Ada*, *Neither the Sea Nor the Sand* and *The Chilian Club* – all budgeted between £100,000 and £150,000. There was a brief period when Tigon became a vertically integrated interest, acquiring the Classic chain of 200 cinemas in 1971.[27]

Until the effect of inflation became more severe from the middle of the decade, British producers seem to have worked to a figure of around £200,000 as the optimum price for a film to be able to recover its costs from the home market. The 'Carry On' films of the early 1970s, for example, were mostly made for a little over this figure: *Carry On Henry* (£214,500), *Carry On At Your Convenience* (£218,805), *Carry On Matron* (£220,257), *Carry On Girls* (£205,962) and *Carry On Dick* (£212,948).[28] In March 1970 Hammer Film Productions announced that *Horror of Frankenstein* and *Scars of Dracula* would be 'the first in the history of Hammer to be produced with 100 per cent British finance': the budget was £200,000 for each film backed by guarantees from EMI Film Distributors.[29] Hammer's rival Amicus also worked to budgets of around £200,000: its films included *The House That Dripped Blood* (£208,330), *From Beyond the Grave* (£203,941) and *The Beast Must Die* (£187,269).[30] Occasionally lower-budget films would score at the box office. *On the Buses* – produced by Hammer for a reported cost of only £89,000 – was the most successful British film of 1971. It was reported to have grossed £511,308 from 244 bookings on general release.[31] And *Confessions of a Window Cleaner* (1974) – produced by Swiftdown (Michael Klinger, Gregg Smith and Norman Cohen) for £150,000 – returned £1,265,954 to the distributor (over half of which came from the home market) and a producer's share of £632,977.[32]

Monty Python and the Holy Grail (1975) highlights the potential for a relatively low-cost film to hit the box-office jackpot. This film had an unusual production history. After it had been turned down by Rank, EMI and the NFFC, producer Mark Forstarter raised the £237,000 budget – the final cost including interest was £282,035 – from a consortium of musical-theatre impresarios, record companies and pop musicians who were encouraged to invest in the film as a means of offsetting income tax. The biggest single investor was theatre producer Michael White, who had produced *Sleuth* on Broadway and staged *Joseph and the Amazing Technicolor Dreamcoat* and *The Rocky Horror Show* in the West End, who put up £78,750. Other investors included the National Westminster Bank (£30,000), Led Zeppelin (£31,500), Pink Floyd (£21,000), Island Records (£21,000), Chrysalis Records (£6,300) and Ian Anderson of Jethro Tull (£6,300), while the members of the Monty Python team – Graham Chapman, John Cleese, Terry Jones, Michael Palin, Eric Idle and director Terry Gilliam – each put up £2,000–£2,500.[33] *Monty Python and the Holy Grail* was picked up by EMI Film Distributors for the United Kingdom. It went on to be a major hit that recouped its cost from the home market and earned substantial revenues overseas: its gross distributors' receipts of £2,358,229 ensured a substantial profit for all investors.[34]

The main new entrant into film finance in the early 1970s was Hemdale Associates. This company had been set up in 1967 by actor David Hemmings and his manager John Daly as an investment trust to avoid personal income tax: Hemmings, who starred in major films in the late 1960s including *Camelot*, *The Charge of the Light Brigade* and *Alfred the Great*, was earning around £100,000 per picture. Hemdale's other clients included actors Peter McEnery, Jack Wild and Mark Lester. Hemdale was cash rich due to its 5 per cent share of the international rights for Lionel Bart's stage musical *Oliver!*. In 1969 its profits were over £175,000.[35] Its investments covered a range of entertainment and leisure industries including film: its first venture into film financing was when it invested £200,000 in *Melody* (1971) – released in Britain as *S.W.A.L.K.* – starring Jack Wild and Mark Lester.[36] Hemmings himself parted company with Hemdale at the end of 1970 when he sold his shareholding to the merchant bank C. P. Choularton.[37] This left John Daly as the prime mover: it was under his direction that Hemdale was transformed from a talent management agency into what became 'essentially a film production and financing company'.[38]

Hemdale was the most expansionist company in the British film industry in the early 1970s. In February 1970, backed by merchant bankers Arbuthnot Latham, it acquired its own production facility (Isleworth Studios) and paid £400,000 for distributor Tigon Pictures.[39] Tigon's chairman Laurie Marsh joined the Hemdale board but became embroiled in a power struggle with Daly which ended when Marsh bought back control of Tigon.[40] In the early 1970s Hemdale dabbled in production and distribution without appearing to know what direction it wanted to take: it made one-off deals with producers including Chilton Films (*Blood on Satan's Claw*, 1971), Josef Shaftel (*Where Does It Hurt?*, 1972) and Mel Ferrer (*Embassy*, 1972).[41] In 1973 Hemdale linked with Los Angeles-based Cinemobile Systems, a subsidiary of Taft Broadcasting, to produce six 'top quality motion pictures' a year under the name of Cinema Artists Investments.[42] The following year it sought to rationalise its various film-related interests under the umbrella of Hemdale Films International.[43]

As a newcomer to the film and entertainment industries, Hemdale was not locked into existing structures and practices: it was therefore more flexible in responding to changing economic circumstances and market conditions. It was also able to diversify its activities into other entertainment media: these included video cassettes and pay-television for hotels. At the end of 1973 it acquired David Frost's Equity Enterprises in a reverse takeover deal as part of a planned move into cinema exhibition.[44] Its biggest success of the decade was in 1974 when it acquired worldwide television rights to the Muhammad Ali–George Foreman heavyweight title fight in Zaire – the famous 'Rumble in the Jungle' – from which it made a profit of over £1 million.[45]

There were mixed fortunes for the established production and distribution groups in the 1970s. The Rank Organisation was scaling back the extent of its production activity: it supported only seven films in 1971 and these were mostly 'Carry On' and Hammer films rather than the ambitious co-productions it had backed during the previous decade.[46] Rank had made profits of £15 million after tax in 1970 but over half of this came from its Rank Xerox subsidiary: film production and distribution now accounted for a relatively minor part of the corporation's business.[47] Rank's scaling down of production left the field open for its putative rival ABPC – taken over by the music industry giant Electric and Musical Industries (EMI) in 1969 – to become the major force in British film production. Bryan Forbes had been appointed head of production and managing director of EMI Elstree Studios. Forbes's production strategy was a throwback to the studio era in the sense that he supported a range of subjects across different genres: EMI's initial programme in 1970–1 included a Peter Sellers comedy (*Hoffman*), a psychological thriller (*The Man Who Haunted Himself*), low-budget horror (*And Soon the Darkness*), a naturalist comedy-drama (*Mr Forbush and the Penguins*) and an adaptation of a children's classic (*The Railway Children*). EMI adopted a flexible approach to financing. For example, *Mr Forbush and the Penguins* (1971) had an unusual tripartite funding arrangement whereby the NFFC and British Lion Films each advanced £201,411 to Associated British Productions, which itself provided the remaining £203,076 towards the aggregate budget of £605,898.⁴⁸ The NFFC praised *Mr Forbush and the Penguins* as an example of 'flexible and effective co-operation'.⁴⁹ In April 1970 the closure of Borehamwood Studios prompted MGM to move its production base to Elstree: EMI terminated its relationship with Warner Bros. and formed a new production and distribution partnership with MGM on a fifty-fifty financing basis.⁵⁰ The first EMI–MGM co-productions, all released in 1971, were Joseph Losey's *The Go-Between*, Mike Hodges's *Get Carter* and Ken Russell's *The Boy Friend*.⁵¹ At the same time Anglo-EMI Film Distributors was formed from the merger of Anglo-Amalgamated Film Distributors and Associated British-Pathé, with Nat Cohen as its chief executive.⁵² Cohen to all intents and purposes oversaw a parallel programme to the EMI–MGM films focused on wholly British-financed films: he described *Villain* (1971) – a violent crime drama starring Richard Burton as a loosely disguised East End gangster Reginald Kray – as 'a great achievement . . . for a British company to be able to make it here and with 100 per cent British finance'.⁵³

Forbes acted as executive producer of all the films produced for EMI under his tenure, and it is clear that fiscal discipline was a high priority. He was at pains to assert that he and studio manager John Hargreaves exercised strict control of budgets and expenditure:

> I am sure you will share my pleasure when I tell you that out of a total of some 15 films inaugurated since May 1969 not one has gone over budget and many of them have not even touched their contingency . . . John Hargeaves and myself don't authorise unrealistic budgets and our methods of cost control are, I believe, second to none and have been proved so over the past eighteen months. We have no policy of proceeding on budgets which bear no relation to the facts of life and once they have been passed by my office you may rest assured that barring total disasters beyond everybody's control, they will be carefully scrutinised along every inch of the way and the projects protected from the more common abuses which, traditionally, have bedevilled our industry.⁵⁴

The context for this letter was that Forbes was seeking a special deal from Film Finances to offer a no-claim bonus for all EMI-produced films regardless of who the individual producers were. Robert Garrett, while acknowledging that such deals had been made with American studios Universal and Fox, replied that Forbes had 'missed the point' and that it would be 'quite impractical commercially to give our No Claim Bonus just on the strength of anybody's record (for example your own) from which we had not previously benefited'.⁵⁵

EMI's major *succès d'estime* in the early 1970s was Joseph Losey's *The Go-Between* (1971). The film's production history demonstrates a commitment to quality but also the imperative of economy. John Croydon felt that the original budget of £701,663 was adequate but that Losey had set himself 'a very tough schedule': in particular he noted that the staging of the cricket match – a pivotal sequence in the film – 'occupies six days which is approximately the number of days by which I consider the schedule to be short'. He recommended the guarantee '[if] we can be satisfied about that either in Losey's ability to shoot the entire script in 11 weeks or to eliminate the cricket match and spread the remainder of the schedule over the week so saved'.[56] The final production budget of *The Go-Between* was reduced to £532,841: this 'large reduction in the total figure has been achieved by the elimination of stars' salaries with the substitution of comparatively low expenses, large cuts in producer's and director's salaries and the elimination of ABPC overheads'.[57] Producer John Heyman deferred his full fee, Losey half his fee, and stars Julie Christie (£4,000) and Alan Bates (£3,000) worked for significantly reduced salaries. Losey's pragmatic contingency planning and ability to adjust his schedule at short notice meant that he was able to overcome the difficulties of an unusually wet summer: *The Go-Between* was finished on schedule and under budget (£468,098) with the cricket sequence intact.[58] The film was regarded as a return to form for Losey and won the Palme d'Or at the Cannes Film Festival.

Forbes, however, reaped no benefit. He resigned as EMI's head of production after two years. His reason, as told to the press, was that 'I did not have enough real influence in the two spheres which perhaps more vitally than the production arm control film – that is, in exhibition and distribution.'[59] Forbes had produced thirteen films in two years but only two – *The Railway Children* and *The Tales of Beatrix Potter* – had scored at the box office. At the time of his resignation in March 1971 Forbes said: 'The final balance sheet will prove there has been an overall success. I refuse to believe that these films will not, in the long run, be seen to be profitable.'[60] Shortly after Forbes's resignation the co-production arrangement between EMI and MGM was strengthened by the formation of EMI–MGM Film Productions, with Nat Cohen as its managing director.[61] Cohen supported low-budget television spin-offs such as *Up Pompeii* (1971) and *Steptoe and Son* (1972). But a change of direction was signalled by EMI Films' chairman and chief executive Bernard Delfont, who evidently had loftier ambitions: 'I'm not saying we wouldn't do a picture for, say, £100,000 if the subject and the people in it appealed to me enormously. But, frankly, I'd rather put our energies into something that has great appeal. And if it costs three, four million dollars, I'd do it.'[62] MGM's decision to withdraw from the co-production deal in September 1973 – occasioned by the Hollywood company's scaling down of production activity – prompted fears about the future of Elstree Studios: closure was averted but the permanent workforce was halved.[63]

EMI's biggest commercial success came with John Brabourne's lavish production of Agatha Christie's *Murder on the Orient Express* (1974). Brabourne, whose previous films included *Sink the Bismarck!* and *Romeo and Juliet*, was the son-in-law of Lord Mountbatten: his connections were seen as crucial to negotiating the screen rights to the work from Christie herself, who had been profoundly disappointed with previous film adaptations of her work.[64] Brabourne assembled an all-star cast including Lauren Bacall, Ingrid Bergman, Jacqueline Bisset, Sean Connery, Albert Finney, John Gielgud, Wendy Hiller, Anthony Perkins, Vanessa Redgrave, Richard Widmark and Michael York. *Murder on the Orient Express* was reported to have cost 'a little over £1 million': Cohen estimated its worldwide distributor's gross at £10 million and averred that it was 'likely to be Britain's biggest foreign currency earning production'.⁶⁵ A film on the scale of *Murder on the Orient Express* would probably have been made for one of the Hollywood studios in the 1960s: this was an instance where the withdrawal of US finance created the opportunity for a British company to plug the gap. For Brabourne: 'The main problem of the British film industry today is the shortage of risk money . . . One used to turn to a big American company which would back a good idea from the word go, but today they are only interested in ready-made packages.'⁶⁶

The other remnant of the old British studio system, British Lion, was looking more and more like a spent force in the 1970s. British Lion had been limping along since its return to private ownership in 1964: its last major successes had been *The Great St Trinian's Train Robbery* and *The Family Way* in the mid-1960s. Shepperton Studios was operating more as an independent production facility than as a film factory: in the late 1960s it was kept busy by big-budget American runaways such as *Oliver!* and *Cromwell*, but the decline of US finance in the early 1970s left its immediate future uncertain. In 1972 British Lion Films recorded a consolidated loss of £1.2 million – against a pre-tax profit of £143,000 the previous year – and there were rumours that Shepperton was to close.⁶⁷ Like ABPC at the end of the 1960s, British Lion's weakness left it a prime target for takeover. In November 1971 it was announced that Star Associated Holdings – owner of the third-largest cinema chain in Britain which controlled 107 cinemas and around 150 bingo halls in the north of England, whose entire share capital was owned by the Eckhart family – was to make a reverse takeover bid for British Lion.⁶⁸ However, British Lion withdrew from the deal when it emerged that the Eckharts were under investigation by the Inland Revenue.⁶⁹

It was at this point, with its shares temporarily suspended pending the merger, that British Lion became a target for John Bentley of Barclay Securities. Bentley was a former stockbroker who had the reputation of being Britain's foremost asset-stripper: he specialised in taking over companies whose assets (particularly in buildings and land) were undervalued on their books and selling them off for a profit. Bentley had no interest in film-making: what he saw in British Lion was 60 acres of land in a London suburb valued at around £5 million (rather more than the value of the studio itself), a cinema advertising business (Pearl & Dean) making profits of £300,000 a year, and a film library worth around £200,000 a year in television sales.⁷⁰ In April 1972 Barclay Securities made a cash offer of £5.5 million for British Lion: this worked out at 135 pence a share, which was slightly below the listed price.⁷¹ It was also rather less than the £9.5 million offered by the Star group only six months earlier. There are conflicting accounts whether British Lion itself welcomed Bentley's interest. A contemporary report in *The Guardian* suggested that the 'deal seems certain to go through', as the directors of British Lion had given an 'irrevocable undertaking' to accept the offer for their own shares which amounted to 53 per cent of the total.⁷² However, Derek Threadgall's history of Shepperton Studios avers that the directors did not want to sell but were obliged to put the sale before shareholders, who voted to accept the offer.⁷³ Either way there was a feeling that Bentley had 'got his timing just right': British Lion was in such a bad way that shareholders were ready to accept any offer, while the NFFC – which still held one voting share in British Lion – 'was ready to countenance a plan which would save *something*, even if it meant presenting the rescuer with a fat profit'.[74]

Bentley's acquisition of British Lion inevitably prompted fears over the immediate future of Shepperton. Derek Threadgall formed the Shepperton Studios Action Committee, mobilising the studio workforce and local residents. Threadgall wrote to Prime Minister Edward Heath 'to oppose vigorously and by any means the closure of Shepperton Studios for re-development . . . It is high time that the ruthless tactics of John Bentley and his merry band of property developers were curbed.'[75] However, the Department of Trade and Industry wanted to keep its distance in order to avoid controversy:

> We cannot be sure what British Lion will do . . . Mr Grant [Anthony Grant – Parliamentary Under-Secretary] believes that the Government must stay clear of the argument for as long as possible. The final solution is bound to be unpleasant, but the NFFC have put the onus on British Lion and it is not for us to take any action which might be construed as helping Mr John Bentley to realise part of his investment in British Lion at a substantial profit.[76]

The Action Committee's campaign was taken up by the national press and there were public statements of support from various film industry luminaries. It even prepared its own bid to buy the studios backed by an Eire-based group called Global Participants. In the event, an agreement was reached between Bentley and the Action Committee whereby part of the site (around 40 acres) would be sold but the studios would be maintained in such a form that they were 'capable of handling production of two major films simultaneously'.[77]

Shepperton had been reprieved; but what the new owners needed was a programme of films to keep the studios operating. Bentley told the press: 'We have great ideas about that – we will find young people with innovative thoughts.'[78] Jeremy Arnold was appointed managing director of British Lion and 32-year-old Canadian Peter Snell became the head of production.[79] Snell produced two films during his brief tenure: *The Wicker Man* and *Don't Look Now*. The horror film *The Wicker Man* (1973) – directed by first-timer Robin Hardy from a script by playwright Anthony Schaffer with a budget of £399,000 – was rushed into production without adequate preparation. John Croydon, assessing the proposition for a guarantee of completion, felt that the script 'is very overlength and very complicated and hazardous and quite impossible to relate to the schedule'. Nevertheless, given that the film was about to start shooting, Croydon concluded his report: 'I think that under these circumstances we have little option but to proceed with this guarantee in the hope that Hardy proves to be a fast Director capable of applying instant modification to the script content and that between them Snell and [production manager Ted] Morley prove capable of extremely difficult production control.'[80] It soon became apparent that this was a forlorn hope. The difficult production of *The Wicker Man* – involving weather delays on location (the film was supposed to be set in the spring but was shot in late autumn) – has become the stuff of legend among cult film aficionados. Croydon believed that 'Snell cannot bring the necessary pressure to bear on the Director to make the necessary cuts and modifications in the script that would enable him to be sure of completion on the due date'.[81] Film Finances had to put Snell on notice that they would not be responsible for overages on cast, music and 'additional shooting at the Caves on which we had no knowledge'.[82] The estimated cost to complete *The Wicker Man* reached £448,300 – an overcost of some £49,300 – but Film Finances told Snell 'that as far as the Guarantee is concerned, the entire overage is your responsibility and that had we been kept fully informed at all times as was your legal obligation to do so, that this film could have been contained within its existing finance'.[83]

Don't Look Now (1973) also proved problematic. Producer Peter Katz had brought the project – to be directed by Nicolas Roeg based on a story by Daphne du Maurier – to British Lion at a time when the company needed films. It was budgeted at £566,501 and was to be shot mostly on location in Venice as an Anglo-Italian co-production with Eldorado Films of Rome. Again there is evidence of hurried preparation: Croydon felt that 'the schedule is a fairly hopeless document . . . I would go as far as to say that if Roeg is to shoot these sequences in the order in which they are scheduled, then, unless he has a very clear and perceptive mind, he, himself, will become muddled.'[84] In the event, the film completed shooting on schedule but experienced delays in post-production which necessitated an extension to the bank credit 'to allow for delayed delivery of the film'.[85] Film Finances advanced an additional £27,636 to secure its completion.[86] Nevertheless *Don't Look Now* was a critical and commercial success – an 'art house' film whose box-office performance was probably enhanced by its erotic love-making scene involving a naked Julie Christie and Donald Sutherland – and was the leading British film at the box office in 1974.

However, the first films of the new British Lion had not even completed shooting before another twist in the ever more complicated saga. At the beginning of 1973 Barclay Securities – whose share value had fallen by half during the protracted negotiations over the future of Shepperton Studios – was itself the subject of a hostile takeover by the banking and finance group J. H. Vavasseur. It has become part of City folklore that John Bentley's first response to the news of Vavasseur's bid for his company was to ask 'Vava-who?'. As *The Economist* noted wryly: 'It is difficult not to repress a hoot of laughter at the sight of Mr John Bentley of Barclay Securities, who made a not entirely deserved reputation as an asset-stripper, being bid for by another financial conglomerate, J. H. Vavasseur.'[87] Barclay Securities, like so many of the companies it had targeted in the past, was in a temporarily weakened position. Bentley decided to take the money. In February 1973, having rejected an offer of £17 million, he accepted Vavasseur's revised offer of £18.5 million.[88] The new owner undertook 'that it will continue to operate a major film studio at Shepperton for so long as this activity may be maintained on a basis of commercial viability'.[89]

However, Shepperton continued operating at a loss and it was not long before the threat of closure re-emerged. There were two particular problems. One was the downturn in British production from 1973: Shepperton was more adversely affected than other studios because in recent years it had depended on the sort of larger-scale films that were now being made in smaller numbers. There was a feeling in the industry at this time that there was a surplus of studio capacity in Britain following the contraction of the production sector: the NFFC's annual report for 1973 suggested that 'with the reduction in the number of big studio-based productions, Elstree, Pinewood and Shepperton comprise an excessive supply of major studio space in relation to the present demand'.[90] The other problem was that Vavasseur was itself experiencing difficulties as a consequence of the Stock Market crash: the group lost £8.8 million in the first six months of 1974.[91] It was a period of much turmoil: Vavasseur's attempt at recapitalisation failed. It opted to turn Shepperton into a 'four-wall' operation: a studio facility with a small permanent staff where producers would rent stages and contract separately for additional facilities and hire technicians on a freelance basis.[92] But only four films were made at the studio in 1975 – *Sinbad and the Eye of the Tiger*, *The Pink Panther Strikes Again*, *The Omen* and *The Adventure of Sherlock Holmes' Smarter Brother* – and its future remained in doubt.

In June 1975 Michael Deeley and Barry Spikings, the joint managing directors of British Lion Films, enacted a management buyout: they raised £1.2 million from five banks and acquired control of Shepperton and British Lion Films.[93] Deeley was the one with the production experience – he had set up Oakhurst Productions in association with actor Stanley Baker and his films as producer included *Robbery* and *The Italian Job* – while Spikings had started out as a pop music promoter. Within the space of barely three years, therefore, ownership of British Lion had passed from one group of film-makers, via two investment companies, and then back to another pair of film-makers. At the start of 1976 Deeley and Spikings signalled a change of direction for British Lion when they told *Screen International* that their production programme would henceforth be oriented towards 'big, star-cast productions clearly aimed at world audiences . . . The rising cost of film production absolutely demands an international thinking among all but the most specialised film-makers.'[94] They specifically cited EMI's success with *Murder on the Orient Express* as the rationale for this decision. *The Man Who Fell to Earth* (1976) – produced by Deeley and directed by Nicolas Roeg starring David Bowie – was the first of these 'big' productions. It was shot entirely in the United States with a reported budget of US $3.5 million.

The first half of the 1970s had therefore witnessed a complete restructuring of the British film industry, in which the last remnants of the studio system that had existed since the end of the Second World War were finally dismantled. There was still to be one last development. The production strategies of EMI and British Lion had put them on converging trajectories by the mid-1970s: the – perhaps inevitable – outcome was the merger of the two companies. The first stage was a financing and distribution deal involving both companies and one of the Hollywood majors. In January 1976 Barry Spikings told Downing Street:

> We, together with EMI, have just closed a deal with Columbia Pictures under which we divide equally the world market for large scale films but Columbia's contribution to the cost of the picture is three dollars to every one we put up. This, I feel, bodes well for the philosophy of gearing up new production funds, even if every deal cannot be quite as good as that one.[95]

In May 1976 it was announced that terms had been agreed for EMI to buy British Lion. The merger made good economic sense. There was simply no longer space for two similar-sized production and distribution interests in the contracting British market, but the merger created a bigger company that it was felt would be able to mount a challenge to Hollywood. EMI paid £730,000 – £230,000 in cash and the balance in shares – for British Lion.[96] Deeley and Spikings became joint managing directors of EMI Film Distributors. The NFFC felt that 'the acquisition of British Lion will substantially add to EMI's management strength and lead to a stimulation and enlargement of EMI's support for and financial involvement in British film production and distribution'.[97] *Screen International* put it more bluntly: it suggested that 'EMI is essentially purchasing the production ability of the two gentlemen concerned'.[98]

EMI's revival in the mid-1970s prompted the Rank Organisation to make one last attempt at a major film production programme. By this time the personalities who had run the organisation since the 1940s had gone: Lord Rank died in 1972 and Sir John Davis finally retired in 1977. In May 1977 the Rank Organisation announced that it again intended to take an 'active interest in film production'.[99] Rank restructured its Leisure and Entertainment Division and appointed Tony Williams as head of production. Williams was more cautious than Deeley and Spikings at EMI: he opted to spread the risk over a programme of middle-budget films rather than aim for two or three potential blockbusters. Over the next two years Rank invested £10 million in the production of eight films: *Wombling Free, The 39 Steps, The Riddle of the Sands, Tarka the Otter, The Lady Vanishes, Eagle's Wing, Bad Timing* and *Silver Dream Racer*.[100] The fact that two of those were remakes of Alfred Hitchcock classics of the 1930s (*The 39 Steps, The Lady Vanishes*) and another two were also period dramas (*The Riddle of the Sands, Eagle's Wing*) would suggest that Rank was seeking to emulate the success of *Murder on the Orient Express*. It was a conservative strategy culturally as well as economically. For Williams: 'You have to go back in time to tell a story that doesn't have to face seventies problems. What people are nostalgic for isn't necessarily any particular period, but the happier values that are missing today.'[101]

Rank's announcement three years later that it was to pull out of film production prompted trade journalist Quentin Falk to quip that 'ripples of shock ran through Wardour Street on a Richter scale of absolute zero'.[102] Edmond Chilton, the Head of Rank's Leisure and Entertainment Division, conceded that 'our return has just not been good enough' and blamed the lack of interest from American distributors: 'We weren't successful in getting a major to take any of our films for the US . . . So we were not helped by the distribution pattern in the US which would have been the key to success.'[103] In fact, it was not only in the American market that the films failed. The published Eady levy returns indicate that only *The 39 Steps* (which by November 1981 had earned £156,302 in Eady payments, suggesting a distributor's gross from the United Kingdom of a little over £400,000) could be adjudged a success. *Bad Timing* (£51,298) was a middling success, but *Tarka the Otter* (£25,905), *The Lady Vanishes* (£25,765) and *The Riddle of the Sands* (£8,200) all performed poorly.[104] Overall Rank had lost £1.6 million on film production. Rank announced that it would provide distribution guarantees of between 10 and 15 per cent for several pictures a year. It would continue as a distributor and exhibitor for another decade, but Rank's days as a major force in the British film industry were over.

NOTES

1. David Pirie, 'New Blood', *Sight & Sound*, 40: 2 (Summer 1971), p. 73.
2. Linda Wood (ed.), *British Film Industry: Reference Guide No. 1* (London: British Film Institute Information and Education Department, 1980), Appendix A, unpaginated.
3. 'The cinema looks to the City', *The Financial Times*, 7 August 1971, p. 13.
4. 'EMI–MGM Link: Elstree, Production and Distribution: Boreham Wood to Close', *Kinematograph Weekly*, 25 April 1970, p. 3.
5. 'American cut-back hits Shepperton', *Kinemetogaph Weekly*, 25 July 1970, p. 6.
6. 'Another studio closure threat for film industry', *The Financial Times*, 3 September 1970, p. 3.
7. 'Britain's film studios wait for work', *The Financial Times*, 7 September 1970, p. 23.
8. 'Future of tv series film production in doubt', *Kinematograph Weekly*, 20 February 1971, p. 12.
9. 'Today's Cinema buys Kine Weekly', *Today's Cinema*, 10 September 1971, p. 5.
10. Sue Harper and Justin Smith, *British Film Culture in the 1970s: The Boundaries of Pleasure* (Edinburgh: Edinburgh University Press, 2012), pp. 261–74.
11. TNA T369/142: Submission by the Board of Directors of the National Film Finance Corporation to the Working Party on the Film Industry, October 1975.
12. 'Film Investment Halved', *CinemaTV Today*, 8 July 1972, p. 18.
13. TNA PREM 16/51: Report from Cinematograph Films Council to Peter Shore (Secretary of State for Trade), 3 April 1974.
14. 'Lower Budgets and Shorter Schedules Keep the Figures Steady', *Kinematograph Weekly*, 25 April 1970, p. 12.
15. Alexander Walker, *National Heroes: British Cinema in the Seventies and Eighties* (London: Harrap, 1985), p. 136.
16. 'Box-office winners of 1970', *Kinematograph Weekly*, 19 December 1970, p. 8.
17. 'Box Office Business', *Kinematograph Weekly*, 6 June 1970, p. 7.
18. 'The American key to British films', *The Economist*, 14 February 1976, p. 176.
19. 'Year of the Blockbuster', *Screen International*, 23 December 1978, p. 1.

20. *National Film Finance Corporation: Annual Report and Statement of Accounts for the year ended 31 March 1974*, Cmnd. 5725 (September 1974), p. 5 (5).
21. 'The Bank Crisis Hits Film Industry', *CinemaTV Today*, 1 September 1974, p. 18.
22. 'The only sane way to make a picture', *Kinematograph Weekly*, 2 January 1971, p. 13.
23. 'Producers are cutting out the wastage', *Kinematograph Weekly*, 28 August 1971, p. 7.
24. *National Film Finance Corporation: Annual Report and Statement of Accounts for the year ended 31 March 1971*, Cmnd 4761 (August 1971), p. 14 (Appendix B).
25. 'The film industry in a City suit', *The Financial Times*, 8 September 1971, p. 16.
26. 'Tony Tenser', *Today's Cinema*, 8 October 1971, p. 8.
27. 'Tigon Planning 200 Classics', *Today's Cinema*, 10 September 1971, p. 10.
28. The BFI Special Collections Unit holds the production budgets for the 'Carry On' films: BFI Thomas GT/3/6 (*Carry On at Your Convenience*), GT/12/6 (*Carry on Dick*), GT/18/6 (*Carry On Girls*), GT/19/5 (*Carry On Henry*), GT/22/6 (*Carry On Matron*).
29. 'Hammer's First Two With All-British Finance From EMI–ABPC', *Kinematograph Weekly*, 14 March 1970, p. 3.
30. FFA General Correspondence Box 197 ('Green Papers'): Robert Garrett to Amicus Productions, 16 May 1973 (*The House That Dripped Blood* and *From Beyond the Grave*); Garrett to Amicus Productions, 21 May 1973 (*The Beast Must Die*).
31. '"On the Buses" rings the bell', *Kinematograph Weekly*, 21 August 1971, p. 3.
32. Andrew Spicer and A. T. McKenna, *The Man Who Got Carter: Michael Klinger, Independent Production and the British Film Industry 1960–1980* (London: I. B. Tauris, 2013), p. 201.
33. TNA FV 81/191: National Film Trustee Company Limited: *Monty Python and the Holy Grail* Trust, n.d.
34. Ibid.: National Film Trustee Company Limited: Allocation of revenues per distributor's statements to 28 February 1979. The allocation of profits was as follows: Python (Monty) Pictures Ltd (£699,319), Michael White (£389,880), Bowerelm Inc. (£184,067), Island Records (£122,711), Pink Floyd Music Ltd (£122,711), Mark Forstarter Productions (£65,321), Chrysalis Records Ltd (£36,815), Ian Anderson Ltd (£36,815) and Christopher Mann (£28,321).
35. 'Hemdale Group Tops 420G Profit Project', *Variety*, 19 November 1969, p. 7.
36. 'Expanding Hemdale plans major production in 1970', *Kinematograph Weekly*, 15 November 1969, p. 3.
37. 'Hemmings to sell stake in Hemdale', *The Financial Times*, 12 November 1970, p. 20.
38. '"Excellent" prospects for Hemdale', *The Financial Times*, 13 August 1971, p. 20.
39. 'Hemdale Now a Renter, Starting Mini-Chain', *Kinematograph Weekly*, 21 February 1970, p. 3.
40. 'Moves to cool down battle for Hemdale group', *Kinematograph Weekly*, 15 August 1970, p. 3.
41. 'Hemdale backing', *Kinematograph Weekly*, 14 August 1971, p. 19.
42. 'Hemdale links with American groups to produce film', *The Financial Times*, 11 April 1973, p. 16.
43. 'Hemdale Consolidating Distrib., Prod., Sales Div. Under New Int'l Umbrella', *Variety*, 18 September 1974, p. 80.
44. 'Dave Frost, John Daly Into British Theaters', *Variety*, 26 December 1973, p. 1.
45. 'Foreman–Ali Fight in Sept. Set By Hemdale for Satellite', *Variety*, 17 April 1974, p. 72.
46. 'Production Review', *Kinematograph Weekly*, 19 December 1970, p. 85.

47. 'Rank Profit Hits a New Peak', *Kinematograph Weekly*, 5 September 1970, p. 3.
48. FFA Realised Film Box 476: *Mr Forbush and the Penguins*: Agreement between Film Finances and British Lion Films, 4 December 1969.
49. *National Film Finance Corporation: Annual Report and Statement of Accounts for the year ended 31 March 1970*, Cmnd. 4402 (May 1970), p. 2 (6).
50. 'EMI–MGM Link: Elstree, Production and Distribution', *Kinematograph Weekly*, 25 April 1970, p. 3.
51. 'EMI–MGM co-production deal', *Kinematograph Weekly*, 4 July 1970, p. 3.
52. 'Anglo-EMI to make new comedy series', *Kinematograph Weekly*, 2 May 1970, p. 3.
53. 'We are going ahead – we have confidence in the industry', *Kinematograph Weekly*, 13 February 1971, p. xi.
54. FFA Realised Film Box 486: *The Go-Between*: Bryan Forbes to Robert Garrett, 30 October 1970.
55. Ibid.: Garrett to Forbes, 2 November 1970.
56. Ibid.: John Croydon to Robert Garrett, 9 March 1970.
57. Ibid.: Croydon to Garrett, 1 July 1970.
58. Ibid.: Statement of Production Cost, 6 December 1970.
59. 'My despair, my disenchantment, by Bryan Forbes', *CinemaTV Today*, 14 October 1972, p. 1.
60. 'Bryan Forbes quits as EMI film chief', *The Financial Times*, 26 March 1971, p. 15.
61. 'EMI and MGM form new production outfit', *Kinematograph Weekly*, 24 April 1971, p. 3.
62. 'In Top Gear – Knowing Course to Take', *Kinematograph Weekly*, 13 February 1971, p. vi.
63. 'This Could Be the End of the Line for Elstree', *CinemaTV Today*, 29 September 1973, p. 6.
64. Mark Aldridge, *Agatha Christie on Screen* (London: Palgrave Macmillan, 2016), p. 125.
65. '"Orient Express" Takings Biggest', *The Financial Times*, 22 January 1975, p. 4.
66. 'Can film-makers Carry On?', *The Observer*, 11 August 1974, p. 11.
67. 'The Crucial Share', *CinemaTV Today*, 3 June 1972, p. 5.
68. 'Why Lion and Star are merging', *CinemaTV Today*, 2 November 1971, pp. 2–3.
69. Derek Threadgall, *Shepperton Studios: An Independent View* (London: British Film Institute, 1994), pp. 120–1.
70. 'The last small picture company show', *The Economist*, 13 May 1972, p. 12.
71. 'Agreed Bid of £5½m. for Brit. Lion', *The Financial Times*, 25 April 1972, p. 36.
72. 'British Lion board backs £5M offer', *The Guardian*, 25 April 1972, p. 15.
73. Threadgall, *Shepperton Studios*, p. 121.
74. 'The Shepperton story', *The Observer*, 12 November 1972, p. 20.
75. TNA PREM 15/1414: Derek Threadgall to Edward Heath, 18 August 1972.
76. Ibid.: L. R. Foxwell (Mrs) to Robin Butler (PM's Private Secretary), 14 September 1972.
77. Ibid.: D. C. Doherty to Butler, 6 November 1972.
78. 'John Bentley and the future of British Lion', *CinemaTV Today*, 20 May 1972, p. 1.
79. 'British Lion Chief of Production', *CinemaTV Today*, 8 July 1972, p. 1.
80. FFA Realised Film Box 530: *The Wicker Man*: John Croydon to Robert Garrett, 4 October 1972.
81. Ibid.: Croydon to Garrett, 6 November 1972.

82. Ibid.: Garrett to British Lion Film Productions, 27 February 1973.
83. Ibid.: Garrett to British Lion Film Productions, 6 April 1973.
84. FFA Realised Film Box 536: *Don't Look Now*: Croydon to Garrett, 11 October 1972.
85. Ibid.: Roger A. Lew to William Croft, 10 September 1973.
86. Ibid.: Croft to Neville Breeze, 23 July 1974.
87. 'Well, well', *The Economist*, 27 January 1973, p. 83.
88. 'Bentley accepts Vavasseur bid', *The Financial Times*, 22 February 1973, p. 1.
89. Threadgall, *Shepperton Studios*, pp. 138–9.
90. *National Film Finance Corporation: Annual Report and Statement of Accounts for the year ended 31 March 1973*, Cmnd. 5422 (August 1973), p. 9 (17).
91. Threadgall, *Shepperton Studios*, p. 137.
92. Ibid. p.141.
93. Ibid. p.143.
94. 'What They Predict for '76', *Screen International*, 24 January 1976, p. 24.
95. TNA T 369/142: Barry Spikings to Lady Falkender, 20 January 1976.
96. 'British Lion, EMI merge', *Screen International*, 28 August 1976, p. 1.
97. *National Film Finance Corporation: Annual Report and Statement of Accounts for the year ended 31 March 1976*, Cmnd. 6633 (September 1976), p. 6 (26).
98. 'Shock Merger as EMI Buy Up British Lion', *Screen International*, 22 May 1976, p. 1.
99. 'UK Production: Double Boost', *Screen International*, 21 May 1977, p. 1.
100. 'Losses of £1.6m sound the knell for cinema production', *The Times*, 7 June 1980, p. 17.
101. 'The lucrative case for believing in yesterday', *The Guardian*, 18 December 1978, p. 11.
102. 'How It All Turned So Sour', *Screen International*, 14 June 1980, p. 10.
103. 'Why I Pulled the Plug Out', *Screen International*, 14 June 1980, p. 1.
104. 'British Film Fund ("Eady" levy) distributions', *British Business*, 2 April 1982, p. 679.

CHAPTER 16

The Changing Landscape of Film Finance

> The old concepts of major studio financing, production and distribution are outmoded. Excessive overheads, the cost of maintaining vast studio complexes, the star system, antiquated distribution methods – all must be changed radically if the industry is to survive. (Josef Shaftel)[1]

The changing structural and economic landscape of the film industry in the 1970s inevitably impacted on the provision of film finance. The major development during the decade was the shift from the traditional model of producers raising their finance against the security of a guarantee from one of the major British or American distributors that had prevailed since the 1940s to a new model based on the pre-sale of distribution rights on a territorial basis. This was largely an outcome of the inability of the two main British distributors, Rank and EMI, to fill the gap created by the retrenchment of the major Hollywood studios in the early 1970s. Another consequence of these developments was the emergence of new players in the field of film finance. In particular, the early 1970s saw an increasing presence by merchant banks as providers of equity capital for film production. As a spokesman for the banking house Samuel Montagu – which backed a consortium involving David Frost's production company Paradine Productions and the Norton Simon talent agency of New York – explained: 'This is our first venture into film finance. Like a lot of merchant banks we are approached from time to time to put up money for films. So far our answer has always been "No" because we did not know enough about it. This idea takes a lot of the risk out of it because we will only offer a commitment provided the film is pre-sold.'[2]

To some extent the changing fiscal landscape of the British film industry reflected developments in the United States. The losses sustained by the major studios on production in the late 1960s brought about a radical restructuring of film finance. Hitherto the studios' production programmes had been funded from their rolling box-office revenues and lines of credit with commercial banks: in the early 1970s this gave way to a model based on the pre-sale of distribution rights (including both theatrical and television) and raising finance from 'outside' providers.[3] It was a model particularly suited to independent production, which flourished during the years of the 'Hollywood

Renaissance' between 1968 and 1975. As an article in the *New York Times* in July 1970 explained:

> Independent producers – who were, in the past, largely limited to the major American motion picture distributors – have been turning in increasing numbers to other sources, such as venture capital, Wall Street investment houses and, what has come to be a vital element in stimulating production by independents, film distributors throughout the world.[4]

From the middle of the decade, following the success of New Hollywood blockbusters such as *Jaws* and *Star Wars*, the majors would once again resume the role of financer-distributors as the US film industry became locked more than ever into a blockbuster mentality whereby the revenues of one or two big box-office hits would sustain a programme of 10–12 films per year. In Britain, however, where the production sector was smaller and more fragmented than in the United States, the practice of distribution pre-sales became the norm even for the large corporations as well as for independent producers. As an official report in 1979 observed: 'Both ACC [Associated Communications Corporation] and EMI have to a greater or less extent used a financial technique that has become common in the 1970s, that is, of pre-selling films to distributors in each country. Thus a film can be, to a greater or less degree, substantially underwritten in advance, thereby reducing the risk to the producing company.'[5]

The practice of raising production finance through territorial pre-sales of distribution rights was not in itself a new phenomenon but hitherto it had tended to be the preserve of producers of low-budget films working at the margins of the industry. Euan Lloyd – a former publicist for Warwick Films who became an independent producer in his own right in the 1960s – pioneered territorial pre-sales for his production of *Shalako* (1968). Lloyd claimed that '*Shalako* was put together in what was then a unique fashion, in that it was presold to most of the countries in the world before a foot of film went through the camera.'[6] The film was originally budgeted at £1,457,338.[7] Lloyd had been unable to interest any of the Hollywood studios in his big-budget European Western, even with a star cast headed by Sean Connery and Brigitte Bardot, so instead he raised the budget by securing promissory notes from distributors in 35 separate territories which he then discounted with the London-based merchant bank Morgan Grenfell. Most of the distributors were independent concerns: the largest advance (US $1,375,000) was from the American Broadcasting Company – which distributed theatrically through the Cinerama Releasing Corporation – for North American rights, while the smallest ($10,000) were from distributors in Finland, Israel and Thailand.[8] The advantage to the producer in this arrangement was that more of the risk was passed to the distributors: as payment was due upon delivery of the film then the producer should – provided the film had been completed on budget and schedule – be able to repay investors sooner and so claim for himself a larger share of the profits.[9]

The advantages for independent distributors, whose advances were based on their estimates of the commercial potential of the film in their own territories, was that they had access to the sort of high-end product that had usually been the preserve of the majors. *Shalako* seems to have performed well at the box office except in North America. According to Lloyd: 'The picture has recovered its money but we are still paying the bank interest, so it's questionable whether we will get a profit for many years.'[10]

Shalako became the model for the packaging of British-made international films by independent producers during the early 1970s. Dimitri de Grunwald, who had been involved in negotiating the bank loan for *Shalako*, set up the International Film Consortium in 1968. This was an alliance of independent distributors in 33 countries – including Chevron Pictures in the United States, Eurofilms of Holland, Juneau International of Argentina and Mallah Films of Israel – which took a share of the profits in proportion to their investment. The aim was to provide continuity in finance by not having to make separate arrangements for each picture. De Grunwald explained:

> In the past, other producers, especially in Europe, have lined up distributors in various countries to provide minimum guarantees in advance for a particular film that can be used to obtain production funds. What we've done is to set this up on a permanent basis through our International Film Consortium for a specific number of films every year.[11]

De Grunwald set up London Screenplays as his production arm: its first film was *The Virgin and the Gypsy* (1970). Shortly later London Screenplays announced a 50 per cent co-financing and distribution deal with the Winthrop Lawrence Corporation of Washington.[12] London Screenplays produced a programme of films in 1970–1 – including *Perfect Friday*, *The McMasters* and *Murphy's War* – through a revolving credit of £10 million from Morgan Grenfell.[13] It was heralded as 'the largest programme of film production for one year ever announced by an independent company in Britain'.[14] Morgan Grenfell's managing director Lord Catto asserted that his primary consideration was economic rather than artistic: 'As a banker I do not deal with the content or artistic control. I am interested in the figures in the end column which show how much money is going to come back. If the money is not going to be forthcoming then I will not allow the film to go ahead.'[15]

London Screenplays was a bold experiment but it did not last. De Grunwald left his own company towards the end of 1970 following disagreements with the bankers over its production programme: he was replaced as chairman by Michael Flint, producer of *The Virgin and the Gypsy*.[16] Thereafter the company oriented more towards distribution, picking up the rights to outside films such as the Kirk Douglas Western *A Gunfight* (1971).[17] De Grunwald's next venture was to set up a company called Script Development Limited in collaboration with theatre producer Peter Hall and writers Robert Bolt, Anthony Harvey, John Hopkins and Christopher Miles in order to develop projects that could be pitched to distributors and financiers: members would provide their services free for twelve months in return for a share of the profits. Hall explained: 'We are not a producing company: we plan to make projects available for others to finance. We are providing that odious word "product".'[18] The initiative resulted in two films, both directed by Christopher Miles: the comedy-dramas *A Time for Loving* (1972) and *That Lucky Touch* (1975). The latter – budgeted at £899,858 and completed for £960,858 – was the last film produced by De Grunwald.[19]

American producer Josef Shaftel was the other important pioneer of distribution pre-sales and consortium financing. Shaftel, best known as producer of the television series *The Untouchables*, came to Britain in the mid-1960s and produced the 'swinging' comedy *The Bliss of Mrs Blossom* (1968) for Paramount. Early in 1970 Shaftel announced a deal with the Cinerama Releasing Corporation for a programme of films 'largely to be made in Britain' that would entail an investment of US $14 million: the films included *The Last Grenade* (already completed), *Ask Agamemnon*, *Say Hello to Yesterday* and *The Statue*. His credit was provided by the Bank of America and London-based merchant bank Hill Samuel.[20] Shaftel evidently felt that the problems of the industry also represented an opportunity:

> New opportunities exist now as never before – particularly for those film-makers who are able to assemble the right elements, budget them sensibly and realistically, provide independent financing, and take the whole package to a major distributor. It places all the controls, financial and artistic, directly in the hands of the producer (who also arranges for a guarantee of completion to satisfy the banks providing the financing) and the result is a film made with greater efficiency and at lower cost. Needless to say, this increases the possibility of profits for all parties concerned.[21]

Shaftel's programme was eclectic in the extreme: it ranged from a historical-political drama (*The Assassination of Trotsky*) to a fantasy musical (*Alice's Adventures in Wonderland*). During production of the latter, Shaftel explained how consortium finance reduced the costs of production: 'It is all working in a marvellous co-operative way – with no big bread up first. If a studio had made it, the cost would have been at least $4 million. As a totally independent production, with 30 separate deals covering the negative cost, we are making it for far less.'[22]

The Assassination of Trotsky (1972) demonstrated the increasing complexities of film financing when a range of different parties was involved. *The Assassination of Trotsky* was shot on location in Mexico by Joseph Losey with Richard Burton and Alain Delon. Shaftel raised the budget of £1 million (US $2.4 million) through a consortium including the Greyhound Corporation ($600,000), the First National Bank of America ($465,000), the French distributor Valeria ($550,000) and the Italian producer Dino de Laurentiis ($400,000), with the balance provided by the production company and deferments. The completion guarantor Film Finances was evidently instrumental in securing the financing. The vice-president of the Bank of America's Entertainment Division, which made the loan to Valeria, wrote appreciatively: 'I should like to take this opportunity to thank you and everybody at Film Finances for the great co-operation and flexibility which you have shown in this transaction, without which we could surely never have proceeded.'[23] The film ran slightly over budget due to the inclusion of a crowd scene that was added during shooting. EMI Film Distributors picked it up for the United Kingdom after its completion.[24]

By and large, however, single-picture financing remained the norm. For Losey's *A Doll's House* (1973) – his film of Henrik Ibsen's play shot entirely on location over one month during the Norwegian winter – the budget was a modest £366,048 (US $912,850). *A Doll's House* was a co-production between Reindeer Films and Les Films La Boetie, which paid $100,000 for distribution in Francophone territories. The American National Bank and Trust Association of Chicago advanced $650,000, with the balance provided by the producer. Tomorrow Enterprises of New York – a subsidiary of the General Electric Corporation – held the option of a negative pick-up for North American distribution for an agreed sum of $500,000, while World Film Services distributed in other territories.[25] Losey, acting as both producer and director, deferred half his total fee, while Jane Fonda agreed to play Nora for only $40,000 in return for a percentage of the gross receipts on a sliding scale starting at 3.5 per cent.[26]

Losey's next film was *The Romantic Englishwoman* (1975) for veteran producer Daniel Angel. A third of the financing came in the form of a loan from the National Film Finance Corporation (£250,000): other substantial contributions came from Rank Film Distributors (£150,000), Rizzoli Films of Italy for Italian and South American distribution rights (£172,000) and Gaumont for France (£135,000).[27] The main expense was Michael Caine, who was paid £105,172 (US $250,000): Losey received £60,000 for directing and Angel £30,000 for producing. Like *A Doll's House*, Losey brought *The Romantic Englishwoman* in slightly under budget: its final cost was £759,474.[28] The records of the National Film Trustee Company reveal that £438,867 was recovered from pre-sales revenue and that the film's total theatrical receipts amounted to £784,476.[29]

The shift to pre-sales for raising finance was made possible by the entry of merchant banks into the field of film finance. Unlike the traditional model, where producers raised their finance as an interest-bearing loan from one of the clearing banks, with the bank holding a mortgage on the film until repayment of the loan, at which point their interest in the film ended, the merchant banks usually invested equity capital in return for a share of the profits. For a brief period in the early 1970s, merchant banks seemed to be falling over themselves to invest in film production. *The Financial Times* reported in 1971:

> City money has been forthcoming in varying amounts. Morgan Grenfell backed Dimitri de Grunwald heavily for a time. The two have now parted company and the bank is taking a breather, albeit temporarily. Hill Samuel put cash behind Mr Josef Shaftel. Rothschilds and Warburgs have tinkered in a smallish way, while the Bank of America has rather more extensive interests. Scotia Investments and Samuel Montagu – in league with David Frost (Paradine) – are quite deeply involved.[30]

The main reason why merchant banks were drawn into the film business was the incentive, supported by the NFFC and the major British distributors, that the three main sources of film revenue – domestic receipts, Eady payment and overseas receipts – should be pooled into a single fund that would be shared between the investors (75 per cent) and the distributor (25 per cent) on a *pari passu* basis. This was intended to provide a faster return on investment: one of the factors that had long deterred private equity finance was the slow return from film exhibition. As the NFFC noted in its annual report for 1970: 'The private investor will not be induced to accept the hazards until the financing of film production offers reasonable prospects of being remunerative in the long term . . . In the present scheme of things the risks shared by the producer, distributor and financier certainly do not favour the financier.'[31]

In the early 1970s the London-based merchant banks had to some extent filled the gap left by the withdrawal of American finance. However, by 1972 there were already signs that the City was looking to downscale its investment in films. Like so many private investors before, the merchant banks had learned the hard way that the film industry was not a pot of gold. In June 1972, for example, Scotia Investments sold its stake in the distributor Scotia-Barber and announced that it was 'withdrawing gradually from film production'.[32] Morgan Grenfell, which had been one of the first in the field, persisted longer than most. Its biggest commitment was to *The Slipper and the Rose* (1975) – Bryan Forbes's film of the Cinderella story which he directed for David Frost's Paradine Productions – for which Morgan Grenfell advanced the full budget of £2,153,042.[33] The film performed well enough at the British box office – no doubt helped by being chosen for the Royal Film Performance of 1976 – but its cost was way in excess of what could be recovered from the home market.

An important context for attracting new investment into the film industry was the Budget of 1971. The aim of the Budget – the first since the election of the Conservative government of Edward Heath the previous summer – was to reduce taxation: this involved the reform of capital allowances – the practice of allowing companies to offset expenditure on capital items against their pre-tax income – by treating long- and short-term investments in the same way and reducing the rate of capital gains tax to a standard 30 per cent. It also allowed companies to write off up to 60 per cent of a capital investment in the first year.[34] The main consequence for the film industry was that companies with no background in the film business were encouraged to invest in film-making as a means of reducing their tax liabilities: capital allowances would usually be spread over a fixed period, which made them particularly amenable to the film industry where profits from a film venture might not accrue for several years. Among the more unlikely investors drawn into the film business at this time were the American pharmaceutical giant Bristol Meyers (manufacturer of Mum deodorant), which backed Joseph L. Mankiewicz's film of Anthony Shaffer's play *Sleuth* (1972).[35] Roman Polanski's film of *Macbeth* (1972) was bankrolled by Playboy Magazine Enterprises. Polanski – who exceeded the £1 million budget by 20 per cent – averred that the backers had little knowledge or understanding of the film industry: 'Playboy felt a little bit like a virgin who was very interested in sex but a little bit scared.'[36]

From the mid-1970s all the more ambitious British producers were raising their finance from the international money market. The Cannes Film Festival, held every year in May, became the hub of international film sales. In 1974 *Variety* reported that Cannes 'is a global sales convention of unparalleled proportions'. 'Indeed,' it added, 'the activity outside the competition proper has put the main event into the shade: trade gossip is hardly concerned with which film may get the grand prix, but which pictures are available in the sidebar market.'[37] There is much anecdotal evidence of the importance of Cannes for making deals. Michael Klinger, who produced two major films based on adventure novels by Wilbur Smith, *Gold* and *Shout at the Devil*, 'has lifted himself into the league of must-see British producers, and Cannes is where he figures he must be seen'.[38] *Gold* (1974), starring Roger Moore and Susannah York, was budgeted at £1 million (US $2.4 million): Klinger had raised $1,725,890 through pre-sales to territories other than Britain and the United States before shooting started. The balance was provided by a consortium of South African business interests who saw the film as an opportunity to encourage the local production industry.[39] Klinger told Film Finances that 'the film is tremendous and the sales are going extremely well.'[40] *Gold* was produced without a US distributor in place – Klinger preferred not to be tied to any of the majors – but was picked up by Allied Artists. It did not perform well at the US box office, though it made a profit from its international sales.

Shout at the Devil (1976), starring Lee Marvin and Roger Moore, was a much bigger production. It was budgeted at £2,385,554, which Klinger raised through a combination of pre-sales and a negative pick-up of US $2.5 million from American International Pictures for US rights.[41] Film Finances, which had guaranteed the film, was not impressed by Klinger's handling of the production: it was soon chasing him for cost reports and for payment of the guarantee fee. Klinger's excuse that the reports sent from South Africa had been lost at Rome airport was met with incredulity: 'What can one make of Klinger? Is he the most inefficient fool or a crook, or both?'[42] Film Finances did not usually like cancelling a guarantee once it had been entered into, but in this case it was made easier by Klinger's failure to meet his responsibilities under the agreement. In the event, *Shout at the Devil* was completed £166,862 over budget.[43] It performed well in Britain (Hemdale International Films handled the British distribution) but was only a moderate success in America.

Euan Lloyd was another British stalwart of Cannes. When he was setting up his action-adventure *The Wild Geese* (1978), Lloyd said: 'Cannes turned the tables for me. I did five million dollars worth of business there which made this picture work for me.'[44] *The Wild Geese* was a mercenary adventure based on a novel by Daniel Carney: Lloyd's star cast of Richard Burton, Roger Moore and Richard Harris allowed him to pre-sell the picture to Allied Artists (North America), Rank (Britain), Avis (Germany), Europa (Scandinavia) and Shochiku (Japan). In addition, the American television network NBC offered US $2.5 million to screen the film two years after its theatrical release.[45] The budget – reported in the trade press as US $12 million but actually $7.9 million – was raised from British merchant bank Guinness Mahon (20 per cent) and the Franco-Swiss Banque de Paris et des Pays-Bas (60 per cent), with further contributions from the Lamitas Property and Investment Corporation and private South African interests.[46] Film Finances was satisfied that 'this is an adequate budget and through the contingency gives us reasonable protection'.[47] *The Wild Geese* was completed on budget and was a box-office success. Lloyd invested some of his profits in the preparation of *The Sea Wolves* (1980), a Second World War adventure starring Gregory Peck, Roger Moore and David Niven. He again raised the budget (reported as $12 million) through pre-sales, with the television producer Lorimar advancing 50 per cent for US rights.[48]

The most expensive British film of the 1970s was Joseph E. Levine's production of *A Bridge Too Far* (1977). This was an epic war movie with a reported budget of £12.6 million (US $22 million). (Levine had a habit of inflating costs when speaking to the trade press, but this seems to be the generally accepted figure.) *The Economist* – remembering the escalating production costs of the late 1960s – feared that 'the film industry shows every sign of taking the road to ruin once again . . . Few very expensive films make money.'[49] *A Bridge Too Far* was based on a book by Cornelius Ryan, author of *The Longest Day*, and was very much a personal project for Levine, who had promised Ryan's widow he would make the film.[50] According to screenwriter William Goldman: 'What Levine planned to do was to try to assemble a package that would eventually prove so appealing to the chains and distributors that they would pay him record-breaking sums of money in advance of receiving the film, and with those advances he would pay for the film as it went along.'[51] To this end, Levine assembled a stellar cast including Dirk Bogarde, James Caan, Michael Caine, Sean Connery, Edward Fox, Elliott Gould, Gene Hackman, Anthony Hopkins, Hardy Kruger, Ryan O'Neal, Laurence Olivier and Robert Redford. Levine offered each of the major actors a fee of $1 million ($2 million for Redford), which he paid from his own pocket.[52] It was a gamble for Levine, who had invested his own money up front. He explained that he had to offer such high fees as there were too many stars to offer anyone a percentage of the profits: 'The reason I paid Redford and some of the others so much money is that they are used to having an interest. But there were 14 [*sic*] stars, and I couldn't afford to give one a share without the others, so nobody has a piece of the picture.'[53]

A Bridge Too Far demonstrated both the advantages and disadvantages of pre-sales agreements. For Levine it was a triumph: he and director Richard Attenborough brought the logistically highly complex film in on schedule and under budget.[54] The star names attached to the film allowed Levine to sell *A Bridge Too Far* to major distributors. Fuji Eioga of Japan (a subsidiary of the Shochiko combine) advanced the additional funding to secure Redford, while United Artists paid US $17 million for North America, the United Kingdom, Australia, New Zealand, South Africa, Germany and Austria.[55] Levine's energetic pre-selling meant that the film had covered its cost before it was even shown in cinemas. Yet the film was ultimately regarded as a box-office failure. It performed well enough in Britain and

Europe, but not in the all-important American market where its rentals amounted to $20 million – a respectable return but far from blockbuster status in the age of *Jaws* and *Star Wars*.[56] Its disappointing performance in America was attributed variously to the preponderance of British actors and to the fact that unlike *The Longest Day* it was a narrative of failure rather than triumph. United Artists had sold the film to exhibitors on the same basis as they had taken it themselves as an unseen advance purchase.[57] One disappointed American exhibitor called it 'a prime example of a blind booking disaster'.[58]

By the late 1970s the British majors were also financing most of their films through pre-sales agreements: this was largely a consequence of the inflation of costs, which obliged producers to look to the international market. EMI had a dual strategy of producing domestic pictures with 100 per cent British financing while looking for international pre-sales for its bigger productions: distribution advances were staggered with part being paid up front, part when the film started shooting and the rest upon delivery of the negative. EMI was liable to pick up any overcost. For *Death on the Nile* (1978) – its follow-up to the highly successful *Murder on the Orient Express* – EMI secured a deal with Paramount for North American rights reported to be worth between US $4.5 million and $5 million.[59] This accounted for around three-fifths of the budget, with the balance forthcoming from another 23 distributors from different countries.[60] Like its predecessor, *Death on the Nile* was sold largely on its star cast, which this time included Peter Ustinov, David Niven, Bette Davis, Mia Farrow, Angela Lansbury and Simon MacCorkindale: it was successful (grossing $14 million), though not to quite the same extent as its predecessor. Even so, EMI was forced to scale back its production activities following overcosts on *Convoy* (1978) and *The Deer Hunter* (1978).[61]

However, it was Lew Grade's Associated Communications Corporation (ACC) which embraced the strategy of international sales more wholeheartedly than any other film-producing organisation.[62] Grade was the older brother of EMI's Bernard Delfont (both men were raised to the peerage in 1976) but temperamentally they were very different: Grade was flamboyant and a risk-taker, whereas Delfont was reserved and cautious. A contemporary profile described Grade as 'the last of the red-hot showmen': his largesse – ranging from his trademark cigars to the salaries he was prepared to pay for talent – was legendary in the industry.[63] Grade was chairman of Associated Television (ATV), which had produced, through its subsidiary the Independent Television Corporation (ITC), a successful cycle of British-made telefilm adventure series since the mid-1950s, including *The Adventures of Robin Hood*, *William Tell*, *Sir Francis Drake*, *Danger Man*, *The Saint*, *The Baron*, *Man in a Suitcase*, *The Prisoner* and *The Persuaders!*. With the returns for telefilm series declining in the 1970s, ITC made the decision to move into theatrical film production: in September 1974 Grade – never one to do anything by halves – announced an investment of £20 million in an ambitious film programme. ITC provided 100 per cent financing for *The Return of the Pink Panther* (1975) – a successful revival of the comedy series written and directed by Blake Edwards and starring Peter Sellers – which was distributed by United Artists.[64]

Like others before him, including Korda and the Rank Organisation, Grade set his sights on the world market with a cycle of international pictures in the late 1970s: these included *The Cassandra Crossing* (1976), *The Eagle Has Landed* (1976), *March or Die!* (1977), *The Boys from Brazil* (1978), *Capricorn One* (1978) and *Escape to Athena* (1979). There are certain parallels with Korda's London Film Productions in the 1930s. Grade's expansion was financed through loans: ACC – the parent company of ITC Films – increased its borrowing from £10 million in 1975 to £22 million by 1977.[65] This loan capital was not just for film production: ACC also had interests in property and in the music publishing industry. In 1979 Grade also acquired control of the 130-screen Classic cinema circuit. Grade recognised that raising the production finance was insufficient in itself if there was no prospect of a wide release in the US market. To that end he concluded a deal with the General Cinema Corporation – the largest cinema circuit in the United States – whereby General Cinemas committed to pre-production exhibition contracts (a form of blind booking) and a minimum number of play dates for films released under the aegis of the jointly owned Associated General Films. For Grade the deal offered a guaranteed US release, while for General Cinemas it offered a supply of high-end product.[66]

Grade was essentially a salesman rather than a producer: *Variety* reported that 'ITC continues to sell films in advance to the highest bidder (without any of the make-weight concession designed to ease the hurt in regard to previous distributor losses). The assumption is that a hit, when it comes, will make everybody rich.'[67] He enthusiastically embraced the strategy of pre-sales: he made deals with US majors including Columbia (*The Eagle Has Landed*), Warner Bros. (*Capricorn One*) and Twentieth Century–Fox (*The Boys from Brazil*) for American rights, and with independent distributors in other territories. However, while Grade's programme included some successful films, there was no outright blockbuster: the most successful was *The Muppet Movie* (1979) – Grade's ATV had produced *The Muppet Show* for television – which earned $14.6 million in North America.[68] The trade journalist Simon Perry felt that Grade's method of financing resulted in bland, conservative product:

> The pre-sale mentality, as evidenced by Grade, demonstrates more and more persuasively that chucking however many expensive ingredients into a tepid container does not result in cordon bleu cooking. And as pursuit of that elusive winner leads the dauntless entrepreneur more hectically into what the jargon calls the mega-budget league (*Raise the Titanic* was due to cost $33,000,000 at the latest count), the need to limit risks becomes even more pressing. The legacy of *The Boys from Brazil*, *Movie Movie*, *The Big Sleep*, *The Cassandra Crossing* and *Escape to Athena*, to name not all that have come and quickly gone, is a reduction of flexibility and opportunities to experiment.[69]

As the films were pre-sold, however, it was the distributors who carried the loss rather than the production company, provided that no significant overcosts were incurred. ACC reported a profit of £13.7 million in 1978: £2.3 million of this came from its film production activity and £5.3 million from its television interests, with the rest from property (£2.5 million), music publishing (£2 million) and other subsidiary businesses.[70]

In 1978 ACC and EMI combined their overseas sales divisions to form Associated Film Distributors: this was yet another attempt by British producers to gain a stronger foothold in the US market by setting up their own Stateside distribution network. It was prompted by what both partners regarded as the unsatisfactory returns from the distribution of their films in the United States. Associated Film Distributors was capitalised at US $38.5 million, with credit from the First National Bank of Boston.[71] Grade was chairman, Delfont vice-chairman, and the directors also included Jack Gill (Grade's senior accountant) and Barry Spikings. The company was nothing if not ambitious: ACC and EMI planned to make twelve films a year. However, the move into distribution meant that ACC was now exposed if its films lost money. Associated Film Distributors was effectively killed off by two films that became bywords for disaster: ACC's $35 million *Raise the Titanic!* (1980) – Grade famously quipped that 'it would have been cheaper to lower the Atlantic' – and EMI's $24 million *Honky Tonk Freeway* (1981). The escalation of costs on both these films was probably due as much to the spiralling inflation at the end of the 1970s which overtook their original budgets as it was to the mismanagement of production. *Raise the Titanic!*, for example, had originally been estimated as costing $18–20 million.[72] But their dismal performance at the box office spelled the end for Associated Film Distributors. *Raise the Titanic!* returned only $7 million from the US market and *Honky Tonk Freeway* a mere $2 million. Grade was the worst affected: ACC lost £26.4 million in 1980 – following a profit of £13 million the previous year – and was carrying another £15 million of loans and overdrafts.[73] Grade was able to make good some of his losses by selling the television contracts for *The Muppet Show* to American interests and disposing of Classic cinemas.[74]

There were conflicting opinions about the reasons for ACC's troubles. *The Financial Times* suggested the corporation's losses arose directly from film production and distribution: 'The poor returns on film-making, the cash demand of the distribution operation and the decline of cinema earnings were the main contributors to a severe liquidity crisis that hit ACC last autumn.'[75] However, City analyst William Phillips of the *Investor's Chronicle* felt there were underlying problems with the management of the company under its autocratic 75-year-old chairman and chief executive:

> I have great admiration for Lord Grade; but his big figures and buying spurs, which enthral the showbiz press, often alarm the City. He should put more, younger executives with broad managerial experience on his main board . . . Too many British showbiz empires lost their way under aged supremos who lost their way: think of Sir Ted Lewis's Decca, Sir John Davis's Rank, Sir John Reid's EMI, Sir Philip Warter's ABPC. The stock market is sending ACC a message for its own ultimate good.[76]

The sharp fall in ACC's share value, which halved in a year, was due not only to the losses of *Raise the Titanic!* but also to uncertainty over the renewal of ATV's television franchise and the view that Grade had paid too much for the Inter-European Property Group in 1979. In the event, Grade was forced out of ACC following a hostile takeover by the Australian tycoon Robert Holmes à Court in 1982. But ACC was no longer an active player in the film industry: it sold off its television interests after ATV lost its franchise in 1982. ITC Films remained active as a distributor for a few years until it was wound up in 1987.

The rise and fall of the Grade empire was perhaps the most spectacular instance to date of a British film-producing organisation whose fate was sealed by an overambitious international strategy. Grade's move into distribution spelled the end for ACC: it was ironic in the extreme that it was a film whose very title recalled a historic disaster that proved to be his downfall. *Raise the Titanic!* provided journalists with ample opportunity for metaphors of hitting icebergs and sinking ships. But ultimately the demise of ACC was not down to losses (no matter how large) on one film but rather to a flawed overall strategy: it demonstrated yet again that the British film industry lacked both the cultural and more to the point the economic capital to compete with Hollywood on its own turf.

NOTES

1. FFA General Correspondence Box 76: Cinerama News press release: 'Fourteen Million Dollar Boost for British Film Production', n.d. (c. January 1970).
2. 'Frost, Bennett to head consortium', *Kinematograph Weekly*, 21 November 1970, p. 8.
3. David A. Cook, *Lost Illusions: American Cinema in the Shadow of Watergate and Vietnam 1970–1979* (Berkeley: University of California Press, 2000), p. 1.
4. 'Financing the Films: New Ideas', *New York Times*, 2 July 1970, p. 100.
5. *The Financing of the British Film Industry: Second Report of the Interim Action Committee on the Film Industry*, Cmnd. 7597 (June 1979), p. 2 (10).
6. 'Euan Lloyd's link with Louis L'Amour', *CinemaTV Today*, 28 October 1972, p. 6.
7. FFA General Correspondence Box 43: Robert Garrett to Kingston Film Productions, 12 September 1967.
8. 'Euan Lloyd's Coin Tactics on "Shalako"; Area Rights Click', *Variety*, 5 February 1969, p. 5.
9. 'The Mystery of Movie Financing', *Los Angeles Times*, 4 June 1968, p. F1.
10. 'Lloyd returns to pre-selling', *CinemaTV Today*, 18 March 1972, p. 14.
11. 'Financing the Films', p. 100.
12. 'De Grunwald secures US backing for consortium', *Kinematograph Weekly*, 22 November 1969, p. 3.
13. '£10m start for de Grunwald consortium', *Kinematograph Weekly*, 1 March 1969, p. 3.
14. '£10m film boost for Britain', *The Times*, 27 February 1969, p. 18.
15. 'The film industry's quest for funds', *The Financial Times*, 22 December 1969, p. 23.
16. 'Flint replaces de Grunwald at London Screenplays', *Kinematograph Weekly*, 7 November 1970, p. 3.
17. 'Lon. Screenplays Accents Distrib of Film Backlog', *Variety*, 30 December 1970, p. 4.
18. 'The League of Gentlemen', *CinemaTV Today*, 15 January 1972, p. 9.

19. FFA Realised Film Box 577: *Heaven Save Us From Our Friends*: Statement of Production Cost No. 6, 6 April 1975.
20. 'Cinerama backs Shaftel in 14 million dollar programme', *Kinematograph Weekly*, 10 January 1970, p. 3.
21. FFA General Correspondence Box 76: 'Fourteen Million Dollar Boost for British Film Production'.
22. 'Shaftel in Wonderland', *CinemaTV Today*, 8 April 1972, p. 22.
23. FFA Realised Film Box 511: *The Assassination of Trotsky*: David L. Carrington to William Aikin, 12 October 1971.
24. 'EMI's flexible film policy: now it backs Losey's "Trotsky"', *Today's Cinema*, 5 October 1971, p. 3.
25. FFA Realised Film Box 533: *A Doll's House*: Robert Garrett to World Film Services, 20 October 1972.
26. Ibid.: Edward Sands to Jayne Productions Corporation, 9 October 1972.
27. FFA Realised Film Box 576: *The Romantic Englishwoman*: Dial Films: Production Budget, 8 October 1974.
28. Ibid.: Statement of Production Cost No. 1, 31 March 1975.
29. TNA FV 81/191: National Film Trustee Company Ltd: Allocation of revenues per distributor's statements to 31 December 1978.
30. 'No love lost behind the scenes', *The Financial Times*, 27 January 1971, p. 15.
31. *National Film Finance Corporation: Annual Report and Statement of Accounts for the year ended 31 March 1970*, Cmnd. 4402 (May 1970), p. 10 (24).
32. 'Scotia Investments', *CinemaTV Today*, 24 June 1972, p. 22.
33. FFA Realised Film Box 586: *The Slipper and the Rose*: Stuart Lyons to Bernard Smith, 2 May 1975.
34. Alan A. Tait, 'Political Economy: The British Budget of 1971', *Public Finance Analysis*, New Series 30: 3 (1972), pp. 489–504.
35. '"Mum's" money backs Olivier', *CinemaTV Today*, 29 January 1972, p. 22.
36. 'Polanski', *CinemaTV Today*, 5 February 1972, p. 28.
37. 'Global Sales Conclave Sans Peer', *Variety*, 2 May 1974, p. 7.
38. 'Film Hits Present Britain's Cannes Pix', *Variety*, 14 April 1976, p. 37.
39. Andrew Spicer and A. T. McKenna, *The Man Who Got Carter: Michael Klinger, Independent Production, and the British Film Industry, 1960–1980* (London: I. B. Tauris, 2013), p. 108.
40. FFA Realised Film Box 558: *Gold*: Michael Klinger to Robert Garrett, 24 January 1974.
41. FFA Realised Film Box 583: *Shout at the Devil*: John Croydon to Robert Garrett, 29 May 1974.
42. Ibid.: Garrett to Bernard Smith, 17 June 1975.
43. Ibid.: Statement of Production Cost, 12 June 1975.
44. '"Wild Geese" take off', *Screen International*, 1 October 1977, p. 12.
45. 'The coup behind "The Wild Geese"', *Screen International*, 7 January 1978, p. 15.
46. FFA Realised Film Box 603: *The Wild Geese*: Film Finances to Elite Film (Zurich), 25 October 1977.
47. Ibid.: Croydon to Garrett, 5 September 1977.
48. '"Sea Wolves" nightmare has a happy ending', *Screen International*, 24 May 1980, p. 17.
49. 'A budget too big', *The Economist*, 29 May 1976, p. 96.
50. Sally Dux, *Richard Attenborough* (Manchester: Manchester University Press, 2013), p. 74.

51. William Goldman, *Adventures in the Screen Trade: A Personal View of Hollywood and Screenwriting* (London: Macdonald, 1984), p. 283.
52. A. T. McKenna, 'Joseph E. Levine and *A Bridge Too Far* (1977): A Producer's Labour of Love', *Historical Journal of Film, Radio and Television*, 31: 2 (2011), p. 215.
53. 'Levine: Why I Paid "Bridge" Stars So Much', *Screen International*, 25 June 1977, p. 20.
54. Goldman, *Adventures in the Screen Trade*, pp. 293–4.
55. 'UA signs deal on "Bridge"', *Screen International*, 14 April 1976, p. 1.
56. 'UA's Film Rental Highlights of 1977', *Variety*, 11 January 1978, p. 3.
57. 'UA Crosses Joe Levine's Costly Bridge', *Variety*, 19 January 1977, p. 7.
58. Quoted in McKenna, 'Joseph E. Levine and *A Bridge Too Far*', p. 222.
59. 'Hint Par. To Distrib "Nile", EMI's Christie Whodunit', *Variety*, 17 August 1977, p. 25.
60. 'Twenty-three countries attend "Death on the Nile" premiere', *Screen International*, 4 November 1978, p. 14.
61. 'Hint Cutback In EMI Pix Prod. As Corporate Parent's Net Slips', *Variety*, 28 December 1977, p. 29.
62. The best overview of the rise and fall of Grade's film empire remains Alexander Walker, *National Heroes: British Cinema in the Seventies and Eighties* (London: Harrap, 1985), pp. 192–215.
63. 'Lew Grade's ITC Ballyhooliks Mark Cannes Film Festival', *Variety*, 26 May 1976, p. 30.
64. 'ATV to spend £20m. on films', *The Financial Times*, 17 September 1974, p. 12.
65. 'ATV film finance', *The Financial Times*, 13 August 1977, p. 12.
66. 'General Cinema Joins ATC in Feature Financing Equity', *The Independent Film Journal*, 29 October 1975, p. 3.
67. 'British In Smilingly', *Variety*, 9 May 1979, p. 333.
68. '50 Top-Grossing Films', *Variety*, 23 July 1980, p. 9.
69. Simon Perry, 'Finance for Local Talent', *Sight & Sound*, 49: 3 (Summer 1980), p. 146.
70. 'Associated Communications Corporation', *The Economist*, 16 September 1978, p. 113.
71. 'Time Is Ripe for Distrib Co., Bernard Delfont', *Variety*, 3 January 1978, p. 8.
72. 'Grade Empire Sweeps Europe', *Screen International*, 19 May 1979, p. 1.
73. 'The script Lord Grade should have filmed', *The Economist*, 23 January 1982, p. 117.
74. 'Muppets come to the rescue', *Screen International*, 4 July 1981, p. 26.
75. 'Titanic losses fail to sink Lew Grade', *The Financial Times*, 27 June 1981, p. 15.
76. 'Why the City gives ACC a low grade', *Broadcast*, 10 November 1980, p. 16.

CHAPTER 17

The National Film Finance Consortium

> We'd very much like to see the NFFC give us a million out of successful trading, instead of us giving it a million! We'd like to see it attracting private money instead of public money . . . There doesn't seem to me to be any reason why films shouldn't get their finance from the market like everything else does in the long run. (Nicholas Ridley)[1]

If the 1970s was a turbulent decade for the British cinema industry, this was especially true for the National Film Finance Corporation. It was a difficult time for the state-owned film bank. The corporation had not made a profit since 1964. Its statement of accounts for 1970 reported a loss of £386,126 for the year and an accumulated deficit of over £5.3 million.[2] At the turn of the decade the NFFC was caught on the horns of a dilemma. On the one hand the withdrawal of a large amount of American capital from the British film industry presented an opportunity for the corporation: there would be more need of its support than at the height of the 'Hollywood UK' boom during the 1960s when the corporation had been looking more and more redundant as a lender to British producers. On the other hand the increasing demand for its support came at a time when the corporation's resources were severely depleted. The NFFC's ability to support the ailing British production sector was also compromised by wider political uncertainty over official film policy. The 1970s was a period of considerable economic and political instability: the toing and froing between a Labour Party inclined to supporting the film industry and a Conservative Party opposed in principle to public subsidy made this an especially difficult period for the NFFC, which had to respond to frequent and often sudden shifts in government policy.

The new decade had in fact started on an auspicious note for the NFFC. The Films Act of 1970 extended the corporation's lending powers until the end of 1980 and, moreover, made provision for a further advance of £5 million from the public purse to be provided in instalments over the ten-year period. This was the first injection of new funds into the NFFC since 1950 and raised the total advanced by the government from £6 million to £11 million. In addition, the NFFC was relieved of its liability to pay interest on advances made before 1965. Although it was recognised on both sides of the House that the economic conditions of the film industry were very different from the circumstances that had led to the establishment of the corporation in the 1940s, there were nevertheless uncanny echoes of the debate at the time during the discussion of the Films Bill: speeches made reference to film as a medium of national projection, export earnings and the role of American interests in the British industry. Gwyneth Dunwoody, the Parliamentary Under-Secretary for the Board of Trade, argued in moving the legislation that 'the continued existence of the Corporation is a very desirable measure of support for the industry'. She also suggested that there was 'every reason to hope that the Corporation, with the increased scope provided in this Bill, will in future at least break even'.[3] The government's case smacked of hope rather than expectation: Dunwoody's optimistic assessment of the immediate economic prospects of the film industry flew in the face of most trade and business commentators. The Opposition spokesman was Sir Keith Joseph: he explained that the Conservative Party would not oppose the Bill but that they did not see further state funding for the NFFC as desirable in the longer term: 'We realise that any thought of ending its operation abruptly – particularly at present – would be entirely wrong. But we still adhere to the hope . . . that in the right circumstances the film industry will be self-financing from private enterprise sources.' He added that the Conservatives would look to 'phase out or taper off the corporation' if the conditions were right.[4]

The NFFC was pleased to have the additional funding but cautioned that it would not go far in making up for the withdrawal of American capital. Its report for 1970 stated that 'the Corporation's new fund of £5 million is small having regard to the gap to be filled, but it should be sufficient to enable it to make a significant contribution to the maintenance of British film production, albeit production of a smaller volume than in recent years, and certainly on a less expensive scale'.[5] John Terry requested an immediate advance of £1.5 million of the new funds as soon as the Films Act became law: he was advised there would be 'considerable difficulty in meeting that request' and that the best he could expect was for £1 million of the new funds to be made available.[6] However, the election of a Conservative government in June 1970 fundamentally changed the context of the debate over the future of the NFFC. The new government was ideologically hostile to state subsidy: one of its first acts was to abolish Labour's Industrial Reorganisation Corporation, and it soon became apparent that there was no interest in propping up failing industries. Its ethos was expressed in a speech by John Davies, the former Director General of the Confederation of British Industries who served as Secretary of State for Trade and Industry in the early 1970s, who declared 'that the essential need of the country is to gear its policies to the greatest majority of people, who are not "lame ducks", who do not need a hand, who are quite capable of looking after their own interests and only demand to be allowed to do so'.[7] The film industry must have seemed like one of those so-called 'lame ducks'. The Conservatives' promise to 'phase out or taper off' the NFFC was confirmed in principle early in 1971:

> Ministers here have confirmed – as they indicated that they would when in Opposition during debates on the Films Bill in Parliament – that their eventual aim is to transfer the Corporation's activities to the private sector. It is not, however,

their purpose simply to abolish the Corporation or in the meantime to discontinue Government financing. Mr Ridley has made this plain, both to the Corporation itself and to the industry. The question is one of method and timing.[8]

Nicholas Ridley was Parliamentary Under-Secretary at the Department of Trade and Industry with specific responsibility for the film industry (sometimes informally referred to as 'films minister') between 1970 and 1972: he would play a key role in the negotiations between the NFFC and the government that secured funding from the private sector.

The future of the NFFC was discussed as part of the government's expenditure review early in 1971. It was soon apparent that its future depended upon it receiving the additional funds provided for by the Films Act: a Treasury minute records that 'the NFFC is apparently viewed as such an unpromising financial prospect that the Clearing Banks will only lend it money on condition that DTI give an assurance that they are advancing further funds to the Corporation'.[9] The new government was opposed in principle to making further advances to the NFFC. One Treasury official questioned 'whether the objective of getting the Corporation into a financial condition which would make it an attractive take-over proposition is *remotely realistic*. The Corporation has lost on average about £175,000 annually since it began. Preliminary indications are that the year ending 31 March, 1971 will be slightly worse than average.'[10] Patrick Jenkin, the Financial Secretary to the Treasury, poured further cold water on the idea when he suggested 'that continuing (and even more, increasing) investment of public funds in unprofitable activities, in order to make those activities profitable enough to dispose of them to the private sector, is a pretty chancey business. It may not come off; and even if it does, the higher price may not justify the resources spent to get it.'[11]

Nicholas Ridley's announcement in June 1971 that the government's aim 'is gradually to withdraw from the financing of the production of films' prompted a letter to *The Times* from a dozen leading film-makers – including Lindsay Anderson, Richard Attenborough, Michael Balcon, Joseph Losey, Karel Reisz, Tony Richardson and John Schlesinger – voicing their 'dismay that the 1970 Films Act . . . should be disregarded' and arguing that the withdrawal of American finance 'offers an opportunity at last to achieve [our] independence. But money has not been and will not be easily obtained from British banks by independent producers. Only the vigorous functioning of a National Film Finance Corporation can guarantee this.'[12] Roy Boulting averred that the government 'cannot see the trees for what appears to be dead wood' and accused Ridley of acting 'in a manner that did not allow either examination or debate'.[13] Ridley was seen at the time (and since) as the prime mover in the drive for the abolition of the NFFC – an impression lent further credence by his later association with the free-market policies of Margaret Thatcher's government in the 1980s. However, the official records cast a slightly different light on the debates that went on behind the scenes. It is clear that there were disagreements between the Department of Trade and Industry on the one hand and the Treasury on the other. Ridley did not, in fact, advocate the dismantling of the NFFC: he wanted to see it transferred to the private sector but he realised that in order to achieve this 'it is essential that they should be given adequate resources in time to make it feasible'.[14] He argued privately that further public funding for the NFFC in the short term would give the corporation the opportunity to demonstrate that it could make a profit and therefore smooth its transfer to the private sector. The real hostility towards the NFFC came from the Treasury: its line was that 'support of the NFFC from public funds is something of an anachronism in this day and age . . . And there is a limit to how far one can throw good money after bad.'[15] Maurice Macmillan, the Chief Secretary to the Treasury, is reported to have remarked that the NFFC should be 'for the chopper as soon as possible, I hope'.[16] Even more moderate voices such as the civil servant Leo Pliatzky, who had served on the Film Industry Working Group in 1964–5 and a Keynesian not in principle opposed to state subsidy, felt that the end might be in sight for the NFFC: 'There is no good economic case for this expenditure. I regard it as a *largely political* issue. From that point of view, abolition of the corporation might be a candidate for announcement in the proposed White Paper on the outcome of the review of functions.'[17]

In the event the proposal that emerged – suggested by the NFFC itself and supported by the Department of Trade – was to put together a consortium of private investors who would supplement public funding for the corporation. The consortium idea reflected the arrangements already emerging in the private sector pioneered by producers such as Dimitri de Grunwald and Josef Shaftel. And it is surely no coincidence that the initiative to bring merchant banks into the proposed consortium followed the arrival of a new chairman of the NFFC: Robert Clark, appointed in 1969, came from a private banking background (Hill Samuel). The NFFC had originally suggested that 'the proposed consortium would normally provide 50 per cent of the budget finance required for selected feature films when the other 50 per cent was being provided by British Lion or Anglo-EMI or any other British distributor which accepted the scheme'.[18] The Department of Trade supported the consortium idea in principle on the grounds that 'the scheme offers the NFFC a chance of achieving viability within two or three years [in order that] the Corporation can be sold or in some other way painlessly phased out of the public sector'.[19] However, the Treasury was concerned that the NFFC wanted to spend all the £5 million provided for it under the Films Act. Therefore it agreed to advance only £1 million, and that was to be provided only on the condition that the corporation raised a further £4 million from the private sector.[20] This was always likely to be a difficult proposition given the deteriorating economic state of the film industry in the early 1970s. As an incentive to encourage private investment, therefore, it was proposed that the three main sources of film revenue – domestic receipts, Eady payments and overseas receipts – should be combined in a single fund which would be shared between the distributor (25 per cent) and investors (75 per cent) on a *pari passu* basis. The aim was 'to place the film financier in a more advantageous, or perhaps one should say a less disadvantageous position than he has hitherto enjoyed' by ensuring a quicker return on the investment.[21] The scheme had a cautious welcome from the industry: it was accepted in principle by EMI and British Lion, while the Rank Organisation 'indicated a willingness to pursue discussions'.[22]

The NFFC prepared the ground for the consortium by looking for outside investment partners in a couple of films it had already agreed to support: *Up Pompeii* (1971) and *Under Milk Wood* (1972). The fact that these were very different projects – a television comedy spin-off and a Dylan Thomas adaptation – demonstrates the cultural uncertainty of the NFFC's policy in the early 1970s. A Cabinet paper records:

> The NFFC opened negotiations with prospective contributors to the consortium in the early part of 1971 and did so on the assumption that the consortium would be offered two films which were then under consideration and which were promising but not yet assured of success. These were *Up Pompeii* and *Under Milk Wood*. The former has covered its costs and will show a profit if only of modest proportions. It is too early to estimate the results of *Under Milk Wood*. The offer of these films to the consortium was undoubtedly an inducement to potential contributors but how important an inducement it was or what the effect of its withdrawal at this stage would be it is impossible to say. In spite however of the delay in establishing the consortium the NFFC feel under a moral commitment to maintain the offer; and if the expectations of the films are realised they should get the consortium off to a reasonably good start.[23]

Under Milk Wood was an unusual arrangement in so far as the merchant bank Hill Samuel provided one-third of the £300,000 budget, with the NFFC making up the remaining two-thirds. The NFFC described the unique arrangement, which did not involve any distributor finance, as an 'imaginative departure from precedent, which augurs well for the future'.[24] The cast, including Richard Burton, Elizabeth Taylor and Peter O'Toole, took modest fees and profit participations. Director Andrew Sinclair told the trade press: 'All the stars – and those in support make impressive reading I think – are doing it for virtually nothing so we have a £300,000 picture with every penny there on the screen.'[25] However, *Under Milk Wood* was not a success. Sinclair brought the film in under budget at £273,297 but it sank at the box office with total distributor's receipts of only £16,233. The NFFC (£10,575) and Hill Samuel (£5,288) each recovered only 5.5 per cent of their investments.[26]

Contrary to the NFFC, therefore, the case of *Under Milk Wood* did not augur well for the provision of private equity capital for the new consortium. *The Economist* was sceptical that sufficient private investment would be forthcoming:

> Will the City stump up? As every star-struck investor knows, the major American film companies, which dominate the British film industry, have been going through two years of decline – from which they have emerged healthier, but still facing a market that continues to contract. When companies that really know the business fall flat on their faces, sceptics will ask what chance there is of recouping an

> investment made through a British film bank whose record is one of continuing losses . . .
>
> In England there have been one-off financings by a hardy few, but the only substantial investment was that by Morgan Grenfell in London Screenplays; it ended unhappily when the bank learned how tricky the business was.[27]

Arthur Sadler, who had succeeded Nicholas Davenport as the film business specialist for *The Financial Times*, put it rather more bluntly: 'It is understood that the City has been more than nervous about investment in an industry which has the outward appearance of a Mad Hatter's tea party.'[28]

Indeed, it soon became apparent that the consortium scheme was not going to be able to attract private equity capital on the scale initially envisaged. In April 1971 Ridley reported to the Treasury: 'The Corporation now say that they are not as sanguine of raising as much from private sources as they were a few months ago, since when the climate in which a consortium might be formed has worsened.'[29] Crucially, the merchant banks investing in the film industry who were seen as the most likely partners for the consortium scheme were already starting to get cold feet. Ridley asked the Treasury to reduce the sum required from the private sector while still advancing £1 million to the NFFC. For the Treasury this was 'a somewhat unwelcome response . . . The Corporation, therefore, evidently with Mr Ridley's acquiescence, reject all the Chief Secretary's conditions.'[30] This is further evidence that Ridley was rather more of a pragmatist regarding the NFFC than the ideologue so often portrayed. Following a meeting between Ridley and Patrick Jenkin on 28 April, it was agreed that the NFFC could draw up to £1 million on a 1:3 ratio with private investment: in other words, the full £1 million would be dependent upon it raising £3 million from the private sector. This came with the warning that if it 'could not live up to these arrangements, the NFFC could not look forward to even this limited continuation of an active role'.[31]

In March 1972 Ridley was finally able to present a paper to the Cabinet outlining the shape of the consortium. He explained that the delay in establishing the consortium 'no doubt reflects the City's caution about investment in film production after unhappy experiences in the past'.[32] However, the NFFC had not been able to raise the full £3 million it needed to meet the Treasury's conditions. It had 'commitments in principle' from eleven investors amounting to £750,000 in total: the major contributors were the National Westminster Bank (£250,000), the Industrial and Commercial Finance Corporation (£100,000), Hill Samuel (£50,000), Howard and Wyndham (£50,000), the Charterhouse Group (£50,000) and the Philip Hill Investment Trust (£50,000). Nevertheless, the Treasury agreed to advance the full £1 million, which brought the total consortium fund to £1,750,000. This came on the strict condition that there would be no further advances.[33] The way the consortium would work in practice was that in order to receive funding a project would have to be recommended by the NFFC and approved by a majority of members of the consortium: the revenues would be shared by all members in proportion to their respective contribution to the fund.[34]

The consortium came into effect in June 1972: the NFFC set up a subsidiary company – the National Film Finance Consortium – in order to administer the scheme, which hereafter became the only channel through which the corporation made loans to producers. The NFFC averred that the policy of making loans 'on a strictly commercial basis' mandated a more fiscally cautious and culturally conservative outlook: after the first year of the consortium it reported that 'the Corporation has had to adopt a tight-fisted policy in place of the more open-handed attitude of the past since, if the Consortium were to fail commercially, not only would the Corporation have to close its doors but the private sector investors would become discouraged for a very considerable time'. 'Accordingly,' it added, 'the Corporation is acting as a small commercial investment group and tries to select for financing only those film projects which seem to have a particularly good chance of achieving profitability.'[35] In the first full year of the consortium it approved loans amounting to £356,437 in total for three features – *Ooh . . . You Are Awful*, *Steptoe and Son* and *The Final Programme* – and one short (*The Cobblers of Umbridge*).[36] The fact that two of the first three features approved were low-brow comedies of a sort popular in the early 1970s demonstrates that the consortium had indeed adopted a safety-first policy. The National Film Trustee Company was set up to administer the collection of revenues.

The financing arrangements for *Ooh . . . You Are Awful* (1972) – a vehicle for television comedian Dick Emery directed by Cliff Owen for British Lion Films – demonstrated how the consortium worked in practice. The consortium advanced £62,500 – one-third of the film's budget of £185,000 – with the same amount put up by EMI Films and the remaining third made up from contributions from other investors: Launder Gilliat & Co. (£15,000), Douglas Bernhardt (£10,000), Alfred Black (£10,000), Cassius Film Productions (£10,000), Carlton Films (£5,000), Silverdea Films (£5,000) and Dick Emery (£5,000). The final cost was £201,443: the overcost was provided by the completion guarantor Quintain Productions (£5,899) and investor Silverdea Films. *Ooh . . . You Are Awful* returned total distributors' receipts of £267,173, which meant that it made a profit. The NFFC and EMI each received £82,582 and the other investors also made profits in relation to the size of their investment except for Silverdea Films (the company of producer E. M. Smedley-Aston) whose profit was reduced by having made up part of the overcost.[37] A profit of 32 per cent on its investment represented a very good return for the consortium and justified the NFFC's new policy of backing films deemed likely to have good commercial prospects.

The consortium meant that the NFFC supported fewer films: it functioned more as a specialised investment trust than as a film bank. For the science-fiction drama *The Final Programme* (1973) – produced by John Goldstone and Sandy Lieberson and directed by Robert Fuest for Anglo-EMI Film Distributors – the NFFC and EMI each advanced 50 per cent of the budget of £291,885. For the musical comedy *Bugsy Malone* (1976) – produced by Alan Marshall and directed by Alan Parker for David Puttnam and Sandy Lieberson's Goodtimes

Enterprises – the NFFC and Rank Film Distributors each contributed £193,500, with an additional £111,810 from the Alan Parker Film Company to make up the budget of £498,810. *Bugsy Malone* would prove to be the consortium's most successful investment. John Terry averred that '*Bugsy Malone* is a film I wish we might have financed 100 per cent when we had the opportunity to do so'.[38] From the mid-1970s the consortium seems to have been open to supporting less obviously commercial projects. For example, *Overlord* (1975) was a low-budget (£89,951) war picture written and directed by Stuart Cooper for which the NFFC loaned £28,500, with the Imperial War Museum contributing £14,850 and the balance in deferments. *Akenfield* (1975) – Peter Hall's film of the novel by Ronald Blythe shot on location using non-professional actors – cost £122,705: the NFFC headed the list of 'first schedule creditors' with £15,000 alongside Petard Productions (£12,000) and a long list of individual investors (including Vera Lynn, who contributed £200), with a 'second schedule' of service companies who either deferred or reduced their fees.[39] For these projects the NFFC's risk was less than the more expensive films as its contribution as a percentage of the budget was smaller and they were in any event produced on lower budgets.

These diverse examples demonstrate that the NFFC was willing to contemplate a flexible approach to financing arrangements through the consortium. At the same time there is some suggestion that the corporation was not entirely happy with the operation of the fund. The involvement of commercial partners in contributing part of the finance tied the NFFC's hands in project selection. In its second full year of operation, the consortium supported only one film: the rock musical *Stardust* (1974). This was an evidently commercial proposition – a sequel to the successful *That'll Be the Day* with the same producers (David Puttnam, Sandy Lieberson) and star (David Essex) – for which the NFFC and EMI each put up 50 per cent of the budget: the consortium's investment was £126,820. According to the NFFC's report:

> This was the only project out of 134 subjects submitted to the Corporation during the year which was ready to go into production and which seemed to have an outstanding chance of commercial success. Of those 134 subjects only 38 had reached a stage of development at which some of the ingredients, including finance from other sources, necessary to enable the film to go into production were present, and of these it is probable that the Corporation would have approved advances in a number of other cases if it had been in a position to pursue a less restrictive policy.[40]

There is a slight undertone here implying that the NFFC felt constrained by the operation of the consortium. It added that £1,250,000 of the consortium fund remained uncommitted and expressed the hope that 1974–5 'may be more stimulating and rewarding'. The following year the NFFC approved loans totalling £321,432 for eight features (*The Man Who Fell to Earth*, *The Romantic Englishwoman*,

Akenfield, Overlord, Bugsy Malone, Dual Blade, James Dean: The First American Teenager, Lisztomania) and one television serial (*Sam and the River*): its report again referred to 'the extremely cautious policy which the Corporation has felt obliged to adopt in advising the Consortium'.[41]

So how successful was the National Film Finance Consortium? Between 1972 and 1978 the consortium backed nineteen feature films and one television serial. The NFFC supported significantly fewer films through the consortium than it had done before but usually made bigger investments in those it supported. By 1978 the total value of loans made through the consortium amounted to £2,822,612, of which less than half (£1,274,042) had been repaid. The consortium's total receipts in respect of its investments were £1,782,784.[42] The NFFC reported that of the nineteen films, 'two have made serious losses and three modest losses, two have broken even and two more are likely to break even, two have made satisfactory profits and three have made exceptional profits'.[43] It was too early to predict the success of the remaining five. The report did not identify which films were which and it is not clear whether profits and losses were calculated as gross receipts above the consortium's investment or as a percentage of the investment. *Bugsy Malone* was the most successful of the films for which distribution receipts are available: the NFFC's gross profit was £184,766 or a 95 per cent profit on its investment. The other profitable consortium films were *Ooh . . . You Are Awful* (£20,882/32 per cent), *The Romantic Englishwoman* (£30,918/11 per cent) and *James Dean: The First American Teenager* (£6,935/21 per cent). There are no receipts for *Stardust*, but it is listed in the corporation's 1975 report as making 'substantial profits'.[44] The records are incomplete, so it is difficult to distinguish the 'modest losses' from the break-even films. It seems likely that *The Man Who Fell to Earth* and *At the Earth's Core* broke even, while *The Final Programme*, *Lisztomania* and *Overlord* were probably loss-makers. *Akenfield*, while entailing a relatively modest investment (£15,000), was also a big loss-maker as the consortium made back only 6.4 per cent of its investment (£971).[45]

The consortium made very little difference to the NFFC's balance sheet overall. The corporation continued to operate at a loss during the early 1970s: it lost £709,512 in 1972, £399,631 in 1973, £457,244 in 1974 and £286,164 in 1975.[46] At best the corporation could point to higher receipts from film distribution (partly due to taking a higher percentage) and a smaller loss in 1975. But this could hardly be considered a success and certainly fell a long way short of the government's ambition of returning the corporation to profitability in order to facilitate its transfer to the private sector.

It might have been expected that a change of government – the Labour Party had formed a minority administration following the general election of February 1974 and would win a small majority in another poll in the autumn – would have thrown the NFFC a lifeline. Indeed, the Department of Trade suggested that a short-term measure 'providing breathing space for the industry would be to allow the NFFC to draw forthwith on the balance of £1m which the Treasury agreed to put up for the NFFC consortium'.[47] However, a note by the Private Secretary to the Chief Secretary to the Treasury (Joel Barnett) was not encouraging:

> ... the Chief Secretary has considerable reservations about the proposal that the NFFC be allowed the balance of the £1m which remains with it under the consortium arrangements. He considers that a thorough examination of the NFFC and the failure of the consortium approach is needed before the NFFC is given a new lease of life. Its record in recent years had been far from impressive, and the Chief Secretary doubts whether it is necessarily the right channel for further public financing of the film industry – if there is to be any.[48]

To this extent the attitude of the new government towards the NFFC seems initially to have been little different from its predecessor. There was certainly no enthusiasm at the Treasury for further funding for the NFFC whether in association with private capital or not.

By the mid-1970s the consortium was under pressure. In 1975 it was reported that one of the consortium partners had decided to withdraw.[49] The consortium fund now amounted to only £500,000. At a time when inflation was beginning to bite, this would not go very far. In April 1976 John Terry proposed to the Department of Trade that the NFFC should resume the policy of investing in films from its own resources as well as through the consortium:

> My Board is anxious to retain the Consortium Fund in its present form so long as our private sector partners are willing to continue. We accordingly came to the conclusion that we ought in future to offer to the Consortium any and all projects in which my Board believed that an investment should be made. In every case where the Consortium accepted the recommendation of the NFFC Board, the investment in question should be provided as to one-third thereof by the Consortium Fund and as to two-thirds thereof by NFFC, and the recovery position and the share of profits attributable to the whole investment would be shared as to one-third to the Consortium and as [to] two-thirds to NFFC. However, in any case recommended by the NFFC Board where the Consortium declined to proceed, we feel it should be open to NFFC to proceed on its own.[50]

In 1976 the NFFC approved loans for two films through the consortium (*Jabberwocky* and *The Duellists*) and another three from its own resources (*Tarka the Otter*, *Black Joy* and *The Disappearance*). A distinction was now emerging between higher-cost films that received consortium funding and lower-budget films in which the NFFC made a smaller investment. For *Jabberwocky* (1977) – the surreal fantasy comedy produced by Sandy Lieberson and John Goldstone and directed by Terry Gilliam for Columbia–EMI–Warner – the NFFC was the largest single investor (£200,000), followed by EMI Films (£137,001) and Michael White Ltd (£162,999). The distributor's receipts were £479,219 and the NFFC lost £22,031 on its investment. However, for *Black Joy* (1977) – Antony Simmons's comedy-drama about the experiences of a Guyanese immigrant in London – the NFFC advanced only £15,000 but this represented 50 per cent of the budget. The distributor's receipts were modest (£87,576) but the NFFC's share (£43,788) represented a profit of 191 per cent.

The NFFC's resumption of loans not channelled through the consortium also signalled a shift back towards the policy of supporting new talent as it had in the 1960s, rather than concentrating on purely commercial projects. Its report for 1977 emphasised the cultural rather than commercial value of the films it had sponsored:

> *The Duellists*, which marked Ridley Scott's first venture as the director of a first-feature film, was selected as one of the official British entries at the Cannes International Film Festival in May 1977 where it won the Special Jury Award; *Black Joy*, directed by Anthony Simmons, achieved the distinction of being the other official British entry at Cannes; *Jabberwocky*, which marked Terry Gilliam's first venture as the director of a first-feature film, was selected as the official British entry at the Berlin International Film Festival in June 1977; and *The Disappearance*, directed by Stuart Cooper, the first film to be part-financed by the Corporation and its sister organisation the Canadian Film Development Corporation, was selected as the official Canadian entry at the San Sebastian International Film Festival in September 1977.[51]

It was a similar tale in 1978 when the NFFC approved three loans through the consortium (*The Thief of Bagdad*, *The Riddle of the Sands*, *Black Jack*) and two less commercial projects from its own resources (*The Sailor's Return*, *The Shout*) for which it put up 50 per cent of the budget. Its report pointed out that *The Sailor's Return* (1978) 'was awarded a main prize at the Karlovy Vary International Film Festival' and that *The Shout* (1978) won the Special Jury Prize at Cannes and 'has received unusually wide critical acclaim'.[52] The NFFC received £52,109 in respect of *The Shout* and £23,076 for *The Sailor's Return*: its total investment in the two films had been £620,000. No films were recommended to the consortium in 1979 or 1980: the last film in which the consortium invested was *Memoirs of a Survivor* in 1981.[53]

The National Film Finance Consortium never became the major player in the field of film finance that had been envisaged in the early 1970s. Its resources were insufficient to support more than a handful of films and its investment strategy was conservative in the extreme. Its two most successful choices were *Stardust* and *Bugsy Malone*, and even the latter of those seems to have been a happy accident rather than an outcome of shrewd commercial judgement. The spiralling inflation of the later 1970s meant that the consortium fund was wholly inadequate for the industry's needs. As the decade drew to an end, the idea that the NFFC might return to profitability seemed as remote a hope as it had ever been.

Notes

1. Quoted in 'Freedom for the Flicks', *Kinematograph Weekly*, 19 December 1970, p. 4.
2. *National Film Finance Corporation: Annual Report and Summary of Accounts for the year ended 31 March 1970*, Cmnd. 4402 (May 1970), p. 3 (7).

3. *Parliamentary Debates: House of Commons*, 5th Series, vol. 795, 2 February 1970, cols 84–8.
4. Ibid. col. 94.
5. *NFFC Annual Report 1970*, p. 6 (20).
6. TNA T 224/2035: F. Morris Dyson (Films Branch): Note of a meeting held on 20 May 1970.
7. *Parliamentary Debates: House of Commons*, 5th Series, vol. 805, 4 November 1970, col. 1211.
8. TNA T 224/2203: H. Bailey to Leo Pliatzky, 4 February 1971.
9. Ibid.: C. W. Kelly to Norton, 27 January 1971.
10. Ibid.: Addendum by C. J. Carey, 4 May 1971 (emphasis in original).
11. Ibid.: J. B. Unwin to Leo Pliatzky, 29 April 1971.
12. 'Financial support for film-makers', *The Times*, 5 August 1971, p. 13.
13. 'Finance for film-making', *The Times*, 30 July 1971, p. 15.
14. TNA T 224/2203: Nicholas Ridley to Patrick Jenkin, 28 April 1971.
15. Ibid.: W. J. E. Norton to Carey, 4 May 1971.
16. Ibid.
17. Ibid.: Handwritten note by 'L. P.' (Leo Pliatzky – emphasis in original).
18. *National Film Finance Corporation: Annual Report and Summary of Accounts for the year ended 31 March 1971*, Cmnd. 4761 (August 1971), p. 2 (11).
19. TNA T 224/2203: C. J. Carey to Pliatzky, 23 February 1971.
20. Ibid.: Pliatzky to Bailey, 16 March 1971.
21. Ibid.: Robert Clark to Nicholas Ridley, 18 January 1971.
22. 'NFFC scheme to boost film financing', *Kinematograph Weekly*, 23 January 1971, p. 3.
23. TNA CAB 130/574: Cabinet paper 91 (72): 'The Future of the National Film Finance Corporation', 24 March 1972.
24. *NFFC Annual Report 1971*, p. 4 (19).
25. 'Enchantment on Llaregyb Hill', *Kinematograph Weekly*, 6 March 1971, p. 12.
26. TNA FV 81/191: National Film Trustee Company Ltd: *Under Milk Wood*: Allocation of revenues as per distributor's statements to 30 December 1978.
27. 'Star money', *The Economist*, 11 September 1971, p. 66.
28. 'No love lost behind the scenes', *The Financial Times*, 27 January 1971, p. 15.
29. TNA T 224/2203: Nicholas Ridley to Patrick Jenkin, 28 April 1971.
30. Ibid.: Norton to Pliatzky, 29 April 1971.
31. Ibid.: Jenkin to Ridley, 6 May 1971.
32. TNA CAB 130/574: 'The Future of the National Film Finance Corporation', 24 March 1972.
33. '£1 Million – And No More', *Today's Cinema*, 13 May 1972, p. 1.
34. *National Film Finance Corporation: Annual Report and Statement of Accounts for the year ended 31 March 1972*, Cmnd. 5080 (August 1972), p. 1 (1).
35. *National Film Finance Corporation: Annual Report and Statement of Accounts for the year ended 31 March 1973*, Cmnd. 5422 (August 1973), p. 5 (2).
36. Ibid. p. 5 (3).
37. TNA FV: 81/191: National Film Trustee Company: *Ooh . . . You Are Awful*: Allocation of revenues per distributor's statement, December 1978.
38. 'The strings on film aid', *The Guardian*, 21 October 1976, p. 9.
39. TNA FV 81/191: National Film Trustee Company: *The Final Programme* Trust.

40. *National Film Finance Corporation: Annual Report and Statement of Accounts for the year ended 31 March 1974*, Cmnd. 5725 (September 1974), p. 2 (4).
41. *National Film Finance Corporation: Annual Report and Statement of Accounts for the year ended 31 March 1975*, Cmnd. 6235 (September 1975), p. 1 (1).
42. *National Film Finance Corporation: Annual Report and Statement of Accounts for the year ended 31 March 1978*, Cmnd. 7370 (September 1978), p. 7 (13).
43. Ibid. p. 7 (12).
44. *NFFC Annual Report 1975*, p. 1 (1).
45. TNA FV 81/191: National Film Trustee Company Limited: Allocation of revenue statements relating to films administered under Trust Deeds.
46. *NFFC Annual Report 1975*, p. 6 (12).
47. TNA PREM 16/51: Neil Hirst to Robin Butler, 31 July 1974.
48. Ibid.: Peter Denison to Nick Stuart, 22 August 1974.
49. *National Film Finance Corporation: Annual Report and Statement of Accounts for the year ended 31 March 1976,* Cmnd. 6633 (September 1976), p. 2 (13).
50. TNA FV 81/103: John Terry to Mary Lackey, 12 April 1976.
51. *National Film Finance Corporation: Annual Report and Statement of Accounts for the year ended 31 March 1977*, Cmnd. 7041 (December 1977), p. 7 (17). NFFC Annual Report 1978, p. 6 (10).
52. *NFFC Annual Report 1978,* p. 6 (10).
53. *National Film Finance Corporation: Annual Report and Statement of Accounts for the year ended 31 March 1981*, HC 466 1981-82 (July 1982), p. 8 (22).

CHAPTER 18

The Prime Minister's Working Party and its Aftermath

> A cynic said recently that there was nothing wrong with the British film industry that a miracle couldn't cure. The Prime Minister has worked a miracle, if only just in time. (John Terry)[1]

On the face of it the election of a Labour government in 1974 augured well for the British film industry (Labour had formed a minority government in March 1974: they won a small majority following another general election in October). Returning Prime Minister Harold Wilson had been the 'father' of the National Film Finance Corporation and was sympathetic to the problems of the film industry. Early in his second administration, Wilson decided 'that it may be time to take a new look at the financing of the film industry'.[2] However, Wilson's narrow parliamentary majority and the worsening economic outlook – brought about by a combination of severe inflationary pressure and increasing unemployment – limited his room for manoeuvre. There is also evidence that his government was not united behind him: the official records reveal a state of what almost amounted to undeclared warfare between Downing Street and the Treasury when it came to the provision of further support for film production. Wilson's skill as a political manager would be tested to its utmost as he attempted to use his influence to help the ailing production industry. On 26 November 1974 Prime Minister's Questions included a planted question from Gwyneth Dunwoody 'whether he is satisfied with interdepartmental co-ordination in the provision of finance for film-making for cinema and television': this was clearly meant as a warning shot across the Treasury's bows that Wilson intended to do something about the film industry.[3]

For perhaps the first time in its history the British film industry felt that it had the Prime Minister's ear. In May 1975 Wilson hosted a working dinner at 10 Downing Street: among those present were Sir Richard Attenborough ('A likeable and helpful character, very successful personally and without any particular axe to grind'), Stanley Baker ('Believed to be known personally to the Prime Minister'), John Brabourne ('Very active and a diplomatic asset'), Nat Cohen ('Very influential in the film industry'), Michael Deeley, Bernard Delfont, Carl Foreman, Harry Saltzman, Michael Relph and Sir John Woolf, with representatives of the NFFC (chairman Robert Clark and managing director John Terry) and the unions (Alan Sapper of the Federation of Film Unions and Peter Plowicz of British Equity).[4] Several of the producers at the dinner submitted memoranda outlining their proposals for actions the government could take to assist the film industry.

The discussion was evidently wide-ranging: Brabourne and Woolf advocated the provision of pre-production finance to assist producers in developing projects; Saltzman suggested setting up a private bank on the Italian model; Cohen argued for the production of films for the international market. Terry argued that 'the industry needed a continuous source of finance' and urged that as a first step the remaining funds available to the NFFC under the Films Act of 1970 should be released immediately. Attenborough suggested that the NFFC should focus on 'fostering talent among new writers and producers' and that a separate film bank should be established 'which should take a commercial view about backing productions for the international market'. A suggestion from Michael Deeley of EMI to combine the functions of the NFFC, the British Film Fund Agency and the British Film Institute Production Board into a new national film body would gain traction in the discussions that followed.[5] Wilson himself suggested 'that the picture of the industry which had been presented was of a high-powered car which lacked the petrol to make it go'.[6]

The outcome of the Downing Street dinner was the setting up of what was originally intended as 'a small working party of six or seven people': a minute by Wilson's Private Secretary Lady Falkender records 'that the Prime Minister would want Mr Stanley Baker and Mr Deeley to be members'.[7] Deeley had suggested that Lady Falkender should chair the Working Party, as 'her presence as chairman would give the film industry much more confidence of your personal involvement in the planning of its future'.[8] The Department of Trade suggested Sir Richard Powell (a former senior civil servant and now a partner in Hill Samuel) as chairman, as he had 'long experience of the organisational and financial relations between industry and Government . . . He is also known to be sympathetic to the world of arts.'[9] In the event, the Working Party would be chaired by John Terry and its membership expanded to nearly twice the original number: Wilson personally nominated Attenborough, Brabourne, Deeley, Delfont, Foreman, Hugh Orr (President of the Association of Independent Cinemas), Sapper, Woolf and Sir John Ryder (chairman of the National Enterprise Board). Michael Relph, President of the Film Production Association of Great Britain, who had been at the dinner, protested at not being included in the Working Party.[10] In fact, none of the trade associations were represented: this might have been a legacy of Wilson's experience of dealing with them in the late 1940s. The Working Party had wide-ranging terms of reference: it was to consider the scale of film production in the light of markets at home and abroad, the associated financial needs and resources of the industry, and the relationship between the film and television industries. Evidence that Wilson wanted the Working Party to produce concrete proposals rather than simply being another talking shop can be seen in the directive to consider 'the organisational implications of their conclusions, including the relationships of the industry with its sources of finance, and the relations between industry and Government'.[11] In other words, Wilson seems to have expected the Working Party to put forward recommendations for an entire new policy for film finance rather than cosmetic or piecemeal changes to the existing set-up.

The Working Party received submissions from various interested parties including the main trade associations and trades unions as well as the British Film Institute and the Writers' Guild of Great Britain. The Guild's President, Carl Foreman, wrote personally to Wilson hoping 'that with the [European Economic Community] Referendum behind us, it will now be possible to implement the simple legislation necessary for the immediate help the industry needs so desperately'.[12] The NFFC proposed 'a new and substantial film financing fund' including a government contribution which 'should ideally be large enough to enable major international production to be financed from UK sources, if necessary in partnership with US and/or European distributors'.[13] The Cinematograph Films Council recommended that a proportion of the Eady levy (it suggested up to £200,000) should be set aside to support script development and pre-production. And Michael Deeley revived a proposal previously made in the summer of 1974 that allocation of Eady money should be changed so that rather than being distributed in arrears as a percentage of box-office receipts, it should be provided up front as a grant equivalent to 25 per cent of below-the-line production costs, with the British Film Fund Agency recouping after investors and producers. Deeley suggested that this would be 'an immediate and practical way of stimulating local production, and in some ways combines the merits of the French Aide system and the British Eady system'.[14]

The Working Party reported in January 1976: its recommendations were far-reaching and in some respects quite radical. The main proposals were that a new interest-free equity fund of £5 million should be created for investment in film production, with the option to draw upon additional funds in subsequent years; that this fund should be provided in part by a levy on the excess profits of the ITV companies; that one-fifth of Eady levy receipts up to a maximum of £1 million a year should also be allocated to the NFFC; and that a new British Film Authority (BFA) should be set up in order to combine the roles of the NFFC, the British Film Fund and the Cinematograph Films Council. Other recommendations included putting aside £200,000 of Eady money to create a fund for pre-production and script development, increasing the grant to the Children's Film Foundation, encouraging independent television companies to invest in film production by allowing them to discount such investment from the levy they paid on advertising receipts, the establishment of a loan fund for independent exhibitors to make improvements to their cinemas, mandating a three-year minimum period before the television broadcast of films, and the statutory deposit of prints of all British films with the National Film Archive. The report attempted to head off objections to such a substantial investment of public money by arguing that short-term investment would secure longer-term benefits: 'We fully acknowledge that this is an exceptionally difficult time to seek financial support from the public purse, but we believe that for the reasons we have given British film production would bring to the national economy and to the community at large a variety of rewards which would far exceed the financial support now required.'[15]

The report provided a detailed context for its proposals. It estimated that production investment of £40 million a year (the total amount invested in 1975 amounted to £25 million) 'could support a small but significant nucleus of higher-cost features of international appeal, as well as a steady output of lower-cost films, many of which might also be successful on the world market'.[16] It argued that support for film production was essentially a form of equity investment rather than a loan and that the new British Film Authority should operate on those principles: the uncertainty of the industry was such that state finance was necessary because '[the] private sector cannot be expected to carry the weight of the new financial resources required in current economic conditions and having regard to the traditionally speculative nature of the business in the short-term'.[17] It highlighted the greater levels of state support for the film industry offered by other European Economic Community members. Some parts of the report harked back to the debates in the 1920s and 1930s in their rhetoric of protecting the British film industry from American imperialism:

> Britain, though it owes much to the enterprise and example of the US film industry, has for too long been an economic and cultural colony of Hollywood. In economic terms, many of the greatest successes of British film talent have assisted the US economy far more than they have the British. In cultural terms, the continuing dominance of the British film industry by Hollywood had militated against the development of a characteristically British cinema. The school of realism which characterised our great war-time films and the school of comedy developed by Ealing stand out as recognisable British traditions. Many important and successful British films have been made since those days (e.g. *Room at the Top*, *Saturday Night and Sunday Morning*, *Lawrence of Arabia*, *If . . .*, *Oliver!*, *Murder on the Orient Express*), but these have been exceptions to the general trend rather than landmarks in a developing British tradition.[18]

It is ironic that three of the six films the report named as representing a distinctively British national cinema had been financed by American money, given that its argument was that Hollywood's influence had militated against such a cinema.

The trade's response to the Terry Report, as it was soon known, was positive. Michael Relph, evidently no longer smarting over his exclusion from the Working Party, felt that the significance of the proposals 'lies not in the fact that they will succeed in financing a lot of small budget British films, but that they will give an investment in big international films to British interests and give them the necessary muscle to initiate production from Britain and not merely to be a service industry for subjects that are initiated abroad'.[19] Other commentators, however, were less enthusiastic. In particular, members of the Cinematograph Films Council – which the Terry Report recommended should be merged with the proposed British Film Authority – were sceptical about its proposals. David Goodliffe, the deputy economic editor of *The Economist*, felt that the suggestion of an authority to co-ordinate all aspects of film policy was ill-considered: 'The working party hoped that an animal with lots of spots could turn out to be a leopard. It seems more likely to be a spotty camel.'[20] Vincent Porter – also a member of the Cinematograph Films Council – felt that the report had 'failed to give any careful analysis to the long-term future' of the industry. He also felt that its recommendations for reforming state provision of film finance fell between two stools:

> Sometimes there is an assumption that all that is necessary is more capital to make the industry commercially viable and that this could be solved by a Government *loan* to the film industry . . . On other occasions, the assumption is that what the industry needs is *aid*. If this is the case, then it will be necessary to assess the cultural and social value of the aid. Unfortunately, the proposals outlined in the Terry Report do not help to clarify this crucial ambiguity – indeed they make it worse. The Report rejects the concept of a loan – arguing that the new capital fund it proposes should not be saddled with interest payments. It proposes instead government *investment* in the industry. Government revenues would come from profits, not from interest.[21]

Porter made the point, not acknowledged in the report, that government investment would need to be offered on commercial terms that were 'no less favourable' than the terms offered by private sector investors: this would in effect put it in competition with the private sector rather than being a specialist investor supporting the sort of projects that private investors deemed uncommercial. However, one of the founding principles of the NFFC had been that its role was to supplement private finance rather than be in direct competition with it.

One of the proposals of the Terry Report was quickly adopted. In 1976 the NFFC reported that it was to make provision for a fund of £200,000 per year 'for script preparation and other proper pre-production purposes'.[22] This initiative – which had been supported by John Brabourne and Sir John Woolf during the Working Party's deliberations – would enable producers to commission scripts and prepare budgets in order to be able to offer pre-packaged films to distributors and financiers: the retreat of the major corporations from active film production meant that development costs more often had to be borne from producers' overheads. The National Film Development Fund was overseen by an advisory committee whose members were drawn from the film industry and appointed by the Secretary of State: the fund could loan up to £12,500 per project, to be repaid from the profits if the film went ahead. After two years the fund had received 289 applications and had approved loans for 71 projects totalling £509,900. 'The Fund has stimulated a great deal of activity and the Corporation welcomes its continuation,' the NFFC reported in 1978. However, it also sounded a cautionary note in so far as it 'foresees dangers and frustrations arising if there is a regular and continuing output of good screenplays at a time when the sources of finance for the production of British films continue to be scarce and spasmodic and when the creation of a strong public fund, to give hope to individual film-makers and confidence to private-sector investors, is still apparently uncertain or remote.'[23]

The NFFC was right to be cautious about the prospects of the new equity investment fund proposed by the Terry Report. Harold Wilson had got what he wanted: a wide-ranging and comprehensive set of proposals to inject new life into the British film industry. He was personally enthusiastic about the plan: 'To me, the significant fact is that for the first time since I have had anything to do with the Industry, i.e. over nearly 30 years, the various sections of the film trade have reached a level of agreement, far more, for example, than has ever been reached at any meeting of the statutory Cinematograph Films Council which has been in existence since pre-war days.'[24] However, the Prime Minister's enthusiasm was not shared by either the Treasury or the Department of Trade. The Treasury felt that the report 'provides only the sketchiest analysis of the industry's problems, not helped by the fact that it contains hardly any statistics': it even tried to block publication of the report 'because it is bound to stir up pressure for the Government to do something substantial for the film industry'. Instead it felt that 'it ought to be considered by officials in the first instance . . . In this way we are more likely to succeed in staving off the Report's wilder proposals than if it is taken immediately by Ministers.'[25] This was clearly an attempt to kick the report into the long grass. A Department of Trade group set up to consider the report produced a set of watered-down proposals which included placing a ceiling of £5 million on new loans to the NFFC which should be on 'more onerous' terms. Peter Shore, the Secretary of State for Trade, told Wilson outright: 'There is no prospect, I am afraid, of finding the funds out of my Department's resources. Much as the proposed investment would be welcomed, there are no programmes which [we] could realistically prune to produce the necessary surplus.'[26]

There was clearly a move afoot in Whitehall to block the implementation of the Terry Report. Wilson, however, was having none of it. He rejected the Department of Trade's response to the report and wrote a long self-justifying memorandum to Shore:

> I have to confess that I have seen this document before, three times in fact. The first was in the 1940s when an almost identical document proved that the National Film Finance Corporation project could not possibly work. In fact it saved the film industry for a period of nearly 30 years at very little cost to the taxpayer – far less than had been estimated. Moreover, that was at a time when it appeared that £3 million (out of a total of £5 million) would have to go to save the independent producers under Korda and would almost certainly go down the drain to meet past losses.
>
> The second time I saw the document was when similar arguments were adduced to prove that the NRDC [National Research and Development Corporation] would not work. Apart from having 833 income-earning inventions, some of them of world importance, including Hovercraft, the world's first digital computer, and the 'wonder-drug' cephalosporin (which has grossed at least $20 million from the United States in royalties to Britain), and netting total licence income from all sources of £39 million, the warnings were, for the rest, well conceived.
>
> The third time I saw this was when it was proved conclusively that the Open University would not work and that a vast proportion of those who enrolled would drop out within months. It is now earning foreign exchange, and British drop-outs have been lower than in any public or private official scheme in the free world.

> Senator Hubert Humphrey has told me that by the end of this decade every State in the Union will have their own scheme, many of them taking our material.
>
> I have referred to these analogies because there is always the thought that devoted and dedicated work might come up with the wrong conclusion – for there can be no doubt that this document is a steer against adoption of the Working Party proposals. Because also, more modestly, I have occasionally been proved right.[27]

Wilson even suggested that the ingrained hostility to supporting the film industry, when the state provided generous subsidy for more high-brow cultural activities via the Arts Council – he calculated current subsidy for the film industry at 0.4 pence per head compared to 33 pence per head for theatre and £4.29 per head for opera – reflected a form of class prejudice: 'It seems to be based on the unspoken thought that it is vastly preferable to provide massive amounts of public money for Covent Garden etc, which in fact are enjoyed to a considerable extent – though not exclusively of course – by richer members of the community.'[28]

By this time it was evident that a serious rift had emerged between Downing Street and the Treasury. Wilson urged moving ahead with the establishment of the British Film Authority, 'otherwise, as I have said, we shall lose, perhaps for a year or more to come, all the momentum that has been established and accepted by a most representative Committee of senior Ministers'.[29] Wilson took the initiative by setting up a Ministerial Group on the Film Industry which met for the first (and last) time in March 1976: it agreed to make available to the NFFC immediately the remaining £2.3 million still available under the Films Act of 1970 and approved in principle further direct assistance of £5 million up to 1980.[30] It would be one of Wilson's last acts as Prime Minister. He had already announced his intention to leave office in April 1976. The Treasury accepted the additional funding for the NFFC reluctantly but understood that on political grounds it would be difficult to block. An internal memorandum of March 1976 makes this very point: 'From the Treasury's point of view it is unfortunate that Cabinet discussion will take place in the coming week, given the present Prime Minister's personal engagement with the subject: a full-blooded presentation of the case against assistance might be thought unreasonable and even opportunistic.'[31] Treasury ministers and civil servants instead decided to play a longer game: to wait for Wilson's departure before making any further attempt to block the implementation of the Terry Report. Evidence of the undisguised contempt in which the outgoing Prime Minister was held can be found in one Treasury memorandum of July 1976: 'In trying to limit expenditure on this lame duck industry (we have Sir H. Wilson, in his "Final Days", to thank for a new tranche of £5m which has recently been approved), the Treasury have had a strong ally in the Department of Trade, who as sponsor for the industry take about as sceptical a view of its claims on public funds as we do.'[32]

Following Wilson's resignation the NFFC – and the film industry as a whole – lost their most influential advocate. Wilson's successor James Callaghan did not share Wilson's personal interest in the film industry. As a sop to his predecessor, Callaghan appointed Wilson to chair an Interim Action Committee on the Film

Industry to consider how best to implement the Terry Report. However, it was soon clear that this was to be more of an inaction committee. Much time was spent in agreeing its membership and terms of reference: Sir John Woolf and Michael Deeley both declined to serve (Deeley later changed his mind) and there was controversy over the role of Lady Falkender due to her inclusion in the outgoing Prime Minister's Honours List.[33] The Department of Trade argued that 'it would be a good idea to introduce a distinctive younger element' and suggested David Puttnam (aged 35), Richard Craven (30) or Beryl Vertue (40) as well as the inclusion of a film critic (Nigel Andrews or Jonathan Miller were suggested) in order 'to have someone concerned with the audience's point of view or with a concern for the artistic element'.[34] Wilson, for his part, felt that the people recommended by the Department of Trade were 'inadequate for the task' and accused the department of adopting blocking tactics: 'I am aware that there is in the Department a strong resistance movement to the implementation of the Working Party's Report: this is widely known and was evidenced by the official comments on the Working Party report made in January and February, *before* the Government's acceptance of the Report, and, no less, by the first proposed terms of reference.'[35] Edmund Dell, the new Secretary of State for Trade, told Wilson bluntly that his objections 'are frankly nonsense' and stuck to his guns over the membership of the committee: 'I am not prepared to have a Committee over-weighted with industry people in the way you suggest. The Committee has to command the confidence not merely of the industry but of the public, not to mention mine as Secretary of State.'[36] The final membership of the committee was a compromise between Wilson's and the department's nominees that reflected a mixture of established industry figures and relative newcomers: David Berriman, John Brabourne, Sir Max Brown, Edmund Chilton, Michael Deeley, Sir Bernard Delfont, Lady Falkender, David Gordon, Allan Grant, Lord Lloyd of Hampstead QC, Anthony Mallinson, Alasdair Milne, David Puttnam, Alan Sapper, Professor Geoffrey Sims, Sir John Terry, Brian Tesler and Alexander Walker. Its diverse composition was an advantage in terms of hearing different points of view but a disadvantage when it came to speedy progress or unanimous recommendations.

The Interim Action Committee finally reported in January 1978: this was a full two years after the Terry Report, during which time the problems affecting the film industry had if anything become only more acute. Its first report focused on the establishment of the British Film Authority. It covered the constitution of the BFA, recommending that it should include a balance of civil servants and members of the film community appointed by and responsible to a minister; that there should be no fewer than seven and no more than nine members, of whom at least two should have experience of working in the film industry and one who 'should have particular concern for the interests of the consumer'; and that it should have recourse to an advisory committee drawn from all sectors of the industry which the BFA itself would appoint. It also covered the role and operation of the BFA, which would become 'the principal advisory body to the Government on all matters relating to film'.[37] It would be responsible for the supervision and allocation of new financial resources for film production recommended by the Terry Report and for recommending any changes to the size of the film fund. It was authorised to provide incentives for producers and exhibitors of short films and for 'films of outstanding artistic merit' as well as to approve loans for the improvement and modernisation of cinemas. It would also become the official agency for the reporting and publication of statistical information relating to the film industry. To this end it would assume the responsibilities currently invested in the Cinematograph Films Council, NFFC and British Film Fund Agency, which would all be dissolved. However, the one very notable absence from the report was any rationale for why the BFA was needed beyond an assertion 'that the fragmentation of Government responsibilities in relation to film had contributed to the present weakness of the British film industry'.[38]

The report met with a cool response to say the least: one Treasury official dismissed it as 'a flimsy and ill-argued document'.[39] The Department of Trade was equally unimpressed. Indeed, it seems that the idea was kept alive merely to appease the former Prime Minister:

> DOT officials recognise the weakness of the case for supporting the film industry and simply wish that the whole subject would go away. DOT Ministers take much the same view but feel boxed in. On the one hand they accept (or anyway Mr Dell did) that there is no case for any of the Terry/Wilson proposals; but, on the other, they are continually harassed by Sir H. Wilson and feel themselves committed to the 1976 statements to (at least) the establishment of a BFA . . . We do not know what attitude Mr Smith [John Smith, the new Secretary of State for Trade] will be taking to the whole nasty mess.[40]

The departmental papers give the impression of ministers and officials looking for reasons to block the report rather than any serious discussion of its proposals. One of the arguments marshalled against it was 'that the EEC has become noticeably tougher on film aids since the publication of the Terry Report . . . I do not think we can assume that any proposal to set up a BFA – certainly if associated with new financial aids to the industry as is recommended – will have an easy ride in Brussels.'[41]

However, Wilson was not easily deterred. He lobbied Callaghan for legislation to be included in the parliamentary session for 1978–9.[42] The Privy Council Office felt 'that it would be unrealistic to expect it to reach Royal Assent next session' – it was already known in government circles that Callaghan intended to hold a general election the following spring – and 'there are still a number of difficult policy points outstanding and the Bill itself could be very substantial'.[43] The Interim Action Committee made a second report in December 1978: this was rather more wide-ranging than the first report and focused on the provision of finance. It concluded:

> The major problem for the British film industry is that so few films, especially those of character and originality, see the light of projection. Thus the means of support for the film industry should be adapted to help bring about a significant

improvement in the situation of feature film production in this country. Hence the need for a properly financed and flexible film-financing division of a British Film Authority. This should not be a specifically cultural institution: the barriers between the minority film and the mass market are being broken down, as the cinema audience itself is becoming more selective. Several years ago it would have been inconceivable that a film like *Annie Hall* would be a commercial hit. But the BFA must be a body concerned with the quality of production and not just the quantity.[44]

Its specific recommendations included modifying the operation of the Eady levy so that only half would be returned to producers, with the other half to be allocated to the BFA to be used at its discretion on production and (to a lesser extent) on cinemas. It envisaged allowing the BFA as much discretion as possible in how it spent its funds: for example, it might offer funding either as investments against a share of the gross receipts or as interest-bearing loans. Or it might advance credit to a film-maker to be cashed in for their next film or give some money as prizes. 'In other words,' the report suggested, 'the BFA could be eclectic and pick and choose from the variety of schemes now in use in Britain and in other countries.'[45]

The second report also addressed the question of tax relief – the subject of a growing campaign in the trade during the later 1970s – which had been outside its original terms of reference. Income tax had become so punitive under the Labour government – up to 90 per cent for the highest earners – that many high-earning British actors and film-makers had left the United Kingdom and were living abroad as tax exiles: a list prepared for the Department of Trade in 1976 included film-makers Ken Annakin, John Boorman, Joseph Losey, Nicolas Roeg, John Schlesinger and Peter Yates, and actors Richard Burton, Marty Feldman, Christopher Lee, Roger Moore, David Niven and Michael York.[46] The Interim Action Committee argued that 'financial penalties of the present system of United Kingdom tax – both in terms of high marginal rates and of the period for which they can work in the United Kingdom without attracting these rates – are such that those whose presence is so vital go abroad and often cannot be persuaded to work in the UK even on an individual film'.[47] It recommended that the period for which individuals should be able to work in the United Kingdom without paying personal income tax should be extended from 90 to 120 days. It also recommended provision for tax relief on losses incurred on film production in order to encourage more inward investment and suggested that 'the cash flow of film production companies and partnerships would be assisted if revenue expenditure becomes fully deductible as incurred instead of the present revenue practice whereby this expenditure is deductible over a period commencing after UK film exhibition begins'.[48]

The Interim Action Committee's second report was no more enthusiastically received than the first. The Chief Secretary to the Treasury effectively scotched it:

> We have made no provision in our existing public expenditure plans for expenditure on films of anything like that amount. I doubt myself whether there would be a case for doing so; since the work done in 1976 – the last time we looked at these

questions – suggested that there was no economic, industrial or employment case for increasing our support for the film industry. In any event, until we have decided what if any additional sums to devote to the film industry, we are in no position to publish White Papers or raise the expectations of the film lobby.[49]

The government made some concession to making a statement in principle about reviewing the funding of the film industry. But the issue was about to be overtaken by the tide of events: the Terry Report and the establishment of the British Film Authority were finally laid to rest when Labour lost the general election of May 1979. Wilson's Interim Action Committee continued to sit – and made three further reports – until 1985.

Overall, the 1970s was a decade of uncertainty and instability regarding official policy towards the film industry. Successive governments adopted very different policies, but in the end neither succeeded in providing the stimulus the industry needed. On the one hand the Conservative government had wanted to end state subsidy and transfer the NFFC to the private sector: however, its economic pragmatism proved ineffective when the corporation was unable to raise sufficient funds from private investors to make it a viable concern. On the other hand the Labour government remained committed to the principle of subsidy and had even been willing to increase the level of state investment: but its major initiatives, the Prime Ministerial Working Group and the Terry Report, failed to materialise into anything concrete. It is impossible to say whether the NFFC would have been any more successful during these years had there been a more stable policy. It had backed significantly fewer films in the 1970s than in either of the previous two decades – of course this was to some extent a consequence of the contraction of the British production sector – and had operated at a loss throughout the decade. In fact, the corporation had not made an annual operating profit since 1964. At the end of the 1970s its position seemed more parlous than ever: it made a loss of £1,191,066 in 1979 and its annual report remarked glumly that 'if the Corporation adheres to the old solutions it will surely fail, for it is those old ways and practices that have led the industry to the position which it is now in'.[50]

Notes

1. '"Miracle Man Harold" – Terry', *Screen International*, 3 April 1976, p. 1.
2. TNA PREM 16/51: Robin Butler to John Wakeling, 16 July 1974.
3. *Parliamentary Debates: House of Commons*, 5th Series, vol. 882, 26 November 1974, col. 115.
4. TNA PREM 16/355: 'Guest list for PM's dinner on 13 May 1975', unsigned but probably annotated by Wilson's Private Secretary Baroness Falkender.
5. Ibid.: Michael Deeley to Baroness Falkender, 1 May 1975.
6. Ibid.: Note of a discussion at a working dinner at 10 Downing Street on Tuesday 13 May for representatives of the film industry.
7. Ibid.: Baroness Falkender to A. C. Hutton, 14 May 1975.
8. Ibid.: Michael Deeley to Harold Wilson, 20 June 1975.

9. Ibid.: A. Taylor to Robin Butler, 23 May 1975.
10. Ibid.: Michael Relph to Wilson, 7 August 1975.
11. Ibid.: 'Working Party – Terms of Reference', n.d.
12. Ibid.: Carl Foreman to Harold Wilson, 9 June 1975.
13. TNA T 369/142: Submission by the Board of Directors of the National Film Finance Corporation to the Working Party on the Film Industry, October 1975.
14. TNA PREM 16/51: Michael Deeley to Baroness Falkender, 30 July 1974.
15. *Future of the British Film Industry: Report of the Prime Minister's Working Party*, Cmnd. 6372 (January 1976), p. 12.
16. Ibid. p. 10.
17. Ibid. p. 12.
18. Ibid. pp. 4–5.
19. 'Relph speaks out on the Terry Report', *Screen International*, 14 February 1976, p. 1.
20. 'In the Picture', *Sight & Sound*, 45: 2 (Spring 1976), p. 82.
21. Vincent Porter, 'British Film Culture and the European Economic Community', *Sight & Sound*, 47: 3 (Summer 1978), pp. 136–7.
22. *National Film Finance Corporation: Annual Report and Statement of Accounts for the year ended 31 March 1976*, Cmnd. 6633 (September 1976), p. 4 (16).
23. *National Film Finance Corporation: Annual Report and Statement of Accounts for the year ended 31 March 1978*, Cmnd. 7370 (November 1978), p. 10 (26).
24. TNA T 369/142: Prime Minister's Personal Minute to Secretary of State for Trade, 6 January 1976.
25. Ibid.: T. P. Lamkaster to Norton, 5 January 1976.
26. TNA FV 81/92: Handwritten note by Peter Shore attached to a minute to the Prime Minister, n.d.
27. TNA T 369/142: Harold Wilson to Peter Shore, 23 February 1976.
28. Wilson based his calculation for the film industry on a subsidy of £5 million against 119 million admissions: this was the level of admissions for the late 1940s rather than the mid-1970s. He alleged a subsidy of £3,289,000 for theatre (10 million admissions) and £4,292,000 for opera (1 million admissions).
29. TNA FV 81/92: Wilson to Shore, 8 March 1976.
30. TNA PREM 16/824: MISC 123 (76) 3, 18 March 1976.
31. TNA T 369/142: Lavelle to Personal Secretary to Chief Secretary to the Treasury, 19 March 1976.
32. TNA T 369/705: W.J.E. Norton to Phillips, 8 July 1976.
33. TNA PREM 16/1994: Ken Stowe to A. C. Hutton, 10 February 1977.
34. Ibid.: Edmund Dell to Harold Wilson, 22 October 1976.
35. Ibid.: Wilson to Dell, 27 October 1976.
36. Ibid.: Dell to Wilson, 4 November 1976.
37. *Proposals for the setting up of a British Film Authority: Report of the Interim Action Committee on the Film Industry*, Cmnd. 7071 (January 1978), p. 3 (10).
38. Ibid. p. 13 (Appendix A).
39. TNA T 366/681: M. A. Cowdy to D. J. L. Moore, 22 November 1978.
40. Ibid.
41. TNA PREM 16/1994: Edmund Dell to James Callaghan, 5 December 1977.
42. Ibid.: Wilson to Callaghan, 2 October 1978.
43. Ibid.: Charlotte Egerton to Philip Wood, 9 October 1978.

44. *The Financing of the British Film Industry: Second Report of the Interim Action Committee on the Film Industry*, Cmnd. 7597 (June 1979), p. 10 (50).
45. Ibid. p. 9 (45).
46. TNA FV 81/110: John Coote to M. Pulvermacher, 3 September 1976.
47. *The Financing of the British Film Industry*, p. 11 (52).
48. Ibid. p. 12 (57).
49. Ibid.: Joel Barnett to John Smith (Secretary of State for Trade), 11 April 1979.
50. *National Film Finance Corporation: Annual Report and Statement of Accounts for the year ended 31 March 1979*, HA 456 1978-79 (3 March 1980), p. 6 (9).

CHAPTER 19

Revising Eady

> Admissions have shown a steady decline almost without a hiccup for twenty years. The figures for 1978/79 are known to be the direct result of the successive [*sic*] *Star Wars, Saturday Night Fever, Close Encounters, Midnight Express, Grease, Moonraker* and *Superman*. There is no present reason for believing that the decline will not continue, albeit with occasional boosts from blockbusters. On the present formula it is therefore virtually inevitable that the levy will continue to decline in real terms and perhaps in £s. (Department of Trade)[1]

The late 1970s was an unusual period for the British film industry. On the one hand the decline in admissions was reversed (albeit temporarily) and box-office returns increased. Annual cinema admissions hit a low of 107 million in 1976 before rising to 108 million in 1977 and 127 million in 1978.[2] This upturn was attributed in large measure to the popularity of American blockbusters such as *Star Wars* (the top film at the British box office in 1978), *Close Encounters of the Third Kind*, *Grease* and *Saturday Night Fever*.[3] The total paid at the box office increased from £75 million in 1976 to £118 million in 1978: this was due partly to rising ticket prices as well as the upturn in admissions.[4] The capital invested in the British production sector was also increasing: again this was partly a consequence of inflation, but it also reflected the preponderance of bigger-budget films later in the decade. In 1976, for example, total production investment in Britain amounted to £58 million in 53 films: this was nearly twice the amount for the previous year and was attributed to a 'combination of galloping inflation and the huge budget of Joseph Levine's *A Bridge Too Far*'.[5] The most active producers in Britain in 1976 were EMI (five films), United Artists (four including the Bond picture *The Spy Who Loved Me*), ITC Films and Twentieth Century–Fox (with three each). Over the next three years the trend was upwards: £74 million in 1977 (58 films), £94 million in 1978 (58 films) and nearly £100 million in 1979 (61 films).[6] These figures included American films shot in Britain that did not qualify for British quota, such as *Star Wars*. Twentieth Century–Fox was the most active: it invested £18 million over three years in the production of *The Omen, Star Wars, Julia* and *Alien*.[7]

On the other hand the increasing box-office takings and investment disguised the fact that the British production sector had contracted to a size not seen since the mid-1940s. More money was being spent but fewer films were being made: the number of eligible British quota films was 42 in 1977, 51 in 1978 and 37 in 1979. It was in the late 1970s that British cinema finally gave up the ambition of being a mass-production industry: the bread-and-butter genre film produced for the home market – with the exception of the last television spin-offs such as *Porridge* (1979) and *Rising Damp* (1980) – was becoming a thing of the past. The uneconomic nature of film production was highlighted by the case of *Carry On Emmannuelle* (1978). The Rank Organisation had withdrawn its financing for the 'Carry On' series following the poor performance of *Carry On England* in 1975: Peter Rogers therefore turned to Hemdale Film Distributors and raised the budget from a commercial investment trust (Cleve Investments). By this time inflation had pushed the budget up to £349,302: *Carry On Emmannuelle* – a spoof of the French soft-core drama *Emmanuelle* that had been fifth at the British box office in 1975 – was the most expensive of the 'Carry On' films but it looks the cheapest of the lot.[8] Rogers accepted Hemdale's terms of 60 per cent of the distributor's receipts and a third of the producer's profits with characteristic good humour: 'The time has come, the walrus and John Daly said, and I and my co-what's-it have great pleasure in confirming the arrangement arrived at between us that you should receive 16⅔ of 100% of the film's blood being exactly one third of the producer's blood, bearing in mind that the writer's 5% comes first. Hoping that this satisfies your vampire instincts.'[9] On this occasion the vampire would be malnourished: *Carry On Emmannuelle* was a box-office flop and marked the end of the series that had begun with *Carry On Sergeant* in 1958.

The increasing production investment in the late 1970s was due to British studios hosting a number of major American films (for example, *Star Wars* was shot at Elstree in 1976). Unlike the runaway boom of the 1960s, however, such films were not made in Britain in order to benefit from the Eady levy. The Department of Trade calculated that inflation had decreased the value of the levy in real terms: 'It is hard to believe that a levy whose total value is a fraction of what it was 10 or 15 years ago is a decisive factor in having films made in the UK.'[10] The US trade paper *Variety* concurred: 'With the adverse effects of a strengthening pound, and with registration as a British film generally reckoned as lessening in value now that the UK market on which box office subsidy (Eady money) is based has shrunk to less than 5% of the world, most foreign producers agree that the financial incentive to come to Britain has been eroded.'[11] There were effectively now two film industries in Britain: a small domestic production sector and a larger service industry for international films. As the Interim Action Committee on the Film Industry observed in 1979: 'It has for many years been generally recognised that the film industry is both a service industry, providing the skills, amenities and facilities for film-making, and a generator of native production. As a service industry it is doing well. It is as an originator, promoter and producer of British films that it is failing.'[12]

From 1978 the British Film Fund Agency published details of the Eady payments for individual films. These reveal the wide difference in box-office returns between the most popular films and the rest. At this time the levy was paid at a rate of 38 per cent of the distributor's gross receipts: therefore it is possible to calculate the distributor's gross (from which distribution fees of 25 per cent and expenses had to be deducted before producers received their share) based on the

Eady payment. In 1977 *Screen International* indicated that 'a film has to be a considerable success in order to gross £300,000 in the UK market and very often first feature pictures gross considerably less than £100,000'.[13] The Eady data reveals that for 37 'high cost' films (defined under the legislation as those where the labour costs exceeded £50,000) released during the eighteen months to September 1979, nine grossed over the £300,000 deemed the benchmark of a 'considerable success' while 22 grossed less than £100,000.[14]

Film	Eady payment	Distributor's gross
Superman (Warner)	£1,025,727	£2,699,281
Moonraker (UA)	£828,680	£2,180,736
Watership Down (CIC)	£490,528	£1,290,863
Death on the Nile (EMI)	£246,875	£649,671
Midnight Express (Columbia)	£240,562	£633,057
The Wild Geese (Rank)	£188,352	£495,633
The 39 Steps (Rank)	£138,485	£364,434
The World is Full of Married Men (New Realm)	£129,353	£340,403
Porridge (ITC)	£119,224	£313,747
Force 10 From Navarone (Columbia)	£101,085	£266,013
Revenge of the Pink Panther (UA)	£84,410	£222,131
The Thief of Bagdad (Columbia)	£53,636	£141,147
The Spaceman and King Arthur (Disney)	£46,050	£121,184
The First Great Train Robbery (UA)	£40,879	£107,624
Alien (Rank)	£40,591	£106,818
Warlords of Atlantis (EMI)	£36,982	£97,321
The Legacy (Pethurst)	£29,103	£76,586
Sweeney 2 (EMI)	£24,729	£65,076
The Water Babies (Pethurst)	£23,287	£61,282
The Europeans (NFTC)	£21,050	£55,394
Tarka the Otter (Rank)	£20,673	£54,403
The Stud (Brent-Walker)	£20,216	£53,200
Quadrophenia (The Who Films)	£19,091	£50,239
The Lady Vanishes (Rank)	£18,666	£49,121
The Medusa Touch (ITC)	£18,174	£47,826
The Hound of the Baskervilles (Hemdale)	£14,975	£39,408
The Golden Lady (Target International)	£14,505	£38,171
Carry On Emmannuelle (Hemdale)	£9,783	£25,745
The Music Machine (Target International)	£8,986	£23,647
International Velvet (CIC)	£8,944	£23,537
Agatha (Brent-Walker)	£8,731	£22,976
The Big Sleep (ITC)	£6,266	£16,489
The Riddle of the Sands (Rank)	£5,867	£15,439
Stevie (Enterprise Pictures)	£2,746	£7,266
The Class of Miss MacMichael (Rank)	£1,941	£5,108

The Four Feathers (Trident-Barber)	£1,580	£4,158
Power Play (Rank)	£678	£1,784

It needs to be borne in mind that the receipts of the most successful films would be inflated by longer runs at more cinemas: hence the fact that the distributor's gross for the least successful film (*Power Play*) was only 0.7 per cent of that for the most successful (*Superman*) is not a like-for-like comparison. A better example to illustrate the gulf might be that two similar Rank-produced films such as *The 39 Steps* and *The Riddle of the Sands* which enjoyed a circuit release through Rank's cinemas grossed 17 per cent and 0.3 per cent of the amount taken by the most successful film exhibited on the Rank circuit (the Bond picture *Moonraker*).

The publication of Eady payments renewed the debate over the purpose and effectiveness of the levy. The most striking fact was that the top ten films accounted for 88 per cent of the levy payments for high-cost films: total Eady disbursements for the top ten amounted to £3,629,095 of the £4,119,999 paid out in that category. The top two films, *Superman* and *Moonraker*, took 45 per cent of the levy for high-cost films. These statistics highlight two issues. One is that more than ever the greatest benefit from the Eady levy was going to the films that needed it least: *Superman* and *Moonraker* were blockbuster releases that were not dependent upon Eady money (as welcome as it no doubt was) in order for their producers to see a profit. Or as the Department of Trade put it, 'the only films that can under the existing scheme get a worthwhile sum, in film makers' terms, are the only ones that don't need them'.[15] The other point is that most of the films at the top of the scale were essentially international productions that happened to be British-based: indeed, only two of the films in the top ten – *The 39 Steps* and *Porridge* – had been entirely British-financed. The Eady levy had been introduced to stimulate the British production sector but the benefits were now accruing mostly to US distributors. *The Economist* observed that 'Eady is meant to be an incentive to British film makers, and not as it is now, a boon to major distributors and American producers of "British" films . . . The British film industry is now largely a production centre for foreign-financed films.'[16]

The British nature of some films such as *Superman* and *Alien* might not have been readily apparent to anyone outside the industry. *Superman* (1978) was shot at Pinewood and Shepperton in 1977–8 with locations in North America. It was produced by the British-registered subsidiary (Dovemead Films) of a Swiss-registered middle company (Film Export AG) which itself was a subsidiary of the Panama-based production company (Film Production International) owned by producers Alexander and Ilya Salkind. The Salkinds raised the production finance through pre-sales, with Warner Bros. offering US $25 million for a negative pick-up and investing more as the budget increased.[17] Unlike the Bond pictures, there was no British connection in the source material, while the director (Richard Donner), credited writers and most of the principal cast were American. The British production base presumably ensured that *Superman* met the criteria for British quota in terms of labour costs even when the salaries of US stars Marlon Brando and

Gene Hackman were taken into account.[18] *Alien* (1979) was shot at Shepperton with the model miniatures at Bray Studios: it had a British director (Ridley Scott) and a largely British production crew but a mostly American cast (excepting John Hurt and Ian Holm). There was some controversy when the Department of Employment issued work permits for two American supporting actors against the wishes of the actors' union Equity.[19] Co-producer Gordon Carroll suggested that the deciding factor to shoot in Britain was a combination of lower cost (*Alien* was budgeted at US $8.5 million) and the technical skills of British studios: 'I very much wanted to make the picture here, because I think the craftsmanship in Britain is extraordinary. Cost makes some difference, but it's really the quality that makes you want to shoot here.'[20]

Another criticism made of the levy beyond the amount drawn by 'foreign-financed' films was that the kind of indigenous British films it subsidised were the wrong sort of cinema. There was a separate category for 'low cost' films (those where the labour costs were under £50,000): the Eady payment for these films was multiplied by 2.5 either until it matched the total labour cost or reached £18,750, whereafter the standard rate applied. This category included a fair proportion of 'X'-certificate sex comedies which were at the lower end of the budget range. The highest Eady payments in this category were for *Adventures of a Private Eye* (£60,779), *The Playbirds* (£56,359), *What's Up Superdoc?* (£29,832), *Come Play With Me* (£29,072), *Can I Come Too?* (£25,732), *I'm Not Feeling Myself Tonight* (£23,015), *Confessions from the David Galaxy Affair* (£19,990), *Adventures of a Plumber's Mate* (£14,175) and *Let's Get Laid* (£13,882). Ken Maidment, President of the British Film Producers' Association, was prompted to write to Labour MP Michael Meacher in order to rebut a claim made during a parliamentary debate that 60 per cent of levy payments went to films 'which are manifestly pornographic':

> The reference to pornographic films must relate to some of the low cost films like *The Lusty Vicar* or *The Lustful Lady*. In this context, I assume that the British Board of Film Censors will be surprised to know that they have been giving Certificates to pornographic pictures, but to talk about 60% of the entire Eady payments going to films which are manifestly pornographic is utter rubbish and irresponsible . . . The substantial part of the Levy allocated to high cost films has been paid to those such as *Superman, Midnight Express, Death on the Nile, Wild Geese, Force 10 from Navarone* and I hardly think that these films can be considered as 'pornographic'.[21]

A Lustful Lady was one of the least successful films in this category, with an Eady payment of only £3,214. (*The Lusty Vicar* would seem to have been an apocryphal film, though there was a Swedish sex film of 1970 whose English title was *The Lustful Vicar*.) The low-cost category did not exclusively comprise sex comedies: it also included the musical documentary *To Russia With Elton* (£39,942) and art films such as Derek Jarman's *Jubilee* (£232).

Another anomaly of the Eady levy was demonstrated in the case of a short documentary called *Hot Wheels*. This drew an astonishing £249,925 from the Eady levy (the next highest film in the category received less than £25,000 and many shorts drew less than £1,000) on account of having been shown as a supporting item to the mammoth hit *Grease* (the second most popular film of 1978): 6 per cent of the distributor's programme receipts were allocated to supporting films, which also qualified for the 2.5 per cent multiplier for low-cost films. There was concern that such a high payment should be made to the distributor Cinema International Corporation, a subsidiary of Paramount, which had produced *Grease* and picked up *Hot Wheels* (produced by James Street Productions) presumably on the grounds that its subject matter matched the main feature. Nor was *Hot Wheels* an entirely exceptional case: in 1979 *The Ledyard* (about three-day eventing) drew 'a staggering £77,805' due to being on the same bill as *Jaws 2*.[22] As a letter to *Screen International* put it: 'The Eady levy was set up to assist British production, particularly the producers of low-cost films. I find it hard to believe that money was ever intended to be handed over to distributors who have no part in the making of the film, nor its finance.'[23]

There was clearly a case for reform of the Eady levy. But there was no consensus on what that reform should be. The various sectors of the trade all had different views about the levy. The exhibitors had always disliked it. Most producers, especially those in the medium and lower cost range, were still dependent upon Eady income which it was estimated accounted on average for around 8.5 per cent of production costs (more for films in the 'low cost' category). The Interim Action Committee weighed up the pros and cons of Eady as an incentive to production:

> The effect on film production is to alter the risk/reward ratio for those British films that qualify for Eady. The average domestic gross is automatically boosted by between two-fifths and three-fifths. The moderate or low-budget British film still looks to the home market for a significant part of its revenue, and without Eady many films in these categories would not be made at all. However, as an incentive it has its disadvantages: any amount of Eady money cannot be counted on in advance and thus the usual feature of an incentive scheme – certainty – is not present. The eventual return from the Eady fund depends not only on (a) the overall size of the box office gross, and its distribution among cinemas, many of which are exempt, but also on (b) how well the film does at the box office, and on (c) how well all the other films eligible for Eady do at the box office during the same period of eligibility.[24]

One criticism of the operation of the levy was that the payments were often made to distributors rather than producers, who would assign their allocation to the distributor as their nominee, though this was defended on the grounds that in most cases the distributor was also the financier. *Variety* commented: 'The major distributors – inc. the Americans – feel with some justification that they are creating the local industry's wealth. Not only are Hollywood studios delivering playable product, their local distrib. divisions have been stumping up whopping ad-promo budgets to (1) sell specific pictures and to (2) push the general idea of catching a movie.'[25]

It was the exhibitors who were most opposed to continuation of the levy. Exhibitors had always regarded the levy as a tax by any other name: they argued that it ate into their profits and prevented them from making much-needed improvements to their premises. The decision to raise Value Added Tax (VAT) from 8 per cent to 15 per cent in the first Budget following the election of the Conservative government in 1979 further increased cinema admission prices without passing any benefit on to the exhibitor. It also had the effect of bringing some cinemas that had previously been exempt from levy payments into the levy. The levy was calculated on a screen-by-screen basis: any screen earning less than £1,400 per week was exempt from paying it. The managing director of the Victoria Playhouse Group complained to the Department of Trade: 'You will appreciate that the marginal levy amount of £1400 has not been adjusted for inflation and the many marginal cinemas who pay the levy some weeks and not others (depending on the films being shown) are obviously being kept in levy when one would have expected them to be exempt.'[26] The Department of Trade had raised the exemption limit but was reluctant to link it to inflation on the grounds that 'there is no obvious index to which we might link film making'. However, according to statistics provided by Her Majesty's Customs and Revenue, which collected the levy on behalf of the British Film Fund Agency, less than a third of all screens actually paid the full levy: they reported that in the levy year 1979–80 there were 1,641 screens in the United Kingdom, of which 427 paid the levy throughout the year, 506 paid the levy some weeks of the year and 708 did not pay any levy at all.[27]

The increase in the number of screens that were either exempt from the levy or paid it only some of the time was due to changes in the exhibition sector during the 1970s. The growth of multi-screen complexes whereby larger cinemas were converted into multiples of two or more smaller screens impacted on the levy, which was collected on a screen-by-screen basis. In 1972 there had been 97 multi-screen complexes in Britain, whereas by the end of the decade there were 340, accounting for around two-thirds of all screens. The average seating capacity of a single-screen cinema in 1978 was 691, while the average capacity of a screen in a complex was only 319: consequently the multiples had a higher average levy yield per seat per annum (£10.97 for a twin-screen complex and £15.29 for a triple-screen compared to £6.80 for a single screen). However, the increase of complexes had created more small screens that were likely to fall below the exemption limit, especially given as the average attendance per screen was only 22 per cent of seating capacity (a figure that once again highlights the gulf between the most successful films and the rest). R. F. Coker, an under-secretary at the Department of Trade, explained that 'this division of large cinemas into smaller units has resulted in some of the constituent screens escaping liability for levy payments because their weekly takings did not reach the threshold. This may be a reflection of their limited seating capacity rather than of their poor commercial performance; and it has been suggested that some complex screens will never exceed the current threshold although they are both successful themselves and part of a successful complex.'[28]

The mini-boom in cinema-going in the late 1970s had seen the annual levy yield increase: it raised £5.5 million in 1976–7, £6.7 million in 1977–8 and £7.5 million in 1978–9. Following statutory payments to the National Film School and Children's Film Foundation, the amount disbursed to producers in 1978–9 was £6.5 million.[29] The view within government was that on balance the levy was a successful instrument of film policy that benefited the industry:

> Over the years, the Eady levy (for which, notwithstanding the name, Sir Harold Wilson claims parenthood) has formed an important part of the films policy of successive Governments. Though its value and efficacy have been questioned, the consensus in the industry is that the levy does serve a useful purpose in stimulating the making of more films in the UK, even though many of these have a mid-Atlantic flavour; and because the Eady formula rewards success as measured at the box office, it should promote the making of films people want to see.[30]

However, there were some caveats. There was already evidence that the boom in attendances had peaked: the estimated levy yield fell to £6.2 million for 1979–80. And the total available for distribution to producers would also be reduced by the Films Act of 1980, which made provision for the allocation of a share of the Eady fund to the National Film Finance Corporation.

The Department of Trade could make changes to the operation and collection of the levy without the need for primary legislation through the agency of the Cinematograph Films Council. The Council was the body established under the Cinematograph Films Act of 1938 to advise the Secretary of State for Trade on matters concerning the film industry. In November 1979 it was announced that a maximum limit of £500,000 on the amount of Eady money that could be paid to a single film would be imposed and that the category of 'low cost' films would be removed. The multiplier for shorts was retained but the level at which a flat rate was paid was reduced.[31] There was some concern that the imposition of a maximum cap for individual films would deter producers of would-be blockbusters from producing in Britain: the next Bond film (*For Your Eyes Only*), slated for production in 1980–1, was mentioned as a possible casualty.[32] In the event, however, this fear was not realised. The removal of the 'low cost' category was accepted reluctantly by the producers concerned: it was preferable to the possibility of excluding sex films entirely, which had been mooted in some quarters but rejected by the Department of Trade as too cumbersome and politically difficult. John Nott, the Secretary of State for Trade and Industry, stated: 'In recent years, a growing number of low cost films have been of the "sexploitation" genre, and while I do not see the levy as an appropriate medium for censorship, few will regret that this type of film will no longer benefit from the multiplier.'[33]

In September 1980 the Department of Trade decided that 'it is timely to consider the whole question of the way levy is calculated and applied'.[34] This was prompted by the continued decline of the Eady yield and was particularly focused on changing the Eady formula to take into account multiple-screen cinemas. R. F. Coker prepared a paper suggesting various alternatives to the existing system: these included basing the levy on the box-office receipts of a whole complex rather than on individual screens, aggregating the levy to calculate an average across all screens in a complex, decreasing the threshold for smaller screens in a complex or increasing the threshold to take into account the total number of seats in a complex. He also suggested a radical alternative: 'The present complicated formula could be dropped and levy could be paid as a straight percentage of every ticket – just as VAT is paid on every sale (and is paid by the customer, not the seller).'[35] However, none of these suggestions gained any traction with the Cinematograph Films Council, which wanted to stick with the existing system but raise the exemption threshold. Coker told a colleague: 'I have used kilograms of paper with suggestions to get Council started, so far without success. A rejection of the next plea for a raised threshold until the levy system is properly examined might do the trick?'[36]

In 1981 the Department of Trade made a determined attempt to force the Cinematograph Films Council's hand. At the start of the year Norman Tebbit, the Parliamentary Under-Secretary for Trade, wrote to Dame Elizabeth Ackroyd, the incoming chair of the Council, that 'we must now reconsider the formula by which the levy yield is to be raised' and tasking the Council with coming up with recommendations.[37] The CFC set up a sub-committee to consider alternatives. It rejected Coker's suggestion of collecting the levy as a straight percentage of ticket sales 'because it would bring into levy those perhaps least able to pay [i.e. the smallest cinemas] while those currently paying would benefit from a considerable reduction in their contribution'. It also felt that aggregating the levy across complexes would be too difficult to administer. The sub-committee initially favoured a 'stratified system', basing the levy on an increasing percentage of box-office receipts starting at 1 per cent up to £400 up to a ceiling of 8 or 9 per cent. It felt that the advantage of this proposal was that it 'would ensure that those least able to pay would be only marginally affected whilst those currently paying would continue to pay approximately the same as they do now and would also ensure that everybody attending the cinema contributed to the levy'.[38] Vincent Porter, an academic member of the CFC, proposed an alternative stratified system with a reduced rate (one-fifteenth rather than one-twelfth of the box office for cinemas with weekly takings under £1,500).[39] In the event, the formula agreed by the sub-committee was based on 'capacity utilisation' – a hybrid between the straight percentage of ticket sales and the stratified system – whereby the levy would be calculated at one-eleventh of net box-office takings less 'relief' for small screens, calculated as £3,000 multiplied by the screen capacity where the figure of £3,000 'represents the average utilisation of single screens which would have the effect of excluding those screens with small admissions and average or below average seat prices without excluding those screens with high capacity utilisation'. This would produce an estimated levy yield of £7.5 million and 'satisfies the criteria laid down by the Minister in his letter of 1 January to the Chairman – namely it is easy to understand and simple, and therefore economical to administer'.[40]

These changes to the operation of the Eady levy took place against the background of a worsening economic outlook for the British film industry in the early 1980s. The upturn in cinema attendances in the late 1970s proved to be temporary. In 1980 total admissions fell to 101 million: this was a decline of 20 per cent on only two years previously and marked a new low since reliable records began in the 1930s.[41] This inevitably impacted on the yield from the levy. The amount returned to producers – already reduced by the decision to divert £1.5 million a year to the NFFC – fell from £5.3 million in 1980 to £4.6 million in 1981 and £2.1 million in 1982.[42] Film-makers – including Bryan Forbes, Mike Hodges, Sandy Lieberson, Nicolas Roeg and John Schlesinger – lobbied the government to extend the levy to films shown on television in order to raise much-needed extra funds to invest in production: 'All signs indicate that a mere handful of British feature films will be produced in the coming year, a cultural and economic outlook which we believe to be a disastrous state of affairs.'[43] Michael Relph also supported the extension of the levy to television screenings but added a caveat that more of the burden should be borne by the major cinema circuits rather than the dwindling number of independents: 'I am afraid that independent exhibitors will never be able to support British production whereas strong monopolistic groups at least have the power to do so if they be constrained to accept their responsibilities . . . If they do not finance some British production the last possible excuse for the existence of the monopolies disappears.'[44] And in 1983 the British Film Producers' Association argued that 'the retention of the fund is vital to British pictures which depend for their success on the home market and to aid producers who are starting their careers'.[45]

However, it is questionable whether the levy any longer made a significant difference to the box-office returns of British films. While the cap of £500,000 as a maximum levy payment for an individual film went some way towards reducing the gulf between blockbusters and other films, it nevertheless remained the case that the films which drew most from the levy were those that needed it least. Following the introduction of the cap in February 1980, five films drew the maximum Eady payment of £500,000: *Monty Python's Life of Brian* (1979), *Superman II* (1980), *For Your Eyes Only* (1981), *Gandhi* (1982) and *Octopussy* (1983). Only one of those films was wholly British-financed (*Monty Python's Life of Brian*), while the two Bond pictures and the Superman sequel were as close to guaranteed hits as could ever be expected in the film industry. Otherwise the value of the Eady levy was being eroded by a combination of rising production costs and diminishing box-office returns. By the early 1980s its days were numbered.

Notes

1. TNA PJ 9/13: R. F. Coker to D. L. Gatland, 8 December 1980.
2. 'UK admissions set 4-year high', *Screen International*, 14 April 1979, p. 1.
3. 'Upsurge in UK admissions to continue', *Screen International*, 13 May 1978, p. 5.

4. 'A guide to UK cinema figures', *Screen International*, 2 February 1980, p. 4.
5. 'Who made what in 1976', *Screen International*, 25 December 1976, p. 2.
6. 'Production', *Screen International*, 22 November 1985, p. 97.
7. '"Alien" leads new Fox film plans', *Screen International*, 28 January 1978, p. 1.
8. BFI Thomas GT/15/11: L. S. Lee to Gerald Thomas, 23 November 1977.
9. BFI Thomas GT/15/7: Peter Rogers to John Daly, 24 April 1978.
10. TNA PJ 9/13: Coker to Gatland, 8 December 1980.
11. '70 Titles Spell UK "Upturn"', *Variety*, 9 May 1979, p. 333.
12. *The Financing of the British Film Industry: Second Report of the Interim Action Committee on the Film Industry*, Cmnd. 7597 (June 1979), p. 1 (2).
13. 'All you ever wanted to know about Eady but were afraid to ask', *Screen International*, 30 April 1977, p. 18.
14. '"Superman" tops Eady '79', *Screen International*, 19 January 1980, pp. 16–17.
15. TNA PJ 9/13: Coker to Gatland, 8 December 1980.
16. 'All about Eady', *The Economist*, 24 November 1979, p. 45.
17. '"Superman": Rare Look at Film Finances', *Los Angeles Times*, 3 April 1980, p. B-1.
18. Unfortunately there is no 'evidence of British nature of a film' record for *Superman* at the National Archives. The Salkinds were notorious for their opaque financing and accounting practices.
19. Equity approved stars Sigourney Weaver and Tom Skerritt but objected to Yaphet Kotto and Harry Dean Stanton on the grounds that the parts could as easily have been played by British actors. 'Union Row Over "Alien" Actors', *Screen International*, 1 July 1978, p. 1.
20. 'Why "Alien" is staying under wraps', *Screen International*, 9 September 1978, p. 30.
21. TNA FV 81/190: K. L. Maidment to Michael Meacher, 11 April 1979.
22. '"The Ledyard" stuns Eady', *Screen International*, 10 November 1979, p. 28.
23. 'Eady probe is overdue', *Screen International*, 3 March 1979, p. 4.
24. *The Financing of the British Film Industry*, p. 6 (29).
25. 'Recent Habit of Hits Fails To Cure British Exhibs' Timidity', *Variety*, 18 October 1978, p. 187.
26. TNA PJ 9/13: T. W. Clarke to R. F. Coker, 4 July 1980.
27. Ibid.: R. J. Graham to Coker, 9 December 1980. The original numbers provided were incorrect, amounting to only 1,023 screens. When Coker queried this, Graham provided the correct figures in a telephone call on 14 January 1981.
28. Ibid.: Coker, 'The Application of the Levy', 5 September 1981.
29. Ibid.: 'British Film Fund: Levy yield and Distribution'.
30. Ibid.: Derek Eagers to Knighton, 17 December 1980.
31. '. . . and for Eady too', *Screen International*, 1 December 1979, p. 1.
32. 'Eady threat to foreign investors', *Screen International*, 9 February 1980, p. 4.
33. Ibid.
34. TNA PJ 9/13: R. F. Coker, 'The Application of the Levy', 5 September 1980.
35. Ibid.
36. Ibid.: Coker to Gatland, 20 November 1980.
37. Ibid.: Norman Tebbit to Dame Elizabeth Ackroyd, 1 January 1981.
38. Ibid.: Cinematograph Films Council Sub-Committee on Collection of Levy: Aide-memoire of points discussed on 23 January 1981.
39. Ibid.: Vincent Porter to Ackroyd, 25 February 1981.

40. Ibid.: Cinematograph Films Council Sub-Committee on the Collection of the Levy: Report to the Council, 7 April 1981.
41. 'All-time low for UK admissions', *Screen International*, 28 March 1981, p. 1.
42. *Film Policy*, Cmnd. 9319 (July 1984), p. 12 (5.12).
43. 'UK Film-Makers Plea: "Save Our Industry"', *Screen International*, 18 April 1981, p. 1.
44. 'Rider to that levy', *Screen International*, 28 March 1981, p. 1.
45. 'Case for retaining a cinema levy', *Screen International*, 23 April 1983, p. 2.

CHAPTER 20

The British Are Coming!

> The present tragedy of the British cinema – and you could call its whole history a series of tragedies – is that the cinema audience has largely disappeared at a point in time when the product itself is undergoing a very real revival . . . But that is not much use to an industry which still depends on an out-moded exhibition system, and which has failed so far to convince the government that it has a case for some kind of coherent encouragement. Thus the future remains as clouded and uncertain as it has always been. (Derek Malcolm)[1]

The early 1980s was seen at the time as a moment of cultural renewal for British cinema. A number of critically acclaimed and (in several cases) commercially successful British films – including *The Long Good Friday, The French Lieutenant's Woman, Gregory's Girl, Chariots of Fire, Gandhi, Local Hero, Educating Rita* and *The Killing Fields* – led to talk of a 'renaissance' of British film-making that for once was not entirely hubristic. The mood was famously expressed by screenwriter Colin Welland, who upon collecting his Academy Award for Best Screenplay for *Chariots of Fire* at the Dorothy Chandler Pavilion in Los Angeles on 29 March 1982, held it aloft and declared: 'The British are coming!'[2] *Chariots of Fire* also won the Academy Award for Best Film: it was the first British film to triumph since *Oliver!* in 1968. Its success was surpassed the following year, when Richard Attenborough's *Gandhi* won eight Academy Awards, including Best Film and Best Director. While pointing out that, like other periods of revival and renewal, the renaissance of British film culture turned out to be short-lived, John Hill nevertheless contends that 'the British cinema which emerged in the 1980s did contain a number of genuinely novel and distinctive aspects and did, at least temporarily, overcome some of the difficulties which beset British film-making in the 1970s'.[3]

However, the new-found cultural vitality of British cinema in the 1980s once again disguised the underlying structural and economic weaknesses of the film industry. It was not a good time for exhibitors. The upturn in admissions in the late 1970s proved to be short-lived: it was followed by the most severe decline in cinema-going for a quarter of a century as annual attendances fell from 112 million in 1979 to an all-time low of 54 million in 1984.[4] The decline was as precipitous as it had been in the late 1950s: the cinema audience halved in the space of only five years. Among the reasons suggested for the decline in cinema-going were the impact of video cassettes, including illegal or 'pirate' copies of films, the age and condition of some cinema buildings, and the effects of a continuing economic recession.⁵ As in the late 1970s, the biggest box-office attractions of the early 1980s tended to be American films: *The Empire Strikes Back*, *Kramer vs. Kramer* and *Star Trek: The Motion Picture* were the top three films at the British box office in 1980, *Arthur* was first in 1982, *E.T. the Extra-Terrestrial* and *Return of the Jedi* were first and second in 1983, *Indiana Jones and the Temple of Doom* was first in 1984 and *Ghostbusters* first in 1985. Unlike the 1970s, however, the success of these films did not reflect a wider box-office trend. Indeed, the opposite seems to have been the case. In 1982 the National Film Finance Corporation suggested that the popularity of American films overall was declining: 'One reason for the latest decline in attendances is a diminishing interest in American films ... Unfortunately, too few films have been produced in the UK in recent years to provide alternatives to the American product.'⁶

At the same time, the domestic production sector contracted severely: the number of British feature films fell from 61 in 1979 to 31 in 1980 and 24 in 1981 before staging a modest recovery to 53 in 1984. This needs to be qualified in so far as British studios also provided a production base for some major American films, including *The Empire Strikes Back*, *Raiders of the Lost Ark*, *Return of the Jedi*, *Indiana Jones and the Temple of Doom* and *Legend*. For indigenous production, however, the outlook was bleaker than at any time since the mid-1920s. Ken Maidment, President of the British Film and Television Producers' Association, cautioned in 1981 that 'the extent of the decline can only give cause for alarm. Only seven British pictures have commenced shooting since the beginning of the year, and it is doubtful if more than a dozen will have started by the end of the year.'⁷ At the end of the year *Screen International* saw both positive and negative signs: 'For the UK film industry in 1981, the silver lining was the performance of British films in the Top 20 money-making chart. The clouds are that this past 12 months is on course to register an all-time low in cinema admissions as well as being the worst ever year for indigenous production.'⁸ British films (albeit American-financed) took the top three places in 1981 (*Superman II*, *For Your Eyes Only*, *Flash Gordon*), with another two (*Clash of the Titans*, *The Elephant Man*) and one Anglo-French co-production (*Tess*) in the top ten. However, other than the Bond pictures, now entering their third decade with their box-office appeal in Britain as strong as ever, it was a lean period for British films: the only others in the annual top ten between 1980 and 1985 were *Chariots of Fire*, *Gregory's Girl*, *Who Dares Wins*, *Gandhi*, *Superman III*, *Monty Python's The Meaning of Life*, *Educating Rita*, *Greystoke: The Legend of Tarzan, Lord of the Apes*, *Santa Claus – The Movie*, *A Passage to India* and *The Killing Fields*.

For this period there are published figures for the box-office receipts of British films. Between 1979 and 1983 the most successful British films in terms of the distributors' grosses in the domestic market (including Eady payments) were *Moonraker* (£3,714,130), *Octopussy* (£3,131,579), *Gandhi* (£2,664,974), *Superman II* (£2,583,333), *For Your Eyes Only* (£2,583,333), *Alien* (£2,444,577), *Monty Python's Life of Brian* (£2,310,889), *Flash Gordon* (£2,258,852), *Superman III* (£1,909,211), *Chariots of Fire* (£1,859,480), *Midnight Express* (£1,420,735), *The Shining* (£1,276,344), *The French Lieutenant's Woman* (£1,224,15), *The Elephant Man* (£1,202,617), *Quadrophenia*

(£1,193,054), *Clash of the Titans* (£1,102,825), *Tess* (£962,974), *Gregory's Girl* (£801,65), *Monty Python's The Meaning of Life* (£713,186), *The Dark Crystal* (£686,267), *The Bitch* (£664,126), *The Spaceman and King Arthur* (£640,161) and *An American Werewolf in London* (£511,715). Any film grossing over £500,000 would have been considered a box-office hit, but there was a wide gulf between the top-grossing films and the rest. Even some British films that featured in the annual top twenty box-office attractions – including *Local Hero* (£487,437), *The Long Good Friday* (£426,308), *Time Bandits* (£403,672), *Who Dares Wins* (£388,521), *Educating Rita* (£364,554), *Lady Chatterley's Lover* (£362,057), *Heat and Dust* (£358,359), *The Sea Wolves* (£335,220) and *Evil Under the Sun* (£315,746) – would not have returned a profit from the home market.[9]

Indeed, the domestic market had now contracted to such an extent that even medium-budget films were dependent upon overseas revenues if they were to return a profit to the producer. *Chariots of Fire* (1981) is a case in point. This film – a heritage drama about British athletes competing at the Paris Olympics of 1924, produced by David Puttnam and directed by Hugh Hudson – was the 'sleeper' of the early 1980s. It did moderately well on its initial release in Britain in 1981, when it had long runs at selected locations including the Odeon Haymarket (where it ran for 23 consecutive weeks) and the Odeon Kensington (18 consecutive weeks) and finished the year as the twelfth most successful film overall.[10] It was on its reissue in 1982 – following its Academy Award triumph and riding a wave of patriotic fervour during the Falklands War (though the film itself was very far from being a jingoistic flag-waver!) – that *Chariots of Fire* really scored with the public: it was the top-grossing British film of the year and second overall behind the Dudley Moore comedy *Arthur* (this was a year without either a Bond picture or a major Spielberg–Lucas epic).[11] By any standard *Chariots of Fire* was a major box-office hit; but even so its total UK distributor's receipts of £1,859,480 (£740,363 earned in 1981 and £1,119,117 in 1982) amounted to less than half of the film's negative cost of £4,032,859.[12] In order to keep the budget down, Puttnam had instituted a profit participation scheme where the producer's share of the profits was divided between key personnel and artistes: Puttnam would receive 20.5 per cent on the first $1 million, with phased reductions to 15.5 per cent on anything over $3 million, Goldcrest Films (which had contributed £17,000 of 'seed money' for script development) a flat rate of 7.5 per cent, Colin Welland and director Hugh Hudson would receive 5 per cent each, there was 1 per cent each for associate producer James Crawford, cinematographer David Watkins, editor Terry Rawlings and production manager Joyce Herlihy, while actors Ian Charleson, Ben Cross, Ian Holm and Nigel Havers received up to 2 per cent.[13]

It is no coincidence that most of the biggest-grossing films in Britain had also done well in America. Sarah Street's study of the reception of British films in the United States identifies the top British rental earners between 1980 and 1985 as *Superman II* ($65.2 million), *Superman III* ($37.2 million), *Octopussy* ($34 million), *Chariots of Fire* ($30.6 million), *Never Say Never Again* ($28.2 million), *For Your Eyes Only* ($26.6 million), *A View to a Kill* ($25.3 million), *Gandhi* ($25 million),

Time Bandits ($20.5 million), *The Killing Fields* ($16 million), *A Passage to India* ($13.9 million), *The French Lieutenant's Woman* ($11.3 million), *Monty Python's The Meaning of Life* ($7.3 million), *Eye of the Needle* ($6.7 million), *The Mirror Crack'd* ($5.5 million), *Brazil* ($4.5 million), *1984* ($4.4 million) and *Evil Under the Sun* ($4 million).[14] Six of the top ten British films in America were either Bond or Superman (*Never Say Never Again* was a rival Bond picture produced outside the Eon Productions series in 1983), while for the most part the rest of the list features heritage and costume subjects. For independent producers, the necessity of interesting a major US distributor was more essential than ever, though it often took a long time for the producer to see any return. This was the case with *Chariots of Fire*, where Colin Welland's agent wrote 'to express both my and Colin's disgust . . . that our September [1982] profit statement would yield no money at all. I presume Fox think they are being tremendously clever in standing on their rights and holding up payment of the money, but it yet again emphasises the impossibility of doing any sort of sensible deal with an American company.'[15]

The British production sector was weaker than ever in the early 1980s. The majors which had dominated the industry in the 1970s were no longer significant players. In 1979 the new NFFC managing director Mamoun Hassan averred that 'EMI and Rank were sick companies and their forward distribution programmes were filled with American product . . . ACC was kept going only by its TV interests.'[16] Rank had all but withdrawn from film production: it would part-finance a small number of films a year with distribution guarantees between 10 and 15 per cent. ACC never recovered from its losses on *Raise the Titanic!*: Lew Grade lost control of the company to Australian tycoon Robert Holmes à Court in 1982. Grade's last venture into film-making was as chairman and chief executive of the newly formed Embassy Communications International: Embassy's first (and last) British film was *Champions* (1984), based on the true story of jockey Bob Champion winning the 1981 Grand National after recovering from cancer.[17] That left EMI (Thorn-EMI following the merger of its parent company with Thorn Industries in late 1979) as the last British 'major'. In mid-1981 EMI announced a production programme of some US $60 million, though most of this was based in America.[18] Eighteen months later, however, the company announced Verity Lambert's appointment as head of production. Lambert came from a television background – she had been head of drama for Thames Television and chief executive of Thames's film-making subsidiary Euston Films – and her appointment at EMI was seen as refocusing on the domestic market, in contrast to the outgoing Barry Spikings: 'A desire to increase the number of indigenous films made for medium-to-low budgets rather than take huge risks on mega-budgeted US productions such as *Honky Tonk Freeway* and *Can't Stop the Music* (both enormous flops) seemed to be behind Lambert's appointment.'[19]

Paul Moody contends that EMI in the 1980s exemplified a 'paradoxical dichotomy' in so far as it was 'trying to create "British" cultural films while at the same time establishing an international company'.[20] EMI's output under Lambert prioritised comedy – *Comfort and Joy* (1984), *Morons from Outer Space* (1985), *Clockwise* (1986) – and was pitched in the middle-budget range. For example, *Morons from Outer Space* was budgeted at £4,016,424: the 'above the line' costs for director Mike Hodges and actor-writers Mel Smith and Griff Rhys Jones (£197,500) amounted to only 5 per cent of the budget, with EMI's overheads (£435,497) accounting for 12.5 per cent.[21] EMI's biggest success during this period was *A Passage to India* (1984). Despite the pedigree of the film – producers John Brabourne and Richard Goodwin had made the successful Agatha Christie adaptations and director David Lean was a double Academy Award-winner for *The Bridge on the River Kwai* and *Lawrence of Arabia* – EMI was reluctant to provide 100 per cent financing following its experience with big-budget films in the late 1970s. EMI advanced US $6.5 million in return for international distribution, with the rest of the budget put up by the American cable television station Home Box Office ($8.5 million) and Columbia Pictures ($1.5 million).[22]

In December 1984 EMI sought to raise a new fund for film production: it looked to raise £18 million from the City through loan stock and preference shares which it would match-fund from its own resources. The security offered was five films – *A Passage to India*, *The Holcroft Covenant*, *Dream Child*, *Morons from Outer Space* and *Wild Geese II* – and was 'in effect raising money on the films to help finance future production'.[23] John Reiss, finance director of Thorn-EMI Screen Entertainment, reported a 'very satisfying' uptake: most of the £18 million was raised from ten British finance institutions.[24] However, the raising of the fund would prove to be a false dawn. Thorn-EMI's decision not to renew Verity Lambert's contract in 1985 signalled the scaling back of its film production activities. In May 1986 Thorn-EMI Screen Entertainment was sold to the Cannon Group for a reported £175 million. Cannon – owned by the Israeli entrepreneurs Menahem Golan and Yoram Globus – was a producer and distributor of mostly low-budget exploitation films: its interest in EMI seems to have been to acquire its chain of 296 cinemas in the United Kingdom.[25]

The withdrawal of the major corporations from an active interest in production left the British production sector more fragmented than it had ever been since the silent era. A report by the British Screen Advisory Council in 1990 calculated that there had been a total of 342 production companies active during the 1980s: 250 of them made only one film.[26] The most acute problem for British producers was access to production finance. *Screen International*'s monthly reports document declining production investment in the early 1980s: for example, in September 1981 the total was £16.4 million compared to £42.2 million for the same month the previous year.[27] On the one hand there were some – such as the veteran director Val Guest, who made his last theatrical feature, *The Boys in Blue* (1982), some forty years after his first – who pooh-poohed the idea of a crisis: 'There has always been a crisis in this business. I must have worked through six of them at least. I simply don't have any time for people who say we are going down the drain. If you have a good project and a good track record, it is not that hard to get a film off the ground with British finance.'[28] And Euan Lloyd was also able to raise the finance for *Who Dares Wins* (1982) – an action picture inspired by the Iranian embassy siege of 1980 – from mostly British sources:

> The joy of this film is that the City has responded so well, which is surprising when the fortunes of the industry are so low . . . I've got a conglomerate of three major banking entities who are backing me. It's all British money except for a small amount from Switzerland and Sweden. So for the first time, the profits will come back here . . . The best thing about the City arrangement, though, is that I've not had to pre-sell in the States.[29]

On the other hand the NFFC reported in 1982 that 'film producers are finding it harder and harder to raise the necessary finance'.[30] The trade press in the early 1980s was full of reports of investors pulling out of the film industry and of projects that collapsed due to lack of finance. In December 1981, for example, the brewer Arthur Guinness & Co. announced that it would no longer invest in film production after losing £3.9 million over the last six years.[31] Perhaps the most high-profile abandoned film project was Don Boyd's *Gossip*: Boyd thought he had secured financing from the Martini Foundation in 1982 but the promised money was never deposited with the bank and Boyd had to shut down the film having borrowed £100,000 in anticipation of the funds to build sets at Twickenham Studios.[32]

The precarious nature of finance affected independent producers more severely than ever. There were numerous instances of films that nearly collapsed during production when their financing arrangements unfolded: in such circumstances a guarantee of completion was of little help as the guarantor's responsibility was to the investor rather than to the producer. *The Return of the Soldier* (1982) – produced by Simon Relph and directed by Alan Bridges from the novel by Rebecca West with a reported budget of £1,750,000 – ran out of money when its American finance was cut off midway into the shooting period. Brent Walker Film Distributors, which had advanced money for the development of the script, stepped in to furnish the completion money.[33] *The Return of the Soldier* was the British entry for the 1982 Cannes Film Festival but its US release was held up for three years due to a dispute between Barry Cooper, one of the original investors, and Brent Walker: the High Court in London ruled that Brent Walker should retain all distribution rights but that Cooper was entitled to an executive producer credit with George Walker.[34] *The Jigsaw Man* (1983) – a spy picture produced by Ron Carr and Benjamin Fisz and directed by Terence Young for the United Film Distributing Company with a budget of US $9 million – was financed by a combination of Irish and American interests. However, the American funds again did not materialise: the film was faced with either having to find $4 million to complete or abandon production. Carr believed that 'confidence in the British film industry would be severely damaged' if the film collapsed.[35] On this occasion it was Pakistani shipping magnate Mahmud Sipra who provided the completion money in return for a 100 per cent interest in the picture.[36]

The contraction of the domestic market meant that British producers again adopted a policy of cost reduction. The early 1980s saw a resurgence of the low-budget picture that had been priced out of the market by inflation in the late 1970s. ITC's *Rising Damp* (1980) – a late entry in the television spin-off cycle – was 'modestly budgeted at around £400,000'.³⁷ A survey of British production by *Sight & Sound* in 1981 found that there were broadly two groups of films. On the one hand there were expensively budgeted films all produced with American finance: *For Your Eyes Only* ($28 million), *The Dark Crystal* ($25 million), *Gandhi* ($20 million), *The Great Muppet Caper* ($14 million) and *The Pirates of Penzance* ($12 million). On the other hand the average cost of British films excluding the high-end budgets was only £650,000: the representative range included *Bad Blood* (£900,000), *Brimstone and Treacle* (£900,000), *An Unsuitable Job for a Woman* (£750,000), *Angel* (£420,000), *Take It Or Leave It* (£400,000) and *Ascendancy* (£250,000).³⁸ The lower end of the budget scale was exemplified by Peter Gregg's *The Trespasser* (1981), a D. H. Lawrence adaptation reportedly shot on a budget of £120,000 provided by the record company Polytel and a consortium of private investors. *The Trespasser* was shot as a television film but had a low-key theatrical release: this anticipated the entry of Channel 4 – the new public television service which began broadcasting in 1982 – into film production.³⁹

The changed landscape of the British film industry following the withdrawal of the majors created space for new entrants to the fields of production and finance. The emergence of several independents – including Goldcrest Films, HandMade Films, Virgin Films and Palace Pictures – had seemed for a while to herald a new dawn for British cinema in the early 1980s. As James Park reported for *Variety* in 1984:

> As the British film biz has struggled off the floor in recent years, several new production companies have made a mark with an impressive debut – Goldcrest's *Gandhi* and HandMade's *Time Bandits*, for example. Latest new entrant is Palace Pictures, whose *The Company of Wolves* fantasy pic stole everyone's thunder when it opened at the Odeon circuit's flagship last month.⁴⁰

HandMade Films had been set up by ex-Beatle George Harrison and his business partner Denis O'Brien in 1978 specifically to produce *Monty Python's Life of Brian* when EMI withdrew its offer to finance the film. HandMade followed it with two other successful projects: John Mackenzie's violent gangster film *The Long Good Friday* (1980) – which HandMade picked up for distribution after the original distributor ITC wanted to make drastic cuts that Mackenzie and producer Barry Hanson resisted – and Terry Gilliam's *Time Bandits* (1981).⁴¹ Virgin Records had invested in the Sex Pistols film *The Great Rock'n'Roll Swindle* (1980): its success again drew the Virgin Group – founded by entrepreneur Richard Branson in the 1970s – further into the industry through the formation of Virgin Films in 1984, which co-financed *Electric Dreams* (1984) with MGM and provided the full budget of £4 million for Michael Radford's film of George Orwell's *1984* (1984). Palace Pictures had started out distributing video cassettes, including cult films such as *Diva* and *The Evil Dead*. It ventured into film distribution with Neil Jordan's debut feature *Angel* (1982), which was co-financed by the Irish Film Board (IR£100,000) and Channel 4 (IR£416,767).⁴² Palace's first venture into production was Jordan's *The Company of Wolves* (1984): the £2 million budget came from distribution pre-sales (ITC Entertainment picked up the rest of the world with Palace handling the UK distribution) and an equity investment from the NFFC.⁴³ However, none of these companies were large enough to invest in more than one or two films a year: therefore they were vulnerable if they backed one big loss-maker, as happened to Virgin with *1984* and HandMade with *Shanghai Surprise* (1986).

The most successful new entrants into film finance and production in the 1980s were Channel 4 and Goldcrest. As these two companies represented the two divergent production strategies that the British film industry had adopted since the 1930s – low-cost films for the home market on the one hand versus expensive films aimed at the international market on the other – they are deserving of more detailed consideration. Channel 4 was the fulfilment of the recommendation of the Committee on the Future of Broadcasting (the Annan Committee) to create a fourth public service television channel in order to 'encourage productions which say something new in new ways'.⁴⁴ Channel 4 was funded by a combination of advertising revenue and a levy on the ITV companies: its Royal Charter specified a remit to encourage innovation in programme content and to cater for minority audiences not represented by the BBC/ITV duopoly. One of the ways in which it did this was to commission films that would be made for television but with the possibility of a theatrical release. There were precedents for this: Peter Hall's *Akenfield* had been produced for London Weekend Television but also had a small-scale theatrical release in 1975. However, this put Channel 4 at loggerheads with the Cinematograph Exhibitors' Association (which upheld a three-year embargo on theatrical films being shown on television) and the trades unions (as pay rates were lower for television productions than for theatrical films). It was not until 1986 that the CEA agreed to lift its embargo for films costing less than £1,250,000 and that an accommodation was reached with the Association of Cinema and Television Technicians whereby the existing agreement that allowed lower rates for theatrical shorts was extended to made-for-television films provided they were fully financed by Channel 4.⁴⁵ Colin Gregg's *Remembrance* (1982) was the first film commissioned by Channel 4: it had a limited theatrical release before the channel had launched, prior to its television screening on 10 November 1982.⁴⁶

Channel 4's commissioning editor David Rose explained that the broadcaster's policy would be to commission around 20 films a year 'made for comparatively modest budgets . . . written and directed by established film-makers and introducing new writing and directing talent'.⁴⁷ In its first year Channel 4 commissioned nineteen features: these included films by established film-makers Stephen Frears (*Walter*), Michael Apted (*P'Tang Yang Kipperbang*) and Desmond Davis (*The Country Girls*) and first-time directors including Karl Francis (*Giro City*), Bill Bryden (*Ill Fares the Land*) and Richard Eyres (*The Ploughman's Lunch*). There were also first features from experienced television directors Mike Leigh (*Meantime*) and Philip Saville (*Those Glory, Glory Days*). The budget range was from £300,000 to a top end of £700,000 for *The Country Girls* and £800,000 for *Red Monarch*, with the average around £400,000–£450,000.⁴⁸ David Drury, who directed *Forever Young* (1983), testified to the creative freedom that film-makers enjoyed under Rose: 'It's a great feeling being given a budget of between £450,000 and £500,000 and told to get on with it. It's indicative of David's trust, really. He is very good at letting people he trusts get on with it.'⁴⁹

Channel Four Films – the subsidiary responsible for film commissioning and finance – adopted different funding strategies. It provided full funding for relatively few films and these were mostly towards the lower end of the budget range: in its first year the fully funded films were *Remembrance* (£320,000), *Hero* (£350,000), *Nelly's Version* (£400,000), *The Disappearance of Harry* (£400,000) and *Accounts* (£400,000).⁵⁰ A more common arrangement was for Channel Four Films to be a co-production partner with another investor (or investors). In these cases Channel 4 would pre-purchase the United Kingdom television rights (£200,000 seems to have been the ball-park figure) as well as providing an additional equity investment up to £100,000. Its total investment was around £2 million per year. Larry Coyne, head of business development, explained the importance of the theatrical market and ancillary sales: 'If we do not get back a penny, that means we are effectively paying £300,000 for the UK [television] distribution rights of each film which may prove unacceptable. At the other extreme, if we get back £4 million, twice our investment, that would reduce the picture price for the UK rights to £100,000 and release extra money for more films.'⁵¹ The financing arrangements varied from one film to another. For *Another Time, Another Place* (1983) – produced by Simon Perry and directed by Michael Radford – Channel 4's total commitment was half the budget of £500,000, with the rest from distributor Rediffusion Films and the Scottish Arts Council.⁵² Peter Greenaway's *The Draughtsman's Contract* (1983) was co-financed by Channel 4 and the British Film Institute Production Board at a total cost of £320,000. *Wetherby* (1985) – produced by Simon Relph and directed by David Hare – was jointly financed by Channel 4 and Central Television subsidiary Zenith Productions at an agreed budget of £995,322. Richard Soames of Film Finances explained the financing arrangements: 'As it stands at present Channel 4 and Zenith together are advancing £950,000 and there is therefore a shortfall of £45,322 . . . I understand there will be a meeting tomorrow to decide how the shortfall will be met, either by taking whole or part of the overheads or by Channel 4 advancing the difference.'⁵³

Channel 4's investment in film was a welcome boost for the ailing British production sector: in 1982–3 it amounted to an injection of £12.5 million into the industry.⁵⁴ However, the advent of this new source of film finance was not a panacea. Some producers complained that Channel 4 had entered a field it did not understand: the commissioning of television content was a more straightforward process than negotiating theatrical distribution, often involving several financing and distribution partners, and there was a view that producers often got a poor deal. A particular issue was the tension between producers and distributors who wanted longer theatrical windows for their films and the broadcaster who wanted the films to be available for television at the earliest opportunity.⁵⁵ This was demonstrated by *She'll Be Wearing Pink Pyjamas* (1985), produced by Adrian Hughes and Tara Prem, and directed by John Goldschmidt with a budget of £954,893.[56] The trade press reported 'huge interest' in the film from Rank and EMI: *She'll Be Wearing Pink Pyjamas* was in a similar vein to the popular *Educating Rita* with the same star (Julie Walters). Hitherto Channel 4 films had been accorded limited releases on the 'art-house' circuit, so the prospect of a major circuit release needed to be taken seriously. However, the circuits wanted a three-year hold-back before it was shown on television in the expectation that (like *Educating Rita*) it would have 'legs' at the box office. Adrian Hughes explained the dilemma from the producer's perspective: 'We are concerned C4 gives *Pyjamas* a proper theatrical release. At the same time, why should C4 pay for and commission a really good piece of filmed drama and yet by the time it comes on the box everyone has seen it?'[57] In the event, *She'll Be Wearing Pink Pyjamas* was released on the ABC circuit but fell short of expectations: Channel 4 was therefore able to negotiate an earlier television première after two rather than three years, where it turned out to be one of the most popular 'Film on Four' screenings.[58]

Laura Mayne argues that Channel Four Films' 'core business of showcasing specially commissioned new feature films provides a valuable index of the changes in the Channel's policy and identity as a film financier over time'.[59] Its early commissions demonstrated some affinity with the traditional television single play – to this extent it is surely no accident that the original broadcast slot of the 'Film on Four' strand was on Wednesday evenings at 9 p.m., recalling the BBC's drama showcase *The Wednesday Play* of the 1960s – but within a few years it also included more self-consciously 'cinematic' films and was embracing a more commercial outlook. The trade paper *Broadcast* pointed to three films released in 1985–6 – *Letter to Brezhnev*, *My Beautiful Laundrette* and *Supergrass* – as evidence 'that C4 does not just commission high-brow movies for limited art house release, but also widely popular pictures that can earn a lot of money'.[60] *Letter to Brezhnev* (1985) – produced by Janet Goddard and directed by Chris Bernard at a final cost of £480,000 – had not been a Channel 4 commission: it was underwritten by Channel Four Films who picked it up when it ran out of funds during production.[61] *My Beautiful Laundrette* (1985) – produced by Sarah Radclyffe and directed by Stephen Frears – was commissioned by Channel Four Films under its television agreement at a budget of £650,000: it was only after the critical acclaim the film received at the Edinburgh Film Festival that it was afforded a theatrical release (by the independent distributor Mainline Pictures) which necessitated renegotiation with the unions. For a low-budget independent film it had what amounted to a very successful theatrical release: it was also an art-house success in the United States, where it was picked up by independent distributor Orion Pictures and returned US $751,465 by June 1986.[62] *Supergrass* (1985) – produced by Elaine Taylor and directed by Peter Richardson – was the first feature for the 'Comic Strip' team. On this occasion Channel 4 bought television rights only, with the theatrical rights held by executive producer Michael White. *Supergrass* opened strongly, grossing £340,108 from 93 cinemas after two weeks, and eventually earned over £1 million.[63]

By the mid-1980s 'Film on Four' had built up a reputation for showcasing original, independent film-making ranging from art cinema (*The Draughtsman's Contract*) to social realism (*Letter to Brezhnev*) and state-of-the-nation films (*The Ploughman's Lunch*). Assessments of its contribution to the British film industry – as opposed to the artistic and cultural merits of the films – were, however, divided. On the one hand Derek Malcolm, film critic of *The Guardian*, felt 'that C4 has completely altered the course of British film-making in the Eighties and provided the most effective springboard there is for the current revival, recognised almost everywhere but in its country of origin'.[64] On the other hand Philip Purser (*The Sunday Telegraph*) felt that 'Film on Four' was 'a senseless diversion of funds from television drama into a moribund film industry'.[65] On balance, the truth is probably somewhere in between. There was no real economic revival for the British film industry; but rather than propping up a moribund industry, the principal significance of Channel 4 was that it collapsed the distinction between cinema and television not only in terms of their aesthetics but also in relation to the provision of production finance.

Goldcrest Films – a co-production partner in a number of Channel 4 films – was the largest new financing and production group of the 1980s. Goldcrest had been founded in 1977 by Canadian merchant banker Jake Eberts in association with the Pearson Longman Group and the Electra Finance Company.[66] Its remit was to provide development funding for producers to be able to commission scripts and put together the packages that would enable them to pitch their films to investors and distributors, in return for which it would receive a percentage of the producer's share: among the films it supported in this way were *Watership Down*, *Black Jack*, *Breaking Glass* and *Chariots of Fire*. It has sometimes been suggested that it was the success of *Chariots of Fire* that persuaded Eberts to move Goldcrest into direct financing of film production. In fact, Eberts was already, separately, involved in the US-based International Film Investors, which had been set up in 1978. And, moreover, Goldcrest's move into direct financing occurred before the release of *Chariots of Fire*. Goldcrest Films International (GFI) was formed in 1980: it raised a fund of £8 million – subscribed by several investment trusts (Murray Johnstone, J. Henry Schroder Wagg & Co. and Noble Grossart) and the National Coal Board Pension Fund – which it would use to invest in six to eight films a year over five years. Its maximum investment would be 50 per cent of the budget and it would not invest more than 20 per cent of its funds in any one film.[67]

Goldcrest's first substantial investment was in Richard Attenborough's epic historical biopic *Gandhi* (1982). Attenborough had been struggling to raise the finance for this project for over a decade. Joseph Levine had been on the verge of committing to the film twice, first in 1973, when a script was written by Robert Bolt, and again in 1978, following *A Bridge Too Far*, which Attenborough had directed, though he withdrew when the Indian government formally recognised the Palestine Liberation Organisation.[68] Goldcrest had already provided £1 million of development funding, which enabled Attenborough to buy back Levine's interest in the film and to commission a screenplay from John Briley. In 1980 Attenborough secured a financial contribution of 30 per cent of the £9.5 million budget from the

National Film Finance Corporation of India. GFI agreed to provide 60 per cent, with the balance from private investors. Goldcrest was taking a calculated risk: the investment was more than the self-imposed 50 per cent maximum (a guideline that seems not to have been observed) and there was no distribution deal in place. In the event, Columbia agreed a negative pick-up after seeing a rough cut and then agreed to spend US $12 million on international distribution.[69] *Gandhi* won both critical and popular acclaim: Columbia estimated that its Academy Award success was worth an additional US $20 million to the international box office.[70]

In the early 1980s all went well for Goldcrest. It was a well-capitalised group and had sufficient funds to invest in a portfolio of films that allowed it to spread its risks. At the lower end of the budget range it partnered with Channel Four Films for some of the early 'Film on Four' productions including *P'Tang Yang Kipperbang* (£400,000) and *Moonlighting* (£600,000). Goldcrest's James Lee explained the financing arrangements:

> The first Films on Four that we did, *P'Tang Yang Kipperbang*, *Secrets* and *Experience Preferred But Not Essential*, were made for very low cost and the Channel Four contribution was very generous – under, but close to half the budget. The subjects were good and proved popular . . . Now costs have risen, from, say £400,000 to £600,000, while the Channel Four contribution has not increased in proportion. It's gone up a bit, but where before it might be £200,000 of a £400,000 budget, it's now £250,000 of a £600,000 budget. The gap that we have to fill has been doubled.[71]

However, the returns on low-budget films were modest. Goldcrest sought to diversify its portfolio by investing in medium-budget films such as *Local Hero* and *Another Country*. It put up the full budget of £2.3 million for *Local Hero* (1983), while *Another Country* (1984) was a co-production with the NFFC and Virgin Films with a total budget of £1.6 million.[72] Goldcrest's next high-budget film was *The Killing Fields* (1984), produced by David Puttnam and directed by Roland Joffé, for which GFI advanced the full budget of £8,419,000. Puttnam expressed his appreciation for Goldcrest's flexible approach; 'Roland never went over budget but we made adjustments. The important thing was that the financier allowed me to have the 10% contingency as a cash sum to spend as I saw fit.'[73]

As had happened so often before, Goldcrest's early success drove it towards a more ambitious strategy. James Lee – who succeeded Jake Eberts as chief executive when Eberts resigned due to his concern over the company's new direction – oversaw a restructuring and share issue that raised £22 million of new capital. *Screen International* averred that the share issue – subscribed by existing shareholders and several new corporate investors – 'indicates confidence on the part of City financial institutions in the future of the film industry – in spite of the Government's planned phasing out of capital allowances [that] could do considerable damage'.[74] Goldcrest Holdings was formed to bring together the various subsidiaries and partnerships, with a credit facility of £10 million from the Midland Bank. Lee explained the rationale behind the share issue: 'We now have enough funds to move ahead on our own resources. In the future we'll be able to finance projects partly with our own money and partly by simple borrowing from the bank. Then, as soon as we have a good track record, we'll go public. We need two or three good years.'[75] Sandy Lieberson, a successful producer of British films in the 1970s, became the new chief of production.[76]

What happened next is an all-too familiar story. At the Cannes Film Festival in May 1984, Goldcrest announced 'one of the most ambitious British production programmes ever': a total investment of £60 million in ten feature films.[77] These included four high-budget films: *Revolution, Absolute Beginners, The Mission* and *Mandrake the Magician*. *Revolution* (1985) – produced by American Irwin Winkler and directed by Hugh Hudson – was quite possibly the most ill-conceived British film ever made: a historical epic about the American War of Independence shot on British locations. Goldcrest agreed to a total budget of £11.3 million, 'including 6% completion fee and US $1.5m above-the-line cast allowance'.[78] Although there were reservations about Hudson ('a very talented director [who] displayed insufficient regard to budget and schedule') and Winkler ('whose last film had gone considerably over budget'), Goldcrest backed the film as it 'presented us with the desperately needed opportunity of making a film of international potential based in England . . . [We] all came to the conclusion that with a strong executive producer and the supervision of Garth Thomas [production manager] we were justified in undertaking the financing of the film'.[79] A further $4 million was raised from Norwegian sources, which increased the total budget to £14.6 million. The casting of Al Pacino, whose fee of $3 million was twice the amount allocated for above-the-line cast, also added an estimated £600,000 to the below-the-line cost as Pacino's availability pushed back the start of principal photography by several weeks.[80]

Goldcrest soon had cause for alarm. After four weeks the cost reports indicated that the film was around £3 million over budget. Lieberson concluded that most of the additional cost 'is a result of attempting to increase the scale of the film over the agreed concept and approved budget'.[81] A month later James Lee informed Winkler that 'the existing situation is intolerable'. He explained the consequences of the escalating overcosts for Goldcrest:

> We are a comparatively small company with limited resources of bank financing. The overshoot on *Revolution* has caused us to exceed our existing credit facilities. The impact on our company has been severe, and the repercussions are serious for the British film industry as a whole. We have already had to delay the start of our next major production. We have withdrawn from another long-time commitment to a very attractive small film; and worse still I personally have been forced to ask one of our clients and closest trading partners to agree to a rescheduling of one of our obligations.[82]

Winkler – claiming (incorrectly) that the overcost was much less – replied dismissively that '[if] our £625,000 overage is a "detriment to the British film industry and those employed in it", I am truly shocked by its lack of resources'.[83] Goldcrest, which as well as financing the film was also acting as completion guarantor in partnership with Entertainment Connections, placed Garth Thomas in overall control of the production. However, Thomas reported 'that Goldcrest's instructions were being largely ignored. It was recognised that because most production costs were already committed there was only limited scope for containing the cost on the remainder of the film'.[84] Goldcrest estimated its final commitment to *Revolution* (including its liability for the completion guarantee) at £19,833,000.

Revolution premièred in New York in December 1985: it was panned so severely by the critics and performed so poorly at the box office that there was immediately chatter in the City about Goldcrest's future. Jake Eberts, who had been brought back as chief executive, tried to allay the fears: 'It's been blown out of all proportion by the national press and television. We're a small, privately-owned film and television boutique operation. The way they're carrying on you'd think we were Westland Helicopters. They have exaggerated the size of our problems and the importance of the company.'[85] Even so, Eberts worked behind the scenes to limit the damage. An internal memorandum records that 'Jake has agreed that for both publicity and business purposes, *Revolution* should be considered £2 million over budget. Although this is a "rounded out" figure, it was calculated by including into the budget a 10% contingency, a sum of £560,000 to cover the three weeks delay in starting, and the extra money involved in the more elaborate ending that Warner Brothers requested.'[86] The actual additional cost to Goldcrest against the agreed budget was closer to £5.2 million. Eberts was also obliged to put together a rescue plan: this involved reducing the company's 'inflated' operating overheads and accelerating the licensing of its films to television. And in the process several film projects (including *Mandrake the Magician*) were abandoned.

The box-office failure of *Revolution* meant that more was riding on Goldcrest's other films than had ever been intended. *Absolute Beginners* (1986) – a musical produced by Chris Brown and Stephen Woolley, directed by Julien Temple – had been a co-production between Goldcrest, Palace Pictures and Virgin Films. Goldcrest and Virgin each advanced half the £6 million budget, but Goldcrest as completion guarantor ended up with most of the £2.2 million overcost.[87] And *Absolute Beginners* was another critical and commercial flop. That left *The Mission* (1986), a second collaboration between producer David Puttnam and director Roland Joffé. Goldcrest had put up the full cost of £15.1 million for this epic costume drama, which unlike the other two films was produced with a modest overcost (£879,920, or 5.8 per cent of the budget) and was a critical success.[88] However, the failure of *Revolution* and *Absolute Beginners* had left Goldcrest over-exposed on this one film: the company therefore sold an equity interest in *The Mission* to a third party (Kingsmere Productions) in order to reduce its losses.[89] While *The Mission* fared better at the box office than the other two films, it still failed to recover its production cost. Goldcrest's shareholders agreed to write off £20 million in losses, including £10 million on *Revolution* alone. The departed James Lee 'is now being blamed for every wrong turn made by the company in its short but eventful history'.[90] Eberts came out of it as the voice of prudence: 'It doesn't make sense for any independent to make films of that size, and certainly not two at a time. That is a judgement I would make whether or not we were in our current difficulties. You need a substantial cash basis to finance those kinds of films.'[91]

The consequence of its losses was that Goldcrest withdrew from direct financing and reoriented its business towards sales and marketing. In 1986 its board of directors, having previously rejected an offer from New York-based property developer Earl Mack, accepted an offer from Masterman, a joint venture between the Brent Walker Group, with interests in leisure and property (it had ceased its involvement in film distribution some years before), and the Ensign Trust, an investment trust acting on behalf of the Merchant Navy Pension Fund.[92] Post-Goldcrest, there were mixed fortunes for the *dramatis personae*: Eberts enjoyed a successful career as an independent producer, whereas David Puttnam's tenure as head of production for Columbia Pictures in the late 1980s was anything but.

The fate of Goldcrest came to define the British film industry in the 1980s in much the same way as London Film Productions in the 1930s, the Rank Organisation in the 1940s and the Associated Communications Corporation in the late 1970s: a narrative of initial success encouraging a more ambitious international strategy leading to over-investment in expensive films in pursuit of the elusive American market whose failure at the box office spelled disaster. Yet again the City had burnt its fingers in film finance: the Pearson Longman Group, as a major shareholder in Goldcrest, bore £8.5 million of its losses in 1985.[93] The consequences – as so often before – were a loss of confidence in the film industry, falling share values and the retreat of equity capital. It was a recurring pattern that the British film industry seemed doomed to repeat throughout its turbulent history.

Notes

1. Quoted in Archie Tait, 'Distributing the Product', in Martyn Auty and Nick Roddick (eds), *British Cinema Now* (London: British Film Institute, 1985), p. 74.
2. 'Winged chariot', *The Guardian*, 31 March 1982, p. 9.
3. John Hill, *British Cinema in the 1980s: Issues and Themes* (Oxford: Clarendon Press, 1999), p. 3.
4. David Docherty, David Morrison and Michael Tracey, *The Last Picture Show? Britain's Changing Film Audience* (London: British Film Institute, 1987), pp. 1–7.
5. 'Cinema decline and its causes', *Screen International*, 9 October 1982, p. 23.
6. *National Film Finance Corporation: Annual Report and Statement of Accounts for the year ended 31 March 1982*, HC 384 1981-82 (February 1983), p. 6 (11).
7. 'Film industry – the pointers to decline', *Screen International*, 17 October 1981, p. 148.
8. '1981 UK Top 20', *Screen International*, 19 December 1981, p. 1.
9. The identical figures for *Superman II* and *For Your Eyes Only* were attributed to incomplete figures being available due to the maximum cap on Eady payments. 'Top Grossing British Films in the UK Market '80–'81', *Variety*, 13 January 1982, p. 191.
10. '1981 UK Top 20', p. 1.
11. '1982 UK Top Twenty', *Screen International*, 18 December 1982, p. 1.
12. BFI Puttnam 70: 'Chariots of Fire Participation Report' to 30 June 1982.

13. BFI Puttnam 68: Letter from Puttnam to members of the Profit Participation Fund, 21 June 1980.
14. Sarah Street, *Transatlantic Crossings: British Feature Films in the United States* (London: Continuum, 2002), p. 195.
15. BFI Puttnam 16: Anthony Jones to David Puttnam, 10 August 1982. Twentieth Century–Fox's distribution statements (BFI Puttnam 68) reveal that to 31 December 1983 it had earned total receipts of US $13,769,497 from *Chariots of Fire* in the United Kingdom, Europe and other international territories. Following deduction of Fox's distribution fee ($5,066,063) and expenses relating to shipping, duties, advertising and dubbing ($4,587,061), the original advance made to the producers ($1,014,699), interest on the advance ($1,445,026) and an additional 'supervisory fee' ($50,000), however, there still remained a deficit of $403,322.
16. TNA FV 81/194: Record of a meeting at Sanctuary House, 14 August 1979.
17. 'Lew's Back – and Embassy's Got Him!', *Screen International*, 26 June 1982, p. 1.
18. 'EMI launches $60m programme', *Screen International*, 23 May 1981, p. 1.
19. 'Spikings: A Job in US?', *Screen International*, 8 January 1983, p. 1.
20. Paul Moody, *EMI Films and the Limits of British Cinema* (London: Palgrave Macmillan, 2018), p. 202.
21. FFA Copy File General Correspondence Box 175: David Korda to Bob Storer, 25 April 1984.
22. 'Thorn EMI provides the key to critical and commercial success of Lean's "India"', *Screen International*, 16 March 1985, p. 24.
23. 'Thorn seeks film finance', *The Financial Times*, 1 December 1984, p. 4.
24. 'Success for Thorn's £18m film fund', *The Financial Times*, 10 January 1985, p. 6.
25. 'Cannon Grabs Screen Entertainment', *Variety*, 7 May 1986, p. 5.
26. BFI Reuben Library: Richard Lewis, *Review of the UK Film Industry: Report to BSAC* (London: British Screen Advisory Council, 1990), unpaginated mimeograph.
27. 'September cash guide', *Screen International*, 17 October 1981, p. 152.
28. 'Production UK', *Screen International*, 31 May 1980, p. 13.
29. 'New faces for $8m adventure', *Screen International*, 13 March 1982, p. 19.
30. *National Film Finance Corporation: Annual Report and Statement of Accounts for the year ended 31 March 1981*, HC 466 1980-81 (July 1982), p. 7 (18).
31. 'Guinness to quit film production', *Screen International*, 19 December 1981, p. 1.
32. Dan North, 'Don Boyd's *Gossip*', in Dan North (ed.), *Sights Unseen: Unfinished British Films* (Newcastle: Cambridge Scholars Publishing, 2008), pp. 169–88.
33. 'Brent Walker to the Rescue!', *Screen International*, 21 November 1981, p. 1.
34. '"Soldier": Court ruling', *Screen International*, 26 June 1982, p. 4.
35. '"Jigsaw Man" Hit By Cash Crisis', *Screen International*, 12 June 1981, p. 1.
36. 'Why I Saved "Jigsaw Man"', *Screen International*, 4 December 1982, p. 1.
37. 'Skeggs – in defence of the television spin-off', *Screen International*, 29 March 1980, p. 13.
38. Antoinette Moses, 'British Productions 1981', *Sight & Sound*, 51: 4 (Autumn 1982), p. 260.
39. 'Breaking down the old barriers', *Screen International*, 8 November 1980, p. 15.
40. 'Palace Pix Leaps Into Limelight With Smash "Company of Wolves"', *Variety*, 24 October 1984, p. 361.

41. Robert Murphy, 'Three companies: Boyd's Co., HandMade and Goldcrest', in Auty and Roddick (eds), *British Cinema Now*, pp. 48–55.
42. FFA Realised Film Box 735: *Angel*: John Boorman and Barry Blackmore to David Korda, 7 October 1981.
43. 'Macabre fairytale "Wolves" signals Palace's debut as production company', *Screen International*, 26 May 1984, p. 17.
44. Hill, *British Cinema in the 1980s*, p. 30.
45. Laura Mayne, 'Channel 4 and British Film: An Assessment of Industrial and Cultural Impact, 1982–1998' (PhD thesis, University of Portsmouth, 2014), pp. 105–6.
46. 'Producers at loggerheads over films on Four', *Screen International*, 11 June 1983, p. 50.
47. 'The Saviour of the Silver Screen', *Broadcast*, 28 October 1983, p. 13.
48. Ibid. p. 17.
49. 'The image problem of television films', *Screen International*, 9 April 1983, p. 9.
50. 'The Saviour of the Silver Screen', p. 16.
51. Ibid. p. 17.
52. 'UK finance backs success', *Screen International*, 14 May 1983, p. 13.
53. FFA Copy File Box 175: Richard Soames to Bob Storer, 23 May 1984.
54. 'The Saviour of the Silver Screen', p. 14.
55. 'Producers at loggerheads over films on Four', p. 50.
56. FFA Copy File Box 175: David Korda to Pink Pyjama Productions, 19 April 1984.
57. 'Channel Four Faces Dilemma', *Broadcast*, 1 February 1985, p. 9.
58. *She'll Be Wearing Pink Pyjamas* drew the second-highest audience (7.59 million viewers) of the 'Film on Four' strand when it was first shown in March 1987 (two years after its theatrical release), behind *Mona Lisa* (7.82 million) and ahead of *Wish You Were Here* (6.67 million), *Dance With a Stranger* (6.02 million) and *The Company of Wolves* (5.8 million). 'Film one-offs that prove a turn-off', *Broadcast*, 27 July 1990, p. 25.
59. Mayne, 'Channel 4 and British Film', p. 47.
60. 'Coyning it in for our film industry?', *Broadcast*, 14 March 1986, p. 24.
61. 'Finding the right formula', *Screen International*, 7 November 1987, p. 18.
62. 'Film Four cleans up', *Screen International*, 7 November 1987, p. 10.
63. 'Supergrass – traditional and unusual approach', *Screen International*, 30 November 1985, p. 15.
64. 'Flying the film flag', *Broadcast*, 18 September 1987, p. 26.
65. Quoted in 'Film one-offs that prove a turn-off', p. 25.
66. The best account of the history of Goldcrest is Jake Eberts and Terry Ilott, *My Indecision is Final: The Rise and Fall of Goldcrest Films* (London: Faber & Faber, 1990).
67. 'City Links for Major Line-Up', *Screen International*, 19 July 1980, p. 1.
68. Sally Dux, *Richard Attenborough* (Manchester: Manchester University Press, 2013), pp. 105–20.
69. 'Columbia Sets $12m on "Gandhi"', *Screen International*, 28 November 1981, p. 1.
70. 'Columbia adds $20m on Gandhi sales', *Broadcast*, 9 May 1983, p. 7.
71. 'Goldcrest raises £22m for new production', *Screen International*, 12 May 1984, p. 246.
72. Eberts and Ilott, *My Indecision is Final*, p. 126.
73. 'Puttnam makes a "Killing"', *Screen International*, 1 December 1984, p. 68.
74. 'Goldcrest Boost to UK Production', *Screen International*, 5 May 1984, p. 1.
75. 'Goldcrest raises £22m for new production', p. 246.
76. 'Lieberson Goes to Goldcrest', *Screen International*, 7 January 1984, p. 1.

77. 'Goldcrest presents its biggest ever line-up', *Screen International*, 1 June 1985, p. 46.
78. BFI Lieberson 14: Goldcrest Films and Television Management Committee Minutes, 17 December 1984.
79. Ibid.: 'Revolution', memorandum for Goldcrest Board of Directors, July 1985.
80. BFI Lieberson 17: James Lee to Sandy Lieberson, 23 January 1985.
81. Ibid.: Lieberson to Garth Thomas, 4 April 1985.
82. BFI Lieberson 14: James Lee to Irwin Winkler, 24 May 1985.
83. Ibid.: Winkler to Lee, 5 June 1985.
84. Ibid.: Management Committee Minutes, 20 May 1985.
85. 'Business as usual as Goldcrest board backs Eberts' survival plan', *Screen International*, 25 January 1986, p. 1.
86. BFI Lieberson 17: Thomas to Lieberson, 12 November 1985.
87. BFI Lieberson 2: Statement of Production Cost: *Absolute Beginners*, 5 October 1985.
88. BFI Lieberson 9: Statement of Production Cost: *The Mission*, 18 August 1985.
89. 'Kingsmere becomes owner of Goldcrest's £17m The Mission', *Screen International*, 12 April 1986, p. 4.
90. 'Shareholders could face £20m write-off in Goldcrest rescue', *Screen International*, 1 February 1986, p. 1.
91. 'Business as usual as Goldcrest board back Eberts' survival plan', p. 12.
92. 'Goldcrest board supports offer from joint venture', *The Financial Times*, 25 August 1987, p. 6.
93. 'Pearson profits hit by share of Goldcrest loss', *The Financial Times*, 25 August 1985, p. 6.

CHAPTER 21

The Retreat of the State

> The notion that we leave film-making to the market-place is simply ignorant. The market-place is just not big enough when you're talking about very high-risk investment... I'm afraid that unless there is government intervention then we won't have a cinema industry. Basically we will just see America on the big screen – on the few big screens left. (Mamoun Hassan)[1]

The decline of cinema admissions, the dominance of American films at the box office and the contraction of the domestic production sector in the early 1980s inevitably impacted upon the National Film Finance Corporation. In hindsight there is a sense that the corporation had been living on borrowed time ever since the election of the Thatcher government in 1979: the decision to wind up the NFFC – along with the other remaining instruments of state support for the film industry, the Eady levy and the quota – now seems an inevitable consequence of the ideological climate of the 1980s. For those on the Tory right the NFFC was a relic of the past that no longer served a useful purpose: its continued existence was incompatible with the ethos of private enterprise and free market economics. For others – especially though not exclusively on the political left – the dissolution of the NFFC and the abolition of the Eady levy symbolised the doctrinaire economics and cultural philistinism of Thatcherism. As Julian Petley observed in 1986: 'They are simply the application to the film industry of the Conservatives' avowed free market economic principles. The present government is hostile to the very notion of subsidy, and reserves a special contempt for arts subsidies.'[2] Alexander Walker was even more outspoken in his book *National Heroes*, published in the year of the NFFC's abolition: 'The Conservatives had made no secret – but rather boasted – of their intention to see subsidised undertakings pass into private hands. How ruthless they could be emerged one General Election, two Films Ministers and a great deal of fretful waiting later.'[3]

Yet as so often the story revealed by the archival record is rather more complex. Walker's suggestion that the NFFC's fate was determined from 1979 is not borne out by the official records: indeed, the new administration initially proved to be rather less ideologically hostile towards the existence of the NFFC than the previous Conservative government of Edward Heath in the early 1970s. At the outset the Thatcher government showed no interest in dismantling the NFFC. Shortly after the election, John Nott, the Secretary of State for Trade, affirmed that the government 'accepts in principle that there is a continuing role for a body to help mobilise finance for the production of British films of an indigenous character... I therefore propose to carry out more detailed consultations with a view to a financial reconstruction enabling the NFFC to carry on with a clean sheet.'[4] It was not until the Thatcher government's second term (1983–7) – the period now regarded as the high-water mark of Thatcherism – that the corporation came into the firing line. Thatcher's first term (1979–83) was less ideologically doctrinaire: the government was less secure, and the hard-line Thatcherites had yet to establish complete hegemony over the so-called Tory 'wets'.

There is even a case to be made that the new government's policy towards the film industry demonstrated some continuity with the previous Labour administration. The immediate decision that confronted Nott in 1979 was whether to replenish the capital of the NFFC or to set up a new British Film Authority on the basis suggested by the Interim Action Committee chaired by Sir Harold Wilson. For the NFFC it must have seemed like a case of *déjà vu*. On two previous occasions – in 1951 and 1970 – an outgoing Labour government had approved further funding, only for an incoming Conservative government to make changes in policy that affected the basis on which that funding was offered. However, Nott proved to be not unsympathetic to the NFFC. He recognised that the corporation had become integral to the industry and still had a role to play in supporting British production. His preference was to find other ways of financing it rather than outright abolition:

> I have come to the conclusion that there is a case on merits for a NFFC-type body to help mobilise finance for indigenous British feature films and that it would be a political mistake to do away with the NFFC and put nothing in its place. The NFFC has been part of the landscape since post-war days. On the other hand, in view of our general policies on public expenditure, I should be reluctant to propose even a small amount of continuing government finance for this purpose, or even government guarantees which should present less difficulty, if a workable alternative can be found not involving further public funds.[5]

'The interest in this subject, and the potential political difficulty if we mishandle it, is disproportionate to the amount of money involved,' Nott added. An official noted: 'We should take the maximum advantage of the breathing space the Summer Recess will give us – assuming that the recent announcement does not stimulate a lot of off-season activity.'[6]

Nott commissioned a review of the NFFC and its functions from Sir Leo Pliatzky, the senior civil servant (retired) who had been tasked with undertaking a wide-ranging review of non-departmental public bodies that would lead to the abolition of such bodies as the New Town Development Corporations, the Agricultural Wages Board and the Eggs Authority in what was dubbed the 'bonfire of the quangos'.[7] 'The review of the Government's policy towards the film industry is being conducted at an exalted level by Sir Leo Pliatzky,' a Treasury note recorded. 'Discussions have been held in the City with a view to seeing whether largely private money rather than Government money could be used to place the NFFC on a sounder footing.'[8] Pliatzky himself was a Keynesian who had no particular axe to grind with the NFFC: he had served on the Working Group on the Film Industry in 1964–5 before moving to the Treasury, where he had been involved in the previous Conservative government's review of the NFFC. There was some urgency to the review as the corporation was (as so often) desperately short of funds: in May 1979 'there was £500,000 in the kitty of which the NFFC could draw on £200,000 (40%); an Act of Parliament was required to enable the NFFC to draw the rest of the money'.[9] Pliatzky met trade representatives and Mamoun Hassan, the newly appointed managing director of the NFFC, who 'thought that the NFFC needed sufficient funds to enable it to back around ten films each year; this would enable risks to be spread'. Hassan suggested that the NFFC should look to provide between 40 and 60 per cent of the budget: as the average cost was now around £500,000, a realistic annual budget for the corporation would be in the region of £2.5 million.[10]

The outcome of Pliatzky's review was more favourable for the corporation than might have been expected. He put forward a seven-point plan for the reconstruction of financial support for the NFFC: that the government should write off all interest owed to it by the corporation (by the 1970s interest payments amounted in some years to more than the receipts from films); that it should make another £1 million available to the NFFC for 1980–1; that £1.5 million a year should be allocated to the NFFC from the proceeds of the Eady levy for a period of five years; that the Eady money would subsume the present allocation of £250,000 a year for the National Film Development Fund, which should be ended as a separate item; that the NFFC should be allowed to borrow up to £5 million from non-government sources; that this amount should be provided by the Finance Corporation for Industry following negotiation of the loan with the NFFC; and that the NFFC should either remain in being as a statutory corporation or be replaced by a limited company in which the Department of Trade would initially be the sole shareholder.[11] A key aspect of Pliatzky's reconstruction plan was that it adopted the recommendations of both the Terry Report and the Interim Action Committee to divert Eady money into funding the NFFC. However, it made no reference to the proposed British Film Authority: another non-governmental body was not likely to be on the cards at a time when the role of such bodies was under review. It was not a blueprint for the winding up of the NFFC: the corporation's future was left open and unlike the early 1970s there was no haste in wanting to transfer it to the private sector.

John Nott accepted a modified version of Pliatzky's proposals. The Department of Trade would make 'a parting gift of £1 million' to the NFFC, 'leaving them with only an increased allocation of Eady money and what they can borrow against it on the open market'. It was a compromise of sorts: the NFFC was to be cut free from public purse strings but it would continue to receive funding raised through a statutory levy. It was understood that this would in effect extend the NFFC more autonomy in deciding how to spend its funds:

> This policy decision means that the Mark II NFFC will be a very different kind of financial creature from the present one, which in turn implies some change in the existing balance of power between the Corporation and the Department. To put it crudely, we are no longer going to pay the piper (or be accountable for so doing); and this raises questions about our calling the tune.[12]

It was suggested that the NFFC might be able to borrow money from Finance for Industry (FFI), the successor to the Industrial and Commercial Finance Corporation.[13] However, Mamoun Hassan was reported to be 'not particularly enthusiastic' about this suggestion 'and was accordingly seeking to tap other sources (including equity participation)'.[14] In particular, he felt that the cost of borrowing from FFI at 2 per cent over base rate was too expensive and that '[no] film company financed high risk film production in this way'.[15] The National Westminster Bank was willing to invest but wanted a seat on the board. A representative of the National Film Finance Consortium reported that 'its record to date was not bright enough to suggest that its members would rush to invest further moneys in film production'.[16]

Pliatzky had suggested that the Eady funding should be guaranteed for five years but had not made any recommendation about the NFFC's future beyond that period. One civil service memo acknowledged that 'we clearly have to extend the powers of the NFFC to make loans to the industry . . . When we last extended the NFFC's life (in 1970) we did so for 10 years and I would advise a similar period this time. An extension of this order would inspire greater confidence in the continued existence of the NFFC; and it would, without overtly stating the Government's opposition, make Ministers' intentions absolutely clear to the pro-BFA faction.'[17] Nott had already decided against setting up the British Film Authority, but it was evidently not politic to acknowledge this directly as it was supported by former Prime Minister Sir Harold Wilson whose Interim Action Committee was still sitting. In the event, the decision was that the NFFC should be extended for five years. Another memo records: 'I think our Bill is somewhat simpler than that of 1970, but in current circumstances may well be more contentious *unless* it is possible to defuse much of the disagreement by pretending that the question of a BFA is still open (difficult when we are extending the powers of the NFFC for 5 years).'[18] Norman Tebbit, the junior minister at the Department of Trade responsible for preparing the Films Bill, remarked that 'the film industry has little economic importance but it does arouse surprisingly strong passions in various quarters.'[19]

There was evidently some urgency attached to the passage of the Films Bill. It was reported that the NFFC was 'down to its last £232,000' and it was feared that if 'the NFFC will effectively have to suspend its operations for several months while the Bill progresses through Parliament there could well be key resignations from the Corporation'.[20] The Department of Trade was anxious to move ahead with expediency in order not to deter private sector investors: 'The financial position of the NFFC is already precarious and any further delay could prove fatal to our plans . . . The balance of £128,000, plus whatever income it can achieve, will not sustain the Corporation for long.'[21] Nott urged 'that this short Bill be given priority both in drafting and during subsequent stages . . . Needless to say if our little scheme fails the NFFC will be dissolved and there could be no question of bailing it out with government money. I would prefer to avoid this difficult situation, if we possibly can.'[22] Norman St John-Stevas, the Cabinet minister responsible for planning the government's legislative programme, was sympathetic but felt that other legislation had priority.[23]

The Films Act was finally passed in July 1980. The NFFC's statutory life was extended for five years; the corporation was relieved of all its existing liabilities in respect of previous government loans; and it was to receive a final grant of £1 million with a guaranteed £1.5 million a year from the Eady levy (or 20 per cent of the annual levy yield, whichever was the greater). The NFFC welcomed the Act but at the same time cautioned that the sums 'that are, and will be, available to the Corporation are limited'. It amplified:

> The Corporation cannot therefore presume to take on the responsibility of financing the British film industry. There is no purpose in the Corporation's operating as yet another low-funded film company; nor would it be useful for it to make small token contributions to a large number of films. Instead, the Corporation has a crucial role to play in giving financial assistance to those films which seek a wide audience but which the industry considers too risky to support.[24]

In other words, the corporation was putting down a marker that it would take the opportunity offered by a more arm's-length relationship with the Department of Trade to prioritise films that struggled to raise finance on their own. This signalled a shift of policy from the National Film Finance Consortium, which had mostly favoured commercial subjects that in some cases could probably have raised their finance without the NFFC. It might also be seen as a return (of sorts) to the corporation's original remit of providing funding for producers who were unable to secure their finance through orthodox commercial channels.

Under these new conditions, even allowing for the limited funds at its disposal, the NFFC was able to contemplate a more ambitious lending policy than had been possible at any time since the early 1960s, when it had backed most of the key British new wave films. The driver of this new policy was Mamoun Hassan, who had been appointed managing director of the corporation at the beginning of 1979. Hassan, born in Saudi Arabia, had previously been head of the British Film Institute's Production Board, in which role he had supported low-budget experimental films including Bill Douglas's autobiographical trilogy (*My Childhood*, *My Ain Folk*, *My Way Home*, 1972–8) and Kevin Brownlow and Andrew Mollo's *Winstanley* (1975). Hassan liked to point out that he was the first NFFC chief from a film-making background: his three predecessors had been a banker, an accountant and a lawyer. A contemporary profile described Hassan as 'the nearest thing to a whizz-kid that this country's film Establishment has yet produced'.[25] His appointment was a radical move, as Hassan had been a vocal critic of the NFFC in the 1970s, and not all sections of the trade were enthusiastic. Ken Maidment of the British Film Producers' Association said that he 'personally was opposed to Mr Hassan's appointment, but he did not know how the BFPA felt about it. He himself felt that Mr Hassan lacked commercial experience.'[26] And W. A. Grant, chairman of the Cinematograph Films Council, thought that Hassan 'was ideologically motivated and wanted to make "social realism" films rather than "fantasy" films. Mr Grant said that he did not necessarily disapprove of the way he thought the NFFC would go under Mr Hassan's leadership; he would reserve judgement.'[27]

Unlike the urbane John Terry, Hassan was not afraid to ruffle feathers in the industry or in government. He had a public battle of words with Ken Maidment over the question of whether Eady money should be channelled through the NFFC rather than paid to distributors: 'The only way you can guarantee that Eady money will go into production is to give it to us . . . The NFFC's *raison d'être* is film production, and we would use the money solely for that purpose and not put it into bowling alleys or hotels as one suspects happens at present.'[28] His suggestion that distributors – the reference to bowling alleys and hotels makes it clear that he was referring to the Rank Organisation – did not reinvest Eady money in film production prompted a strongly worded response from Maidment, describing Hassan as 'ill-informed' and suggesting that his statements were 'wrong, misleading and mischievous . . . To say that the purpose of the Eady levy has been misunderstood, misrepresented and subverted is a slur, and an objectionable one at that, at the vast number of people and companies who over many years played a responsible part in our production activities.'[29] Hassan retorted: 'All I can say is that Ken Maidment is better at finding needles in haystacks than I am.'[30]

The loosening of the relationship between the NFFC and the Department of Trade allowed Hassan the space to impose his own views on the corporation's lending policy. The corporation's report for 1979 (not delivered for nearly a year as its future was under review) amounted to a manifesto for a new approach to state investment in the film industry. It bears Hassan's *imprimatur* much more overtly than the rather dull and straightforwardly factual reports submitted by his predecessor. Hassan argued that the traditional distinction between 'commercial' and 'art' films was mistaken as 'most film-makers operate in the indefinable area in between' and that 'the term "commercial" defines an attitude rather than a realistic expectation of returns'.[31] He further suggested that 'the Corporation's brief should be to make not only films that appeal to a popular audience, but also films that will feed ideas and innovation'.[32] Hassan suggested that the NFFC should invest in up to ten films a year, otherwise 'it would be difficult to play an effective role in improving the climate for British cinema'.[33] It would look to support films in the budget range between £500,000 and £1.5 million: its minimum investment would be 25 per cent and it was prepared to advance over half the budget for features and the full budget for shorts.

The NFFC's new direction had been signalled by its decision – in fact made shortly before Hassan's appointment but embraced enthusiastically by the new managing director – to back Merchant-Ivory Productions' *The Europeans* (1979). Indian producer Ismail Merchant and American director James Ivory were a well-established partnership who had worked together since the 1960s and were particularly associated with quality heritage films and literary adaptations. The NFFC had put up half the £450,000 budget of *The Europeans*, with additional finance from the German record company Polytel and other private investors.[34] The NFFC's significant level of support for *The Europeans* provoked some complaints that it was not a sufficiently 'British' film: its director and star (Lee Remick) were Americans, it was based on an American novel (Henry James) and most of the locations were in Massachusetts. A Department of Trade memo recorded that 'when [the] NFFC decided to support *The Europeans* it was on the understanding that Miss Vanessa Redgrave would be available to play the female lead; in the event, she withdrew for reasons not unconnected with her political actions'.[35] The NFFC felt obliged to defend its investment on cultural grounds:

> *The Europeans* was considered very carefully, particularly as to whether it was sufficiently involved in a British cultural tradition to justify the Corporation's support . . . It is important to clarify our position. The Corporation is not limited, by its terms of reference, to supporting only 'British' films, however defined. The Corporation is determined to play its part in supporting British cinema, but our commitment is not a narrow one . . .
>
> *The Europeans* was scripted by a distinguished British writer, adapted from a book by a major novelist of American origin who contributed to a British literary tradition, produced and directed by a team which has made numerous films inflecting British life, and crafted by British technicians.[36]

The Europeans met the legal definition for British quota; it also met the selection criteria for the Cannes Film Festival, where it was the official British entry in 1979. The NFFC's investment was justified on commercial grounds: *The Europeans* was reported to have earned back its negative cost from its London and Paris releases.[37]

Under Hassan's leadership, the NFFC adopted a policy of supporting emergent film-makers. The romantic comedy *Gregory's Girl* (1980) was the second feature by Scottish writer-director Bill Forsyth: it was co-financed by the NFFC and Scottish Television and was made on a 'shoestring budget' of £189,000.[38] Its commercial success meant that Forsyth was able to attract private sector investment for his next film, *Local Hero*. *Babylon* (1980) was the first feature of documentary director Franco Rosso: the budget of £300,000 was shared between the NFFC and Chrysalis Records.[39] *Memoirs of a Survivor* (1981) was the first film directed by former editor David Gladwell and the script had been supported by a grant from the National Film Development Fund: the NFFC advanced half the £800,000 budget, with EMI (which had initially rejected it) providing the other half.[40] *An Unsuitable Job for a Woman* (1982) was the second feature of Chris Petit, whose debut feature *Radio On* had been supported by the BFI Production Board: on this occasion the co-investors were Boyd's Company and Goldcrest Films. *Britannia Hospital* (1982) was an exception in so far as its director Lindsay Anderson was already established (though he had not made a film for some years): the NFFC advanced £450,000 towards the budget of £2.5 million.[41] Hassan had also wanted to support *Moonlighting* (Jerzy Skolinowski), *Heat and Dust* (Merchant-Ivory) and *Merry Christmas, Mr Lawrence* (Nagisa Oshima) but was overruled by his board.[42]

These films all to a greater or lesser degree reflected the NFFC's policy of supporting projects 'which the industry considers too risky to support'. The Eady payments give some indication of the relative success of the films: *Gregory's Girl* was by some distance the most successful (£136,859), *The Europeans* moderately so (£39,170), but there were poor returns for *Babylon* (£13,069), *Britannia Hospital* (£7,999) and *Memoirs of a Survivor* (£1,694).[43] Hassan averred that the least successful film (*Memoirs of a Survivor*) had been considered a commercial project as it was based on the work of a well-known writer (Doris Lessing) and featured a major British star (Julie Christie): 'It was aimed, as all our films are, at the popular market place. It was a gamble, as all films are. But it was the kind of gamble I felt we should take.'[44] He blamed the failure of *Britannia Hospital* on a combination of the weather and the fact that its release coincided with the outbreak of the Falklands War.[45] One correspondent to *Screen International* complained that except for *Gregory's Girl*, all the films financed by the NFFC 'since the commencement of Mamoun Hassan's reign as the managing-director have been distributed on the art-house circuit . . . All Mr Hassan is achieving with his evasive excuses that their failure is due to the general decline of cinema admissions is to drive another – if not the final nail – in the coffin of the British film industry.'[46]

Yet despite the disappointing returns of most of these films, the NFFC had in fact returned to profit. In 1981 the corporation recorded its first annual profit since the early 1960s, amounting to £2.7 million. However, this was due to the restructuring of its finances by the Films Act of 1980 rather than to its earnings from films. The profit arose largely from an 'extraordinary item of £1,965,756 due to bringing back into accounts provision for interest due but no longer owed'.[47] After the interest write-off, the profit was £737,742. More of the corporation's income came from the Eady levy (£994,303) than film receipts (£388,278). Against this were debited operating costs (£295,130) and provision for loss (£295,130). It was a different story in 1982, when the corporation recorded an operating profit of just over £1 million. This time there was no extraordinary item to distort the balance sheet. The NFFC's income amounted to £1.9 million – the full amount of £1.5 million from Eady and profits from films amounting to £460,613 – against operating costs of £374,871 and provisions for loss of £599,657.[48] And in 1983 the operating profit was £1.2 million: income had risen to £2.2 million, with profits from films amounting to £702,204, while operating costs (£454,822) and provisions for loss (£355,464) had reduced slightly overall.[49] The corporation could point to increasing profits from films in the early 1980s as evidence of the efficacy of its new investment policy, though these were due in large measure to the success of one film (*Gregory's Girl* enjoyed a highly successful reissue in 1982).

The additional funding from the Eady levy meant that the NFFC was able to make a more significant contribution to the industry than it had at any time since the 1960s. In 1982, for example, it advanced over £1 million, twice the amount available the previous year and significantly more than the limited loans it had been able to make during the 1970s. A lower total the following year (£258,931) was due to two films for which loans had been approved not being made, leaving the corporation to invest in just two features: Derek Jarman's art-house biopic *Caravaggio* and Richard Eyre's odd-couple road movie *Loose Connections* (for which the NFFC provided a third of the budget with Virgin Films making up the rest).[50] In 1984 the corporation invested £2.2 million in six features: *Dance with a Stranger*, *Defence of the Realm*, *Another Country*, *Secret Places*, *When the Wind Blows* and *The Company of Wolves*.[51] An upbeat Hassan told the press that 'for the first time since I've been with the corporation, we've got the sort of money we need to do the job properly – that is, to invest in a portfolio of films, rather than investing in one film at a time'.[52]

With the NFFC operating at a profit, with its historic debts written off, and with no further call upon public money, the corporation's dissolution in 1985 might therefore seem to run against the grain of government policy. Why did a government so committed to market forces abolish a non-government body that was operating economically and making profits? While the preferred explanation is that the dissolution of the NFFC was a political decision, the underlying reason was economic. The government had thrown the NFFC a lifeline by allocating it a share of Eady money; but in so doing it had also linked the corporation's future to the wider economic fortunes of the industry. It had not anticipated the precipitous decline in cinema admissions that followed in the early 1980s. Cinema admissions 'plummeted to a new all-time low in 1982'.[53] One of the consequences was a diminished Eady yield: the levy had peaked at £6.6 million in 1979 but collections fell to £4.5 million in 1981 and £2.7 million in 1982.[54] The NFFC's report for 1982 highlighted the extent to which production investment was now being subsidised by the exhibition sector: 'One unforeseen consequence of linking the Corporation's funding to the Eady levy is that, in straitened times, the effect of supporting one section of the industry would be to place a burden on the other. The choice is seen by some as either the survival of the cinemas or a wider spectrum of support of production, albeit at a low level, but not both.'[55]

The first indication that the future of the NFFC might be in doubt came in a Department of Trade memorandum in late 1982 regarding the reappointment of banker Graham Williams as chairman of the corporation for one year only rather than the full term: 'Unfortunately the future of the film industry in this country is particularly uncertain at present – this indeed is the principal reason why this letter seeking the Prime Minister's authority to reappoint has been delayed.' 'Moreover,' it added, 'the levy on cinema admissions, which forms the basis of the Corporation's finance, is giving rapidly declining proceeds, matching declining cinema attendance, and it is by no means clear that in light of this the current financial arrangements could continue for long.'⁵⁶ This would suggest that it was the declining pot of money from the Eady levy that put the corporation's future in doubt rather than ideological hostility from government. At the same time, films minister Iain Sproat announced a wide-ranging review of film legislation. This included the suggestion of extending the levy to video cassettes and the introduction of tax-shelter schemes along the lines of those in operation in Canada and Australia.⁵⁷ However, it was the suggestion that the levy might be scrapped that grabbed the headlines. Fiona Halton of the Association of Independent Producers responded robustly: 'The Department of Trade has shown its complete indifference to British film in the present time of crisis . . . Left to the Department of Trade, Britain looks set to lapse back to the servicing industry we have fought so hard to transcend.'⁵⁸

It was not so much that Sproat was hostile to the film industry (as sometimes claimed) but rather that he was more sympathetic to the views of exhibitors than producers. The first outcome of the review was the decision to suspend the quota with effect from 1 January 1983. This was a response to the declining number of British films, which in the early 1980s had fallen to the lowest level since the 1940s. This put pressure on exhibitors to meet their quota obligations. In 1981 the Cinematograph Films Council had reported that exhibitors were on average exceeding their quota (32 per cent compared to the statutory level of 30 per cent) but that 96 exhibitors had been reported for defaulting (none were prosecuted).⁵⁹ The Council recommended that the quota should remain at 30 per cent but the Department of Trade decided to reduce it to 15 per cent as it felt that otherwise 'shortage of British films would leave nearly every cinema in the country technically breaking the law'.⁶⁰ Sproat's subsequent decision to suspend it entirely was explained in terms of allowing more choice for exhibitors and reducing red tape: 'Taking into account the parlous state of the film industry and the serious shortage of films, I do not think the behaviour of exhibitors in showing all British and Community films they can will change, but they will be relieved of the formidable and unnecessary administrative burden.'⁶¹ Sproat lost his seat in the general election of June 1983 (one of the few Conservative MPs to do so), but the Cinematograph Exhibitors' Association continued its long-standing campaign for abolition of the levy.⁶²

In July 1984 the government published its White Paper entitled simply *Film Policy*: it was presented by Norman Tebbit (Secretary of State for Trade and Industry) and as might be expected it reeked of Thatcherite dogma. Its preamble averred that 'the bulk of the legislation currently applicable . . . is wholly inappropriate to the changed situation' of the film industry in the 1980s.⁶³ It highlighted the 'new market opportunities' for film offered by video, cable television and satellite broadcasting, and maintained that the existing support apparatuses for the industry had been 'introduced when protectionist instincts were stronger than today'.⁶⁴ It weighed up the pros and cons of the levy, but in the end resolved that 'the existing Eady levy is an unreasonable burden on the cinema exhibitors, and [we] have decided that it should be removed completely'.⁶⁵ (The White Paper considered – and rejected – two alternatives to abolition. One was to reduce the amount of the levy: this was not considered appropriate as it would provide no more than temporary respite for exhibitors and would reduce the amounts available for the National Film and Television School and the BFI Production Board. The other was to find replacement funding from other sources: however, the television companies were spared because it was felt the ITV companies were already paying a significant levy on their advertising receipts.) It recognised that abolition of the levy would cut off the main source of funding for the NFFC, whose primary role it understood to be the support of new talent: therefore it proposed that the government would contribute £1.5 million a year for five years towards a private company in association with other industry partners to continue this aspect of the corporation's activities. The White Paper intended that the company 'will be run on commercial lines, although it is recognised that the rates of return required may be somewhat below those normally sought and therefore a correspondingly higher level of risk may be taken with some of the projects supported'.[66] Other recommendations included the abolition of the Cinematograph Films Council, maintaining the film development fund with a grant of £500,000 per year, and to find alternative finance for the National Film and Television School from the BBC and ITV companies.

The White Paper marked a fundamental shift in film policy: it proposed nothing less than the dismantling of the entire apparatus of state support for the film industry that had been built up since the Cinematograph Films Act of 1927. It was full of rhetoric about enabling creative enterprise by removing bureaucratic impediments and state controls. It sought to place its recommendations in the wider context of government policy:

> It is part of a new outlook in which the Government intends to shift its approach to the film industry away from the statutory intervention of the last 30 years and towards the creation of the right business investment. This policy is part of, and wholly consistent with, the Government's approach to industry generally ... The package of measures now proposed is designed to consolidate the change that has taken place, and to encourage its development. It will remove the need to take money away from any part of the industry itself and thus avoid cumbersome and bureaucratic regulatory mechanisms.[67]

The conclusion – that the paper was intended 'to free the creative talents and business skills of those involved in the providing of entertainment by way of feature films and to ensure that new talent is encouraged to come forward' and that the policies it laid out 'are policies of freedom and challenge' – reflected the very essence of the Thatcherite project.

Responses to the White Paper from the industry were more or less as expected. The Cinematograph Exhibitors' Association welcomed the abolition of the levy, which it regarded as moribund, but the unions and producers' associations were unhappy. Ken Maidment told *Screen International*: 'By sweeping away the existing legislation relating to films (eight Acts of Parliament and 25 statutory implements are scheduled to be repealed) we will end up with there being no such thing as a British picture ... [We] will lose the identity of the British film industry.'[68] Mamoun Hassan, who announced his resignation following publication of the White Paper, made a stinging critique accusing the government of bad faith:

> To subject us all to a review when the decision had already been made and all that was being sought was the language of the execution is pretty disgraceful because we are dealing with people's lives and careers. I never felt that anyone took a blind bit of notice of anything I said. The evidence was never sifted, it was simply blocked, and any outside view was taken as evidence of delinquency.[69]

The NFFC had been subject to many previous reviews and had come close to being abolished several times before, under both Labour and Conservative governments; but this time there was no R. B. Tippetts or Leo Pliatzky to argue the case for its continuation.

The White Paper formed the basis of the Films Bill presented to Parliament early in 1985. *The Financial Times* described it as a 'simple seven-clause Bill'.[70] It passed through Parliament with little controversy. Labour's trade spokesman Bryan Gould argued in favour of continued state support – 'It is unusual, even for this Government, to introduce a measure that has received such a hostile reception from those whose interests it is meant to advance' – but the government's large majority would always have carried the day even if had been more of a priority for the Opposition.[71] The House of Commons asked for more information about the proposed successor company – which the new Secretary of State for Trade and Industry Norman Lamont referred to as 'the son of NFFC' – and suggested that it should be a 'partnership' rather than a limited company.[72] An amendment proposed in the House of Lords that the NFFC should be retained funded by a levy on the sale of films to television was defeated.[73] For Sarah Street – co-author of a history of British film policy entitled *Cinema and State* published in 1985 – the Films Bill 'seeks to expose the industry to the chill winds of market forces by dismantling all state support for British film'.[74] However, John Hill argues that the dissolution of the NFFC was a consequence of the historic failure 'to lay the foundations for a commercially successful film industry'.[75]

The passing of the Films Act had left unresolved the nature of 'the son of NFFC'. In May 1985 the Department of Trade informed the Treasury 'of the general intention of the Department to enter into an agreement with a private successor body to the National Film Finance Corporation. The new body has not yet been formed, but it is intended that it will go by the name of the British Screen Finance Consortium and will be a limited partnership under English law.'[76] The plan was for the Department of Trade to provide an annual grant of £1.5 million for a period of five years, plus a further £500,000 a year for the same period to support pre-production development and short films. Therefore the government that had wanted to end state subsidy for the film industry committed itself to providing another £10 million over five years. A month later, Norman Lamont was able to confirm more details:

> [It is] my intention to dissolve the National Film Finance Corporation with its functions being largely carried by a private successor-company. Channel Four, Thorn-EMI, the Rank Organisation and the British Videogram Association are forming a company (The British Screen Finance Consortium) for this purpose. They intend to put finance into BSFC which will be used, together with a £1.5 million per annum contribution from DTI and the income which is generated in the portfolio of rights in the films financed by the NFFC, to make loans to film producers to make new films.[77]

The Department of Trade reinforced the point that 'the £1.5 million annual grant is for five years only and we would be opposed to the continuation of any grant beyond this time'.[78] The consortium was set up as a private company, rather than as a limited partnership as first proposed, to allow it to qualify for tax relief under the terms of the Finance Act of 1981.[79] A further nuance was that the Department of Trade's £1.5 million per annum would be in the form of a loan rather than a grant: this was actually a way of reducing the tax liabilities of the BSFC as a grant would have incurred a tax penalty. A memorandum of agreement was drawn up between the Department of Trade and the BSFC whereby the latter would take over the assets and liabilities of the NFFC upon its dissolution.[80]

The setting up of the BSFC highlighted one of the weaknesses of the Conservative government's faith in the free market. In introducing the Films Bill, Lamont had spoken of 'the impressive strength of the British film industry' – he specifically mentioned *Local Hero*, *Educating Rita* and *The Dresser* as 'notable successes' – and referred to Thorn-EMI as 'one of our major production companies . . . investing up to £25 million in new films this year'.[81] However, within a year Thorn-EMI would announce its withdrawal from film financing and the sale of its Screen Entertainment Division to the Cannon Group: the new owner did not continue with the investment. And at the end of 1985 there was still some doubt about the participation of the British Videogram Association in the consortium.[82]

The NFFC was formally dissolved on 31 October 1985. Ironically its last full year of operation had been one of its most successful. In 1985 the NFFC returned a profit of over £1.5 million. In the same year it had invested £1.6 million in four features: *Comrades*, *No Surrender*, *The Girl in the Picture* and *A Room With a View*. Merchant-Ivory's *A Room With a View* (1986) – continuing the producers' cycle of heritage films and the first of a triptych of adaptations of E. M. Forster – turned out to be one of the most successful films in the corporation's history. *A Room With a View* exemplified the complex political economy of the film industry by this time in so far as it was a six-way co-production between Merchant-Ivory Productions, the NFFC, Goldcrest Films, Film Four International, Curzon Film Distributors and Cinecom. The last partner put up the largest share (45 per cent) of the production budget of £2.2 million.[83] The NFFC's contribution is not included in its annual report but would not have been less than 25 per cent. *A Room With a*

View had also received a grant of £15,000 from the National Film Development Fund to support the writing of the screenplay. After six months on release, the film returned a distributor's gross of £2,026,304 in Britain.[84] It also returned US $14 million from North America and was reported to be 'the most profitable art-house picture ever shown in the United States'.[85]

The success of *A Room With a View* highlights the anomaly of a body such as the NFFC by the 1980s. On the one hand the film's success demonstrated that the corporation was capable of backing winners and justified its approach of investing in a portfolio of films in so far as the profits of *A Room With a View* made up for losses on the other films it had supported at the same time. On the other hand the film's success could be cited in support of the argument that the NFFC was no longer needed as here was an example of a film standing on its own feet in the marketplace. Ismail Merchant regretted the demise of the NFFC but felt that the outlook for the film industry was positive: 'Things are certainly improving in Britain, even if it's a shame that the Government has changed the character of the NFFC, which was so important for we independent producers.'[86]

Yet in truth the success of *A Room With a View* was both too little and too late for the NFFC. It had been involved in only seventeen completed features between 1980 and 1985: this was significantly less than the ten films a year envisaged by Mamoun Hassan in 1979. It highlighted what a marginal role the corporation now played in British film finance compared to the days when it had supported between a half and a third of all British features. While critics deplored the philistinism of a government that considered the film industry as a commercial activity first and foremost, and paid scant regard to its cultural and artistic status, this is to ignore the fact that the origin of the NFFC had been rooted in an entirely economic context and that any cultural remit it had acquired over the decades had arisen through its own funding priorities. The NFFC had been set up to provide temporary relief for a beleaguered production sector that was desperately short of finance: the fact that the same shortage persisted four decades later demonstrates the long-term failure of the film policy of successive governments to create a more stable economic base for the British film industry.

Notes

1. 'Hassan slams Government attitude to UK film industry', *Screen International*, 13 October 1984, p. 16.
2. Julian Petley, 'Cinema and State', in Charles Barr (ed.), *All Our Yesterdays: 90 Years of British Cinema* (London: British Film Institute, 1986), p. 40.
3. Alexander Walker, *National Heroes: British Cinema in the Seventies and Eighties* (London: Harrap, 1985), p. 267.
4. *Parliamentary Debates: House of Commons*, 5th Series, vol. 971, 26 July 1979, cols 395–6.
5. TNA FV 81/194: John Nott to Geoffrey Howe, 19 July 1979.
6. Ibid.: D. Doyle to R. F. Coker, 27 July 1979.
7. Michael Cole, 'Quangos: The Debate of the 1970s in Britain', *Contemporary British History*, 19: 3 (2005), pp. 321–52.

8. TNA FV 81/194: Doyle to Haddinott, 18 July 1979.
9. TNA FV 81/190: Note of Sir Leo Piatzky's meeting with Mr Hassan on 21 May 1979.
10. Ibid.
11. TNA FV 81/194: 'Financial Reconstruction of the National Film Finance Corporation: Outline Plan', n.d.
12. Ibid.: A.C.G. Lewis to Doyle, 2 August 1979.
13. 'NFFC Looks to Private Funds', *Screen International*, 28 July 1979, p. 8.
14. TNA FV 81/194: Derek Eagers to Doyle, 14 August 1979.
15. Ibid.: Record of a meeting at Sanctuary Buildings on 14 August 1979.
16. Ibid.: Eagers to Coker, 28 August 1979.
17. TNA FV 81/199: K. M. Long to Doyle, 6 September 1979.
18. Ibid.: Long to Eagers, 9 October 1979.
19. Ibid.: Norman Tebbit to Norman St John-Stevas, 14 September 1979.
20. Ibid.: Long to Eagers, 9 October 1979.
21. Ibid.: Eagers to Private Secretary, Secretary of State for Trade, 11 October 1979.
22. Ibid.: John Nott to Norman St John-Stevas, 17 October 1979.
23. The Films Bill was also delayed pending the outcome of an action brought by the European Commission – the executive arm of the EEC – which had been threatening for some time to refer state subsidies for film production to the European Court of Justice under Article 169 of the Treaty of Rome. It was not just Britain in the dock: subsidy schemes in France, Italy, Denmark and the Federal Republic of Germany were also deemed to be in breach of EEC regulations regarding free movement of labour, as they stipulated a minimum percentage of labour costs should be paid to citizens of a specific country. The British government got around this by amending the quota regulations to extend eligibility to include any films produced in an EEC member state. 'Eady Inquiry Halts Films Bill', *Screen International*, 1 March 1980, p. 4.
24. *National Film Finance Corporation: Annual Report and Statement of Accounts for the year ended 31 March 1980*, HC 793 1979-80 (October 1980), p. 5 (7).
25. Nigel Andrew, 'New direction for film-makers', *The Financial Times*, 2 June 1979, p. 8.
26. TNA FV 81/190: Note of Sir Leo Pliatzky's meeting with Mr Maidment on 24 May 1979.
27. Ibid.: Note of Sir Leo Pliatzky's meeting with Mr Grant, n.d.
28. 'Hassan speaks out on Eady', *Screen International*, 3 March 1979, p. 11.
29. 'The BFPA replies to Mamoun Hassan', *Screen International*, 24 March 1979, p. 4.
30. 'Eady cash: Hassan hits back at all the critics', *Screen International*, 7 April 1979, p. 64.
31. *National Film Finance Corporation: Annual Report and Statement of Accounts for the year ended 31 March 1979*, HC 456 1978-79 (March 1980), p. 5 (4).
32. Ibid. p. 5 (5).
33. Ibid. p. 6 (7).
34. 'ICM has "Europeans"; Merchant-Ivory for Cannes Fest', *Variety*, 18 April 1979, p. 4.
35. TNA FV 81/190: Derek Eagers to Sir Leo Pliatzky, 23 May 1979.
36. *NFFC Annual Report 1979*, p. 9 (26–8).
37. 'See Fast Recoup on "Europeans"; Producer Rues British Put-Down', *Variety*, 26 December 1979, p. 4.
38. 'Keeping flag flying with black comedy', *Screen International*, 5 September 1981, p. 31.
39. 'Patois and mike', *Screen International*, 8 March 1980, p. 41.
40. 'Anatomy of a "Survivor"', *Screen International*, 24 January 1981, p. 25.

41. Antoinette Moses, 'British Production 1981', *Sight & Sound*, 51: 4 (Autumn 1981), p. 260.
42. 'NFFC To Step Up Investment', *Screen International*, 1 October 1983, p. 2.
43. 'Eady Distributions', *Screen International*, 12 March 1983, p. 14. I was not able to find the Eady payment for *An Unsuitable Job for a Woman*.
44. 'NFFC – taking a chance', *Screen International*, 5 June 1982, p. 19.
45. 'NFFC – our fears for the future', *Screen International*, 31 July 1982, p. 24.
46. 'NFFC evasion' (L. Lloyd), *Screen International*, 28 August 1982, p. 4.
47. *National Film Finance Corporation: Annual Report and Statement of Accounts for the year ended 31 March 1981*, HC 466 1980-81 (March 1982), p. 5 (3).
48. *National Film Finance Corporation: Annual Report and Statement of Accounts for the year ended 31 March 1982*, HC 384 1981-82 (February 1983), p. 5 (3).
49. *National Film Finance Corporation: Annual Report and Statement of Accounts for the year ended 31 March 1983*, HC 545 1982-83 (July 1984), p. 5 (3).
50. 'The Italian connection', *The Guardian*, 7 July 1983, p. 11.
51. *National Film Finance Corporation: Annual Report and Statement of Accounts for the year ended 31 March 1984*, HC 512 1983-84 (July 1985), p. 5 (2).
52. 'NFFC investment plans', *Screen International*, 24 September 1983, p. 2.
53. 'New UK admissions low, but US looks rosy', *Screen International*, 15 January 1983, p. 1.
54. *British Film Fund Agency: Annual Report and Statement of Accounts for the fifty-two weeks ended 15 October 1983*, HC 616 1982-83 (23 October 1984), p. 5 (4).
55. *NFFC Annual Report 1982*, p. 6 (10).
56. TNA T 488/160: John Whitlock to Tim Flesher, 25 November 1982.
57. 'The end of Eady?', *The Economist*, 13 November 1982, p. 52.
58. 'Shock Review Stuns Industry', *Screen International*, 13 November 1982, p. 1.
59. *Cinematograph Films Council: Forty-third Annual Report for the year ended 31 March 1981*, HC 468 1980-81 (20 October 1981), p. 5 (17).
60. 'Quota danger', *Screen International*, 8 August 1981, p. 2.
61. 'Quota Is Axed!', *Screen International*, 24 July 1982, p. 1.
62. 'CEA to fight on over levy', *Screen International*, 18 June 1983, p. 2.
63. *Film Policy*, Cmnd. 9319 (July 1984), p. 1 (1.2).
64. Ibid. p. 5 (3.1).
65. Ibid. p. 12 (5.11).
66. Ibid. p. 15 (7.4).
67. Ibid. pp. 12–13 (5.12–5.13).
68. 'White Paper brings immediate response from unconvinced industry', *Screen International*, 28 July 1984, p. 6.
69. 'Hassan slams Government attitude to UK film industry', p. 16.
70. 'A £10m five-year programme', *The Financial Times*, 7 November 1985, p. 15.
71. *Parliamentary Debates: House of Commons*, 6th Series, vol. 68, 19 November 1984, col. 29.
72. *Parliamentary Debates: House of Commons*, 6th Series, vol. 72, 5 February 1985, col. 755.
73. *Parliamentary Debates: House of Lords*, 6th Series, vol. 460, 7 March 1985, col. 1451.
74. Sarah Street, 'A Bill to kill the British film industry', *The Guardian*, 1 February 1985, p. 19.
75. John Hill, 'Government Policy and the British Film Industry 1979–90', *European Journal of Communications*, 8: 2 (1993), p. 222.
76. TNA T 631/140: I. K. Mathers to Lucas, 24 May 1985.

77. TNA T 631/92: Norman Lamont to John Moore, 24 June 1985.
78. Ibid.: Eileen Conn to Moore, 25 June 1985.
79. Ibid.: Lamont to Moore, 31 July 1985.
80. TNA T 631/140: Draft Agreement between the Secretary of State for Trade and Industry and the British Screen Finance Consortium, n.d.
81. *Parliamentary Debates: House of Commons*, 6th Series, vol. 68, 19 November 1984, col. 29.
82. 'Video industry input for BSFC confirmed', *Screen International*, 14 December 1985, p. 32.
83. 'Merchant-Ivory's "Room" continues long-standing producer-director-scriptwriter collaboration', *Screen International*, 8 June 1985, p. 24.
84. 'Room passes £2m', *Screen International*, 18 October 1986, p. 2.
85. 'Britain's film industry discovers that small is profitable', *The Economist*, 28 February 1987, p. 81.
86. 'Merchant-Ivory's "Room" continues . . .', p. 24.

Conclusion

> At one time, film and cinema used to go together like, well, Laurel and Hardy. No longer. Film financing has been hard hit. Film production, similarly. The government's White Paper on Film Policy is the culmination of a series of blows. At the other end of the distribution chain, film exhibition is fragmented and helpless. (*Sight & Sound*)[1]

There was a sense in the mid-1980s that the fortunes of the British film industry had reached a new nadir. The vanishing cinema audience, the contracting domestic production sector, the collapse of Goldcrest and the withdrawal of Thorn-EMI from the film business contributed to a general sense of malaise. The dismantling of state support represented by the abolition of the Eady levy and the winding up of the National Film Finance Corporation confirmed that the government had finally abandoned any policy of continuing to prop up the ailing industry. There was no better indication of the decline of the British film industry since the heyday of Alexander Korda and the Rank Organisation than the fact that the most active financing and production group in the mid-1980s was the film arm of a television broadcaster specialising in low-cost films (Channel Four Films). British cinema was a shadow of its former self: it had become little more than a cottage industry producing a handful of films a year for a domestic market that more than ever was dominated by American interests.

Against this background the promotion of 'British Film Year' in 1985–6 now seems at best ironic and at worst utterly hubristic. This was an industry-led initiative to promote the idea of cinema-going: its aim was 'to attract the lost millions back to the cinemas'.[2] British Film Year involved a series of events – screenings, exhibitions, festivals and workshops – co-ordinated through the British Film Institute and the network of regional film theatres across the United Kingdom. In many respects it recalled the 'British Film Weeks' of 1924, not least in that it offered a cultural response to what was really an economic crisis in the film industry.[3] It would probably be fair to say that the sort of film culture promoted by British Film Year was as much rooted in the heritage of British cinema than its contemporary present: the first official event was the royal première of David Lean's *A Passage to India* – a recent example of the tradition of quality literary adaptation that represented the culturally respectable face of British cinema – and its chair Sir Richard Attenborough, Academy Award-winning producer and director of *Gandhi*, was a respected elder statesman whose career as an actor and film-maker represented a link back to British cinema's 'golden age' of the 1940s.

Indeed, British Film Year can be seen as reflecting the history of the film industry in Britain. For one thing, it was precariously financed. As a commentator in *Sight & Sound* wryly observed: 'For some months the BFY organisers struggled to put together an act which looked like being crippled by shortage of cash and uncertainty about when funds would come through. (The government, criticised for offering only a measly £325,000, at least stumped up on time.)'[4] In that sense it resembled the production of so many independent British films. The campaign's budget of slightly over £1 million came from a consortium that as well as the government's contribution included distribution interests (£500,000), exhibitors (£100,000) and 'other film interests' (£121,000).[5] With most British distributors scaling back their operations by the mid-1980s, the lion's share of the distributors' contribution came from American interests whose hegemony of the distribution sector was one of the consequences of the eclipse of the large British producer-distributors. And there were very different assessments of how successful (or not) British Film Year was. On the one hand its advocates could point to an increase in cinema attendances during 1985 as evidence that the campaign to attract the public back into cinemas had met with some success; on the other hand the fact that this increase was largely on the back of American films – including *Back to the Future*, *Rambo: First Blood Part II* and *Ghostbusters* – suggested that there was no real revival for British film-making. This reflected a wider uncertainty over the objectives of British Film Year: it was never entirely clear whether the aim was to promote cinema-going in general or to raise awareness of British films. As a correspondent to *Screen International* wrote: 'I can only presume that the apparent lack of awareness [of British Film Year] is largely attributed to media indifference to the film industry.'[6]

It may be debated whether the crisis of the mid-1980s was really any different from the other crises that have characterised the history of the British film industry and have been documented in this book. The withdrawal of state support was a unique factor: this had been threatened several times before but for various reasons had never materialised. And added to the challenge of television – a thorn in the side of the film industry since the 1950s – was the rise of the market for home video cassettes. In other key respects, however, the crisis shared many common features with others that had gone before. British producers, buoyed by the success of a few exceptional films, overreached themselves in an ultimately futile attempt to compete with Hollywood on its own terms; investors burned their fingers and became wary of the film industry; consequently the production sector was faced with a shortage of capital and all producers experienced difficulty in raising their finance. And underlying it all was the perennial paradox of the British film industry: that the domestic market was simply too small to return a profit to producers. Even Channel 4 looked to ancillary markets (video, television) and international sales when budgeting its low-cost films.

In the introduction I set out the three interlinked themes of *The Money Behind the Screen*: the institutional and economic structure of the British film industry; the sources of film finance; and the role of government in supporting the British domestic production sector. It will be clear from this study that all those aspects of the British cinema landscape underwent profound and far-reaching changes between the end of the Second World War and the 1980s. From a structural perspective the British film industry was transformed during this period from a duopoly where two combines (the Rank Organisation and ABPC/EMI) held a hegemony over production, distribution and exhibition to a much more fragmented industry. The combines had ensured a certain degree of stability for the industry in so far as they had been able to sustain their own production programmes – whether through direct financing or, more usually, through provision of distribution guarantees for independent producers – while their extensive exhibition interests allowed them to offset losses incurred on film-making. The combines had adjusted to previous crises by instituting economies in production and by closing their less remunerative cinemas. But even the combines could not stave off the effects of the decline of cinema-going forever: diminishing revenues from their cinemas eventually brought about their withdrawal from production. Thorn-EMI was the last vertically integrated British film corporation: its decision to sell off its Screen Entertainment Division was due as much to declining profits from exhibition as it was to losses on production.

The sources of film finance also changed fundamentally over this period. In the 1940s the vast majority of British films were wholly British-financed – either by one of the major production groups from their own resources or through distribution guarantees – with only a small number of British quota films funded by American distributors. The conditions for the increasing level of US investment in the British production sector were established by the Anglo-American Film Agreement of 1948 and the introduction of the Eady levy in 1950: the availability of what in effect amounted to a subsidy for British-based production through the levy was a more important factor here than the utilisation of Hollywood's frozen funds. Over the following two decades the political economy of the British film industry was transformed to the extent that by the mid-1960s American finance accounted for the majority of British films, including most of the commercially successful films. However, the scaling down of US investment in the early 1970s left the British industry economically impoverished as British financial sources (including the NFFC) were not able to fill the gap left by the Americans. In the 1970s the shift to distribution pre-sales and consortium financing brought new players including merchant banks and investment trusts into the field of film finance. A consequence of this process was the emergence of what might be described as a polyglot financing model: it is now a rare occurrence that a British film has only one source of finance.

The period covered by *The Money Behind the Screen* also spans the entry – and subsequent withdrawal – of the state into the provision of film finance. A comprehensive history of the National Film Finance Corporation remains to be written, but it is possible here to make some general observations. The circumstances that brought the NFFC into existence were historically specific: it was intended to be a measure of temporary support until the production sector was put onto a more secure economic footing. The fact that it became a semi-permanent feature of the fiscal structure of the British film industry was as much a consequence of the industry's weakness as the corporation's success. It undoubtedly saved the British Lion Film Corporation from halting production entirely – and as British Lion was the main alternative to the Rank/ABPC duopoly its survival at this point was necessary for the continuation of a competitive industry – and it was credited with encouraging a more economical approach to production as well as supporting independent producers through the provision of end money loans. There is no doubt that the NFFC was a major player in film finance throughout the 1950s: indeed, it may be argued that producers became too dependent upon it. From the 1960s, however, its importance declined and the NFFC became a marginal presence in the industry: it supported fewer films and was insufficiently resourced to make more than a token contribution to the financing of film production. It was probably fortunate to survive successive reviews in the 1960s and early 1970s. The NFFC had been conceived in response to one crisis in the industry and it was disbanded as a consequence of another: in truth, it had outlived its usefulness long before the axe fell in 1985.

The history of the British film production industry has been one of recurring crises. At the heart of all those crises has been the shortage of production finance. A recurring theme of *The Money Behind the Screen* is that most British films have been loss-makers: to this extent the question is not so much why British producers have so often struggled to raise finance but rather why investors have continued to invest in film production at all given the uncertainty of public taste and the ratio of success to failure. The Bond pictures are the only British films for which box-office success is guaranteed. Otherwise the most successful British films – including *The Private Life of Henry VIII, The Red Shoes, Hamlet, The Dam Busters, The Bridge on the River Kwai, The Guns of Navarone, Lawrence of Arabia, Tom Jones, Chariots of Fire* and *Gandhi* – were all in some way exceptional: they exemplify what the American screenwriter William Goldman described as the 'non-recurring phenomenon'.[7] What I hope *The Money Behind the Screen* has demonstrated is that there is more to the history of British film finance than just the exceptional films that feature so prominently in most histories of British cinema and that the politics of film finance have played a much more important role in shaping the history of British cinema than has hitherto been acknowledged.

Notes

1. John Howkins, 'British Film Year', *Sight & Sound*, 54: 1 (Winter 1984), p. 8.
2. 'British Film Year officially underway', *Screen International*, 23 March 1985, p. 4.

3. See Andrew Higson, 'The Discourses of British Film Year', *Screen*, 27: 1 (1986), pp. 86–110.
4. 'Kockenlocker', 'Double Takes: British Film Year', *Sight & Sound*, 55: 2 (Spring 1986), p. 95.
5. 'Deloitte Hoskins & Sells report says British Film Year has been a success', *Screen International*, 21 December 1985, p. 10.
6. 'British Film Year – still a mystery to the public' (letter from John Wolstenholme of United Media), *Screen International*, 6 July 1985, p. 6.
7. William Goldman, *Adventures in the Screen Trade: A Personal View of Hollywood and Screenwriting* (London: Macdonald, 1984), p. 50.

APPENDIX I

Production Costs and Revenues of Selected Feature Films in the Late 1940s

Early in 1950 the Board of Trade requested details of production costs, distributors' receipts and producers' shares from the four main production groups: the Rank Organisation, British Lion Film Corporation, the Associated British Picture Corporation and Ealing Studios. There were some differences in how the groups presented the information: for example, Rank included both domestic and overseas receipts, whereas the others presented receipts for the home market only.

THE RANK ORGANISATION

Source: TNA BT 64/4490: J. Arthur Rank Organisation Ltd: Memorandum regarding information required by the Board of Trade regarding Film Production and Distribution, Schedule VI. The films included in the schedule were (a) the most profitable film for each quarter (or the least unprofitable where no film made a profit), (b) the closest film to the average for the quarter, and (c) the biggest loss-maker per quarter. The 'UK receipts' listed here are the producers' shares from the home market, 'overseas receipts' are the producers' shares from other markets. The combined producer's share must be more than the cost of production for the film to have made a profit.

Film	Cost	UK receipts	Overseas receipts	Total
Great Expectations (1946)	£391,600	£222,600	£190,200	£412,800
Green for Danger (1946)	£202,400	£114,700	£61,100	£175,800
The Hungry Hill (1947)	£375,600	£133,200	£40,800	£174,000
The Man Within (1947)	£161,800	£81,000	£74,200	£155,300
The Root of All Evil (1947)	£155,000	£71,300	£19,400	£90,700
Take My Life (1947)	£211,800	£75,200	£51,700	£126,900
The Upturned Glass (1947)	£196,000	£156,000	£85,800	£241,000
Holiday Camp (1947)	£150,400	£141,900	£24,500	£166,400
The Brothers (1947)	£162,900	£73,500	£33,700	£107,200
End of the River (1947)	£217,400	£69,600	£69,800	£139,400
The Woman in the Hall (1947)	£201,200	£97,900	£19,900	£117,800
Uncle Silas (1947)	£366,300	£70,500	£12,200	£82,700
Easy Money (1948)	£116,800	£98,600	£20,400	£119,000
Blanche Fury (1948)	£382,200	£145,300	£101,500	£246,800

Film				
The Mark of Cain (1948)	£253,400	£70,000	£5,800	£75,800
Miranda (1948)	£170,400	£143,400	£32,600	£176,000
Broken Journey (1948)	£197,000	£91,300	£41,800	£133,100
One Night With You (1948)	£236,200	£53,700	£9,500	£63,200
My Brother's Keeper (1948)	£113,600	£81,200	£23,000	£104,200
Mr Perrin & Mr Traill (1948)	£190,700	£67,200	£18,900	£86,100
London Belongs To Me (1948)	£271,300	£93,400	£19,700	£113,100
Oliver Twist (1948)	£371,500	£277,300	£103,100	£380,400
The Weaker Sex (1948)	£175,200	£92,700	£13,100	£105,800
Esther Waters (1948)	£338,600	£33,600	(£700)	£32,900
Portrait from Life (1949)	£132,800	£93,000	£43,900	£136,900
The Passionate Friends (1949)	£346,800	£83,500	£135,900	£219,400
The History of Mr Polly (1949)	£253,500	£70,900	£10,500	£81,400
The Blue Lagoon (1949)	£311,100	£186,500	£164,900	£351,400
Marry Me (1949)	£117,900	£38,200	£12,100	£50,300
The Bad Lord Byron (1949)	£223,900	£31,200	£13,500	£44,700

Another two 'exceptional' films were listed separately:

The Red Shoes (1948)	£505,600	£179,900	£1,111,400	£1,291,300
Hamlet (1948)	£572,500	£187,800	£1,164,400	£1,352,200

BRITISH LION FILM CORPORATION

Source: TNA BT 64/4493: British First Feature Films Released Through British Lion Film Corporation Ltd during 30 months to 30 June 1949. 'UK revenues' here refer to the distributor's gross receipts: no overseas revenues were included.

Film	Cost	UK revenues	Producers' share
The Shop at Sly Corner (1947)	£76,715	£124,197	£92,877
White Cradle Inn (1947)	£135,000	£99,666	£72,473
The Courtneys of Curzon Street (1947)	£315,810	£328,668	£238,731
Man About the House (1947)	£304,521	£166,075	£111,820
An Ideal Husband (1948)	£506,000	£215,155	£149,559
Mine Own Executioner (1948)	£295,000	£143,632	£101,963
Nightbeat (1948)	£175,118	£118,578	£90,028
Anna Karenina (1948)	£553,000	£135,341	£95,687
Call of the Blood (1948)	£66,295	£45,713	£33,401
Spring in Park Lane (1948)	£238,000	£370,000	£280,193
The Winslow Boy (1948)	£425,915	£216,000	£159,034
The Fallen Idol (1948)	£397,568	£203,000	£150,553
The Small Voice (1948)	£121,000	£80,000	£59,844
Bonnie Prince Charlie (1948)	£760,000	£155,570	£94,327

Elizabeth of Ladymead (1949)	£298,654	£129,700	£84,073
The Small Back Room (1949)	£232,972	£104,00	£75,537
Forbidden (1949)	£100,000	£68,400	£50,680

ASSOCIATED BRITISH PICTURE CORPORATION

Source: BT 64/4492: Associated British Pathé: UK Distribution: Analysis of contracts played to 1 April 1950. 'UK revenues' are the distributor's gross receipts.

Film	Cost	UK revenues	Producers' share
While the Sun Shines (1947)	£110,840	£98,984	£62,807
Temptation Harbour (1947)	£133,174	£106,226	£72,026
Silver Darlings (1947)	£94,731	£33,783	£21,836
Brighton Rock (1947)	£192,436	£147,124	£94,902
My Brother Jonathan (1948)	£193,851	£226,362	£142,813
Bond Street (1948)	£163,629	£104,588	£59,611
Noose (1948)	£136,500	£119,229	£74,918
The Guinea Pig (1948)	£252,418	£173,052	£121,824
Silent Dust (1948)	£149,854	£105,859	£66,979
Queen of Spades (1948)	£232,500	£47,282	£17,678
For Them That Trespass (1948)	£150,232	£71,954	£38,467
Man on the Run (1948)	£110,090	£64,453	£35,947
Private Angelo (1948)	£218,713	£36,994	£19,489

EALING STUDIOS

Source: BT 64/4491: Ealing Studios Ltd: Collection of information about overhead costs and earnings of British films. The 'UK receipts' refer to distributor's gross receipts.

Film	Cost	UK receipts	Producers' share
Nicholas Nickleby (1947)	£146,069	£139,313	£106,427
Hue and Cry (1947)	£104,222	£96,812	£87,796
The Loves of Joanna Godden (1947)	£167,073	£82,908	£59,642
Frieda (1947)	£168,435	£227,017	£184,055
It Always Rains on Sunday (1947)	£180,936	£229,834	£188,247
Against the Wind (1947)	£202,330	£94,995	£81,436
Saraband for Dead Lovers (1948)	£371,205	£87,338	£59,034
Scott of the Antarctic (1948)	£371,599	£214,223	£165,967
Another Shore (1948)	£180,936	£35,371	£24,804
Eureka Stockade (1948)	—	£55,855	£40,258
Passport to Pimlico (1949)	£276,787	£104,444	£81,436
Whisky Galore! (1949)	£128,715	—	—
Kind Hearts and Coronets (1949)	£224,853	—	—

Train of Events (1949)	£144,978	—	—
A Run for Your Money (1949)	£141,221	—	—
The Blue Lamp (1950)	£142,304	—	—
Dance Hall (1950)	£167,749	—	—

APPENDIX II

National Film Trustee Company: Production Costs and Receipts

The National Film Trustee Company was set up in 1971 to collect revenues for NFFC-sponsored films, though it was also used by distributors of some non-NFFC films. The table lists the production costs and distributor's receipts (combined domestic and overseas) to 31 December 1978.

Source: TNA FV 81/191.

Film	Cost	Distributor's receipts
Under Milk Wood (1971)	£273,279	£15,862
Fright (1971)	£127,555	—
Ooh . . . You Are Awful (1972)	£201,443	£267,173
Endless Night (1972)	£250,197	£345,269
The Lovers (1972)	£62,228	£177,649
The Love Ban (1973)	£98,121	£110,093
The Final Programme (1973)	£222,143	£291,885
Akenfield (1974)	£120,094	£931
Overlord (1975)	£89,951	£41,007
The Romantic Englishwoman (1975)	£784,476	£844,198
Monty Python and the Holy Grail (1975)	£282,035	£2,358,229
Bugsy Malone (1976)	£574,953	£1,373,964
Jabberwocky (1976)	£587,668	£479,219
James Dean: The First American Teenager (1976)	£99,558	£148,618
Black Joy (1977)	£31,720	£87,576
The Sailor's Return (1978)	—	£46,152
The Shout (1978)	—	£176,806
Carry On Emmannuelle (1978)	£349,302	£48,003

APPENDIX III

Budgets and Costs of Selected British First Features Guaranteed by Film Finances

The Film Finances Archive includes budgets and cost reports for most of the films for which it provided a guarantee of completion. The budget figures listed here are those identified as the 'agreed budget' in the letter of intent issued by Film Finances (an undertaking in principle to guarantee the film) which was sometimes adjusted from the budget submitted by the producer. The cost is the last 'estimated final cost' from the cost reports supplied by producers, except in cases marked with an asterisk (*) where it is a certified final cost from a chartered accountant. The final cost is not included where the archival materials are incomplete or contradictory.

Film	Budget	Cost
The Woman in Question (1950)	£129,986	—
Another Man's Poison (1951)	£93,844	£106,096
High Treason (1951)	£154,850	£168,325
Valley of Eagles (1951)	£134,977	£136,113
Angels One Five (1952)	£144,208	£143,222
Curtain Up (1952)	£83,736	£67,945
The Gift Horse (1952)	£167,272	£218,784
Moulin Rouge (1952)[1]	£300,000	£434,264*
Women of Twilight (1952)	£47,280	£49,216
Albert, RN (1953)	£84,292	£88,378
Appointment in London (1953)	£136,244	£125,689
The Beggar's Opera (1953)	£300,631	£379,697
Cosh Boy (1953)	£37,160	£38,537
Decameron Nights (1953)	£83,897	£94,552
Genevieve (1953)	£114,937	£124,658
Innocents in Paris (1953)	£140,158	£161,462
The Red Beret (1953)[2]	£176,328	£209,980*
The Beachcomber (1954)	£182,351	£171,776
The Black Knight (1954)[3]	£297,728	—
Dance Little Lady (1954)	£74,895	£76,669
Eight O'Clock Walk (1954)	£47,958	£49,216
Father Brown (1954)	£135,585	£122,018
Hell Below Zero (1954)[4]	£211,000	£247,512
Lilacs in the Spring (1954)	£239,971	£297,746
The Sea Shall Not Have Them (1954)	£162,420	£165,857

Star of India (1954)[5]	£111,135	£133,185
The Stranger's Hand (1954)[6]	£125,516	£164,200
Above Us the Waves (1955)	£165,772	£158,772
Cockleshell Heroes (1955)[7]	£240,473	£267,406
Footsteps in the Fog (1955)[8]	£115,000	£112,118
Josephine and Men (1955)	£129,905	£123,345
A Kid for Two Farthings (1955)	£197,889	£198,120
King's Rhapsody (1955)[9]	£380,215	£403,718
Oh . . . Rosalinda!! (1955)	£276,328	£255,445
A Prize of Gold (1955)[10]	£203,954	£209,671
Three Men in a Boat (1955)	£191,579	£247,137
Richard III (1955)	£443,209	£452,057
The Gamma People (1956)	£71,177	£85,060
The Iron Petticoat (1956)[11]	£187,595	£189,803
The Man Who Never Was (1956)[12]	£227,262	£212,274
Odongo (1956)	£102,500	£121,093
Private's Progress (1956)	£143,647	£161,069
Reach for the Sky (1956)	£326,630	£365,499
Safari (1956)[13]	£274,372	£299,609
Three Men in a Boat (1956)	£191,579	£247,517
Action of the Tiger (1957)[14]	£183,734	£248,383
The Admirable Crichton (1957)	£202,819	£221,884
The Battle of the River Plate (1957)	£274,071	£275,348
Lucky Jim (1957)	£165,186	£172,289
Quatermass II (1957)	£113,421	£117,731
The Smallest Show on Earth (1957)	£135,279	£144,834
Time Without Pity (1957)	£104,906	£108,875
Yangtse Incident (1957)	£261,090	£290,374
Behind the Mask (1958)	£169,776	£164,162
The Key (1958)	£376,163	£412,843
The Man Who Wouldn't Talk (1958)	£135,762	£127,582*
Orders to Kill (1958)	£173,552	£170,832
tom thumb (1958)[15]	£184,027	£235,415
Blind Date (1959)[16]	£137,328	£139,841
The Bridal Path (1959)	£158,717	£162,634
Carlton-Browne of the FO (1959)	£219,276	£211,633*
Danger Within (1959)	£197,181	£178,111*
Dentist in the Chair (1959)	£97,935	£86,033
Expresso Bongo (1959)	£149,468	£156,082
Room at the Top (1959)	£227,779	£231,387*
The Battle of the Sexes (1960)	£135,175	£133,435
The 'Beat' Girl (1960)	£76,919	£79,840
City of the Dead (1960)	£44,966	£47,341
Cone of Silence (1960)	£132,129	£139,342

Title	Cost	Final
The Entertainer (1960)	£196,628	£205,870*
The League of Gentlemen (1960)	£175,434	£179,602
Peeping Tom (1960)	£130,921	£133,394
Saturday Night and Sunday Morning (1960)	£114,980	£116,848*
A Terrible Beauty (1960)	£250,000	£241,732
The Trials of Oscar Wilde (1960)	£269,546	£296,500
Tunes of Glory (1960)	£271,165	£267,731
Two-Way Stretch (1960)	£115,500	£118,677
A Change of Heart (1961)	£127,968	£121,457
The Day the Earth Caught Fire (1961)	£190,818	£213,581
The Kitchen (1961)	£26,983	£27,246
A Taste of Honey (1961)	£120,940	£120,329
Dr No (1962)	£321,227	£392,022*
A Kind of Loving (1962)	£148,000	£145,820
Lancelot and Guinevere (1962)	£494,746	£690,970*
The Valiant (1962)	£181,000	£245,439
The Wrong Arm of the Law (1962)	£220,852	£233,570
Billy Liar (1963)	£209,000	£219,227
French Dressing (1963)	£171,664	£179,467
The Leather Boys (1963)	£106,000	£106,271
The Mind Benders (1963)	£210,781	—
The Servant (1963)	£141,725	£138,005
Tom Jones (1963)[17]	£412,374	—
The VIPs (1963)	£982,142	£1,071,314
What a Crazy World (1963)	£130,161	£121,191
Dr Terror's House of Horrors (1964)	£107,375	£105,209
King and Country (1964)	£82,728	£85,785*
Nothing But the Best (1964)	£176,500	£175,594
Zulu (1964)	£688,672	£653,439
Darling (1965)	£353,949	£392,449
Dr Who and the Daleks (1965)	£135,000	£159,054
The Ipcress File (1965)	£309,261	£304,978
Cul de Sac (1966)	£129,974	£170,938
Deadlier Than the Male (1966)	£540,683	£588,597
Kaleidoscope (1966)	£475,737	£482,109
Morgan: A Suitable Case for Treatment (1966)	£164,913	£191,674
Passage of Love (1966)	£169,200	—
The Quiller Memorandum (1966)	£956,359	£912,757
The Sandwich Man (1966)	£250,000	£189.334
Accident (1967)	£299,772	£281,555
Battle Beneath the Earth (1967)	£116,110	£156,307
The Bobo (1967)	£985,061	c. £1,117,000
The Jokers (1967)	£228,725	£275,512
The Long Duel (1967)[18]	£1,056,211	£1,069,669

Maroc 7 (1967)[19]	£316,000	£399,835*
Poor Cow (1967)	£242,607	£228,206
Pretty Polly (1967)	£589,434	£601,841
Robbery (1967)	£357,143	£395,338
The Terrornauts (1967)	£86,792	£85,332
Ulysses (1967)	£222,269	—
The Bofors Gun (1968)	£165,000	£171,058
Boom! (1968)	£1,531,224	£1,913,650
Can Heironymous Merkin Ever Forget Mercy Humppe and Find True Happiness? (1968)	£443500	£486,790
Charlie Bubbles (1968)	£324,151	£318,483
Isadora (1968)	£1,283,942	£1,484,021
A Touch of Love (1969)	£282,389	£304,512
Age of Consent (1969)[20]	£371,451	—
Lock Up Your Daughters (1969)	£755,423	£878,986
The Last Grenade (1970)	£1,203,574	£1,126,552
The Go-Between (1971)	£532,841	£468,098
Mr Forbush and the Penguins (1971)	£564,725	£625,113
Straw Dogs (1971)	£922,710	£1,055,829

Notes

1. *Moulin Rouge* was a dual-budget picture: the additional dollar budget was $160,000 covering the fees of director John Huston and stars José Ferrer and Zsa Zsa Gabor.
2. *The Red Beret* was a dual-budget picture: the additional dollar budget was $315,000, which covered star Alan Ladd, producers Irving Allen and Cubby Broccoli, screenwriter Richard Maibaum and American publicity costs.
3. *The Black Knight* was a dual-budget picture: the additional dollar budget covered star Alan Ladd (who deferred his fee of $450,000), director Tay Garnett and producers Irving Allen and Albert R. Broccoli. There is no recorded final cost as the guarantee was cancelled by agreement between Film Finances and Columbia Pictures.
4. *Hell Below Zero* was a dual-budget picture: the additional dollar budget covered star Alan Ladd, producers Irving Allen and Albert R. Broccoli, director Mark Robson and screenwriter Richard Maibaum.
5. *Star of India* was a treble-budget picture: in addition to the sterling budget there was an Italian budget (35,689,000 lire) and a dollar budget in an unspecified amount that covered star Cornel Wilde and director Arthur Lubin.
6. *The Stranger's Hand* was an Anglo-Italian co-production: the sterling budget was £77,525, with the balance provided in lira by the Italian co-production partner. The certified sterling cost came to £92,235.
7. *Cockleshell Heroes* was a dual-budget picture: the additional dollar budget covered star/director José Ferrer and producers Irving Allen and Albert R. Broccoli.
8. *Footsteps in the Fog* was a dual-budget picture: the additional dollar budget of $453,000 covered the cost of stars Stewart Granger and Jean Simmons, director Arthur Lubin and screenwriters Leonora Coffee and Dorothy Davenport. It is not clear from the file

whether co-producer Mike Frankovich was included in the dollar or sterling budget. Maxwell Setton appears to have been the effective producer.

9. *King's Rhapsody* was a treble-budget picture in which the sterling budget was £227,680, with Errol Flynn's fee paid in dollars and a Yugoslavian contribution towards location costs.
10. *A Prize of Gold* was a dual-budget picture: the additional dollar budget covered star Richard Widmark and producers Irving Allen and Albert R. Broccoli. The sterling budget included location expenditure in German Marks (equivalent to £9,070).
11. *The Iron Petticoat* was a dual-budget picture: the additional dollar budget of $500,000 covered stars Bob Hope and Katharine Hepburn. Independent Film Distributors advanced the full sterling budget and $100,000 of the dollar budget, which was converted into sterling.
12. *The Man Who Never Was* was a dual-budget picture: the additional dollar budget 'not to exceed $280,400' included the story rights and services of producer André Hakim and stars Clifton Webb and Gloria Graham. The living expenses of Hakim, Webb and Graham were included in the sterling budget.
13. *Safari* was a dual-budget picture: the additional dollar budget covered stars Victor Mature and Janet Leigh and producers Irving Allen and Albert R. Broccoli.
14. *Action of the Tiger* was a dual-budget picture: the sterling budget included location expenditure in Spanish pesetas. The dollar budget was $750,000.
15. *tom thumb* was a dual-budget picture: MGM agreed to increase the sterling budget from £184,027 to £194,027 and the dollar budget from $180,000 to $205,275 after shooting had commenced. The dollar budget was again adjusted upwards to $226,022 after completion of filming.
16. *Blind Date:* Film Finances' letter of intent (19 March 1959) includes a clause that the budget 'will be adjusted so as to provide for the period of studio occupation to be over a full 8 weeks'.
17. *Tom Jones*: the completion guarantee was cancelled by mutual agreement between Film Finances, United Artists and Woodfall Films. The film is estimated to have cost £480,000 to complete.
18. *The Long Duel*: the final cost included an unspecified amount (possibly up to £46,000) arising from an abortive plan to shoot in India.
19. The budget of *Maroc 7* was adjusted upwards to £326,000 during production in order to allow a sequence planned for the studio to be shot on location.
20. *Age of Consent*: the budget is in dollars (US $1,040,062): £371,451 was the sterling equivalent in 1969. There is no record of the final cost.

APPENDIX IV

National Film Finance Corporation: Accounts, 1950–1985

This appendix summarises the accounts provided in the annual reports of the National Film Finance Corporation between 1950 and 1986. The accounts refer to the twelve months ending 31 March, except for the first year where it covers the eighteen months from 1 October 1948 to 31 March 1950. The table includes: the total number of films (features and shorts) for which advances were made each year; the total value of loans; the corporation's profit or loss for the year; and the accumulated year-on-year balance of the corporation's lending history.

The NFFC had no capital of its own: it was funded by loans from the Board of Trade (later the Department of Trade) plus whatever income it received from interest on loans and its share in the box-office receipts of films. Its borrowing history may be summarised as follows:

Cinematograph Film Production (Special Loans) Act 1949:	£5 million
Cinematograph Film Production (Special Loans) Amendment Act 1950:	£1 million
Cinematograph Film Production (Special Loans) Amendment Act 1952:	£2 million*
Films Act 1970:	£5 million+
Films Act 1980:	£1 million

* The additional £2 million made available under the Cinematograph Film Production (Special Loans) Amendment Act of 1952 was to be borrowed from non-government sources.
+The £5 million made available by the Films Act 1970 was over a period of ten years.

Year	Films	Loans	Profit/Loss	Balance
1948–50	63	£3,743,325	- £702,252	N/A
1950–1	73	£1,467,897	- £675,850	- £699,345
1951–2	78	£1,210,967	+ £10,891	- £1,375,195
1952–3	73	£1,468,698	- £45,851	- £1,410,155
1953–4	55	£1,545,246	- £158,573	- £2,600,495 *
1954–5	54	£1,730,901	- £211,020	- £3,750,515 +
1955–6	39	£1,125,767	+ £79,132	- £3,682,813
1956–7	67	£1,414,037	+ £84,727	- £3,598,086

1957–8	65	£1,941,213	- £116,443	- £3,714,529
1958–9	58	£1,788,135	- £222,367	- £3,936,896
1959–60	67	£1,575,515	- £194,095	- £4,130,997
1960–1	35	£927,504	+ £18,441	- £4,112,550
1961–2	53	£1,034,396	+ £49,564	- £4.062,986
1962–3	47	£1,687,964	- £219,867	- £4,282,853
1963–4	20	£473,149	- £701,120	- £4,209,989 #
1964–5	15	£464,102	- £265,555	- £4,359,844
1965–6	23	£1,083,592	- £292,245	- £4,563,561
1966–7	17	£936,161	- £369,699	- £4,933,260
1967–8	9	£258,851	- £199,098	- £5,092,358
1968–9	8	£778,208	- £149,239	- £5,158,564
1969–70	11	£861,622	- £386,126	- £5,344,674
1970–1	14	£687,063	- £189,277	- £5,536,858
1971–2	2	£438,371	- £709,512	- £6,246,370
1972–3	4	£356,437	- £399,631	- £6,646,001
1973–4	1	£126,820	- £457,244	- £7,100,338
1974–5	8	£321,432	- £286,164	- £7,386,502
1975–6	1	£364,039	- £331,660	- £7,718,162
1976–7	5	£432,500	- £403,789	- £8,121,951
1977–8	5	£927,982	- £432,566	- £8,554,517
1978–9	6	£600,149	- £1,191,060	- £9,745,583
1979–80	2	£468,657	- £1,296,050	- £11,041,633
1980–1	5	£592,318	+ £2,703,498	- £8,338,135
1981–2	6	£1,031,831	+ £1,032,520	
1982–3	3	£258,931	+ £1,391,918	
1983–84	8	£2,207,604	+ £1,018,513	
1985	11	£1,645,168	+ £1,520,794	

* The significant increase in the accumulated deficiency in 1953–4 over the previous year was due to the NFFC increasing its anticipated provision for loss on its loan to the British Lion Film Corporation.

+ The significant increase in the accumulated deficiency in 1954–5 over the previous year was due to the NFFC underwriting the share issue of the restructured British Lion Films.

The reduction of the overall deficiency in 1963–4 despite the large loss for the year was due to the sale of the NFFC's interest in British Lion Films.

The NFFC's debts were written off by the Films Act of 1980 and therefore no longer included in the corporation's annual reports after 1980–1.

APPENDIX V

Feature Films supported by the National Film Finance Corporation, 1949–1985

This appendix is a chronological list of all the completed feature films supported by loans from the National Film Finance Corporation (and its predecessor the National Film Finance Company) between its inception in 1948 and its abolition in 1985. It does not include loans agreed for films but not taken up. The NFFC's annual reports listed films by distributor and production company (until 1955) and then by production company: here they are listed alphabetically by title. Note that the year in which a loan was approved does not necessarily correspond to the year in which the film was released.

1948–50: Loans to distributors and producers approved to 31 March 1950

The Adventurers; The Adventures of PC 49; Angel With the Trumpet; Blackmailed; The Body Said No; Cairo Road; Celia; Children of Chance; The Clouded Yellow; The Cure for Love; Dark Interval; The Dark Light; Double Confession; The Elusive Pimpernel; The Galloping Major; Give Us This Day; Golden Arrow; Gone to Earth; The Happiest Days of Your Life; Happy Go Lovely; Her Favourite Husband; Honeymoon Deferred; I'll Get You For This; The Interrupted Journey; The Last Days of Dolwyn; The Late Edwina Black; The Man in Black; Maria Chapdelaine; Maytime in Mayfair; Meet Dr Morelle; Meet Simon Cherry: Midnight Episode; Miss Pilgrim's Progress; Morning Departure; Mr Drake's Duck; My Daughter Joy; Odette; Old Mother Riley – Headmistress; Over the Garden Wall; Pandora and the Flying Dutchman; The Romantic Age; Saints and Sinners; School for Randle; Seven Days to Noon; Shadow of the Eagle; She Shall Have Murder; Skimpy in the Navy; State Secret; That Dangerous Age; The Third Man; The Third Victorian; Tony Draws a Horse; The Twenty Questions Murder Mystery; Up for the Cup; Waterfront; What a Carry On; The Woman in Question; The Woman With No Name; The Wonder Kid: The Wooden Horse; Your Witness.

1950–1: Loans to distributors and producers approved since 31 March 1950

Angels One Five; Appointment With Venus; Blind Man's Bluff; The Browning Version; Circle of Danger; Cheer the Brave; The Chelsea Story; Cry the Beloved Country; The Dark Man; Flesh and Blood; Green Grow the Rushes; Hell is Sold Out; High Treason; Hotel Sahara; Into the Blue; Laughter in Paradise; Lilli Marlene; The Long Dark Hall; Madame Louise; The Magic Box; Murder in the Cathedral; Never Take No for an Answer; Night Without Stars; No Resting Place; Old Mother Riley's Jungle Treasure; Outcast of the Islands; The Scarlet Thread; The Second Mate; So Little Time; Take Me to Paris; The Tales of Hoffmann; There is Another Sun; White Corridors; Tom Brown's Schooldays; Worm's Eye View.

1951–2: Loans to distributors and producers approved since 31 March 1951
The African Queen; The Armchair Detective; Brandy for the Parson; The Brave Don't Cry; The Card; Come Back, Peter; Cosh Boy; The Cruel Sea; Curtain Up; Derby Day; Distant Trumpet; The Fake; Emergency Call; Father's Doing Fine; The Gentle Gunman; The Gift Horse; Hammer the Toff; The Holly and the Ivy; Home at Seven; Hot Ice; Hunted; I Believe in You; I'm A Stranger; The Importance of Being Earnest; It Started in Paradise; Judgement Deferred; Lady Godiva Rides Again; The Lady With a Lamp; Little Big Shot; The Love Lottery; Made in Heaven; Mandy; Meet Me Tonight; Miss Robin Hood; Mr Denning Drives North; Moulin Rouge; Night Was Our Friend; No Haunt for a Gentleman; Old Mother Riley Meets the Vampire; The Penny Princess; The Planter's Wife; Private Information; Reluctant Heroes; The Ringer; Salute the Toff; Scrooge; The Second Mrs Tanqueray; Sing Along With Me; Something Money Can't Buy; Song of Paris; The Sound Barrier; South of Algiers; Time Gentlemen, Please!; The Titfield Thunderbolt; Top Secret; Tread Softly; Treasure Hunt; Trent's Last Case; Twice Upon a Time; Venetian Bird; Who Goes There?; The Woman's Angle; Women of Twilight; The Yellow Balloon; You're Only Young Twice.

1952–3: Loans to distributors and producers approved since 31 March 1952
Alf's Baby; All Halloween; Always a Bride; The Angel Who Pawned Her Harp; Appointment in London; Background; The Beggar's Opera; The Broken Horseshoe; The Captain's Paradise; Child's Play; Circumstantial Evidence; The Conquest of Everest; Death Goes to School; Desperate Moment; The Final Test; Flannelfoot; Folly to be Wise; Front Page Story; The Girl on the Pier; The Heart of the Matter; Hindle Wakes; House of Blackmail; Innocents in Paris; The Intruder; Laxdale Hall; The Long Memory; The Maggie; The Malta Story; Man of Africa; The Man Between; Meet Mr Lucifer; Meet Mr Malcolm; Murder at 3 a.m.; The Night Won't Talk; Operation Malaya; The Oracle; The Queen's Colours; Royal Heritage; Small Town Story; The Square Ring; The Story of Gilbert and Sullivan; The Straw Man; Street Corner; There Was a Young Lady; They Who Dare; Three Steps in the Dark; Top of the Form; Turn of the Key; The Wedding of Lilli Marlene; West of Zanzibar.

1953–4: Loans to distributors and producers approved since 31 March 1953
Albert, RN; Bang! You're Dead; The Beachcomber; Beautiful Stranger; The Belles of St Trinian's; The Blue Parrot; Burnt Evidence; Conflict of Wings; The Constant Husband; Dance Little Lady; Dangerous Cargo; The Devil Girl From Mars; Devil on Horseback; The Devil's Pass; The Divided Heart; The End of the Road; Eight O'Clock Walk; Forbidden Cargo; Golden Ivory; The Good Die Young; The Green Scarf; The Harassed Hero; Hobson's Choice; An Inspector Calls; Lease of Life; Make Me an Offer; Malaga; The Man Who Loved Redheads; The Master Plan; Profile; The Sea Shall Not Have Them; The Stranger's Hand; Three Cases of Murder; A Time to Kill; Tomorrow is Sunday; The Traitor; Trilby; The Weak and the Wicked.

1954–5: Loans to distributors and producers approved since 31 March 1954
Above Us the Waves; Aunt Clara; Before I Wake; The Blue Peter; Break in the Circle; Carrington, VC; Charley Moon; Cloak Without Dagger; The Colditz Story; The Delavine

Affair; Double Cross; Escapade; Fairy Story; The Feminine Touch; Final Appointment; The Gelignite Gang; Geordie; Heir at Large; I Am A Camera; John and Julie; Josephine and Men; King's Rhapsody; The Ladykillers; The Long Arm; The Love Match; Miss Tulip Stays the Night; Mr Pastry; The Naked Flame; Oh . . . Rosalinda!!; Port of Escape; The Quatermass Experiment; Raising a Riot; Room in the House; See How They Run; Stock Car; The Teckman Mystery; They Can't Hang Me; To Dorothy a Son; Touch and Go; Who Done It?; A Yank in Ermine; You Lucky People.

1955–6: Loans to producers approved since 31 March 1955

The Baby and the Battleship; Breakaway; Child in the House; Dry Rot; The Extra Day; Fun at St Fanny's; The Gentleman Corsican; Guilty; A Hill in Korea; High Terrace; Home and Away; I'll Take the High Road; It's a Great Day; It's a Wonderful World; It's Never Too Late; Keep it Clean; Loser Takes All; Man in the Road; The March Hare; My Teenage Daughter; The Narrowing Circle; Pacific Destiny; Private's Progress; Ramsbottom Rides Again; Return to the Desert; The Secret Tent; Stars in Your Eyes; Stolen Assignment; Table in the Corner; Three Men in a Boat; Tons of Trouble; The Weapon; Yield to the Night.

1956–7: Loans to producers approved since 31 March 1956

The Abominable Snowman; After the Ball; At the Stroke of Nine; The Birthday Present; The Booby Trap; Brothers in Law; Carry On Admiral; Clean Sweep; The Crooked Sky; The Curse of Frankenstein; Davy; Face in the Night; Kill Me Tomorrow; Law and Disorder; Light Fingers; Lucky Jim; The Mailbox Robbery; The Man From Tangier; The Man in the Sky; Manuela; Mark of the Pheonix; Morning Call; Next To No Time; Not Wanted on Voyage; The Passionate Stranger; The Scamp; The Shiralee; The Smallest Show on Earth; The Steel Bayonet; Stormy Crossing; Stranger in Town; The Surgeon's Knife; Suspended Alibi; That Woman Opposite; These Dangerous Years; Time Without Pity; The Tommy Steele Story; A Touch of the Sun; The Traitor; The Truth About Women; Vicious Circle; West of Suez; Woman in a Dressing Gown; You Pay Your Money; Yangtse Incident.

1957–8: Loans to producers approved since 31 March 1957

The Bank Raiders; Barnacle Bill; Battle of the V1; Behemoth the Sea Monster; Behind the Mask; Black Ice; Blind Spot; Blood of the Vampire; The Camp on Blood Island; Carry On Sergeant; Cat Girl; The Crowning Touch; Death Over My Shoulder; The Diplomatic Corpse; Dracula; Dublin Nightmare; The Duke Wore Jeans; Dunkirk; The End of the Line; Family Doctor; Fiend Without a Face; The Golden Disc; Happy is the Bride; The Haunted Strangler; The Heart Within; Hidden Homicide; House in the Woods; I Was Monty's Double; In the Wake of a Stranger; Intent to Kill; The Key; The Lady is a Square; The Man in the Room; The Man Who Liked Funerals; The Man Who Wouldn't Talk; Murder at Site 3; The Nightcomers; No Cover for Harry; No Trees in the Street; Nowhere To Go; Orders to Kill; The Passionate Summer; The Revenge of Frankenstein; Room at the Top; Sea of Sand; The Secret Man; The Silent Enemy; 6.5 Special; She Didn't Say No; Shamus; The Snorkel; The Spaniard's Curse; Them Nice Americans; Tread Softly Stranger; The Trollenberg Terror; Undercover Girl; Up the Creek; Virgin Island; The Whole Truth; Wonderful Things; Zoo Baby.

1958–9: Loans to producers approved since 31 March 1958

And the Same to You; Beyond This Place; Breakout; The Bridal Path; Broth of a Boy; Carlton-Browne of the FO; Carry On Nurse; Carry On Teacher; Danger Within; Deadly Record; The Doctor's Dilemma; Follow That Horse; Friends and Neighbours; Further Up the Creek; The Heart of a Man; The Hound of the Baskervilles; I Only Arsked; I'm All Right, Jack; Jack the Ripper; Jet Storm; Left, Right and Centre; Long Distance; Life in Danger; Life in Emergency Ward 10; Life is a Circus; The Man Who Could Cheat Death; The Mummy; The Rough and the Smooth; Sapphire; Serious Charge; The Siege of Pinchgut; S.O.S. Pacific; The Stranglers of Bombay; Subway in the Sky; This Other Eden; Tiger Bay; Tommy the Toreador; A Touch of Larceny; The Ugly Duckling; Violent Moment; Winter Quarters; Yesterday's Enemy.

1959–60: Loans to producers approved since 31 March 1959

The Angry Silence; The Beat Girl; Beyond the Curtain; The Big Day; Bottoms Up; Carry On Constable; Cone of Silence; The Challenge; City of the Dead; Danger Tomorrow; Dentist in the Chair; Desert Mice; Don't Panic Chaps!; Echo of Barbara; The Entertainer; Faces in the Dark; The Flesh and the Fiends; Foxhole in Cairo; The French Mistress; The Full Treatment; The Hand; Hell is a City; His and Hers; Just Joe; The League of Gentlemen; Linda; The Long and the Short and the Tall; The Man in the Back Seat; The Man Who Couldn't Walk; Never Let Go; Never Take Sweets from a Stranger; The Night We Dropped a Clanger; Not a Hope in Hell; Peeping Tom; Piccadilly Third Stop; Please Turn Over; The Professionals; Saturday Night and Sunday Morning; The Savage Innocents; The Siege of Sidney Street; Snowball; Sword of Sherwood Forest; The Terror of the Tongs; Too Young to Love; The Trouble with Eve; The Two Faces of Dr Jekyll; The White Trap.

1960–1: Loans to producers approved since 31 March 1960

The Breaking Point; The Damned; The Day the Earth Caught Fire; Don't Bother to Knock; Double Bunk; Fury at Smugglers' Creek; The Gentle Trap; Hair of the Dog; The Hellfire Club; The Impersonator; Jungle Street; The Kitchen; A Matter of Who; Nearly a Nasty Accident; Out of the Shadow; Over the Odds; A Question of Suspense; Rag Doll; The Sleepwalkers; Spare the Rod; Taste of Fear; Ticket to Paradise; Two and Two Make Six; A Weekend With Lulu; What a Carve Up!; What a Whopper!; The Wind of Change.

1961–2: Loans to producers approved since 31 March 1961

Ambush in Leopold Street; The Amorous Prawn; Bank Raid; Band of Thieves; The Barber of Stamford Hill; The Boys; Break; Dead Man's Evidence; Decoy; Dock Brief; Doomsday at Eleven; Enter Inspector Duval; Emergency; Flight for Singapore; Freedom to Die; The Golden Rabbit; A Guy Called Caesar; The Iron Maiden; Jailbreak; Jigsaw; Journey to Nowhere; Live Now, Pay Later; The Man Who Finally Died; Mix Me a Person; Mrs Gibbons' Boys; Night Without Pity; Operation Snatch; The Painted Smile; The Pirates of Blood River; Pit of Darkness; The Playboy of the Western World; Private Potter; A Prize of Arms; Serena; Seven Keys; Some People; Stranglehold; Take Me Over; Tomorrow at Ten; The Traitors; We Joined the Navy.

1962–3: Loans to producers agreed since 31 March 1962
Bomb in the High Street; Breath of Life; Calculated Risk; The Comedy Man; Danger By My Side; Dilemma; Echo of Diana; The Eyes of Annie Jones; Farewell Performance; The Fur Collar; The Girl in the Headlines; Hide and Seek; It's All Happening; Impact; The King's Breakfast; Ladies Who Do; The Leather Boys; Live it Up!; Lunch Hour; Maniac; The Marked One; The Mind Benders; Night of the Prowler; Nightmare; Nothing But the Best; The Old Dark House; The Party's Over; A Place to Go; The Scarlet Blade; The Servant; The Silent Playground; Sparrows Can't Sing; Station Six – Sahara; Summer Holiday; The Switch; Touch of Death; Two Left Feet; Wanted for Money; West 11; The World Ten Times Over.

1963–4: Loans to producers approved since 31 March 1963
Blind Corner; Catacombs; The Curse of the Mummy's Tomb; The Devil-Ship Pirates; Devils of Darkness; Dr Terror's House of Horrors; Four in the Morning; French Dressing; The Gorgon; The Hijackers; Saturday Night Out; Shadow of Fear; The Sicilians; The Soldier's Tale; The Uncle; Where Has Poor Mickey Gone?

1964–5: Loans to producers approved since 31 March 1964
Be My Guest; Darling; Dr Who and the Daleks; Joey Boy; The Little Ones; Morgan – A Suitable Case for Treatment; The Night Caller; Rotten to the Core; Smokescreen; Three Hats for Lisa; 24 Hours to Kill; Up Jumped a Swagman.

1965–6: Loans to producers approved since 31 March 1965
Accident; Cul-de-Sac; Daleks' Invasion Earth 2150 AD; The Great St Trinian's Train Robbery; He Who Rides a Tiger; I Was Happy Here; Maroc 7; The Projected Man; Romeo and Juliet; The Sandwich Man; A Study in Terror; Theatre of Death; They're a Weird Mob; The Trap; We're Wrestling Tonight; The Yellow Hat.

1966–7: Loans to producers approved since 31 March 1966
Don't Lose Your Head; The Family Way; Miss Mactaggart Won't Lie Down; Night of the Big Heat; Poor Cow; Press for Time; Run With the Wind; Stranger in the House; Two Weeks in September; The Witches; Ulysses.

1967–8: Loans to producers approved since 31 March 1967
The Girl on a Motorcycle; The Green Shoes; Negatives; Taste of Excitement; Till Death Us Do Part; Two Gentlemen Sharing.

1968–9: Loans to producers approved since 31 March 1968
The Body; A Hole Lot of Trouble; The Intrepid Mr Twigg; Long Road South; The Pale Faced Girl; Sex and the British; Spring and Port Wine; The Violent Enemy.

1969–70: Loans to producers approved since 31 March 1969
Bartleby; Entertaining Mr Sloane; Every Home Should Have One; Loot; Mr Forbush and the Penguins; One Brief Summer; Three Sisters.

1970–1: Loans to producers agreed since 31 March 1970
Churchill the Man; The Darwin Adventure; Family Life; Fright; I, Monster; The Lonely Sea and Sky; Pass of Arms; Praise Marx and Pass the Ammunition; A Touch of the Other; Under Milk Wood; Up Pompeii.

1971–2: Loans to producers approved since 31 March 1971
Captain Kronos – Vampire Hunter; Endless Night.

1972–3: Loans to producers approved since 31 March 1972
The Final Programme; Ooh! . . . You Are Awful; Steptoe and Son Ride Again.

1973–4: Loans to producers approved since 31 March 1973
Stardust.

1974–5: Loans to producers approved since 31 March 1974
Akenfield; Bugsy Malone; Dual Blade; James Dean: The First American Teenager; Lisztomania; The Man Who Fell to Earth; Overlord; The Romantic Englishwoman.

1975–6: Loans to producers approved since 31 March 1975
At the Earth's Core.

1976–7: Loans to producers approved since 31 March 1976
Black Joy; The Disappearance; The Duellists; Jabberwocky; Tarka the Otter.

1977–8: Loans to producers approved since 31 March 1977
Black Jack; The Riddle of the Sands; The Thief of Bagdad; The Sailor's Return; The Shout.

1978–9: Loans to producers approved since 31 March 1978
Babylon; The Europeans; That Summer; Radio On.

1979–80: Loans to producers approved since 31 March 1979
Memoirs of a Survivor.

1980–1: Loans to producers approved since 31 March 1980
Britannia Hospital; Gregory's Girl.

1981–2: Loans to producers approved since 31 March 1981
An Unsuitable Job for a Woman.

1982–3: Loans to producers approved since 31 March 1982
Caravaggio; Loose Connections.

1983–4: Loans to producers approved since 31 March 1983
Another Country; Dance With A Stranger; Defence of the Realm; Secret Places; When the Wind Blows.

1984–5: Loans to producers approved since 31 March 1984
Comrades; The Girl in the Picture; No Surrender; A Room With a View.

Bibliography

PRIMARY SOURCES

Archival sources

Bank of England Archive, London:
EC: Exchange Control Commission
SMT: Securities Management Trust

Barclays Group Archive, Manchester:
Barclays Bank Advance Registers, 1934–50

British Film Institute, London:
Michael and Aileen Balcon Collection (BFI Balcon)
Sandy Lieberson Collection (BFI Lieberson)
London Films Collection (BFI London Films)
David Puttnam Collection (BFI Puttnam)
Karel Reisz Collection (BFI Reisz)
Gerald Thomas Collection (BFI Thomas)

Film Finances Archive, London:
Realised Films: records of the finance and production of individual films including budgets, scripts, schedules, progress and cost reports, and miscellaneous correspondence.
General Correspondence: internal company records and accounts, and 'Green Papers' (copies of letters of intent including unmade films) and films not guaranteed.
Minute Book M. 104.

Lloyds Banking Group Archive, London:
Advances and General Purposes Minute Book, 1950.

The National Archives, Kew, London:
BT: Board of Trade Manufactures Department, including records of the National Film Finance Corporation, the British Film Production Fund and general film policy.
CAB: Cabinet Office, including papers relating to loans to the film industry.
FO: Foreign Office records, including miscellaneous files relating to film.
FV: Records created or inherited by the Department of Trade and Industry, including policy towards the film industry and revision of the British Film Production Fund.
PJ: Records created or inherited by the Department of Trade, including policy towards the film industry and revision of British Film Production Fund.
PREM: Prime Minister's Office, including correspondence relating to the sale of Shepperton Studios and the Prime Minister's Working Party on the Film Industry (1976).

T: Treasury records, including correspondence relating to the Anglo-American Film Agreement and the provision of loans for the National Film Finance Corporation.

Stanley Kubrick Archive, University of the Arts, London:
SK 12: Production records of *2001: A Space Odyssey* including distribution and financing contracts.

Other sources:
British Film Producers' Association: Executive Council minute books, 1937–40, 1953–66 (in author's possession).
Film Production Association of Great Britain Executive Committee minute book, 1967–72 (in author's possession).

Statutory legislation

Cinematograph Films Act, 1948 (11 & 12 Geo.6 c.23)
Cinematograph Films Act, 1957 (5 & 6 Eliz.2 c.21)
Cinematograph Film Production (Special Loans) Act, 1949 (14 Geo.6 c.20)
Cinematograph Film Production (Special Loans) Amendment Act, 1950 (14 Geo.6 c.18)
Cinematograph Film Production (Special Loans) Amendment Act, 1952 (15 & 16 Geo.6 & 1 Eliz.2 c.29)
Cinematograph Film Production (Special Loans) Act, 1954 (2 & 3 Eliz.2 c.15)
Films Act, 1960 (8 & 9 Eliz.2 c.57)
Films Act, 1966 (1966 c.48)
Films Act, 1970 (1970 c.26)
Films Act, 1985 (1985 c.21)

Official reports

British Film Fund Agency: Annual Report and Statement of Accounts for the fifty-two weeks to 31 October 1983, HC 616 1982-83 (23 October 1983).
Cinematograph Films Council: Annual Report for the year ended 31 March, 1939–83: HC Paper No. 160 1938-39 (July 1939); HC 183 1945-46 (24 October 1946); HC 62 1949-50 (May 1950); HC 190 1950-51 (20 May 1951); HC 184 1951-52 (8 May 1952); HC 181 1952-53 (18 May 1953); HC 202 1953-54 (30 June 1954); HC 14 1954-55 (21 June 1955); HC 344 1955-56 (25 July 1956); HC 241 1956-57 (25 July 1957); HC 236 1957-58 (8 July 1958); HC 246 1958-59 (8 July 1959); HC 301 1959-60 (28 July 1960); HC 268 1960-61 (25 July 1961); HC 300 1963-64 (28 July 1964); HC 306 1964-65 (3 August 1965); HC 507 1966-67 (21 June 1967): HC 284 1967-68 (24 June 1968); HC 301 1968-69 (26 June 1969); HC 291 1969-70 (27 May 1970); HC 372 1972-73 (18 July 1973); HC 127 1973-74 (22 January 1975); HC 673 1974-75 (4 November 1975); HC 638 1975-76 (12 October 1976); HC 218 1978-79 (30 October 1979); HC 708 1979-80 (28 July 1980); HC 468 1980-81 (20 October 1981); HC 145 1981-82 (18 January 1983).
Distribution and Exhibition of Cinematograph Films: Report of the Committee of Enquiry appointed by the President of the Board of Trade, Cmd. 7837 (November 1949).
The Distribution of Films for Exhibition in Cinemas and by Other Means: Fifth Report of the Interim Action Committee on the Film Industry, Cmnd. 8536 (March 1982).
Film Policy, Cmnd. 9319 (July 1984).
Film and Television Co-operation: Fourth Report of the Interim Action Committee on the Film Industry, Cmnd. 8227 (April 1981).
Films: A Report on the Supply of Films for Exhibition in Cinemas, HC 206 1965-66 (28 October 1966).
The Financing of the British Film Industry: Second Report of the Interim Action Committee on the Film Industry, Cmnd. 7597 (June 1979).
Future of the British Film Industry: Report of the Prime Minister's Working Party, Cmnd. 6372 (January 1976).

National Film Finance Corporation: Annual Report and Statement of Accounts for the year ended 31 March, 1950–85: Cmd. 7927 (April 1950); Cmd. 8193 (April 1951); Cmd. 8523 (April 1952); Cmd. 8816 (April 1953); Cmd. 9166 (June 1954); Cmd. 9464 (May 1955): Cmd. 9751 (May 1956); Cmnd. 176 (May 1957); Cmnd. 448 (June 1958); Cmnd. 799 (July 1959); Cmnd. 1096 (July 1960); Cmnd. 1398 (June 1961); Cmnd. 1793 (July 1962); Cmnd. 2079 (July 1963); Cmnd. 2453 (September 1964); Cmnd. 2770 (September 1965); Cmnd. 3066 (August 1966); Cmnd. 3418 (October 1967); Cmnd. 3716 (July 1968); Cmnd. 4094 (June 1969); Cmnd. 4402 (May 1970); Cmnd. 4761 (August 1971); Cmnd. 5080 (August 1972); Cmnd. 5433 (August 1973); Cmnd. 5725 (September 1974); Cmnd. 6235 (September 1975); Cmnd. 6633 (September 1976); Cmnd. 7048 (December 1977); Cmnd. 7370 (November 1978); HC 456 1978-79 (3 March 1980); HC 793 1979-80 (27 October 1980); HC 466 1980-81 (26 July 1982); HC 384 1981-82 (13 May 1983); HC 545 1982-83 (23 July 1984); HC 512 1983-84 (22 July 1985); HC 188 1984-85 (4 February 1986).

Proposals for the setting up of a British Film Authority: Report of the Interim Action Committee on the Film Industry, Cmnd. 7071 (January 1978).

Review of Films Legislation: Report of the Cinematograph Films Council, Cmnd. 3584 (March 1968).

Report of the Working Party on Film Production Costs (1949).

Structure and Trading Practices of the Film Industry: Recommendations of the Cinematograph Films Council, Cmnd. 2324 (April 1964).

Parliamentary proceedings (Hansard)

Parliamentary Debates: House of Commons, 5th Series (1909–81), 6th Series (1981–)
Parliamentary Debates: House of Lords, 5th Series (1909–)

Newspapers and periodicals

British Business; Daily Herald; Daily Mail; The Daily Telegraph; The Economist; The Financial Times; The Guardian; Los Angeles Times; New York Times; The Observer; The Sunday Times; The Times.

Film journals and trade papers

Broadcast; CinemaTV Today; Daily Cinema; Daily Film Renter; Films and Filming; The Independent Film Journal; Kinematograph Weekly; Motion Picture Herald; The Penguin Film Review; Screen International; Sight & Sound; Today's Cinema; Variety.

Yearbooks

British Film and Television Year Book (London: BA Publications, 1953–82)
Kinematograph Year Book (London: Kinematograph Publications/Odhams Press, 1945–71)

Memoirs and diaries

Ackland, Rodney, *The Celluloid Mistress; or, The Custard Pie of Dr Caligari* (London: Allan Wingate, 1954).

Attenborough, Richard, *In Search of Gandhi* (London: The Bodley Head, 1982).

Baker, Roy Ward, *The Director's Cut: A Memoir of 60 Years in Film and Television* (London: Reynolds & Hearn, 2000).

Balcon, Michael, *Michael Balcon presents . . . A Lifetime of Films* (London: Hutchinson, 1969).

Box, Betty, *Lifting the Lid: The Autobiography of Film Producer Betty Box OBE* (Lewes: Book Guild, 2000).

Box, Sydney, *The Lion That Lost Its Way and Other Cautionary Tales of the Show Business Jungle*, ed. Andrew Spicer (Lanham, MA: Scarecrow Press, 2005).
Broccoli, Albert R., with Donald Zec, *When the Snow Melts: The Autobiography of Cubby Broccoli* (London: Boxtree, 1998).
Danischewsky, Monja, *White Russian – Red Face* (London: Victor Gollancz, 1966).
Davenport, Nicholas, *Memoirs of a City Radical* (London: Weidenfeld & Nicolson, 1974).
Forbes, Brian, *Notes for a Life* (London: Collins, 1974).
Gilbert, Lewis, *All My Flashbacks* (London: Reynolds & Hearn, 2010).
Goldman, William, *Adventures in the Screen Trade: A Personal View of Hollywood and Screenwriting* (London: Macdonald, 1984).
Guest, Val, *So You Want To Be in Pictures?* (London: Reynolds & Hearn, 2001).
Hepburn, Katharine, *The Making of 'The African Queen'; or How I Went to Africa with Bogart, Bacall and Huston and Almost Lost My Mind* (London: Century Hutchinson, 1987).
Jackson, Pat, *A Retake Please!: 'Night Mail' to 'Western Approaches'* (Liverpool: Liverpool University Press/ Royal Naval Museum Publications, 1999).
Minney, R. J., *'Puffin' Asquith: A Biography of the Hon. Anthony Asquith, Aesthete, Aristocrat, Prime Minister's Son and Film Maker* (London: Leslie Frewin, 1973).
Pascal, Valerie, *The Disciple and His Devil* (London: Michael Joseph, 1971).
Picker, David V., *Musts, Maybes and Nevers: A Book About Movies* (North Charleston, SC: CreateSpace Independent Publishing, 2013).
Powell, Michael, *A Life in Movies: An Autobiography* (London: William Heinemann, 1987).
Powell, Michael, *Million Dollar Movie* (London: William Heinemann, 1992).
Saville, Victor, *Evergreen: Victor Saville in His Own Words*, ed. Roy Moseley (Carbondale: Southern Illinois University Press, 2000).
Wilcox, Herbert, *Twenty-Five Thousand Sunsets: The Autobiography of Herbert Wilcox* (New York: A. S. Barnes 1969).

Secondary Sources

Books and monographs

Aldgate, Anthony, and Jeffrey Richards, *Britain Can Take It: The British Cinema in the Second World War* (Oxford: Basil Blackwell, 1986).
Aldridge, Mark, *Agatha Christie on Screen* (London: Palgrave Macmillan, 2016).
Allen, Robert C., and Douglas Gomery, *Film History: Theory and Practice* (New York: McGraw-Hill, 1985).
Armes, Roy, *A Critical History of British Cinema* (London: Secker & Warburg, 1978).
Arts Enquiry, *The Factual Film: A Survey Sponsored by the Dartington Hall Trustees* (Oxford: Geoffrey Cumberledge/Oxford University Press, 1947).
Auty, Martin, and Nick Roddick (eds), *British Cinema Now* (London: British Film Institute, 1985).
Baillieu, Bill, and John Goodchild, *The British Film Business* (Chichester: John Wiley & Sons, 2002).
Barber, Sian, *The British Film Industry in the 1970s: Capital, Culture and Creativity* (Basingstoke: Palgrave Macmillan, 2013).
Barnett, Correlli, *The Audit of War: The Illusion and Reality of Britain as a Great Nation* (London: Macmillan, 1986).
Barr, Charles, *Ealing Studios* (London and Newton Abbot: Cameron & Tayleur/David & Charles, 1977).
Bernstein, Irving, *Hollywood at the Crossroads: An economic study of the motion picture industry* (Los Angeles: Hollywood Association of Film Labor, 1957).
Betts, Ernest, *The Film Business: A History of British Cinema 1896–1972* (London: George Allen & Unwin, 1973).

Briggs, Asa, *The History of Broadcasting in the United Kingdom. Volume V: Competition 1955–1974* (Oxford: Oxford University Press, 1995).

Burrows, Jon, *The British Cinema Boom, 1909–1914: A Commercial History* (London: Palgrave Macmillan, 2017).

Caute, David, *Joseph Losey: A Revenge on Life* (London: Faber & Faber, 1994).

Chanan, Michael, *The Dream That Kicks: The Prehistory and Early Years of Cinema in Britain* (London: Routledge & Kegan Paul, 1980).

Chapman, James, *The British at War: Cinema, State and Propaganda, 1939–1945* (London: I. B. Tauris, 1998).

Chibnall, Steve, *J. Lee Thompson* (Manchester: Manchester University Press, 2000).

Chibnall, Steve, *Quota Quickies: The Birth of the British 'B' Film* (London: Palgrave Macmillan/British Film Institute, 2007).

Chibnall, Steve, and Brian McFarlane, *The British 'B' Film* (London: Palgrave Macmillan/British Film Institute, 2009).

Cook, David A., *Lost Illusions: American Cinema in the Shadow of Watergate and Vietnam, 1970–1979* (Berkeley: University of California Press, 2000).

Curran, James, and Vincent Porter (eds), *British Cinema History* (London: Weidenfeld & Nicolson, 1983).

Dickinson, Margaret, and Sarah Street, *Cinema and State: The Film Industry and the British Government, 1927–84* (London: British Film Institute, 1985).

Docherty, David, David Morrison and Michael Tracey, *The Last Picture Show? Britain's Changing Film Audience* (London: British Film Institute, 1987).

Durgnat, Raymond, *A Mirror for England: British Movies from Austerity to Affluence* (London: Faber & Faber, 1970).

Dux, Sally, *Richard Attenborough* (Manchester: Manchester University Press, 2013).

Eberts, Jake, and Terry Ilott, *My Indecision is Final: The Rise and Fall of Goldcrest Films* (London: Faber & Faber, 1990).

Farmer, Richard, Laura Mayne, Duncan Petrie and Melanie Williams, *Transformation and Tradition in 1960s British Cinema* (Edinburgh: Edinburgh University Press, 2019).

Floud, Roderick, *The Cambridge Economic History of Modern Britain Volume 3: Structural Change and Growth, 1939–2000* (Cambridge: Cambridge University Press, 2004).

Geraghty, Christine, *British Cinema in the Fifties: Gender, Genre and the 'New Look'* (London: Routledge, 2000).

Geraghty, Christine, *My Beautiful Laundrette: A British Film Guide* (London: I. B. Tauris, 2005).

Gillett, Philip, *The British working class in postwar film* (Manchester: Manchester University Press, 2003).

Glancy, H. Mark, *When Hollywood loved Britain: The Hollywood 'British' film 1939–45* (Manchester: Manchester University Press, 1999).

Guback, Thomas, *The International Film Industry: Western Europe and America Since 1945* (Bloomington: Indiana University Press, 1969).

Hammond, Michael, *The Big Show: British Cinema Culture in the Great War 1914–1918* (Exeter: University of Exeter Press, 2006).

Harper, Sue, and Vincent Porter, *British Cinema of the 1950s: The Decline of Deference* (Oxford: Oxford University Press, 2003).

Harper, Sue, and Justin Smith, *British Film Culture in the 1970s: The Boundaries of Pleasure* (Edinburgh: Edinburgh University Press, 2012).

Higson, Andrew (ed.), *Young and Innocent? The Cinema in Britain 1896–1930* (Exeter: University of Exeter Press, 2002).

Hill, John, *Sex, Class and Realism: British Cinema 1956–1963* (London: British Film Institute, 1986).

Hill, John, *British Cinema in the 1980s: Issues and Themes* (Oxford: Clarendon Press, 1999).

Hunter, I. Q., Laraine Porter and Justin Smith (eds), *The Routledge Companion to British Cinema History* (London: Routledge, 2017).

Johnson, Tom, and Deborah Del Vecchio, *Hammer Films: An Exhaustive Filmography* (Jefferson, NC: McFarland, 1996).

Kennedy, Paul, *The Realities Behind Diplomacy: Background Influences on British External Policy, 1865–1980* (London: Fontana, 1981).

Kinden, Gorham (ed.), *The American Movie Industry: The Business of Motion Pictures* (Carbondale: Southern Illinois University Press, 1982).

Klingender, F. D., and Stuart Legg, *Money Behind the Screen: A Report prepared on behalf of the Film Council* (London: Lawrence & Wishart, 1937).

Kulik, Karol, *Alexander Korda: The Man Who Could Work Miracles* (London: W. H. Allen, 1975).

Lewis, Richard, *Review of the UK Film Industry: Report to BSAC* (London: British Screen Advisory Council, 1990).

Low, Rachael, and Roger Manvell, *The History of the British Film 1896–1906* (London: George Allen & Unwin, 1948).

Low, Rachael, *The History of the British Film 1906–1914* (London: George Allen & Unwin, 1949).

Low, Rachael, *The History of the British Film 1914–1918* (London: George Allen & Unwin, 1950).

Low, Rachael, *The History of the British Film 1918–1929* (London: George Allen & Unwin, 1971).

Low, Rachael, *The History of the British Film 1929–1939: Film Making in 1930s Britain* (London: George Allen & Unwin, 1985).

McFarlane, Brian (ed.), *An Autobiography of British Cinema* (London: Methuen, 1997).

McFarlane, Brian (ed.), *The Cinema of Britain and Ireland* (London: Wallflower Press, 2005).

MacKillop, Ian, and Neil Sinyard (eds), *British Cinema of the 1950s: A Celebration* (Manchester: Manchester University Press, 2005).

Macnab, Geoffrey, *J. Arthur Rank and the British Film Industry* (London: Routledge, 1993).

Macnab, Geoffrey, *Delivering Dreams: A Century of British Film Distribution* (London: I. B. Tauris, 2016).

Monaco, Paul, *The Sixties: History of the American Cinema, 1960–1969* (Berkeley: University of California Press, 2001).

Moody, Paul, *EMI Films and the Limits of British Cinema* (London: Palgrave Macmillan, 2018).

Morgan, Kenneth O., *The People's Peace: British History 1945–1990* (Oxford: Oxford University Press, 1990).

Murphy, Robert, *Realism and Tinsel: Cinema and Society in Britain 1939–48* (London: Routledge, 1989).

Murphy, Robert, *Sixties British Cinema* (London: British Film Institute, 1992).

Murphy, Robert (ed.), *The British Cinema Book* (London: British Film Institute, 1997).

Oakley, Charles, *Where We Came In: Seventy Years of the British Film Industry* (London: George Allen & Unwin, 1964).

Petrie, Duncan, Melanie Williams and Laura Mayne (eds), *Sixties British Cinema Reconsidered* (Edinburgh: Edinburgh University Press, 2020).

Perry, George, *The Great British Picture Show* (London: Pavilion Books, 1985).

Political and Economic Planning, *The British Film Industry: A report on its history and present organisation, with special reference to the economic problems of British film production* (London: Political and Economic Planning, 1952).

Porter, Vincent, *On Cinema* (London: Pluto Press, 1985).

Ramsden, John, *The Dam Busters: A British Film Guide* (London: I. B. Tauris, 2003).

Richards, *The Age of the Dream Palace: Cinema and Society in Britain 1930–1939* (London: Routledge & Kegan Paul, 1984).

Richards, Jeffrey (ed.), *The Unknown 1930s: An Alternative History of the British Cinema, 1929–1939* (London: I. B. Tauris, 1998).

Roth, Andrew, *Sir Harold Wilson, Yorkshire Walter Mitty* (London: The Book Service, 1977).

Schatz, Thomas, *Boom and Bust: American Cinema in the 1940s* (Berkeley: University of California Press, 1999).

Seagrave, Kerry, *American Films Abroad: Hollywood's Domination of the World's Movie Screens* (Jefferson, NC: McFarland, 1997).

Sedgwick, John, *Popular Filmgoing in 1930s Britain: A Choice of Pleasures* (Exeter: University of Exeter Press, 2000).

Spicer, Andrew, *Sydney Box* (Manchester: Manchester University Press, 2006).

Spicer, Andrew, and A. T. McKenna, *The Man Who Got Carter: Michael Klinger, Independent Production, and the British Film Industry, 1960–1980* (London: I. B. Tauris, 2013).

Spraos, John, *The Decline of the Cinema: An Economist's Report* (London: George Allen & Unwin, 1962).

Street, Sarah, *British National Cinema* (London: Routledge, 1997).

Street, Sarah, *Transatlantic Crossings: British Feature Films in the United States* (London: Continuum, 2002).

Taylor, A. J. P., *English History 1914–1945* (Oxford: Oxford University Press, 1965).

Taylor, Philip M. (ed.), *Britain and the Cinema in the Second World War* (London: Macmillan Press, 1988).

Thompson, Kristin, *Exporting Entertainment: America in the World Film Market 1907–1934* (London: British Film Institute, 1985).

Threadgall, Derek, *Shepperton Studios: An Independent View* (London: British Film Institute, 1994).

Vincendeau, Ginette (ed.), *The Encyclopedia of European Cinema* (London: Cassell, 1995).

Walker, Alexander, *Hollywood, England: The British Film Industry in the Sixties* (London: Michael Joseph, 1974).

Walker, Alexander, *National Heroes: British Cinema in the Seventies and Eighties* (London: Harrap, 1985).

Walker, Alexander, *Icons in the Fire: The Decline and Fall of Almost Everybody in the British Film Industry 1984–2000* (London: Orion, 2004).

Wasko, Janet, *Movies and Money: Financing the American Film Industry* (Norwood, NJ: Ablex Publishing, 1982).

Wood, Alan, *Mr Rank: A Study of J. Arthur Rank and British Films* (London: Hodder & Stoughton, 1952).

Wood, Linda (ed.), *British Film Industry: BFI Information Guide No. 1* (London: British Film Institute Information and Education Department, 1980).

Wood, Linda (ed.), *British Film 1927–1939: BFI Research Guide* (London: BFI Library Services, 1986).

Wood, Linda (ed.), *British Film 1971–81: BFI Research Guide* (London: BFI Library Services, 1983).

Articles and book chapters

Aldgate, Anthony, 'Defining the Parameters of "Quality" Cinema for "the Permissive Society": The British Board of Film Censors and *This Sporting Life*', in Anthony Aldgate, James Chapman and Arthur Marwick (eds), *Windows on the Sixties: Exploring Key Texts of Media and Culture* (London: I. B. Tauris, 2000), pp. 19–36.

Anderson, Lindsay, 'Get Out and Push!', in Tom Maschler (ed.), *Declaration* (London: Macgibbon & Kee, 1957), pp. 154–78.

Bakker, Gerben, 'The Decline and Fall of the European Film Industry: Sunk Costs, Market Size and Market Structure, 1890–1927', *Economic History Review*, 58: 2 (2005), pp. 310–51.

Barr, Charles, '*Straw Dogs, A Clockwork Orange* and the Critics', *Screen*, 13: 2 (1972), pp. 17–32.

Bignell, Jonathan, 'Pinter, Authorship and Entrepreneurship in 1960s British Cinema: The economics of *The Quiller Memorandum*', *Historical Journal of Film, Radio and Television*, 40: 3 (2020), pp. 533–50.

Chapman, James, 'A Short History of the *Carry On* Films', in I. Q. Hunter and Laraine Porter (eds), *British Comedy Cinema* (London: Routledge, 2012), pp. 100–15.

Chapman, James, 'The Trouble With Harry: The Difficult Relationship of Harry Saltzman and Film Finances', *Historical Journal of Film, Radio and Television*, 34: 1 (2014), pp. 43–71.

Chapman, James, 'Film Finances and *The Trial* (1963): Alexander Salkind, Orson Welles, and European co-production in the 1960s', *Historical Journal of Film, Radio and Television*, 40: 4 (2021), pp. 788–807.

Chapman, Llewella, '"They wanted a bigger, more ambitious film": Film Finances and the American "Runaways" That Ran Away', *Journal of British Cinema and Television*, 18: 2 (2021), pp. 176–97.

Chibnall, Steve, 'Rome, Open for British Production: The lost world of "Britalian" films, 1946–1954', *Historical Journal of Film, Radio and Television*, 33: 2 (2013), pp. 236–69.

Chibnall, Steve, 'Hollywood-on-Thames: The British productions of Warner Bros.-First National, 1931–1945', *Historical Journal of Film, Radio and Television*, 30: 4 (2019), pp. 687–724.

Cole, Michael, 'Quangos: The Debate of the 1970s in Britain', *Contemporary British History*, 19: 3 (2005), pp. 321–52.

Collinson, Naomi, 'The Legacy of Max Schach', *Film History*, 15: 3 (2003), pp. 376–89.

Drazin, Charles, 'Film Finances: The Early Years', *Historical Journal of Film, Radio and Television*, 34: 1 (2014), pp. 2–22.

Dux, Sally, 'Allied Film Makers: Crime, Comedy and Social Concern', *Journal of British Cinema and Television*, 9: 2 (2012), pp. 198–213.

Ellis, John, 'Art, Culture, Quality: Terms for a Cinema in the Forties and Seventies', *Screen*, 19: 3 (1978), pp. 9–49.

Gruner, Olly, '"Good Business, Good Policy, Good Patriotism": The British Film Weeks of 1924', *Historical Journal of Film, Radio and Television*, 32:1 (2013), pp. 41–56.

Hall, Sheldon, 'African Adventures: Film Finances Ltd and actor-producers on safari', *Historical Journal of Film, Radio and Television*, 34: 4 (2014), pp. 546–67.

Harper, Sue, 'The Price of Oysters: *Tom Jones* (1963) and Film Finances', *Historical Journal of Film, Radio and Television*, 34: 1 (2014), pp. 72–84.

Higson, Andrew, 'The Discourses of British Film Year', *Screen*, 27: 1 (1986), pp. 86–110.

Hill, John, 'Government Policy and the British Film Industry 1979–90', *European Journal of Communications*, 8: 2 (1993), pp. 203–24.

Hodson, John, '"Who Wrote *Lawrence of Arabia*?": Sam Spiegel and David Lean's Denial of Credit to a Blacklisted Writer', *Cineaste*, 20: 4 (1994), pp. 12–18.

Lovell, Alan, 'The Unknown Cinema of Britain', *Cinema Journal*, 11: 2 (1972), pp. 1–8.

McKenna, A. T., 'Joseph E. Levine and *A Bridge Too Far* (1977): A Producer's Labour of Love', *Historical Journal of Film, Radio and Television*, 31: 2 (2011), pp. 211–27.

Mayne, Laura, 'Whatever Happened to the British "B" Movie? Micro-budget film-making and the death of the one-hour supporting feature in the early 1960s', *Historical Journal of Film, Radio and Television*, 37: 3 (2017), pp. 559–76.

Mayne, Laura, 'An Uncompetitive Cinema: The British Fiction Short Film in the 1960s', *Historical Journal of Film, Radio and Television*, 38: 1 (2018), pp. 119–32.

Mayne, Laura, 'A World on His Shoulders: Nat Cohen, Anglo-EMI and the British Film Industry', *Journal of British Cinema and Television*, 18: 1 (2021), pp. 34–49.

Moody, Paul, 'Verity Lambert's Thorn-EMI Films', *Journal of British Cinema and Television*, 18: 1 (2021), pp. 96–120.

Morris, Nathalie, 'An Eminent Series: *The Adventures of Sherlock Holmes* and the Stoll Film Company', *Journal of British Cinema and Television*, 4: 1 (2007), pp. 18–36.

North, Dan, 'Don Boyd's *Gossip*', in Dan North (ed.), *Sights Unseen: Unfinished British Films* (Newcastle: Cambridge Scholars Publishing, 2008), pp. 169–88.

Petley, Julian, 'Cinema and State', in Charles Barr (ed.), *All Our Yesterdays: 90 Years of British Cinema* (London: British Film Institute, 1986), pp. 31–46.

Petrie, Duncan, 'Resisting American Dominance in Sixties British Cinema: The NFFC/Rank joint financing initiative', *Historical Journal of Film, Radio and Television*, 36: 4 (2016), pp. 548–68.

Petrie, Duncan, 'Bryanston Films: An Experiment in Co-operative Independent Film Production and Reception', *Historical Journal of Film, Radio and Television*, 38: 1 (2018), pp. 95–115.

Popple, Simon, 'Group Three: A Lesson in State Intervention?', *Film History*, 8: 2 (1996), pp. 131–42.

Porter, Vincent, 'Feature Film and the Mediation of Historical Reality: *Chance of a Lifetime* – a case study', *Media History*, 5: 2 (1999), pp. 181–99.

Porter, Vincent, 'The Robert Clark Account: Films released in Britain by Associated British Pictures, British Lion, MGM, and Warner Bros.', *Historical Journal of Film, Radio and Television*, 20: 4 (2000), pp. 469–511.

Porter, Vincent, 'All Change at Elstree: Warner Bros., ABPC and British Film Policy, 1945–1961', *Historical Journal of Film, Radio and Television*, 21: 1 (2001), pp. 5–35.
Rowson, Simon, 'A Statistical Survey of the Cinema Industry in Great Britain in 1934', *Journal of the Royal Statistical Society*, 99: 1 (1936), pp. 67–119.
Shail, Robert, 'Stanley Baker and British Lion: A Cautionary Tale', in Paul Newland (ed.), *Don't Look Now: British Cinema in the 1970s* (Bristol: Intellect, 2010), pp. 33–41.
Small, Pauline, 'Anglo-Italian Co-Production in the 1950s and 1960s: Film Finances, the Prince and Venice', *Historical Journal of Film, Radio and Television*, 37: 2 (2017), pp. 220–41.
Smith, Justin, 'Glam, Spam and Uncle Sam: Funding Diversity in 1970s British Film Production', in Robert Shail (ed.), *Seventies British Cinema* (London: Palgrave Macmillan/British Film Institute, 2008), pp. 67–80.
Smith, Justin, 'Une Entente Cordiale? – A brief history of the Anglo-French Film Co-Production Agreement, 1965–1979', in Lucy Mazdon and Catherine Wheatley (eds), *Je t'aime . . . moi non plus: Franco-British Cinematic Relations* (Oxford: Berghahn, 2011), pp. 49–64.
Smith, Justin, 'Calculated Risks: Film Finances and British Independents in the 1970s', *Historical Journal of Film, Radio and Television*, 34: 1 (2014), pp. 86–102.
Street, Sarah, 'Alexander Korda, Prudential Assurance and British film finance in the 1930s', *Historical Journal of Film, Radio and Television*, 6: 2 (1986), pp. 161–79.
Street, Sarah, 'Stepping Westward: The distribution of British feature films in America, and the case of *The Private Life of Henry VIII*', in Justine Ashby and Andrew Higson (eds), *British Cinema, Past and Present* (London: Routledge, 2000), pp. 51–62.
Street, Sarah, 'Film Finances and the British New Wave', *Historical Journal of Film, Radio and Television*, 34: 1 (2014), pp. 23–42.
Stubbs, Jonathan, '"Blocked" Currency, Runaway Production in Britain and *Captain Horatio Hornblower* (1951)', *Historical Journal of Film, Radio and Television*, 28: 3 (2008), pp. 335–51.
Stubbs, Jonathan, 'The Eady Levy: A Runaway Bribe? Hollywood Production and British Subsidy in the Early 1960s', *Journal of British Cinema and Television*, 6: 1 (2009), pp. 1–20.
Tait, Alan A., 'Political Economy: The British Budget of 1971', *Public Finance Analysis*, New Series, 30: 3 (1972), pp. 489–504.
Thumim, Janet, 'The "popular", cash and culture in the postwar British cinema industry', *Screen*, 32: 3 (1991), pp. 245–71.

Unpublished papers and theses

Barber, Sian, '1970s British Film: Capital, Culture and Creativity' (PhD, University of Portsmouth, 2009).
Bolton, Anne, 'Independent Producers Ltd: A Case Study of an Independent British Production Group in the 1940s' (PhD, University of Leicester, 2020).
Lovell, Alan, 'The British Cinema: The Unknown Cinema', British Film Institute Education Department, 13 March 1969, typescript held by the BFI Reuben Library.
Mayne, Laura, 'Channel 4 and British Film: An Assessment of Industrial and Cultural Impact, 1982–1998' (PhD, University of Portsmouth, 2014).
Romer, Stephen, 'The Decline of the British Film Industry: An Analysis of Market Structure, the Firm and Product Competition' (PhD, Brunel University, 1993).

Index

ABC (US television network), 261
ABC cinema circuit, 69, 130, 181, 216, 316, 321
Abdul the Damned, 18
Absolute Beginners, 324–5
Accounts, 320
Ackroyd, Elizabeth, 308
Acres, Birt, 14
Action of the Tiger, 171
ad valorem duty, 21, 24, 34–6, 39
Adelphi Films, 104
Adventure of Sherlock Holmes' Smarter Brother, The, 254
Adventures of a Plumber's Mate, The, 304
Adventures of a Private Eye, The, 304
Adventures of Quentin Durward, The, 162, 167
Adventures of Robin Hood, The (TV series), 214, 268
Adventures of Sherlock Holmes, The, 15
Adventures of Tartu, The, 51, 161–2
African Queen, The, 123, 131–2, 150–1
Against the Wind, 72
Agatha, 302
Akenfield, 281–2, 318
Alan Parker Film Company, 281
Albion Film Distributors, 215
Aldgate Trustees, 18, 48
Alfie, 197, 200, 229
Alfred the Great, 235, 247
Alien, 300, 302, 304, 313
All-Industry Tax Committee, 181
Allen, A. G., 53
Allen, Irving, 138, 167–70
Allen, Robert C., 12
Allied Artists, 266
Allied Film Makers, 183, 185–6, 207
Allport, F. W., 38, 164
Altria, William G., 179, 235, 237
Amalgamated Studios, 19, 22, 166; *see also* Borehamwood Studios
Amazing Quest of Mr Bliss, The, 144
Ambler, Eric, 173

American Broadcasting Company: *see* NBC
American National Bank and Trust Association, 264
American Werewolf in London, An, 314
Amicus Films, 219, 247
Amorous Adventures of Moll Flanders, The, 232
Anderson, Ian, 247
Anderson, Lindsay, 1, 110, 187, 191, 229, 276, 337
Anderson, Michael, 118, 136, 203
Angel, 318–19
Angel, Daniel, 148–9, 180, 204, 264
Angel With the Trumpet, 129–30
Angels One Five, 110, 117
Anglo-Amalgamated Film Distributors, 104, 183, 190, 204–5, 224, 249
Anglo-American Film Agreement (1948), 39–42, 83, 162–3, 349
Anglo-American Film Agreement (1950), 43, 113
Anglo-EMI Film Distributors, 249, 280
Angry Silence, The, 123, 185
Anna Karenina, 54, 72
Annakin, Ken, 136, 155, 206, 296
Annan Committee, 319
Another Country, 323, 338
Another Man's Poison, 148–50
Another Shore, 72–3
Another Time, Another Place, 320
Antonioni, Michelangelo, 196, 228
Apted, Michael, 319
Appointment With Venus, 115
Arbuthnot Latham, 248
Archers, The, 20, 117
archives, 3, 5, 7n
Ardmore Studios, 166, 216
Arthur, 313–14
Arthur Guinness & Co., 317
Arliss, Leslie, 88, 117
Arts Council, 293
Arts Enquiry, 19

Ascendancy, 318
Ask Agamemnon, 263
Asquith, Anthony, 1, 54, 56, 72, 88, 115, 147–8
Assassination of Trotsky, The, 263–4
Associated British Film Distributors (ABFD), 72, 88, 121
Associated British-Pathé, 58, 87–8, 104, 117, 130, 249
Associated British Picture Corporation (ABPC), 13, 20, 22, 24–5, 46–7, 51, 53–4, 65–6, 73–4, 117–18, 120, 128, 181, 187, 206–7, 248, 349–50
Associated Communications Corporation (ACC), 261, 268–71, 315, 326
Associated Film Distributors, 270–1
Associated General Films, 269
Associated-Rediffusion, 138, 180
Associated Talking Pictures, 24, 47, 73, 118–19, 180
Associated Television (ATV), 268, 271
Association of British Independent Film Producers, 69
Association of Cine Technicians, 22, 67, 89
Association of Cinema and Television Technicians, 319
Association of Independent Producers, 339
Association of Specialised Film Makers, 100
Astonished Heart, The, 66
At the Earth's Core, 282
Attenborough, Richard, 1, 66, 152, 185, 207, 267, 276, 287–8, 312, 322–3, 347–8
Attlee, Clement, 90
auteur theory, 2–3
Avis, 266

Baby and the Battleship, The, 123, 135
Babylon, 336–7
Bacall, Lauren, 250
Back to the Future, 348
Bad Blood, 318
Bad Lord Byron, The, 71
Bad Timing, 256
Baird, Edward, 56, 88, 115, 147
Baker, Leslie, 186
Baker, Peter, 84
Baker, Reginald, 119
Baker, Roy, 116
Baker, Stanley, 203, 254, 287
Balcon, Michael, 23, 65, 72, 87–8, 119–20, 184, 192, 208–10, 276
Bank of America, 7n, 57, 134, 148, 206, 263

Bank of England, 3, 5, 18, 22, 32, 41, 46, 48–9, 52, 78, 128, 132, 246
Bankers Investment Trust, 52
Banque de Paris et des Pays-Bas, 267
Barclay, Clifford, 236–7
Barclay Securities, 251, 253
Barclays Bank, 144
Bardot, Brigitte, 223, 261
Baring, Aubrey, 56, 88, 117, 184–5
Barnacle Bill, 120
Barnett, Joel, 283
Baron, The (TV series), 268
Barr, Charles, 1
Barretts of Wimpole Street, The, 167
Barton, Harold, 101
Bates, Alan, 250
Bates, H. E., 83
Battle of Britain, 234, 236, 244–5
Battle of the River Plate, The, 111, 117, 136
Battle of the Sexes, 184
Baxter, John, 88, 120–1
BBC, 81, 119, 138
Beachcomber, The, 155
Beaconsfield Studios, 88, 122
Bean, Robin, 223
Beast Must Die, The, 247
Beat the Devil, 132
Beau Brummell, 162, 167
Beaver Films, 185, 207
Becket, 200
Beggar's Opera, The, 133
Belles of St Trinian's, The, 110, 134, 182
Bennett, Compton, 152
Bentley, John, 251–3
Bergman, Ingrid, 250
Bernard, Chris, 321
Bernstein, Sidney, 42
Best Years of Our Lives, The, 21
Betts, Ernest, 12
Bevin, Ernest, 38
BFI *see* British Film Institute
Bhowani Junction, 167
Big Sleep, The, 302
Biggles, 236
Billings, R. H., 109, 116, 118, 169, 174
Billy Liar, 190–1, 196
Birth of a Nation, The, 15
Bisset, Jacqueline, 250
Bitch, The, 314
Black Jack, 322
Black Joy, 283–4

Black Knight, The, 169–70
Black Narcissus, 21
Blakely, John, 86
Blanche Fury, 71
BLC Films, 139
Bliss of Mrs Blossom, The, 263
blocked sterling, 32, 39–41, 161–4
Blow-Up, 196, 228
Blue Lagoon, The, 70–1
Blue Lamp, The, 72, 109, 118
Blue Murder at St Trinian's, 182
Board of Trade, 3, 5, 34–43, 48–50, 55, 62, 65–9, 78, 80, 83, 113–14, 119, 120, 131, 132–4, 146, 163, 174–5, 198, 201, 208, 219–21, 230, 277, 332; *see also* Department of Trade, Department of Trade and Industry
Bobo, The, 196, 232–3
Bogarde, Dirk, 116, 203–4, 205, 210, 267
Bogart, Humphrey, 31–2, 132, 150
Bolshoi Ballet, The, 182
Bolt, Robert, 175, 262, 322
Bond, Ralph, 22
Bond Street, 73
Bonnie and Clyde, 235
Bonnie Prince Charlie, 4, 5, 23, 54, 63, 72, 81
Boom!, 204, 231
Boorman, John, 296
Boothby, Robert, 31–2
Borehamwood Studios, 166, 171, 230, 236, 243, 249; *see also* Amalgamated Studios
Born Free, 197, 200
Boulting, John, 57–8, 66, 85, 89, 135, 137–8, 208–9, 224, 231
Boulting, Roy, 57–8, 66, 135, 137–8, 208–9, 224, 276
Bowie, David, 254
Bowring-Skimming, Edward, 144
Box, Betty, 88, 115–16
Box, Muriel, 155
Box, Sydney, 62, 65, 122, 206, 208
Boxall, Harold, 66
Boy Friend, The, 249
Boyd, Don, 317
Boyd's Company, 337
Boys from Brazil, The, 269
Boys in Blue, The, 316
Brabourne, John, 250–1, 287–8, 316
Brain, The, 216
Brando, Marlon, 216, 303
Branson, Richard, 318

Brauer, Artur, 216
Bray Studios, 244, 304
Brazil, 315
Breaking Glass, 322
Brent Walker Film Distributors, 317
Brent Walker Group, 326
Brickhill, Paul, 118
Bridge on the River Kwai, The, 110, 172–3, 182, 316, 350
Bridge Too Far, A, 267–8, 300, 322
Bridges, Alan, 317
Brief Encounter, 3
Brighton Rock, 73
Briley, John, 322
Brimstone and Treacle, 318
Bristol Meyers, 265
Britannia Film Distributors, 215
Britannia Hospital, 337
British Actors' Equity Association, 67, 287
British and Dominions Film Corporation, 24
British Broadcasting Corporation *see* BBC
British Electric Traction, 130
British Film Authority, 289–90, 293–5, 297, 331–3
British Film Fund Agency, 288, 295, 301, 306
British Film Institute (BFI), 3, 347
BFI Production Board, 288, 320, 334, 336, 340
British Film Makers, 88–9, 115–16, 221
British Optical and Precision Engineers, 52
British Film Producers' Association (BFPA), 25, 40–1, 64–5, 69, 77, 96, 98–100, 121, 164, 201, 246, 304, 309, 313, 335
British Film Production Fund, 6, 7, 37, 74, 101, 164, 230; *see also* Eady levy
'British Film Weeks', 15, 347
'British Film Year', 347–8
British Lion Film Corporation, 11, 20, 24–5, 51, 53–5, 57, 64, 72, 78–9, 82, 90, 95, 104, 112, 114, 121, 123, 128–39, 140n, 147, 350
British Lion Films, 134–9, 207–10, 215, 224, 251–4, 278, 280
British Lion Production Associates, 129–30
British Lion Studio Company, 129, 137–8
British National Films, 24, 47, 51
British new wave, 186–92
British Screen Advisory Council, 316
British Screen Finance Consortium, 341–2
British Videogram Association, 342
Broadcast, 321
Broccoli, Albert R., 167–70
Broken Journey, 71

Bromhead, Michael, 208
Brothers, The, 71
Brown, C. M. P. 218
Brown, Chris, 325
Brown, David, 216
Brown, George, 88, 184
Browning Version, The, 148
Brownlow, Kevin, 237, 334
Bryan, John, 184
Bryanston Films, 4, 138, 183–5, 191–2, 199, 215
Bryden, Bill, 319
Bugsy Malone, 280–1
Bunny Lake is Missing, 228
Burton, Richard, 203, 231, 249, 263, 266, 278, 296
Burtt, V. L., 109
Butch Cassidy and the Sundance Kid, 235
Butcher's Film Services, 104
Butler, R. A., 91, 133

Caan, James, 267
Cabaret, 4
Caesar and Cleopatra, 21–3, 64
Caine, Michael, 264, 267
Cairo Road, 102
Call of the Blood, 72
Callaghan, James, 293, 295
Calling Bulldog Drummond, 167
Can Heironymous Merkin Ever Forget Mercy Humppe and Find True Happiness?, 229, 231
Can I Come Too?, 304
Can't Stop the Music, 315
Canadian Film Development Corporation, 284
Cannes Film Festival, 266, 317, 323, 336
  Palme d'Or, 196–7
Cannon Group, 316, 342
Capitol Film Productions, 18
Capricorn Corporation, 42
Capricorn One, 269
Captain Horatio Hornblower, RN, 162, 166
Caravaggio, 338
Card, The, 115
Cardboard Cavalier, 23
Cardiff, Jack, 89
Carlton Films, 280
Carr, Ron, 317
Carreras, James, 202
Carroll, Gordon, 304
Carry On At Your Convenience, 246
Carry On Camping, 197, 205–6
Carry On Cleo, 197

Carry On Constable, 196, 197
Carry On Cruising, 197
Carry On Dick, 246
Carry On Doctor, 197
Carry On Emmannuelle, 301–2
Carry On England, 301
Carry On Girls, 246
Carry On Henry, 246
Carry On Nurse, 110, 123, 183, 214
Carry On Matron, 246
Carry On Sergeant, 183, 301
Carry On Teacher, 183
Carry On Up the Jungle, 245
Carry On Up the Khyber, 197, 205
Carter, A. L., 88–9, 109
Cartier, Rudolf, 129
Casino Royale, 230
Cassandra Crossing, The, 269
Cassius Film Productions, 280
Catherine the Great, 18
Catto, Lord, 262
Central Office of Information, 120
Central Television, 320
Chaffey, Don, 139
Champions, 315
Chance of a Lifetime, 69–70
Channel 4, 318–22, 348
  Channel Four Films, 320, 347
  'Film on Four', 321–2, 328n
Chaplin, Charles, 15
Chapman, Graham, 247
Chappell, Connery, 35, 37
Charge of the Light Brigade, The, 230, 235–6, 247
Chariots of Fire, 312–14, 322, 350
Charleson, Ian, 314
Charlie Bubbles, 229, 231
Charter Film Productions, 135
Charterhouse Group, 279
Chase Bank, 41
Chester, Hal, 214
Chevron Pictures, 262
Chibnall, Steve, 173
Children of Chance, 129
Children's Film Foundation, 104, 307
Chilian Club, The, 246
Chilton, Edmond, 255–6
Chilton Films, 248
Chitty Chitty Bang Bang, 235
Christie, Agatha, 250, 316
Christie, Julie, 191, 196, 250, 253, 337
Chrysalis Records, 247, 336

Churchill, Randolph, 40
Cinecom, 342
Cineguild, 20
Cinema Artists Investments, 248
cinema attendances, 17, 19–20, 62, 104, 110, 162, 179–80, 243, 300, 312–13, 338, 348
Cinema International Corporation, 305
Cinematograph Exhibitors' Association (CEA), 23, 33, 35, 63–4, 68–9, 77, 96, 100, 104, 180, 319, 339–40
Cinematograph Film Production (Special Loans) Act (1949), 80–1
Cinematograph Film Production (Special Loans) Amendment Act (1950), 128
Cinematograph Film Production (Special Loans) Amendment Act (1952), 224
Cinematograph Film Production (Special Loans) Act (1954), 113
Cinematograph Films Act (1927), 2, 6, 14, 16–17, 33, 161, 340
Cinematograph Films Act (1938), 46, 48, 307
Cinematograph Films Act (1948), 23, 41, 69–70, 163
Cinematograph Films Act (1957), 122–3
Cinematograph Films Council, 4, 25–6, 46, 48, 50–1, 68, 244, 289–90, 292, 295, 307, 335, 339–40
CinemaTV Today, 244
Cinemobile Systems, 248
Cinerama Releasing Corporation, 261, 263
Circuit Management Association, 69
Citadel, The, 161
City of the Dead, 214
City Shares Trust, 224
Claridge Productions, 171
Clark, James, 237
Clark, Robert (producer), 66, 118
Clark, Robert (merchant banker), 277
Clash of the Titans, 313–14
Class of Miss MacMichael, The, 302
Classic cinema circuit, 246, 269
Clayton, Jack, 136, 153, 187
Cleopatra, 197
Cleese, John, 247
Cleve Investments, 301
Clockwise, 316
Clockwork Orange, A, 3–4
Close Encounters of the Third Kind, 300
Clouded Yellow, The, 102
Clydesdale Bank, 47
Cockleshell Heroes, The, 169

Coe, Peter, 233
Cohen, Nat, 204, 249–51, 287–8
Cohen, Norman, 247
Coker, R. F., 306, 308, 310n
Colditz Story, The, 123, 134, 182–3
Colonel Bogey, 64
Columbia-EMI-Warner, 283
Columbia Pictures, 41–2, 139, 157, 164, 167–72, 230, 233–4, 237, 244, 269, 316, 323, 326
Come Play With Me, 304
Comfort and Joy, 316
Commercial Bank of Scotland, 47
Committee on the Future of Broadcasting *see* Annan Committee
Companies Act (1948), 79
Company of Wolves, The, 319, 338
completion guarantees, 2, 121, 143–58, 216, 218, 317, 325
Comrades, 342
Concanen Films, 57, 89
Confessions from the David Galaxy Affair, 304
Confessions of a Window Cleaner, 245, 247
Cone of Silence, 185
Confederation of British Industries, 275
Connery, Sean, 250, 261, 267
Conquest of Everest, The, 121
Conspirator, 167
Constellation Films, 56, 144
Continental Film Distributors, 188, 190
Convoy, 268
Cook, David A., 235
Cool Mikado, The, 219
Cooper, Barry, 317
Cooper, Rod, 245
Cooper, Stuart, 281
Cornelius, Henry, 114, 116
Country Girls, The, 319
Courtauld, Stephen, 46–7, 73, 119
Courtenay, Tom, 196
Courtneys of Curzon Street, The, 21, 62, 72, 130
Cox, Vivien, 170
Coyne, Larry, 320
C. P. Choularton, 247
Craigie, Jill, 69
Craven, Richard, 294
Crawford, James, 314
Crichton, Charles, 184, 217
Crimson Pirate, The, 166
Cripps, Stafford, 33, 35, 37, 42, 86, 98
Cromwell, 236, 245, 251
Cross, Ben, 314

Crown Film Unit, 86–7, 114, 121
Croydon, John, 7n, 139, 147–8, 151–3, 155–7, 168–70, 172–4, 185, 188–91, 199, 203–4, 215, 222, 229, 233, 249–50, 252–3
Cruel Sea, The, 110, 118
C. T. Bowring & Co., 47, 144
Cullen, William, 146–7
Cunliffe-Lister, Philip, 14, 16
Cure for Love, The, 129–30
Curse of Frankenstein, The, 123, 202
Curzon Film Distributors, 342
Cyclone Films, 222
Czinner, Paul, 18, 223

Dad's Army, 245
Daily Express, 80
Daily Film Renter, 119
Daily Mail, 40
Dalton, Hugh, 20, 33, 35–7
'Dalton duty' *see ad valorem* duty
Dalrymple, Ian, 129, 133
Daly, John, 247–8, 301
Dam Busters, The, 110, 118, 136, 203, 350
Dance Hall, 72
Dance With a Stranger, 338
Dancing Years, 118
Danger Man (TV series), 268
Dangerous Moonlight, 161
Danischewsky, Monja, 184
Danziger, Edward, 214–15
Danziger, Harry, 214–15
Dark Crystal, The, 314, 318
Dark Man, The, 102
Darling, 204–5
Davenport, Nicholas, 46, 48, 57, 78–9, 81, 111–12, 130
David Newman Films, 218
Davies, John, 275
Davis, Desmond, 222, 319
Davis, Bette, 148,, 268
Davis, John, 1, 4, 52–3, 65–6, 70, 116–17, 120, 128, 133, 191, 201–2, 205–6, 217, 223–4, 255
Davy, 120
Day the Earth Caught Fire, The, 202, 215
Dearden, Basil, 155, 180, 185
Death on the Nile, 268, 301
Deeley, Michael, 254–5, 287–8, 293
Deer Hunter, The, 268
Defence of the Realm, The, 338
Del Giudice, Filippo, 51, 56, 69, 77

Delfont, Bernard, 207, 250, 268, 287
Dell, Edmund, 294
Dell, Jeffrey, 88
Delon, Alain, 263
Denham Studios, 17, 22, 66, 115, 161
Dent, David, 184
Dentist in the Chair, 138–9
Department of Trade, 292, 295, 303, 306–9, 331–3, 336, 339–42
Department of Trade and Industry, 252, 276, 282
Derby Day, 132
Desperate Moment, 115
Deutsch, David, 233–4
Deutsch, Oscar, 20, 51
Diamonds Are Forever, 244
Dickinson, Margaret, 2, 36, 95, 104
Dickinson, Thorold, 65, 88, 115
Disappearance of Harry, The, 320
distribution guarantees, 2, 48–9, 55–8, 86, 134, 164, 221, 260
Distributors Corporation of America, 136
'Distribution and Exhibition of Films' *see* Plant Report
Diva, 318
Dmytryk, Edward, 82
Doctor at Large, 111
Doctor at Sea, 111
Doctor Dolittle, 236
Doctor in Love, 196
Doctor in the House, 110, 116
Dr No, 7n, 196–7, 199, 202
Doctor Zhivago, 197
Doll's House, A, 264
Domino Productions, 234
Don't Look Now, 245, 253
Don't Lose Your Head, 205
Donat, Robert, 89
Donner, Richard, 303
Doomwatch, 246
Double Confession, 102
Douglas, Bill, 334
Dovemead Films, 303
Dracula, 2, 123
Drake, Charlie, 206
Draughtsman's Contract, The, 320
Drayton, Harold, 90, 130–2
Dream Child, 316
Dresser, The, 342
Drum, The, 18
Drury, David, 320

Dryhurst, Edward, 56
Dulles, Allen, 37
Duncan, Andrew, 50–1
Dunkirk, 111, 120
Dunwoody, Gwyneth, 275, 287
Durgnat, Raymond, 1, 110

Eadle, Richard, 23
Eady, Wilfrid, 37–8, 40, 54, 78, 86–7, 90, 91, 95–105, 118
Eady levy, 6, 95–105, 114, 118, 122, 136, 153, 164, 189, 214, 229–30, 265, 289, 296, 301–9, 330, 332–8, 349; *see also* British Film Production Fund
Eagle Has Landed, The, 269
Eagle Star Insurance Company, 52
Ealing Studios, 23–4, 51, 55, 72–3, 87, 116, 118–20, 147, 180
Easy Money, 70
Easy Rider, 235
Eberts, Jake, 322–6
Eclipse Film Productions, 83
Economist, The, 131, 135, 139, 218, 236, 253, 267, 278–9, 290, 303
Educating Rita, 312, 314, 321, 342
Edwards, Bill, 173, 182
Edwards, Blake, 268
EEC *see* European Economic Community
Eldorado Films, 252
Eldridge, John, 121
Electra Finance Company, 322
Electric and Musical Industries *see* EMI
Electric Dreams, 318
Electrical Trades Union, 67
Elephant Man, The, 313
Elizabeth of Ladymead, 72
Ellman, Louise, 216
Elstree Distributors, 203, 206
Elstree Studios, 19, 22, 88, 117, 207, 250
Elusive Pimpernel, The, 23, 129, 132
Elvin, George, 67
EMB Film Unit *see* Empire Marketing Board
Embassy Communications International, 315
Embassy Pictures, 203–4
Emery, Dick, 280
EMI, 207–8, 248–51, 254–5, 261, 268, 315–16, 318, 336, 349
EMI Film Distributors, 246–7, 255, 264
EMI-MGM Film Productions, 250
Emmanuelle, 301
Empire Marketing Board, 86–7, 120

Empire Strikes Back, The, 313
'end money', 2, 56–7, 80, 85, 220
End of the River, The, 71
Endfield, Cy, 203, 246
Ensign Trust, 326
Entertainer, The, 123, 187–8, 202
Entertainment Connections, 325
Entertainment Tax, 19, 25, 62, 67, 95–100, 114, 180–1
Eon Productions, 315
Epstein, Brian, 209
Equity Enterprises, 248
Eros Films, 148, 165, 214
Escape to Athena, 269
Essex, David, 281
Essoldo cinema circuit, 182
Esther Waters, 71
E.T.: The Extra-Terrestrial, 313
Eurofilms, 262
Europa Films, 266
European Economic Community (EEC), 289–90, 295, 344n
Europeans, The, 302, 336–7
Euston Films, 315
Evans, Edith, 65
Evil Dead, 318
Evil Under the Sun, 314–15
Exclusive Films, 79, 83–4
Expresso Bongo, 138–9
Extra Day, The, 155
Eye of the Needle, 315
Eyre, Richard, 319, 338

Facett Productions, 170
Fahrenheit 451, 228
Fairchild, William, 155
Falkender, Lady, 288, 294, 297n
Fall of the Roman Empire, The, 197
Fallen Idol, The, 11, 23, 54, 63, 72
Fallow Land, The, 83
Fame is the Spur, 58
Family Way, The, 197, 209, 224, 251
Famous-Lasky Film Service, 161
Far From the Madding Crowd, 229
Farrow, Leslie, 47
Farrow, Mia, 268
Father Brown, 170–1
Father's Doing Fine, 117
Federation of Film Unions, 287
Feldman, Charles K., 230
Feldman, Marty, 296

Fennell, Albert, 184
Ferrer, José, 153, 174
Ferrer, Mel, 248
Ferry to Hong Kong, 117, 182
Festival Film Productions, 89
Field, Mary, 104
Film Finances, 3, 5, 7n, 135–6, 139, 143–58, 168–72, 184–5, 187–91, 196, 199–200, 205, 215–16, 218, 224, 231–4, 249, 252–3, 266–7, 320
Film Four International, 342
Film Industry Defence Organisation (FIDO), 180–1
Film Policy (White Paper), 339–41
Film Production Association of Great Britain, 236–7, 288
Films Act (1970), 274–6, 288, 293
Films Act (1980), 307, 333–4, 337
Films Act (1985), 341–2
Films and Filming, 223
Films La Boetie, 264
Final Act of the United Nations Charter on Trade and Employment *see* Havana Charter
Final Programme, The, 280, 282
Finance Act (1981), 342
Finance Corporation for Industry, 78, 91, 332
Financial Times, The, 40, 84–5, 242, 246, 264, 270, 279, 341
Finney, Albert, 189, 196, 250
First Great Train Robbery, The, 302
First National Bank (Boston), 270
First National Bank of America, 263
First World War, 14–15, 95, 161
Fisz, Benjamin S., 206, 234, 317
Flash Gordon, 313
Flint, Michael, 262
Fly Away, Peter, 64
Flynn, Errol, 136
Fonda, Jane, 264
For the Love of Ada, 246
For Them That Trespass, 73
For Your Eyes Only, 307, 309, 313–14, 318
Forbes, Bryan, 185, 207, 248–50, 265, 309
Forbidden, 72
Force 10 From Navarone, 302
Foreman, Carl, 171, 173, 289
Forever Young, 320
Forstarter, Mark, 247
Forsyth, Bill, 336
Foster, Maurice, 156

49th Parallel, 19, 21
Four Feathers, The (1939), 18, 156
Four Feathers, The (1978), 303
Four Weddings and a Funeral, 4
Fox, Edward, 267
Fox Film Corporation, 15
Foxwell, Ivan, 88, 117, 134, 182–3, 203
Foy Investments, 52
Francis, Karl, 319
Francovich, Mike, 173
Frears, Stephen, 319, 321
Free Cinema, 110
Freedom Group, 208–9
French, Henry, 66, 99, 101, 103, 164
French Lieutenant's Woman, The, 312–13, 315
Frend, Charles, 184–5
Frieda, 21, 72–3
From Beyond the Grave, 247
From Russia With Love, 197, 199, 201
'front money', 2, 56, 82, 85, 143
Frost, David, 248, 260, 265
Fuest, Robert, 280
Fugie Eioga, 267
Fuller, W. R., 35, 40, 100
Furie, Sidney J., 206, 216
'Future of the British Film Industry' *see* Terry Report

Gabor, Zsa Zsa, 153
Gale, John, 222–3
Galloping Major, The, 148
Gainsborough Pictures, 21, 51–2, 63, 65–6
Gaitskell, Hugh, 33, 90, 103
Gamma People, The, 170
Gandhi, 309, 312–13, 318, 322–3, 347, 350
Garrett, Robert, 56, 143, 144–56, 168–72, 187, 199–200, 203–4, 216, 218, 234, 249
Garrick Film Distributors, 216
Gater, Henry, 66
Gater Report, 66–7; *see also* Working Party on Film Production Costs (Board of Trade)
Gaumont cinema circuit, 63, 69, 181
Gaumont-British Picture Corporation (GBPC), 18, 20, 24, 46–7, 52, 147
General Cinema Corporation, 269
General Cinema Finance Corporation (GCFC), 19, 47, 51–2, 68
General Film Distributors (GFD), 47–8, 52, 58, 72, 86, 88, 104, 115, 147
General Post Office Film Unit *see* GPO Film Unit

General Theatre Corporation, 52
Genevieve, 4, 114, 116, 123
Geordie, 135
Gershwin, Jerry, 232
Get Carter, 249
Ghost Goes West, The, 18
Ghostbusters, 313, 348
Gielgud, John, 250
Gift Horse, The, 114, 150–3, 155
Gilbert, Lewis, 116, 229
Gill, Jack, 270
Gilliam, Terry, 247, 283, 318
Gilliat, Sidney, 20, 129, 133, 137–8, 182, 208–10, 230, 236
Gilling, John, 170
Girl in the Picture, The, 342
Give Us This Day, 82, 102
Gladwell, David, 336
Globus, Yoram, 316
Go-Between, The, 249–50
Goddard, Janet, 321
Golan, Menahem, 316
Gold, 245, 266
Goldcrest Films and Television, 13, 314, 318, 322–6, 337, 342, 347
Goldcrest Films International, 322–3
Goldcrestt Holdings, 323
Golden Lady, The, 302
Goldfinger, 197, 199, 201
Goldman, William, 267, 350
Goldschmidt, John, 321
Goldstone, John, 280, 283
Gomery, Douglas, 12
Gone to Earth, 129, 132
Gone With the Wind, 68
Gonks Go Beat, 196
Goodbye, Mr Chips (1939), 161
Goodbye, Mr Chips (1969), 235
Goodliffe, David, 290
Goodtimes Enterprises, 280–1
Goodwin, Richard, 316
Gordon, Richard, 116
Gossip, 317
Gould, Bryan, 341
Gould, Elliott, 267
GPO Film Unit, 120
Grade, Leslie, 207
Grade, Lew, 13, 268–71, 315
Graduate, The, 235
Graf, William, 171
Granada cinema circuit, 182

Grant, Cary, 144
Grant, W. A., 335
Grease, 245, 300, 305
Great Caruso, The, 110
Great Expectations, 11, 21, 70–1
Great Muppet Caper, The, 318
Great Rock'n'Roll Swindle, The, 318
Great St Trinian's Train Robbery, The, 209, 251
Greatest Show on Earth, The, 110
Green, Guy, 185
Green for Danger, 71
Greenaway, Peter, 320
Greene, Graham, 132
Gregg, Colin, 319
Gregg, Peter, 318
Gregory's Girl, 312, 314, 336–7
Greyhound Corporation, 263
Greystoke: The Legend of Tarzan, Lord of the Apes, 313
Grierson, John, 87–8, 120–1
Griffith, D. W., 14, 15
Griffith, Hugh, 233–4
Group Holdings, 52
Group production scheme (NFFC), 88–9, 115–18, 120–2, 221–2
Group 3, 88–9, 120–2, 126n
Grunwald, Anatole de, 83, 129, 203
Grunwald, Dimitri de, 236, 262–3, 277
Guardian, The, 322
Guest, Val, 139, 215, 316
Gulf + Western, 235
Guinea Pig, The, 58, 63, 66, 69, 73
Guinness, Alec, 173–44, 203
Guinness Mahon, 267
Guns of Navarone, The, 139, 172–3, 197, 206, 350

Hackman, Gene, 267, 304
Haggar, William, 14
Hair of the Dog, 215
Hakim, André, 167
Half a Sixpence, 230
Hall, Peter, 262–3, 281
Halton, Fiona, 339
Hambros Bank, 209
Hamer, Robert, 170
Hamlet (1913), 14
Hamlet (1948), 11, 21, 70–1, 157, 350
Hammer Film Productions, 173, 202, 244, 246–7
Hanbury, Jack, 190
Hancock, Tony, 206

HandMade Films, 318–19
Hanson, Barry, 318
Happiest Days of Your Life, The, 110, 129, 131
Happy Ever After, 118
Happy Go Lucky, 118
Happy is the Bride, 138
Hard Day's Night, A, 197, 199–200, 202, 219, 234
Hardy, Robin, 252
Hare, David, 320
Hargreaves, John, 249
Harper, Sue, 111
Harris, Richard, 196, 266
Harrison, George, 318
Hart-Davis, Rupert, 222
Harvey, Anthony, 262
Harvey, Laurence, 204
Hassan, Mamoun, 315, 330, 332, 334–8, 341, 343
Havana Charter, 39
Havelock-Allan, Anthony, 20, 55–6, 88, 115, 129, 144, 147
Havers, Nigel, 314
Hawkins, Jack, 185
Haxell, Fred, 67
HBO, 316
He Who Rides A Tiger, 217–18
Heald, Lionel, 209
Heart of the Matter, The, 133
Heat and Dust, 314, 337
Heath, Edward, 252, 265, 330
Heathcoat-Amory, Derrick, 181
Heathfield Investment Society, 47
Hell Below Zero, 169–70
Hellions, The, 155, 215
Hellman, Marcel, 88, 117
Hello, Dolly!, 236
Help!, 197, 199–200, 219
Hemdale Associates, 247–8
Hemdale Films International, 248, 266, 301
Hemmings, David, 247
Henry V, 21, 51, 157
Hepburn, Katherine, 132, 150–1
Hepworth, Cecil, 14
Her Favourite Husband, 109
Her Majesty's Customs and Revenue, 306; *see also* Inland Revenue
Herlihy, Joyce, 314
Here Come the Huggets, 63
Hero, 320
Heroes of Telemark, The, 206

Heyman, John, 250
High Treason, 115, 150
Highbury Studios, 24, 115, 147
Hill, John, 312, 341
Hill Samuel, 263, 278–9, 288
Hiller, Wendy, 250
History of Mr Polly, The, 23, 71
Hitchcock, Alfred, 17, 42
Hoare, Victor, 208
Hobson's Choice, 135
Hodges, Mike, 249, 309, 316
Holcroft Covenant, The, 316
Holiday Camp, 21, 70
Holm, Ian, 314
Holmes à Court, Robert, 271, 315
Home Box Office *see* HBO
Honeymoon Deferred, 129
Honky Tonk Freeway, 270, 315
Hope, Peter, 146–7, 151, 155
Hopkins, Anthony, 267
Hopkins, John, 262
Horizon Pictures, 150–1, 172–3
Horror of Frankenstein, 246
Hot Wheels, 304–5
Hound of the Baskervilles, The, 302
Hour of 13, The, 167
House That Dripped Blood, The, 247
Houston, Penelope, 228
How the West Was Won, 197
Hudson, Hugh, 314, 324
Hue and Cry, 72
Hughes, Adrian, 321
Hughes, Howard, 168
Hume, Nutcombe, 208
Hungry Hill, The, 71
Hunted, 115
Huston, John, 132, 150, 153–4
Huth, Harold, 155

I Accuse!, 167
I Was Happy Here, 222, 224
I'm All Right, Jack!, 110, 123, 138, 214
I'm Not Feeling Myself Tonight, 304
Ideal Husband, An, 54, 72
Idle, Eric, 247
if . . ., 196, 229
Ill Met By Moonlight, 117
Imperial War Museum, 281
Importance of Being Earnest, The, 115
In Which We Serve, 19, 51, 66
Independent Artists, 191

Independent Television Corporation *see* ITC
Independent Film Distributors, 130, 132, 135–6, 152–3, 181
Independent Frame, 66
Independent Producers, 20, 70, 185
Indiana Jones and the Temple of Doom, 313
Individual Pictures, 20
Industrial and Commercial Finance Corporation, 78, 91, 113, 279, 333
Industrial Finance and Investment Corporation, 47
Industrial Reorganisation Corporation, 225, 275
Inland Revenue, 251; *see also* Her Majesty's Customs and Revenue
Interim Action Committee on the Film Industry, 12, 293–7, 301, 305, 331, 333
International Film Consortium, 262
International Film Investors, 322
International Velvet, 302
Interrupted Journey, The, 102, 130, 144
Intolerance, 15
Inverchaple, Lord, 38–9
Invitation to the Dance, 167
Ipcress File, The, 206
Irish Film Board, 318–19
Isadora, 229, 231
Island Records, 247
Islington Studios, 24, 115
It Always Rains on Sunday, 72–3
It Started in Paradise, 115
It's Great to be Young, 118
It's Trad, Dad!, 219
ITC, 268, 318
Ivanhoe, 110, 162, 166–7
Ivory, James, 336

J. Arthur Rank Film Distributors, 117
J. Arthur Rank Organisation *see* Rank Organisation
J. Arthur Rank Overseas Distributors
Jabberwocky, 283
Jackson, Pat, 116
Jaffe, Leo, 170
James Dean: The First American Teenager, 282
James Street Productions, 304
Janni, Joseph, 129, 190, 204–5, 209–10, 224
Jarman, Derek, 304, 338
Jarratt, Arthur, 63, 78, 101, 129, 134, 137
Javelin Films, 56, 147
Jaws, 245, 261
Jaws 2, 305

Jay, Douglas, 221
Jay Lewis Productions, 82, 151–3
Jenkin, Patrick, 276, 279
Jethro Tull, 247
J. H. Vavasseur, 253–4
Jigsaw Man, The, 317
Joffé, Roland, 323, 325
John, Rosamund, 67
John and Julie, 122
Johnston, Eric, 35, 37–40, 42
Jokers, The, 219, 229, 231
Jones, Griff Rhys, 316
Jones, Jennifer, 132
Jones, Terry, 247
Jordan, Neil, 318–19
Joseph, Keith, 275
Jubilee, 304
Judgement Deferred, 121
Julia, 300
Juneau International, 262

Kantner, Jay, 229–30
Kastner, Elliott, 232–3
Katz, Peter, 252
Keeling, John, 133–4
Kennedy, Arthur, 174
Kennedy, Paul, 32
Kerkorian, Kirk, 235
Key, The, 170
Keynes, John Maynard, 31
Khartoum, 210
Kid for Two Farthings, A, 156–7
Killing Fields, The, 312–13, 323
Kind Hearts and Coronets, 3, 72–3, 118
Kind of Loving, A, 190, 196
Kinden, Gorham, 1
Kinematograph Renters' Society (KRS), 68–9, 180
Kinematograph Weekly, 11, 20, 22, 25, 36, 77–80, 84, 88–9, 91, 109, 111, 115, 119–20, 122, 137, 161, 164–5, 169, 179, 236, 238, 244
King, Alexander, 23, 40, 99
King, George, 72
King and Country, 203–4
King's Rhapsody, 136
Kingsley, David, 122, 134–6, 137, 207–9, 214
Kingsmere Productions, 325
Kinney National Services, 235
Kipps, 161
Klement, Otto, 144
Klingender, F. D., 5, 18, 47

Klinger, Michael, 247, 266–7
Knack, The, 196, 200
Knight, Castleton, 110
Knight Without Armour, 18
Knights of the Round Table, 162, 167
Korda, Alexander, 3, 5, 13, 17, 20–1, 47, 53, 65, 78, 90, 129, 156–7, 347
Kramer vs. Kramer, 313
Kruger, Hardy, 267
Kubrick, Stanley, 196, 228, 230
Kulik, Karol, 54

L-Shaped Room, The, 207
Ladd, Alan, 168–9
Ladies Who Do, 219
Lady Chatterly's Lover, 314
Lady Vanishes, The, 256, 302
Lady With a Lamp, The, 132
Lambert, Verity, 315–16
Lamitas Property and Investment Corporation, 267
Lamont, Norman, 341–2
Lancelot and Guinevere, 232
Lansbury, Angela, 268
Last Days of Dolwyn, The, 129, 130
Last Grenade, The, 262
Laughter in Paradise, 110
Launder, Frank, 20, 64, 129, 133, 137–8, 182, 208–9
Lavender Hill Mob, The, 118
Laverstoke Investment Trust, 47
Lawrence of Arabia, 172, 174–5, 196–7, 200–1, 316, 350
Lawrie, James, 55, 57, 68, 79, 81, 83, 85, 91, 117, 146, 149–50
Lazenby, George, 246
Leacock, Philip, 121
League of Gentlemen, The, 185–6
Lean, David, 1, 20, 66, 129, 172, 174, 316, 347
Leather Boys, The, 216–17
Lee, Christopher, 296
Lee, Frank, 57, 90, 113, 138
Lee, James, 323–5
Led Zeppelin, 247
Ledyard, The, 305
Legacy, The, 302
Legend, 313
Legg, Stuart, 5, 18, 47
Leigh, Mike, 319
Lesslie, Colin, 184

Lester, Mark, 247
Lester, Richard, 219
Let's Get Laid, 304
Letter to Brezhnev, 321
Lever, Harold, 113–14
Levine, Joseph E., 203–5, 267, 300, 322
Lewis, Jay, 152–3
Lieberson, Sandy, 3, 280–1, 283, 309, 324
Life for Ruth, 186
Lime Grove Studios *see* Shepherd's Bush Studios (Lime Grove)
Lindenberg, Paul, 47
Lion Has Wings, The, 19
Lion International Films, 135
Lisztomania, 282
Live and Let Die, 244
Lloyd, Euan, 261–2, 266–7, 316–17
Lloyds Bank, 47, 57, 144, 148, 184, 188–91, 224, 227n
Lloyds of London, 144
Loach, Ken, 1, 3, 224
Local Hero, 312, 314, 323, 336, 342
Lock Up Your Daughters, 233–4
Lolita, 228
London and Yorkshire Trust, 133
London Film Productions, 3, 47, 144, 156–7, 269, 326
London Belongs To Me, 70–1
London Screenplays, 262
London Town, 4, 21, 23
Long Duel, The, 206
Long Good Friday, The, 312, 314, 318
Long Memory, The, 115
Longest Day, The, 197, 268
Loneliness of the Long Distance Runner, The, 4, 186, 196
Look Back in Anger, 186, 190
Loose Connections, 338
Lorimar, 267
Losey, Joseph, 1, 3, 196, 203–4, 210, 231, 249–50, 263–4, 276, 296
Love in Waiting, 64
Love Match, The, 122
Loves of Joanna Godden, The, 72
Lovell, Alan, 7
Low, Rachael, 1, 13–15
Lucky Jim, 183
Lustful Lady, A, 304
Lustowe Corporation, 136
Lynn, Vera, 281
Lyttelton, Oliver, 46, 51, 81, 84, 90

MacCorkindale, Simon, 268
McCreath, Hugh, 53
McEnery, Peter, 247
McFarlane, Brian, 1
McMasters, The, 262
MacPhail, Angus, 14
MacQuitty, William, 155, 208
Macbeth, 265–6
Mack, Earl, 326
Mackendrick, Alexander, 173
Mackenzie, John, 318
Macmillan, Harold, 47
Macmillan, Maurice, 277
Macnab, Geoffrey, 95
Made in Heaven, 115
Magic Box, The, 89
Maidment, Ken, 304, 313, 335, 340–1
Mainline Pictures, 321
Major Barbara, 22, 48–50
Malcolm, Derek, 312, 322
Mallah Films, 262
Malta Story, The, 116
Man About the House, 72
Man for All Seasons, A, 196, 210, 236
Man in a Suitcase (TV series), 268
Man in the Moon, 186
Man in the Sky, The, 120
Man on the Run, 73
Man Who Could Work Miracles, The, 18
Man Who Fell to Earth, The, 254, 282
Man Who Never Was, The, 167
Man With the Golden Gun, The, 244–5
Man's Fate, 236
Mancunian Film Corporation, 83, 86
Mandrake the Magician, 324–5
Mankiewicz, Joseph L., 265
Mannock, P. L., 17, 22
Manorfield Investments, 52
Maria Chapdelaine, 129
Mark of Cain, The, 71
Markey, Gene, 129
Marney, Derrick de, 89
Maroc 7, 222–3
Marry Me, 71
Marsh, Laurie, 248
Marshall, Alan, 280
Marshall Plan, 37–8
Martell, Edward, 208
Martini Foundation, 317
Marvin, Lee, 266
Mary Stuart, 236

Master of Ballantrae, The, 162, 166
Matter of Life and Death, A, 21
Matthews, Jessie, 18
Mature, Victor, 169
Maxwell, Catherine, 53–4
Maxwell, John, 53–4
Mayflower Pictures Corporation, 56
Mayne, Laura, 321
Maytime in Mayfair, 129, 130
MCA *see* Music Corporation of America
Meacher, Michael, 304
Mears, Harry, 104
Medusa Touch, The, 302
Meet Me Tonight, 115
Melina Productions, 215
Melody, 247
Memoirs of a Survivor, 284, 336–7
Men of Two Worlds, 21
Merchant, Ismail, 336, 343
Merchant-Ivory Productions, 336, 342
Merry Christmas, Mr Lawrence, 337
Merton Park Studios, 204
Metro-Goldwyn-Mayer *see* MGM
Metropolis and Bradford Trust, 52
MGM, 12, 120, 157, 161, 164, 166–7, 171–2, 203, 230, 234, 236–7, 243, 249–50, 318
Middleton, Drew, 39
Midland Bank, 47, 323
Midnight Cowboy, 235, 237
Midnight Express, 302, 313
Miles, Bernard, 69
Miles, Christopher, 262–3
Millichip, Roy, 222
Millions Like Us, 19
Mills, John, 23
Milos Films, 132
Mine Own Executioner, 72
Ministry of Defence, 234
Miniver Story, The, 166
Minney, R. J., 21, 65
Miranda, 63, 70
Mirror Crack'd, The, 315
Mission, The, 325–6
Mr Forbush and the Penguins, 248–9
Mr Perrin & Mr Traill, 71
Mrs Christopher, 148
Mitchum, Robert, 166
Modesty Blaise, 204, 209–10, 231
Mollo, Andrew, 334
Molton Films, 153
Monty Python and the Holy Grail, 4, 245, 247

Monty Python's Life of Brian, 309, 313, 318
Monty Python's The Meaning of Life, 313–14
Moody, Paul, 315
Moonlighting, 323, 337
Moonraker, 244, 302–3, 313
Moore, Dudley, 314
Moore, Roger, 266–7, 296
Morgan Grenfell, 261–2, 265
Morning Departure, 82, 102, 151
Morons from Outer Space, 316
Morris, Oswald, 153
Morton, Monty, 201–2
Motion Picture Export Association, 35, 38, 40, 43, 164
Motion Picture Herald, 40, 89
Motion Picture Producers and Distributors of America, 15
Moulin Rouge, 123, 132, 153–5
Mudlark, The, 162, 167
Muppet Movie, The, 269
Muppet Show, The (TV series), 269–70
Murder on the Orient Express, 250–1, 254–5, 268
Murphy, Robert, 2, 196
Murphy's War, 262
Music Corporation of America, 235
Music Machine, The, 302
Muson, Chris, 229
My Beautiful Laundrette, 4, 321
My Brother Jonathan, 73
My Brother's Keeper, 70–1
My Daughter Joy, 129
My Fair Lady, 197
Mycroft, Walter, 88

National Archives, 3, 5
National Association of Theatrical and Kinema Employees, 67
National Broadcasting Company: *see* NBC
National Coal Board Pension Fund, 322
National Circuit, 182
National Film Archive, 290
National Film Board of Canada, 120
National Film Development Fund, 291, 332, 336, 343
National Film Finance Company, 24, 79–81, 130
National Film Finance Consortium, 274–84, 334
National Film Finance Corporation (NFFC), 1, 5, 6, 7, 37, 55, 57, 68, 74, 77–92, 95, 102, 111–14, 119, 121, 128–30, 131, 133–4, 136–8, 146, 149–50, 179, 183, 185–6, 198, 208–9, 214, 216, 218–25, 228, 231, 238, 244, 249, 252, 264–5, 274–84, 289, 291, 295, 307, 313, 317, 323, 330–43, 347, 349–50; *see also* British Film Makers; Group production scheme; Group 3; National Film Development Fund; National Film Finance Company; National Film Finance Consortium
National Film Finance Corporation of India, 323
National Film School, 307, 340
National Film Trustee Company, 264
National Provincial Bank, 41, 46–8, 50, 57, 147–8, 185–6, 190, 214–16, 221
National Westminster Bank, 247, 279, 333; *see also* National Provincial Bank; Westminster Bank
National Telefilm Associates, 138
NBC, 266–7
Neagle, Anna, 18, 68, 136
Neame, Ronald, 20, 23, 88, 115, 167, 184
Neame Enterprises, 209
Neither the Sea Nor the Sand, 246
Nell Gwynn, 18
Nelly's Version, 320
Nettlefold Studios, 24; *see also* Walton Studios
Never Let Go, 167
Never Say Never Again, 314
Never Take No For An Answer, 150
New Elstree Studios, 215
New World Pictures, 148
New York Times, 261
Newbrook, Peter, 222
Newley, Anthony, 229
Newman, David, 217–18
Night and the City, 167
Night Without Stars, 148
Nightbeat, 72
1984, 315, 318
Niven, David, 267–8, 296
No Orchids for Miss Blandish, 63
No Resting Place, 148
No Room at the Inn, 63
No Surrender, 342
Nolbandov, Sergei, 88
Noose, 73
Norman, Montagu, 32, 49
North West Frontier, 182
Norton Simon, 260
Nott, John, 307, 330–4

Nova (distributor), 215
Now, Barabbas, 83
Nowhere to Go, 120

O'Brien, Denis, 318
O'Brien, Tom, 67
O'Hara, Gerry, 222
O'Neal, Ryan, 267
O'Toole, Peter, 174, 196, 278
Oakley, Charles, 12
Octopussy, 309, 313–14
Odd Man Out, 21
Odeon cinema circuit, 69, 181
Odeon Theatres, 20, 24, 51–2
Odette, 109, 129, 131–2
Oh . . . Rosalinda!!, 118, 156
Oliver!, 196–7, 230, 234, 245, 251
Oliver Twist, 11, 63, 70
Olivier, Laurence, 21, 157, 188, 267
Omen, The, 254, 300
On Her Majesty's Secret Service, 245
On the Buses, 245, 247
One Night With You, 71
One Wild Oat, 148
Ooh . . . You Are Awful, 280, 282
Open Road Productions, 171, 173
Orion Pictures, 321
Ornstein, George H., 198–200, 235
Orr, Hugh, 288
Osborne, John, 4, 187, 209
Ostrer, Maurice, 63
Outlook Films, 69
Overlord, 281, 282
Overton, Arnold, 134
Oxford University Film Society, 64

P'Tang Yang Kipperbang, 323
Pacino, Al, 324
Pal, George, 171–2
Palace Pictures, 318–19, 325
Palache Report, 20, 69
Palin, Michael, 247
Pallos, Stephen, 215, 231
Pandora and the Flying Dutchman, 102
Panton Film Guarantees, 143
Paradine Productions, 260, 265
Paramount Pictures, 12, 161, 206, 232, 234–5, 263, 268, 305
Park, James, 318
Parker, Alan, 280–1
Parkin, Leslie, 184

Parrish, Robert, 232
Parthian Productions, 83
Pascal, Gabriel, 21, 22, 29n, 48, 50, 65
Pascal Film Productions, 48
Passage to India, A, 313, 316, 347
Passionate Friends, The, 23, 70–1
Passport to Pimlico, 72–3, 118
Paul, R. W., 14
Pax Films, 215
Pears, S. J., 79, 129
Pearson Longman Group, 322, 326
Peck, Gregory, 166, 266
Peeping Tom, 202
Penington, Jon, 139
Penny and the Parnell Case, 64
Perfect Friday, 262
Perkins, Anthony, 250
Perry, George, 12, 17–18
Perry, Simon, 320
Persuaders!, The (TV series), 268
Petard Productions, 281
Petit, Chris, 336
Petley, Julian, 12, 330
Philip Hill Investment Trust, 279
Phillips, Leslie, 222–3
Phillips, William, 270
Piccadilly Incident, 21
Piece of Cake, 64
Pilgrim Pictures, 56, 66, 69, 77
Pinewood Studios, 17, 19, 22, 88, 115, 170, 303
Pink Floyd, 247
Pink Panther Strikes Again, The, 245, 254
Pinnacle Productions, 56–7
Pinter, Harold, 203
Pirates of Penzance, The, 318
Pirie, David, 243
Plant, Arnold, 68–9
Plant Report, 55–6, 69, 96
Plantagenet Films, 82
Playbirds, The, 304
Playboy Magazine Enterprises, 265
Pliatzky, Leo, 218, 277, 331–3, 341
Plowicz, Peter, 287
Plummer, Christopher, 233
Polanski, Roman, 196, 265–6
Political and Economic Planning, 11, 104, 161
Polytel, 318, 336
Pommer, Erich, 18
Ponti, Carlo, 236
Poor Cow, 197, 224
Porridge, 301–2

Portal, Lord, 47, 68–9
Porter, Edwin S., 14
Porter, Vincent, 111, 116, 290–1, 308
Portrait from Life, 63, 70
Power Play, 303
Powell, Michael, 1, 17, 20–2, 66, 116–17, 129, 132, 156, 222
Powell, Richard, 288
Prem, Tara, 321
Preminger, Otto, 228
Pressburger, Emeric, 20–1, 116–17, 129, 132, 156
Pretty Polly, 231
Priggen, Norman, 184, 203
Prime Minister, The, 161
Prime Minister's Working Party on the Film Industry, 288–90; *see also* Terry Report
Prisoner, The (TV series), 268
Private Angelo, 69, 74
Private Life of Don Juan, The, 18
Private Life of Henry VIII, The, 17–18, 47, 350
Private Life of Sherlock Holmes, The, 236
Private's Progress, 111, 123, 135
Prize of Gold, A, 169–70
Production Facilities, 64
Provincial Cinematograph Theatres, 24, 52
Prudential Assurance Company, 3, 18, 47, 52, 91
Public Accounts Committee, 90
Pure Hell of St Trinian's, The, 207
Purser, Philip, 322
Puttnam, David, 3, 280–1, 294, 314, 323, 325–6
Pygmalion, 22

Quadrophenia, 302, 313–14
Queen is Crowned, A, 110
Queen of Spades, 23, 65–6, 74, 83
Quiller Memorandum, The, 203
Quinn, Anthony, 174
Quintain Productions, 280
quota, 6, 16–17, 23, 32, 40–1, 43, 49, 77, 90, 122
Quota Act *see* Cinematograph Films Act (1927)
'quota quickies', 16–17, 161

Radclyffe, Sarah, 321
Radford, Michael, 318, 320
Radio On, 336
Railway Children, The, 245, 250
Rains, Claude, 174
Raise the Titanic!, 4, 270–1, 315
Raising a Riot, 135

Rambo: First Blood Part II, 348
Ramsaye, Terry, 89
Rank, Joseph Arthur, 19, 25, 33, 46–7, 51–2, 62–4, 104–5, 205
Rank Film Distributors, 191, 202, 264, 266
Rank Film Distributors of America, 117, 182, 231
Rank Organisation, 1, 11, 13, 19–20, 51–2, 57, 64–5, 70–1, 86, 110, 114–17, 144, 181–2, 203, 205–6, 221–4, 234, 248, 255–6, 260, 278, 301, 326, 335, 347, 349–50; *see also* General Cinema Finance Corporation; General Film Distributors; J. Arthur Rank Film Distributors; J. Arthur Rank Overseas Distributors; Odeon Theatres; Rank Film Distributors; Rank Film Distributors of America; Rank Xerox
Rank Xerox, 205, 248
Raphael, Frederick, 205
Rapper, Irving, 148
Ratoff, Gregory, 129
Rattigan, Terence, 174
Rawlings, Terry, 314
Rawnsley, David, 66
Reach for the Sky, 110
Reade, Walter, 209–10, 224
Red Beret, The, 167–8
Red Monarch, 319
Red Shoes, The, 2, 11, 21, 63, 70–1, 173, 350
Redford, Robert, 267
Redgrave, Vanessa, 231, 250, 336
Reed, Carol, 1, 17, 54, 72, 129, 130, 156–7, 171
Reindeer Films, 264
Reiss, John, 316
Reisz, Karel, 3, 187–9, 191, 229, 231, 276
Reith, John, 81–2, 87–8, 90, 120
Relph, Michael, 155, 185, 287–8, 309
Relph, Simon, 317, 320
Rembrandt, 18
Remembrance, 319–20
Remick, Lee, 336
Remus Films, 187
Rescued by Rover, 14
Return of the Jedi, 313
Return of the Pink Panther, The, 245, 268
Return of the Soldier, The, 317
Revenge of the Pink Panther, 245
Revolution, 4, 324–5
Richard, Cliff, 197, 206, 210
Richard III, 156–7

Richardson, Tony, 1, 4–5, 187–90, 199–200, 209, 276
Riddle of the Sands, The, 256, 302–3
Ridley, Nicholas, 274, 276–9
Riley, W. G., 77–8
Rising Damp, 301, 318
Rittenberg, Saul, 171–2
Riverside Studios, 24
Rizzoli Films, 264
RKO Radio Pictures, 13, 41, 163–4, 168
Rob Roy, the Highland Rogue, 163
Robinson, David, 229
Robson, Mark, 170
Roeg, Nicolas, 253–4, 296, 309
Rogers, Peter, 183, 205–6, 301
Romantic Age, The, 102
Romantic Englishwoman, The, 264, 282
Romeo and Juliet, 223
Romulus Films, 57, 82, 132, 136, 150
Room at the Top, 110, 186–7
Room With a View, A, 342–3
Rose, David, 319–20
Rosenberg, Max, 214
Rosso, Franco, 336
Rowson, Simon, 13–14, 16
Roy, Ernest G., 24–5
Ruggles, Wesley, 21
Run for Your Money, A, 72
runaway production, 161–75, 198–201, 228–38
Russell, Ken, 1, 249
Ryder, John, 288

Sadler, Arthur, 279
Safari, 169–70
St John, Earl, 88, 116
St John-Stevas, Norman, 334
Sailor Beware!, 135
Sailor of the King, 167
Sailor's Return, The, 284
Saint, The (TV series), 268
Saints and Sinners, 129–30
Salkind, Alexander, 303
Salkind, Ilya, 303
Saltzman, Harry, 187–90, 206, 234, 287–8
Sam and the River, 282
Sammy Going South, 191
Samson and Delilah, 110
Samuel Montagu, 260
Sanders of the River, 18
Sandwich Man, The, 222, 224
Santa Claus – The Movie, 313

Santana Pictures, 132
Sapper, Alan, 287
Sapphire, 123, 182
Sapphire Films, 214
Saraband for Dead Lovers, 72–3
Sassoon, Arthur, 144
Saturday Night and Sunday Morning, 4, 123, 138, 186, 188–90, 196, 202, 207, 214
Saturday Night Fever, 245, 300
Saunders, Colin, 53
Savigny, Peter de, 115
Saville, Philip, 319
Say Hello to Yesterday, 263
Scarlet Pimpernel, The, 18
Scars of Dracula, 246
Schach, Max, 18
Schaffer, Anthony, 252
Schlesinger, John, 187, 190–1, 204–5, 209, 229, 237, 276, 296, 309
School for Scoundrels, 214
Schute, Martin, 223
Schwartz, Frederick J., 246
Scotia Investments, 265
Scott, C. H., 79
Scott, Ridley, 304
Scott of the Antarctic, 23, 63, 72–3
Scottish Arts Council, 320
Scottish Television, 336
Screen International, 254–5, 316, 323, 337, 340, 348
Scrooge, 110, 148
Sea Wolves, The, 267, 314
Seagulls Over Sorento, 167
Séance on a Wet Afternoon, 186
Second World War, 5, 18–20, 48–52, 161–2, 243, 349
Secret Places, 338
Sedgwick, John, 17
Sellers, Peter, 184, 232–3, 245, 248, 269
Selznick, David O., 21, 132, 166
Sequence (magazine), 110
Serious Charge, 123
Servant, The, 203
Setton, Maxwell, 56, 88, 117, 184
Seven Arts, 191
Seven Days to Noon, 58, 109, 129
Seventh Veil, The, 21
Shadow of the Eagle, 102
Shaftel, Josef, 165, 248, 260, 263, 277
Shalako, 261–2
Shanghai Surprise, 319

Sharif, Omar, 174
Shaw, George Bernard, 22, 48
Shawcross, Hartley, 89–90
She'll Be Wearing Pink Pyjamas, 321
Shepherd's Bush Studios (Lime Grove), 24, 115
Shepperton Studios, 137, 139, 173, 208, 230, 236, 244, 251–4, 303; *see also* Sound City Studios
Sherriff, Paul, 153
Shining, The, 313
Shipman-King cinema circuit, 182, 207
Shiralee, The, 120
Shochiku, 266
Shop at Sly Corner, The, 72
Shore, Peter, 292
Shot in the Dark, A, 199
Shout, The, 284
Shout at the Devil, 266
Siege of Pinchgut, The, 120
Sight & Sound, 110, 347
Silent Dust, 73
Silver Darlings, 73
Silverdea Films, 280
Sim, Sheila, 66
Simmons, Antony, 283
Sinbad and the Eye of the Tiger, 254
Sinclair, Andrew, 278
Sink the Bismarck!, 196, 250
Sipra, Mahmud, 317
Sir Francis Drake (TV series), 268
Sirius Film Productions, 114
633 Squadron, 199
Sixty Glorious Years, 18
Skutezky, Victor, 88
Skyfall, 2
Sleuth, 265
Slipper and the Rose, The, 265
Small Back Room, The, 72
Small Voice, The, 72, 144
Small World of Sammy Lee, The, 191
Smallest Show on Earth, The, 155, 180
Smedley-Aston, E. M., 155, 280
Smith, Gregg, 247
Snell, Peter, 252
So Little Time, 117
Soames, Richard, 320
Some Like It Cool, 219
Somervell, Rupert, 39, 49, 97–8
Something Money Can't Buy, 115
Somlo, Joseph, 153
Song for Tomorrow, A, 64

Soskin, Paul, 88, 119
Sound Barrier, The, 110, 131
Sound City Studios, 17, 20, 53; *see also* Shepperton Studios
Sound of Music, The, 197, 235–6
South African Story, 148
Spaceman and King Arthur, The, 314
Spiegel, Sam, 150–1, 172–5
Spikings, Barry, 254–5, 270, 315
Spraos, John, 180
Spring in Park Lane, 21, 63, 68, 72
Sproat, Iain, 339
Spy Who Loved Me, The, 244, 300
Stack, Robert, 152
Standard Industrial Trust, 208
Star!, 236
Star Associated Holdings, 251
Star of India, 165–6
Star Trek: The Motion Picture, 313
Star Wars, 245, 261, 300
Stardust, 245, 281–2, 284
State Secret, 129
Statue, The, 263
Steptoe and Son, 250, 280
Stevie, 302
Stewart, Hugh, 88
Stoll Film Company, 15
Stop Press, 66
Stopford, Richard, 57, 79, 112–13
Storm Over the Nile, 157
Story of Gilbert and Sullivan, The, 133
Story of Robin Hood and His Merrie Men, The, 115, 162–3
Stranger's Hand, The, 132
Straw Dogs, 3
Street, Sarah, 1, 12, 36, 95, 104, 314–15, 341
Strick, Joseph, 224
Stross, Raymond, 165–6, 216–17
Stubbs, Jonathan, 175
Stud, The, 302
Summer Holiday, 197, 206
Summertime, 156
Sunday Telegraph, The, 322
Supergrass, 321
Superman, 302–4
Superman II, 309, 313–14
Superman III, 313–14
Sutherland, John, 253
Sutro, John, 216
Sutton, Dudley, 216
Swiftdown, 247

Taft Broadcasting, 248
Take It Or Leave It, 318
Take My Life, 71
Tales of Beatrix Potter, The, 245, 250
Tales of Hoffmann, The, 132
Tarka the Otter, 256, 302
Tarzan's Peril, 164
Taste of Honey, A, 4, 190, 196, 202
Taylor, A. J. P. 17
Taylor, Elaine, 321
Taylor, Elizabeth, 203, 231, 278
Taylor, Gilbert, 66
Taylor, Robert, 166–7
Tebbit, Norman, 308, 339
Teddington Studios, 19, 51, 83, 161, 166
Temple, Julien, 325
'Tendencies to Monopoly in the Cinematograph Film Industry' *see* Palache Report
Tenser, Tony, 246
Terrible Beauty, A, 166
Terry, John, 198, 218–22, 224, 227n, 275, 281, 283, 287–8, 335, 340
Terry Report, 289–95, 297, 332
Tess, 314
Thames Television, 207, 315
That Dangerous Age, 129–30
That Lucky Touch, 263
That'll Be the Day, 281
Thatcher, Margaret, 276, 330–1
They're A Weird Mob, 222–4
Thief of Bagdad, The, 19
Third Man, The (film), 11, 21, 130
Third Man, The (TV series), 138
39 Steps, The (1959), 182
39 Steps, The (1979), 256, 302–3
This Happy Breed, 19, 51
This Sporting Life, 191, 196
Thomas, F. L. 202
Thomas, Garth, 324–5
Thomas, Gerald, 3, 183
Thomas, Ralph, 116
Thompson, J. Lee, 173
Thorn-EMI Screen Entertainment, 316, 342, 347, 349; *see also* EMI
Thorn Industries, 315
Thorncroft, Antony, 230
Thorneycroft, Peter, 113, 122
Thorpe, Richard, 166–7
Threadgall, Derek, 251–2
Three Men in a Boat, 136
Thunderball, 197, 199, 234

Tiger Bay, 182
Tigon Film Productions, 246, 248
Till Death Us Do Part, 197
Time Bandits, 314–15, 318
Time for Loving, A, 263
Times, The, 276
Tippetts, R. B., 221, 341
Titan International Pictures, 222
To Russia With Elton, 304
Today's Cinema, 244
Todd, Derek, 217, 230
Todd, Richard, 136
Toeplitz, Giuseppe, 47
Toeplitz, Ludovico, 18, 47
Tofosky, James, 235
Tom Brown's Schooldays, 148
Tom Jones, 2, 4–5, 191–2, 196–7, 199–200, 210, 220, 231, 232, 234, 350
tom thumb, 171–2
Tomorrow Enterprises, 264
Tony Draws A Horse, 102
Train of Events, 72
Transamerica Corporation, 235
Transatlantic Pictures, 42
Treasure Island, 41, 110, 162–3
Treasury, 5, 31, 37–9, 43, 85–7, 96, 101–2, 111, 128, 133–4, 137, 146, 161, 276–7, 279, 293
Trent's Last Case, 132
Trespasser, The, 318
Trouble in the Air, 64
Truffaut, François, 196, 228
Truman, Harry S., 31, 39
Tufnell, Satterthwaite & Co., 147
Tunes of Glory, 198, 202
Tushingham, Rita, 196
Twentieth Century-Fox, 12, 51, 161, 164–5, 167, 203–4, 210, 236, 269, 315
Twickenham Studios, 189, 317
Two Cities Films, 21, 51, 77, 144
2001: A Space Odyssey, 230, 234–5
Two-Way Stretch, 207
Two Weeks in September, 223

Ulysses, 224
Under Capricorn, 42
Under Milk Wood, 278–9
United Artists, 4–5, 7n, 41, 48, 157, 161, 165, 192, 198–202, 219, 234, 235–6, 244, 267–8
United Film Distributing Company, 317
Universal Pictures, 15, 52, 161, 204, 206, 229, 232, 236

Universal Soldier, 246
Unsuitable Job for a Woman, An, 318, 336–7, 345n
Up Pompeii, 245, 250, 278
Up the Junction, 197
Upturned Glass, The, 70
Ustinov, Peter, 268

Valeria (distributor), 263
Valiant, The, 198, 202, 215
Variety, 34, 266, 269, 318
Venetian Bird, 115
vertical integration, 12–13, 46, 246; *see also* Associated British Picture Corporation; Rank Organisation
Vertue, Beryl, 294
Very Edge, The, 216
Vic Films, 190, 224
Victim, 186
Victoria Playhouse Group, 306
Victoria the Great, 18
video cassettes, 312, 348
View to a Kill, A, 314
Villain, 249
VIPs, The, 203
Virgin and the Gypsy, The, 262
Virgin Films, 318–19, 323, 325, 338
Vitti, Monica, 210

Walbrook, Anton, 65
Walker, Alexander, 2, 198, 201, 216, 231, 245, 294, 330
Walker, George, 317
Walker-Smith, Derek, 32–3
Wallace, Edgar, 53, 147
Walt Disney Productions, 41, 163–4
Walter Heller & Co., 151
Walters, Julie, 321
Walton Studios, 214; *see also* Nettlefold Studios
Warlords of Atlantis, 302
Warner Bros., 12, 51, 53, 161,164, 166, 232–3, 236, 249, 269, 303, 325
Warner-Seven Arts, 207, 235
Warning to Wantons, 66
Warter, Philip, 53, 70, 73–4, 117–18
Water Babies, The, 302
Watership Down, 302, 322
Watkins, David, 314
Warwick Film Productions, 167–70, 261
Wasco, Janet, 1
Waterfront, 102

Waterloo Road, 19
Way Ahead, The, 19, 51
Way to the Stars, The, 19, 51
Weaker Sex, The, 71
Wednesday Play, The (TV), 321
Weinstein, Hannah, 214
Welland, Colin, 312, 314–15
Wembley Studios, 51, 161
West 11, 219
Westminster Bank, 18, 48; *see also* National Westminster Bank
Wessex Film Distributors, 215
What's Up Superdoc?, 304
When the Wind Blows, 338
Where Eagles Dare, 234, 245
Where No Vultures Fly, 110, 118
Whirlpool, 182
Whisky Galore!, 72–3, 118
Whistle Down the Wind, 186, 207
White, Eirene, 12, 217
White, Michael, 247, 321
White Corridors, 148
White Cradle Inn, 72
Who Dares Wins, 313–14, 317
Wicked Lady, The, 21, 63
Wicker Man, The, 252–3
Widmark, Richard, 169, 250
Wilcox, Herbert, 21, 64, 68, 72, 129–30, 132–3, 136–7, 174
Wild, Jack, 247
Wild Geese, The, 266–7, 302
Wild Geese II, 316
Wilde, Cornel, 165, 232
Wilding, Michael, 68
William Tell (TV series)
Williams, Graham, 338
Williams, Tony, 255
Willis, Lord, 200–1, 228
Wilson, Charles, 103
Wilson, Harold, 12, 25, 37–8, 40, 42–3, 64–5, 77–8, 81, 83, 87, 96–7, 99, 105n, 113, 220, 286–8, 291–3, 331, 333
Wilson, Michael, 175
Wilson, Roy, 200
Winckles, Kenneth, 235
Winkler, Irwin, 324–5
Winner, Michael, 219, 229
Winslow Boy, The, 54, 63, 72, 83
Winstanley, 334
Winthrop Lawrence Corporation, 262

Wintle, Julian, 88, 184
Wisdom, Norman, 118, 206
Woman Alone, A, 144
Woman in Question, The, 102, 147–8
Woman With No Name, The, 102
Woman's Angle, The, 117
Wonder Kid, The, 129
Wonderful Life, 206
Wood, Alan, 52
Wooden Horse, The, 109–10, 129, 131
Woodfall Film Productions, 4, 187–90, 199–200
Woolf, C. M., 51
Woolf, James, 132
Woolf, John, 132, 135–6, 150–1, 153–4, 187, 208, 287–8, 294
Woolley, Stephen, 325
Wootton, Baroness, 209
Working Party on Film Production Costs (Board of Trade), 64, 66–7; *see also* Gater Report
World Film Services, 264
World is Full of Married Men, The, 302
World is Ours, The, 147
World Ten Times Over, The, 219
Wrong Arm of the Law, The, 202
Wrong Box, The, 207

Yangtse Incident, 136
Yank at Oxford, A, 161
Yates, Peter, 296
Yeabsley, Richard, 132
Yellow Balloon, The, 117
Yield to the Night, 118
York, Michael, 250, 296
York, Susannah, 266
You Must Be Joking!, 219
You Only Live Twice, 197, 230
Young, Terence, 317
Young Mr Pitt, The, 161
Young Ones, The, 197, 206, 216
Your Witness, 102
Yule, Lady, 46

Zampi, Mario, 88, 117
Zanuck, Darryl F., 167
Zenith Productions, 320
Zinnemann, Fred, 236
Zulu, 203, 210

EU representative:
Easy Access System Europe
Mustamäe tee 50, 10621 Tallinn, Estonia
Gpsr.requests@easproject.com

www.ingramcontent.com/pod-product-compliance
Lightning Source LLC
Chambersburg PA
CBHW080922300426
44115CB00018B/2918